D0529458

# REMEMBERING EMMETT TILL

*Remembering*

# EMMETT TILL

## DAVE TELL

*The University of Chicago Press*
*Chicago and London*

The University of Chicago Press, Chicago 60637

The University of Chicago Press, Ltd., London

© 2019 by The University of Chicago

Published 2019

Printed in the United States of America

28  27  26  25  24  23  22  21  20  19      1  2  3  4  5

ISBN-13: 978-0-226-55953-7 (cloth)

ISBN-13: 978-0-226-55970-4 (e-book)

DOI: https://doi.org/10.7208/chicago/9780226559704.001.0001

Library of Congress Cataloging-in-Publication Data

Names: Tell, Dave, 1976– author.
Title: Remembering Emmett Till / Dave Tell.
Description: Chicago ; London : The University of Chicago Press, 2019. | Includes bibliographical references and index.
Identifiers: LCCN 2018043686 | ISBN 9780226559537 (cloth : alk. paper) | ISBN 9780226559704 (ebook)
Subjects: LCSH: Till, Emmett, 1941–1955—Anniversaries, etc. | Till, Emmett, 1941–1955—Anniversaries, etc.—Economic aspects. | Murder victims—Monuments—Mississippi—Delta (Region)—History. | Murder victims—Monuments—Mississippi—Tallahatchie County—History. | Delta (Miss. : Region)—Social conditions. | Tallahatchie County (Miss.)—Social conditions. | Delta (Miss. : Region)—Race relations. | Tallahatchie County (Miss.)—Race relations. | Civil rights movements—United States—History.
Classification: LCC E185.93.M6 T45 2019 F347.M6 | DDC 364.1/34—dc23
LC record available at https://lccn.loc.gov/2018043686

♾ This paper meets the requirements of ANSI/NISO Z39.48–1992 (Permanence of Paper).

FOR THE EMMETT TILL MEMORIAL COMMISSION
OF TALLAHATCHIE COUNTY, INC.

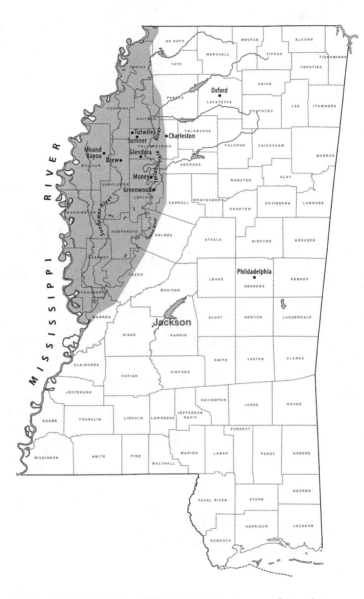

The shaded area is the Mississippi Delta. Map by Hammons and Associates.
Used by permission.

I have a dream this afternoon that there will be a day that we
will no longer face the atrocities that Emmett Till had to face or
Medgar Evers had to face, that all men can live with dignity.
*Martin Luther King Jr., Detroit, June 23, 1963*

# CONTENTS

# ACKNOWLEDGMENTS

If the quality of a book may be calibrated to the extent of its debts, *Remembering Emmett Till* will be incredible. Initial funding was provided in generous measure by the Hall Center for the Humanities at the University of Kansas, and a fellowship from the National Endowment for the Humanities provided the leisure to write. Between the Hall Center at the beginning of the project and the NEH down the homestretch, my research and writing have been supported by an incredible array of institutions, libraries, foundations, nonprofits, state agencies, commercial enterprises, and colleagues of all stripes.

At the Hall Center for the Humanities, I thank Sarah Bishop, Clarence Lang, Eliott Reeder, Bobbi Jo Rahder, and Victor Bailey. Without Sally Utech's commitment to the public humanities or Kathy Porsch's ability to fund them, this book would not exist.

I fear I've called upon every librarian at the University of Kansas. In particular, Pam Lach, Brian Rosenblum, Rhonda Houser, Sara Morris, Karna Younger, Carmen Orth-Alfie, Scott McEathron, Ada Emmett, Josh Bolick, LeAnn Meyer, Marianne Reed, and Jeromy Horkman have lent their expertise to this project. I'm particularly indebted to Julie Petr's ability to answer my crazy questions (How high was the Tallahatchie River in 1955?).

At the University of Kansas, I thank Jay Childers, Tom Beisecker, Ben Chappell, Emily Ryan, Anne Dotter, Elizabeth MacGonagle, Beverly Mack, David Roediger, Shawn Alexander, Jonathan Lamb, Ed Healy, Laura Mielke, Frank Farmer, Carl Lejuez, Danny Anderson, Jim Mielke, Germaine Halegoua, Bill Tuttle, Andy Anderson, Ludwin Molina, John Fackler, Sheyda Jahanbani, Erik Scott, Marta Vicente, Maryemma Graham, Randal Jelks, Henry Fortunato, Dorthy Pennington, Cheryl Lester, Sherrie Tucker, Hannah Britton, Tamara Falicov, Joy Ward, Steven Epstein, Beth Innocenti, Jeremy Shellhorn, Nathan Wood, Robin Rowland, Rick Hellman, Christine Metz Howard, Kristi Henderson, and Mary Lee Hummert. Thanks to Lindsay Harroff for fantastic research assistance and to Jenea Havener for reading a draft and making the book more precise, less repetitive, and more compelling!

While my list of debts runs long in Kansas, it runs still longer in Mississippi. At the University of Mississippi, I thank Jennifer Ford, Leigh McWhite, Ted Ownby, Bill Rose, and Jody Skipper. At the William Winter Institute for Racial Reconciliation, I thank Susan Glisson, Charles Tucker, Jennifer Stollman, April Grayson, and Portia Espy. At the Mississippi Department of Archives and History, I thank Mingo Tingle, Bill Gatlin, Ken P'Pool, and, above all, Alieen de la Torre. At the Mississippi Development Authority, I thank Sarah McCullough, Joy Foy, Mary Margaret Miller, and director Craig Ray. At Belinda Stewart Architects, I thank Belinda Steward and Holly Hawkins. At Hammons and Associates, I appreciate the support of Wanda Clark and the steady guidance of president Allan Hammons. In addition to these, I benefited from a wide range of indispensable Mississippi contacts. Included are Rolando Herts, Tim Kalich, David Rae Morris, W. Ralph Eubanks, Richard Dickson, Reilly Morse, John R. Hailman, Patrick Magennis, John Elzey, Clay McFerrin, James W. Powers, George Schimmel, Temita Davis, Jim Abbott, Kate Hackett, Allan Barton, Susan Neiman, Kathryn Green, Mary Annette Morgan, Patrick McDonough, Ellen Whitten, and Charles Weir.

This project never would have happened without the unceasing support and collaboration of the Emmett Till Memorial Commission of Tallahatchie County, Inc. In particular, thanks to John Wilchie, Willie Williams, Frank and Judith Mitchener, Martha Ann Clark,

Sykes Sturdivant, Devante Wiley, Benjamin Saulsberry, Betty Pearson, Jessie Jaynes, and Mayor Johnny B. Thomas. Above all, thanks to Patrick Weems, whose passion, energy, and Rolodex kept the work humming along. If this book achieves nothing else, it has already given me a close friend and trusted colleague in the pursuit of commemorative justice. Many, many thanks to Patrick!

Among the rewards of writing this book was the pleasure of working with a world-class group of Emmett Till scholars. In a world of dog-eat-dog scholarship, this group stands out for their sheer generosity. Here I thank Devery Anderson, Keith Beauchamp, Jerry Mitchell, Alvin Sykes, Chris Benson, Plater Robinson, Dale Killinger, David Beito, Luther Brown, Steve Whitaker, and Steve Whitfield. Above all, thanks to Davis Houck who would not let me say no to this project. My debts to Davis grow with every passing year.

I've also enjoyed the support of a wide range of scholars, colleagues, and friends from across the country. The following lent assistance and/or friendship at critical points in the project: James Young, Doug Blackmon, Tanner Colby, Gene Dattel, Neil Padden, David Trowbridge, Garnette Cadogan, Elizabeth Stigler, Howard Blount, Katie McCormick, Chris Spielvogel, Leslie Von Holten, Bob Hariman, Tony Corbeill, David Frank, Paul Stob, Kassie Lamp, Keith Miller, Ersula Ore, Kirt Wilson, Mike Hogan, Steve Browne, Jeremy Engels, Mary Stuckey, Barbara Biesecker, Bjorn Stillion-Southard, Carole Blair, Brad Vivian, Greg Dickinson, Jess Enoch, Jennifer Courtney, Kundai Chirindo, Vanessa Beasley, Stephen Schneider, Art Walzer, Brent Steele, Debra Hawhee, Catherine Waggoner, Kristan Poirot, Michael Shaw, Mitch Reyes, Meg Handler, Greg Clark, Gerard Hauser, Susan Jarratt, John Lucaites, Maegan Parker-Brooks, Stephen A. King, Allison Prasch, Kyle Jensen, Jay Tolson, Marc Havener, Matt and Kori Podszus, Mark and Brenda Brown, Caleb Stegall, Jason and Jenny Lichte, Leah Henry, Bryan Banz, Josh McBain, Tyler Clements, Kevin Lee, and Deborah Dunn. Thanks to Greg Spencer for teaching me the art of rhetoric and to Rosa Eberly for long-dormant lessons in the public humanities. Thanks to Jack Selzer for the unending support. And thanks to Ned O'Gorman, for his investment in so many aspects of my life.

I am fortunate to work with talented and generous photographers: Ashleigh Coleman, Pablo Correa, and Maude Schuyler Clay.

The University of Chicago Press has lived up to its reputation as a world-class publishing house. I'm grateful Doug Mitchell took a chance on the project and, as it came to fruition, peppered even the most administrative of emails with a lively erudition! The book never would have come to fruition without the professional shepherding of Kyle Wagner. Portions of this book are derived in part from an article published in *Advances in the History of Rhetoric* 20, no. 2 (2017); © Taylor & Francis, available online: http://www.tandfonline.com/ https://doi .org/10.1080/15362426.2017.1325414. Portions of chapter 4 were first published in *Southern Cultures* 23, no. 3 (Fall 2017); southerncultures .org.

I am particularly touched to have the support of members of the Till family. While I have been thinking about Emmett Till commemoration for the past fifteen years, Wheeler Parker has borne the memory of his cousin since 1955. I count my time driving through the Mississippi Delta with Wheeler and his wife, Dr. Marvel Parker, as a highlight of my life. They are a talented and powerful couple, deeply committed to protecting the truth of Till's murder.

I am surrounded by wonderful family: Jeff and Aubrey Tell, Bill and Sue Tell, and Branch and Jaylene Fields have all taken an active interest in the project and its author. Finally, no matter how much I have invested in this book, I find the love of Jack, Ashlyn, and Hannah dearer still. Especially Hannah.

# REMEMBERING EMMETT TILL

On May 5, 2011, the Tourism Division of the Mississippi Development Authority (MDA) announced the creation of the Mississippi Freedom Trail, a multisite cultural initiative designed to commemorate twenty-five places that played a significant role in the state's civil rights history. Of the twenty-five sites, the MDA was convinced that none were more important than Bryant's Grocery and Meat Market in Money, Mississippi. A country store in the heart of the Mississippi Delta, Bryant's Grocery was the site where Emmett Till whistled at Carolyn Bryant in August 1955.[1] Three days after the whistle, Bryant's husband, his kin, and an array of accomplices snatched the fourteen-year-old boy from his uncle's home, tortured him, shot him, attached his body to a cotton-gin fan with a length of barbed wire, and sank him in a Mississippi river.

From the perspective of the MDA, the "murder and funeral of Emmitt [sic] Till" was "the genesis of the [civil rights] movement, giving Rosa Parks the strength to sit down and Reverend Martin Luther King, Jr. the courage to stand up."[2] In a symbolic gesture to the sheer impact of Till's murder on the American racial landscape, the MDA made Bryant's Grocery the first stop on the Mississippi Freedom Trail. On May 18, 2011, surviving members of the Till family joined veterans of the Mississippi freedom struggle at the long-abandoned grocery to unveil the first Freedom Trail marker (see figure 1).[3] The well-

**FIGURE 1.** This is the first sign on the Mississippi Freedom Trail. It suggests that Till's murder and, by extension, the civil rights movement started at Bryant's Grocery and Meat Market. The trees in the background hide the ruins of the store. Photograph by Ashleigh Coleman. Used by permission.

publicized event announced the investment of the MDA in civil rights commemoration, the national consequences of Till's murder, and the central role of Bryant's Grocery in the history-bending homicide.

The 2011 ceremony had a strong undercurrent of irony. The MDA seemed unaware that their decision to cast Bryant's Grocery as the origin of the Till murder was a strategy once tainted by racism. In September 1955, at the trial of Till murderers Roy Bryant and J. W. Milam, the grocery functioned as the origin of the murder only for those who sought to justify racial violence. Indeed, those prosecuting the murderers argued that the Till affair began, *not* at Bryant's Grocery and Meat Market, but rather at the site of the abduction, the homestead of Till's uncle Moses Wright on Dark Fear Road.[4] By starting their story at the Wright residence, three days *after* the events at the grocery, the prosecution was trying to keep Till away from Carolyn Bryant, keep Bryant herself from testifying, and thereby prevent the suggestion that Till's murder was a "justifiable homicide"—a fitting punishment for a black boy who insulted a white woman.[5]

It was the counsel for the defense that championed the importance of Bryant's Grocery. In the interest of getting Carolyn Bryant on the witness stand, they argued that the events of Bryant's Grocery formed the "essential background for a later happening."[6] Judge Curtis Swango ruled in their favor. While he mandated that the jury leave the room, he allowed Bryant to tell her story. Although she confessed in 2008 that none of it was true, she testified in court that Till forcibly held her hand, asked her for a date, grabbed both of her hips, and propositioned her with "unprintable words."[7] The jury did not need to be in the room. They heard Bryant's tale by other means, and they acted on it. Nine of the twelve jurors later confided that they voted to acquit the murderers not because they believed the men were innocent (they did not) and not because they doubted the identity of the body (the open argument of the defense), but rather because of what happened at Bryant's Grocery. "The simple fact was that a Negro had insulted a white woman. Her husband would not be prosecuted for killing him."[8]

By May 2011, however, the partisan history of Bryant's Grocery had been long lost. If, in 1955, the possibility of justice hinged on whether or not Bryant's Grocery was the "essential background" of the murder, by 2011 the contest over the site was drowned out amidst the pomp and circumstance of the Mississippi Freedom Trail. From a bitterly contested site, the process of commemoration transformed the grocery into the unquestioned origination point of the murder. Irony of ironies, when the Till family gathered at the remains of the grocery to unveil the Freedom Trail, they unwittingly endorsed the same argument that once convinced nine jurors to acquit two murderers. The old racially charged geography that once assured the undeserved freedom of Till's killers was now advanced by the MDA and put in the service of the state's "epic struggle for equality."[9]

The late emergence of Bryant's Grocery as the unquestioned starting point of the murder perfectly captures the primary storyline of *Remembering Emmett Till*: the deep intertwining of race, place, and commemoration. Because the "simple fact" that a black boy insulted a white woman hinged on the establishment of the grocery as the origination point of the murder, the act of commemorating the grocery registered in the domains of both geography and race. The moment the Freedom Trail sign went up, it was no longer racist to say that the murder began at the grocery. This lesson holds across time: since 1955, practices of Emmett Till commemoration have been calibrated to both racial commitments and the ever-changing meaning of the Mississippi Delta. Race, place, and commemoration always shift in tandem.

*Remembering Emmett Till* tells five stories about race, place, and memory. Together, they tell the complete story of Till's commemoration in the Mississippi Delta, accounting for long silences and brief, passionate outbursts of memorial investment. They tell the backstories of the signs and museums that now punctuate (portions of) the land where Till was killed. They reveal a world of controversy, patronage, nepotism, and enduring racism lurking just behind the placid surface of polished historical markers. At times, these controversies were fueled by intellectual debates over what precisely happened to Emmett Till. More often, the controversies were motivated by the simple fact that stories of Till's death are one of the few remaining Delta commodities not controlled by agribusiness. More often still, however, financial despair has driven intellectual debate: the desperate pursuit of revenue in the Delta has fueled an even more desperate creativity with Till's story, with the result that the imperative of economic development has unsettled the plotline of a murder that was ambiguous from the very start. If I pay exorbitant attention to the funding schemes that have underwritten the Delta's commemorative investment, it is because these schemes did not simply disseminate a settled story; they also transformed the story in the interest of making it fundable. In the process, the commemoration of Till's murder has transformed most of what we think we know about the night Till was killed.

The stories of *Remembering Emmett Till* are not only exhaustive, covering the full range of the Delta's commemorative investment. They are also locally textured, full of heroes and villains whose names have never graced the pages of our civil rights histories. They are dramatic, alive to the human virtues and vices that have, since 1955, driven the on-again, off-again industry of Emmett Till storytelling. Most importantly, they are stories in which it is virtually impossible to tell where practices of commemoration end and old-fashioned racial politics begin. Much like the MDA's Freedom Trail, the stories of *Remembering Emmett Till* are, simultaneously, stories about race, about the Mississippi Delta, and about the never-settled legacy of a murder.

If the unsettled legacy of Till's murder teaches us anything about the practice of commemoration, it is surely the fact that commemoration is not a discrete cultural practice. At least in the Delta, commemoration has always worked in and through the domains of race and place. I refer to the interanimating force of race, place, and commemoration as the *ecology of memory*.[10] In recent years, "ecology" has emerged as a critical term to designate, on the one hand, the active participation of humans in processes once set apart as natural (e.g., global warming) and, on the other hand, the active participation of the surrounding environment in processes once reserved for humans (e.g., memory). In short, ecology has become a shorthand term for the interdependence of domains that once seemed independent.[11] Just as ecologists proclaim the deep relevance of human action on weather patterns, I am suggesting that race, place, and commemoration are as interconnected as deforestation, fossil fuel consumption, and global temperatures.[12] If this is true, the histories of racism, of Till commemoration, and of the Mississippi Delta cannot even be *described* (let alone understood or analyzed) apart from the ways that race, place, and commemoration work through each other—and transform each other.[13]

At its most basic level, *Remembering Emmett Till* is simply the first description of the entanglement of commemoration, racism, and the Delta in the wake of Till's murder.[14] It follows the legislators, county supervisors, funding boards, nonprofit organizations, private foundations, small-town mayors, anonymous citizens, ex-cons, and midlevel bureaucrats who, since 2005, have overseen an unevenly distributed $5 million investment in the Mississippi Delta's commemorative infrastructure. Drawing on untapped archives, a thousand pages of never-before-seen Freedom of Information Act documents, reams of grant records, competing maps, and extensive on-site experience, *Remembering Emmett Till* presents the murder from the perspective of those who live in its shadow and, all too often, survive economically through the desperate repackaging of Till's story. It tells the sometimes-inspiring, more-often-heartbreaking, always-unlikely backstories of the Delta's twenty-first-century investment in Till's story.

Lest description seem too meager a goal for yet another book on Till's murder, I stress that there has never before been a comprehensive account of the people, things, and places that have molded our memory of Till's murder. Most of what we think we know about the murder has been shaped, at times in dramatic fashion, by the racial culture, natural environment, and built infrastructure of the Mississippi Delta. Even such basic components of the story as the number of accomplices, the site of the killing, and Till's supposedly overconfident personality seem uncontestable (and basic) only because of the ways that racism and the natural environment of the Delta have shaped our collective memory. *Remembering Emmett Till* thus tells the unlikely stories of how the rivers, soils, hills, judicial districts, sidewalks, playgrounds, county lines, courthouses, and service stations of the Delta have become agents of racism and memory at the same time, transforming the story of Till's murder in elementary ways.

It is no exaggeration to say that *Remembering Emmett Till* will transform everything we think we know about the murder of Emmett Till. It does so not by uncovering new facts from 1955—which by this point are relatively well known—but rather by demonstrating the differential intensities with which various facts have circulated since 1955. While seemingly major components of Till's story (such as his murder site) have gone uncommemorated, relatively minor components have achieved a massive, affectively charged afterlife in the Delta. Where was Till's body dropped in the water? Where was it recovered? From where was the gin fan stolen that weighted his body in the river? If these questions have been debated (and commemorated) with an intensity out of proportion with their historical significance, this is because the economic well-being of entire towns hinges on the answers given (see chapters 2 and 5). To put things rather too bluntly, if the question of the cotton gin from which the fan was stolen has received far more attention in Mississippi than the murder site, it is because the cotton gin is surrounded by poverty and the murder site is not. With slightly more nuance, we can say with certainty that as Till's story has been passed down through the generations, its plot has been reshaped by the ever-pressing, always-urgent conditions of remembrance in the Delta as much as by the distant facts of 1955. Thus while the murder site intuitively seems as if it deserves the premier commemorative investment, the conditions of twenty-first-century remembrance have given the cotton gin a dearer value. There is an unsettling suggestion here. Much of what we know—or think we know—about Till's murder derives from the unequal intensity with which various components of his story have been commemorated. The stories of Till's remembrance must not be separated from the story of his murder; they *are* the story of his murder.[15]

Given the importance of the Mississippi Delta to the stories I tell (and to the story of Till's murder that we think we know), *Remembering*

*Emmett Till* is organized spatially. The first chapter begins with a basic geographical fact: the erasure of the murder site in Sunflower County from every map of Till's murder published between 1956 and 2005. By retelling Till's story from the perspective of the long-excluded county, the chapter does two things. For those who need it, it provides a careful historical review of the murder. More than a review, however, the chapter demonstrates that as the geospatial coordinates of Till's murder shifted (where was he killed?), so also did the mechanics of racism, the possibility of justice, the size of the murder party, the identities of the perpetrators, and the roster of those who fought for justice. Indeed, virtually every variable in Till's story shifts with the movement of Sunflower County in and out (mostly out) of Till's story.

Chapters 2 and 3 focus on Tallahatchie County, Mississippi—the site of the greatest concentration of Till memorials anywhere in the world. Just as Sunflower County was written out of Till commemoration despite its significance in 1955, Tallahatchie County is filled with memorials despite the fact that it has little historical claim to Till's story beyond serving as the accidental site of the trial. The latter county now boasts over twenty historical signs, a museum, a park, an interpretive center, a community building, and—at the center of it all—a multimillion-dollar renovation to the county courthouse designed to return the building to its 1955 appearance. An investment on this scale required the collaboration of committed activists and unlikely champions. Chapter 2 tells their story and, as it does so, attends to the improbable role of the Delta's natural ecology in bringing this investment to pass. In the Delta, both racism and commemoration are calibrated to the composition of the soil, the flatness of the land, and—above all—the management of rivers. Explaining the ways that Till's story has been shaped by the natural-aquatic-political history of the Delta, the chapter suggests that even soils and rivers are agents of memory and racism.

Chapter 3 considers the relationships between Till's murder and the civil rights movement. Until the twenty-first century, the civil rights movement generally began with the Montgomery bus boycott or *Brown vs. Board.* The Mississippi Delta was virtually—if not totally—

ignored. Starting in 2005, however, under the imperative of raising money to commemorate Till's murder, local memory workers wrote Tallahatchie County into the history of the civil rights movement. Insisting that Rosa Parks was thinking of Emmett Till when she refused to cede her seat (which may or may not be true), and posting signs to this effect across the county, activists made Tallahatchie County what they needed it to be: the origin of the movement. Situated as the long-ignored starting point of the freedom movement, locals found themselves with a powerful argument for state funds.

Chapter 4 focuses on the hamlet of Money, Mississippi, the site of Bryant's Grocery and Meat Market. I recover the forgotten history of Young's Grocery and Market, the country store that inhabited the shell of Bryant's Grocery during the 1980s. Although Bud and Rita Young have never appeared in a book on Till's memory, they controlled the famous building during the first revival of Till commemoration, and the history of their store provides a powerful critique of the assumptions that have long governed Till commemoration. When the Youngs were bought out in the mid-1980s, the building that once housed Bryant's Grocery began to fall into disrepair. Hurricane Katrina claimed the roof and a story-sized portion of the north wall, and, to this day, the building is little more than four crumbling brick walls, held up by vines, filled with rubble, and surrounded by a cheap, plastic construction fence designed to protect visitors from falling bricks. The ruin of the grocery is made all the more conspicuous by the pristine restoration of the adjacent gas station, Ben Roy's. This chapter tells the scandalous story of how and why money earmarked for the preservation of civil rights sites transformed Ben Roy's but left Bryant's in ruin. It is a story about how materiality, memory, money, and racism transformed the meaning of the Mississippi Delta.

Finally, chapter 5 focuses on the village of Glendora, Mississippi. The tiny town in the heart of the Mississippi Delta has only five streets but eighteen markers related to Till's murder. In addition to an unparalleled density of historical signs, Glendora is also a site of staggering poverty, even by the standards of the already impoverished

Mississippi Delta. I trace the links that bind these two facts together, suggesting that the impoverishment of the town has bound the commemoration of Emmett Till to questions of municipal infrastructure and welfare programs. In Glendora, it is no exaggeration to say that the poverty of the community has transformed Till's story. The story has been attached to (and funded by) poverty-driven projects like the construction of sidewalks and the provision of internet service, and, as a result, the site of the murder and the size of the murder party have shifted once again.

Across all of these stories, I stress the ecology of memory, the deep intertwining of Till's story with the contours (natural and otherwise) of the Mississippi Delta. Lurking behind the stories told in each chapter is a resolute insistence that Till commemoration bears the imprint of the Delta, that the physical, cultural, and symbolic landscape of the Delta has been permanently altered by the memory of Till's murder, and that racism works most powerfully at those moments in which it is difficult to distinguish racism from the natural environment, when historical revisionism is driven by soils and prejudice at the same time, and when intolerance seems to be a function of a river's path through the Delta. Given the fundamental nature of these entanglements, the stories of *Remembering Emmett Till* assume a newfound urgency. They are not simply a record of long-past racial atrocities; they are also an index to the continuing ways in which race works in and through the Delta, its natural environment, and its built infrastructure. It is not too much to say that the story of Till's commemoration is, quite simply, the story of race and the Mississippi Delta.

## THE MISSISSIPPI DELTA

The Mississippi Delta is shot through with contradictions. It is a place of rich land and poor people. It is a bioregion where the contours of the natural environment (flooding rivers, deep soils) weigh heavily on day-to-day life, and yet it is also a place known for its cultural production (the blues, southern literature). It is a place of vast, sometimes unimaginable poverty, and yet there remains to this day a wealthy planter class with second homes in Oxford and escapes on the gulf shore. Finally, it is a place of genteel extravagance, gracious manners, and southern charm, all of which flowered in the vice-like grip of Jim Crow racism. The Delta was a place, Yvette Johnson writes, where planters "wore suits when they lynched you. They drank illegal whiskey from a clean glass. They delicately wiped their mouths on monogrammed handkerchiefs after they spat on you."[16]

Geographically speaking, the Mississippi Delta is a diamond-shaped expanse of land in the northwest corner of Mississippi, not to be confused with the *river delta* to the south where the Mississippi River fans out to meet the Gulf of Mexico (see map in front of book). For those who know it, the Mississippi Delta can be distinguished by any number of features. Geographically, it sits between the Mississippi River and its eastern tributaries; ecologically, it is a massive alluvial floodplain; agriculturally, is was the site of the second cotton kingdom; economically, it is defined by the extremes of exceptional white wealth and extensive black poverty; culturally, it is the "taproot of black culture" and ground zero of white southern literature; and racially, it has inherited the legacy of once being known as the "worst place in the entire country for Negroes."[17] With distinctiveness in virtually every register, locals refer to the area simply as "the Delta." In Mississippi, James C. Cobb explains, people don't go to Clarksdale, Greenwood, or Greenville. Rather, they simply go "into the Delta"—a region so overdetermined with meaning that the significance of one's specific destination is overwhelmed by layer-upon-layer-upon-layer of meaning proper to "the Delta."[18]

The best-known geographic coordinates of the Delta come from the patriarch of the region's white literati, David Cohn. Two hundred miles north to south, Cohn wrote, "the Mississippi Delta begins in the lobby of the Peabody Hotel in Memphis and ends on Catfish Row in Vicksburg."[19] Bounded by the Mississippi River on the west and the Coldwater, Tallahatchie, and Yazoo Rivers on the east, the Delta stretches seventy miles across at its widest point. In between are 4.5 million acres of the best land and starkest poverty anywhere in the country. Cohn's oft-cited coordinates are telling. The boundaries of the Delta are marked by rivers, an upscale Memphis hotel ("the London Savoy of this section"), and a fictional black business district called "Catfish Row" that never existed.[20] We might think of these natural-cultural-racial boundaries as a reminder of the ties that, at least in the Delta, bind the natural environment, the distribution of wealth, and racial injustice. Although Cohn would be the last to admit it, both the land-forms and infrastructure of his beloved Delta were entangled with a deep commitment to white supremacy. In the Delta, it is simply impossible to talk about nature—especially rivers and soils—without also talking about race.[21]

For ecologists such as Mikko Saikku, the Delta is first and foremost a bioregion, an alluvial floodplain created by the annual flooding of the Mississippi River and its tributaries. The drainage area of the Mississippi, Saikku writes, "covers some 1.2 million square miles, or more than 40 percent of the coterminous United States, from New York to Wyoming." The great river carries the minerals from this vast swath of land and, in Cohn's words, "hurls them against the levees of the Delta."[22] The magnitude of the great river and the wealth it brought to the Delta were so grand that they inspired not only ecologists like Saikku but also novelists such as William Faulkner, who wrote lyrically in *Go Down, Moses* of the floods that left Delta land ever richer.[23] Flattened and enriched by the mineral deposits carried by annual floods, the soil of the Delta achieved a mythical status. It is flat enough, some say, to render the curvature of the earth visible and fecund enough to be the stuff of legend.[24] The "thick, chocolate-colored, near-magical sludge," Yvette Johnson writes, had the Delta's earliest settlers "drunk on dreams of the extreme riches all but guaranteed to those with capital and perseverance to endure the land and tame the river."[25]

Dreams of untold fortune were bound up with the unrivaled capacity of the Delta's soil to grow cotton. Known as "white gold," cotton dominated US exports from 1803 through 1937 and generated staggering amounts of wealth for the greater Mississippi valley.[26] By the time the Civil War arrived, Walter Johnson writes, "there were more millionaires per capita in the Mississippi valley than anywhere else in the United States."[27] Indeed, it was the sheer financial promise of cotton that transformed the Delta from a panther-infested jungle to a stretch of virtually uninterrupted farmland. Still 70 percent hardwood forest in 1860, by 1890 the Delta was inhabited by 273,000 blacks (77 percent of the population), nearly all of whom were lured by the fact of abundant labor and the fiction of well-distributed wealth.[28] As agents recruited black labor from other sections, they stressed the fecundity of the soil and the possibility of riches. It was "a place where cotton grew so tall it could be picked only from horseback" and where "money could be gathered from trees."[29] They failed to mention that those who picked the cotton were not the ones who harvested the fortune. "For whites, the Delta was a place of immense profits, for blacks it was a place of unspeakable horrors."[30] As Gene Dattel has noted, the Delta marked the "quintessential intersection between cotton and race."[31] Cotton covered the land, blacks dominated the population, and fortunes built on the backs of black labor flowed to white planters. Indeed, while the storied soil of the Delta has long been treated as either natural or mythical, its flatness and its fecundity are also racial. As I note in the conclusion, the only reason the Delta is flat enough to reveal the curvature of the earth is a history of black men clearing forests to expose soil, the richness of which routed wealth to some and oppression to others.

But it was profitable. "White privilege on an unprecedented scale was wrung from the lands of the Choctaw, the Creek, and the Chickasaw and from the bodies of the enslaved people brought in to replace them."[32] Just as in antebellum Mississippi the price of an enslaved person was calibrated to the price of cotton, so in the postbellum Delta sharecropping turned "lashes into labor into [cotton] bales, into dollars."[33] A lot of dollars. Between 1890 and 1920—a time frame that corresponds precisely with the post-Reconstruction disenfranchisement of African Americans—the Delta earned its moniker as the second cotton kingdom.[34] At the heart of this kingdom was the ecology of the Delta: soil, flatness, and cotton distributing violence and wealth along racially coded lines.

Perhaps because of its extremes of violence and wealth, the Delta has always fancied itself as an autonomous region unmoved by the

cares of the world. As the *Atlanta Constitution* put it in a 1962 editorial, the Delta has "its ears closed to any story save its own, with its
conviction that it has a God-given right to do as it pleases unshaken
by history or events."[35] In truth, however, the proud independence
of the Delta has always been a strategy for resisting particular en-
croachments (often around issues of racial diversity) and not others.
Tallahatchie County sheriff H. C. Strider is the perfect example. On
the one hand, his isolationism is the stuff of legend. Virtually every
Emmett Till documentary replays a grainy video of Strider's racist defense of local mores: "We never have any trouble until some of our
Southern niggers go up North and NAACP [National Association for
the Advancement of Colored People] talks to 'em and they come back
home. If they would keep their nose and mouths out of our business,
we would be able to do more when enforcing the laws of Tallahatchie
County and Mississippi."[36] On the other hand, Strider was not just
the county sheriff, he also farmed 1,500 acres of Tallahatchie County
land with the assistance of thirty-five sharecroppers.[37] If Tallahatchie
County was truly as isolated as he suggested—if it could get along
without northern interference—then his cotton would have left him
none the richer. Cotton was "the first complex global business" and,
while New York City may have been home to the NAACP, it was also
the end point of 40 percent of cotton revenue.[38] Without ports in New
Orleans, markets in New York City, or factories in Liverpool, Strider's
farm never would have turned a profit. The so-called isolationism of
the Delta, in other words, never had a basis in fact; it was always little
more than a reactionary mechanism designed to stay the forces of
cultural change, especially when those forces upset the racial norms
on which the southern aristocracy depended.[39] And, as the thirty-five
black families that farmed Strider's land remind us, no one benefited
from the global markets or local racial norms more than the sheriff
himself.

Its intensity notwithstanding, the cotton kingdom was short-lived.
The international market for cotton collapsed in the 1930s, and, as
Gene Dattel has it, the once-vibrant Delta was transformed into "a
permanent ward of the federal government."[40] From a war-driven

price of 35.5 cents a pound in 1919, cotton dropped to 5.5 cents a pound in 1931, the lowest price since 1894. Exacerbating the problem, mechanical pickers were introduced in the 1930s, and, by 1950, 7 percent of Delta cotton was picked by machine.[41] A job that once took scores of laborers (thirty-five families for the Strider Plantation) was now done by machine. The mechanical picker upended the sharecropping economy and devastated the Delta. When the kingdom fell, so too did the region's basic economic infrastructure.

At the heart of it all was Greenwood, the self-proclaimed "Cotton Capital of the World." The town where Emmett Till spent his last free night surged into a bustling destination in the early decades of the century. Driven by cotton factors on Front Street, Greenwood teemed with life. Staplcotn, one of the largest cotton marketing cooperatives in the world, was founded in Greenwood in 1921, and the town perpetually felt as if it was "on the verge of something huge." But when the cotton markets collapsed, Greenwood "took just a few decades to crumble to the ground." The smaller towns in the Delta suffered even more dramatically. By the twenty-first century, the economic devastation of the Delta was so complete that Richard Grant labeled the region a "study in American ruin," and Yvette Johnson speculated that it "takes a stranger driving through the Delta only an hour or two to see the human misery."[42] The Delta is a region in which "human suffering and institutional deficiencies [reach] staggering proportions."[43]

All of this would indelibly mark the life, death, and commemoration of Emmett Till, who traveled to Mississippi at the tail end of the cotton kingdom. Although he surely would not have recognized it at fourteen years old, his trip into the heart of the Delta was shaped by factors from both sides of the region's economic transition. On the one hand, his uncle Moses Wright was a sharecropper, and Greenwood had not yet succumbed to the poverty of the postcotton Delta. Till's cousin Simeon Wright remembered a still-vibrant downtown scene on Till's last night in Greenwood.[44] As the young boys gazed at the segregated nightclubs on Johnson Street and negotiated the bustling crowds, they were witnessing the final throes of a way of life made possible by the annual flooding of the river, the richness of the soil, and the racially coded economics of sharecropping. On the other hand, his murderer J. W. Milam occasionally serviced mechanical cotton pickers—an omen that the end of the cotton kingdom was near at hand.[45] If Cobb is correct that the decrease in the need for black labor (occasioned by the advent of mechanical pickers) led to a corresponding *increase* in racial hostility, there is a note of tragic, capitalist irony in the fact that Till was killed by a mechanic.[46] He was a victim of both the cotton kingdom (which reinstitutionalized racial hierarchy after Reconstruction) and its failure.

Unlike the murder, which came at a time when sharecroppers and planters alike still placed their hopes in cotton, the commemoration of the murder is set in the context of an economically devastated Mississippi Delta. By the time the first academic treatment of Till's murder was written in 1963, the International Harvester Company had a mechanical picker that commanded 64 percent of the market share.[47] This is a handy way to remember that Till's commemoration has never known anything but a postcotton Delta.[48] Indeed, the Delta's first memorial to Till's murder came thirteen years *after* Cobb announced that human suffering in the Delta had reached "staggering proportions." No wonder questions of commemoration insistently circle around questions of economic development. And no wonder that Till's commemoration has too often been a desperate, back-against-the-wall attempt to generate revenue in a region where there were no longer sufficient jobs (chapters 2 and 5).

And yet, the postcotton Delta is not simply the setting of Till commemoration. With its rivers, infrastructure, misery, flatness, and racial stratification, it is an active ingredient in shaping the processes of commemoration and, as a result, shaping the collective memory of Till's murder. If memory is ecological, entangled with its natural and cultural environments, then the Delta itself must be listed alongside memory commissions, museums, and state archives as a shepherd of Till's story.[49]

## COMMEMORATION AND RACE IN THE DELTA

"We are witnessing a world-wide upsurge in memory."[50] By the time the celebrated memory scholar Pierre Nora wrote these words in 2002, the sentiment was widespread. Two years earlier, Andreas Huyssen noted a "contemporary obsession with memory," and, two years earlier still, sociologists Jeffrey K. Olick and Joyce Robbins noted that public culture and academic writing were "saturated" with notions of public memory.[51] Some scholars trace the surge in commemoration as far back as 1982, the year Maya Lin's controversial Vietnam Veterans Memorial was dedicated on the National Mall.[52] However the surge is dated, Erika Doss captures the situation in her aptly named *Memorial Mania*. Contemporary American culture, she argues, is marked by an "obsession with issues of memory and history and an urgent desire to express and claim those issues in visibly public contexts."[53] This remarkable cultural investment in commemoration is most often figured as a form of cultural compensation for the destabilizing effects of late capitalism, mass immigration, or postmodernism.[54]

In one respect, the Mississippi Delta is no different than the mass culture indexed by Nora, Huyssen, and Doss. It too is obsessed with memory. In another respect, however, I am convinced that this obsession must not be explained with recourse to broad social transformations like global capitalism or postmodernism. To be sure, global capitalism shaped the Delta in profound ways. As noted above, cotton was the world's "first complex global business" (Friedrich Engels was a cotton magnate).[55] In the Delta, however, the urge to commemorate was never the product of an existential need to shore the community against the ever-accelerating pace of the world. There were nearer, more compelling motives driving longtime Delta residents to break their habits of silence and circulate Till's story. Throughout *Remembering Emmett Till*, I chart the ways that tourism, racism, poverty, economic development, old-fashioned local politics, and even the path of the Tallahatchie River played a more formative role in the region's commemorative obsession than the much-rumored destabilizations of postmodernity or global capitalism.[56]

I first traveled to the Delta to understand Till's murder, but my time there has transformed my understanding of commemoration more broadly. This broader transformation is a consequence of four particularities of Till commemoration in the Delta: the delayed chronology of commemoration, the disregard of the Delta in virtually every extant account of Till's murder, the intersections of race and commemoration, and the fact that Till commemoration in the Delta was a cultural import. In what follows, I elaborate on each of these observations, before drawing this introduction to a close with a working definition of commemoration.

### Emmett Till, the Mississippi Delta, and Chronologies of Commemoration

Any consideration of Emmett Till commemoration in the Mississippi Delta must confront the basic question of what, precisely, counts as commemoration. If poetry, song, theater, creative nonfiction, novels, and the arts count as commemoration, then Till's murder has lived in memory virtually uninterrupted since 1955. Gwendolyn Brooks, James Baldwin, Bob Dylan, Langston Hughes, Audre Lorde, Toni Morrison, and Lewis Nordan each did their part to give Till's story a home in the "literary imagination" long before the murder was taken up by historians or recalled by public memorials.[57] Indeed, for thirty years following Till's murder, artists were virtually the only keepers of Till's story.[58]

None of the aforementioned artists were writing in the Delta, and there is no evidence to suggest that their work circulated therein. Indeed, there is significant evidence to the contrary, suggesting that Till's murder was rarely, if ever, publicly talked about inside the Delta. When the first memorials began emerging in the Delta in the twenty-first century, so too did accounts of a long-enforced silence. In her gripping *Coming of Age in Mississippi*, Anne Moody tells of how she was haunted by Till's murder, but never allowed to speak of it openly.[59] Likewise Sumner's Betty Pearson grew up with the murder, but never spoke of it across racial lines. Although Pearson attended all five days of the Till trial in 1955, she was "struck by the fact that no one in the ... community discussed it." When the Emmett Till Memorial Commission (ETMC) was formed in 2006, she confided to her friend Susan Glisson that "this is the first time in 50+ years that there has been any open dialogue about the Till murder and trial." While the Till murder was certainly an object of cultural fascination, and while it was certainly talked about in hushed tones in safe spaces, it was seldom discussed openly inside the Delta.[60] While Brooks, Baldwin, Morrison, and others may have done their part to put Till's murder in the *national* literary imagination, their efforts did little to break the taboo that reigned inside the Delta. Anderson refers to this fact as the region's "long, concerted effort to forget the horror and injustice of the Till case."[61]

The thirtieth anniversary of the murder in 1985 marked a turning point in the history of Till commemoration. In July of that year, Rich Samuels unveiled the first Till documentary for WMAQ Chicago, and, one month later, Till's murder was back in the national news for the first time in thirty years.[62] In 1987, Henry Hampton made the Till murder a central part of his massively influential *Eyes on the Prize*— a six-hour documentary that dominated the civil rights education of an entire generation.[63] One year later, Stephen J. Whitfield published *A Death in the Delta*, the first monograph dedicated exclusively to Till's murder. With the exception of Hugh Stephen Whitaker's 1963 thesis at Florida State University—an important but long-overlooked text— Whitfield's 1988 volume was the first academic treatment of the murder. At this point, the floodgates were open. The 1990s saw a steady treatment of Till's murder by academics (Clenora Hudson-Weems, Charles Payne, and John Dittmer), artists (Endesha Ida Mae Holland and Lewis Nordan), and radio personalities (Plater Robinson). In the twenty-first century, the steady flow of academic and artistic engagement increased tenfold. Two new documentaries ushered in the new millennium, and books (for academics, children, and the public) appeared with ever-increasing regularity.

But still, none of this commemorative energy seemed to register inside the Delta. It is, of course, difficult to know just when and where stories of Till's murder circulated. As *Coming of Age in Mississippi* makes plain, simply talking about Till was considered a subversive act, and, for this reason, we must assume that those who did talk about the murder took care to ensure that their conversations would not circulate broadly. The fact that the *Chicago Defender* was smuggled into the Delta by porters on the Illinois Central Railroad suggests both a demand for racially subversive stories and the effort expended to keep that demand off the public radar.[64] The experience of Anne Moody can likely be generalized; she spoke of Till in safe spaces but never mentioned his name in public.

The difficulty of tracking subversive stories notwithstanding, the experience of Betty Pearson suggests that the relative openness of the region can be calibrated to its investment in commemorative infrastructure. According to Pearson, Deltans did not speak openly of the Till murder until they began the process of creating historical markers. In her experience, it was only when the ETMC was formed to erect historical signage and restore the courthouse to its 1955 condition that the murder was spoken of across racial lines. Her testimony is confirmed in rather dramatic fashion by the minutes from one of the earliest meetings of the commission. On June 20, 2006, member after member, both white and black, spoke against the long silence that had prevailed in the Delta on the subject of Till's murder. One claimed that the silence was enforced by the White Citizens Council, another suggested that the "Klan had a hold on [the] county" and "harassed" those who broke the silence; another complained that children in the Delta didn't know the story, and still another complained that he had to "bite his tongue." By the end of the meeting, there was a palpable sense that the commission's "1st order of business" was simply to "acknowledge what happened."[65] To the extent that the experience of Pearson and the commission are indicative of larger trends, we can assume that the relative silence of the Delta persisted until, in 2006, the commission jump-started a period of intense commemorative labor inside the Delta.

To measure the impact of this silence, one need only note the discrepancy between the pace of civil rights commemoration more broadly and the pace of Emmett Till commemoration. According to the official histories, the civil rights movement began to be commemorated across the South in the 1970s. Initially, commemorative efforts were focused in "Alabama, Georgia, and other places where the great, telegenic mass demonstrations were held, rather than, say, in Mississippi, the scene of quieter, less visible efforts and of more sinister, more random, and less restrained violence."[66] By 1989, however, historian Dell Upton notes that commemoration had moved beyond the sites of grand demonstrations to a local, "rank-and-file" approach to commemoration. Renee C. Romano and Leigh Raiford provide a similar chronology, identifying the late 1980s as the beginning of a widespread investment in civil rights commemoration. By 2006, they argue, "the civil rights movement of the 1950s and 1960s [had] assumed a central place in American historical memory."[67]

The disjunction between the standard chronologies of commemoration and the Delta's investment in Till's memory is difficult to overstate. In 1989, the year in which Upton claims that civil rights commemoration moved into its popular phase, the Mississippi Delta was still sixteen years removed from its first experiment with Till commemoration. By 2006, by which time Raiford and Romano suggest that the civil rights struggle had obtained a "central place" in American memory, Mississippi had only a single Till memorial, and it was only six months old. While the remainder of the South had civil rights monuments aplenty by 2006, the newly formed ETMC had barely gotten off the ground—they were still venting their frustrations over the Delta's culture of silence and were still two years away from installing their first commemorative marker. Indeed, so removed is the calendar of Till commemoration from the standard arc of southern commemorative practices that neither Upton nor Romano and Raiford address a single instance of Till commemoration.

A particularly compelling example of our habits of writing Emmett Till out of public memory can be found in the epigraph to this book. On June 23, 1963, Till's murder had a prominent place in the single most iconic speech of the civil rights movement, Martin Luther King Jr.'s "I Have a Dream" speech. On that day in Detroit, King dreamed of world in which the atrocities of the Till murder would be a thing of the past. Till, however, would not last long in the speech. Ironically, King eliminated the reference to Till on the eighth anniversary of his murder, August 28, 1963, when he made the speech famous at the March on Washington. That is, Till was written out of the speech at the very moment it became a civil rights primer for generations of American grade-school students. Although it would have been impossible to predict at the time, King's choice to feature Stone Mountain of Georgia and cut Emmett Till would be, for the remainder of the century, perfectly mirrored in the distribution of memorials.

All told, forty-nine years and eleven months passed between the murder of Emmett Till and its first public commemoration in the Delta. On July 1, 2005, the nearly fifty-year silence was broken with two blue roadside markers erected thirty miles apart from each other outside the towns of Greenwood and Tutwiler. The intervening stretch of Highway 49E was rechristened the "Emmett Till Memorial Highway." In the years that followed the renamed highway, the Delta experienced an unprecedented memory boom. Since July 1, 2005, the Delta has invested well over $5 million in the production of an entire Emmett Till commemorative infrastructure. The Delta now boasts dozens of roadside markers, a museum, two restored buildings, an interpretive center, a walking park, and a community building. This newfound commemorative infrastructure is uncoordinated, unevenly distributed, ideologically inconsistent, and frequently vandalized. For all these limitations, however, the infrastructure ensures that the memory of Emmett Till has something it never had before: a material presence on the landscape of the Delta.

### The Mississippi Delta and Till's Story

The long silence of the Mississippi Delta on the murder of Emmett Till is matched only by the equally long (if not longer) disregard of the Mississippi Delta by the artists, historians, and storytellers of all stripes who, since 1955, have ensured that Till's story circulated for a national audience. Indeed, perhaps the single most surprising fact about the cultural practice of Till storytelling is the complete disregard for the ways in which the contours of the Mississippi Delta—a place of intense cultural specificity—have shaped practices of commemoration and, more importantly, reshaped our basic knowledge of what happened the night Till was killed. From academic books to public television documentaries and everything in between, the stories that have circulated through our culture about Till's murder have never considered the Delta as anything more than the incidental place of the murder.

To be sure, as a geographically bounded region, the Delta allows writers to locate the crime in a rural portion of northwest Mississippi. For this reason, the Delta is mentioned in virtually every telling of Till's story, but its function is restricted to the establishment of the geospatial coordinates of the murder. In this regard, the groundbreaking work of Stephen Whitaker is illustrative. Explaining the location of the trial in his 1963 thesis, he wrote of Tallahatchie County that it was little more than an intensified version of the Deep South. While Mississippi functioned synecdochically for the entirety of the "deep south," he argued, Tallahatchie County functioned synecdochically for the state of Mississippi: it is, as it were, the deepest of the "deep south."[68] While descriptions of Delta counties as the epitome of the Deep South are common, such logics imply that the particularities of a given locale are relevant only insofar as they resemble the so-called mind of the South.[69] In this sense, Whitaker set the tone for generations of Till scholarship. The Delta is always mentioned, but it never mattered. Or, more precisely, there was nothing about the particularity of the Delta that mattered for the remembrance of Till's murder.[70]

If any feature of the Delta is highlighted in Till remembrance, it is the intensity of its racism. This is particularly evident in the Emmett Till documentaries that flourished in the years surrounding the fiftieth anniversary of the murder. Both Stanley Nelson's *The Murder of Emmett Till* (2003) and Keith Beauchamp's *The Untold Story of Emmett Louis Till* (2005) use the setting of the murder in the heart of Mississippi to capture the severity of racism. Yet even here the particularities of the Delta are lost. While it is true that the racism of the Delta was particularly intense, that intensity resulted not simply in *more* racism, but in racism of a very precise sort, paternalism.[71] When Nelson and Beauchamp invoke the Ku Klux Klan and the history of lynching, they capture the *intensity* of southern racism, but they miss the *form* of racism proper to the Delta. Although the Delta's white planters were unquestioned champions of white supremacy, they considered their opposition to lynching as a badge of moral superiority. Alexander Percy, for example, in many ways the epitome of the Delta's white planter class, used the same book to describe his opposition to the Klan and his refusal to rescue black laborers from a levy on which they were trapped in the great flood of 1927. To his mind, there was no contradiction between the imperatives of white supremacy and his moral disapproval of the Klan.[72]

Percy's convictions, of course, do not make Till's murder any less a lynching.[73] They do, however, explain the long tradition of blaming the acquittal on the racist convictions of the jurors, most of whom lived outside the Delta (see chapter 2). While Percy's convictions had little basis in fact, they were so widespread that the planters of the Delta could only make sense of the murder by blaming it on the outsiders who sat at the heart of the legal proceedings. If we are to understand the history of Till commemoration, then we must attend to the racial distinctions that have long structured life in the Delta—even if those distinctions have always been self-serving. Beauchamp's and Nelson's documentaries and, more broadly, the long history of marginalizing these distinctions, suggest that the Delta has never yet been taken seriously as the setting of Till's murder and commemoration.

And yet, *Remembering Emmett Till* is dedicated to the proposition that the particularities of the Delta have shaped virtually every facet of Till remembrance. To take only one example, consider the signs of the Mississippi Freedom Trail. The markers are cast aluminum signs, forty-two by forty-seven inches, mounted on seven-foot posts, with an oval-shaped crest emerging from the top. The front features a raised-letter surface (see figure 1); the back is a printed, black-vinyl sheet featuring photographs and explanatory prose (see figures 14 and

15). On both sides, the oval crest is an etched plate featuring silhouetted civil rights marchers above the title: "Mississippi Freedom Trail." At a cost of approximately $8,000 each, the signs were designed by Hammons and Associates, a graphic design firm in Greenwood, and cast by Sewah Studios in Ohio.

My point in rehearsing these details is that *none* of them—from the funding scheme, to the dimensions of the markers, to the seven-foot post, to the crest on the top, to the raised-letter front or the black-vinyl back, to the local design firm or the distant industrial forge—were developed for Emmett Till's memory, or even for civil rights memory. They were borrowed from the well-established practice of blues commemoration in the Mississippi Delta. Years before Hammons and Associates designed the Mississippi Freedom Trail, they designed the Mississippi Blues Trail—a massively successful experiment in tourism and economic development. Indeed, the Freedom Trail was originally proposed as an extension of blues commemoration.[74] The oval crest that now crowns Freedom Trail signs hearkens back to the circular crest on the top of Blues Trail signs, a crest designed to replicate the shape of an LP vinyl record.

In some respects, the oval-shaped crest at the top of the Freedom Trail markers is an odd fit for a project designed to commemorate "sites central to the [civil rights] struggle here in Mississippi."[75] While marchers have unquestionably become a symbol of civil rights protest, they do not capture the specificity of the Mississippi movement. Indeed, as Charles Payne argued in his magisterial *I've Got the Light of Freedom*, the Mississippi struggle was not characterized by high-profile media events, marches, legal action, or public speeches. Until very late in the 1960s (when marches did come to Mississippi), the Mississippi struggle was a low profile, under-the-radar effort comprised of "organizing"—door-to-door canvassing and the development of local leadership.[76]

In another sense, however, the oval etch-plate is a perfect way to remember that the commemoration of Emmett Till in the Mississippi Delta did not happen in a vacuum. It was shaped—in this case literally—by the history of the blues, the Delta's premier cultural export.

In this sense, the Freedom Trail signs are reminiscent of the Emmett Till Historic Intrepid Center (ETHIC) in Glendora, Mississippi, a museum designed to commemorate both Till's murder *and* the legendary harmonica sensation Sonny Boy Williamson. The ETHIC museum once sold T-shirts with Till on the front and Williamson on the back. Taken together, the signs, the museum, and the T-shirts are reminders that Till commemoration always bears the imprint of the Mississippi Delta. While the effects of this imprint are sometimes trivial (T-shirts and the dimensions of a sign), at other times they have altered the basic plotlines of Till's story.

### Race, Commemoration, and the Ecology of the Delta

Perhaps the easiest way to convey just how deeply the landscape of the Delta has shaped practices of commemoration is to consider once more the issue of racism. From the murderers, to the five lawyers who defended them, to the white press that championed the acquittal and demonized Mamie Till-Mobley—the stories of Till's murder are chock-full of racists. Above all, there is Tallahatchie County sheriff H. C. Strider, the Delta's own Bull Connor, who greeted the black press with daily slurs and ensured the acquittal of the murderers by changing his mind on the race of the body that was pulled from the water.[77] No fire hoses, dogs, or nightsticks are needed to round out the image of Strider as a caricature of southern bigotry.

And, yet, the sheer racism of Strider, the murderers, and their lawyers has long occluded the more subtle ways that racism has controlled our memory of what happened to Emmett Till. As Michelle Alexander explained in *The New Jim Crow*, racism is too often indexed to high-profile examples of bigotry (e.g., Strider) rather than "the way it functions naturally, almost invisibly . . . when it is embedded in the structure of a social system."[78] While Till's murder was made possible by bigots such as Strider, the commemoration of the murder has been transformed by a racism that, as Alexander suggests, is virtually invisible because it appears as natural as the storied landforms of the Mississippi Delta itself.

A major premise of *Remembering Emmett Till* is that racism and commemoration have, from the very beginning, been entangled with the natural, cultural, and built environments of the Delta. Consider, for example, the differential forms of racism on either side of the Talla-hatchie River. On the west side of the river, in the Delta, where flood-ing flattened the land and enriched the soil, planters such as Percy tended to reject the virulent racism of the Klan, if only because the character of the soil (flat and rich) meant that the instability of black labor was the weakest link between themselves and fortune. The Klan flourished east of the river, in the hills, not because racism was there more stringent, but rather because the contours of the land meant that black labor registered as a form of competition rather than as the key to wealth. As I explain in chapter 2, these different forms of racism have dramatically shaped our memory of Till's murder. There could hardly be a better example of Michelle Alexander's thesis that racism works most powerfully when it seems to function naturally. In Tallahatchie County, racism seemed as natural as the north-to-south path of the river and, for this reason, exerted an outsized but invisible influence on Till commemoration. The very landforms of the Delta are the transfer points through which questions of race came to influ-ence commemoration and by which commemoration came to serve the interests of the planter class.

### Commemoration as a Cultural Import

While the Delta has profoundly shaped our sense of the murder, this must not suggest that Till commemoration was the end result of a local, homegrown memorial culture. Nothing could be further from the truth. Till commemoration in the Mississippi Delta was a cultural import both financially and intellectually. While commemoration was transformed by the Delta, the money that funded it and the ideas to which it gave expression originated outside the region. Financially, the vast majority of the money came from federal earmarks (secured by Senator Thad Cochran and Representative Bennie Thompson), federal organizations (e.g., National Park Service, US Department of

Agriculture [USDA]), or state institutions based in Jackson (e.g., the Mississippi Department of Archives and History [MDAH], the Mississippi Humanities Council). Indeed, apart from a one-time gift of $15,000 from Delta native Morgan Freeman and a measured commitment from the Delta Center for Culture and Learning (Cleveland, MS), the vast majority of the budget for Till commemoration in the Delta originated outside the region.

Intellectually speaking, the same pattern prevailed. Because there was astonishingly little published on the Till murder between 1955 and the twenty-first century, the vast majority of commemorative projects in the Delta lean on a standard set of historical sources, none of which are native to the Delta.[79] Usual suspects include William Bradford Huie's 1956 account of the murder for *Look* magazine; Hugh Stephen Whitaker's 1963 thesis, "A Case Study in Southern Justice"; Stephen Whitfield's 1987 *A Death in the Delta*; Mamie Till-Mobley and Christopher Benson's 2003 *Death of Innocence*; and Christopher Metress's 2003 *The Lynching of Emmett Till*. If these sources reappear time and again in the creation of the Delta's commemorative infrastructure, it is because there was not much else to go on. When in 2004 Dale Killinger assumed the role of the lead FBI agent reinvestigating the murder, the first thing he did was run to the Oxford, Mississippi, public library to pick up a copy of Whitfield and Metress.[80] When, in 2007, the ETMC assembled a bibliography to guide their reconstruction of the courthouse, sources were so slim that they listed Wikipedia alongside the FBI report compiled by Killinger.[81] Although the Delta did have native Till experts (Luther Brown and Henry Outlaw, both at Delta State University; see chapter 5), these authorities never published on the Till murder and were thus astonishingly invisible, even to the Delta's professional memory makers. When Tallahatchie County sought a local Till expert to advise them on the content of roadside markers, the closest authority they could find was Plater Robinson—an independent scholar living in New Orleans (see chapter 3).

In sum, the more one looks at the commemoration of Till's murder in the Delta, the more porous the boundaries of the region seem. Choose any Till memorial in the Delta, look closely at either its intellectual or financial history, and you will find a trail of either footnotes or receipts—all of which lead straight out of the Delta. From the high-profile recreation of the Sumner courthouse, to the cheap roadside markers produced by the commission, to the Till museum in Glendora, the Delta's commemoration boom has been funded (both financially and intellectually) by imported goods.

### COMMEMORATION REFIGURED

The ways in which Till commemoration was imported into the Delta, entangled with its landforms, and transformed by the particularities of its racism suggest two broad lessons regarding the nature of commemoration. First, the history of Till commemoration in the Delta challenges a common academic distinction between history and memory. Among academics there is, to put it mildly, a pronounced anxiety about the relationship of memory to history. The contest between the two terms has not served memory well. Predictably, whenever "memory" is set off against "history," the former is cast as subjective and transient while the latter—history—is dignified with an aura of objectivity. The most direct formulation comes from Pierre Nora, whose work is considered by some to be the "crowning moment" of memory studies.[82] Nora writes, "Memory and history, far from being synonymous, appear now to be in fundamental opposition." Memory is vulnerable to manipulation and plagued by forgetting; it is in "permanent evolution." History, by contrast, requires "analysis and criticism" and is for this reason a source of "universal authority."[83] While Nora's formulation is exceptional for the starkness with which he opposes the two terms, a basic opposition between memory and history remains a standard feature of much academic work—at times deployed by professional historians decrying the untrained productions of those who create public memorials.[84]

Even a cursory examination of the Delta's memory work, however, quickly calls into question Nora's thesis. For the fact is that virtually every commemorative enterprise in the Delta drew its authority from the work of professional historians—mostly Whitfield, Whitaker, and

Metress. This is not to suggest that the various historical authorities agreed, or even that the public memorials that took form in the Delta gave faithful voice to academic histories—they did not. Rather, the intellectual genealogies of the Delta's commemorative efforts suggest that there can be no hard-and-fast line between, say, the public memorials in Sumner or Money and the historical treatises read by those who crafted them. To those who did the work of commemoration, Whitaker's thesis, Whitfield's monograph, Metress's edited collection, and, later, Devery Anderson's tome, registered neither as "universal authorities" nor as specifically academic treatises. Quite the contrary. In the context of the Delta's long silence, Whitaker and Whitfield were precious resources who had kept Till's story alive in the long interval between the murder and its public commemoration. Although the memorialists felt no compunction to heed every detail advocated by Whitaker or Whitfield, they recognized these men as fellow laborers in the work of commemoration.

In this respect, it is telling that, like me, Christopher Metress had his assumptions about memory and history remade by the stories of Till's murder. When he first began studying the murder, he intended to write an authoritative historical account against which he could weigh competing versions of Till commemoration. He quickly concluded, however, that both history and memory were built out of the various narratives that circulated about Till's death. "I soon realized," he wrote, "that I would be betraying the process of how we determine what history is and how it comes to have meaning for us, especially in the case of Emmett Till." Without denying that some of these narratives had more validity than others, he concluded that memory was "the very stuff of history."[85] Not only were the public memorials of the Delta built on narratives first circulated by historians, but now historians of Till's murder regularly visit memorials before publishing their work. The sheer fluidity between academic history and public memory is nowhere more evident than in the writing and circulation of Devery Anderson's *Emmett Till*. Before he published the book in 2015 with the University Press of Mississippi, he spent years touring the Delta's burgeoning memory sites. Upon publication, the book immediately became a key source for public memory. In Nora's stark terminology, this fluidity between academic history and popular commemoration could only be described in circular terms: history influencing memory influencing history.

To avoid such circularity, I follow the lead of Christopher Metress and regard all stories of Till's murder as a form of commemoration. I use memory and history as interchangeable terms, for both are little more than the selective appropriation and recirculation of narratives of Till's death. I tend to use the word "memory" because, unlike history, its popular usage includes conations of impermanence—and, as we shall see, Till's story is remarkable for the sheer range of its variation. I also use *storytelling* as a heuristic for the basic activity of commemoration. I do so in part because the circulation of Till's story is the commonality that binds academic writing and public commemoration. More personally, however, I rely on the figure of storytelling because the ETMC—the largest, most influential body of Till commemorators in the world—figures their own identity as storytellers. As they seek to use Till's memory for social justice in the Delta, their call is to "engage in the story of Emmett Till, explore your own story, and create a new emerging story."[86] When we recall that the commission considered its "1st order of business" to be the public acknowledgment of historical injustice, we can appreciate the camaraderie they felt with the historians who, like themselves, sent Till's story into a world that wasn't paying it much attention.

Finally, the experience of commemoration in the Delta is a lesson in the ecology of memory and the rhetorical power of place. As I have been at pains to emphasize, Till's commemoration cannot even be described without attending to the particularities of the Mississippi Delta or the varieties of racism to which it has long been home. From the Freedom Trail to Delta-styled paternalism, stories of race, place, and commemoration are accurate only to the extent that they are told as a single tale. Just as the Freedom Trail marker in front of Bryant's Grocery is also a claim about geography (about the path of the murder party) and about race (the geography was designed to exonerate white men), so paternalism is both a feature of the Delta's landforms and a powerful agent shaping the stories passed down about Till's murder. The Freedom Trail and paternalism are not unique in this regard. If *Remembering Emmett Till* is filled with objects that seem at first glance far afield from Till's memory (e.g., gas stations, public housing, hills, soils, bridges, and broadband wireless service), it is because accuracy demands that stories of race, place, and commemoration be told together.

All of this suggests that the Mississippi Delta plays a role in Till's story well beyond the provision of geographical coordinates. If race, place, and commemoration are truly as intertwined as the history of Till commemoration suggests, then we must rethink the role of place in American cultural politics. Scholars have long noted that while time and history have been figured as dramatic forces shaping cultural politics, place has been reduced to the inert backdrop of historical action.[87] At least in the case of Emmett Till, such a view is not only untenable, but it also keeps us from describing the work of commemoration and the effects of race. The very landforms of the Delta were the mechanism through which racism found a purchase point on the story of Till's murder and by which particular stories of Till's murder came to seem as natural as the path of the Tallahatchie River through the heart of the Delta.

## CHAPTER ONE

# RACE, GEOGRAPHY, AND THE ERASURE OF SUNFLOWER COUNTY

On September 21, 1955, the *Memphis Press-Scimitar* published one of the first maps of Emmett Till's murder (see figure 2). It was a hand-drawn map of three counties: Leflore County, where Emmett Till whistled and from which he was kidnapped; Tallahatchie County, where the trial of killers Roy Bryant and J. W. Milam was then in session; and Sunflower County, where, one day later, Willie Reed would testify that he heard J. W. Milam beat Emmett Till. Every detail of the map was contested. The counsel for the defense argued that the entire Till affair should be confined to Leflore County. Their version of the story began and ended at Bryant's Grocery and Meat Market in Money, Mississippi. It was there, they argued, that Till "assaulted" Carolyn Bryant. And it was there, they argued, that Carolyn's husband Roy and his half brother J. W. Milam turned Till loose after kidnapping him two and eight-tenths miles away.[1]

The prosecution offered a different itinerary. As I noted in the introduction, the prosecution rooted the Till affair, not at the Bryant store in Money, but rather at the homestead of Till's uncle Moses Wright on Dark Fear Road (see figure 3).[2] From this site in rural Leflore County, the prosecution argued, the killers took Till to a barn in Sunflower County where they killed him. It was outside this barn that Reed testified that he "heard the cries of a boy" and "noted with anxiety of soul that the cries gradually decreased until they were heard no

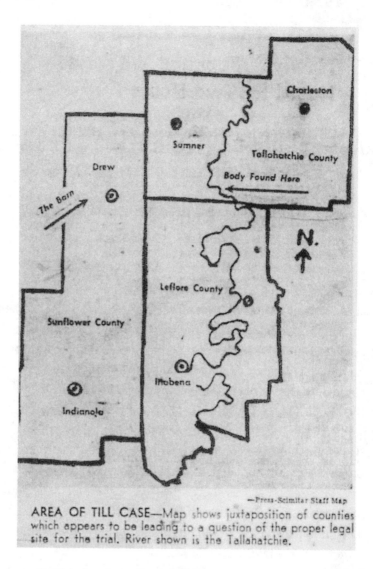

AREA OF TILL CASE—Map shows juxtaposition of counties which appears to be leading to a question of the proper legal site for the trial. River shown is the Tallahatchie.

—Press-Scimitar Staff Map

**FIGURE 2.** Published on September 21, 1955, in the *Memphis Press Scimitar*, this is one of the first maps of Emmett Till's murder.

more."[3] After Till fell silent, the prosecution continued, the murderers wrapped his body in a tarpaulin and drove it to Tallahatchie County where they attached it to a cotton-gin fan with a length of barbed wire and sank it in the Tallahatchie River.

From the perspective of the defense, the geography of the mur-

FIGURE 3. The Wright home in 1955. Although it was only 2.8 miles from Bryant's
Grocery, the prosecution insisted that the murder started here (and not at the grocery)
in an attempt to keep Carolyn Bryant from testifying. The home was destroyed by a
tornado in 1971. Special Collections Department, University of Memphis Libraries.
Used by permission.

der was inextricably bound to the race of the victim. Defense lawyer
Sidney Carlton instructed the jury that there was "nothing reasonable about the state's theory that Bryant and Milam kidnapped Till
in Leflore County, drove several miles to a plantation in Sunflower
County, then doubled back into Tallahatchie County to dump the
body."[4] His colleague John Whitten then added, "Every last Anglo-
Saxon one of you has the courage to free these men."[5] Thus it was that
the jury retreated to their chambers to consider two arguments, one
about race and the other about geography. When they emerged sixty-
seven minutes later, their acquittal was a referendum on both counts:
the disposability of black lives was confirmed, and Sunflower County
was officially excised from the itinerary of Till's murder. It would not
appear on another map of Till's murder for nearly fifty years.

The long erasure of Sunflower County perfectly captures the complex entanglements of race, geography, and memory. The presence or absence of Sunflower County in Till's story has never been purely a question of geography. In the wake of the trial, the earliest commemorative efforts were driven by a young cadre of black writers for whom the inclusion of Sunflower County was a mechanism of protesting the Jim Crow legal process. The pattern held. For the next six decades, while Sunflower County moved in and out of Till's story (mostly out), its presence was indexed to far more than geospatial coordinates. As the location of Till's death shifted, so too did the mechanics of racism, the possibility of justice, the size of the murder party, and the identities of the perpetrators, as well as the roster of those who fought for justice. Indeed, there is hardly a variable in the entire story of Till's murder that is not modified by the presence or absence of Sunflower County. More than any other place in Mississippi, Sunflower County has served as a shorthand heuristic for the competing memories of Till's death.

As the memory of Till's lynching developed over the course of the century, questions of geography and racism were always at hand—and they were always interrelated. Sunflower County functioned as the relay point through which the variables of race, place, and memory bled one into the other. Through Sunflower County, questions of geography—of miles driven, of ground covered, of sites defiled, and of borders crossed—had elementary effects in the domain of race. The geospatial coordinates of Till's murder, for example, were always connected to the size of the murder party. As the geographic range of the murder fluctuated among one, two, or three counties, so too did the size of the murder party and, by extension, the percentage of that party who were never even brought to trial. Geography, in other words, was fundamentally indexed to the category of race, because the question of whether or not racial justice was even pursued hinged on the question of where, precisely, Till was killed. In the case of Sunflower County, racism has been, quite literally, measured in miles.

Just as geographic uncertainty had racial consequences, the particular story of Till's murder made possible by the exclusion of Sunflower County has had lasting effects on the landscape of the Delta. To this day, Sunflower County remains the only relevant county in the Delta without a single built memorial to Emmett Till. Unlike the two counties to its east, the spaces of which are fairly planted with memorials, Sunflower County has nothing. Its still-barren commemorative landscape is a material reminder of how memory, race, and place are bound together. Without a single memorial, it is as if the landscape of Sunflower County is shaping the contours of Till's story, limiting the murder party to no more than two, already acquitted men.

I tell the story of Sunflower County in three parts. I start by attending to the first posttrial commemorative work through which Sunflower County emerged as a topos of racial resistance. Although the jury did its best to eliminate the county from Till's itinerary, an impressive array of journalists refused to let the jury have the last word. In October 1955, after the black press had retreated to the safety of the urban North, they reinstated Sunflower County in order that they might expand the size of the murder party and thereby bring a greater range of injustice into view. From a space dismissed in the name of Anglo-Saxon courage, Sunflower County became a powerful argument for racial reform. It remained so until January of 1956.

While October 1955 was a brilliant moment of reemergence for Sunflower County, it would not last. Even as black journalists were forcibly reinserting the county into the narrative of Till's death from the safety of New York and Chicago, plans to eliminate the county for a second time were afoot in the Delta. Indeed, the same lawyers that once convinced the jury that the inclusion of Sunflower County was "not reasonable" were at it again, developing a memorial strategy that sanitized the murder and truncated the murder party—all by eliminating Sunflower County. This time it worked, and the second section explains how and why.

In the third section, I attend to the third attempt to eliminate Sunflower County from the memory of Till's murder. Here I track a gradually increasing disregard for the category of geography. Eventually, in the final decades of the twentieth century, the categories of race and place were disentangled. For the first time in the history of Till commemoration, it was possible to adjust the size of the murder party without adjusting the murder site. The effect of this *was not* to neutralize questions of geography by detaching them from questions of race. Rather, by pretending that geography was an autonomous field, it empowered geography by rendering its work less conspicuous. The sheer cultural power of a suddenly inconsequential geography came home to me in a very personal way in the summer of 2014. Till's cousin Simeon Wright told me that, in the grand scheme of things, it didn't matter *where* Till was killed; it only mattered that he was killed and that he was killed for being the wrong color at the wrong time in the wrong place. While I have great respect for the late Simeon Wright and the countless hours he invested in shepherding Till's memory, in this instance he was wrong. The erasure of Sunflower County provides compelling answers to the very questions about which Wright cared: questions of racism and justice. In the case of Till's commemoration, if we care about race, we also must care about geography—the two have always moved in tandem.

I conclude with the unlikely story of Ellen Whitten, granddaughter of defense lawyer John Whitten Jr. There is a strong note of irony here, as the Whitten family played a long and direct role in the repeated erasure of Sunflower County. It is, then, with a strong sense of poetic justice that, in 2005, Ellen Whitten reanimated Sunflower County and, for the first time in fifty years, put it back on a map of Till's murder.

## THE REBIRTH OF SUNFLOWER COUNTY

The earliest posttrial commemorations of Till's murder were driven by an insistence on the relevance of Sunflower County—and all the implications that county brought with it. This crusade to remember Sunflower County was conducted primarily by one white journalist and a corps of black writers and activists who were in Mississippi for the trial. The white journalist was Clark Porteous of the *Memphis Press-Scimitar*. Because he was white, Porteous was able to publish the story of Sunflower County during the trial—in late September 1955. To be sure, the story was not his; he learned of Sunflower County only after the black press gave him the scoop. The group of black writers included the celebrated *Afro-American* correspondent James L. Hicks, Simeon Booker from Johnson Publications (*Ebony-Jet*), Moses Newson and L. Alex Wilson for the *Tri-State Defender*, Olive Arnold Adams, and the legendary Mississippi civil rights activist Dr. T. R. M. Howard. Although Hicks, Booker, Howard, and others (Ruby Hurley, Medgar Evers) discovered Sunflower County—and even went undercover as sharecroppers to substantiate its relevance—they could not publish their story during the trial simply because they were black. It would need to wait until October.

Hicks was haunted by his decision to withhold the story of Sunflower County. Eleven days after the trial ended, safely back in New York City, he explained, "I did not write it while in Mississippi for fear of bodily harm to myself and my colleagues." Although he was "ashamed" that he did not "throw caution to the wind" and tell the story as it was unfolding, he still believed that it could have cost him his life. "If I had tried this, I would not be here in New York to write this."[6]

Right or wrong, Hicks and his colleagues did not publish the story as it emerged during the trial in September 1955. Although they fed portions of the story to Porteous, and although Porteous published an early map of Sunflower County (see figure 2), the majority of the story did not emerge until October 1955, two weeks after the trial. This means that the story of Sunflower County has always been historical revisionism. It was a form of commemoration designed to radically alter the terms of Till's story and, critically, those who participated in it. At the heart of the Sunflower County story was a fundamental rejection of the one-county theory offered by the defense, allowed to stand by the prosecution, and accepted by the jury. As I retell the story of Sunflower County's emergence in the weeks following the trial, I stress that more than geography was at issue. By moving the murder site and expanding the geographic range of the murder, the black press used Sunflower County to provide eyewitnesses to the murder, to expand the roster of perpetrators, and to demonstrate the prejudice of Jim Crow justice.

From the perspective of Till's murder and his memory, Sunflower County was born at midnight on September 18, 1955 — just eight hours before the trial was scheduled to begin. It was then that a plantation worker named Frank Young arrived at T. R. M. Howard's Mound Bayou home. Howard was an unparalleled force for racial justice in Mississippi. Although he is generally remembered for his 1951 founding of the Regional Council of Negro Leadership, his civil rights credentials were vast.

> Four years before the Montgomery Bus Boycott, he founded a mass nonviolent movement in the Mississippi Delta. From 1952–1955 he organized annual civil-rights rallies that sometimes attracted crowds of ten thousand, led a successful statewide boycott, and publicly faced down a segregationist governor. He not only hired Medgar Evers for his first job out of college but was instrumental in introducing him to the Civil Rights Movement.[7]

In addition to his civil rights resume, by the time of Till's death, Howard was also the chief surgeon at the Taborian Hospital and an entrepreneur so wealthy that he drove only the latest model Cadillac.

From the perspective of Frank Young (and Till commemoration more broadly), the most important thing about Howard was his guns.[8] Howard employed two security guards around the clock, stashed firearms "in every corner of every room," and kept a pistol lashed to his own waist. For these reasons, Howard's home in Bolivar County became the "black command center" during the trial, and it was, for the same reason, the preferred lodging for Till's mother, Mamie Bradley; African American congressman Charles C. Diggs; and other blacks whose connections to the Till trial rendered them potential targets of racial violence. The home provided shelter for black witnesses, space for strategy meetings, and, above all, safety.[9]

As a witness to Till's murder, Frank Young must have known that, just as much as Diggs and Bradley, he too was a potential target of racial violence. When he arrived at the Howard home seeking safe harbor, he told Howard that Till had been killed inside a barn on the

Sturdivant Plantation just west of the town of Drew, Mississippi, in Sunflower County. This was the first time Sunflower County had been mentioned in the context of Till's murder, and it had the potential to rewrite Till's itinerary in fundamental ways. "These revelations," historians write, "were earthshaking. They could provide eyewitness evidence of the kidnapping and possibly murder and shift the trial venue to Sunflower County."[10]

Young's ability to locate the murder in Sunflower County would have come as a breath of fresh air to the prosecution, whose inability to locate the site of the murder was widely understood as a significant limitation. In articles written on the first and third day of the trial, Porteous reported that the state was "expected to have difficulty proving where the slaying took place" and that this difficulty was understood by the prosecution as a "weakness of its [own] case."[11] Simeon Booker noted that a white reporter told him that the trial would be over quickly: "The State doesn't even know where this boy was killed."[12] Before the trial even began, defense lawyer J. J. Breland predicted victory based in part on the prosecution's inability to prove that the murder "happened in the second judicial district of Tallahatchie County."[13] This was indeed a difficult point to prove. As late as the second day of the trial—some thirty-six hours after Young appeared at Howard's home but still twenty-four hours before his story broke publicly—the print media was speculating that the trial may shift to Leflore County, the site of the whistle and kidnapping.[14]

Young's testimony put many of these anxieties to rest, if only momentarily. He told Howard that Till had been conveyed via a crowded green pickup truck to the headquarters barn on the Ben W. Sturdivant Plantation (see figure 4).[15] J. W. Milam knew the plantation well. Until May 1, 1954, he had an ownership stake in the plantation, and, at the time of the murder, his brother Leslie worked there as the "operating manager of farming operations."[16] It was in the Sturdivant barn, Young believed, that Till was killed. In a written statement conveyed via Porteous to prosecuting attorneys Gerald Chatham and Robert Smith, and which Porteous eventually printed verbatim, Howard summarized Young's tale:

FIGURE 4. Emmett Till was tortured and, most likely, killed in the room at the north end of this barn, through the door that is just behind the bed of the truck and the gas pump. © Ed Clark / The LIFE Picture Collection / Getty Images. Used by permission.

I am informed that a 1955 green Chevrolet truck with a white top was seen on the place [Sturdivant Plantation] at 6. A.M. Sunday, Aug. 28, the last time Till was seen alive. There were four white men in the cab and three negro men in the back. Photos of Till have been identified. He was in the middle in the back.

There are witnesses who heard the cries of a boy from the closed shed. They heard blows. They noted with anxiety of soul that the cries gradually decreased until they were heard no more.

Later a tractor was moved from the shed.

The truck came out with a tarpaulin spread over the back.

The Negroes who went into the shed were not seen at this time and have not been seen around the plantation since.[17]

The essential thing to note in Howard's summary is that the size of the murder party ("four white men in the cab and three negro men in the back") was expanded by shifting the murder site. If Till was killed in Sunflower County, more persons than simply Roy Bryant and J. W. Milam were involved. To the four white men and three black men (one of whom was Till) mentioned by Young, one also needs to add Leslie Milam—as manager of the Sturdivant Plantation he would have already been there when the truck arrived.

While Young could not identify anyone but Till (and that only with the assistance of photographs),[18] Willie Reed could. Reed was a farm-hand on the adjacent Clint Shurden Plantation and, on the morning of the August 28, was cutting across Sturdivant property when he heard, from the barn, "some licks like somebody was whipping somebody."[19] He saw J. W. Milam emerge from the shed, gun on his hip, get a drink of water, and reenter the shed. Reed then retreated to the home of Mary Amanda (Mandy) Bradley (who lived on the Sturdivant Plantation) where he rendezvoused with Frank Young.[20] Together, the two of them advanced toward the barn under the pretense of going to the well for water. Weeks later, during the trial, Reed found himself at a loss for words to describe the agony he and Young heard coming from the barn: "[Till] was just hollering, 'Oh.'"[21] Based on the accounts of Reed and Bradley (both of whom testified in trial) and Frank Young's story (as recounted by Howard), a journalist writing under the pseudonym "Amos Dixon" reconstructed the scene inside the Sunflower County barn for the *California Eagle*: "Emmett fell to the floor, still crying and begging. Their frenzy increased. The blows fell faster. The frenzy mounted higher. The killers kicked and beat their victim. Finally, the cries died down to a moan and then ceased."[22]

If Howard had any doubts about the veracity of Young's tale, they would not have lasted long. The same day Young arrived with the news of Sunflower County, James Hicks arrived in Mound Bayou with a compatible story, independently sourced. Looking for a pretrial head-line, Hicks had intended to spend the day in Sumner, the site of the trial. He stopped by the funeral of "Kid" Townsend—a well-liked black man who had recently passed of a heart attack. Outside the church, a stranger approached him, asked if he was covering the Till trial, and, upon learning that he was, urged him to walk behind a nearby car and talk to the woman he found there. Hicks did as he was told. The woman behind the car confided that a local black man known to her only as "Too Tight" was with Emmett Till the night of the murder, but had not been seen since. Should Hicks want more information, she told him to go to King's Place, the only African American dance hall in Glendora.[23]

Hicks drove directly to King's Place. He asked the manager about the mysterious "Too Tight" and was directed to a woman with whom he flirted in order to gain information. He danced with her, asked her if he could take her out for drinks, and promised to come back to see her (which he never did). The seduction worked. By the time Hicks left King's Place around dinner time, he had learned a number of important facts about the Till murder—facts that were true but which would be disregarded in the trial and, in large part, written out of public memory along with Sunflower County. The woman told Hicks that Levi "Too Tight" Collins lived with her and her common-law husband, Henry Lee Loggins. Both Collins and Loggins worked for "one of those white men who killed that boy from Chicago [Milam]." She then confided that both Collins and Loggins had been in jail since the previous Monday.[24] When Hicks later retold the story of his King's Place adventure, he said, "I knew then that I was on the trail of something big."[25] Indeed he was.

Hicks left his informant at King's Place in Glendora and returned to Mound Bayou to share his story with T. R. M. Howard. Howard, for his part, had just heard Frank Young's tale of screams in Sunflower County. When the two men compared notes late on the evening of September 18, they quickly realized that their stories were compatible. Frank Young had spoken of two unidentified black men on the back of the truck in Drew. Hicks and Howard quickly came to the conclusion that Collins and Loggins were the two men with Till in the back of the truck that Young and Reed had seen in Sunflower County.[26]

Hicks and Howard may have only been half right. Even among proponents of Sunflower County, there is some uncertainty as to whether or not Collins and Loggins were in fact the men flanking Emmett Till. Although all agreed that Loggins "was along to see that Emmett Till didn't jump off the truck and run once he was placed there," there is less certainty regarding the identity of Loggins's assistant.[27] Well after the trial was over, "Dixon" and Adams suggested that a certain Willie Hubbard helped Loggins hold Till down. On this latter account, Collins remains a part of the story, but he doesn't enter the action until Milam needs a black field hand to clean out his truck. Regardless of who guarded Till on the drive to Sunflower County, the crucial thing to note is that Loggins and Collins were essential witnesses for Howard and the black press precisely because they appear in—and only in—the Sunflower County version of the story.[28] And because the Sunflower County version of the story included eyewitnesses and an expanded murder party, it is hardly surprising that Loggins and Collins were quickly booked under false names in a distant jail. Their mere presence at the trial would have called into question the venue of the trial, the geography of the murder, and the number of men being tried.

The reason Collins and Loggins appear only in stories of Till's murder that include Sunflower County is simple. Their essential role—as Hicks, Howard, "Dixon," and Adams understood it—was to guard Emmett Till in the back of the truck during the thirty-mile journey to the Sturdivant Plantation.[29] If the murderers never took Till on what "Amos Dixon" would call a "long ride," they would have had no need for field hands to guard Till in the back of the truck.[30] This is why Hicks was incensed that prosecutors Chatham and Smith refused to sufficiently investigate the tip from his King's Place informant that Collins and Loggins were being held in a distant jail.[31] Had these men been found, they could have borne witness to a radically different account of Till's murder.

While they couldn't reach Collins and Loggins, Howard, Hicks, and others from the black press identified five other witnesses to the events in Sunflower County who could, theoretically, testify in court. The evening after Young broke the news of Sunflower County, Howard called a strategy meeting at his home in Mound Bayou. Held on the evening of the first day of the trial, the meeting was attended by NAACP field secretary Ruby Hurley and three influential members of the black press: James Hicks, L. Alex Wilson, and Simeon Booker. Although Hurley, Booker, and Hicks wanted to go public with the story of Sunflower County immediately, Howard prevailed upon them to hold the presses until the safety of the five witnesses could be assured.[32] They agreed to contact the prosecuting lawyers through a trusted member of the white press, the *Memphis Press-Scimitar*'s Clark Porteous. Porteous came immediately and met the group at Howard's Magnolia Mutual Insurance Company, also in Mound Bayou. Although Porteous unexpectedly brought with him James Featherston and W. C. Shoemaker from the "staunchly segregationist *Jackson Daily News*," Howard proceeded to retell Young's story.[33] After Porteous convinced the *Daily News* reporters not to go public until the safety of the witnesses could be assured, they agreed on a plan. Porteous would invite District Attorney Gerald Chatham and his assistant Robert Smith to a meeting at Howard's home at 8 p.m. the following day. Medgar Evers and his NAACP colleagues would don "cotton picking clothes" and go "undercover as sharecroppers" to inform the black witnesses of the meeting.[34] Once everyone was assembled, Howard would tell Young's story, produce the five witnesses, and prevail upon the lawyers to "stop the trial and move it to Sunflower County."[35]

The meeting never happened. After Porteous conveyed the news to Chatham and Smith during Tuesday's lunch recess, officials from Sunflower County headed immediately to the Sturdivant Plantation and inadvertently spooked the witnesses. When the witnesses failed to show up for the meeting, the black press and white establishment joined forces in what Simeon Booker later called "Mississippi's first interracial manhunt." Leflore County sheriff George Smith and three white reporters (Porteous, Featherston, and Shoemaker) teamed up with Hicks, Booker, and Wilson to round up the witnesses. From midnight until 3 a.m., this cadre of writers and lawmen divided themselves by race (with whites and blacks in each group) and fanned out across the back roads of Sunflower County. It was a frantic search. "Before you could say Jackie Robinson," Hicks wrote, "cars were moving out in all directions."[36] Booker found himself following Sheriff Smith "in a 70-mile-an-hour chase along dusty backwoods roads" in pursuit of Willie Reed.[37] By 3:00 a.m., the group had made contact with each of the five Sunflower County witnesses.[38] Howard assured the witnesses they would be kept safe (Willie Reed moved in with Howard that night) and promised each of them jobs in Chicago in exchange for their testimony.

Porteous kept his word. The following day, Wednesday, with the witnesses now in Howard's safekeeping, Porteous filed the first public story of Sunflower County. On that day Porteous published the only twentieth-century map of Emmett Till's murder that included Sunflower County (figure 2). On Thursday, Willie Reed, Add Reed, and Mandy Bradley testified in court to the Sunflower County beating, the cries for mercy, and the tarpaulin covered body. With his testimony, Willie Reed became an essential part of the Sunflower County version of Till's death.[39] Much like Levi Collins, Henry Lee Loggins, and Leslie Milam, Willie Reed's significance stems from the fact he is only relevant if Till was murdered in Sunflower County. His mere presence in Till's story reroutes the murder and implicates a wider range of murderers.

These two days—Wednesday and Thursday, September 21 and 22, 1955—mark the high point of Sunflower County's existence in twentieth-century Till memory. Papers around the country quoted the Porteous exposé, and, for at least these two days, it seemed difficult to argue with the right of Sunflower County to be included in Till's commemorative geography.

But this was a fleeting moment. The next day, September 23, 1955, marked the beginning of a long, intermittent campaign to purge Sunflower County from the collective memory of Till's murder. The first attempt to eliminate Sunflower County was, as I noted in the introduction, defense attorney Sidney Carlton's argument that there was "nothing reasonable about the state's theory that Bryant and Milam kidnapped Till in Leflore County, drove several miles to a plantation in Sunflower County, then doubled back into Tallahatchie County to dump the body." Until the end, Carlton and the rest of the defense team insisted that the Till affair was confined to Leflore County: Till assaulted Carolyn Bryant, was kidnapped, and released in or near

Money, Mississippi. This particular geography, of course, obligated the defense to make a bizarre, hard-to-believe argument that the body pulled from the river in Tallahatchie County did not belong to Emmett Till. In support of this theory, John Whitten suggested that the NAACP had planted the body in the river as a mechanism for disrupting southern mores. He even hinted that they obtained the body with the help of Howard and his Taborian Hospital in Mound Bayou.[40] To counteract Mamie Bradley's identification of her son's body, Carlton weakly suggested that "sometimes mothers believe what they want to believe."[41]

The jury certainly believed what it wanted to believe. They voted unanimously for the one-county theory in which Till could not have been murdered because there was no corpus delicti—no body-as-evidence-of-crime. While the jury thus robbed Sunflower County of legal status in Till's story, it did nothing to stem the determination of Howard and the black press to spread the word of Sunflower County. Indeed, due to the posttrial commemorative labor of Hicks, Booker, Howard, Wilson, Adams, and "Dixon," Sunflower County did far more than survive the decision of the jury. It thrived. During the trial proper, the story of Sunflower County depended entirely on the three white reporters who were privy to Howard's information—primarily Porteous, but also Featherston and Shoemaker. Starting eleven days after the trial, however, when Hicks filed his first dispatch, the story of Sunflower County surged. Multipart, serialized versions of the story ran in black papers across the country. From the *California Eagle*, to the *Atlanta Black Star*, to the *Baltimore Afro-American*, to the *Cleveland Call and Post*, to the *Chicago Defender*, the black press provided retroactive, play-by-play accounts of the trial. These accounts rehearsed the legal proceedings, but challenged those proceedings with stories of Sunflower County. Between October 4, 1955, and February 23, 1956, the aforementioned newspapers ran no less than twenty distinct articles about the relevance and consequences of Sunflower County. Alongside the black press was the lecture circuit of Howard, though which thousands of people (Martin Luther King Jr. and Rosa Parks included) heard the Sunflower County version of Till's murder. All told, during the months following the trial, the commemoration of Sunflower

County became a form of black resistance, a mechanism for both re-membering Emmett Till and challenging the terms on which his story had theretofore been told.

As Sunflower County became a technique of countercommemora-tion, it cast in bold relief the potential of spatial questions to register racial commitments. When the murder was moved thirty miles west, three interrelated things happened. First, in addition to establishing, ex post facto, the simple fact of the murder, the Sunflower County narrative dramatically expanded the size of the murder party. Second, when the black press moved the murder to Sunflower County, they introduced an entire cast of characters who would, henceforth, serve as proxies for the county. The most significant members of this cast were Leslie Milam, Henry Lee Loggins, Levi Collins, and Willie Reed. From October of 1955 through the present day, these characters have been focal points for controversy precisely because they are relevant only if Till was murdered in Sunflower County by a murder party of more than two people. For these four characters, it is impossible to separate questions of racism from questions of geography: the inten-sity of racism shifts as the murder site moves east or west based on the inclusion of these men in the story of Till's murder.

Finally, the story of Sunflower County opened the possibility of further legal action. Because only J. W. Milam and Roy Bryant had been tried, stories of Sunflower County rendered a new set of actors vulnerable to legal action. From Leslie Milam, to Loggins and Collins, to the mysterious "white men" who were reported to have accompa-nied Bryant and Milam to the Sturdivant Plantation, memories of Sunflower County jeopardized a wide range of participants. Although future legal action was a long time coming, when it did come in 2004, it was accompanied by a resurgence of Sunflower County narratives.

## WILLIAM BRADFORD HUIE AND THE SECOND ERASURE OF SUNFLOWER COUNTY

At 7 p.m. on the evening of October 28, 1955, freelance journalist William Bradford Huie arranged a quiet meeting in the Sumner law offices of Breland and Whitten. Attended by murderers J. W. Milam and Roy Bryant; Roy's wife, Carolyn; and their lawyer, John L. Whitten, the meeting would fundamentally reshape the geography of Till's murder.[42] If the meeting had a sense of urgency to it, it is because everyone in the room had something to gain.

Huie wanted to sell the inside story of Till's murder to *Look* magazine, but the market was already saturated with on-the-scene, exposé-style stories of Till's murder.[43] In this sense, Huie could not have picked a worse time. Late October 1955 was the heyday of the Sunflower County tales being pushed by Hicks, Howard, Booker, and Wilson. In fact, the very next day, the *Baltimore Afro-American* would run Hicks's article under the heading "Unbelievable! Inside Story of Miss. Trial." Hicks regaled his readers with stories of "secret meetings, underground movements, [and] cloak-and-dagger tactics" to get the "inside story of racial conditions in Mississippi."[44] Hicks was simply the tip of the iceberg. His "boasts of originality, authenticity, [daring-do,] and truthfulness would be repeated *ad infinitum* by journalists selling competing versions of Till's story."[45] In the context of so much press, why would *Look* pay for yet another story, written by an outsider who had not even been to the trial?

Huie was not the only one with a problem. Murderers J. W. Milam and Roy Bryant had fallen on hard times. The black sharecroppers who once patronized Bryant's Grocery and Meat Market now refused their patronage. Nine days before the meeting, the Bryants were forced to put the Grocery and Meat Market up for sale.[46] For his part, Milam lost the financial backing needed to farm in the Delta and, within a year, was living in a shack without plumbing.[47] Although financial support from the white establishment flowed liberally during the trial, it dried up quickly thereafter, and the murderers were hard-pressed for money.

While Huie faced an oversaturated market and the killers were newly impoverished, the law firm of Breland and Whitten had their own problems—admittedly of a rather different nature. The lawyers had initially declined to defend Milam and Bryant. But as the publicity mounted, and as the NAACP issued searing—and sometimes false—

attacks on the entire state of Mississippi, the trial came to represent much larger stakes.[48] No longer about the brutal death of a child, the trial was now about the legitimacy of the entire region. Stephen J. Whitfield captured this shift.

> Local pride and self-sufficiency were imperiled, and the capacity of whites to govern themselves . . . came to be the central issue in the Till case. The primacy of states' rights became so urgent, the feelings of defensiveness so raw and exposed, that the murder of an adolescent declined in moral magnitude.[49]

If it was simply a murder trial, Breland and Whitten were uninterested. If, however, the trial became a referendum on the Delta, well, that was a cause worth defending. And defend it they did, either pro bono or at cut rates, depending who you ask.[50]

But the trial did not have its intended effect. In their desperation to defend their home ground, the lawyers concocted widely disbelieved claims: that the body in the river was planted by the NAACP, that it had been there for weeks, and that Emmett Till's mother could not identify her own son. By October of 1955, these claims were widely ridiculed and understood for what they were, the thinnest of cover for a murder and an acquittal that were motivated, in whole, by racism. While the lawyers had set out to defend the Delta and buttress local mores, Tallahatchie County had become a national byword.

In just a few months, the nationally known journalist David Halberstam would skewer Tallahatchie County in the April 1956 edition of *The Reporter*. Halberstam described a county characterized by arbitrary violence and stringent racism. "'There's open season on the Negroes now,' one man said. 'They've got no protection, and any peckerwood who wants to can go shoot himself one, and we'll free him. It gets worse and worse.'" Alongside the arbitrary violence, Halberstam cited the lawyer's far-fetched theories as evidence of pervasive racism. With a heavy dose of irony, he opined that in Tallahatchie County the "good people can tell you in one breath that that wasn't the Till boy's body they fished out of the river."[51] Halberstam's story proved that the lawyers' efforts during the trial had backfired. Instead of justifying the Delta, it opened the region to further ridicule.

Although Huie, the murderers, and the lawyers each arrived in Sumner on October 28 burdened with problems, they capped off the night by sharing a bottle of whiskey. They had just put the finishing touches on a mutually beneficial arrangement. William Bradford Huie would write the story of Till's murder for *Look* magazine. To solve his problem of a saturated market, the lawyers gave him complete access to their clients. For five nights—October 24–28, 1955—Whitten arranged for Huie to meet with the murderers in his Sumner office.[52] In these meetings, Huie told his publishers, the killers told him "everything they knew and felt." Armed with the knowledge and feelings of the murderers, Huie knew that his article could thrive in any market. In his own immodest estimate, a first-person narration of Till's murder would prove "more explosive than UNCLE TOM'S CABIN—and a damn site more honest."[53]

Once Huie had access to the murderers, he was quick to mitigate their financial problems. He promised them 20 percent of the royalties and a $3,150 advance. In addition, as a thank-you to the lawyers for arranging the visits, he promised them 10 percent of the royalties and a $1,269 down payment.[54] He would later explain: "For me to publish the fact that they did commit that murder would be what we call 'libel per se,' meaning I am libeling these men when I say they murdered because they had already been tried and found not guilty of murder . . . therefore, I'll in effect pay them for the right to libel them."[55] It should be noted that Roy Bryant would later claim that "he ain't never made a damn nickel" off the story. In fact, he even claimed that his "only regret" from the murder was that J. W. Milam got all the money.[56] Regardless of whether or not Bryant ever actually received money, it is certain that the promise of $3,000 must have seemed like a lifeline in October of 1955.

Finally, now that Huie had his story and the murderers some money, it remained only to solve the embarrassment of the lawyers—whose concocted account of the murder was transparently false and widely ridiculed. The arrangement reached that fateful night gave them a second chance to craft their own version of Till's murder—a version that minimized the violence done to Till and, critically, limited the murder party to the two people who had already been tried. This last point is critical. At the very moment of their meeting, the wide circulation of Sunflower County meant that Mississippi was being ridiculed not simply for acquitting Bryant and Milam, but also for failing to indict others. Huie was now offering them a second chance. He could sanitize the murder by adjusting the size of the murder party to the number of the acquitted—and all of this by eliminating Sunflower County. Again.

After it was published, Milam would refer to Huie's story as the "Mississippi" version of the story.[57] Indeed, it is only because it was the Mississippi version that Huie could tell his editors at *Look*,

> Publication of this story, with all its revolting details, is exactly what Breland's group in Mississippi *wants*. They want to "put the North and the NAACP and the niggers *on notice*." My proposal strikes them as being a "good propaganda move." They think of me as a "rough writer" who ain't no nigger-lover and who'll "lay it on the line."

In an October 1956 letter, Huie told John Whitten that his writing on Till's murder would be "a bitter dose for the NAACP and the 'liberals.'" He then asked Whitten to pass a message on to his partner: "Tell Mr. Breland I'll send him the [damning army] file on [Emmett's father] Pvt. Louis Till when I'm finished with it, and he can send it around and have it read aloud at all the meetings of the Citizens' Councils."[58] Huie, in other words, suggested to Breland and Whitten that his work on behalf of Till's memory would be a "good propaganda move" for white supremacists. His telling of the story, he suggested, should be considered by the lawyers as a second chance to defend their home ground. The same motivation that led them to defend the murderers in the first place now animated their desire to let William Bradford Huie tell their story.

Although the story Huie printed in *Look* is told in the words of J. W. Milam, scholars have suggested that Milam was simply giving voice to the opinions of lawyers J. J. Breland and John L. Whitten. Near the end of the story, for example, Milam muses philosophically about the relationship of the Till murder to integration and *Brown vs. Board*. Houck and Grindy suggest that Milam simply could not—or would not—have "waxed" with such polish.

> Careful readers might have also been skeptical of Milam's ostensible rhetorical talents. It would take a degree of intellectual abstraction to situate and articulate what he was about to do in the context of a post-*Brown* world—to say nothing of doing it with a loaded pistol, while under the influence, and with a rapidly rising summer sun. By all accounts, Big Milam was not one for abstraction or careful rationalization; no, his talents, by his own admission, were in killing and in working negroes.[59]

If the prose in *Look* magazine was not Milam's, to whom did it belong? Although a certain answer to this question is impossible, the evidence points to the ringleader of the southern defense, J. J. Breland. In Huie's article, "Milam" is intensely local: "Niggers ain't gonna vote where I live." He is devoted to his "folks." He labels Till an outsider: "Chicago boy." And he suggests that Till was sent down, presumably by the NAACP, to "stir up trouble." All of this, down to the level of word choice, resembles nothing so much as Breland's rant against integration and his desire to put the North "on notice"—quoted above in the letter from Huie.

It is no wonder, then, that the lawyers shared a bottle of whiskey with Huie that October evening. Huie was going to write their (new) version of the story. Further, he was going give their version indisputable authority by putting it in the first-person voice of J. W. Milam, and he was going to pay them for the trouble. It was a win-win-win situation. Titled "The Shocking Story of Approved Killing in Mississippi," Huie's story solved three problems at once. Huie got his story, the murderers got their money, and the lawyers got a second chance to control the memory of Emmett Till.

There was only one hitch. Before *Look* editor Dan Mich would touch the story, he required signed "Consent and Release" forms from every person named therein. After all, Huie's story claimed that legally innocent men were in fact guilty of murder. Although Huie understood the need for legal releases, he was unsure how many he could obtain. Critically, it was the technical matter of "Consent and Release" forms that, once again, connected the fate of Sunflower County to the size of the murder party. In an October 12 letter to the NAACP's Roy Wilkins, Huie wrote that there were "four in the torture-and-murder party."[60] However, since only two of these men had been tried and therefore enjoyed the protections of double jeopardy, there was some uncertainty about the willingness of the untried murderers to sign a release. Huie thus asked *Look* editor Daniel Mich how to proceed. "If we do not have their [the two undisclosed murderers] releases, shall we name them in the story or not? Shall we quote them anonymously in any part of the action?"[61] By the time he wrote the Chicago newspaperman Basil Walters on October 18, he had worked out a solution. After telling Mr. Walters that he knew "all four" murderers by name, he suggested the following: "We can, if necessary, omit the names of the other two. We can even avoid all reference to them, though I would urge any publisher to state that they were present, to quote whatever they said at any point in the action, but not to name them."[62]

It is worth stressing that Huie, when he wrote these letters, had not yet met with the murderers or their lawyers. Without yet needing to accommodate himself to their political needs, it is no surprise that he claimed there were four murderers. That number was circulating widely. In fact, on the same day that Huie wrote to Walters—October 18—the *Atlanta Daily World* ran Hicks's tale of the late-night manhunt for witnesses that eventuated in the testimony of Willie Reed—testimony that suggested four white men were involved.[63] Ten days before that, Howard had told the same story to a crowd of 2,500 people in Baltimore's Sharp Street Church. Although Howard changed Reed's name to "Willie Ames" for the protection of the witness, he rehearsed the key points of Reed's testimony: "there were four men on the front seat" of the truck that arrived on Sturdivant Plantation with Till's body in the back. Given this context, the only surprising thing about Huie's October 18 claim is that he could *name* the four white men. No one in the black press was able to do this.[64] Until he met with the lawyers, Huie's updates from Mississippi were consonant with the stories then circulating about Sunflower County.

By the evening of October 23, however, Huie was telling a different story. He had just spent the first of five sessions with Roy Bryant and J. W. Milam in the offices of Breland and Whitten. Upon returning to his room at the Greenwood Holiday Inn, he dashed off an exuberant account of the interview for his editor.

> I have just returned from Sumner where I spent an almost unbeliev-able day in Whitten's office—with Bryant and Milam. We have reached a verbal agreement on all points; and they have told me the story of the abduction and murder. This was really amazing, for it was the *first* time they have told this story of the abduction and murder.... I can't see how it can miss being one the most sensational stories ever published.[65]

In addition to conveying his excitement about the interviews and the potential they had as a magazine story, his letter served a very practical purpose: it reduced the number of "Consent and Release" forms *Look* required. He told Mich that he now believed there were only two people in the murder party. "Of this I am now certain: there were not, after all, *four* men involved in the abduction-and-murder: there were only two. So when we have these releases from Bryant and Milam and the woman, we are completely safe."[66]

While it is impossible to know why Huie changed his mind, scholars have long assumed that the murderers lied to Huie and he believed it.[67] Perhaps he was so taken with the experience of hearing the murder told firsthand in the offices of Breland and Whitten that he uncritically accepted the story they told. As Terry Wagner put it, Huie had "an unjustified faith in every word that J. W. Milam told him."[68] Houck and Grindy put the matter stronger, concluding that Huie was "bamboozled and *Look* hoodwinked."[69] Sharon Monteith puts the matter stronger still: "Huie failed to scent all the bullshit in Milam's account."[70]

If Huie was simply being gullible, however, it is essential to remember that his gullibility was motivated. He had a material interest in believing the two-murderer version of the story for the simple reason that it was publishable. It did not require "Consent and Release" forms from anyone who did not enjoy the protections of double-jeopardy and was, for this reason, far more attractive to *Look*. Quite apart from questions of truthfulness and naïveté, the two-murderer story conveyed to William Bradford Huie in the Sumner law offices of Breland and Whitten offered him an easy road to publication.

Regardless of his motivations, when Huie's "Shocking Story of Approved Murder in Mississippi" came out in January of 1956, it featured only two murderers, Roy Bryant and J. W. Milam. It also featured only two counties: Leflore County, where Till whistled and from which he was abducted, and Tallahatchie County, where he was murdered and his body was recovered. These two facts were connected: any two-murderer version of the story *could not* include Sunflower County. At a bare minimum, the presence of Sunflower County required the presence of J. W. Milam's brother Leslie—who managed the Sturdivant Plantation. But Leslie Milam had not been tried, he did not sign a release form, and thus he could not be implicated in Huie's story. If there were to be only two murderers, there could be only two counties. So Huie moved the murder approximately 19 miles east, to an abandoned spot of riverbank along the Tallahatchie River in Tallahatchie County. By moving the murder site across county lines, Huie limited the range of guilt by limiting the geography involved. Two murderers, two counties.

In order to make this version of the story coherent, Huie fundamentally altered the facts of the murder. In addition to moving the murder site 19 miles, he also eliminated scores of participants, created a stoic, affect-less version of Emmett Till, and invented a fictional location from which the gin fan was stolen.

### A Smaller "Shocking Story"

When Huie's "Shocking Story" is read alongside the other stories of Till's murder circulating in October 1955, one of its most conspicuous features is the range of characters who do not appear. Levi Collins, Henry Lee Loggins, Willie Hubbard, Willie Reed, Frank Young, Mandy Bradley, Add Reed, Medgar Evers, James Hicks, Clark Porteous, and even T. R. M. Howard—by October of 1955, all of these were commonly cited names in the various stories of Emmett Till. Even Dan Wakefield's October 1 report in the *Nation*—not particularly focused on Sunflower County or the exaggerated murder party—mentioned several of these names.[71] Huie, by contrast, wrote every last one of them out of Till's story.

Going through the list of excluded names, one thing becomes clear. The decisive trait each of these characters share is the capacity to route Till's murder through Sunflower County. Every last one of them are relevant to Till's story if—and only if—the murder party passed through Sunflower County. Perhaps the most significant person not mentioned by Huie, however, was Leslie Milam, J. W. Milam's brother and Roy Bryant's half brother. More than anyone else, Leslie Milam was the reason the murder happened in Sunflower County. Just before he died in 1974, Leslie Milam confessed to a local minister, Macklyn Hubbel of Cleveland, Mississippi's First Baptist Church, that he was involved in the murder in Emmett Till.[72] J. W. Milam confessed the same before his death in 1980. In the course of a phone interview during which he thought he was speaking with a young, sympathetic white girl, J. W. told how four white men and two black men took Till to Leslie Milam's farm in Sunflower County. He told her that the murderers—all six of whom he named—drove out to the Mississippi River before taking Till to the Sturdivant Plantation where he was killed and stripped of his clothing.[73] J. W. Milam, in other words, confirmed in detail the stories of Sunflower County that had been circulated by the black press in October of 1955. Finally, in 1985 Roy Bryant was recorded on audiotape boasting of how he "done whopped the son of a bitch." As Devery Anderson relates the story, Bryant confirmed "that Till was tortured and murdered inside of the shed" on the Sturdivant Plantation.[74] In sum, through a series of late-in-life disclosures, Bryant and the two Milams agreed that Till was killed in Sunflower County. Based on all this evidence, the FBI concluded in 2006 that "Till was killed in the barn on Leslie Milam's farm."[75]

The story that William Bradford Huie published in *Look* briefly aligns with the telephone confessions of J. W. Milam. Both accounts agree that the murderers took Till to the Mississippi River, looking for a bluff with which to scare him. As Huie tells the story, the *two* brothers were looking for a bluff near Rosedale known as the "scariest place in the Delta." "Big Milam's idea," Huie relates, "was to stand him up there on that bluff, 'whip' him with the .45, and then shine the light on down there toward the water and make him think you're gonna knock him in."[76] Whether or not such a place exists, both Huie (in *Look*) and Milam (1980 confession) noted that they couldn't find it. And here, critically, is where the two accounts diverge.

Where Milam's deathbed confession suggests that the murder party proceeded directly to Leslie Milam's barn, Huie wrote that "they drove back to Milam's house in Glendora." It was in the shed behind Milam's home that they "began 'whipping' him" and from which they took him to the river where they shot him and left him.[77] Critically, if this is true, the murderers had no need to stop in Sunflower County, and Huie had no need to obtain a "Consent and Release" form from Leslie Milam. The smaller murder party and the Glendora murder site were a package deal; by moving the murder site, Huie was able to write out of his narrative those such as Leslie Milam from whom he could not obtain release forms.

### The Emotional Life of Emmett Till

Henry Lee Loggins and Levi Collins were more difficult to eliminate. These latter two had, according to the black press, been recruited for the precise reason of keeping Till in the back of the truck. This was an important job, as even without Sunflower County, Huie's story still features more miles driven than any other account of the murder. From Money in Leflore County, east to the Mississippi River, and then, when they could not find their bluff, back to Glendora in Tallahatchie County. Before they finally go to the river, however, Huie has them drive back to Boyle (thirty miles to the west) to secure a gin fan before retreating a final time to Tallahatchie County. All told, scholars estimate that Huie's itinerary required the murder party to drive approximately two hundred miles.[78]

The sheer mileage was a problem for Huie. Why would Till lie docile in the back of the truck for so long? Especially when the vast majority of those miles were *before* he was tortured. Huie can't include Collins and Loggins without inflating the murder party, introducing eyewitnesses who did not appear in court, and breaking his promise to the lawyers. But he nonetheless required a mechanism to keep Till in the back of the truck. As Till's mother would later note, according to Huie, "Emmett just sat there and went along for the ride."[79] Huie's account of why Till just "sat there" is the least convincing part of the "Shocking Story."

> At some point, when the truck slowed down, why hadn't Bobo [Till] jumped and run? He wasn't tied; *nobody was holding him.* A partial answer is that those Chevrolet pickups have a wraparound rear window the size of a windshield. Bryant could watch him. But the real answer is the remarkable part of the story. Bobo wasn't afraid of them! He was as tough as they were. He didn't think they had the guts to kill him.[80]

Till wasn't afraid of them? His alleged bravery has gone down as one of the most uncritically accepted parts of the entire lore. In the acclaimed 1987 *Eyes on the Prize*, Huie expands on the point. "Young Till never realized the danger he was in." This is difficult to believe. "It strains credulity," Whitfield wrote, "that Till could have been so impervious to the danger he faced."[81] The sheer persistence of the mythology of a not-scared Till is nowhere more evident than this: the only museum in the world dedicated primarily to the murder of Emmett Till is called the Emmett Till Historic *Intrepid* Center (see chapter 5)—the "intrepid" designating the fact that Till "was fearless in facing death at the hands of his kidnappers."[82] How a fourteen-year-old boy, kidnapped at 2 a.m., tortured, and conveyed around the Delta in the back of a truck could not be scared is simply unfathomable.

It is impossible to know the precise emotions Till felt that night— although fear must have been among them. Regardless of the precise extent to which Till was scared, we can say for certain that Huie's notscared Till was a mechanism for eliminating the participation of Loggins and Collins, who were there only because a scared boy would run. Without a scared boy, there was no reason to keep Collins or Loggins in the story. And this, of course, served Huie just fine, eliminating the need for release forms he could not obtain.

When Willie Reed and Frank Young bore witness to the inclusion of Sunflower County, they also testified to the emotional life of Emmett Till. Until the very end, they reported, Till was crying out, "Oh!" Willie Reed spoke of "hollering," and "Amos Dixon" wrote of moans, of "crying and begging." A Sunflower County witness named Warren Hampton remembers playing by the side of the road as Milam's truck passed near the Sturdivant Plantation. He recalls hollering coming from the back of the truck.[83] *Of course!* Given the conditions of torture, what boy—what man—would not cry out? However, by the time of Huie's "Shocking Story," Till's emotional response to torture had been indexed to an impossible place: Sunflower County. By robbing Till of his emotions, Huie eliminated the need for Loggins and Collins, and by extension Sunflower County.

Even the feelings of Emmett Till were, in the end, a partisan (and racial) tool designed to keep the murder party thirty miles away from Leslie Milam and Sunflower County. His very temperament was falsified, politicized, and racialized: a means of evading Sunflower County, protecting Leslie Milam, and reducing Till's story to two murderers and two counties. Only a stoic Till could be murdered by two people in Tallahatchie County.

## Sunflower County and the Gin Fan

Consider, finally, the origin of the gin fan with which Till's body was weighted in the Tallahatchie River. In Huie's account, after Bryant and Milam (alone) had driven Till over one hundred miles—from Money to the Mississippi River and back to Glendora—the whipping commenced, Till remained stoic, and Milam decided to "make an example" of him. It was then, Huie records, that Milam realized he needed a weight to hold Till's body in the river and thought of a discarded cotton-gin fan at the Progressive Ginning Company outside of Boyle, Mississippi, in Bolivar County. So the three of them set out once more, Milam and Bryant in the front, the unguarded Till in the back. They drove another sixty miles round trip to get the fan before proceeding to the banks of the Tallahatchie River, only a few miles from where they began. At the riverbank, Huie records, Till's last moments were characterized by a refusal to cry out (he "stood silently") and a refusal to be scared ("the youth still thought they were bluffing"). He was then killed on the banks of the Tallahatchie River—stoic and unafraid.[84]

Yet this account, again, strains credulity, and not simply for reasons of unlikely emotional fortitude. If Milam did indeed torture Emmett Till in the shed behind his home in Glendora—as Huie claims—one wonders why he would drive thirty-four miles to the Progressive Ginning Company simply to retrieve an object with which to weight Till's body in the water. This question gains even more urgency when we note that the arrival of daylight made Bryant and Milam nervous. If they were in such a hurry, why travel so far to obtain so common an object?

The question gains more urgency still once we note that Milam's home was next door to the Glendora Cotton Gin—and still more urgency when we realize that Milam's good friend Elmer Kimbell worked at the gin and was likely part of the murder party. When FBI agent Dale Killinger interviewed Carolyn Donham (nee Bryant) in 2004, she claimed that Kimbell was with the murder party when they returned to Bryant's Grocery and Meat Market to have her identify

Emmett Till.[85] When all these factors are considered, a trip to Progressive Ginning Company seems unlikely to say the least. It would have involved an unnecessary sixty-mile round trip, undertaken when the perpetrators were already nervous about the passage of time, and when they already had access to a nearby gin through a friend who was also, according to Carolyn, an accomplice in the murder.

Why, then, did Huie invent the burdensome tale of an unneeded trip to Boyle? Much like Leslie Milam, Elmer Kimbell had not signed a waiver and, any implication that he may have been involved would have jeopardized Huie's ability to print the story. The trip to Boyle, in other words, was one more mechanism for restricting the size of the murder party, this time by eliminating Elmer Kimbell. Huie could tell Till's story only if the fan came from Boyle.

Huie's fictional tale of the Progressive Ginning Company has been so influential that, in 2007, *after* the ETMC decided that the fan was stolen from Glendora, they designed a commemorative marker that referred to the Glendora Cotton Gin as the "Progressive Ginning Company." Plater Robinson caught the mistake; his correction is worth quoting in full.

> The Glendora gin is not the Boyle gin. The killers told Huie that they got the gin fan in Boyle, Mississippi [at the Progressive Ginning Company]. This is a lie, and part of the cover up. This particular lie was designed to distract attention from the Drew, Mississippi, tractor shed, on the Clint Shurden plantation. That plantation was managed by Leslie Milam, brother and half-brother to J. W. Milam and Roy Bryant, and was the setting of Emmett's murder. . . . The Boyle gin was part of the cover up, thrown in the "mix" to explain away those long hours that the killers spent at Drew.[86]

Boyle was part of the cover-up, designed to protect Kimbell and conceal "those long hours that the killers spent at Drew," in Sunflower County.

From the misplaced murder site, to the size of the murder party, to the unlikely stoicism of Emmett Till, to the invention of the Progressive Ginning Company, virtually every aspect of the story now appears as a concerted effort to eliminate all traces of Sunflower County. And why wouldn't it? Huie was working for the white defense lawyers; it should be no surprise that his tales countered those published by the black press. Hicks, Howard, Booker, and their colleagues were using Sunflower County as a principle of black resistance; Huie, the lawyers, and the murderers were using it to minimize, all at once, the size of the murder party, the extent of the racism, and the geographical range of the murder. In both cases, Sunflower County was the relay point through which questions of race attached themselves to questions of commemoration.

### MAPPING THE MURDER: POST-HUIE MAPS AND THE FINAL ERASURE OF SUNFLOWER COUNTY

Until the twenty-first century, Huie's basic narrative of two men, acting alone, killing a not-scared boy on the banks of the Tallahatchie River was seldom challenged.[87] In 2003, however, Mamie Till-Mobley decisively broke with this tradition. Writing with Christopher Benson, she provided a detailed rebuke of Huie's story, noting the racial motivations driving Huie to erase Sunflower County.[88] Two years later, Keith Beauchamp's documentary *The Untold Story of Emmett Louis Till* questioned the veracity of Huie's tale, suggesting that the murder party may have been as large as fourteen people.[89] Finally, in 2006, the FBI's publication of the findings of their 2004 reinvestigation dramatically ended Huie's reign as the official teller of Till's story. Although the bureau did not name fourteen accomplices, it upended the reputation of William Bradford Huie, turning him into "the man who publicized a calculated, largely fabricated confession."[90]

Long before any of this, however, one of Huie's central assumptions was being slowly called into question—and would eventually be discarded altogether. Although the black press and Huie disagreed about virtually every facet of Till's murder, they both agreed that the categories of place and race—of geography and justice—moved in tandem. It was this assumption that has been called into question.

Indeed, the story of Till's post-*Look* memory in the twentieth century is the story of the growing—and for some, total—irrelevance of geography as a category of racial history. While scholars—including me—were quick to challenge the plotline of Huie's story, they gradually allowed geography to function as an independent variable, as if questions of race and place were wholly exogenous concerns. The compelling allure of this logic was made particularly clear to me on a summer day in 2014 as I was standing beside the ruins of Bryant's Grocery and Meat Market. On that day Simeon Wright explained to me why he did not care to accompany my colleagues and I to Sunflower County. He suggested that it did not matter *where* Till was killed as much as the simple fact that he *was* killed, and that he was killed for being the wrong color in the wrong place and the wrong time. For Wright, race and place and had become independent variables; he cared about the racism that motivated the killing, but not about where the killing happened. This capacity to analytically separate race from place was prepared for by a decades-long trend away from the assumptions that once structured the accounts of the black press and Huie's "Shocking Story."

The first post-*Look* map of Till's murder was published in 1963 by Hugh Stephen Whitaker (see figure 5).[91] Whitaker's account of the murder is massively indebted to William Bradford Huie and his hand-drawn map is a faithful rendering of Huie's itinerary. It remains, to this day, the most complete visualization of Huie's tale. Two things need to be stressed about Whitaker's map. First, although Huie was clearly his primary source, Whitaker began the process of disjoining the categories of race and space. Despite the fact that Whitaker offered a two-county, two-person theory of the murder, he also introduced a measure of uncertainty about the size of the murder party without suggesting that this uncertainty could have any ramifications on the map he published. Before narrating Huie's story, Whitaker provided this disclaimer: "It is possible that Milam deviated from the truth in slight detail in order to protect other persons who might have been involved from criminal action."[92] Although he quickly admitted that this was a distant possibility and implied that he in fact trusted Milam's ac-

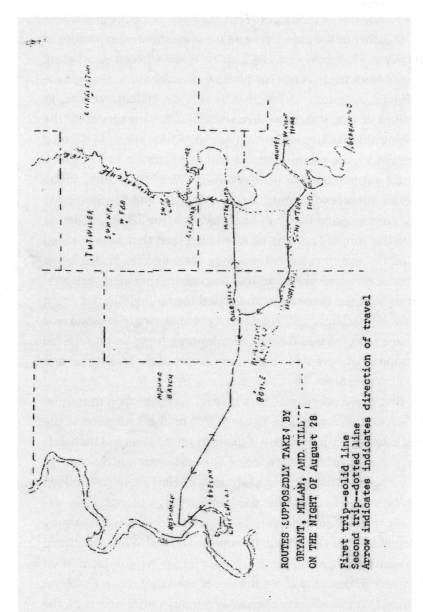

FIGURE 5. Steve Whitaker's 1963 hand-drawn recreation of William Bradford Huie's murder route. The geography recorded here dominated the memory of Till's murder from 1956 to 2005. Note that the murder party passes through Sunflower County (the narrow rectangular county in the middle) but does not stop there. Map by Hugh Stephen Whitaker. Used by permission.

count (as given to Huie), Whitaker nonetheless opened the possibility that the size of the murder party need not be calibrated to the geography of the murder. He cautioned that the size of the murder party might be wrong but gave the reader no analogous warning about the contents of the map. To be sure, this is a subtle move. However slight it may be, its importance stems from the fact that, in the decades that followed Whitaker, the subtle autonomy he gave to questions of geography became more and more pronounced.

Second, Whitaker's map is a good reminder that Huie's is a two-county itinerary only in the sense that the legal events of the episode (the kidnapping and the murder) are located in two counties (Leflore and Tallahatchie).[93] The scope of Whitaker's map is unusually large, stretching from the Mississippi River on the west to the Tallahatchie River on the east. His map covers more square miles than any other published map of Till's murder. He places both the kidnapping and the murder on the east side of the map, on the banks of the Tallahatchie River. Between these two points, he plots the hundreds of miles driven as Huie's truncated murder party was looking for the bluff on the Mississippi, commuting back and forth to Glendora, and retrieving the fan. This journey took them straight through Sunflower County (in one side, out the other) *twice* before finally arriving in Tallahatchie County at daybreak. In 1963—the year of Whitaker's map—these intervening miles between the kidnapping in Leflore County and the murder in Tallahatchie County were legally innocuous and, from the perspective of Till commemoration, irrelevant. Eventually, however, these miles would come to play a critical role in undoing the tendency to treat the categories of race and geography as independent variables. This insight, however, would need to wait until the twenty-first century.

Following Whitaker, the next major telling of Till's story was the landmark 1987 documentary *Eyes on the Prize*. Produced by Henry Hampton over the course of nineteen years, *Eyes on the Prize* has become the "principal film account of the most important American social justice movement of the twentieth century."[94] On the surface, *Eyes on the Prize* followed Huie's account to the letter. It even put an aged, white-haired Huie on the screen, and gave him the privilege of narrating Till's story for yet another generation. Unlike *Look*, however, Hampton did not grant Huie the exclusive rights to the story. He also reintroduced James Hicks—the long-forgotten African American reporter who discovered Collins and Loggins and who, with the help of Howard, first discovered the relevance of Sunflower County. Hicks had not appeared in any version of Till's story since the *Look* confession came out in January 1956. For a 1980s generation, unfamiliar with the legacy of October 1955, *Eyes on the Prize* was the first time Hicks was part of the story. Unfortunately, Hicks did not talk about his undercover work on behalf of Sunflower County. Nor did he talk about Collins or Loggins. Had he done so, the effect would have been similar to that of Whitaker—pushing apart the categories of race and place by suggesting that the insertion of Sunflower County into Till's story need not alter the basic story told by Huie of two murderers acting alone to kill a stoic boy.

As it happened, however, Hicks spoke only of the severity of the racial climate of 1950s Mississippi. With no mention of Sunflower County, *Eyes on the Prize* gave the false impression that there was no essential conflict between the stories of Huie and Hicks. And thus, much like Whitaker, the wedge slipped in between race and place was ever so slim, dependent for its effect on a viewer who knew more about Hicks than Hampton allowed on the screen. The following year, the crack opened by Whitaker and Hampton between the domains of geography and justice would be blown wide open by Stephen J. Whitfield.

In his 1988 *A Death in the Delta*, Whitfield published the next map of Till's murder. The only book on Till's murder published by a university press in the twentieth-century, *A Death in the Delta* departed in important ways from the monolithic geography of Huie and Whitaker. Whitfield reintroduced the lost cast of characters that featured so prominently in October 1955: Leslie Milam, Willie Reed, Levi Collins, Henry Lee Loggins, James Hicks, Ruby Hurley, and Medgar Evers—none of whom had been mentioned by Huie or Whitaker and all of whom fit only the Sunflower County version of the murder. Whitfield also noted that Huie's account was "too narrowly rendered" and that other accomplices may have been involved.[95] Yet, rather than rebuke the Huie/Whitaker narrative as fundamentally misguided—as the inclusion of the above-named suggested he might—Whitfield assimilated the story of Willie Reed into the story of William Bradford Huie. This assimilation was made manifest in the first map of Till's murder to be published with the imprimatur of a university press (see figure 6). Although Whitfield specifically noted that Reed's testimony referenced the Sunflower County plantation managed by Leslie Milam, and although he knew full well that Collins and Loggins fit *only* in Reed's version of the story, his map excluded Sunflower County. Published as a frontispiece opposite the title page, the map featured only Leflore County and Tallahatchie County. Its caption reads: "Emmett Till walked fatefully into a store in Money; he was killed a week later near Glendora."[96] Thus, although Whitfield was careful to *document* the competing versions of Till's death, and although he noted that "the testimony of Wright and Reed . . . is simply too compelling to be discounted," he nonetheless followed the same geography as Huie and Whitaker.[97] While Whitaker had simply acknowledged the possibility of an exaggerated murder party, Whitfield claims that the evidence in favor of such a party is "compelling." He even names names. Yet, like Whitaker before him, he reproduced the two-county geography of William Bradford Huie. Geography and racial justice had become independent categories. For the first time, the two long-entwined, critical debates of Till commemoration—who was involved, where it happened—were treated as if they were unrelated. Whitfield introduced Willie Reed and his testimony of a six-person murder party *without adjusting his map*.

This disconnection between the geography of the murder and size of the murder party reached its climax in the powerful, award-winning documentary *The Murder of Emmett Till*. Released by Mac-Arthur "Genius" Fellow Stanley Nelson in 2003, *The Murder of Emmett Till* was the first documentary treatment of the murder to appear since *Eyes on the Prize*. Much like Hampton, Nelson remained captivated by "the convenience of the *Look* confession as well as the impunity

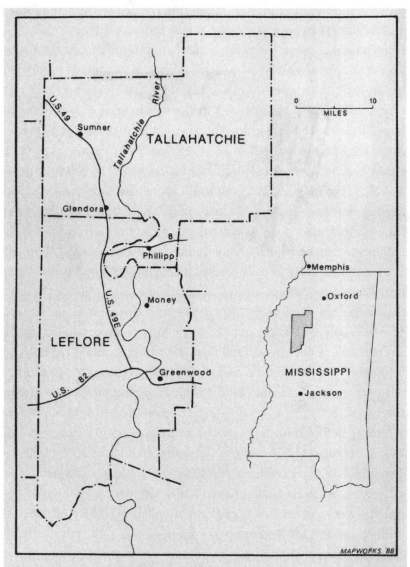

The northwestern wedge of Mississippi is the flat and fertile Delta, where Robert Penn Warren, among others, observed a "sad and baleful beauty." The Delta has historically had the state's highest ratio of blacks to whites. In August 1955, Emmett Till walked fatefully into a store in Money; he was killed a week later near Glendora. Till's corpse was recovered near Phillipp. Less than a month later, the accused killers were tried in Sumner, the county seat of Tallahatchie County. *(Herb Heidt, Mapworks)*

**FIGURE 6.** This 1988 map is the first map of Till's murder to be printed by a university press. Note both the complete absence of Sunflower County and the caption, which indicates that Till was killed in Glendora (Tallahatchie County).

and relish with which Milam told his story."[98] In a move that recalled
Hampton's decision to put Huie on the screen, the closing scene of
Nelson's documentary features a voice actor playing the role of J. W.
Milam narrating the story of the murder. Although the lines are not
a verbatim quotation of the "Shocking Story," the effect is the same.
Huie's version of the story is once again told in the first-person voice
of a murderer. It is a powerful cinematic moment.

As powerful as the moment was, however, it made for a puzzling
end to a documentary that included an interview with Willie Reed.
Twenty-two minutes into *The Murder of Emmett Till*, Reed told his
once-familiar story of hearing screams emerge from the barn. "I could
hear this cryin' and cryin' and beatin', and I'm saying to myself, 'They
beatin' somebody up there.' I heard that beatin' even before I got to,
even before I got to the barn." In a critical and inexplicable move,
however, Nelson's narrator interprets Reed's reference to "the barn"
to mean "Milam's shed" in Glendora.

> Reed spoke in a voice barely louder than a whisper. He'd seen Roy
> Bryant, J. W. Milam and one other white man with Emmett Till early
> that Sunday morning, and had heard the sounds of a beating coming
> from Milam's shed.[99]

This quotation does three key things. First, it moves Reed's testimony
to the home of J. W. Milam in Glendora, Tallahatchie County. This is
unprecedented. There has never been any debate about the location of
Reed's testimony. During the trial he testified that he lived on Shurden Plantation in Sunflower County and that the shed was adjacent to
that plantation.[100] Although the defense lawyers tried to confuse Reed
on a number of factors, they never challenged his claim that the barn
was in Sunflower County. In fact, the defense treated the Sunflower
County location of Reed and his barn as a given fact and simply argued
that it was "unreasonable" to assume that the murderers had traveled
that far out of their way.

Second, much like Whitfield, but in an even more explicit manner,
Nelson treated the size of the murder party and the geography of the

murder as independent variables. The size of the murder party could be adjusted — note his reference to "one other white man" — without also moving the murder to Sunflower County.

Finally, by moving Reed to Tallahatchie County and disengaging the content of his testimony ("one other white man") from the geography of the murder, Nelson domesticated and assimilated Reed's testimony to the dominant, white account of the murder. Until Nelson's PBS documentary, Willie Reed had always been a principle of resistance against the injustice of the trial and the various fabricated accounts (from both the jury and Huie) that sanitized the murder. In fact, Reed was a key part of the accounts circulated by the black press for the precise reason that his simple presence in the story of Emmett Till was a challenge to the dominant narratives. Nelson diffused the charge of Reed's presence and made it seem as though the contributions of Huie and Reed added up to a single coherent narrative.[101]

With this background, consider once more the powerful cinematic conclusion of *The Murder of Emmett Till*. As the voice actor assumed the role of J. W. Milam and told Huie's story as if it was a first-person confession, Nelson rolled footage of a rural Mississippi barn. *But it was footage of the same barn that Nelson earlier placed under Reed's testimony*. To be clear, Nelson was retelling the story of William Bradford Huie. He explicitly placed the murder at "Milam's shed" in Glendora, but, at the climax of the film, at the precise moment that the voice actor described his tool shed "back of the house" (in Glendora), Nelson ran footage of Sunflower County. The *same* barn that, thirty minutes earlier, accompanied Reed's testimony now accompanied Huie's story. Using identical visual cues and geographic references for both Reed and Huie is a profound conflation of two stories that were once at odds with each other. While, earlier in the film, Nelson used a narrator to place Reed's testimony in Glendora, he now used video footage to suggest that Huie's narrative was interchangeable with Reed's.

Perhaps the largest consequence of this confusion is the disentanglement of race from geography. Sunflower County was no longer needed to expand the size of the murder party, and, vice versa, the testimony of those in Sunflower County (e.g., Willie Reed) could be treated as if it originated in Tallahatchie County. We might think of this movement, begun with Whitaker and epitomized in Nelson, as the *third* erasure of Sunflower County. The jury erased it the first time when they endorsed the one-county theory of the murder. Huie erased it a second time, by concocting a two-county version of the murder. Nelson erased it a third time, not by moving the murder, as Huie had done, but rather by suggesting that the precise location of the murder is unrelated to questions of legal import. While the jury and Huie actively evaded Sunflower County, Nelson simply made it irrelevant.

## CONCLUSION

The end of Huie's reign over the cartography of Till's murder contains a strong note of irony. After an absence of nearly fifty years, Sunflower County finally reappeared on a map of Till's murder in 2005. The map was created by Ellen Whitten, granddaughter of John W. Whitten Jr., defense lawyer for Milam and Bryant. For her honors thesis at Rhodes College, Whitten compared Willie Reed's testimony as it appeared in Nelson's *The Murder of Emmett Till* to Huie's account in *Look*. At the heart of her thesis, she quoted the critical moment in Nelson's documentary in which Reed admits to hearing Emmett Till being beaten as he was walking near "the barn." Unlike Nelson, however, who interpreted this "barn" as J. W. Milam's shed in Glendora, Ellen Whitten interpreted Reed's admission as evidence that the murderers "took Till to Leslie Milam's place."[102] Where Nelson registered no inconsistencies between the accounts of Reed and Huie, Ellen Whitten argued forcefully that if Reed's account was true, then Huie's must be false. At the heart of her interpretation were the once-irrelevant miles mapped by Steve Whitaker between the abduction and the murder. As you will recall, in 1963 Whitaker mapped Huie's itinerary in exquisite detail (see figure 5), attending to not only the legal events (the kidnapping and murder) but also the long drive west to the Mississippi River, east to Glendora, back west to Boyle, and finally back east to the Tallahatchie

River. Whitten counted "approximately 200" miles and concluded, as the FBI would one year later, that such a distance was simply not possible and that "Milam's confession must be fabricated."[103]

Thus it was that Ellen Whitten undid the work of her grandfather. John W. Whitten Jr. had a larger role than anyone else in constricting the possibility of justice by constricting the geographic scope of the murder. It was the elder Whitten, after all, who, with the help of his colleagues, developed the bizarre one-county theory of the murder in which there could be no murder because there was no body. It was the same Whitten who, after his colleague Sidney Carlton claimed that there was "nothing reasonable" about Willie Reed's account of Sunflower County, told the jury that "every last Anglo-Saxon one of you has the courage to free these men." Finally, it was Whitten who, in October 1955 arranged for Huie to meet with the murderers to fabricate and publish a two-county, two-murderer story. In some form or other, John Whitten Jr. was behind every intentional attempt to eliminate Sunflower County in the twentieth century.

All of his work, however, could not withstand the careful analysis of his granddaughter. Just as the elder Whitten constricted the geography of the murder to protect the perpetrators of Till's murder, so the younger Whitten reanimated the well-worn category of geography to expose the lies that had for fifty years protected white men. By counting miles and measuring distances, Ellen Whitten speculated that Huie must have been protecting guilty men. Although she wondered only if an unnamed accomplice may have helped toss the body from a bridge, her impulse was dead on: the geography of the murder was in fact intimately connected to the size of the murder party; the number of counties was calibrated to the number of murderers; race and geography shifted in tandem. Her homemade map—a twenty-first century, software-aided analog to Whitaker's pencil-drawn map—thus added Sunflower County back into the relevant geography of Till's murder. In a fitting note of poetic justice, Ellen Whitten became the first person in fifty years to publish a map of Till's murder that included Sunflower County.

Less than one year later, in February 2006, the FBI partially published their "Prosecutive Report"—a summary of their findings from the 2004–5 investigation under the leadership of Dale Killinger. If Ellen Whitten read the report, she must have been pleased. The FBI not only reached the same conclusions she did regarding the fundamental falsity of the *Look* account, but they did so via the same method: counting miles and reengaging the question of geography. When the FBI added up the miles in Huie's account (and on Whitaker's map) they concluded that the mileage was not "physically possible." Although they counted thirty-six fewer miles then Ellen Whitten, their total was nonetheless sufficient to render Huie's account impossible. If the murderers arrived in Boyle by daybreak (5:06 a.m.), they could not have driven 164 miles.[104]

The FBI disproved Huie's account in such a commanding fashion that Terry Wagner claims that they turned Huie into "a largely irrelevant source."[105] This is not quite true. While Huie's plotline has been discredited, he shares with the FBI, both Whittens, and the black press a fundamental assumption about the entanglement of racism and geography. In 1956, Huie shrunk the murder party to J. W. Milam and Roy Bryant by moving the murder to Tallahatchie County. In 2006, the FBI reversed the logic. They disproved Huie's story of Tallahatchie County by taking his own mileage seriously and plotting it against the time of the sunrise. The report then listed ten falsehoods perpetuated by Huie. Of the ten charges, six of them dealt with geography, and the other four dealt with the size of the murder party! By reactivating the old axiom that the categories of geography and race shift in tandem, the FBI proved Huie's plotline untrue.

With the Tallahatchie County tale physically impossible, the FBI reintroduced, with new force, the familiar roster of Willie Reed, Mandy Bradley, Add Reed, Leslie Milam, Levi Collins, and Henry Lee Loggins.[106] This is the same roster introduced by the black press in October 1955 and subsequently written out of Till's memory by John Whitten Jr. and William Bradford Huie. Wherever this cast has been allowed to tell their full story, they have routed the murder through

Sunflower County and thereby expanded the murder party. The FBI's account was no exception. Three pages after disproving Huie's tale and reintroducing the Sunflower County roster, the FBI bluntly concluded, "Till was killed in the barn on Leslie Milam's farm."[107]

It is because the FBI took the geography of the murder seriously, counting miles and measuring distances, that we now know for sure that the violent racism brought to bear on the body of Emmett Till had a broader, more diffuse origination point than Roy Bryant and J. W. Milam. If the black press, Mamie Till-Mobley, Chris Benson, Keith Beauchamp, Steve Whitfield, Ellen Whitten, Davis Houck, and the FBI had not valiantly kept alive the stories of Sunflower County, had they not taken the geography of the murder seriously, we might have lost to history the simple fact that more people killed Till than have ever been brought to trial. The extent of guilt and the range of racism have, historically speaking, been attuned to basic questions of how far the murder party drove and where they were when they killed Emmett Till. Racism has been measured in miles.

Despite all that has happened since 2005, and despite Wagner's suggestion that William Bradford Huie has become an irrelevant source, his story is not yet dead. Huie's influence lives on in the landscape of the Mississippi Delta. To this day, Sunflower County remains the only relevant county in the Mississippi Delta without a single built memorial to Till's memory (see figure 7). Leflore County boasts two memorials, and Tallahatchie County over a dozen. The differential landscapes of the three counties are a material analogue to Huie's story. Simply by driving through the three counties, tourists will be confronted with a material and spatial counterpart of the *Look* confession. While plenty of roadside markers name J. W. Milam and Roy Bryant as the murderers, not a single sign indicates that anyone else may have been involved. The geographic distribution of the roadside markers (none in Sunflower County) combined with the content of those markers (naming only Milam and Bryant) reproduces Huie's two-county, two-murderer theory yet again. The landscape of the Delta has thus become a significant liability to the pursuit of justice. While only students and scholars are likely to read Ellen Whitten's thesis or the FBI's

**FIGURE 7.** This is a 2015 picture of the barn on what was once the Sturdivant Plantation. It remains unmarked. Photo by Pablo Correa. Used by permission.

five-hundred-page report, thousands of tourists make their way to the Mississippi Delta each year to learn of Till's murder through cultural heritage tourism. If they are paying attention to the landscape, this new generation of civil rights activists and young people are being taught the same old two-county theory that for so long shielded people like Leslie Milam and Elmer Kimbell from justice.

## CHAPTER TWO

# OF RACE AND RIVERS:
# TOPOGRAPHY AND MEMORY
# IN TALLAHATCHIE COUNTY

[Till's] story starts at the Tallahatchie River in Money.
*Eyes on the Prize*

The Mississippi Delta is what environmental historian Mikko Saikku has called a "hydraulic regime"—a bioregion in which both cultural and economic power are tied to the management of water.[1] The Delta never would have been the nerve center of the twentieth-century cotton kingdom were it not first a massive alluvial floodplain, a low-lying flatland the soil of which was made rich by the annual flooding of the Mississippi River. Every spring, David L. Cohn wrote, "when the accumulated waters of more than a million square miles of plains and hills and mountains have been gathered together, the Mississippi hurls them against the levees of the Delta," and a "river-sea composed of the gathered streams of America rushes with stupendous force through the Delta."[2] No wonder locals know the Delta as, simply, "river country."[3]

While flooding was the source of the Delta's wealth, it also threatened wholesale destruction. We can gauge just how attuned the political economy of the Delta was to the threat of flooding by a litany of historical-political-aquatic facts. First, the repair of levees was a task for which slaves could be pulled from the fields against the will of otherwise sovereign planters.[4] Second, the Delta's native art form—the blues—has more songs composed about rains and floods than any other natural phenomena.[5] Third, levee-breaking was a war strategy pursued by both Union and Confederate armies.[6] Finally, before the University of Mississippi became the "Rebels" in 1936, they were known simply as "the Flood"—a menacing moniker (and no less racial) for all those who had lived in the Delta in 1927.

Given the centrality of water and its administration to the natural, cultural, and political life of the Delta, it should not be surprising that the commemorative life of the region also bears the imprint of its rivers and their propensity to flood. This is nowhere more true than Tallahatchie County, the site of the 1955 Emmett Till trial and, thanks to *Look* magazine and the commemorative tradition discussed in chapter 1, the oft-supposed site of Till's murder. Yet, the commemorative landscape of Tallahatchie County remained barren for decades. Despite the fact that people had long assumed it was the site of Till's murder, and despite the further fact that the trial was the "first great media event of the civil rights movement," the county did not have a single built memorial to the lynching until 2005.[7] This would change dramatically. As early as 2009, locals referred to west Tallahatchie County as the "Emmett Till National Historic Site."[8] By 2014, the county had a renovated courtroom, a "Civil Rights Driving Tour," an Emmett Till walking trail, and at least eight roadside markers dedicated to Till's memory.

In this chapter, I tell the story of the transformation of Tallahatchie County from a culture of silence to ground zero of Emmett Till commemoration. As I do so, I stress the influence of topography and, above all, the north-to-south path of the Tallahatchie River through the heart of the county. There is, I argue, a direct line of influence from the path of the Tallahatchie River, to flood control, to the largest, most organized attempt to remember Emmett Till on record. This is not to say that Till would still be uncommemorated if there was no river; it is to say, however, that the history of Till commemoration is at the same time a history of the Tallahatchie River, its management, and its cultural, political, and racial effects on the life of the Delta.

Scholars of memory have long fought to keep memory and nature apart from each other.[9] James Young warns against the "sustaining illusion" of memorials, that they are "indigenous, even geological outcroppings in a national landscape." If memorials are disguised as outcroppings, Young cautions, they sustain the illusion that the history they recall is "as naturally true as the landscape in which they stand."[10] While Young's warning is well taken, the reverse lesson also applies. At least in Tallahatchie County, commemorative politics have long accomplished their most powerful work *through the mediation of the natural environment*. If not geological outcroppings, as Young feared, then hills, rivers, floods, and soils. Tallahatchie County's most prominent "natural" features are the very mechanisms through which race, politics, and commemoration mingled and, by mingling, produced the commemorative landscape as we know it. The county's rivers, hills, and soils are, in other words, the transfer points through which questions of race came to influence commemoration and by which practices of commemoration evolved in way that served the racial interests of the planter class. In short, the ecology of the county (its rivers, soils, and hills) undergirds the ecology of memory (the entanglement of commemoration, race, and place).

I tell this story in two parts. In the first section, I explain how the Tallahatchie River has become an important boundary in a variety of different registers: cultural, economic, judicial, and topographical. Above all, I stress the ways in which the river aligns particular modes of racial oppression with particular landforms. The river's history of distributing racisms will prove key in this chapter's long second section, a chronologically organized account of the river's influence on Till commemoration. Through it all, I suggest that the history of Emmett Till in Tallahatchie County provides concrete evidence that the river—and, more broadly, the ecology of the Delta—is a political actor in its own right and that commemoration and racism, while not "indigenous," nonetheless gain force as they are invested by the natural environment.

## RACISM AND THE RIVER

Because of the influence of *Look* magazine, it was widely—nearly universally—assumed that Tallahatchie County was the site of Till's murder. For this reason, the county is mentioned often and highlighted on virtually every map of the murder. But the county is rarely given any agency. It has never been more than an accidental spot on a map, an exogenous set of spatial coordinates. There was nothing about the particularities of the county that made it important for Till's murder, and nothing about Till's murder that made the particularities of the county relevant for memory work. Tallahatchie County is always mentioned, but it has never mattered. Or, more precisely, it never mattered as anything more than the accidental location of the trial.

Yet the topographical features of Tallahatchie County have, from the very beginning, played a massive role in shaping the memory of Emmett Till. In fact, this does not put it quite strongly enough. Even if the influence of the county's topography has seldom been acknowledged, it has played a formative role in all facets of public life from the antebellum period forward. "From the earliest days of its settlement," James C. Cobb writes, "the Delta's physical environment encouraged its residents to believe they were different from other Mississippians."[11] On a smaller scale, the same must be said of Tallahatchie County: its natural features informed its cultural life, and, at the places its cultural life was most intense, the influence of the county's topography was strongest. The county's most distinguishing characteristics—from race to agriculture—could hardly be talked about without invoking the topography of the county. In this regard, the most important feature of the county's physical environment is the fact that it is not entirely within the Delta. The eastern boundary of the Mississippi Delta, marked by the Tallahatchie River and an adjacent string of bluffs, cuts Tallahatchie County in half. Only the western half of the county is in the Delta—the fertile floodplain of the Mississippi known for its aristocratic planters and topsoil. The eastern half of the county is in an area known simply as "the hills."

By the late nineteenth century, the Tallahatchie River was a boundary marker for the county in several different registers. Topographically, it divided the flat alluvial plains of the Delta from the rolling hills of the east. Economically, it divided the affluent cotton kingdom of Delta plantations from the small, poor farms hewed out of the hills.[12] Culturally, it divided the self-styled aristocratic Delta "planters" from the lower-class "farmers" of the hills. Finally, since the opening years of the twentieth century, the river has divided the county juridically, dividing the first from the second judicial districts. All of these distinctions have played identifiable roles in the commemoration of Emmett Till, but none of them have been quite as influential as the sharp distinction in racial attitudes marked by the course of the Tallahatchie River. Racially speaking, the river has divided two different styles of oppression, the paternalistic noblesse oblige of the Delta aristocracy and the open racism of the hills. In practice, of course, these distinctions can hardly be separated: the wealth of the Delta depends on the alluvial plains, reproduces distinctions of class, and engenders paternalism as the preferred form of racism. I list them discretely only to stress the sheer range of cultural divisions made possible by the river. The hills and Delta may both be in Tallahatchie County, but they stand for two entirely different ways of life. There is hardly a domain of public life in the county unaffected by the course of the Tallahatchie River.

The antagonism between the Delta and the hills is so culturally engrained that the two regions use different words to designate the same, all-important activity of agriculture. As Robert Brandfon has written, the sheer money generated by cotton grown in the rich alluvial soil of the Delta produced an increasingly impassioned cultural distinction between the regions. As cotton returned increasing profits, "the Delta farmer was separated from his brother in the hills. One became a *planter*, the other remained a *farmer*, and with the passing years, as the differences became more marked, so the enmity between them grew in like proportion."[13] Capturing the dynamics of both power and race that informed this distinction, Saikku notes that in the antebellum Delta, a "planter" was simply a farmer who owned more than twenty slaves.[14] As the years passed, the term "planter" assumed a near mythical quality. No longer did it indicate simply (and literally) a person who planted seeds; rather, "planter" was shorthand for the gracious and often-extravagant life of the Delta's white elite. Picturing themselves as the "embodiment of southern civility and gentility," planters regarded the Delta as their "fiefdom" and fancied themselves an "aristocracy of wealth and talent surrounded by ignorant blacks [in the fields] and venal rednecks [in the hills]."[15] Although many in this crowd pursued a variety of business interests and very few limited themselves to actual planting, all preferred to be identified as "planters": "the appeal of cotton planting was symbolic of social as well as economic supremacy."[16]

By the end of nineteenth century, the enmity between the hills and the Delta was so basic that all manner of political conflicts could be attributed to the Tallahatchie River and the cultural-political distinctions it made possible. As James Cobb put the matter, "political conflict in Mississippi often followed the geographic, economic, and class lines that separated the Delta from the hills." Controversies over political redistricting, electoral politics, and taxation can be traced to "the bitter antagonism between a flourishing cotton kingdom and the economically declining and morally disapproving 'red-neck' counties of the remainder of the state."[17]

This antagonism has never been much of a secret. By the 1940s, it was the subject of a novel by John Faulkner (William's younger brother). His *Dollar Cotton* uses the journey of hills-farmer-turned-Delta-planter Otis Town to dramatize the animosity between the regions. Once Town became a Delta planter, Faulkner has him add a pretentious silent "e" to his last name (shifting it from Town to Towne).[18] By dramatizing the vanity of Town/Towne, Faulkner "captured the feeling of outrage at the unpunished profligacy and laziness of the Delta that pervaded the hill counties of Mississippi."[19]

If there was one cultural institution in Tallahatchie County that was not confined to a single side of the Tallahatchie River, it was racism. As Cobb explains, there was never, at any point, "any sign of significant disagreement between Delta and hill-country whites about the necessity of maintaining absolute and ironclad supremacy over blacks."[20] In the self-understanding of the Delta aristocracy, however, there was a profound difference at the level of method.[21] Indeed, an essential aspect of the "river planter myth" is paternalism: the planter's belief that their own racial superiority required kindness on their part toward the less fortunate. Noblesse oblige: nobility obliges.

The classic articulation of planter paternalism belongs to David L. Cohn's 1935 *God Shakes Creation*—an impassioned and anecdotal apology for the Old South traditions of the Delta. Like other self-styled aristocrats of his generation, Cohn felt keenly the cultural superiority of the Delta, the impoverishment of the hills, and the fragility of the entire arrangement. He believed that white Delta planters were the arbiters of good manners and the goodwilled guardians of the black labor supply.[22] In the very first sentence of his essay "The White Man's Point of View," Cohn notes that racial attitudes in the Delta break along the Tallahatchie River.

> The point of view of the Delta white man about the Negro varies sharply with his origin and breeding. At one extreme of attitude stand the descendants of the early settlers of the Delta. At the other extreme stand the poor whites who have lately come to the Delta from the hills of Mississippi.[23]

The remainder of the essay—and the remainder of *God Shakes Creation*—then fills out the portraits of these two racial sensibilities, one from each side of the river.

Planters, Cohn explains, extend friendship and protection to the "utterly dependent" black laborers. This was the obligation of nobility. "If, say these men, the whites of the Delta wish to enjoy the rights and privileges that flow to them as members of the dominant race they must be willing to assume those responsibilities which are inseparably attached to enlightened privilege and justified right."[24] First and foremost, these responsibilities entailed preventing the black workforce from sinking "into bottomless pits of despair."[25] For this reason, Cohn records, planters "regard the Negro with affection and sentiment. They have not only tolerance for him, but often a friendly intimacy with him. Many whites of this class maintain life-long friendships with Negros."[26] Cohn was nearly blind to the atrocities and the sheer human dispossession of the plantation-turned-sharecropping economy. He believed that sharecropping, "whatever its defects, was often marked by human tenderness, understanding, and enduring friendships."[27]

Cohn's references to affection, sentiment, and protection must not be mistaken for justice. A planter's "friendship" with his laborers had strict limits. "There is room and welcome in the Delta only for the Negro who 'stays in his place.'"[28] To Cohn's mind, there was no contradiction between paternalism and white supremacy. He could, in the same breath, sing of the "white man's responsibility towards the Negro" and insist on the "white man's dominance socially and politically."[29] There was no irony in his mind when he wrote of the Delta: "This is a pure and true democracy. There is no qualification of property or mental attainment for the franchise of voting. One need be only free, white, and twenty-one."[30]

Cohn was hardly unique. At the heart of the "river planter myth" is the ability to think of oneself as racially tolerant while remaining fully committed to white supremacy. The lynchpin of this otherwise contradictory set of beliefs was the fact that paternalism required only individual acts of kindness. "The problem was," Cobb writes, "that individual whites were normally satisfied that they had fulfilled their obligation to blacks by simply treating fairly those with whom they dealt personally."[31] Thus planters could (and did) fight to maintain systems of white supremacy all while boasting of the fairness with which they treated their laborers. The classic story in this regard belongs to Cohn's friend William Alexander Percy. In his *Lanterns on the Levee*, Percy dedicated an entire chapter to the plight of the Delta's black laborers in the devastating flood of 1927.[32] Planters, he reported, were quick to provide food and medical supplies to the African Americans trapped on the levee. In the midst of the crisis, planters worked at food kitchens, conveyed women and children around on boats, and even built latrines. But, out of fear that the black laborers would not return, the planters did not allow their workforce to be evacuated.[33] The noblesse oblige of the planters, it seems, required both individual acts of kindness and resistance to systematic reform. They ensured the blacks were well fed, but left them on the levee. Through the entire ordeal, "none of us was influenced by what the Negroes themselves wanted: they had no capacity to plan for their own welfare; planning for them was another of our burdens."[34]

Such condescending paternalism was the essence of noblesse oblige: burdened with their welfare, engaged in short-term acts of kindness, all the while maintaining their own supremacy. It is a "delicate" problem, Cohn wrote, "to raise the Negro's standards in every phase of life without disturbing the equilibrium of racial relations, and the *status quo* of the white man's dominance."[35] It is no wonder that the in the six-year gap between the publication of Cohn's *God Shakes Creation* and Percy's *Lanterns on the Levee*, John Dollard published *Caste and Class in a Southern Town* and Hortense Powdermaker published *After Freedom*. The last two books were sociologies that laid bare the staggering racism of the Delta.[36] The simple fact that all four of these books could be published within a six-year span speaks to the sheer power of the "river planter myth": because racial progress was coded as individual kindness it could coexist with widely documented systematic racism.

According to the terms of the river planter myth, the poor whites from the hills were as racially prejudiced as planters were tolerant. Unlike planters, Payne explained, farmers in the hills were "plain mean, and they didn't try to dress it up."[37] Poor whites from the hills are "distinguished by [their] blind hatred of Negroes."[38] Powdermaker ascribed to "poor whites" a "burning resentment against the Negro."[39] Indeed, a commonplace of planter literature — epitomized by *God Shakes Creation* and *Lanterns on the Levee* — is a rehearsal of the racial atrocities visited on blacks by poor white people in the hills. Percy and Cohn seem to take great pleasure in recounting their battles with the Ku Klux Klan.[40] Percy, for example, spends an entire chapter of *Lanterns* describing how he and his father LeRoy chased the Klan from Greenville. For both generations of Percys, the KKK, their lynchings, and their terror had no place in the Delta. LeRoy Percy explicitly linked the "hill country-crowd" with the techniques of racial terror associated with the Klan: they are "unintelligent and slinking . . . the sort of people who lynch negroes."[41]

Historians have not been kind to the likes of Percy and Cohn. While these two self-styled aristocrats believed that their paternalism was born from a class-based sense of human decency, historians have seen in the traditions of noblesse oblige little more than a de facto accommodation to the fact that Delta plantations (and hence white profits) required an astounding amount of black labor.

> More than a romantic residue left over from antebellum times, paternalism was an important feature of plantation life in the New South. It softened the cold impersonality of the contract. No tenant was allowed to go naked for long, if only for the reason that the planter was hard up for his labor and took care of the workers he did have.[42]

Likewise, Cobb notes that it was planters' "obsession" with retaining black labor that curbed the excesses of violence and cruelty that were perpetrated upon blacks in other, less labor-dependent parts of the state. Interpersonal kindness toward black laborers, a concern for their welfare, and actions taken for their protection were, in fact, little more than a side effect of the planters' keen awareness of their own dependency on labor.[43] Even lynching, which planters associated with the "hill-country crowd" did not go away entirely; it was simply calibrated to the calendar of agricultural labor. Most Delta lynchings occurred in June and July—the "laid by" months when black labor was least needed.[44] The summer months thus function as a reminder that the paternalism of the planters was little more than a mechanism of racial subjection.

From the perspective of the black laborers, the paternalism of the planters did not make the Delta a better place to live. Indeed, from the perspective of the movement activists who made a name for themselves in the 1960s, the noblesse oblige of the aristocracy made not an iota of difference. The reputation for paternalism notwithstanding, the Delta remained the single most dangerous place in the state of Mississippi to organize for freedom. Payne wrote, "As blacks from other states feared going to Mississippi, blacks from the hill counties or piney woods of Mississippi were frequently reluctant to venture into the Delta."[45] Dorie Ladner of the Student Nonviolent Coordinating Committee (SNCC) made a similar point in more graphic language: "Whatever was left over from slavery had been left in the Delta."[46] Even the Emmett Till historian Stephen Whitfield called the Delta the "worst place in the entire country for Negroes."[47]

Contrary to David Cohn, who feared that the traditions of noblesse oblige were passing from the Delta by the 1940s, the cultural and racial split between the Delta and the hills was alive and well in 1950s Tallahatchie County.[48] In fact, these traditions received national attention just months after Till was murdered. In December 1955, J. W. Milam's neighbor (and Till murder accomplice) Elmer Kimbell murdered African American gas-station attendant Clinton Melton. Another all-white jury was convened in the Sumner courthouse, and another not-guilty verdict was reached. David Halberstam covered the trial for *The Reporter*. He divided white Mississippians into two camps: "the good people" and the "peckerwoods." Although the terms were different from Cohn's planters and hill people, the racial ideologies were the same: the "good people" talk of "racial harmony" while the "peckerwoods" "kill Negroes."[49]

In sum, by the time Till was killed in 1955, the Tallahatchie River had become a mechanism for distributing various forms of racism. West of the river, in the flatlands of the Delta, the river enriched the soil, fueled the cotton kingdom, and shaped racial domination into the form of interpersonal kindness. In the hills to the east of the river, where such kindness had no economic incentives, racism took a more caustic, straightforward form. In the immediate aftermath of the trial, these attitudes would protect the reputation of the planter class.

### EMMETT TILL AND THE TALLAHATCHIE RIVER

Rivers have long been associated with traditions of remembering and forgetting. Fueled by the classical myth of the River Lethe, which provided complete forgetfulness for all those who drank from it, rivers have become the archetypal metaphor of forgetfulness. From Dante, to Keats, to Byron, to Poe, to Baudelaire, to Ginsberg, the Western tradition has ensured that the ancient connection between oblivion and rivers is regularly updated.[50]

In the American South, however, the entanglement of rivers and forgetfulness has no need of Greek mythology or literary traditions. More practical matters have assured an intimate series of connections among rivers, oblivion, and forgetfulness. Because rivers in the Delta were clouded with silt and guarded by thickets of vegetation so dense as to make them unapproachable except at designated landings, they were often the preferred disposal site of white lynchers and the final resting spot of murdered black bodies. As the bodies accumulated, racism assumed the role once held by the Greek mythology, connecting riverbeds to the possibility of forgetfulness. When Till's killers dumped his body in the Tallahatchie River, for example, they were no doubt hoping that what Faulkner called the "thick, slow, black, unsunned" water of the Tallahatchie River would forever hide the corpse and consign the murder to oblivion.[51] CORE (Congress of Racial Equality) activist Anne Moody recalled her first exposure to Till's murder in terms of rivers. Although she had "heard of Negroes found floating in a river," the Till lynching was her first direct experience of the indignity of racial violence. While whites conveyed a certain respect for the animals they killed, she wrote, "when a man was butchered or killed by man, in the case of Negroes by whites, they were left lying on a road or found floating in a river."[52] By the time Till was kidnapped, the function of rivers as a repository for black bodies was so common that Leflore County sheriff George Smith's first reaction was to look under bridges.[53] During the Till trial in September of 1955, the connection between lynching and rivers was the unspoken assumption of a joke that circulated among the Delta's white youth. As Mamie Till-Mobley remembered:

> These [white boys] would joke about how only a black boy would steal
> a gin fan and then try to carry it across a river. And then say straight-

faced that they didn't know what all the fuss was about. After all, that Tallahatchie River was full of niggers. That's what they would say.[54]

This sentiment was widespread in Sumner. When the *Nation*'s Dan Wakefield arrived to cover the trial, a resident confided to him, "that river's full of niggers."[55] Likewise, defense lawyer J. J. Breland warned that outside pressure to integrate would mean that "the Tallahatchie River won't hold all the niggers that'll be thrown in."[56] Jokes and threats notwithstanding, the fact is that the "chocolate-brown water of the Tallahatchie" did not conceal the body of Emmett Till.[57] On August 31, 1955, seventeen-year-old fisherman Floyd Hodges discovered Till's body protruding from the water.

Hodge's discovery, however, did not mark the end of the river's influence over the memory of the murder. Indeed, if the waters of the Tallahatchie failed to conceal the body by their muddiness, the river had plenty of other mechanisms by which to bend, preclude, or make possible the memory of Till's murder. What follows is a chronologically arranged account of how the river worked as a racially charged agent of memory and how commemoration worked through the mediation of the natural environment. At times the river enabled commemoration and at other times it simply shaped its form, but it always was an essential ingredient in the long afterlife of Emmett Till.

### The Racist Jurors from the Hills!

Before the first day of the trial was over, the course of the Tallahatchie River through the county made its presence felt. Thinking they would be better served by securing jurors unfamiliar with the defendants and thus in a better position to deliver an impartial verdict, the prosecution pursued jurors from the county's police Beat 1, east of the river.[58] This may have been a mistake, as neither J. W. Milam nor Roy Bryant were liked by those who lived closest to them.[59] As David T. Beito and Linda Royster Beito explain, "people who had dealings with the brothers were more likely to dislike them."[60]

Mistake or not, the composition of the jury relative to the Tallahatchie River became a mechanism that allowed the county's planter
class to evade charges of racism and, as it were, push the memory
of Till's murder outside the Delta. In this regard, the distribution of
racial logics between the hills and the Delta is key. Because the white
jury members came from the hills, the logic ran, they felt none of
the noblesse oblige proper to Delta planters and were, for this reason, easily swayed by the race-baiting of the defense. Thus it was
that before the first witness was called, the Delta "responsibles"—as
Huie labeled the planters—had a commemorative logic that exoner-
ated themselves and shifted the burden of the acquittal away from the
Delta, across the Tallahatchie River, and into the hills.[61]

This commemorative rationale appears to have begun with lead defense lawyers, J. J. Breland and John Whitten. In an interview with
Hugh Stephen Whitaker, the first historian to write about the murder,
Breland claimed that "after the jury had been chosen, any first-year
law student could have won the case."[62] Whitaker explained this sentiment in terms of the relative location of the jury members' homes.
He created a hand-drawn map of Tallahatchie County, he subdivided
it into the five police beats, and then drew a line that separated the
Delta from the hills (see figure 8). Although three of the jury members
were from the Delta side of the river, he stressed that none of these
"were considered to have been endowed with any paternalism toward
Negroes."[63] Whitaker thus accepted the racial premise of the river
planter mythology—that planters were more tolerant than farmers
from the hills—and used it as a commemorative logic by which the
responsibility for the acquittal was pushed out of the Delta.

It is difficult to overstate the influence of this argument in the history of Till commemoration. The differential distribution of racial
logics on either side of the Tallahatchie, combined with the location
of the jury vis-à-vis the river, has been a recurrent mechanism for
exonerating the "responsibles" of the Delta. In his 1988 *A Death in
the Delta*, Stephen J. Whitfield repeated Whitaker's blame-the-hill-
country-jury logic. Whitfield acknowledged that the outcome of the
case was a foregone conclusion, "since ten of the jurors came from

TALLAHATCHIE COUNTY

Beat lines are broken.
All land east of heavy
line is hills, to
the west is the
Delta.

**FIGURE 8.** This is Whitaker's police beat map. He created it to demonstrate that the jury came from the hilly (and therefore prejudiced) side of the county. Map by Hugh Stephen Whitaker. Used by permission.

the poor-white, even more Negrophobic hill section of Tallahatchie County, rather than the more paternalistic side of the Delta."[64] Had the trial been in Leflore County, "virtually all in the Delta," John Hailman wrote in 2013, the results "would have been different."[65]

In 2009, Beito and Beito replicated the logic of Whitaker, Whitfield, and Hailman. They conceded that it was "not within the realm of possibility to secure a murder conviction against Milam and Bryant." The "most obvious problem," they continued, was the "composition of the jury": "The prosecution had stumbled badly in the selection process by allowing them to come primarily from the deeply prejudiced hill country section of the county."[66] Beito and Beito were well aware that the Delta was no interracial paradise; they called it a "sea of white supremacy."[67] But this levelheaded assessment of racial politics in the Delta was not inconsistent with the mythology of paternalism. In fact, the authors use the racism of the hill-country jury to deflect another oft-repeated explanation of the acquittal. According to this logic, which also had its start with Whitaker, the acquittal was not simply the result of a racist jury but also because the local establishment was determined to resist outside pressures brought to bear on them by the NAACP. The explanations are not incompatible, and the vast majority

of scholars have advanced both at once.[68] For Beito and Beito, however, the acquittal had nothing to do with a desire to resist outside influence; it was simply the racism of a jury drawn from the hills.[69]

One the most fascinating instances of this logic comes from Ellen
Whitten. Granddaughter of defense lawyer John W. Whitten Jr., Ellen
Whitten grew up in Sumner and learned of the Till case through family
connections. In addition to putting Sunflower County back on the
map (see chapter 1), she also blamed the prosecution for not understanding local politics. "What these men did not understand about
Tallahatchie County," she wrote, "is that it is and always has been divided, half hill country, half Delta land, with distinct differences between the residents and distinct antagonism as well."[70] She then listed
each member of the jury, categorizing them not only by their hometown and their profession (this much was common), but also by which
side of the river they lived on. Next to each name she clarified "East
Tallahatchie County" or "West Tallahatchie County."[71] Of those from
the hills she noted, "Not only was their presence in town unappreci-
ated, their presence on the jury proved beneficial to the defense."[72]

Finally, in 2015, Devery Anderson's *Emmett Till*—the definitive
scholarly history of the murder—repeated the logic yet again. Of the
jurors he wrote, "Most of them were from Beat 1 [the hills] and ran
smaller farms. They were actually less friendly toward blacks because
they usually found themselves competing with them."[73] Anderson
then claimed that the defense recognized the prosecution's mistake
and were, in Whitaker's terms, "happy to capitalize" on the hill-
country origins of jury.[74]

It is important to stress the intellectual genealogy of these claims.
To establish the racist-jury-from-the-hills argument, Anderson, Whitten, Beito and Beito, and Whitfield rely exclusively on Whitaker's
1963 master's thesis (it is unclear on whom Hailman relies).[75] Whitaker, in turn, had two primary sources, both of whom he interviewed:
defense lawyer J. J. Breland and *Look*'s William Bradford Huie. However, because Huie got his story from Breland and his law partner
John Whitten, the ultimate origin of the logic reaches back to two of
the Delta's most established white families, the Whittens and the Bre-

lands. Thus, despite its repetition in a wide variety of respected histories, the claim that the jury was racist because they were from the hills has its ultimate origin in two, white, aristocratic Deltans. When this genealogy is made explicit, it becomes clear that, however real the racism of the hills might be, in the case at hand its application originated with Tallahatchie County's planter class—not the most objective source. This suggests that the endless rehearsal of where the jurors were from was not simply an account of the facts; given its origin, it was also a partisan commemorative strategy geared toward vindicating the Delta's planter class by pushing responsibility for the acquittal eastward, out of the Delta, over the river, and into the hills.

The rhetorical strategy implicit in the planter's rehearsal of the jury's composition is particularly evident when we compare it to accounts of the murder (and even accounts of the jury selection) that do not originate with the planters themselves. Most telling in this category is Mamie Till-Mobley's account of the jury selection. Writing with the accomplished Chicago journalist, professor, and lawyer Christopher Benson, Till-Mobley delves into such details as the occupations of the jurors and the various things that might disqualify them for service, but she never once invokes the hills/Delta schism.[76] For her, the whole of Tallahatchie County "had a reputation for being a mean place, very hostile toward blacks."[77] Before Emmett boarded a train for Mississippi, Till-Mobley spoke to her son for the first time about southern racial mores. She did not warn him to be careful in the hills; she told him to be careful in Mississippi.[78] In other words, from her perspective, racism was hardly confined to the hills, and the fact that the jury was drawn predominantly from east of the river was, to her mind, an inconsequential fact.

Just as much as Breland and Whitten sit at the origin of a long commemorative tradition of blaming the excessive racism in the hills, Till-Mobley sits at the origin of another strand of commemoration. In this strand, the most important commemorations are the two acclaimed documentaries, *The Murder of Emmett Till*, a 2003 PBS documentary by Stanley Nelson, and *The Untold Story of Emmett Louis Till*, released in 2005 by Keith Beauchamp. Although there are significant differences between the two films, both lean heavily on Mamie Till-Mobley's account of the murder, and both spend significant time explaining the racial context in which the Till murder should be situated. Neither film mentions a Delta/hills schism, but both emphasize a racial context that in the Breland-and-Whitten tradition would belong only in the hills: lynching. Nelson notes that seventy-five blacks had been lynched in the state of Mississippi in the seventy-five years leading up to 1955.[79] Likewise Beauchamp provided images of robed Klansmen and black bodies hanging from tree limbs.[80] From the perspective of Tallahatchie County planters, such images had no business describing what *Ebony*'s Cloyte Murdock called the "Land of Till's Murder."[81] Lynching was an activity proper to the hills, not the Delta. Yet, neither Mamie Till-Mobley nor the documentarians were Deltans; none of them saw any point in dividing the racial mores of Tallahatchie County along the river. From their perspective, Mississippi was, in its entirety, racist.

The distribution of racial attitudes along the path of the Tallahatchie is thus only one way to explain the racial context in which Till was murdered. In fact, the myth of the river planter (and the history of noblesse oblige) has been relevant only for those historians who are working, albeit at several levels of remove, from evidence provided by planters themselves. When Tallahatchie County planters needed a commemorative strategy by which to minimize their own culpability, they found a resource in the topographical contours of their own county. The Tallahatchie River had long divided the county in a myriad of registers; in the wake of the acquittal, the planters (and their historians) turned to the path of the river one more time. From the earliest Till history (Whitaker) to the most recent and widely respected (Anderson), the topography of the county has been the relay point through which racism informed commemoration. The very contours of the land have confined racism to a demographic that was at once exogenous and essential: the jury. The river thus provided a mechanism for remembrance without responsibility; much like the planter myth, it acknowledged racism but moved it east, over the river, away from the economic and cultural engines of the plantation economy.

Located in the hills, racism required nothing of Deltans save condemnation. And condemn they did, time and again, those racist jurors from the hills.

*The River and the Renovation of the Emmett Till Courtroom*

Because the flooding of the Tallahatchie River occasionally prevented passage between the Delta and the hills, the county has had two courthouses since 1903, one on each side of the river.[82] The first county seat was in the hills, in the three-thousand-person town of Charleston, the largest town in the county. When the county decided to create a Delta courthouse to accommodate the annual flooding of the river, the town of Sumner competed with the town of Webb to become the second county seat.[83] Although the two towns, separated by less than three miles, were comparable at the turn of the century, the different economic fortunes of the two towns are now immediately recognizable. While Webb is little more than a block of abandoned storefronts in a state of disrepair, Sumner, which won the battle for the courthouse, is one of the county's few thriving towns. The small town square now boasts a number of legal offices, art galleries, and an upscale restaurant. As Harry MacLean explains, the courthouse and the attendant legal industry have given Sumner an appearance of prosperity.[84] This prosperity, of course, was ultimately a function of the Tallahatchie River; the river, which had long distributed various racial intolerances, now, because it was prone to flooding, also distributed the profits of government. It ensured that the Delta would receive its fair share of official business. Just as the western Delta counties along the Mississippi River built levees to ensure the smooth operation of their political economies in the face of flooding, Tallahatchie County built a second courthouse for the same reason.

The fortunes of Sumner, however, were not long secure. In 1949, six years before the Till trial, Tallahatchie County built a throughtruss bridge on State Highway 32 over the Tallahatchie River. The river was now passable year round, and there was no longer a compelling rationale for two courthouses. By the time of the trial in 1955, it was already obvious that the bridge threatened the economic stability of Sumner—a town whose relative prosperity was grounded in a duplicate courthouse. As the *Memphis Press-Scimitar* explained, "Back in the old days, the Tallahatchie River often flooded and folks couldn't get across, so the county has two county seats, though two are not needed now. Sumner is the western district county seat, and there would be little reason for this town of 550, if it were not for the courthouse."[85]

As the Sumner courthouse gradually fell into disrepair, anxieties over the fate of the courthouse—and the future of the town—were only heightened. Residents of Charleston saw in the ill-repaired Sumner courthouse an opportunity for consolidation and a chance to recover the profits of the county's entire legal business.[86] The Charleston courthouse had itself recently been renovated, and "east-siders" saw no reason to duplicate their efforts.[87] As the local paper made explicit, opinions about the future of the Sumner courthouse followed, precisely, the path of the Tallahatchie River. "Eastern Tallahatchie folk" favored "cost-cutting" and consolidation while Delta residents on the west side of the county advocated saving the courthouse. It had become, the *Sun-Sentinel* noted, "a war between the Halves, East against West, with the Tallahatchie River pretty much marking the line of demarcation."[88]

By April of 2004, the condition of the courthouse was so poor that the Tallahatchie County Grand Jury made the "current physical status of the courthouse" the object of its annual report. The grand jury provided a bullet-point list of seventeen items it found objectionable. The list included everything from collapsing ceilings, to broken tiles, to soiled ceilings, to faulty plumbing, to a stairwell that was "in overall terrible general decay."[89] In addition to the visible damage reported by the grand jury, a study of the courthouse by Belinda Stewart Architects revealed that the very structure of the courthouse—its "two central trusses"—were compromised by termite damage and moisture.[90] The Sumner courthouse was "structurally deficient and inadequate for current administrative needs."[91] Given the depths of the repairs needed and the faltering Tallahatchie County economy, residents of

Sumner feared "that if the courthouse is shut down, even temporarily, they will lose their legal infrastructure to the courthouse in Charleston, and Sumner might slip into the same doldrums as other impoverished Delta communities."[92] As the president of the Tallahatchie County Board of Supervisors (and west-side resident) Jerome Little put it, Sumner was "in critical need of assistance."[93]

It was in this context that the commemoration of Emmett Till came to the foreground in Tallahatchie County. If, some fifty-plus years after the murder, the county was finally willing to break the silence that had long enveloped Till's murder, this was because the memory of Emmett Till now answered a "critical need." While there was no tax money to *repair* the courthouse, the memory of Emmett Till could provide grant money to *restore* the courthouse to its 1955 condition.[94] The local newspaper put that matter bluntly. "It is precisely the Till tie-in that is viewed as the long-term hope for solving many local ills, not the least of which is acquiring funds to repair and improve the facility [courthouse]."[95] Little made his case to US senator Thad Cochran. The local courthouse, he explained was in "poor—but repairable—condition." It was plagued by "significant structural damage" and was out of compliance with accessibility requirements. But, he continued, "the story of Emmett Till cannot be forgotten. There are school children all over the country who do not know about Emmett Till. This story must be told—and the significance of these events explained."[96]

This was not the first time the physical condition of the courthouse intersected with the memory of Emmett Till. In 1973, Tallahatchie County hired the Yale-trained preservationist Jack DeCell to modernize the courthouse where Till was tried.[97] Recognized "as one of the leading preservation architects of the south," DeCell "strove for absolute accuracy."[98] Had there been a will in 1973 to commemorate the 1955 trial, the DeCell restoration would have been the perfect opportunity. The courthouse had been the site of the "first great media event of the civil rights movement," and the county now had "leading preservationist" and a "Courthouse Building Fund" of $100,000.[99]

Yet DeCell ignored the building's storied history. He installed elevators, air-conditioning, and inoperable aluminum windows. In the courtroom itself, he installed church-style pews and painted the room purple. He installed a drop ceiling, added hallways on three sides of the gallery, shrank the courtroom by 854 square feet, and dramatically altered the affective experience of the room.[100] The impact of the DeCell renovations was so dramatic that, in 2011, the board of supervisors complained that he was "hiding many of the reminders of the past."[101] Little described DeCell's work as "inappropriate renovations," and some locals have even wondered if DeCell's 1973 "modernization" was an act of intentional forgetfulness. One citizen claimed that DeCell's work "was done to take the curse off the building; I believe that."[102] Fueling these anxieties is the fact that it was during the De-Cell renovation that the cotton-gin fan that once held Till's body in the Tallahatchie River was lost. From 1955 to 1973, the fan was stored in the basement of the courthouse; it has not been seen since.[103]

Little was determined that the next renovation would honor the memory of Emmett Till. Working through Harvey Henderson—defense lawyer for J. W. Milam and Roy Bryant who was still practicing law in Sumner in 2005—Little secured the services of Clarksdale architect Richard "Richie" M. Dickson. Dickson, whose firm had just gone bankrupt, who now operated a "firm of one," and who was slowed by an inability to type, poured himself into the project.[104] Leaning heavily on PBS.org, which until 2017 featured the *Look* confession on its *American Experience* website, Dickson generated a comprehensive report titled "Historical Restoration and Addition, Tallahatchie County Courthouse, Sumner, Mississippi." Dated January 4, 2006, the report included a summary of the Till case drawn from PBS and *Look*, a history of the courthouse, and a $4,280,195 plan to restore "the courtroom to the conditions that existed at the time of the trial of Roy Bryant and J. W. Milam for the murder of Emmett Till."[105]

Dickson's proposal is a fascinating document. It moves seamlessly between the requirements of the legal industry (Americans with Disabilities Act compliance, space for the circuit clerk and tax assessor), the failures of the DeCell renovation (shrinking the courtroom), and the memory of Till's murder. By restoring the courtroom to its 1955 condition, Dickson suggested, the county might solve three problems at once: it could save its legal industry, bring its courtroom into conformity with the standards of the Americans with Disabilities Act, and commemorate the murder of Emmett Till—a murder, he noted (borrowing words from PBS.org), that was "the real spark that ignited broad-based support for the [civil rights] movement."[106] The centerpiece of Dickson's proposal was adding two two-story additions to the east and west sides of the courthouse. On the ground floor, and on the second floor on the west side, these additions would increase office space by 35–50 percent, thus increasing the productivity of the legal industry. On the second floor on the east side, the addition would provide two "exhibition galleries" to "tell the story of Emmett Till." Because the commemorative space was on the second floor, visitors to that space would be able to gaze directly into the second-story courtroom through what were once—before the additions—external windows.

Dickson's scheme never came to fruition. Indeed, he was hardly paid for his efforts; the county offered (and he accepted) a payment of $5,104.40 to satisfy a $96,950.00 invoice.[107] Despite the fact that his plans were never realized, his proposal remains important for two reasons. First, Dickson's research into the murder of Emmett Till and the basic objectives he outlined informed the courthouse restoration from 2007 to 2014. His "Historical Restoration and Addition" was incorporated—in places word for word—into the official 2007 *Tallahatchie County Courthouse Feasibility Study*. The latter document, prepared by Belinda Stewart Architects and purchased by the board of supervisors for $45,750, became a master document in the renovations and was referred to in virtually every grant application that funded the restoration.[108] The very first page of the *Feasibility Study* lays out four objectives for the restoration: they are cut-and-paste, verbatim, from Dickson's "Historical Restoration and Addition."[109] At the heart of these objectives—and at the heart of both the 2006 Dickson report and the 2007 *Feasibility Study*—was the marriage of Till commemoration and economic revitalization: a courtroom restored to its 1955 status promised to save the courthouse, the Delta's share of the county's legal industry, and the town of Sumner.

This marriage of commemoration and commerce is the second reason the Dickson report remains important. It is a material reminder that that earliest expressions of commemoration in Tallahatchie County emerged in the context of what the local paper called a "war between the halves." The Tallahatchie River split the county in half, creating a second courthouse that, with the passage of time, became dilapidated and unnecessary. The aging and unneeded courthouse, in turn, sparked a debate over the future of the Delta's legal industry and the fate of Sumner. It was that debate that, in 2005, brought Till commemoration to the foreground. In this regard it is important to remember that Harvey Henderson—Milam and Bryant's defense lawyer in 1955 and Dickson's first contact in 2005—was no friend of Till commemoration. He claimed that "people don't want it [the courthouse] messed with."[110] Despite this, Henderson was "a realist"; he knew the east-west tension in the county was real, and he was deeply invested in saving Sumner's legal industry, not least because he was an important part of that industry.[111] If commemoration could save the county's second judicial district, it was a price he was willing to pay.

### The River and the ETMC

On January 4, 2006, Dickson presented his plan inside the Sumner courtroom at the first meeting of the Emmett Till Memorial Commission.[112] It did not go well. Although the details of what transpired in that meeting have been lost, we do know that it was Dickson's final appearance in the county's pursuit of Till commemoration. One year later, he would meet County Supervisor Marvin Doss in Charleston to pick up his small check. He remembers the day well. Moments before the transfer was made, Dickson's foot was run over by a car on Charleston's busy square. It was, for him, a fitting conclusion to his work on behalf of Emmett Till. It added injury to the insult of underpayment.

If Dickson did not have a future in Tallahatchie County's commemorative schemes, the ETMC did. In time, the commission would become an eighteen-member, biracial body of enormous influence.

The commission has spent more money on Till commemoration, created more memorials, and had a greater impact on the commemorative landscape of the Delta than any other organization. With a combination of earmarks secured by US senator Thad Cochran, seven grants from the MDAH, and the support of Morgan Freeman, the ETMC transformed the commemorative landscape of Tallahatchie County. They renovated the courtroom (although not to Dickson's specifications), created an eight-site "Civil Rights Driving Tour," and funded an "Emmett Till Interpretive Center" across the street from the courthouse.

Much like Dickson's proposal, however, the ETMC would never have happened were it not for the "war between the halves" that threatened the courthouse and the town of Sumner. The commission itself gained momentum and wielded power only because of the economic issues pressing the western half of Tallahatchie County. This blending of commerce and commemoration was recognized formally in the commission's bylaws. In place by the middle of 2007, the bylaws clarify that the ETMC was founded

> for the purpose of fostering racial harmony and reconciliation and to seek federal, state, and private funds and grants to initially restore the Tallahatchie County Courthouse in Sumner, Mississippi, to explore the restoration of other buildings and sites of historical value.[113]

In what follows I explore the contours of this delicate balance between commerce and commemoration and argue that the fragility of Sumner, caused by the river, was *the* factor that transformed the ETMC from a high-minded commission with little cultural clout to an influential commemorative body.

The bylaws may have made the commercial aims of the commemorative venture explicit, and the ETMC may have been jump-started by the precarity of Sumner, but, at least to Jerome Little's mind, the commemoration of Till's murder was a moral imperative. While local whites such as Harvey Henderson tended to see the commemoration of Till's murder as a last-ditch effort to save the county, Little saw the potential ruin of Sumner as an opportunity to commemorate Till's murder. It is a fine, but important distinction. Henderson was willing to commemorate in order to produce commerce; Little was willing to save Sumner if it meant he could commemorate Till's murder.

Jerome "G" Little was deeply committed to racial justice. He was born in 1952, the son of sharecroppers on the plantation of Frank Mitchener Sr.—a wealthy Sumner planter whose son Frank Jr. would in time influence the memory of Emmett Till in profound ways.[114] Little came of age making twenty-five cents an hour "chopping cotton" on the Mitchener Plantation. Although the plantation was only five miles northeast of the Sumner courthouse, Little did not learn about the murder of Emmett Till until he joined the marines and traveled the world.[115] Apparently, Till's story was better commemorated across the world than it was in Tallahatchie County. It was a lesson he would never forget. He described his efforts on behalf of Till's memory as a "calling"; "Something was just in me," he recalled. As long as he was living, it was his life goal to "make sure that everybody in this county, everybody in this state, and everybody in this nation understands what happened [and] why it happened."[116]

The best evidence that Little cared about more than economic returns is the fact that before the first meeting of the ETMC, he called Susan Glisson and asked her to be involved. Glisson was (and is) something of a specialist in the domain of racial reconciliation in Mississippi. By the time Little called her in 2005, she was already a major player in the state's racial politics. In 1998, she brought President Bill Clinton's "One America: The President's Initiative on Race" to the University of Mississippi—its only southern stop. From the momentum generated by this one-thousand-person conversation in Oxford, and with the support of former Mississippi governor William Winter, in 1999 Glisson established the William Winter Institute for Racial Reconciliation at the University of Mississippi. In 2002, when the University of Mississippi brought James Meredith back to campus, she convinced their reluctant chancellor to issue an apology. In 2003, she helped Newton County, Mississippi, craft an apology to the family of civil rights icon Medgar Evers. Finally, in 2004 she visited the town of Philadelphia, Mississippi, every Monday for three months to form a group of citizens known as the Philadelphia Coalition—a volunteer group that pursued justice for the Freedom Summer murders of Michael Schwerner, James Chaney, and Andrew Goodman (the *Mississippi Burning* murders). In 2005, when Edgar Ray Killen was finally indicted, it was Glisson who wrote the statement that was issued by the coalition. The statement perfectly captures Little's conviction that racial reconciliation requires public acts of memory.

> We challenge our fellow citizens to join us in an honest appraisal of the past. Knowledge brings truth and the truth brings freedom. Today we have a cause for hope because our community came together to acknowledge its sin. But we also have a purpose for the future: to seek the truth, to insure justice for all, and to nurture reconciliation. And so we promise in our own community to see this journey through to the finish line. . . . We must all understand how and why these murders and thousands of others occurred. We must understand the system that encourages it to happen so we can dismantle it. We must never allow it to happen again. We have the power now to fulfill the promise of democracy. Join us in that struggle.

Glisson did not get involved with the Philadelphia Coalition to generate economic returns. She was a memory activist. She wanted to use an "honest appraisal of the past" to generate a better democracy in the present. Beginning with the Meredith event at the University of Mississippi in 2002, every initiative she pursued involved a "ritual of atonement," an honest appraisal of the past (memory work) as the starting point of racial justice. In this regard, Glisson's influence is nowhere more evident than in the fact that the ETMC occasionally referred to themselves as the "Emmett Till Justice Commission of Tallahatchie County."[117] The interchangeability of "memorial" and "justice" perfectly captures Glisson's conviction that the two pursuits are best served together. More importantly, the interchangeability captures Little's conviction that the ETMC was never simply about economic returns.

In 2000, Little became Tallahatchie County's first black president of the board of supervisors. It was the capstone of a political career spent fighting the Delta's white political machine. After his discharge from the marines in 1977, he was the first African American to run for Beat 5 county supervisor. In 1983, he filed the first of several lawsuits against Tallahatchie County, eventually forcing the county to redraw its voting districts. In 1994, he became the second African American to be seated as a supervisor of Tallahatchie County.[118] By 2005, African Americans were well represented in local governance, but wealth and cultural influence still resided with the planter class. For this reason, Glisson and Little were convinced that the cultural power of the ETMC hinged on white participation. As powerful as their own moral commitments were, they required help from people they hardly trusted. As MacLean put the matter, "the whites in town would have to be brought on board."[119] Acting on a tip from Governor Winter, Glisson reached out to Betty Pearson—one of the Delta's few white liberals.

In many ways, Betty Pearson was the glue of the ETMC. In Governor Winter's words, "She's about the only person with the trust of both blacks and whites."[120] As the great-granddaughter of one of the Delta's earliest cotton planters, Pearson had the respect of the white community. Defense lawyer Harvey Henderson was the best man in her wedding. She was also, however, a longtime civil rights advocate. As a student at the University of Mississippi in the summer of 1942, she organized the African American women who ran the university's laundry service to strike. Although the strike resulted in better wages, it also prompted university chancellor Alfred Benjamin Butts to call Betty's father and threaten that further racial agitation would get her expelled.[121] While she maintained a low profile for the rest of her time at Ole Miss, she wrote a paper titled "Why Schools Should Be Integrated." Through the intervention of her philosophy professor, the paper was entered in a national competition and ended up winning her a "full scholarship to do graduate work at Columbia." Her father refused to allow her to move to New York City, and so, as a form of revenge, she drove to Memphis and joined the marines.[122] After the war, she returned to Tallahatchie County, attended all five days of the Emmett Till trial in 1955, was appointed to the Mississippi Advisory Committee to the US Civil Rights Commission in 1959, and, in the 1960s, used her plantation home to shelter activists, lawyers, and "freedom riders" who came to the state to work on voter registration drives.[123]

With her pedigree commanding the respect of the white community and her history earning her the respect of the black community, Pearson was the key to filling the ETMC's eighteen slots—nine for white people, nine for black people. When, in February of 2007, the ETMC decided to have two cochairs, one white and one black, Pearson was elected to serve alongside Tutwiler mayor Robert Grayson. With Pearson as cochair and Glisson as a consultant, the ETMC now had two powerful women pushing the commission to use the memory of Emmett Till for purposes of racial reconciliation. In an undated letter to Glisson, Pearson wrote that her "primary intent in the work of the Emmett Till Commission is not tourism, or marking a 'trail,' or remodeling the courthouse, but in the opportunity it gives us to develop a new kind of bi-racial community here."[124]

For Little, Glisson, and Pearson, the possibility of racial justice motivated their participation in the ETMC. But if they were motivated by justice, they were also savvy enough to pitch the ETMC as a revenue generator. They were well aware that the local white elite spoke the language of commerce: they were driven by money, and, if they could be brought on board, they had the potential to bring in money. In this regard, Betty Pearson's most important recruit was Frank Mitchener Jr.—who grew up alongside Little on his father's plantation and went on to become "one of the wealthiest plantation owners in the county."[125] Mitchener's most important asset was his long friendship with US senator Thad Cochran. By July of 2007, not long after Pearson recruited Mitchener to the ETMC, Mitchener convinced Cochran to provide the first of two $750,000 earmarks for Till commemoration in Tallahatchie County.

While Mitchener and other white community members were central to the success of the ETMC, they were, as a rule, not motivated by racial justice or the possibility of long-overdue commemoration.

Although there are certainly exceptions (e.g., Betty Pearson), for the most part, the white commissioners cared about saving the town of Sumner and generating revenue, and the black commissioners cared about racial justice. As Pearson explained to Glisson: "Jerome [Little] and Senator [David] Jordan and I think all of the blacks focus on how horrible the crime was, and the need for acceptance of responsibility and reconciliation. On the other hand, the white participants . . . primary focus is on the restoration of the courthouse and the tourists that might bring."[126] Sociologists Alan Barton and Sarah J. Leonard spent significant time with the ETMC from 2006 to 2008. In a 2010 article tellingly titled "Incorporating Social Justice in Tourism Planning," they reached the same conclusion as Pearson. While the black commissioners had a "commemorative focus," the white members were motivated by the economic promise of saving Sumner. One of them even went on record, telling Barton and Leonard, "We see this Till thing as a way to get funds to restore the Courthouse, which it needs."[127] Mitchener himself told the *Atlanta Journal Constitution*, "I'm interested in our little town surviving."[128]

While Mitchener may have been the "most prominent member" of the commission, the ETMC records suggest that his motivations were widely shared.[129] In January of 2007, the commission created a bullet-point list of the various reasons Tallahatchie County citizens had joined the ETMC. The answers provided are indicative of how the commission's double charge (commerce and commemoration) functioned to bring together a group of people with fundamentally different goals. On the one hand, several commissioners claimed that racial reconciliation was their primary motivator. Answers included "Reconciliation"; "Closure for black and white after the divisions caused by the Till trial"; "Races coming together"; "Reach out as brothers in Christ for the greater good"; "Want to be more open, more trusting"; and "Bring us as a people together, there are divisions between black and white, need to be honest to get at the root of racism and cut it off, we must teach our children to work together."

On the other hand, there were just as many answers that focused on economic returns for Sumner and the county: "Bringing economic development to Tallahatchie County"; "Fix the courthouse once funds come"; "Economic development and recreation"; "Bring tourism to the county"; "Economic Development"; "To raise money to get all the necessary work done"; "Restore the courthouse"; and "Restoration of the courthouse, wants the community to prosper by having libraries, museums, and things that bring in tourists, education"[130]

As these lists make clear, the marriage of commerce and commemoration was the condition of memory work in Tallahatchie County. If the town was not poised to lose its legal industry, the moral imperatives of Little, Glisson, and Pearson would have fallen on deaf ears. Mitchener never would have reached out to Cochran, and the ETMC would never have gotten off the ground. But Sumner *was* threatened, and the twinned opportunities of commerce and commemoration provided sufficient purchase for community members across the racial spectrum to find meaning and purpose on the ETMC. They also found conflict.[131] Given the racial composition and competing motivations of the ETMC, it is hardly surprising that racism bitterly divided the commission. In addition to the segregated culture in which the commissioners lived, the distrust was also driven by the fact that two of the black commissioners had grown up the children of sharecroppers on plantations owned by two of the white commissioners.[132] At times, the distrust between the races was so severe that commissioners resigned, meetings devolved into shouting matches, and the two halves of the commission (black and white) met separately.[133]

But the center held. The combination of commemorative justice and the path of the Tallahatchie River made the restoration of the courthouse a common good. In pursuit of this good, the ETMC replaced Dickson with Belinda Stewart Architects, a widely respected firm out of Eupora, Mississippi. Just as Dickson had done, Stewart proposed an architectural solution that represented the interests of both Little and Mitchener. Rather than expanding the courthouse with wings to house offices and exhibition space, which would alter the footprint of the building and compromise its potential (now realized) place on the National Register of Historic Places, Stewart proposed purchasing an abandoned grocery store across the street from

**FIGURE 9.** The interior of the second-district Tallahatchie County Courthouse, 1955. © Ed Clark / The LIFE Picture Collection / Getty Images.

the courthouse as an annex.[134] Although plans for the annex changed several times over the years, it was initially designed to house both a tax office and a welcome center/museum space for Emmett Till tourists.[135] In other words, Stewart's plan creatively found ways to extract from the courthouse restoration project both economic development and different ways of telling Till's story.

By 2010, Stewart's firm was also the official grant-writing wing of the ETMC.[136] Charging the ETMC 5 percent of awarded funds, Stewart secured seven grants from the MDAH, which, in addition to earmarks secured by Cochran and a $250,000 grant from the USDA, were sufficient to restore the courtroom to its 1955 condition (see figures 9, 10, and 11) and transform the long-defunct Wong's Grocery into the Emmett Till Interpretive Center—a museum space and community center in which the memory of Emmett Till's murder is a starting point for conversations about racial justice in the twenty-first-century Delta.[137]

In every grant written by Belinda Stewart Architects, the restoration of the courthouse was both a driver of economic revenue and

FIGURE 10. The interior of the second-district Tallahatchie County Courthouse, as it existed between the DeCell renovation in the early 1970s and the Emmett Till Memorial Commission renovation in the twenty-first century. Photo by Belinda Stewart Architects. Used by permission.

FIGURE 11. The interior of the second-district Tallahatchie County Courthouse, 2018. Photograph by Ashleigh Coleman. Used by permission.

a source of racial reconciliation. For example, a successful 2011 application for $210,000 explained, "Restoration and enhancement of the courtroom provides visitors to the historic courtroom a take away message that enhances their understanding of the crucial role that Tallahatchie County and Sumner Mississippi played in the civil rights movement." Without missing a beat, Stewart continued, "Economic development is occurring with new businesses being established on the town square, the establishment of the Emmett Till Memorial Site Welcome Center, enhancement of tour activities and expansion of the vision for the site and especially the museum."[138]

Central to Stewart's success was her vision that the renovated courthouse would be, simultaneously, a fully operating county facility (thus appeasing the white commissioners) and a museum to the racial intolerance that resulted in the murder of Emmett Till (thereby appeasing the black commissioners). To accomplish both tasks at once, she budgeted nearly $600,000 to install a state-of-the-art audiovisual system in the courthouse. The A/V system was to include touch-screen displays featuring interactive video and motion-activated audio near the witness stand and jury box. In addition, large photographs accompanied by explanatory narratives would be displayed throughout the building.[139] All of this was designed to allow the courthouse to function as a municipal business and a museum at the same time. Although the A/V system is yet to be installed, the $600,000 budget line is a material reminder of the unique obligations of the ETMC: they had to feature both commerce and commemoration, and, for this reason, no price was too high for a mechanism that could transform a single space into an engine of legal industry and a focal point for racial justice.

The marriage of commerce and commemoration is expensive and easy to criticize. But for Little, Glisson, and Pearson, it was the cost of doing business. From their perspective, the economic fragility of Sumner was their greatest asset. It provided them the opportunity to recruit the local white establishment, raise unprecedented amounts of money, and transform the commemorative landscape of the county. Without the Tallahatchie River cutting the county in half and creating a will to save Sumner, the moral fervor of Little and his compatriots would have remained admirable but unrealized longings.

### The River and a Public Apology

From the very beginning, one of Jerome Little's great passions was that the ETMC would hold a high-profile national press conference. The press conference would signal, at the highest possible level of visibility, the commemorative intentions of the ETMC. According to a press release circulated in advance, the ETMC would use the press conference to "unveil . . . its plans to develop a national civil rights museum dedicated to the documentation and study of the landmark Till case."[140] Little hoped to attract figures from the upper reaches of government and cultural politics to add gravitas to the ceremony. He wanted Jesse Jackson or Al Sharpton to attend the event and amplify its call for justice. He wanted President Bush to apologize for the indifference of President Eisenhower; he wanted Mississippi governor Haley Barbour to apologize for the indifference of Hugh L. White, governor at the time of Till's murder; he wanted Tallahatchie County sheriff William Brewer to apologize for his 1950s predecessor, Clarence Strider, whose racism during the trial has been well documented; and he wanted an apology from the commissioners on behalf of Tallahatchie County to the family of Emmett Till.[141] In sum, Little envisioned "a commemorative day in which governmental officials and representatives of our justice system will stand with us before the public and media to openly acknowledge this miscarriage [of justice] and pledge to never allow it to trespass our county again."[142] With this vision in mind, the "Tourism Committee" (a subcommittee of the ETMC) proposed that the commission host a national press conference on the steps of the Tallahatchie County Courthouse on September 3, 2007.[143]

Only the apology from the commissioners and the sheriff would find fruition; the rest proved too controversial—and too racial—for the ETMC. At a heated meeting of the ETMC on November 9, 2006, the group almost splintered over the national press conference. At least one of the white commissioners threatened to walk away if Little pursued Jackson or Sharpton.[144] Although Little backed off and agreed not to invite Sharpton or Jackson, "he nourished a flicker of resentment that he couldn't say what he wanted without whites threatening to leave the table."[145]

After postponing the date twice, the ceremony was held on October 2, 2007. It was a moving ceremony by all accounts. The most dramatic part of the morning was a public resolution, signed by all eighteen members of the ETMC and read on the steps of the courthouse by cochairs Betty Pearson and Robert Grayson. With three of Till's cousins seated alongside four hundred celebrants in folding chairs set up on the streets of Sumner, Pearson and Grayson took turns speaking for the ETMC: "We the citizens of Tallahatchie County believe that racial reconciliation begins with telling the truth. We call on the state of Mississippi, all of its citizens in every county, to begin an honest investigation into our history." Then, after briefly rehearsing the facts of the murder, Pearson and Grayson addressed the Till family:

> We, the citizens of Tallahatchie County, recognize that the Emmett Till case was a terrible miscarriage of justice. We state candidly and with deep regret the failure to effectively pursue justice. We wish to say to the family of Emmett Till that we are profoundly sorry for what was done in this community to your loved one. We, the citizens of Tallahatchie County, acknowledge the horrific nature of this crime. Its legacy has haunted our community.[146]

It was moving oratory, made even more so by the fact that it was delivered alternately by Pearson and Grayson. As the local audience would have surely known, Grayson grew up a sharecropper on the Pearson Plantation.[147] When they now stood side by side, proclaiming for the Till family that "racial reconciliation begins with telling the truth," and announcing a "deep regret" and a "profound sorrow" for the county's failure to "pursue justice," it must have seemed as if the ETMC was ushering in a new racial order.

But we must not let the pathos of the moment obscure the county politics that were also at play. Even here, in the most intimate yet most public moment of the ETMC, the path of the Tallahatchie River was making its presence felt. This time, the issue was not fragility of Sumner. By October 2007, Cochran's first earmark had been secured and the courthouse—while still in shambles—was set on the path to renovation. With Sumner secured, the ETMC now faced a basic question over its relationship to the 1955 murder. Should the commissioners—the default custodians of Till's memory in the twenty-first century—apologize? Did the commissioners or other county officials bear some fashion of responsibility simply by residing in Tallahatchie County? These questions were divisive. In one sense, they were resolved in Little's favor; the October ceremony did, after all, feature the ETMC's resolution. In another sense, however, these questions were resolved in favor of Frank Mitchener and other commissioners who saw no reason to apologize. Although the national press conference happened, and although it was widely celebrated, the story of just how it came to be reveals that paternalism was still alive and well in Tallahatchie County.

The public resolution almost didn't happen. In May of 2007, the resolution was drafted by Susan Glisson, but Frank Mitchener refused to sign the document. At issue was the word "apologize." An apology implied guilt, he reasoned, and neither he nor anyone else on the commission had anything for which to apologize.[148] Voicing a widely held opinion among the planters of Tallahatchie County, Mitchener told the *Memphis Commercial Appeal* that "the people who live here resent the fact that the murder was not committed here and the kidnapping did not occur in this county. . . . But because the body washed up on the Tallahatchie (County) side of the river, the trial was held here and we get blamed for it."[149] In order to avoid taking anymore blame, he refused to apologize. "He couldn't be sorrier for what had happened," he said, "but he had nothing do with it."[150] At this, he got up from an ETMC meeting, "walked out of the room, and went home."[151]

It took a private visit from Susan Glisson to change his mind. When she visited his home in the spring of 2007, he explained his case. The Mitchener family had always treated African Americans well, he argued. On this point, all were agreed. Even Jerome Little, who grew up as a sharecropper on the Mitchener Plantation, noted that it was "a place where blacks were treated with dignity and respect."[152] Why should Mitchener, of all people, apologize for a wrong that was committed by other people? From his perspective, the fact that the Mitchener family treated African Americans well meant there was no reason to apologize. For others, Mitchener's hesitation registered as yet another instance of paternalism—a habit of mind that understood racism only in individual terms. As James Cobb reminds us, a hyper-individualized social imaginary in which the category of racism is exhausted by a catalog of benevolent (or otherwise) interpersonal relations is a key tenet of the Delta's paternalism. "The problem," Cobb wrote, "was that individual whites were normally satisfied that they had fulfilled their obligation to blacks by simply treating fairly those with whom they dealt personally."[153] With racism measured as a set of interpersonal relations, there was no way Mitchener was going to apologize. Apologizing for a 1955 murder would have required a sense of the structural (rather than interpersonal) inequities that both enriched Mitchener and deprived Till of his life.

At this point, the line between forgetfulness and commemoration becomes blurry. The paternalism marked off by the Tallahatchie River had long been a source of forgetfulness. Or, more precisely, of exporting responsibility for Till's murder to people in other places. The old tradition of using the hill-country location of jurors' homes has, in the twenty-first century, a counterpart in Mitchener's refusal to apologize. In both instances, paternalism was the foundation of a refusal to accept the burdens of the past. Just as the racist-juror logic exported responsibility to the hills, Mitchener's individualism transferred responsibility to the people (in other counties and other times) who had physically laid hands on Emmett Till. In both instances, the Delta's planter class turned up guilt free.

Although Glisson could not convince Mitchener of structural racism, she did make headway with a more practical angle. The question of whether or not Tallahatchie County deserved its fate was, she reasoned, a moot point. The fact is that the trial was held here, the

eyes of the world are on us, and the reputation—and financial via-
bility—of our county depends on how we respond. Once he understood the document as a strategic move to offset undeserved notori-
ety, and once he edited out the two places in which the resolution said
the word "apologize," he was ready to sign.[154] It was his edited version
of the document that Pearson and Grayson read on October 2, 2007.
Some of Glisson's original prose remained; the document still talked
about telling the truth and about racial reconciliation, but it did not
apologize because, at the end of the day, Mitchener simply could not
be convinced that the people of Sumner had any reason to do so.

In many ways, the resolution was an unalloyed success. Until he
passed on December 14, 2011, at the age of fifty-nine, Jerome Little
was prone to get tears in his eyes as he reflected on the ceremony.[155]
The Till family wholeheartedly embraced the resolution, and media
outlets across the country carried news of a new racial order in Tallahatchie County. Till cousins Simeon Wright, Wheeler Parker, and
Deborah Watts expressed a profound gratitude for the ETMC and their
resolution. "The world has been holding its breath for fifty-two years,"
Watts said, "and now it's exhaling."[156] State Representative David Jordan—who emceed the event when Morgan Freeman proved unavail-
able—called the ceremony a "remarkable event."[157]

And yet, at the heart of the event was the same paternalism that
had long controlled the memory of Emmett Till in Tallahatchie
County. Through the influence of Mitchener, the paternalistic belief
that one's obligation to racial justice could be discharged through
interpersonal kindness shaped the public resolution that was the affective high point of the ceremony. And Mitchener was not alone.
Local high school teacher Joe Young responded to the ceremony in
a similar way: "I downplay the apology because I think that our generation can't apologize for what someone else did. We can only speak
for ourselves." Sheriff Brewer expressed similar sentiments from the
podium: "I've got a resolution all written up, but I'm not gonna read it.
I'm just gonna tell you we apologize. We're sorry for what happened. I
didn't do it; I was just a dream in Mom and Daddy's heart, but I know
how you feel."[158]

It is worth stressing, then, that the ceremony—the apex of ETMC publicity—was controlled by the topography of the Delta in two distinct ways. First, the fragility of Sumner—a fragility born of the river—was the argument Glisson used to overcome the paternalism that was keeping Mitchener from signing the resolution. Second, the paternalism itself had long been an effect of the path of the river through the county. The river divided the county juridically and racially. Juridically, it produced two courthouses and a longing to save Sumner's legal industry. Racially, it divided the paternalism of the Delta from the open racism of the hills. Pearson and Grayson never would have read the ETMC resolution from the steps of the courthouse on October 2, 2007, unless both distinctions were in play.

## CONCLUSION

Writing of the American West's dependence on irrigation, Donald Worster suggests that it is "first and most basically, a culture and a society built on, and absolutely dependent on, a sharply alienating, intensely managerial relationship with nature."[159] Just as much as the canals of the American West, the judicial districting of Tallahatchie County, the construction of its second courthouse, the addition of a bridge on State Highway 32, and, ultimately, the fight to save Sumner are evidence of the empowering entanglement of politics, nature, and culture. While such entanglement can be found anywhere public works have shaped the landscape, the case of Tallahatchie County is particularly complex. There, the management of the river became entwined not only with questions of politics and culture, but also with questions of race and memory. The river did not cause racism, of course, but it did distribute modes of oppression. Indeed, it is not too much to say that river—its path, its management, and the topography it produced—has, from 1955 to the present, been the most significant mediator between race and commemoration. The river was the transfer point, the relay through which questions of race were made ingredient in commemoration and by which questions of commemoration were influenced by race.

The effect of this entanglement of the river, race, and commemoration has blurred the line between politics and nature. The more one considers the commemoration of Emmett Till, the more it seems that the Tallahatchie River is an agent of memory and the more Till commemoration seems as natural as a geological outcropping. The truth, of course, is that commemoration is a hybrid production, inconceivable without contributions from human actors (Pearson, Glisson, Little) and nonhuman agents (soils, riverbeds).[160] In the words of Donna Haraway, the commemoration of Till's murder in Tallahatchie County is a "natural-technical object," the force of which is a function of the blurriness of the line that divides nature from culture.[161] It is almost as if the river itself, including the hills to its east and the soils to its west, has conspired to exonerate Delta elites of responsibility. After all, it was the political-aquatic distribution of racism that first blamed the murder on hill-country jurors and subsequently let the planter class evade a formal apology.

And yet, even as race inhabited the river and made possible the exporting of responsibility, the river was also the mechanism by which Glisson, Pearson, and Little pursued racial reconciliation. Had the county's long history of river management not threatened the town of Sumner, they would have had no leverage with which to bring the local power structure into the ETMC. Without the river, in other words, the landscape of Tallahatchie County would remain what it was until 2005, a barren commemorative desert.

In sum, in Tallahatchie County, the explosion of commemoration since 2005 has been inextricably bound up with river. The river both made possible the elementary fact of commemoration (it happened!) and shaped the racial contours of that commemoration. In this regard, it is perhaps not surprising that images of the muddy, serpentine river are among the most circulated visual backdrops for Till's story. Every documentary treatment of Till memories—including documentaries produced in 1985, 1987, 2003, and 2005—prominently feature panoramic shots of the river. In Rich Samuels's 1985 documentary, the slow-moving river is the backdrop for the opening of every segment and the backdrop over which the credits roll. Three years later, the narrator of *Eyes on the Prize* made this visual logic explicit: "[Till's] story starts at the Tallahatchie River in Money." Whether or not Till's story *started* at the river is a matter of debate, but it is certain that the river has shepherded Till's story for over sixty years. Without the river's influence, the stories we know of Till's murder, his acquittal, and his commemoration in Tallahatchie County would be profoundly different.

## CHAPTER THREE

# EMMETT TILL, TALLAHATCHIE COUNTY, AND THE BIRTHPLACE OF THE MOVEMENT

When Richard M. Dickson submitted his "Historical Restoration and Addition" to the ETMC in January 2006, he concluded with three elegant paragraphs copied verbatim from PBS.org. Citing the influence of Till's murder on Rosa Parks and Martin Luther King Jr., Dickson wrote, "The murder of Emmett Till was a watershed in the development of the nascent movement for civil rights. Some historians describe it as the real spark that ignited broad-based support for the movement."[1] There was nothing original about such sentiments. Dickson was reproducing the prose of PBS, and PBS, in turn, was simply giving voice to the conventional wisdom. Since the mid-1960s, there has been a vibrant tradition of dating the origin of the civil rights movement to the murder of Emmett Till. While there has never been consensus on the matter—plenty of scholars still prefer the Montgomery bus boycott or *Brown v. Board*—Till's murder is a well-respected option. Consider, for example, the testimony of Joyce Ladner, a Mississippi activist involved with SNCC.

> When I met people in SNCC in 1962 . . . all of us remembered the photograph of Emmett Till's face, lying in the coffin, on the cover of *Jet* magazine. . . . Everyone of my SNCC friends I've known 40 years can recall that photograph. That galvanized a generation as a symbol—that was our symbol—that if they did it to him, they could do it to us.[2]

The causal relationship Ladner posited between Till's murder and the civil rights movement has been reinforced by statuary, poetry, roadside markers, oral histories, dissertations, novels, and every documentary film ever produced on Till's murder.[3] The last book-length treatment of the lynching that did *not* draw a causal connection between the murder and the movement was Hugh Steven Whitaker's master's thesis in 1963. While some scholars have been more measured than others, since the early 1960s it has literally been impossible to engage the Till murder without treating it, in Dickson's words, as a "watershed in the development of the nascent movement for civil rights."[4] Even the volunteers who flooded to Mississippi and fought for civil rights in the 1960s are now routinely identified as the "Emmett Till generation."[5]

While Till-sparked-the-movement claims were a matter of course by the twenty-first century, Dickson's "Historical Restoration and Addition" was not simply a reflection of conventional wisdom. As an architect hired by Tallahatchie County to provide schematic drawings for the restoration of the second-district courthouse, Dickson's ultimate investment was not in the historical significance of the murder per se, but rather in the historical significance of the county courthouse. For this reason, where PBS concluded that Till's murder was the "real spark" of the movement, Dickson added a proviso.

> The location the spark occurred is the Tallahatchie County Courthouse in Sumner, Mississippi. It is the place where people can come and remember. The Courthouse must be restored so future generations can kindle the spark, learn from our past and move forward in freedom.[6]

For Dickson and the ETMC, the point was not simply that Till sparked the movement, but, rather, that the spark came from the second-district Tallahatchie County Courthouse (see figure 12). The ETMC's insistence on the centrality of Tallahatchie County was rooted neither in pride nor in an intellectual calculus of etiological factors. It was rooted, rather, in the simple fact that the influence of Tallahatchie County was the *condition of commemoration.* If the movement did not

FIGURE 12. The second-district Tallahatchie County Courthouse, 1955. Special Collections Department, University of Memphis Libraries. Used by permission.

start in the county—or, if that argument could not be sold—there would be no grant money with which to commemorate Till's murder. Tallahatchie County would remain as barren as its neighbor to the west, Sunflower County.

For this reason the ETMC made a remarkable decision. Although they had no interest in the particular "restorations" or "additions" proposed by Dickson, they nonetheless included his "Historical Restoration and Addition" as part of their application for a 2006 Community Heritage Preservation grant from the MDAH.[7] Funded at $36,600, the grant financed a study assessing the feasibility of restoring the Sumner courthouse to "the 1955 condition when it housed the Emmit [*sic*] Till trial."[8] From the perspective of obtaining MDAH money, it was not enough that Till's murder was a "watershed" moment in the "nascent movement for civil rights." Nor was it enough that it was the "real spark that ignited broad-based support." In addition to these claims, the ETMC needed Dickson's conclusion that the "location the spark occurred is the Tallahatchie County Courthouse."

No one understood the economic ramifications of etiology more acutely than Johnny B. Thomas, mayor of Glendora and the original treasurer of the ETMC. In 1998, Thomas oversaw the purchase of the Glendora Cotton Gin, the site from which many believe the fan that held Till's body in the river was stolen. Despite control of the site, his applications for funding to do commemorative work have been repeatedly rejected (see chapter 5). In fact, Thomas was one of only three applicants to be turned down for a 2011 Mississippi Civil Rights Historical Sites (MCRHS) grant. This was a strikingly noncompetitive grant program that funded a number of Emmett Till historical sites, including Ben Roy's Service Station (chapter 4), a site with no civil rights history at all.[9] Beyond his failure to secure grant money, the state also declined to endorse his application to list the gin on the National Register of Historic Places. He suffered both setbacks because the MDAH could not verify his claim regarding the origin of the fan. The MDAH's architectural historian, Bill Gatlin, wrote the department's 2010 report on the Till case. He concluded, "nothing establishes that the gin fan came from Glendora."[10] And, on the basis of this uncertainty, Mayor Thomas found both his application for funding declined and his request for historical status rejected.

Although different in outcome, the experiences of Dickson and Thomas with the MDAH underscore a basic point about money, memory, and geography: it pays to be on site. The most conspicuous difference between the ETMC application for the courthouse and the

Thomas application on behalf of the cotton gin is geographical authenticity. The MDAH believed the ETMC's claim that the courthouse "is the location the spark occurred" but did not trust Thomas's gin-fan itinerary. The differential results are painfully obvious. The courtroom has been beautifully restored with over $4 million in grant money and has become the central hub of Emmett Till tourism, with 3,500 visitors in 2015.[11] The cotton gin, by contrast, is languishing; until it won an earmark from a friendly legislator, it was little more than a homemade museum surviving on money generated from low-income housing (see chapter 5).

It is difficult to predict what kind of money, if any, the courthouse would have received had the ETMC not consistently peddled Dickson's line about the causal importance of Tallahatchie County. The fact is, however, that they did peddle it. Relentlessly. The claim that Tallahatchie County—and the courthouse in particular—is the origin of the American civil rights movement is the single most repeated (and well-funded) claim across eleven years (2006–17) of grant writing. Virtually every dollar spent by the county on Till commemoration—and they have spent millions from 2006 to the present—was awarded in response to an appeal based first and foremost on the causal influence of Tallahatchie County.

These numbers are even more impressive when they are contextualized by the fact that no history of the civil rights movement has ever bestowed significant attention on Tallahatchie County. While the Till trial was undeniably a major media event, Tallahatchie County had significantly less movement activity than most other Delta counties.[12] Leflore County was bustling with movement activity; Fannie Lou Hamer gave the movement a beachhead in Sunflower County; Aaron Henry was headquartered in Coahoma County; and Amzie Moore and T. R. M. Howard led the fight in Bolivar County. With all this activity in nearby counties, Tallahatchie County is conspicuous primarily for its *lack* of movement activity. This is nowhere more evident than in the two magisterial works published on the Mississippi movement in the mid-1990s. Charles Payne's *I've Got the Light of Freedom* mentions the county only twice in five hundred pages—and both times only as an incidental location of passing interest. His map identifies not a single site of civil rights interest in Tallahatchie County.[13] Likewise, John Dittmer's *Local People*, an exhaustive account of on-the-ground organizing in Mississippi, could not identify a single "center of Civil Rights activity" in Tallahatchie County.[14] Dittmer's map suggests that Tallahatchie County was one of the few Delta counties without *any* movement activity.

None of this was an impediment to Dickson or the ETMC. In 2006 they began crafting the story of Tallahatchie County's centrality to the civil rights movement, inserting it into every grant application they filed. Regardless of its historical merits, the claim that the origin of the movement was now languishing provided powerful leverage on the coffers of state and federal funders. Beginning in 2006, grant money began pouring into the ETMC and, via the ETMC, into western Tallahatchie County. And, slowly but surely, as the ETMC oversaw the construction of an entire commemorative infrastructure (restored courthouse, museum, roadside markers), the county assumed a status that would have been unthinkable in the 1990s: it became the origin of the civil rights movement. For example, a sign unveiled on the historic courthouse lawn during the national press conference in 2007 concludes, "Till's murder, coupled with the trial and acquittal of these two men, drew international attention and galvanized the Civil Rights Movement in Mississippi and the nation" (see figure 13). With signs such as this posted across the county, the ETMC made Tallahatchie County into what they needed it to be: the birthplace of the civil rights movement.

Precisely speaking, then, the causal status of Tallahatchie County as the origin of the movement is a *product* of commemoration rather than an *object* of commemoration. Till was not remembered because Tallahatchie County *was* the birthplace of the civil rights movement, it *became* the birthplace of the movement in order that the Till might be remembered and the courthouse might be restored. In this chapter, then, I tell the story of how Tallahatchie County—a site that barely registered in the dominant histories of the 1990s—became the origin of the civil rights movement. It is yet one more example of the ecology

**EMMETT TILL MURDER TRIAL**

In August 1955 the body of Emmett Till, a 14-year-old black youth from Chicago, was found in the Tallahatchie River. On September 23, in a five day trial held in this courthouse, an all-white jury acquitted two white men, Roy Bryant and J. W. Milam, of the murder. Both later confessed to the murder in a magazine interview. Till's murder, coupled with the trial and acquittal of these two men, drew international attention and galvanized the Civil Rights Movement in Mississippi and the nation.

MISSISSIPPI DEPARTMENT OF ARCHIVES AND HISTORY, 2007

**FIGURE 13.** Dedicated in October 2007 in Sumner, MS, this was the first sign erected by the Emmett Till Memorial Commission. Photograph by Ashleigh Coleman. Used by permission.

of memory. The ETMC had to rewrite the racial history of their county before commemorative work could move forward; the entanglement of race, place, and commemoration was a condition of memory work. Although the ETMC is, strictly speaking, a *memory* commission, in this instance, the work of the commission was as creative as it was recollective. They created a past for Tallahatchie County in order that they might restore the courthouse, save their town, and remember Till. In this sense, the first task of commemoration was to make Tallahatchie County worthy of remembrance.

### EMMETT TILL'S BODY AND THE
### BIRTH OF THE MOVEMENT

One of the earliest commemorative projects to connect Till and the civil rights movement came in 1976. In September of that year, at a ceremony in Denver City Park, local officials unveiled a statue that made the linkages between the Emmett Till murder and the civil rights movement explicit. The bronze statue depicted Martin Luther King Jr. and Emmett Till standing side by side.[15] Although King and Till never knew each other in life, the twenty-foot, $110,000 statue joined them via the history of the movement. As many have noted, "Till's August 28, 1955 murder and King's 1963 'I Have a Dream' speech occurred exactly eight years apart."[16] The inscription on the pedestal of the Denver statue explicitly links Till, King, and the wider movement: "Lynched in Mississippi in 1955, his death and the Montgomery Bus Boycott launched what became a non-violent revolution for freedom."

Although the statue would not last long in Denver, the connection it forged between Till and the civil rights movement would.[17] By the second half of the 1980s, such a connection was commonplace. In 1985, for example, Rich Samuels produced the first of several Till documentaries. Created for WMAQ Chicago, the documentary opened with a shot of Denver's statue and then juxtaposed the murder of Emmett Till and King's "I Have a Dream" speech—a connection on which, many years later, the ETMC would capitalize. Lest his audience miss the connection latent in the juxtaposition of the Till murder with the single most iconic speech of the civil rights movement, Samuels made the lesson explicit by titling his documentary *The Murder and the Movement*. Two years later, in 1987, *Eyes on the Prize* turned to the Till story only eleven minutes into its six-hour rehearsal of the movement, suggesting, at least by placement, that Till's murder sparked the movement.[18] One year after *Eyes on the Prize*, Clenora Frances Hudson completed a Ford Foundation–funded dissertation titled "Emmett Till: The Impetus for the Modern Civil Rights Movement." The Denver statue and the high-profile documentaries notwithstanding, Hudson argued that the Till murder "has been vastly underappreciated as a main stimulus for the Civil Rights Movement."[19]

Much to the chagrin of Hudson (publishing as Hudson-Weems since 1994), who insists that the civil rights influence of Emmett Till is her own, unique insight, the claim has become a matter of course since the mid- to late 1980s. In fact, Devery Anderson's definitive 2015 *Emmett Till* is subtitled *The Murder That Shocked the World and Propelled the Civil Rights Movement*. One measure of just how commonplace the claim has become is the tremendous effort Hudson-Weems has exerted to claim the insight as her own. In self-published books of 2006 and 2007, Hudson-Weems accused a wide range of scholars of plagiarism. In her view, she "holds the research rights" to Till's story, and anyone who suggests a link between Till and the movement without giving her credit is guilty of intellectual property theft.[20] She even suggested an analogy between the lynching of Emmett Till by white murderers and the stealing of her ideas by other scholars, what she characterized as a "cruel act of public intellectual lynching."[21] Her claim has no merit. She was not the first to make the connection, and her analogy grossly distorts the nature and severity of plagiarism.[22] Her protests notwithstanding, the claim that Emmett Till sparked the civil rights movement has become one of the most widely circulated claims in the entirety of the Till literature. If Anderson does not cite Hudson-Weems to justify his subtitle, this is because the claim is so general, so widely disseminated, and so unoriginal that it hardly requires a citation.

Until the 2006 efforts of the ETMC, the connection of Till to the civil rights movement hinged, in particular, on the vast circulation and sheer influence of a photograph of Till's mutilated face that appeared in *Jet* magazine.[23] Taken by photographer David Jackson at A. A. Rayner's mortuary in Chicago and reprinted in the *Chicago Defender* and the *Pittsburgh Courier*, the photograph inspired what Charles Payne called the "Till generation"—the generation of activists who came to the fore in the 1960s but who were moved to action by the 1955 photograph. In a way that nothing else could, Jackson's photograph of Till's beaten body captured the sheer violence visited on the body—and especially the face—of Emmett Till. Although the brutality of the picture is difficult to describe, the words of John Edgar Wideman come close. He described a face "crushed, chewed, [and] mutilated."[24] A face "with all the boy, all the human being battered out of it."[25]

Jackson's photograph of Till's body in its Chicago casket has always been a lightning rod of controversy, even among those who share a commitment to commemorating the murder. Some, such as the ETMC's Johnny Thomas, argue that every commemoration of Till's murder must include the photograph—how else to capture the truth of what happened? After all, Thomas notes, did not Till's mother insist on an open-casket funeral, famously proclaiming her desire that "the world . . . see what I've seen"?[26] Others, such as historian Robin D. G. Kelley are more circumspect, arguing that the photograph is so explicit that its display reproduces the terror it depicts.[27] In March 2017, the controversy flared at New York City's Whitney Museum of American Art. Artist Dana Schutz's "Open Casket," an abstract rendering of Till's body with similarities to Jackson's photograph, inspired a multinational controversy about the prerogative of white artists to circulate images of Till's body.[28] Regardless of how the controversy is settled, it does suggest the continued relevance of Payne's old category, the "Till generation."[29] Just as the photograph moved people to action in the 1960s, it continues to do so today.

Virtually everyone *outside* of Tallahatchie County agrees that the Jackson photograph transformed the Till murder from one more 1955 Mississippi lynching—alongside the forgotten lynchings of Lamar

Smith and George W. Lee—into the unforgettable spark of the civil rights movement. Frederick Harris proved the point with quantitative data. He concluded that 66 percent of respondents remembered the murder of Emmett Till, a percentage not terribly different from those that remembered the Montgomery bus boycott, *Brown v. Board*, or the Scottsboro trials. However, Harris concluded that the Till murder had a greater influence on the civil rights movement than these other iconic events. This, he suggested, could be traced to the influence of the Jackson photograph.[30] Art historian Maurice Berger would likely agree. In *For All the World to See: Visual Culture and the Struggle for Civil Rights*, he suggested that of all the events that fostered political activism, Till's murder was the most dependent on photography.[31]

Movement veterans dramatically confirm the sensibilities of Harris and Berger. In the late 1980s, African American congressman Charles Diggs claimed that the Jackson photograph was "the greatest media product in the last forty or fifty years, because that picture stimulated a lot of interest and anger on the part of blacks all over the country."[32] Expressing a similar sentiment, Delta activist Amzie Moore claimed that the photograph made Till's murder "the best advertised lynching I had ever heard."[33]

No one, however, has thought about the Jackson photograph and its influence on the civil rights movement as carefully as Christine Harold and Kevin DeLuca. Taking the influence of Till's murder on the civil rights movement as a matter of course, they asked in 2005, "What *exactly* is it about this case that evoked such a dramatic response?" Their answer? The grainy photograph from *Jet* magazine. The image, they explained, "articulated the ineffable qualities of American racism in ways words simply could not do" and, for that reason, "served as a political catalyst for black Americans in the then-fledgling civil rights movement."[34] There is, then, wide consensus that, to the extent that the Till murder sparked the civil rights movement, it did so because of Jackson's photograph of Till's mutilated corpse. From Rich Samuels, to *Eyes on the Prize*, to a wide range of historians, to the testimony of movement veterans—it was Jackson's photograph, taken in Chicago, which made the Till murder the spark of the movement.[35] As recently as 2016, *Time* magazine called it "the photo that changed the civil rights movement."[36]

This is not good news for Tallahatchie County. The stronger the consensus that it was David Jackson's photograph that made Till's murder a galvanizing event for the civil rights movement, the more difficult it is to identify Tallahatchie County as ground zero of the movement. The photograph was, after all, taken in Chicago, at the corner of Forty-First and Cottage Grove, the site of A. A. Rayner and Sons funeral home. When tens of thousands of onlookers saw the body displayed during the open-casket funeral, Harold and DeLuca report that "any comforting geographical boundaries were forever punctured."[37] The photograph of the broken body made clear that Till's murder could not be confined to the South—it could happen to anyone, anywhere. This much was clear to the fifteen-year-old Julian Bond, living in Pennsylvania. "I felt vulnerable for the first time in my life—Till was a year younger—and recall believing that this could easily happen to me."[38] Till's mother learned the same lesson, "The murder of my son has shown me that what happens to any of us, anywhere in the world, had better be the business of us all."[39]

Among its other effects, the Jackson photograph nationalized—if not globalized—the violence done to Till's body. The affective power of the photograph stems from its juxtaposition of youthful innocence and brutal torture. It was a picture of a boy, beaten. Shelby Steele put it best, Till was "the quintessential embodiment of black innocence, brought down by a white evil so portentous and apocalyptical, so gnarled and hideous, that it left us with a feeling not far from awe."[40] Because the visceral grip of the photograph stemmed from the combination of innocence and brutality, its effects were decoupled from the county in which the beating occurred. As Mamie Till-Mobley noted, the beating could have happened "anywhere in the world." From the perspective of a nascent movement needing volunteers, this was the need of the hour, an image that stressed the threat against even the most innocent, the most removed from the political to-and-fro of agitation in the Jim Crow South. It was precisely *because* the image "punctured" comforting geographical boundaries that it galvanized the civil rights movement. Had Jackson's photograph been easily localized, its terror confined to southern agitators, it never would have "changed the civil rights movement."

From the perspective of the ETMC, however, the geographical dislocation of the Jackson photograph was no boon. To the extent that it was the photograph that transformed Till's murder into the spark of the civil rights movement, the ETMC could claim no special status for Tallahatchie County. And, without originary status, the county had no purchase on grant money; ETMC treasurer Johnny B. Thomas had learned this in his dealings with the MDAH's Bill Gatlin. If the ETMC had any hope of grant money, they needed Tallahatchie County, not Chicago or the dislocated threat of violence, to register as the birthplace of the movement. To make Tallahatchie County worthy of remembrance, they focused not on the photograph but rather on the trial, which was, of course, held in their very own second-district courthouse.

The shift in emphasis from the photograph to the trial is particularly evident in the sign erected by the ETMC on the courthouse lawn in Sumner, Mississippi, in 2007 (see figure 13). In this regard, it is important to stress that the *initial* draft of the sign focused on the open-casket funeral Mamie Till-Mobley held in Chicago "to show what had been done to her son."[41] It was at the funeral, of course, that tens of thousands of onlookers—David Jackson included—saw Till's body and were moved to action. The draft of the sign acknowledged as much, "The resulting public outcry is deemed one of the main sparks that ignited the Civil Rights Movement."[42] But this sign was never created. Before it was cast by Sewah Studios and unveiled at the national press conference, the ETMC shifted the origin of the movement from Chicago to Sumner. The final copy—standing to this day on Sumner Square—focused neither on the photograph, nor the funeral, nor the body. Rather, it focused on the "five day trial" held in Tallahatchie County: "Till's murder, coupled with the trial and the acquittal of these two men, drew international attention and galvanized the Civil Rights Movement in Mississippi and the nation."

Although the ETMC has erected nine signs across the county, the one on the courthouse lawn in Sumner is the only one that is officially part of the MDAH's state historical marker program. Because it is part of this program, the ETMC was required to submit documentation to verify the sign's prose. They submitted page 148 of Whitaker's 1963 thesis—the page that talks about the international significance of the trial. They also submitted a page printed from the PBS website about the impact of the trial (the same page Dickson had copied). Finally, and most importantly, they included a portion of Dickson's 2006 "Historical Restoration and Addition." It apparently did not matter (and it certainly was not noted) that Dickson's report was commissioned and paid for by the ETMC (and thus was not the most trustworthy form of documentation). The important part was Dickson's conclusion: "The location the spark occurred is the Tallahatchie County Courthouse in Sumner, MS."[43]

The sign that now stands on Sumner Square—and the documentation preserved in the archives—set the pattern for Till commemoration in Tallahatchie County. In both the grant writing that funded the work and in the signs erected by the ETMC, there is marked emphasis on the trial and, more generally, on Tallahatchie County as the site that sparked the civil rights movement. In 2010, Mayor Johnny B. Thomas even erected a sign to this effect in a small park on the outskirts of Glendora on the southern edge of the county. The sign read, "It's a pleasure to be given the opportunity to serve this Historic Community that SPARKED THE CIVIL RIGHTS MOVEMENT." Or, as Mississippi senator David Jordan explained to a group of citizens gathered in the Sumner courthouse, "Like the start of the civil war, [the Till trial] was the start of the civil rights movement."[44]

The historical accuracy of these arguments may be disputed. Whether such claims stand up under inspection or not, one thing is certain: the promise of money made the meaning of the county fungible. Although one might suppose that the grant writers simply leveraged the history of Tallahatchie County to make Till commemoration possible, *the particular history peddled by the applicants did not predate the applications themselves.* For this reason, commemoration did not so much recall the history *of* Tallahatchie County as it did cre-

ate a new, fundable history *for* Tallahatchie County. Sometimes commemoration requires a new racial history.

## ROSA PARKS AND A NEW BIRTHPLACE
## FOR THE MOVEMENT

The Tallahatchie County Courthouse in Sumner has received seven
grants from the MDAH. The first of these was in 2002, three years before the creation of the ETMC and well before the plans to renovate
the courthouse to its 1955 condition. At the time of the 2002 application, the only leverage Tallahatchie County had on MDAH money was
the sheer disrepair of its courthouse. Virtually the only document preserved in connection with this grant is the April 2004 grand jury report
on the "physical status of the courthouse."[45] Submitted to the MDAH
after the grant was won, the report provides an itemized account of a
courthouse in shambles. From ceilings to tiles to plumbing to stair-
ways—the report documented decay and neglect in every recess of the
facility. Apparently moved by such dire conditions, the MDAH provided $100,000 with which the county paid Richard M. Dickson and
Kermit B. Buck and Sons to weatherize the exterior of the building.[46]

While $100,000 is a sizeable investment, this money did not even
begin to address the problems listed in the grand jury's report. It did
not address the failing structures, the collapsing plaster, or the leaky
plumbing. It simply funded the application of Thorocoat to the exterior masonry of the building in the hopes that further decay could
be forestalled. In order to actually restore the courthouse, the county
would need a more powerful argument than physical disrepair. When
Jerome Little founded the ETMC in late 2005, the county suddenly
found themselves with a new claim on MDAH money. In every grant
submitted after the creation of the ETMC, the county emphasized that
the courthouse—and the county more generally—was the site where
the civil rights movement was born.

Using the memory of Emmett Till's murder to locate the origins
of the civil rights movement in Tallahatchie County proved to be a
lucrative strategy. In grant applications submitted in 2006 and 2007,

the county made both arguments—stressing both the physical decay of the courthouse and the historical importance of the site. By 2009, however, the historical/commemorative argument became so successful that the physical status of the courthouse dropped out of grant applications altogether.[47] Indeed, from 2009 forward, every grant application from the ETMC to the MDAH contained the same typo-riddled paragraph, cut and pasted from one application to the next, that contained a variant of the awkward courthouse-and-spark metaphor first deployed by Dickson: "The courthouse is the site of the Emmett Till murder trial, which has received national and international attention as the 'spark that started the civil rights movement in America.'"[48] Ultimately, the courthouse was restored not because it was in disrepair, but because Till's murder provided the county the evidence needed to root the civil rights movement in the Sumner courthouse. This was dramatically confirmed in January 2017, when the National Park Service awarded the ETMC $500,000 to preserve an already-repaired courthouse. The first sentence of the National Park Service grant narrative ran, "The 1955 lynching of Emmett Till is widely regarded as a catalyst for the Civil Rights Movement."[49]

At the center of the ETMC's fund-raising campaign was a figure of unquestioned civil rights credentials: Rosa Parks. The Montgomery bus boycott of December 1955 is often cited as the beginning of the civil rights movement. But why did Rosa Parks refuse to give up her seat? If her motivation could be traced back three months to the murder of Emmett Till, then the origin of the civil rights movement could be traced, not to Montgomery County, Alabama, but to Tallahatchie County, Mississippi. The mere possibility that the legendary Montgomery activist could be linked to Tallahatchie County was so seductive that even though doubts circulated about whether or not Rosa Parks had in fact any historical connection to the Delta, her story nonetheless became the ETMC's most prominent, most repeated, and perhaps even its most lucrative fund-raising strategy. After all, Parks provided the ETMC with a mechanism to connect Till's murder to the movement *without* the David Jackson photograph. Unlike the photograph, which connected Till to the movement via Chicago, the story of Parks's growing commitment to activism flowed through Tallahatchie County and thus provided the ETMC the history they needed to secure funding. Parks rooted the movement in Tallahatchie County, and Tallahatchie County, now understood as the birthplace of the movement, had the history it needed to command money with which to commemorate Till's murder.

Between 2007 and 2009, the ETMC had its best fund-raising years ever. Largely due to commissioner Frank Mitchener's relationship with US senator Thad Cochran, the ETMC was able to secure two federal earmarks—for $700,000 and $750,000—for the restoration of the courthouse. On January 7, 2008, to help Cochran secure the funds, Jerome Little provided him with a detailed summary of ETMC's work, the first paragraph of which stressed that the events of the Tallahatchie County Courthouse "changed the course of history."

> The Tallahatchie County Courthouse in Sumner, Mississippi is nationally significant because of events occurring there at the beginning of the civil rights movement in the United States. In September 1955, J. W. Milam and Roy Bryant were tried for the brutal murder of fourteen-year-old Emmett Till. The case was highly publicized internationally and the acquittal of the defendants changed the course of history for this nation. . . . Three months later, Rosa Parks refused to give up her seat on a bus in Montgomery. Mrs. Parks has stated that she was thinking of Emmett Till during her arrest.[50]

Note that Parks links Till to the movement via the trial (in Tallahatchie County) rather than the David Jackson photograph. In a 2006 interview two years before the letter to Cochran, Little made the Rosa Parks logic even more explicit. "Rosa Parks stated," he claimed, "that the death of Emmett Till was the beginning of the civil rights movement."[51]

It is difficult to know whether Rosa Parks did, in fact, make such statement. Although there is no place in her published writing where such a claim might be found, it is *possible* that she was motivated by Till's murder. We know, for example, that four days before she initiated the boycott, she was in the congregation at Martin Luther King's

Dexter Avenue Baptist Church when Dr. T. R. M. Howard visited and told the story of Till's murder for the black population of Montgomery. Given Howard's role in the trial, and his role in the racial politics of the Delta, it is hardly surprising that his narrative of the murder featured the trial in Tallahatchie County but made no mention of the Chicago funeral or the David Jackson photograph.[52] The timing of the talk was evidence enough for historians David T. Beito and Linda Royster Beito, who, like the ETMC's Jerome Little, concluded that "Till's murder was central to her thinking at the time of her arrest."[53]

However, while it is of course possible that Parks was "thinking of Emmett" at the time of her arrest, it is far from certain. The claim can be traced no further back than Jesse Jackson's 2003 introduction to Mamie Till-Mobley and Chris Benson's *Death of Innocence*. In that volume, and again while speaking at Park's funeral in 2005, Jackson argued that "Emmett Till was 'the big bang,' the Tallahatchie River was 'the big bang' of the civil rights movement." As proof, he told of a personal conversation with Parks. When asked why she refused to cede her seat, she responded, "I thought of Emmett Till and I couldn't go back."[54] Although Jerome Little was not at Parks's funeral, he may have gotten the story from the longtime Greenwood politician David Jordan. Jordan was instrumental in the early stages of the ETMC, and, in 2014, he too claimed that Rosa Parks had confided in him privately about the importance of Till's murder.[55] "I remember engaging in a conversation with Rosa Parks and hearing from her own mouth that the death of Emmett Till is what triggered her refusal to give up her bus seat to a white man."[56]

While the independent recollections of similar sentiments by Jackson and Jordan do make the Parks lore plausible, it nonetheless remains true that the claim that Parks was "thinking of Emmett" in her moment of famous disobedience is, as Devery Anderson put it, "only a secondhand statement."[57] In fact, in September 2017 the Parks quotation was *removed* from the Mississippi Freedom Trail marker in front of Bryant's Grocery and Meat Market (compare figures 14 and 15). Allan Hammons—whose Hammons and Associates oversees the production of the Mississippi trail initiatives—had received so many

**FIGURE 14.** This is the first sign on the Mississippi Freedom Trail (Money, MS) as it existed until the summer of 2017. Note the quotation from Rosa Parks in the top right of the sign. Photo by Pablo Correa. Used by permission.

**FIGURE 15.** This is the first sign on the Mississippi Freedom Trail (Money, MS) after it was replaced in 2017. Note the top, right corner. The quotation from Rosa Parks has been replaced with a quotation by Mamie Till. Photo by Pablo Correa. Used by permission.

questions about the historical legitimacy of the Parks quotation that he decided there was not sufficient historical evidence to include it on the sign.

From the perspective of the Delta, however, the Parks story might as well be gospel truth. While Hammons recently redacted the Parks quotation from the state marker, the same quotation was integral to funding the marker in the first place. Indeed, the very first sentence of the official proposal for the Freedom Trail got right to the point.

> Among the most significant and seminal sites in the American Civil Rights Movement can be found in Mississippi. Many believe that the 1955 murder and funeral of Emmitt [*sic*] Till and the subsequent trial and later confession may well be the genesis of the Movement, giving Rosa Parks the strength to sit down and Reverend Martin Luther King, Jr. the courage to stand up.[58]

Less than a year after this proposal, the MDA unveiled the Freedom Trail marker outside of Bryant's Grocery and Meat Market in Money, Mississippi. On the top right-hand side of the north face of the marker, Hammons and Associates inserted the "quotation" from Rosa Parks: "I thought of Emmett Till and when the bus driver ordered me to move to the back, I just couldn't move" (see figure 14). The "second-hand statement" had become state-approved history. It needed to be, for if Till did not inspire Parks who in turn sparked a national movement, there would be no justification for making Bryant's Grocery and Meat Market the first stop on the Freedom Trail. After all, over three hundred communities in Mississippi lobbied the MDA for a chance to participate in the trail.[59] But because funding was premised on the claim that Till gave Parks "the strength to sit down," the state made the Till marker the first stop on an itinerary of freedom.

Formally unveiled at 3 p.m. on May 18, 2011, with members of the Till family in attendance, the Freedom Trail marker in front of Bryant's Grocery was dedicated, and the Parks lore became official history. Neither the legislative proposal nor the sign gave any indication that the Parks quotation was anything other than verified truth. Even though the prose was crafted by a task force composed of scholars and movement veterans, and even though the task force was led by the highly capable Luther Brown of Delta State University, no one seemed to notice that the act of commemoration (from funding through execution) authorized an unverified tale. There could hardly be a clearer example of how practices of commemoration are often forced to *create* a history worthy of commemoration. Without turning the legend of Parks into a direct quotation, without bracketing the uncertainty of their claim, the MDA might never have gotten the funding needed to launch the Freedom Trail. Perhaps the only way to remember one's history is to produce it on a fundable model.

The ETMC, for their part, found the Rosa Parks lore equally lucrative. Beyond Little's appeal to Senator Cochran, which deployed the Parks story and netted well over a million dollars, the ETMC's next two grants leaned heavily on the Parks connection. In applications for Community Heritage Preservation grants in 2009 and 2011, the ETMC inserted the Parks story into form letters, signed by a wide variety of dignitaries and submitted to the MDAH as supporting documents. The letter claimed, "Mrs. Parks has stated that she was thinking of Emmett Till during her arrest."[60] The most moving invocation in these applications, however, was an undated letter from Suanne Strider Buttrey, the great-granddaughter of H. Clarence Strider, the openly racist sheriff of Tallahatchie County who, in 1955, played a crucial role convincing the jury that the NAACP had planted a body in the Tallahatchie River to stir up trouble. At the "risk of causing resentment" within her family, Buttrey wrote a courageous letter about her desire to be involved in the ETMC. She concluded by claiming that Till's murder inspired Rosa Parks's refusal to move to the back of the bus.[61]

The 2009 application included a four-page, full-color brochure created by Belinda Stewart Architects called "Emmett Till National Site Development" (see figure 16). This brochure is the ETMC's most-polished, most-nuanced argument that the civil rights movement can be traced to Tallahatchie County. The first page of the brochure is a full-page picture of Till's uncle Moses Wright standing erect with his left hand extended, pointing his finger. This posture replicates the

**FIGURE 16.** Brochure created by Belinda Stewart Architects for the Emmett Till Memorial Commission, 2007. Belinda Stewart Architects. Used by permission.

famous moment in the Till trial when Wright extended his left arm and pointed at J. W. Milam and Roy Bryant, accusing them of kidnapping his nephew. Also on the first page are three inset pictures: Emmett Till, Rosa Parks, and Martin Luther King Jr. The inset of King is on the bottom right of the page. It is a photograph taken from the

Detroit version of the "I Have a Dream" speech, the not-as-famous precursor to his performance on the National Mall. King's posture mirrors the posture of Moses Wright: he stands with his right arm extended, pointing. The visual continuity from the pointing Wright, through Parks, to the pointing King (who is in the act of giving a version of the iconic address) alludes to the influence of the Till trial on the civil rights movement. Not content with allusion, the text on the front page of the brochure makes the lesson explicit. Quoting, verbatim, the language of the letter from Jerome Little to Senator Thad Cochran (quoted above), the text read, "The case was highly publicized internationally and the acquittal of the defendants changed the course of history for the nation." Like the Freedom Trail marker, the brochure then put the ubiquitous Rosa Parks lore between quotation marks: "I thought about Emmett and I couldn't go back." Finally, the brochure quotes King's Detroit speech: "I have a dream this afternoon. I have a dream that there will be a day that we will no longer face the atrocities that Emmett Till had to face or Medgar Evers had to face, that all men can live with dignity." Although these references to Till and Evers were removed by Dr. King before he made his "I Have a Dream" speech famous on the National Mall, the ETMC reinserted them on its brochure. By doing so, the brochure drew a straight line of influence from the trial in Sumner where Moses Wright stood and pointed to the most iconic moment of the civil rights movement: Dr. King standing and pointing, delivering his "I Have a Dream" speech.

Following two pages of pictures, the brochure concluded by reflecting on the consequences of a county remade as the origin of the movement. It will "create jobs, jumpstart the region's economy and prepare the people of the area for the 21st century by spurring private investment potential for the area and job growth." The four-page brochure is thus a perfect example of why it was so important to the ETMC that Tallahatchie County was the birthplace of the civil rights movement. Beyond its proven status as a lucrative fund-raising strategy, it also proved correct the convictions of both factions of the ETMC. On the one hand, for those who wanted to use Till's memory for economic returns, what could be better than promoting the central business district of Sumner as the starting point of the freedom movement. The brochure explained, "Economic stimulus applied here [in Tallahatchie County] will increase the opportunity for private investment, bring job creation and retention, allow for renewable energy retrofit and provide an educational opportunity as a 21st century living classroom." On the other hand, for those who were invested in Till commemoration as a means of racial reconciliation, what could be better than connecting Till's murder to King's dream of a day in which "all men can live with dignity."[62]

If Tallahatchie County could become the birthplace of the civil rights movement, everyone in the county would win. The legacy of the movement, the history of racial justice, economic investment, and Till's memory were all bound up with a "secondhand" statement from Rosa Parks or, more broadly, with a geographically partisan history of the movement. Everyone on the ETMC had an investment in seeing their county turned into the natal grounds of civil rights. And, for this reason, it is hardly surprising, not only that every single grant application from 2007 forward makes just this case, but also that the case is made with increasing energy, culminating in the glossy production of the "Emmett Till National Site Development" brochure— a brochure that, in its very title, betrayed the fundamental logic of Till commemoration. The ETMC invested their energy in the rebranding of their own "site," and commemoration naturally followed. Indeed, as the money flowed into the ETMC, their vision of Tallahatchie County began to take material form on the landscape.

## TALLAHATCHIE CIVIL RIGHTS DRIVING TOUR

The historical marker unveiled by Jerome Little in October 2007 on the northwest corner of the courthouse (figure 13) was the first of nine roadside markers that would, within six months of the ceremony, be erected by the ETMC around the west (Delta) side of Tallahatchie County. Collectively, the ETMC refers to the signs as the "Tallahatchie Civil Rights Driving Tour." The tour is the ETMC's most visible mechanism for shaping the story of Emmett Till's murder. As the commission put it at their October 24, 2006, meeting, the driving tour was their chance to "write the story and write it right."[63]

The commission took this chance seriously. In the interest of "writing it right," they obtained $15,000 in funding from Morgan Freeman and relied on the research of Plater Robinson, education director at the Southern Institute for Education and Research, a nonprofit associated with Tulane University.[64] Robinson is something of a local legend in the Delta's Emmett Till circles. He is "considered by many to be the foremost authority on the case," and the ETMC leaned heavily on his expertise as they crafted their tour.[65] Robinson spent four years trolling the back roads of Mississippi, reconstructing, moment by moment, the murder of Emmett Till. In February of 1994, he attended the final trial of Byron De La Beckwith (murderer of Medgar Evers) in Jackson. From there, he drove directly to the Delta and, by talking to locals and consulting a phonebook, found the home of Roy Bryant. When Bryant's "mentally handicapped" sister inadvertently invited him into the family home, Robinson heroically captured an unrepentant Bryant on audiotape. With De La Beckwith's belated conviction in the news cycle, Bryant was visibly concerned that he was next. "So to hell with them." "I'm sick of it," he said. "Forty years old; they need to let that stuff go." His only regret, he claimed, was that "he ain't never made a damn nickel."[66]

On the same trip that Robinson caught Bryant on tape, he also met Maude Schuyler Clay, an accomplished Delta photographer whose 1999 *Delta Land* was dedicated "to the memory of Emmett Till."[67] Driving on gravel roads near Webb, Mississippi (just south of Sumner), in 1994, Robinson stumbled upon black and white children playing together. Taken aback by the sight, Robinson stopped and introduced himself. He met MayJean Waters McShane, an African American woman who kept Clay's three children while she pursued photography. Through McShane, Robinson eventually met Clay herself who was so impressed with his firsthand knowledge of the Till murder that she once claimed that "he's done more research on this story than anyone I've ever met." Clay, in turn, introduced Robinson to her friend Betty Pearson (see chapter 2), and Pearson introduced him to the ETMC. Upon meeting the ETMC, Robinson discovered still another unexpected connection. His boarding school acquaintance Sykes Sturdivant was a commissioner; they both attended Virginia's prestigious Woodberry Forest School.

On the basis of these unlikely connections, Robinson became the ETMC's chief authority on the Till murder and wielded a profound influence in the creation of the driving tour.[68] The minutes of the ETMC are filled with emails from Robinson to Susan Glisson, who, from her post at the William Winter Institute in Oxford, was helping to organize the ETMC and draft the prose for the signs. The commission thought through the content of their signs so carefully that the archives are filled with discarded prose once intended for the roadside markers. In addition to the revisions prompted by Robinson's feedback, the ETMC also preserved historical documentation for every sign but one. Because they hoped that the state would eventually sponsor all nine markers, and because the state required all prose on state-sanctioned signs to be connected to the historical record, the ETMC painstakingly vetted their claims about Till's murder, ceasing to do so only after it became apparent that Mississippi would not sponsor more than a single marker (their private contractor Signs Unlimited required no verification). Because the Civil Rights Driving Tour is a product of such careful revision and historical documentation, we may look to the roadside markers—and especially their inconsistencies—for a lesson in the ETMC's preferred history of Tallahatchie County. As we might expect, it is a history that foregrounds the historical importance of Tallahatchie County, minimizes the Chicago side of the story, and, in general, makes good on the claim announced on the courthouse lawn: "Till's murder, coupled with the trial and acquittal of these two men, drew international attention and galvanized the Civil Rights Movement in Mississippi and the nation."

All nine stops on the Tallahatchie Civil Rights Driving Tour are in Tallahatchie County. It was not always intended to be so. The first time the ETMC discussed a driving trail, on March 23, 2006, they circulated among themselves a list of ten potential sites, four of which were not in the county. In Sunflower County, they considered a marker at the barn on the Sturdivant Plantation near Drew where Till was tortured. In Leflore County, they considered signs for Bryant's Grocery and Meat Market where Till whistled, the Leflore County Courthouse in Greenwood where Milam and Bryant were first detained, and the home of Moses Wright from which Till was abducted.[69] The commission even drafted prose for the signs at the Sturdivant barn, the Wright home, and the Money store.[70] Although it is unclear why these three signs were never produced, it is likely a consequence of the fact that the ETMC was appointed by the Tallahatchie County Board of Supervisors and was, by virtue of both its bylaws and mission statement, focused on Tallahatchie County.[71] For whatever reason, despite the fact that these sites were crucial to the murder of Emmett Till, they were not included on the driving tour. In their place are two distinctly less significant sites: the site of King's Place juke joint where reporter James Hicks's worked undercover (see chapter 1) and, at Robinson's suggestion, the murder site of Clinton Melton, the Glendora gas-station attendant who was killed ten weeks after Till. While these two sites are certainly deserving of historic markers, they pale in comparison to the historical importance of Bryant's Grocery and Meat Market, the Drew barn where Till was killed, and the Wright home. The effect of these substitutions not only leaves the Till story incomplete (and internally inconsistent), it also makes it seem as if the Till saga was confined to Tallahatchie County.

Nothing reveals the Tallahatchie County–centric Till history offered by the driving tour with as much clarity as the composition history of the signs themselves. The correspondence with Plater Robinson and the painstaking effort to document each claim has left a fascinating paper trail of how, precisely, Tallahatchie County became the exclusive site of Emmett Till's murder and the origin of the civil rights movement.

*Two Signs in Glendora*

Near the eastern end of Thomas Street in Glendora, Mississippi, an ETMC sign marks the site of J. W. Milam's home. The sign claims that

Milam's backyard shed was the site of Till's torture, which, as we know from chapter 1, it was not. Unsurprisingly, when the ETMC prepared to submit the copy of this sign for approval by the MDAH in April of 2007, they included photocopies of William Bradford Huie's *Look* magazine account—a particularly useful version of the story for the ETMC because it moved the torture and murder site from Sunflower County to the shed behind the Milam home, in Tallahatchie County.

Of the nine original ETMC signs, two of them are justified with recourse to Huie's *Look* article, and another four are justified with recourse to Whitaker, whose 1963 thesis leans almost exclusively on Huie's account.[72] The commission's reliance on Huie is so profound that their first draft of the sign that now stands in front of the Glendora gin misidentified the gin as the "Progressive Ginning Company"—a mistake that was corrected by Plater Robinson but which only could have originated with Huie's account.[73] Another early draft even claims that the "Glendora gin" was "in Boyle."[74] While this is obviously false (the Glendora gin is in Glendora), it reveals the extent to which the ETMC relied on Huie's tale. Robinson's correction is also telling, as it reminds us why, precisely, Huie moved the murder site to Tallahatchie County.

> The Glendora gin is not the Boyle gin. The killers told Huie that they got the gin fan in Boyle, Mississippi [at the Progressive Ginning Company]. This is a lie, and part of the cover up. This particular lie was designed to distract attention from the Drew, Mississippi, tractor shed, on the Clint Shurden [actually, Sturdivant] plantation. That plantation was managed by Leslie Milam, brother and half-brother to J. W. Milam and Roy Bryant, and was the setting of Emmett's murder. . . . The Boyle gin was part of the cover up, thrown in the "mix" to explain away those long hours that the killers spent at Drew.[75]

Despite the fact that the ETMC received this correction from Robinson, and on his advice removed the reference to the "Progressive Ginning Company" from the sign in front of the Glendora gin, they nonetheless retained the story about the shed in the back of Milam's yard—a shed that was just as much a cover-up, and just as much "thrown in the 'mix' to explain away those long hours that the killers spent at Drew," as was the Progressive Ginning Company.

In fact, Robinson explicitly told the commission that Till was not beaten in Milam's shed. "Milam told Huie that he and Roy Bryant whipped Emmett at the shed behind Milam's house in Glendora. This is a lie." Robinson then explained the actual relevance of Milam's home. After Till was murdered and his body discarded, "Milam's employees" were made to wash out his truck, which was parked at his home. This is all true; the reference is to Henry Lee Loggins and Levi Collins, black accomplices in the torture, murder, and cover-up of Till's murder (chapter 1). They do not appear in the *Look* article for the simple reason that, as eyewitnesses to the murder, they would undermine Huie's attempt to "explain away" those hours spent at Drew. Although they only cited Huie, on this count the commission chose to follow Robinson's advice, inserting his euphemistic language of "employees" into the final copy of the sign.[76] The sign thus points to two historical sources, neither of which can be reconciled with each other. It claims that the Till was beaten in the backyard shed, which the commission knew was *false* because of Robinson's input. But the sign also claims that the Milam house was the scene of the truck's washing, which the commission knew to be *true* because of Robinson's advice. The commission thus waivered on which historical authority they chose to trust. On the matter of the beating, they chose to trust Huie, who Robinson correctly noted was wrong. But on the matter of the truck washing, they chose to follow Robinson. The only overarching principle seems to be: root the story of Till's murder in Tallahatchie County to the greatest extent possible. For, by following Robinson on the truck washing and Huie on the torture, they were able to place both events in Tallahatchie County. The fact that, until the ETMC's driving tour, the two events were considered mutually exclusive and never appeared in the same text is further evidence that the ETMC's most important criterion was geographical location: if an event could be traced to Tallahatchie County, it merited inclusion on the tour.

The plot only thickens when we consider the ETMC sign that sits five hundred feet west of the one marking Milam's home. This sign marks the location of King's Place, a juke joint where the celebrated African American reporter James Hicks went undercover and learned for the first time about the involvement of Loggins and Collins. As evidence, the ETMC cited a Hicks article from the October 8, 1955, *Cleveland Call and Post*.[77] In the article, Hicks tells how an anonymous tip lead him to the club where he danced with a woman, learned of eyewitnesses, and started down a path of inquiry that eventuated in evidence that placed the murder in Sunflower County. The ETMC sign, however, doesn't tell the entire story. It simply notes: "Here a young woman revealed to Hicks the real name of Leroy [*sic*] 'Too Tight' Collins, as well as Henry Lee Loggins, alleged witnesses in the Till trial who had been incarcerated in the Charleston jail under false names and false charges." Without telling the rest of the story (as Hicks did), the ETMC sign creates the false impression that the presence of Collins and Loggins was perfectly compatible with the story set five hundred feet east about the beating in Milam's shed.[78] This in turn suggests that the presence of Collins and Loggins—and the undercover work done by Hicks and celebrated by the ETMC—was perfectly compatible with a Tallahatchie County murder. In truth, these two signs are mutually exclusive: *If* Collins and Loggins were key witnesses, *then* King's Place is a historic site *but* Milam's shed is not. Concomitantly, *if* Milam's shed is a historic site, *then* Collins and Loggins were red herrings *and* King's Place was the site where the black press lost the story.

The ETMC did not submit the original *Cleveland Call and Post* version of Hicks's article to the MDAH. Rather, they submitted an excerpt reprinted from Christopher Metress's 2002 book, *The Lynching of Emmett Till*. As the ETMC duly noted, the Hicks excerpt begins on page 154. They do not note that page 154 also argues that Huie's account of the Till murder has been "widely challenged" since the mid-1980s.[79] There are two issues here. First, the two signs, located less than a baseball throw apart from each other on Thomas Street in Glendora, cannot both be true. Second, although the average tourist may not realize the two accounts are mutually exclusive, it is difficult to believe that whoever prepared the supporting documents submitted to the MDAH did not realize that the documentation for the King's Place sign, down to the page, cast doubt on the documentation for the sign marking Milam's home. Again, the only principle of selection seems to be a commitment to heed only those historical sources that centered the story on Tallahatchie County.

## The Tutwiler Sign

Fifteen miles northwest of the signs in Glendora, the ETMC erected a sign outside Chester Nelson's funeral home in Tutwiler, Mississippi. It is the only sign besides the one on the courthouse lawn in Sumner that explicitly makes the case that the Till murder "is considered to be one of the main sparks that ignited the Civil Rights Movement." There was never any question whether the Tutwiler funeral home would be included on the ETMC tour. Tutwiler mayor Robert Grayson was an original cochair of the commission (alongside Betty Pearson) and a champion of the Tutwiler site. In the fall of 2007, he even asked the ETMC if they would buy the funeral home for $1.5 million and restore it in a manner analogous to the Sumner courthouse (they did not).[80] Most likely as a result of Grayson's influence, the funeral home is the first site listed on the ETMC's original list of significant sites.[81]

However, a commitment to the Tutwiler site did not mean its story would be easy to tell. During the trial in September 1955, Nelson's embalmer Harry D. Malone was an important witness for the defense. He testified that the body was in such poor condition that it must have been in the Tallahatchie River for at least ten days. This, of course, meant that the body could not be Emmett Till and the defendants could not be guilty (because there was no corpus delicti). Along with Sheriff Strider's testimony, Malone's narrative was a key factor in the jury's official rationale for acquitting J. W. Milam and Roy Bryant.[82] The ETMC would not tell this story.

In his closing remarks to the jury, prosecutor Robert Smith suggested that Malone did not personally embalm the body and therefore was not in a position to judge either its condition or the amount of time it was in the river. Although Smith did not suggest an alternative, many believe that Till's body was actually prepared by Malone's black assistant Woodrow Jackson. While filmmaker Keith Beauchamp and historian Paul Hendrickson would both eventually interview Jackson and corroborate his story, the first person to record Jackson's experience was Sister Anne Brooks, DO, a Catholic nun and medical doctor who has lived in Tutwiler since 1984 providing medical care and fighting for civil rights. During her first twenty-five years in Tutwiler, Brooks kept a detailed log of civil rights activity in the county and across the nation. The log is a treasure trove of history, preserving threats made against her by the KKK and a county-specific ledger of racial injustice. In the log, she records the names of the patients at her clinic who were involved in the Till case. She lists J. W. Kellum—the unrepentant defense lawyer who told the jury that their "forefathers will turn over in their graves if the defendants are found guilty"—and Woodrow Jackson.[83] She quotes Jackson, "I'm proud of what I did. It's hard to do a wet body, and they wanted the casket open."[84] The ETMC was proud too; upon his death in November 2007, they issued a formal recognition of his role in Till saga. The recognition insisted that it was Jackson who prepared Till's body for transport to Chicago.[85]

Before he died, Jackson attended an ETMC meeting on June 27, 2006. While the minutes from this meeting are slim, it is clear that the majority of the discussion focused on the driving tour.[86] Given the complicity of the Malone narrative in the acquittal of Milam and Bryant and the presence of Jackson in their midst, it is not surprising that the ETMC chose to commemorate Jackson's version of the story. The first words on the sign betray no hint of controversy: "On August 31, 1955, Woodrow Jackson prepared Emmett Till's body here at the Tutwiler Funeral Home." From there, the sign rehearses the path of Till's body north from Tutwiler to Chicago where Till's mother defied the order not to open the casket and promised "to show the world what was done to her son." The sign concludes, "The public outcry over the condition of Emmett's mutilated body is considered to be one of the main sparks that ignited the Civil Rights Movement."

Critically, this prose was *not* written for the Tutwiler sign. Indeed, this language—nearly verbatim—was developed for the sign on the courthouse lawn in Sumner. As you will recall, however, the language for the courthouse sign was altered, shifting the burden of history (and the spark of the movement) from the display of the body in Chicago to the trial in Sumner.[87] Instead of simply discarding the original courthouse prose, the ETMC recycled it for the Tutwiler sign. This should not suggest, however, that in Tutwiler (unlike Sumner) the ETMC was willing to allow Chicago to be the center of attention. Quite the opposite. Before claiming that the "public outcry" over the condition of Till's mutilated body sparked the civil rights movement, the Tutwiler sign begins by noting the role of Tutwiler's Woodrow Jackson. It thus provided a Tallahatchie County point of origin for a body that would, when it reached Chicago, be photographed and become the "spark" of the civil rights movement.

This insistence on rooting the body in Tallahatchie County is even more evident when we consider an early draft of the sign for the Tutwiler Funeral Home. The draft provided a much fuller itinerary, noting that Till's body "first was taken to Greenwood in Leflore County" before being "moved back to Tallahatchie County" where it was embalmed by Jackson. This early draft also provides far more details about Jackson's experience with the body—from his trip to pick it up in Greenwood, to his police escort back to Tutwiler, to his all-night embalming job that ended at eight the following morning.[88] Because all of these details match the account of Jackson himself, who relayed it to Paul Hendrickson for *Sons of Mississippi*, it is likely that the ETMC drafted the sign based on Jackson's own memory of the story conveyed when he attended their meeting in June 2006.[89]

But Jackson was not their only source. Plater Robinson also weighed in on the Tutwiler sign, stressing the "mutilated, decomposed condition of the body" and the formaldehyde needed to preserve it. He also told the commission that Till's uncle Crosby Smith (from Sumner) signed a document promising that the casket would not be opened.[90]

For the final copy of the sign, the ETMC heavily redacted Jackson's play-by-play narrative, retaining only the simple fact that he prepared the body—this is the first sentence of the sign. They also ignored the majority of Robinson's advice, keeping only the part about Smith signing a will-not-open promise—this is the second sentence. To complete the marker, they added two sentences recovered from the discarded language for the courthouse sign. Although there are a lot of moving parts in the development of the sign, every decision made by the ETMC is consistent with a Tallahatchie County–centric version of Till's story. They kept only that portion of Robinson's advice that featured Crosby Smith—resident of Sumner. Likewise, they kept only that portion of Jackson's narrative that allowed them to start the itinerary of the body at the Tutwiler funeral home. The final copy outside the Tutwiler Funeral Home is a perfect, Tallahatchie County midpoint between the draft of the courthouse sign, which did not trace the body back far enough and thus suggested that the civil rights movement was sparked in Chicago, and the draft of the Tutwiler sign, which traced the body too far back (to Leflore County, where Jackson acquired the body). As it stands, the Tutwiler sign suggests that while the body's destination was Chicago, its origin was in Tallahatchie County. In this telling, Woodrow Jackson not only erases the racist testimony of H. D. Malone, but he also anchors the body of Emmett Till—and, by extension, the civil rights movement itself—in Tallahatchie County.

### Two Signs on the River

The plot grows thicker still. The detailed itinerary of the body (originally intended for the Tutwiler sign) would eventually find a permanent home on the ETMC's sign that marked the site where they believed Till's body was pulled from the water. The drafted-but-discarded prose for the Tutwiler sign describing how the body moved back and forth between Greenwood (Leflore County) and Tutwiler (Tallahatchie County) eventually became the final copy for a sign titled, simply, "River Site." The river site sign is the only ETMC sign for which there are no preserved drafts and no record of revisions. This is likely because the commission made a last-minute decision to post two "River Site" signs—one at the site where they believed the body was pulled from the river (Graball Landing, see figure 24, conclusion) and a second one 2.6 miles north at the Sharkey Bridge. The purpose of the second sign (also titled "River Site") was to direct visitors from the

Sharkey Bridge, down the inconspicuous River Road, toward Graball Landing, the site where the commission believed the body was recovered. Without a second sign, visitors might never venture down the lonely dirt road on the eastern bank of the Tallahatchie River.

Although he is a forgotten figure now, the key actor on the two river site signs is Simon Garrett—an assistant mortician at Greenwood's Century Burial Association at the time of Till's murder. Either Garrett or his boss Chester Miller were involved in every event described on the first river site sign (the body's removal from the water and its subsequent journey from Greenwood to Money to Greenwood to Tutwiler). Moreover, when Woodrow Jackson brought Till's body from Greenwood to Tutwiler, he received the body from the care of either Garrett or Miller.[91] Finally, it was Garrett's memory that is ultimately responsible for the placement of the first river site sign at Graball Landing (the alleged point of recovery) and for the prose of the sign at Sharkey Bridge—both of which are controversial.

The ETMC originally planned for only a single river site sign to mark the spot of the body's recovery. Although they did not know precisely where to put it, they crafted a small, mostly accurate narrative for the sign.[92] The draft noted that the body was discovered by fishermen "at this location" after three days in the water. It noted further that the body was weighted down with a cotton-gin fan and that it was identified by the Till family ring still clinging to the body. The only mistake in the draft, a mistake inspired by Huie's account in *Look*, was the ETMC's claim that "this site is approximately 8 miles downstream from where his body was dumped."[93] The claim that the body floated eight miles was invented by Huie to justify his invented murder site.

Plater Robinson would have none of it. Based on information that he learned firsthand from Simon Garrett, he fundamentally rewrote the sign. In a strongly worded letter to the ETMC, he insisted that, according to Garrett,

the body was never in the river, which was twenty yards away. Instead, the body was rolled down the levee into the "drift" (the area between the river and the levee). Heavy rains had bloated the river. When

the water subsided, Emmett's body was revealed. There was a black
community (houses, church, and cemetery) a few feet away.

This was a novel theory. In the fifty-three years between the murder
and this communiqué, the fact that Till's body was found in the river
had never been questioned. The fact that the ETMC rewrote their sign
according to these suggestions is a measure of just how much they
trusted Plater Robinson. In place of their mostly accurate draft, they
crafted (and installed) a sign that claimed Till's body was never in the
river.

Although it is unclear where the fault lies, the preponderance of
evidence suggests that the body was, in fact, in the river. In an undated follow-up letter to the ETMC, Robinson tried to correct the
record, noting that he had been fed faulty information from Garrett. Whether the letter was received too late, or whether the ETMC
simply preferred the body-in-the-mud theory, they ultimately chose
to go with the story Robinson learned from Garrett. The sign that now
stands where the Sharkey Bridge crosses the Tallahatchie River is the
only ETMC sign with an egregious factual error. Despite what the sign
says, the body was thrown in the river, it was not intended as a warning for an adjacent black community, and there is no evidence that
such a community even existed.

At Robinson's insistence, the ETMC placed the first river site sign—
the sign that marked the spot of the body's recovery—2.6 miles down-
river from the Sharkey Bridge at an old steamboat landing known by
locals as Graball Landing. The FBI disagrees with this location. In a
map published by the bureau in February 2006, they suggested that
Till's body was discovered nearly five miles downstream from Graball Landing. Significantly, the FBI believes that Till's body was discovered in a portion of the Tallahatchie River that briefly dips into Leflore
County.[94] While the ETMC would clearly prefer Robinson's theory
simply because it located the recovery spot in their own county, there
may have been an even more pressing reason for locating the sign 2.6
miles southeast of the Sharkey Bridge.

Graball Landing is at the confluence of the Tallahatchie River and the Black Bayou, a small, cypress-lined body of water that flows through Glendora before emptying into the Tallahatchie River. ETMC commissioner and Glendora mayor Johnny B. Thomas has spent considerable energy arguing that Till's murderers dropped his body into the bayou (not the river) from the Black Bayou Bridge on the south side of Glendora (chapter 5). If Till was indeed dropped from the Black Bayou Bridge—and it is certainly plausible that he was—then it would be a short 1.3 mile float to Robinson's spot.

The ETMC, then, had a twofold reason for going with Robinson's theory. In fact, they may well have persisted with his spot even after they learned that his Garrett-inspired information for the other sign was false. They were well aware of the FBI investigation and even had a personal relationship with agent Dale Killinger. It is difficult to believe that the commission had not read the FBI report by the time they erected the river site signs in 2008—at that time the report had been public for over two years. Regardless of what they did or did not know, it is certain that by sticking with Robinson's location, the ETMC at once relieved themselves of following the FBI's official placement in Leflore County *and* they gave greater plausibility to a theory championed by one of their officers (Thomas; for more on Graball Landing, see the conclusion). While it may be difficult to say for sure where the body was recovered, it is certain that the ETMC had a vested interest in Graball Landing.

In sum, at virtually every stop on the ETMC's Civil Rights Driving Tour, their ambition to root the murder of Emmett Till in Tallahatchie County is dramatically confirmed. While only two signs (at the courthouse and in Tutwiler) explicitly claim that the civil rights movement started in Tallahatchie County, every sign defaults to the version of Till's story that gives the county the greatest historical role. From their composition history, to their location, to their final copy, the signs suggest an opportunism with historical sources: they follow only those sources that confine the murder to Tallahatchie County.

## CONCLUSION

At virtually every possible moment when Till's story could have veered over county lines, the ETMC chose to tell it in such a fashion that placed Tallahatchie County at the heart of the Till murder and, more broadly, at the heart of the civil rights movement. From their fascination with a debatable story about Rosa Parks to the composition history of their driving tour signs, the commission always rooted Till's murder in their own county. In effect, the commission remade the history of the county so that they could win funds with which to remake the history of Till's murder. There could hardly be a better example of the ecology of memory. Place (Tallahatchie County) had to be given a new racial history in order for the murder of Emmett Till to be remembered.

I close this chapter with a story about an ETMC sign that stood briefly on the site of the Delta Inn—the "old hotel" as locals knew it. Built in 1914, the Delta Inn was a mansion that was the center of mid-century Sumner society and, during the trial, the site at which the jury was sequestered. Although the story is sad in many ways, it illustrates the connections between Tallahatchie County, the movement, and the murder. With the help of Maude Schuyler Clay, the ETMC crafted a noncontroversial message about the history of the hotel and its role in the trial. At the urging of Plater Robinson, they inserted a final line that claimed a cross was burned in front of the Delta Inn midway through the trial—an event for which there is modest evidence.[95]

Just before the ETMC was formed, John Whitten III purchased the site of the then-crumbling Delta Inn. According to Clay, the hotel began to deteriorate in the 1980s or 1990s. After a failed attempt to register the building on the National Register of Historical Places, the once-grand mansion was "declared a danger and a menace to public safety."[96] Whitten agreed. The son of John Whitten Jr.—defense lawyer for Roy Bryant and J. W. Milam—Whitten III still works in the same brick office building from which his father defended the murderers; he replaced J. J. Breland in the infamous firm of Breland and Whitten.[97] Much like his father, his record on race relations is poor. In

2009, the NAACP accused him of a hate crime for organizing a vigilante mob to pursue an untried, unarmed African American man whom he believed was guilty of burglary. He chased the man in a World War II era armored tank.[98]

Shortly after purchasing the site of the Delta Inn, Whitten hired a Greenwood firm to take it down brick by brick. A newspaper reporter with a keen eye noted, "Once the structure is demolished and the property cleared, Whitten will be left with a spacious vacant corner lot facing the town's Courthouse Square."[99] Predictably, Whitten was not excited about the prospect of an ETMC sign on his property. Although the sign did not mention his father's role in the injustice, one can imagine that Whitten is not looking for ways to commemorate his father's legacy. Interviewed by NPR, he said, "We didn't do it. It didn't happen here. This was something that was dragged in and left to rot in our courthouse. . . . [It was] a long time ago, part of history. I don't think it should be denied. I don't think it should be honored."[100] Apparently he also did not think it should be marked with a sign. Shortly after the driving tour signs were erected, a drunk Whitten was heard late at night on the square claiming that the Delta Inn roadside marker would end up on the bottom of the Tallahatchie River. Shortly thereafter the sign went missing; the police did not investigate, and it has never been replaced.

The irony is thick. Although the relationship between Whitten and the ETMC has never been close, they shared a common logic. Both tied the possibility of commemoration to the role of Tallahatchie County in the murder. The ETMC argued that the county played an important role in the murder—so important that its legacy could be seen in the Montgomery bus boycott and in the movement that followed. Accordingly, the ETMC became the single largest community organization to ever mobilize for the memory of Till's murder. They have done more for Till's memory than any other group by a large margin. Whitten, for his part, believed that Tallahatchie County was shouldering the blame for events that happened elsewhere. He told me this personally in the spring of 2016, and he may have a point. If the FBI is indeed correct that the body was discovered in Leflore County, then the trial should have been held in Greenwood and the town of Sumner should never have been involved. Regardless, Whitten insists on the county's innocence, and it appears as if he may have stolen the sign. No role for the county, no memory for Till. The undertones of racism notwithstanding, Whitten has given voice to the fundamental logic of the ETMC. For both, the possibility of Till's memory was tied to the racial history of the county. If Whitten won the battle over the Delta Inn, however, the ETMC has won the war. They have raised nearly $5 million and turned the county into what they desperately needed it to be: the birthplace of the movement.

## CHAPTER FOUR

# RUINS AND RESTORATION IN MONEY

The ruins of Bryant's Grocery and Meat Market and the beautifully restored Ben Roy's Service Station stand sixty-seven feet apart from each other on the southern edge of Money, Mississippi, the small hamlet visited by Emmett Till in August 1955. Both buildings are owned by a trio of siblings with a personal investment in the memory of Till's murder. Annette Morgan, Harry Tribble, and Martin Tribble are the three children of Ray Tribble, an unrepentant juror from the 1955 trial of Roy Bryant and J. W. Milam.[1] After the trial, Ray Tribble excelled in business, the family accrued farmland around Money, and, in the mid-1980s, his children purchased the two-story building that once housed Bryant's Grocery.[2] After Annette and Harry purchased Ben Roy's Service Station in 2003, the family owned everything in Money except the Baptist church.[3] While only Bryant's Grocery was directly involved in the murder of Emmett Till, the Tribbles have ensured that both buildings play a large, if competing, role in the commemoration of the murder.

Bryant's Grocery is the site where Till whistled at Carolyn Bryant. Perhaps hesitant to allow the crumbling building to be turned into a monument to their patriarch's complicity in permitting two of Till's killers to walk free, the Tribbles have rejected numerous offers to buy the property and have allowed it to fall into ruin (see figures 17, 18, and 19).[4] The iconic front porch collapsed in the early 1990s, the interior

**FIGURE 17.** Bryant's Grocery and Meat Market, 1955. Special Collections Department, University of Memphis Libraries. Used by permission.

floors were gone by the turn of the century, and Hurricane Katrina claimed the roof and a story-sized portion of the grocery's north wall. And yet, the ruin of the building notwithstanding, the grocery has become a mecca for civil rights tourists wanting to see the place at which many believe an ill-timed whistle set the civil rights movement in motion.[5] Judging by the ever-increasing number of visitors to the site, it seems as if the structural integrity of Bryant's Grocery stands in an inverse relationship to its symbolic value: the greater the ruin, the more potent the memory site.[6] In 2011, without a trace of irony, the state erected a sign proclaiming Bryant's Grocery the origin of the civil rights movement, and, at virtually the same time, the county erected a cheap, orange, plastic fence to protect visitors from falling bricks. The near-simultaneous installation of a historical marker and protective fencing suggests that the site's commemorative value is calibrated to

**FIGURE 18.** Site of Bryant's Grocery and Meat Market, circa 1993. Photo by Plater Robinson. Used by permission.

**FIGURE 19.** Site of Bryant's Grocery and Meat Market, 2018. Photo by Ashleigh Coleman. Used by permission.

its structural disrepair—as if the quick ruin of a life could be recalled in the slow ruin of a building.

Sitting sixty-seven feet south of the ruined grocery, Ben Roy's Service Station has followed a starkly different trajectory. Although it has no historic connection to Emmett Till's murder, since 2011 it has been actively written into his story. In July of that year, Annette Morgan and Harry Tribble won a Mississippi Civil Rights Historical Sites grant for the restoration of Ben Roy's Service Station. Because Bryant's Grocery was crumbling and because Ben Roy's had a covered portico, Morgan and Tribble reasoned, the gas station had become a default site from which tourists could gaze at the grocery and learn their civil rights history. The application put its case for civil rights money like this: "It is very likely that the events that transpired at Bryant's Grocery . . . were discussed underneath the front canopy of the adjacent service station."[7] The restoration of Ben Roy's, the application continued, would allow a new generation of tourists to "meet under that canopy and discuss the events surrounding the death of Emmitt [*sic*] Till and the civil rights era in a new light."[8] And, with nothing more certain than the possibility that Till's murder was discussed from the adjacent gas station, the MDAH gave $206,360.80 earmarked for civil rights to the restoration of Ben Roy's.[9]

And thus, despite their different trajectories of ruin and restoration, both Bryant's Grocery and Ben Roy's Service Station are now an inescapable part of Till's story. Indeed, the structural integrity of both buildings must be counted as an aftereffect of Till's lynching. Without the murder, Bryant's Grocery would not be in ruin, and Ben Roy's would not be restored.[10] In this chapter I tell the stories of these two buildings, and some of the businesses that inhabited them, and ask what their histories of ruination and preservation might teach us about memory, racism, and the Mississippi Delta.

I attend first to Young's Grocery and Market, that is, to the 1980s business that inhabited the building left behind by Bryant's Grocery. After the acquittal, the black sharecroppers that once kept Bryant's Grocery in business refused to patronize it, and the store was put up for sale less than a month after the trial.[11] For the next three decades, the building was maintained as a country grocery—first as Wolfe's, then as Young's Grocery and Market. Although little is known of Wolfe's, Bud and Rita Young's tenure as owner-operators of the country store coincided with the 1980s resurgence of Till commemoration (see introduction). For this reason, Young's became a pilgrimage site in its own right. Young's Grocery has earned the distinction of the being *most misnamed place* in the history of Emmett Till commemoration. Despite the fact that the grocery featured a large sign over the front door that read "Young's Gro. & Mkt.," and despite the fact that the sign was prominently featured and easily legible (it was virtually unavoidable), a decade's worth of Emmett Till activists visited Young's but called it Bryant's—as if the material history of the place was unrelated to questions of commemoration (see figure 18 above). The history of confusing Young's Grocery with Bryant's Grocery provides the opportunity to see what commemoration looks like when questions of place are ignored. The result is a rigorously forensic form of commemoration, a memory practice consumed with figuring out who did what to whom. If forensics has been the dominant mode of Till commemoration, this is because questions of place have never been taken seriously.

Sometime in the 1980s, the Tribble family bought the building that housed Young's Grocery and, before that, Bryant's Grocery. Unlike the Youngs, the Tribbles neither maintained the building nor kept up the store. As it descended into ruin, the building itself moved into the foreground of the commemorative imagination. No longer the unmarked backdrop of a forensic inquiry, the building itself and its conspicuous disrepair became the focal points of commemorative practice.[12] In the brokenness of the ruins, the building recalled not only the events of 1955, but also the fact that those events had been disregarded, ignored, and untended. While Young's Grocery, materially invisible, focused commemoration exclusively on 1955, the Tribble building, materially inescapable, framed the murder of Emmett Till in light of the enduring racism of the Mississippi Delta. The ruins have, as it were, extended the chronology of Till's story, such that the 1955 murder lives on in twenty-first-century ruin. Just as a decade's

**FIGURE 20.** Ben Roy's Service Station, 2014. Photo by Pablo Correa. Used by permission.

worth of pilgrims visited Young's store and misnamed it, the subsequent generation of pilgrims visited the Tribble building and found it *haunted*. As a ghost carries the past unbidden into the present, so the ruins of the store give visible form to the never-quite-successful will-to-forget Till's story. The more the store crumbles, the greater the evidence of unaddressed racism mounts, and the more potent the indictment of the Delta's long refusal to address the murder directly.

In the sharpest of contrasts to the crumbling grocery, Ben Roy's Service Station has been beautifully restored since 2014 (see figure 20). The contrast goes beyond the relative repair of the buildings. Its funding scheme notwithstanding, the renovation makes no reference to Till's murder, to civil rights history, or to the building to its north. The grant application even suggests that the 1950s Delta was a place of interracial fraternity, a region where the social strictures of Jim Crow were tempered by the communitarian bonds of life in small-town America. Long on Americana but short on race, the renovation of Ben Roy's suggests its own master conceit for the remembrance of Till's murder: nostalgia. The restored service station is an unqualified evocation of a fictional past in which the infrastructure of American life was unmarked by race. The irony is thick: the murder of Emmett Till made the restoration of Ben Roy's possible, but the restoration itself casts a vision of the Mississippi Delta in which the murder can only register as an aberration.

In all three cases—Young's Grocery, the Tribble ruins, and Ben Roy's—practices of commemoration were inextricably bound to the material conditions of the Delta. The well-maintained store provided for the forensic tradition; the ruins transformed commemoration into an insistent-but-always-failing forgetfulness; and the Americana of Ben Roy's robbed the lynching of its gravitas through a nostalgic version of the Delta in which race hardly registered.

As of this writing, Young's Grocery is thirty years gone. All that remains are the ruins and the service station, both of which frame the murder of Emmett Till via the racial mores of the Delta. Either Till's murder still bears witness to the racism of the Delta or it is an aberration from the charms of midcentury America. On this score, Morgan and Tribble were right. The restoration of Ben Roy's Service Station does indeed cast the murder of Emmett Till in a "new light." It counters the haunting experience of the grocery with the nostalgia of midcentury Americana. While Bryant's suggests that the Delta has never adequately dealt with the murder of Emmett Till, Ben Roy's suggests that there was not that much to deal with in the first place. Although they do so in dramatically different ways, both buildings use the memory of Emmett Till to give racial meaning to the Mississippi Delta, and, conversely, they use the experience of race in the Delta to redefine the meaning of Till's murder.

## YOUNG'S GROCERY AND THE FORENSIC TRADITION OF MEMORY

During the 1955 trial, the prosecution tried valiantly to keep Bryant's Grocery and Meat Market out of Till's story. By the second day of the trial, it was widely rumored that Till had "assaulted" Carolyn Bryant when he was alone with her inside the store. By the third day of the trial, defense lawyer Sidney Carlton was previewing the testimony of Carolyn Bryant, their star witness.[13] He told the *Greenwood Morning Star* that Bryant would testify that Till "came into the store and propositioned her," and that "he grabbed her and unsuccessfully tried to assault her."[14] As Davis Houck and Matthew Grindy explain, the defense was implying that the murder was a case of "justifiable homicide": their clients may have murdered Emmett Till, but it was for the "good cause" of protecting southern white womanhood from black sexual aggression.[15] This strategy was not lost on the prosecution. When Carolyn Bryant took the stand to describe the events of August 24, the state quickly objected that the events at the grocery were not part of the res gestae (things done, or the start-to-end period of a felony). "Anything that happened prior to [J. W. Milam and Roy Bryant] going down to Mose [sic] Wright's house is certainly not competent to bring in here."[16] By insisting on a particular chronology, the state was trying to make Bryant's Grocery irrelevant. Any hint of sexual aggressiveness would hurt their case, so they insisted that the crime began late Sunday night, three days after Till visited Bryant's Grocery.

On this score, the failure of the prosecution is of epic proportions. Beyond the fact that they failed to keep Carolyn Bryant from testifying, and thereby forcibly inserting Bryant's Grocery into the legal narrative of Till's death, they failed even to keep the relevance of Bryant's Grocery controversial. Immediately after the trial, the defense's argument that Till's murder began at Bryant's Grocery was treated as an uncontested fact rather than a partisan narrative designed to highlight black sexual aggression. Perhaps the best example of the normalization of Bryant's Grocery comes from the legendary Kansas poet Langston Hughes. By October 1955, just one month after the trial, Hughes wrote "The Money Mississippi Blues." Although the song was intended as a fund-raiser for the NAACP, Hughes collapsed the entirety of Till's story into the town of Money, the one place the prosecution sought to avoid.[17] Clearly, neither Hughes nor the NAACP understood the inclusion of Bryant's Grocery as a win for Sidney Carlton or the legal defense team. The store had become a nonpartisan component of Till's story.

The pattern held. From William Bradford Huie, to Steven Whitaker, to Stephen J. Whitfield, to Devery Anderson, to Timothy B. Tyson—for sixty years the most influential voices shaping Till's story have begun their narratives at Bryant's Grocery. The simple fact that the relevance of Bryant's Grocery was once a controversial point has been all but lost from memory. The site that was once the lynchpin of the legal defense of the murderers has become the state-sponsored origination point of Till's murder. In 2011, the MDA put a sign in front of the grocery, making it the first stop on the Mississippi Freedom Trail (see introduction).

The normalization of Bryant's Grocery should not suggest that Carolyn Bryant's testimony, or the suggestion of justifiable homicide, has been unquestioned. The opposite is rather the case. While the inclusion of Bryant's Grocery in Till's story is no longer controversial, questions about what precisely happened in the store remain as all-consuming as they were in the 1955. Did Till really assault Carolyn Bryant? Did he proposition her? Did he whistle at her? These *forensic questions*—questions focused on determining precisely what happened—have provided the definitive model for Emmett Till commemoration. The most recent, most comprehensive, and most respected scholarship on the Till murder has been motivated by an ever-more-determined investigation to figure out what happened inside the store.

Consider Devery Anderson's 2015 *Emmett Till*, currently the authoritative history of the murder. Anderson's tome began as a detective-style quest to determine precisely what happened inside the store. Seven years before the book was released, Anderson published an essay in *Southern Quarterly* titled "A Wallet, a White Woman, and a Whistle: Fact and Fiction in Emmett Till's Encounter in Money, Mississippi."[18] As the title suggests, Anderson's essay (and later book) is a fundamentally forensic undertaking—committed to discovering what happened in 1955. Tellingly, the book ends with a long appendix titled "Piecing the Puzzle," a question-and-answer guide to the murder's most controversial elements.[19] From the initial essay in *Southern Quarterly* through the final section of the *Emmett Till*, Anderson proceeds as if a detailed ledger of misdeeds exhausts the obligations of memory. So committed was he to this philosophy of memory that he divided his massive list of sources by their proximity to 1955: primary sources were considered in main text; secondary sources were relegated to footnotes.

Timothy Tyson's acclaimed *The Blood of Emmett Till* (2017) is the most recent forensic pursuit. The book began in September 2008, when Carolyn Bryant contacted Tyson and told him that she lied under oath about what happened in Bryant's Grocery. Regarding her courtroom testimony that Till assaulted her, she told Tyson, "That part's not true."[20] Tyson then rewrote the story of Emmett Till based on a new account of the events at Bryant's Grocery. Although Anderson's and Tyson's books are very different, both use Bryant's Grocery to answer a series of forensic questions. As the two most recent and respected books on Till's murder, they demonstrate how thoroughly the forensic approach to commemoration has taken hold.

While Anderson and Tyson circle continuously around Bryant's Grocery, they never feature the store itself. The grocery was the *site* of their inquiry and even the *inspiration* for it, but not the *object* of their inquiry. For both Anderson and Tyson—and by extension the whole of the forensic tradition—Bryant's Grocery was simply the uncontested site of highly contested events. As such the only questions that seemed to register bore on the facts of 1955: What happened in Bryant's Grocery? Who did what to whom? How can guilt, blame, victimhood, and responsibility be distributed?

The placelessness of the forensic tradition is nowhere more evident than in the records of those who visited Young's Grocery and Market, as the building was known in the late 1970s through the middle of the 1980s. The only thing we know about J. L. "Bud" and Rita Young is that they kept a country store in the building that once housed Bryant's Grocery. This simple act, however, had profound commemorative ramifications. Simply by keeping the building in relatively good repair, Bud and Rita enabled a myopic fascination with forensic questions. In good repair, the store itself attracted zero attention, allowing those who visited it to become entirely absorbed in forensic questions.

In fact, one of the most startling oversights in all of Till commemoration is how many people could visit Young's and call it Bryant's—as if the particularities of a place had no bearing on memory.

Consider Rich Samuels. On July 11, 1985, his documentary titled *The Murder and the Movement* aired on Chicago's NBC affiliate WMAQ. After briefly introducing the towns of Greenwood and Sumner, Samuels focused his viewers' attention on Money: "But the story of Emmett Till begins eight miles north of Greenwood in Money, Mississippi, which is just about as small as a town can get."[21] After some historical footage of Bryant's Grocery as it appeared in 1955, the documentary cut to a shot of Samuels standing in front of Young's Grocery. Although the building was clearly uninhabited and, as Samuels noted, "long since abandoned," the building itself remained in relatively good repair. A sign above the porch labeled "Young's Gro. & Mkt." was still clearly legible. As Samuels stood in front of Young's, he contrasted the long-abandoned building with the still-vivid memories of the Till family about the fatal encounter inside Bryant's Grocery. From the Youngs' storefront, Samuels cut directly to interviews with Till cousins Simeon Wright and Wheeler Parker—both of whom were with Till at Bryant's Grocery in 1955. As eyewitnesses to the whistle and abduction, Wright and Parker were expert forensic witnesses.

After Wright and Parker, Samuels featured the one-time *Look* journalist William Bradford Huie. Although Huie has since been discredited, in 1985 he too was considered a forensic authority on Till's murder. As he explained the murder for Samuels, Huie stressed the allure of Carolyn Bryant, calling her one of the "prettiest twenty-one or twenty-two year old women I ever saw in my life." Although this is unsurprising (Huie always stressed the sexual side of the murder), it is particularly fitting for Samuels. The documentarian had just asserted that Till's story "begins . . . in Money," and that claim is historically tied to the sexual appeal of Carolyn Bryant. The logic is circular: the storefront recalls the beauty of Bryant, which, in turn, justifies beginning Till's story in Money. Lost in the circularity of Samuels's claim is the simple fact that he is standing in front of a clearly marked *Young's Grocery*. The irrelevance of the building's current ownership is a testament to the placelessness of the forensic tradition. Consumed with a ledger of historical illegalities, Samuels has no need to consider any witnesses (e.g., Bud and Rita Young) beyond those who could help reconstruct the events of 1955. On this score, there is perhaps no more telling fact than this: to date, Bud and Rita Young have never appeared in Till's story. A tradition blind to the importance of place but enthralled with questions of forensics simply had no use for them.

One year after Samuels's documentary aired, former *Ebony* staffer Clotye Murdock Larsson returned to Money to write a follow-up piece for the magazine. In 1955, she covered the murder for Johnson Publishing Company in Chicago and wrote a well-regarded article titled "Land of the Till Murder." Published in *Ebony* in 1956, the article documented the racial unrest simmering just under the surface of the Mississippi Delta.[22] When she returned thirty years later, she opened her article with a half-page color photograph of herself in the exact spot that Rich Samuels stood for his documentary: in front of the sign reading "Young's Gro. & Mkt."[23] The building appears incrementally worse than when Samuels stood in front it. Windows, portions of the upstairs railing, and a sign on the southeast corner are broken. Much like Samuels, however, Murdock Larsson used the store as a heuristic to recount the events of 1955: "The Emmett Till story began in the summer of 1955 in Money, Miss., a dusty crossroads settlement too obscure to merit a turn-off sign on the main highway." She then proceeded to the classic questions of Till forensics: Till's flirtatiousness, his "wolf whistle," and hints of sexual aggression. Like Samuels, Murdock Larsson ignored the building itself. Neither its relative state of repair nor the fact that it was now, obviously, owned by the Youngs mattered at all to Murdock Larsson. For an article ostensibly about the "land of Till's murder," she pays precious little attention to the material conditions of that land. The building itself was little more than the incidental context of the events in question, a heuristic for memory on the model of forensics. While her story may have begun in Money, it could have happened anywhere.

The most fascinating story from the 1980s, however, is the fiction pedaled by Richard Rubin. Published in 2002, Rubin's *Confederacy of*

*Silence: A True Tale of the New Old South* purports to be the true story of the year he spent in Greenwood, Mississippi, just a few miles south of Money, in 1988. With a newly minted degree in history from the University of Pennsylvania, Rubin headed south to work for the *Greenwood Commonwealth* and experience the Delta for himself. It was to be a personal adventure. Rubin was a New Yorker, an Ivy Leaguer, and a Jew. From his perspective, the Mississippi Delta was "pure mystery, an abyss at the bottom of America."[24] When he arrived, he believed his worst biases were confirmed; he perceived the Delta as a region still shot through with racism. His title is a reference to his sense that he needed to keep his progressive racial views to himself in order to get along in Delta society. Silence, Rubin suggests, was the cost of admission for a liberal in the Delta. Needless to say, Rubin's is the kind of book Deltans have learned to distrust: a northerner dropping in to tell them how racist they are.[25] To this day, *The Confederacy of Silence* ruffles feathers in Greenwood, where locals are quick to point out that Rubin's book tour never brought him back to Greenwood, where he would have had to face questions from the people he featured.

Rubin was "fascinated with the murder of Emmett Till," and *The Confederacy of Silence* repeatedly circles back to Till's story.[26] In fact, Rubin claims that his original motivation to visit the Delta can be traced to the first time he heard Till's story told. As a junior in college in 1987, he saw *Eyes on the Prize*, the celebrated six-hour documentary that stressed the role of Till's murder in instigating the civil rights movement. He was captivated by Till's story and, by the end of the documentary, had a "burning desire" to visit Mississippi for himself.[27] The Till segment of *Eyes on the Prize* was narrated by William Bradford Huie. Intrigued by Huie's account of interracial mingling in Money, Rubin was preoccupied with Bryant's Grocery. He visited the store "every few weeks" during the fall of 1988.[28] The store was still open, he wrote, operating as Young's and selling Vienna sausages, sardines, and deviled ham. Rubin would park across the street from Young's and "just stare at it for a few minutes," before slowly making his way toward the store. The slow walk from his car to the store was a pretext to muse over forensic questions. He would examine the front porch where, he claimed, Till bragged about his biracial sexual prowess (another clue he learned Till's story from Huie). After the deliberately slow walk, he would "saunter on into the store itself and greet the clerk behind the counter." This, he reports, was so much "meaningless conversation," a cover for silent forensic speculation: "she stood there, a little to the left, probably, and he stood here, right on this spot where I am right now."[29]

While he may have parked across the street and stared at the store, much of Rubin's story appears to be fabricated. By the time he arrived in the Delta in the summer of 1988, Young's had been closed for at least three years. The 1985 video of Rich Samuels and the 1986 *Ebony* photograph of Clotye Murdock Larsson provide visual evidence that Young's was, as Samuels put it, "long since abandoned" by the time Rubin arrived. If further evidence were needed, the *Greenwood Commonwealth*—the paper Rubin was working for at the time—later reported that Young's Grocery closed in the "early 1980s."[30]

Although it is unclear why, precisely, Rubin would fabricate a story about visiting a still-operating Young's Grocery, the fact that he did has much to teach us about the relationship between commemoration and the materiality of the building.[31] When he visited in 1988, the store had begun its decline into ruin. According to his own account, the screen was full of holes, the enclosed front porch was sagging, and the sign on the northeast corner of the building was falling and rusty.[32] From Murdock Larsson's earlier account (and pictures), we know further that the porch was no longer enclosed, the sign was entirely gone, and the windows were broken or missing altogether. Rubin, however, could not admit the extent of the damage. His fictional story required an inhabitable store, and so he described the building as if it was in better repair than it actually was. By neglecting the full extent of the disrepair, Rubin allowed the material status of the building (its ownership and relative disrepair) to fade from view. Once more relegated to the role of incidental context, the site was no more than an occasion to ask forensic questions. In fact, so engrossed was he in forensic questions that he occasionally seemed to forget that the building itself had changed hands. This is nowhere clearer than in his fictional one-person boycott of Young's Grocery. After milling about the store and engaging in "meaningless conversation," Rubin claims that he would leave without buying anything. He refused to buy sausages, sardines, and deviled hams from Young's as a protest against Bryant's! "I did not wish to patronize the place, no matter what it was called these days."[33] Young's had become literally interchangeable with Bryant's—an exchange that was only possible by disregarding the building, its ownership, its sign, and its conspicuous age.

The slippage in Rubin's fictional account between the two stores perfectly captures the symbolic logic of the building until it fell into disrepair. So long as it was in good repair (or imagined to be so), the building that housed Bryant's Grocery inspired commemoration on the model of forensics: it encouraged speculation, and even inquiry, into what happened in 1955. For Samuels, Murdock Larsson, and Rubin—and after them Anderson and Tyson—forensic questions filled the full range of their attention. If these authors did not attend to the materiality of the store—or even to the obvious fact that it was now owned by the Youngs—this is because forensic analysis did not require it. The intact grocery was simply a mechanism for rehashing midcentury sexual infractions; it was nothing more than the incidental context for forensic inquiry.

Although Bud and Rita Young have never before appeared in a book about Till's memory, they nonetheless played a major role in determining the meaning of the building that once housed Bryant's Grocery. To be sure, there is no evidence to suggest that the Youngs had any ideological investment in the murder of Emmett Till. Moreover, it is impossible to know if the Youngs were even aware that events in the building they kept as a country store led to a murder with such significance to the civil rights movement. And, yet, simply by maintaining a store in the building, they kept the structure in relatively good repair. From the perspective of Till commemoration, their upkeep of the building enabled the placelessness of the forensic tradition. A maintained building is just one more building. Notable for neither its ruin nor its glamor, the particularities of the building faded into the background. Once in the background, commemoration was interchangeable with forensics.

To be sure, forensic questions are important. But they are not a natural mode of commemoration or even its highest form. If they seem to have taken precedence, this is only because the likes of Bud and Rita Young have been written out of Till's story. Place has been undervalued, and forensics has filled the void. Moreover, *Remembering Emmett Till* is built on the conviction that the facts of 1955 are only half of Till's story, if that. As every chapter has stressed, his story has been indelibly stamped by material conditions of the Delta—from its county lines, to its topography, to its soils, waterways, and landforms. This remained the case in 1980s Money, where the unthinking maintenance of the store enabled the elision of place and a commemorative tradition captivated and exhausted by forensics.[34]

## THE HAUNTED RUINS OF BRYANT'S GROCERY

In the mid-1980s, children of Ray Tribble purchased the building and allowed it to fall into disrepair. As the structure deteriorated, the meaning of the building became more complex. To be sure, the ruins still gestured to the facts of 1955. Just as Young's inspired forensic questions about what happened in and around the store, the Tribble's ruined building continued to prompt such speculation. If anything, such speculation intensified. Locals suggest that every passing year generated an increasing number of tourists descending on Money to see the spot where Till whistled at Carolyn Bryant.[35] In addition, however, the ruins made it obvious that the store and, by extension, Till's story, had not been well tended. Marking an enduring indifference to Till's story, the ruins of the store called into question the racial culture of the Delta writ large. Ruins, Mary Carruthers wrote in a different context, "all but [shout] that they have been preserved for the chastisement of future generations."[36] The ruins of Bryant's Grocery have been chastising tourists since the 1980s, making the racial indifference of the Delta obvious and prompting questions about how a site of such historical magnitude (Annette Morgan calls it the most historic site in the country) could be allowed to fall into ruin? As a commemorative symbol, the meaning of the building was now doubled, pointing to both past and present, to the murder and its willed forgetfulness. As the building fell, forensics gave way to haunting, and commemoration began to feel like the end result of a failed attempt to banish the murder from cultural memory.

By 2000, when Paul Hendrickson profiled the building for a *Washington Post* article titled "Mississippi Haunting," the floors were completely gone. In stark contrast to those who visited the store during the Youngs' tenure, Hendrickson's account was focused on the building itself. No longer relegated to the incidental location of a historical inquiry, the sheer disrepair of the building was the theme of Hendrickson's story. He described the broken plate glass, the rafters that had fallen to the foundation, and the rodents that scurried among the debris. A second-story toilet, still bolted to the brick wall, now hung suspended in space "with only air beneath, a ludicrous sight." While Hendrickson found the ruins beautiful, the "beauty of the building has to do with its look of extreme fragility. A good cough would knock it over." To his mind, the crumbling ruins of Bryant's Grocery were a poignant commentary on the uncommemorated murder and an indictment of the contemporary Delta. "There is no plaque from a state historical commission," he wrote. The absence of a plaque confirmed the obvious meaning of the ruins: Bryant's Grocery was ignored and abandoned. It was "forgotten," a "shrine in ruin." The conspicuous disregard of the store was evidence of what Hendrickson called "nonchange" in American race relations. The same bigotry that was once displayed in the murder of Emmett Till was now manifested in the disregard of the grocery.[37]

And yet, for Hendrickson, forgetfulness and nonchange were only half of the story. The material evidence of disregard notwithstanding, the building still gestured to the murder of Emmett Till. The murder, he wrote, "is why I've come [to Money], why I'm standing now on this spot. I am trying to dream my way into the brutal murder of Emmett Till. I am trying to imagine what some of it was like."[38] Imagine it he did. After contemplating the ruins, Hendrickson proceeded to cover the same ground as Samuels, Murdock Larsson, and Rubin—the whistle, the alleged violation of sexual taboos, and the brutal murder. Unlike the previous writers, however, for whom the store was simply a forensic site and an opportunity to rehearse the facts of the murder, Hendrickson was keenly attuned to the symbolic complexity of the ruins.[39] He saw in them both a call to memory and evidence that the call had been thus far ignored.

If we attend, like Hendrickson, to the complexity of the ruins of Bryant's Grocery, it is possible to see the ruins as a material analogue to the fate of Till's story in the Mississippi Delta. Like the ruined store itself, tales of Till's murder have been ignored but never erased from the cultural landscape. Both the story and the store remain unaddressed but insistent; the longer they are ignored, the more obvious the inattention becomes. And yet, the more obvious the inattention, the more urgently the ruins seem to discharge their commemorative function. While all of this may seem rather philosophical, the ironic complicity of disregard and commemoration has been borne out by the remains of Bryant's Grocery. The state's historical marker and the orange plastic fence were erected at virtually the same time, and, by the Tribbles own reckoning, the number of tourists increases with the extent of the ruin.[40] The greater the ruin, the more urgent the memory.

Hendrickson captured the double meaning of the ruins with the metaphor of *haunting*. In 2003, he republished "Mississippi Haunting" as the prologue to *Sons of Mississippi: A Story of Race and Its Legacy*. As the story shifted from the *Washington Post* to *Sons of Mississippi*, the title shifted from "Mississippi Haunting" to "Nothing Is Ever Escaped." The prologue concluded with a riff on James Baldwin. As Baldwin said of his father's legacy, so Hendrickson said of Till's murder: "nothing is ever escaped." Bryant's Grocery is haunted because disregard and inattention will never be the end of the story. The ruins may be ignored, but they can never be escaped. To say that Bryant's Grocery is haunted, then, is to say that it is half-remembered, or remembered because it can never be totally forgotten. As Hendrickson put it, Bryant's Grocery is "poised between memory and forgetting"; it is simultaneously a call to remember and evidence that the local community has yet to assume the burden.[41]

Hendrickson is hardly alone. As early as the late 1980s, the production team of *Eyes on the Prize* considered opening their film "with ghosts" by centering their story on the "dilapidated store." They pictured the ruined Bryant's as a "haunted landscape overgrown like Auschwitz."[42] As the reference to the infamous death camp suggests, the haunted tradition of commemoration is one-part censure. As Hariman and Lucaites have written, "There is something terribly wrong when a civilization appears to have been abandoned."[43] For both Hendrickson and Else, the ruins of Bryant's Grocery suggested that the endurance of Till's story is in part a function of a failed effort to forget it entirely. Although the ever-increasing stream of tourists bears witness to the failure of this will-to-forget, the effort to leave Till's story untended has itself become part of Till's story. That is why Hendrickson claims that the ruins of the store are evidence of "nonchange" in the Delta's race relations. The same racism that once cost Till his life is now a constituent part of his memory; to remember Till in the ruins of Bryant's Grocery is to experience firsthand the enduring racism of the Delta. This explains the affective charge of the ruins: the more the store crumbles, the more it generates shame, anger, and disbelief.[44]

Curiously, one of the most prominent manifestations of the haunting conceit comes from Richard Rubin who, in 1995, returned to the Delta and took the opportunity to interview the lawyers who had defended Till's murderers and the jurors who had acquitted them. When he returned, he discovered that Young's Grocery—the site of his fabricated boycott—was now little more than "a crumbling building that had once been Bryant's Grocery." Although he did not make up another story about entering the store, he did interview Ray Tribble—juror from the 1955 trial and, for the past ten years, father to the owners of the building that was once Bryant's Grocery. The interview with Tribble appears in a *New York Times Magazine* essay titled "The Ghosts of Emmett Till."

The difference between *Confederacy of Silence* and "The Ghosts of Emmett Till" is instructive. In *Confederacy*, Rubin imagined an intact store and was able to, in striking fashion, obliterate the distance between 1955 and 1988; he walked into Young's (and boycotted it) as if it was Bryant's. As he wrote "Ghosts," however, the store was "crumbling," and Till's murder was now cast as a "burr" that periodically pricked the American conscience. Poised between memory and forgetting, Till's story lay dormant for years, Rubin wrote, only to flare up, inspire outbursts of commemoration, rage, and sorrow, then fade again into the background.[45] The story could not be put to rest and functioned as an indictment of contemporary society. In a remarkable interview with John Whitten, the defense lawyer confided to Rubin that he had "played the race card"—the idiom was a phrase made popular by what was then thought of as the trial of the century:

> And it occurred to me, right then, just how much the defense of O. J. Simpson owed to the defense of Roy Bryant and J. W. Milam, and how little, in some ways, the country had changed in the past 40 years. The issue of race was still so potent that it could overwhelm evidence and hijack a jury, even when the case at hand was a brutal, savage murder.

The similarities with Hendrickson are striking. For both writers, the conceit of haunting captured an inability to completely forget the story of Till's murder. Just as Hendrickson wrote that nothing is ever escaped, so Rubin noted that Till's story occasionally rises from dormancy to prick the American conscience—memory as that which cannot be forgotten. Just as Hendrickson suggested that the unforgotten story functioned as an indictment of the Delta, a measure of nonchange in race relations, so Rubin stressed how little the country changed between the trials of Emmett Till and O. J. Simpson. For both writers, the unforgotten is always damning.

In sum, while the ruins of Bryant's store clearly recall the events of 1955—that is why Rubin and Hendrickson visited them in the first place—they also, in their brokenness, are a conspicuous display of commemorative indifference and an indictment of the racial mores of the twenty-first-century Delta. Beyond the literary work of Hendrickson and Rubin, perhaps the best evidence that the ruins of the store function as an indictment of the community are the various attempts to buy the store from the Tribbles or erect commemorative infrastructure. In 2007, for example, Robert Jenkins, a community development expert from Virginia, learned of the neglected store on a business trip to Jackson. He immediately offered to buy the property and restore it, only to be rebuffed by the Tribble family, who, he claims, proposed selling the bricks one by one to African Americans.[46] One year later, a local insurance agent named Billy Walker was so embarrassed by the crumbling ruins that he tried to buy the store. "It was a disgrace" to the local community, he told a local reporter, evidence of communal apathy toward the past.[47] In 2010, Neil Padden, a Nashville businessman with connections to Congressman John Lewis, offered six figures but could not close the deal.[48] As Sherron Wright (the great-niece of Moses Wright) summed up the situation in 2018, by not selling the store, the Tribbles are, in effect, holding the building hostage. "They just want history to die," she said.[49]

Although a complete history of attempts to buy Bryant's Grocery is difficult to establish, coverage in the local paper does suggest that the ruins of the store, and the sense of shame engendered by the them, have generated a consistent stream of interest in buying the property. In 2007, the *Greenwood Commonwealth* noted that although the property "isn't worth a penny" on Leflore County's budget, the Tribbles offered to sell the property to the county for $40 million. They lowered their price to $4 million, and the county responded with an offer of $50,000 before the negotiations broke off.[50] While these eye-popping figures are difficult to verify (beyond the fact that they were printed by the widely respected Jerry Mitchell), if true, they are an astonishing marker of just how powerfully the ruins of the store signaled an indictment of the community.

The Mississippi Freedom Trail sign that was erected in 2011 in front of Bryant's Grocery has its origins in precisely the sense of shame produced by the ruins of Bryant's Grocery. On October 17, 2009, a retired businessman and a medical doctor from Jackson participated in the

"Great Mississippi Road Trip," a tour of civil rights sites organized by the Mississippi Center for Justice. The tour included a stop at the ruins of Bryant's Grocery in Money. Months after the tour, still bothered by the fact that Bryant's was uncommemorated, the Jackson citizens set up a dinner with their tour guide at the legendary Mississippi blues joint Po' Monkey's. By the time they had finished their round of Bud Lights, $4,000 had changed hands, and the process to commemorate Bryant's was underway. Between the Po' Monkey's dinner in April 2010 and the unveiling of the Freedom Trail in April 2011, the project grew exponentially. What the Jackson citizens intended as a gift to commemorate the grocery blossomed into the gift that jump-started the entire thirty-site Freedom Trail. While the full story of how the Freedom Trail grew from a single gift is complex, the essential point is that the origin of the Mississippi Freedom Trail was the haunting power of the ruins. The ruins were at once a reminder of the 1955 murder, which is why the Center for Justice stopped in Money. But they were also a marker of enduring indifference, which is why the businessman and the doctor set up the dinner at Po' Monkey's.

Since its installation in 2011, the Mississippi Freedom Trail marker has only accentuated the symbolic power of Bryant's Grocery. The sign emphasizes, if not exaggerates, the historical importance of Bryant's Grocery, arguing that the crumbling store was the origination point of the American civil rights movement. By so emphasizing the historic importance of the site, the disregard of the store becomes even more palpable. In June 2017, the Freedom Trail sign was vandalized. The black vinyl was either erased with acid or scraped from the aluminum with a blunt instrument (see figure 21). Although Hammons and Associates quickly replaced the sign (deleting the connection to Rosa Parks, see figures 14–15), the vandalized sign was a perfect analogue to the ruins of Bryant's Grocery. The accomplished journalist Jamil Smith saw this clearly, tweeting that the vandal "tried to, quite literally, erase history."[51] Tried to, but could not. Much like the ruins of the store, the vandalized sign preserved Till's story alongside its attempted erasure. This doesn't quite put it strongly enough. Both the ruined store and the defaced sign signaled that the attempts to erase

**FIGURE 21.** Mississippi Freedom Trail sign, Money, MS, summer 2017.
Photo by Allan Hammons. Used by permission.

Till's story (either through vandalism or inattention) had become part
of the story itself. Till could no longer be remembered without also
remembering the Delta's failed will-to-forget.

From Hendrickson, to Rubin, to Walker, to Jenkins, to Padden, to
the anonymous Jackson citizens, the rubble of Bryant's Grocery has
consistently been interpreted as both a marker of Till's murder and an
indictment of the present-day Delta. The ruins have made the indifference of the community painfully obvious, they have given tangible
form to willed forgetfulness, and, for a wide range of writers and visitors, they have functioned as an indictment of the Mississippi Delta
itself. In their brokenness, the ruins of Bryant's Grocery are a double
indictment of the Delta; they bear witness to a racist past and an indifferent present.

## BEN ROY'S SERVICE STATION AND NOSTALGIA

The restoration of Ben Roy's Service Station would have been impossible without the murder of Emmett Till or the ruins of Bryant's Grocery. The historic importance of Bryant's Grocery generated a booming tourist industry, but ruins left tourists with nowhere to go. Ben Roy's was in the right place at the right time. It became the default destination of those who had come to see the grocery but were turned away by the danger of the ruins and the restrictions of the orange fence. And yet, while the violent and racially coded history of Bryant's Grocery made the restoration of Ben Roy's possible, the restoration itself reframed the racial history of the Delta. While the ruins hinted at a Delta community too callous to remember Till's murder, the restored Ben Roy's focused on the charms of day-to-day life in the midcentury Delta.

Although the restored Ben Roy's is, quite literally, built on the legacy of racism and funded by Emmett Till tourism, the gas station eliminates all evidence of segregation, racism, and violence. The restored service station contains not a single gesture to Till's murder, the civil rights movement, or the building just to its north. Rather, it is stocked with 1950s Americana, a heavy dose of nostalgia, and an explicit attempt to minimize the violence of segregation in the Delta. Ben Roy's thus stands as a countermemory to Bryant's Grocery and Meat Market. While the grocery suggested an ongoing indifference to matters of racism, Ben Roy's invokes the charm of rural life; while the grocery reminds passersby of the violence of the midcentury Delta, Ben Roy's suggests that that violence was out of keeping with time and place. In sum, while Bryant's Grocery stands as an indictment of the Delta, Ben Roy's is an apology for it.

The story of Ben Roy's begins with its funding mechanism, the MCRHS grant program—a one-time initiative timed to coincide with the fiftieth anniversary of the freedom rides. Among other sites, the program funded the creation of the Mississippi Freedom Trail, the headquarters of the Council of Federated Organizations in Meridian, the Medgar Evers house in Jackson, the Amzie Moore house in

Cleveland, the Vernon Dahmer house in Hattiesburg, and the second-district Tallahatchie County Courthouse in Sumner (site of the Till trial). Ben Roy's was the *only* funded project that was not a civil rights site. While the Glendora Cotton Gin was denied funding because its claim to be the origin of the fan that held Till's body in the water could not be verified (see chapter 5), Ben Roy's was funded despite its total lack of civil rights history. Unlike the unfunded Glendora gin, which at least had a plausible claim to civil rights history, Ben Roy's had nothing. Nothing, that is, except its proximity to Bryant's Grocery.

Without a civil rights history of its own, Ben Roy's was funded by tourism. The MCRHS grant program was funded under House Bill 1701, a 2010 bill designed to fund projects that demonstrate "the state's attractiveness as a tourism destination."[52] The same bill that funded the restoration of civil rights sites also funded a horse show on the gulf coast, renovations to the home of Elvis Presley, and the restoration of the home of J. Z. George—a nineteenth-century Confederate politician who signed the ordinance of succession, defended the disenfranchisement of African Americans, and supported the racist state constitution of 1890. With tourism as the ultimate driver of state funding, the capacity of Ben Roy's to attract visitors was just as important as its linkages to the civil rights movement. Indeed, in the case of Ben Roy's, its potential to attract tourists *was* its link to the civil rights movement. Tourists did not come to Ben Roy's *because* it was a civil rights site. Rather, they came to Bryant's, ended up at Ben Roy's, and by their presence gave the old service station the one thing it needed before it could claim state money: a link to the civil rights movement.

Well aware that Ben Roy's had no civil rights history apart from its connection to Bryant's Grocery, Mary Annette Morgan (granddaughter of Ray Tribble and the family's grant writer) used the indiscriminate movement of tourists between the two buildings to build her case for civil rights money.

> In this day and age, tourists to Mississippi and to the Delta region want to get "off-the-beaten-path." They want to experience history hands-

on and see places where events took place and where legends lived and died. Today, without any investment in the site, hundreds of visitors travel to the site just to see the ruins of the Bryant Grocery building and to experience the nostalgia of small town Money. Just imagine if we could make Money, Mississippi more of a destination, instead of just a disappearing ghost town. How many more visitors would travel to Money if there was actually some type of cultural center for them to see and to experience?[53]

Morgan was talking about *Ben Roy's*. The gas station was not "the place where events took place." Nor was it true that "hundreds of visitors travel to the site." These claims could be true only if Ben Roy's and Bryant's Grocery counted as the same site. And this was the importance of tourists. With Bryant's Grocery in ruin—unsafe to approach, let alone enter—visitors tended to congregate under the canopy of Ben Roy's. It was precisely the penchant of tourists to wander between buildings that allowed Morgan to move seamlessly between Bryant's Grocery ("where the events took place") and Ben Roy's Service Station (which she wanted to restore). As the visitors wandered, they became the mechanism by which Morgan wrote the service station into the history of civil rights.

The lead architectural firm on the Ben Roy's project was the Greenwood firm of Beard and Riser. Partner Dale Riser wrote portions of the grant application and helped Morgan build her case that tourism could provide Ben Roy's with a retroactive civil rights history. He wrote,

It is not inconceivable, in fact it is very likely, that the events that transpired at Bryant's Grocery on that day in August of 1955 were discussed underneath the front canopy of the adjacent service station; rehabilitating that service station will allow new and future generations of Mississippians, Americans, and others to meet under that canopy and discuss the events surrounding the death of Emmitt [sic] Till and the civil rights era in a new light.[54]

Like Morgan, Riser relied on visitors to give Ben Roy's a civil rights charge and a claim on state money. By talking about the murder under the canopy, visitors drew Ben Roy's into the ever-expanding orbit of the civil rights movement.

Morgan and Riser both concluded that Ben Roy's could serve as a "visitor center," an "interpretive space," or "cultural center" from which tourists could engage the history of civil rights and discuss the murder of Emmett Till in a "new light."[55] The key question is how the "new light" of by Ben Roy's will reframe the murder. Looking again at Morgan's proposal provides our first hint. Writing of a "more comprehensive" commemoration of Till's murder, she writes:

> Today, without any investment in the site, hundreds of visitors travel to the site just to see the ruins of the Bryant Grocery building and to experience the nostalgia of small town Money. Just imagine if we could make Money, Mississippi more of a destination, instead of just a disappearing ghost town.

A "ghost town" was unacceptable. A ghost town, after all, is precisely what Hendrickson had found when he visited Money in 2000 and used it as a study in enduring American racism. As a (slowly) disappearing ghost town, Money functioned as an indictment of the community, a material reminder of their failure to properly commemorate the murder. Against this vision of Bryant's Grocery, Ben Roy's posits "the nostalgia of small town Money."

The pursuit of nostalgia did not have to entail the elision of race. In order to make Ben Roy's into an "interpretive space," the Tribble family promised that the renovation would restore the segregated bathrooms on the north side of Ben Roy's. During the 1950s, Ben Roy's had two exterior bathrooms, one for whites and the other for blacks. The bathrooms were marked "colored" and "white," and opened to the outside. Sometime later—the date is not known—these bathrooms were changed. The signs were taken down, the exterior doors were removed, and the bathrooms were reoriented to the inside of

Ben Roy's—one accessible from a storage room, the other from an office. At a cost of $6,000, the application promised that the "segregated bathrooms will be restored to their original state. *They will display the reality of segregation in the Jim Crow South before the enforcement of Civil Rights legislation.*"[56]

The promise to restore the segregated bathrooms was the family's *only* mechanism connecting Ben Roy's to the Delta's racial history. They chose not to install interpretive signage or placards that could speak to the history of civil rights or the memory of Emmett Till. As Morgan explained to *Leflore Illustrated*, "We're going to set it up exactly as it would have looked in the 1950s. . . . It's not going to be a museum with panels and reinterpretations. It's none of that. It's the real thing. You see it the way it was, completely renovated." Without interpretive panels, the commemorative labor of Ben Roy's would be borne exclusively by the building itself and the collection of midcentury artifacts it housed. Such artifacts included "the original furniture, signage, and memorabilia of the service station and its attached house."[57]

And yet, the artifacts do not display the "reality of segregation." Two things about the Tribbles' collection of southern artifacts deserve mention. First, their collection did not involve the Jim Crow signage that once marked the bathrooms "colored" and "white." While they refurbished the bathroom fixtures and reoriented the doors to open to the outside, they did not reinstall the Jim Crow signage. Without the signs, the restored but unmarked bathrooms do not "display the reality of segregation." To the contemporary tourist, the twin bathrooms would likely register simply as a men's and women's room.

Second, in addition to the original artifacts preserved by the Tribbles and returned to the store, the family collected a variety of extra midcentury items to help refashion Ben Roy's as a "period piece." These items included a "vintage sofa," circular washtubs, a sewing machine, a Hobart meat slicer, Coca-Cola signs, midcentury wheelbarrows, and a variety of decorative trunks.[58] While they refused to add signage that could have connected their gas station to civil rights, they were quick to add a variety of artifacts that connected their building to the charms of midcentury rural America. The cumulative effect is that the restored Ben Roy's is far more powerful as a period piece than it is as a civil rights cultural center.

This much was by design. While the grant application acknowledged that the restored building would be both "an authentic time period exhibit and [a] visitor's center," the emphasis of the application—and the renovation—was squarely on Ben Roy's as a "reminder of an era in the history of Mississippi." Both Morgan and Riser emphasized the nostalgic value of Ben Roy's as an "unspoiled authentic exhibition of a 1950s-era service station." If renovated, Morgan wrote, the service station will "allow visitors to step back in time to the summer of 1955 and to rural Money, Mississippi."[59] Riser too emphasized the nostalgic value of Ben Roy's. In the "small-town South," he argued, service stations such as Ben Roy's were far more than functional necessities. Ben Roy's was "the hub of social activity and offered a visible 'front stoop' for the community," a place where locals went for refreshments, conversation, or "just to visit with the station's proprietors."[60] Although the application occasionally nodded to the "reality of segregation" (and promised to mark it with Jim Crow bathrooms), it also made segregation itself seem rather charming. A jukebox once stood on the porch, Morgan wrote, and on weekend nights blacks and whites alike gathered to "shed their work-week blues and enjoy the Jukebox at Ben Roy's."[61]

Thus we have nostalgia and ruins sixty-seven feet apart from each other. But if the ruins of Bryant's Grocery bear witness to the endurance of racism in the Delta, the nostalgia of Ben Roy's minimizes the impact of midcentury racism. According to the restoration of Ben Roy's, the Delta may have been marked by segregation, but segregation did not seem to impinge on the social experience of sharing music and conversation on a Saturday night. The distribution of material artifacts at the service station underscores just this point; racism is left wholly unmarked while the affective experience of stepping back in time is supported by a wide range of southern things: vintage couches, sewing machines, and Coca-Cola signs. It was in just this sense that Dale Riser concluded that a restored Ben Roy's could cast "the death of Emmitt [sic] Till and the Civil Rights era in a new light": it contextualized the undeniable violence of the ruins with the unlikely nostalgia of interracial Saturday nights.[62]

In sum, while the Tribbles *won* the civil rights grant by using tourists to blur the distinction between Bryant's Grocery and Ben Roy's Service Station, they *spent* the money in such a way that Ben Roy's appears, not as an extension of Bryant's Grocery, but as a countervailing force to the symbolic power of the ruined store. While Bryant's recalls the force with which racism impacts practices of memory, Ben Roy's suggests that the realities of segregation were overmatched by the charm of small-town living: the Jim Crow bathrooms were erased, and the juke-box-quickened front porch was cast as a haven from the cultural norms that once kept blacks from socializing (or whistling) across racial lines. When all the erasures of race and the investments in nostalgia are accounted for, it almost seems as if Ben Roy's took civil rights money and used it to create a period piece designed to evoke nostalgia for racially promiscuous front-stoop Saturday nights that may well have never happened.

Although it is impossible to know for sure whether or not Ben Roy's ever hosted interracial social gatherings, two well-established contexts make it seem unlikely. First, the very first businesses in the Delta to be boycotted during the civil rights movement were white-owned service stations.[63] With the help of Medgar Evers, the Regional Council of Negro Leadership (T. R. M. Howard's operation) distributed fifty thousand bumper stickers with the phase "Don't Buy Gas Where You Can't Use the Restroom." Although Ben Roy's did provide Jim Crow facilities, and thus would not have been a target of the campaign, David and Linda Beito report that the campaign "galvanized ordinary blacks in the Delta."[64] As early as 1952, before sidewalks, lunch counters, bus stations, or swimming pools were contested, gas stations were among the first lighting rods of black inequality in the Delta, and it is difficult to imagine that a front-porch jukebox could overcome the racial charge attached to them. Although Richard Rubin is not always a trustworthy guide, his insight that the Delta had separate gas stations for blacks and whites might itself be a legacy of Howard's boycott and a reflection of the racial charge attached to service stations.[65]

Second, we know the recreational habits of one black family from Money: the Wright family. On weekends, this family went not to Ben Roy's Service Station, just two and eight-tenths miles away, but to the segregated streets of downtown Greenwood. Not only did Greenwood have more to offer, but the family also believed that Ben Roy's wife failed to treat blacks with respect.[66] Thus, on the night of Saturday, August 27, 1955, the Wright boys took their cousin to Greenwood for a night of big crowds, drinking, and gazing at nightclubs.[67] That same Saturday night, Till's killers were socializing, not at Ben Roy's but at their own family store. The second party confronted the first at the Wright home at 2 a.m., and Emmett Till would never again see the light of day.

Regardless of whether or not the historic front porch of Ben Roy's was ever the site of promiscuous socialization, one thing is certain. With old-fashioned gas pumps and a litany of Americana, the restored Ben Roy's is wholly given over to the nostalgia of midcentury, small-town life. It is a beautiful building, but its beauty was funded by unacknowledged racial violence. I cannot look at it without imagining what red-capped Trump supporters might see when they look backward to a once-great America. They see gas stations and, more broadly, an entire American infrastructure made possible by economies of race but unmarked by legacies of violence. And this is the tragic irony of Ben Roy's: its restoration was paid for, literally, by the memory of Till's murder, but the finished product recodes the racial history of the Mississippi Delta and makes Till's murder seem like an aberration.

Even a gas station is an agent of memory. Without saying a word — or posting a sign — Ben Roy's just stands there, beautifully restored, evidence for those who need it of the charms of midcentury Delta life.

## CONCLUSION

Young's Grocery, the ruined Tribble building, and Ben Roy's Service Station — these three structures provide three different examples of how race, place, and commemoration shift in tandem. At Young's Grocery, place was minimized, memory was forensic, and race was confined to the past. For the Tribble ruin, the enduring racism of the Delta is an ingredient part of an unforgotten murder. And for Ben Roy's Service Station, the memory of Till's murder funded a vision of the Delta in which the social strictures of race were tempered by the sheer charm of midcentury living.

For sixty years and counting, the forensic tradition of inquiry has dominated the commemoration of Till's murder. From the 1950s probes of Jimmy Hicks to the exhaustive work of Devery Anderson in the twenty-first century, Till storytelling has been nothing short of obsessed with forensic questions. If Timothy Tyson's 2017 *The Blood of Emmett Till* has rocked the Emmett Till community despite its modest historical revelations, it is because it challenged the very wellspring of commemoration. Announcing that Carolyn Bryant confessed to lying under oath about what Till did to her inside the grocery struck at what must be counted as Till commemoration's most sacred space. Precisely because of the mystery that has shrouded the events inside Bryant's Grocery, the store has always functioned as ground zero of the murder (despite the fact that it was simply the location of the whistle). From Langston Hughes's 1955 "The Money Mississippi Blues," to Rich Samuels's 1985 *The Murder and the Movement*, to Anderson's 2015 *Emmett Till*, a tradition long charmed by forensic questions has been nothing short of spellbound by Bryant's Grocery.

There is nothing wrong with forensic questions. After all, the forensic model of inquiry has funded a vibrant commemorative tradition that shows no signs of slowing. With that said, the history of Money, or, more precisely, the structural histories of the town's two remaining storefronts, puts the forensic tradition of inquiry in context. To the extent we can trust these buildings (and they have no reason to lie), a thriving forensic tradition requires certain material conditions. As soon as the Bryants' store was allowed to crumble, the forensic fascination of who-did-what-to-whom was reframed by the enduring racism of the Delta. The onset of ruin, in other words, transformed the basic focus of commemorative inquiry: the inattention of the local community was now a part of the meaning of Till's murder. At least in this instance, forensic questions required a rigorous bracketing of place. As soon as the building crumbled and the *place* of commemoration transformed the *object* of commemoration, forensic inquiry suddenly seemed insufficient.

That is to say, the Mississippi Delta is not simply the place where Till was killed or the setting where memory work happens. It is an ingredient part of memory work itself. Indeed, in the case at hand, the ruins of the store and the preservation of the gas station—that is, the material infrastructure of the Delta—are the precise means through which racism came to alter the meaning of Till's murder. Without the ruined grocery, Till's murder would never have haunted the Delta. Without the preserved Ben Roy's, the murder would never be entwined with small-town nostalgia. The lesson here is about the intractability of place and the capacity of racism to alter the past through an investment in things as mundane as grocery stores, fallen bricks, and gas stations.

## CHAPTER FIVE

# MEMORY AND MISERY IN GLENDORA

On September 19, 2006, the town of Glendora celebrated the simultaneous opening of the Emmett Till Historic Intrepid Center (ETHIC) and the Johnny B. Thomas Adult Continuing Education and Training Center.[1] The former was a museum dedicated to the memory of Emmett Till; the latter was a ten-station computer lab. Both were novelties. ETHIC was the first Till museum in the world and the Delta's first commemorative site of any kind besides the stretch of Highway 49E designated as the "Emmett Till Memorial Highway." The creation of the computer lab marked the first time that broadband internet had been available in and around the impoverished town of Glendora.[2]

The computer lab quietly funded the ETHIC museum. On September 27, 2005, the USDA awarded a Community Connect broadband grant to the village of Glendora. Funded at $325,405, the grant was intended to "bring broadband connectivity to the Mississippi Delta community of Glendora—a small village socially and geographically isolated from the mainstream." Unbeknownst to the USDA, the grant also funded the Delta's first Emmett Till museum.[3] From the USDA's perspective, the grant was exclusively about the provision of internet access to an impoverished population. As a state, Mississippi ranks dead last in household access to high-speed internet, and, as with most social inequities, the effects of the digital divide weigh heaviest on those with the least resources. In Mississippi, this means that un-equal access to the internet is yet another strike against those living in the Delta.[4]

While the Community Connect program was designed to temper the effects of the digital divide, it was never intended to fund a museum. Indeed, in the 647 pages of records preserved by the USDA, including the application, labor contracts, invoices, and correspondence, the name of Emmett Till is never once mentioned. The poverty of the community is stressed, as are the social and economic benefits of the internet. With an USDA-funded computer lab, for example, Glendora residents could take correspondence courses, apply for jobs, secure prescription medicines, and complete GEDs. Finally, the grant promised to revolutionize municipal services by connecting "the public library, health clinic, police department, and volunteer fire department."[5] But if the USDA knew that an Emmett Till museum was part of the deal, there is no record of that fact.

Just down the road from the museum is the "Emmett Till Memorial Park and Interpretive Nature Trail." The park features a playground built out of repurposed tires and a 3,100-foot asphalt walking trail adjacent to the Black Bayou on the south side of town. The trail is lined with fifteen interpretive signs, eleven of which expressly recall the murder of Emmett Till. Much like the ETHIC museum, however, funding for the park was *not* driven by the importance of remembering Till's murder. Rather, the funding hinged on the opportunity to provide basic municipal services, in this case a sidewalk and a playground. The sidewalk was funded by a $65,625 grant administered by the Mississippi Department of Wildlife, Fisheries, and Parks as part of their Recreational Trails Program. From the perspective of the Recreational Trails Program, the grant was about the creation, maintenance, and accessibility of a walking trail in an impoverished community. The *content* of the signs that lined the walking trail was incidental, unrelated to the project funding. The playground was added by Partners in Development, a Boston nonprofit that works with impoverished communities. Neither the Department of Wildlife, Fisheries, and Parks nor Partners in Development had any investment in Till's memory. Like the USDA, they were invested only in arresting poverty and mitigating its effects.

In addition to the ETHIC museum and the park, the village of Glendora boasts a wide array of Till-themed signage, giving it the greatest density of Till memorials anywhere in the world. In the heart of town, Glendora hosts four roadside markers produced by the ETMC as part of their Tallahatchie Civil Rights Driving Tour (chapter 3). The four signs are in such close proximity that from any one of them at least one additional sign is always in view. Adding these to the signs in the park, the small sign directing traffic toward the park, and two additional ETMC signs on the outskirts of town, the tiny village of five streets has a total of *eighteen* historical signs dedicated to the memory of Emmett Till. There is nowhere else in the Delta (or the world) that even approaches this density of Till commemoration.

And yet, as extensive as it may be, Glendora's investment in Till commemoration has never been a product of its history with the Till murder or a moral imperative to remember a local injustice. While the museum, the park, and the signs give eloquent voice to a local history of injustice, the deprivation of human life, and the urgency of civil rights, these moral imperatives have never compelled the investment required to build public memorials. In the years between the opening of the ETHIC museum in 2006 and its renovation in 2011, Glendora's mayor, Johnny B. Thomas, tried three times to fund memorial work based solely on the fact that, in some form or another, virtually every version of Till's story routes the murder party through Glendora. Each of the mayor's three initiatives failed. In retrospect, his efforts seem hopelessly naive; they were grounded in the noble-but-mistaken conviction that historical injustice was a sufficient rationale for commemorative labor. The failure of Thomas's three initiatives is a trenchant reminder of a comment made by the art historian Kirk Savage: "Public monuments do not arise as by natural law to celebrate the deserving; they are built by people with sufficient power to marshal (or impose) public consent for their creation."[6] In Glendora, the commemorative worthiness of the town is a moot point. If the town now boasts the greatest density of Till memorials in the world, this is not a reflection of historical facts, moral imperatives, or the geography of Till's murder.

The creation of the ETHIC museum and the park hold the key to understanding commemoration in Glendora. Neither of these efforts used Till's story to command public money. The USDA didn't even know about the connection to Emmett Till, and the Mississippi Department of Wildlife, Fisheries, and Parks did not consider it a relevant factor in funding decisions. In both cases, it was the poverty of the community and the compelling necessity of public goods (e.g., sidewalks, broadband) that, via a circuitous route, brought Till commemoration to Glendora. The success of the museum and the park combined with the mayor's three failed attempts to use Till's story as leverage for funding illustrate this chapter's primary theme: without poverty, there would be no Till commemoration in Glendora. In this respect, the computer lab and the sidewalk are just the beginning. Till commemoration in Glendora has come into existence only through its enabling links with low-income housing, temporary low-paying jobs, and welfare remediation. In Glendora, it is a simple historical fact that poverty is the condition of commemoration, that commemoration functions as welfare, and that the intertwining of poverty, municipal programs, and memory has reshaped the basic plotline of Till's murder. The harshest of Glendora's critics go even further, suggesting that the commemorative work in the town exacerbates the already dire poverty of the village.

In this chapter, I explore these lessons in detail. By telling the story of how, why, and for whom Glendora developed its remarkable commemorative infrastructure, I trace the connections binding memory, poverty, and municipal services. In Glendora, commemoration is so entwined with the basic operation of the town that things as otherwise innocuous as sidewalks, broadband service, apartments, and playgrounds appear as agents of memory. Indeed, while municipal infrastructure may seem an unlikely hero, in Glendora questions of infrastructure have wielded far more power over the commemorative landscape than have the heartbreaking stories of local injustice. While the town has tried to leverage the sheer horror of Till's story, it has managed to create memorials only when the horror of the story was routed through such mundane city services as sidewalks, broadband, and low-income housing. Glendora is thus a perfect example of the ecology of memory: commemoration thrived only when it was indexed to poverty and the infrastructure of a failing town.

This entanglement of commemoration, poverty, and infrastructure has consequences not only for Glendora—which gains and loses city services with the ebb and flow of commemorative efforts—but it also impacts what we think we know about the night Till was killed. Critically, the efforts to commemorate Till's murder in Glendora introduced two structures that appear fleetingly, if at all, in mainstream accounts of Till's death: the Glendora Cotton Gin and the Black Bayou Bridge. Mayor Thomas uses the park and the museum to argue that the murderers stole the cotton-gin fan that held Till's body in the water from the Glendora gin and that Till's body was dropped into the Black Bayou (and not the Tallahatchie River) from a bridge on the south side of town. If true, these claims would dramatically revise the conventional wisdom: they would alter the murder path, definitively implicate Milam's friend Elmer Kimbell who worked at the gin, and resolve a long-standing uncertainty regarding the body's disposal site.[7] My goal in this chapter is not to resolve these questions, but rather to demonstrate that their likelihood is calibrated to the municipal infrastructure of Glendora. It is neither an exaggeration nor a figure of speech to say that Kimbell's inclusion in Till's story is indexed to the sidewalks, apartments, and internet service of Glendora.

## MISERY AND MEMORY

The five streets of Glendora are lined with breathtaking poverty. When the museum was founded in 2005, 272 of the village's 285 people were African American, and 271 of these were on some form of welfare.[8] When the MDA reviewed the economic status of the town in 2009, they described Glendora as a town with "no hope, no pride of community, [and] no willingness to make it better."[9] Indeed, the impoverishment of Glendora is astounding, even by Delta standards. It's a town where the median household income is 60 percent below the state average, 86 percent of children live below the poverty line, one-fifth (18 percent) of the adults have a high school education, only a quarter of the population has a car, fewer still have drivers' licenses, and almost no one has a job.[10] The MDA listed Glendora's "top employers" as the Benevolent Aid and Burial Society, which is open only on an as-needed basis and provides zero jobs, and a local nonprofit, the Glendora Economic and Community Development Corporation (GECDCO), the tax returns for which list only one paid employee—its founder and executive director, Mayor Johnny B. Thomas.[11] The nearest gas, medical care, and jobs are ten miles away; a grocery store with fresh produce is even farther. While the whole of the Delta is often compared to the "third world," the epithet rings particularly true in Glendora, where electricity, plumbing, and floors cannot be taken for granted.[12] The nonprofit organization Partners in Development, committed to helping the "poorest of the poor," has chosen to focus on Haiti, Guatemala, and Glendora, Mississippi.[13]

The sheer poverty of the town and the conspicuous density of its commemorative work are deeply related. In March 2010, the MDA sent a team of economic development specialists to Glendora. Following a day of site visits and conversations with local residents, the specialists prepared a formal report on Glendora. Ostensibly intended to provide "local leadership and citizens [with] an objective appraisal of the town's existing assets," the report is in fact a heartbreaking record of desperate poverty and an overly optimistic—almost ludicrous—assessment of the possibility of Emmett Till–driven tourism to rescue the town from its economic woes.

In terms of identifying assets for economic development, the outlook of the MDA was bleak. One development specialist failed to find any assets in Glendora at all, suggesting that the "intrepid spirit" of the citizens was the town's dearest economic resource. Beyond this, the report noted that several townspeople were good cooks and thus suggested opening a restaurant. Also suggested was turning the trash-strewn and snake-infested "shore" of the stagnant bayou into "waterfront property." These suggestions were neither realistic nor feasible.

They are little more than wishful thinking, unconnected to the demographic realities of the town. The only actionable suggestion was the MDA team's near-universal agreement that the town's most viable asset was Till-driven tourism. This was not news to Thomas. From the dedication of the ETHIC museum in 2006 forward, he has clung to Till's story as though it were the only thing standing between Glendora and wholesale ruin.

While the MDA may be correct that Till's story is Glendora's most valuable commodity, they did not foresee that the marketing of the story would profoundly alter its content. Indeed, while Glendora has always been involved in Till's story in one form or another, it was not until the town's twenty-first-century crusade to remember the murder that the Black Bayou Bridge and the Glendora Cotton Gin came to the forefront of Till's story. In the remainder of this section, I highlight the key historical intersections of Glendora with Till's story.

J. W. Milam lived near the east end of town, and, according some accounts, the scheming began when Roy Bryant and Tallahatchie County sheriff H. C. Strider joined him for a night of drinking in Glendora.[14] This point has become particularly important to Mayor Thomas, who likes to stress that "the premeditated [*sic*] person who premeditated [the murder]" lived in Glendora.[15] While it might be tempting to assume that Thomas would promote *any* version of the story that featured Glendora, this is not true. William Bradford Huie's account in *Look* magazine gave a prominent role to the tiny village, suggesting that Till was tortured in the shed behind Milam's home. Despite the centrality Huie gives to Glendora, Thomas has personal reasons to distrust the *Look* narrative. Quite apart from the fact that Huie used *Look* to disseminate the defense lawyer's version of the story and protect Leslie Milam from prosecution (chapter 1), he also eliminated Thomas's father from the story, cutting Thomas himself off from his only source of inside information.

Thomas claims to be the biological son of Henry Lee Loggins.[16] Loggins, recall, was a Glendora resident, an employee of J. W. Milam, and an oft-rumored accomplice to the murder. He may have been the one who held Till in the back of Milam's truck on the long drive to Sunflower County or washed out the truck after Till was dead. As discussed in chapter 1, Loggins was eliminated from the *Look* narrative because he could tie the murder to the Sturdivant Plantation, implicate Leslie Milam, and thereby prevent *Look* from publishing the story. Loggins himself surely would have raised no objections to Huie's story. Until he died in October 2009, he consistently denied any involvement in the Till murder. Most prominently, he appeared on *60 Minutes* in 2004 and repeatedly told Ed Bradley in no uncertain terms that he had nothing to do with the case.[17]

The issue of Loggins's complicity in the murder has never been quite so simple for Mayor Thomas, whose capacity to tell an inside story requires the involvement of Loggins.[18] With his father providing an otherwise untapped firsthand source of information about the murder, it is hardly surprising that Thomas has never believed Loggins's claim to innocence. In 2005 he told the local paper that his father would confess his involvement if the FBI were to offer him immunity.[19] Although Loggins never did confess, he did call into question the status of his relationship with Thomas, whom he characterized as a "stepson."[20] Undeterred, in 2012, after Loggins passed, Thomas created two YouTube videos titled "My Father Helped Kill Emmett Till."[21] It has always been important to Thomas to stress that if his father (or stepfather) was involved, it was because he was forced to cooperate by J. W. Milam, the violent overseer on the Flautt Plantation on which his family lived.[22]

In addition to eliminating Loggins, Huie also eliminated the Glendora juke joint King's Place, the site where Thomas's mother, Adeline Hill, worked and where an anonymous source told reporter Jimmy Hicks that Loggins and Levi Collins were being held illegally in the Charleston jail to prevent them from testifying in the Till murder trial. Some suggest that Hill may have even been the woman with whom Hicks danced and from whom he learned of Loggins and Collins.[23] If true, this would give Thomas an even tighter relationship to the Till murder, another personal connection to the Sunflower County theory, and a yet another reason to distrust the *Look* account.

With personal connections to Loggins, Hill, and King's Place, it comes as no surprise that Mayor Thomas believes that Till was tortured at the Sturdivant Plantation in Sunflower County, for if Hill and Loggins were involved so were Leslie Milam and the Sturdivant barn. But Thomas takes the theory a step further. Leaning on the authority of Loggins, he claims that after Till was tortured (and perhaps murdered) in Sunflower County, *the murderers returned to Glendora to obtain the cotton-gin fan and dispose of the body*.[24] Milam's close friend and neighbor Elmer Kimbell, an oft-rumored accomplice to the murder, worked at the Glendora Cotton Gin and could have secured the fan. Moreover, the Black Bayou Bridge on the south side of Glendora was decommissioned in 1955, is less than a mile from the gin, and is an undeniably convenient disposal site. If, as Thomas argues, Till was dropped into the Black Bayou, it would have been a short 1.3 mile float through the bayou to the Tallahatchie River where his body was eventually discovered. In fact, if Till's body was indeed pulled from the water at the site of the ETMC's "River Site" sign (chapter 3), then it was almost certainly dropped into the bayou from the bridge on the south side of Glendora.

Logistically speaking, the mayor's tale is eminently reasonable. The Glendora Cotton Gin is a *far* more feasible site from which to obtain a fan than either of the other historically viable options: the gins in Boyle and Itta Bena. In terms of a disposal site, the Black Bayou Bridge is both convenient and the *only* extant theory apart from Huie's widely distrusted account.[25] On these two points, Thomas's account has won the favor of Till expert Keith Beauchamp. When Beauchamp, Whoopi Goldberg, and Frederick Zollo (of *Mississippi Burning* fame) film their long-promised feature-length film on Till's murder, they will have the fan stolen from the Glendora gin and the body dropped off of the Black Bayou Bridge.[26]

And yet, despite the plausibility of the account, there is virtually no publicly available evidence to support it. Outside of a few little-known interviews by Beauchamp with other residents of Glendora, the relevance of the Glendora Cotton Gin and the Black Bayou Bridge hinges largely on Thomas's version of Loggins's account. Thomas thus finds himself in a difficult position. On the one hand, the simple poverty of his town has made him desperate to leverage Till-related tourism as a form of economic development, and this requires a Glendora-centric version of Till's story. On the other hand, his version of the story depends almost exclusively on a deceased witness who while alive disowned all involvement with the case.[27] The result is the circuitous tale of how commemoration came to Glendora. Instead of leveraging the town's history to build a commemorative infrastructure, Thomas leveraged the town's poverty to give the town a new history (that is, to advance a new theory of where and by whom Till was killed). The result is that the contours of Till's story and the guilt of Elmer Kimbell are calibrated to the provision of internet access and sidewalks.

## POVERTY AND THE CREATION OF THE ETHIC MUSEUM

For some, the 2006 emergence of the museum is a story of persistent poverty, political corruption, graft, and welfare dependency. For others, it is a story of Johnny B. Thomas, a champion of the people and a civil servant par excellence. For whatever some may say, it is indisputably true that he has found creative solutions to poverty, created something from nothing, and provided basic, life-sustaining services to an impoverished community. While I will not resolve this debate, one thing is certain: the museum would not have been funded, built, staffed, stocked, or maintained apart from the poverty of Glendora. Poverty made the museum possible, it shaped the story told by the museum, and, in the view of the museum's critics, it perpetuates the poverty of Glendora by setting in motion a cycle of welfare dependency.

### Funding the ETHIC Museum

The intertwining of poverty and commemoration was never as visible as it was the day the ETHIC museum opened. A daylong ceremony set for September 26, 2006, was announced with press releases from both the village of Glendora and the AbsoCom Corporation. AbsoCom was the internet service provider funded by the USDA Community Connect broadband grant. The events of the day alternated between a focus on Till's murder and the social importance of rural broadband service. Presentations were made by Keith Beauchamp, the celebrated producer of the then-just-released *The Untold Story of Emmett Louis Till*, and Ike Fowler, the chief executive officer of AbsoCom. Both men spoke about their passion. Beauchamp focused on the relevance of Till's murder, and Fowler on the importance of the internet. Steve Whitaker—author of the oft-cited 1963 MA thesis on Till's murder—led a walking tour focused on Glendora's connections to the Till murder. This was followed by a "roundtable discussion on the effective use of emerging broadband technologies." Finally, Congressman Bennie Thompson marked the fifty-first anniversary of the Till trial by speaking on the "importance of broadband utilization." From the roster of celebrants, to the itinerary of events, to the topics of speeches, the festivities of the day bore unceasing witness to the ties that made Till commemoration and high-speed internet service a package deal.

Although poverty was not mentioned publicly during the celebration of September 26, it was the driving force behind the day's events. It was the fact of poverty—and the hope of its amelioration—that first brought Ike Fowler to Glendora. Four years earlier, in 2002, Fowler moved from New York to Mississippi to found AbsoCom and "eliminate the negative impact of the digital divide within rural communities."[28] As Fowler's partner (and son) Isaac Fowler explained the company's motivation, "citizens who have access to this type of technology are better prepared to live longer, provide better opportunities for their children, accumulate wealth and participate more effectively in the democratic process."[29] For the elder Fowler at least, providing the rural poor with internet access was a God-given mission. A devout Christian, Fowler printed a bible verse, Luke 1:37, on the bottom of each page of AbsoCom's business plan: "Nothing is impossible with God." Motivated by the Old Testament story of Nehemiah rebuilding the ruined city of Jerusalem, Fowler saw AbsoCom (and the internet) as an instrument for the "reconstruction of decimated communities."

Until President Obama's 2009 American Recovery and Reinvest-

ment Act, which provided $7.2 billion "to help bridge the technologi-
cal divide," AbsoCom's primary funding mechanisms were Community Connect broadband grants from the USDA. In many ways, the
USDA program matched Fowler's vision perfectly. Like Fowler, the
USDA addressed rural poverty with technology. To qualify for a grant,
applicants were required to complete a "Rurality Calculation Table"
and an "Economic Need Calculation Worksheet." Glendora ranked
at the highest (most dire) level in both categories—its 285 residents
made less than 33 percent of the national per capita income and were
exceptionally isolated from basic life resources: food, employment,
and medical care. Glendora's application stressed that the overwhelming poverty of the town was the "overlying factor in any discussion of
local demographics."

The poverty of Glendora motivated both Fowler and the USDA.
Fowler saw AbsoCom as a modern-day Nehemiah and broadband
technology as a mechanism for rebuilding the decimated village of
Glendora. The USDA, for its part, found the application compelling
and, on September 27, 2005, informed Mayor Thomas of the $325,405
award.[30] According to the terms of the grant, the money was to be
used to pursue three goals: establish a broadband communication system, create a community center and computer lab in the cotton gin,
and use the lab to extend economic and educational resources of the
web to the community. Such resources included the potential to apply
for jobs online, submit college applications, pursue GED degrees, or
take correspondence courses. Notably, when the grant application explained the "educational resources" it would fund, it never mentioned
Till, civil rights, or a museum.[31]

It is unclear if anyone at AbsoCom was aware that a Till museum
was part of the Glendora project.[32] Although Fowler passed away in
2011, and the company defaulted soon after, one former employee
speculates Fowler would have loved the idea of connecting a museum
to a computer lab.[33] Adding a museum would transform the computer
lab from a site of practical assistance to a community gathering space.
The museum meant that Fowler was not simply providing technical
services (rural broadband); rather, in the tradition of Nehemiah, he

was providing a practical good that would, in turn, revitalize a broader sense of community. Just as Nehemiah rebuilt a spiritual community by building a wall, Fowler would restore Glendora's sense of community by providing internet service.

Regardless of whether Fowler or anyone else at AbsoCom knew that USDA funds were being used to build a museum, it is unquestionably the case that the ETHIC museum was funded by the poverty of Glendora. There would never have been a museum without a computer lab, and there never would have been a computer lab without the poverty of Glendora, the charitable convictions of Fowler, or the remediation programs of the federal government.

Ironically, although the USDA had no knowledge that their funding was being used to create a museum, the unannounced museum lasted longer than the computer lab. While the USDA application explicitly addressed the long-term sustainability of the broadband service, plans for sustainability were based on wildly optimistic assumptions. In a town with a per capita income of approximately $7,000 per year and in which 40 percent of the households make less than $10,000 per year, the application speculated that "30 of the 69 households will continue their Internet subscriptions [beyond the duration of the USDA grant] at a nominal fee of $40 per month." Moreover, in a town whose population was shrinking at a rate of 17 percent every decade, Thomas predicted that "internet subscriptions will increase by at least 3 subscriptions a year."[34] With assumptions such as these, it should be no surprise that internet service to the town of Glendora was suspended only thirteen months after USDA support was withdrawn.[35] It has never been restored. Thus, among the many ironies of Till commemoration must be included the following fact: although the USDA never knew they funded a museum, ETHIC is the only enduring legacy of the Community Connect broadband grant program.

### Building the ETHIC Museum

Once the computer lab was funded, Mayor Thomas still had a sizeable challenge. He had to transform a defunct cotton gin into a facility that could host the computer lab and a Till museum. This task was made even more daunting by the fact that his USDA-approved budget allocated every last dollar to the creation of an AbsoCom computer lab. After all, it was a computer center, and not a museum, that would satisfy the stated funding goals of the application and the granting program.[36] Between the approved budget and the actual expenditures, however, Mayor Thomas fired the contractor who was slotted to renovate the Glendora Cotton Gin and hired his own nonprofit, GECDCO, in its place. It is important to pause on the work of GECDCO, not only because the museum was constructed by the nonprofit, but also because through the mediation of GECDCO, the ETHIC museum became ever-more entangled with poverty and its satellites: political graft, nepotism, low-income housing, and, some claim, downward cycles of increasingly severe impoverishment.

From 1938 through the early 1980s, the Glendora gin was owned and operated by Martha B. Lowe and was "one of the largest employers in the Glendora community."[37] Mrs. Lowe and her family were known for funding local black farmers.[38] In 1999, GECDCO purchased the gin from the Lowes for $8,500 and, for three years, used the gin to process sweet potatoes. With assistance from a federal grant, GECDCO rented sixty-three acres of farmland, bought a potato combine, and paid approximately twenty-five seasonal laborers to process three thousand bushels of sweet potatoes each year. GECDCO had difficulty selling their potatoes, didn't pay taxes on the gin, and eventually forfeited the property. In an unlikely turn of events, however, the town of Glendora paid the taxes, and the state transferred the forfeited land to the "Town of Glendora" on September 30, 2005—three days after the USDA awarded Glendora a Community Connect broadband grant. After the transfer was complete, Mayor Thomas then counted $8,500 (the price paid by GECDCO in 1999) as a local match on the USDA's investment.[39] Mayor Thomas thus acquired the cotton gin twice: once as the executive director of GECDCO and a second time as the mayor of Glendora. This double acquisition was essential to the USDA grant. Although Glendora was given the land patent for free—through the "intergovernmental transfer" of forfeited lands—Thomas counted the

1999 cost of the entire building as an in-kind match. While $8,500 may have been a fair, if dated, estimate of the gin's value, listing it as an in-kind match suggests that the entire facility was to be used for the computer lab, for in the world of federal grants, an in-kind match is considered the grantee's noncash contribution to a funded project.[40]

In addition to the purchase price of $8,500, Thomas argued that the town's commitment to use one thousand square feet of the gin as a computer lab on an ongoing basis constituted a contribution of $10,000 per year toward the project. Given the fact that the building had been generating zero revenue for years, this is a generous estimate of the worth of those particular square feet.[41] Regardless, over the course of the two-year grant, this added $20,000 to Glendora's match. In addition, Thomas counted the contribution of one acre of land near the gin for the broadband tower as a $5,000 in-kind match. Thus, the in-kind value of the gin far exceeded its actual, revenue-producing value. Simply by pledging to donate a defunct building and unused land to the project, Thomas nearly reached his required 15 percent match.

The financial history of the gin foregrounds an uncomfortable truth: while the building may house the first Till museum in the world, and while it may have been the site from which the murderers stole the fan that held Till's body in the water, *these facts are unrelated to each other*. Although a sign in the parking lot now tells visitors that the fan used to weight Till's body in the water "was taken from this gin," this history—true or false—is incidental to the creation of the ETHIC museum. The gin is not the site of the museum because it may have been involved in the murder; rather, it now houses a museum because of the simple fact that it had room to house a computer lab and, for this reason, could command the investment of the USDA. Likewise, from the perspective of the USDA, the gin was not a historical site. It was simply available space that could be donated to the project, monetized as an in-kind match, and used to offset the total cost incurred by the agency. In this sense, it is helpful to remember that before the gin housed a computer lab and a museum, it housed a sweet potato plant. All three of these of initiatives (sweet potatoes, computer lab, Till museum) were grant-funded enterprises leveraged by the poverty of the community and were intended to spur economic development. None of them were funded by Till's memory, and none of them proved financially viable. The potato factory folded after three years, the broadband service barely outlasted the USDA grant, and the museum, while still in operation, survives only by a complex funding stream grounded in (and perhaps perpetuating) the poverty of the village.

After Thomas arranged for the cotton gin to serve as a museum and computer lab, he still had to do the physical work of renovation. At the time, the gin was simply a cavernous, three-story structure built from corrugated metal retrofitted to process potatoes. To renovate the site, Thomas signed a contract with James Butler, owner of Contractor Services of MS, Ltd., of Jackson, Mississippi. For an agreed-upon price of $39,800, Contractor Services was going to renovate the interior of the gin, including $3,000 for the installation of gypsum-board partitioning walls that would divide the space in half and, in effect, create the room that would house the museum. But three months later, in letters dated June 23, 2006, and July 3, 2006, Thomas informed the USDA that Glendora had terminated Butler's contract. Butler, the letters claimed, was unable to begin work in a timely manner.[42] The letters thus sought the USDA's permission to offer the same $39,800 contract to GECDCO. Thomas was essentially asking permission for the town (of which he was the mayor) to enter into a contract with GECDCO (of which he was the founder, executive director, and only paid employee) to do manual labor in exchange for payment from a federal grant (of which he was the grantee). As an additional perk of the proposed arrangement, he noted that it would allow the community to "realize the benefit of any funds left after the project has been completed."[43]

The USDA apparently approved the mayor's request. For the demolition proposed by Butler's firm, Thomas used prison labor donated as an in-kind contribution (worth $8,540) from the Mississippi Department of Corrections.[44] The irony of using seven prisoners to turn a cotton gin into an Emmett Till museum never seems to have occurred to Thomas. Historically speaking, the economic potential of cheap (or free) convict labor led to the passage of laws across the South designed to imprison black men and thereby re-create the labor pool that was lost with the abolition of slavery. Douglas Blackmon has memorably condemned the practice of convict labor as "slavery by another name," and Michelle Alexander traces a straight line of ever-evolving mechanisms of oppression from slavery, through convict labor, through Jim Crow social norms, to the mass incarceration of black men in contemporary America.[45] One of the most eloquent writers on Till's memory is John Edgar Wideman, who wrote in 2004 that the brutal murder of Till was an expression of the same racial hatred that can be otherwise seen in slavery, black incarceration, and the war on drugs. For Blackmon, Alexander, and Wideman, the racial logic of convict labor was of a piece with the racial logic that led to Till's murder.

All of the history notwithstanding, in the spring and summer of 2006, seven prisoners did the demolition work necessary to turn a cotton gin into a Till museum and a computer lab. In strict economic terms, this was no bargain. The Butler contract designated only $300 toward demolition while the prisoner labor cost in excess of $8,000. The key difference, again, is that the prison labor was donated by the Department of Corrections and thus counted as an in-kind match. As a match, the inflated cost of demolition was a windfall for Glendora. Instead of paying a small amount of money to Butler, they were able to count a significantly larger amount of (donated) money against the required match. From the perspective of Glendora, then, the strategic value of prison labor was precisely the same as the strategic value of the empty gin: both could be counted toward the in-kind match required by the USDA. The historical irony notwithstanding, the prison labor turned out to be an essential component in making the commemoration of the murder possible.

Once the demolition was complete, Thomas used GECDCO to hire local contract labor to complete the renovation. Files recovered by a Freedom of Information Act inquiry include a GECDCO invoice for the same construction services (minus demolition) listed on the original contract with James Butler. The invoice includes a person-by-person account of who, precisely, received USDA money to renovate the cotton gin. The list includes the mayor himself; his wife, Shirley Taylor; two of his children; the local fire chief; and Patricia Brown, whom various grant documents list either as the president of GECDCO, its "librarian," or its "director of childcare" (it is unclear what the "Glendora librarian" position entailed, since the application also noted that "there is no library at all in the village of Glendora").[46]

It is difficult to know whether the last-minute shift from Contractor Services of MS to GECDCO saved money or even if it accelerated the timeline of the renovation. It may have simply been a low-profile form of nepotism or political graft—realizing private gain from funds designated for a public good. It is clear, however, that the switch offered Mayor Thomas an array of benefits: it kept USDA money in his community and, in some instances, in his own family. Moreover, regardless of whether or not the GECDCO contract was a legitimate mechanism to accelerate the renovation, one thing is certain: the physical space of the museum was built by a combination of prison labor and work done by Thomas's own family, members of his board, and a range of contract labor. It was Mayor Thomas's nonprofit— a group with no recorded construction experience—that renovated the Glendora Cotton Gin and built the rooms that housed both the computer lab and the Till museum.

The renovation of the gin was complete by the spring of 2006, but the entanglement of GECDCO and the ETHIC museum had only just begun. To this day, the nonprofit is an essential part of the day-to-day operation of the museum and the key to its financial stability. Decades before Till commemoration came to Glendora, Thomas founded GECDCO as a mechanism to generate revenue in a region with a null tax base. On June 14, 1982, the same year he became mayor, Thomas created the nonprofit "to assist the Governing Body [sic] with up lifting [sic] the community from it's [sic] impoverishes [sic]."[47] Because the village generates insufficient tax revenue ($220 per year as of 2005) for either a mayoral salary or the provision of basic city services, Thomas uses the nonprofit to fill the void.[48] Many see Thomas's creation of GECDCO as a godsend, supplying short-term labor contracts and city management when the town itself was unable to do so.[49]

The key to the financial stability of GECDCO is the provision of low-income housing. In December 2005, just after the USDA awarded

Glendora the Community Connect broadband grant, GECDCO bought the Jack G. Flautt apartments on Gipson Avenue in Glendora. Because the apartments are designated as affordable housing under Section 8, GECDCO collects approximately $100,000 per year in rental subsidies from the federal government.[50] With this money, GECDCO uses seasonal and intermittent contracts with unemployed locals to keep up the apartments, pick up trash, monitor computer labs and childcare facilities, and staff the museum. While these contracts pay less than minimum wage (one source has it as half the minimum wage, another at $3 per hour), Thomas does provide his laborers with IRS 1099 forms with which they can register as self-employed and thereby be eligible for Earned Income Tax Credit—a *refundable* credit that, given the fact that his laborers are otherwise unemployed, would generate a payout from the IRS.[51] And, because the mayorship is an unpaid position in Glendora, Thomas uses GECDCO income to pay himself an annual stipend of approximately $20,000—a figure that, in the impoverished town of Glendora, is approximately twice the per capita income.[52] Even if this were to generate resentment in Glendora (and I have no evidence that it does), such resentment would likely not cost Thomas his job. Some locals explain the continuous reelection of Thomas by citing the temporary contracts handed out by GECDCO. There is some fear that if Thomas were not reelected, he could walk away with GECDCO, essentially stripping the town of its capacity to provide basic services via contracts that, if not lucrative, do provide a meager amount of money and access to IRS refunds. Depending on whom you ask, the entire scheme is either a scam, keeping the village of Glendora perpetually impoverished, or a savvy survival strategy for bringing federal money into an impoverished town. I've heard both versions of the story.

From the perspective of Till commemoration, however, the point I wish to stress is the intimate bonds between memory and misery. Even if we were to take the USDA, AbsoCom, and the prison labor out of the picture entirely, the intricate linkages between GECDCO and the ETHIC museum provide ample evidence that poverty is the condition of commemoration and, at least as some locals see it, commemoration is contributing to poverty. The museum was built by GECDCO, a nonprofit born from and funded by the poverty of Glendora. The nonprofit's only major source of income, and the only reason it can provide municipal services in the first place, is the income generated by the Flautt apartments. The origin of this money, of course, is the poverty of the townspeople, which sets in motion a funding stream that flows from the federal government, through the North Delta Regional Housing Authority, to GECDCO, and ultimately to the museum and other civic projects. The museum then returns the favor, paying its employees for half their labor, ensuring their continued reliance on welfare, and their continued residence in low-income housing, which, in turn, keeps the federal money flowing. While GECDCO has been keeping this cycle going for twelve years, and thus proving its sustainability, one Tallahatchie County employee told me that that the GECDCO-plus-ETHIC combination is essentially keeping the village in poverty. While this last point is controversial and there are many (especially in Glendora) who defend Thomas and are grateful for his remarkable capacity to route federal money into Glendora, one thing is certain: *the impoverishment of Glendora is the condition of memory work*. From the funding of the museum, to its building, to its day-to-day operation—commemoration would be impossible without the poverty of the villagers.

### Filling the ETHIC Museum

GECDCO's renovation of the cotton gin created two climate-controlled rooms inside the Glendora Cotton Gin. The room on the west side of the gin housed the Johnny B. Thomas Adult Continuing Education and Training Center; the eastern room housed ETHIC. Once the gin was renovated and AbsoCom filled the west room with ten computers, Mayor Thomas still needed to acquire artifacts for the museum. Without an acquisitions budget, the primary exhibit in the museum was a thirty-three-foot timeline of Till's murder created by college students at Mississippi Valley State and Prairie View A&M University in Texas. Other items included a plantation bell, a replica gin fan, a cotton sack, a bed "from the era" (the relevance of which is unclear), and various items affixed to poster boards. For example, the *Look* confession was cut out from the magazine (and portions of it printed from PBS.org), laminated, and mounted on white card stock. Similarly, informational webpages on the Ku Klux Klan and socialism were printed, laminated, and mounted. Once the poster boards were filled with printouts, they were hung on walls, leaned against interior columns, or set on top of artifacts (like the bed).[53] An "exhibit" featuring King's Place was simply a midcentury bureau, some old golf clubs (again, relevance unclear), and several dilapidated guitars hung on the wall. The museum had not a single original artifact. Visitors who paid the $7 entry fee would see the printed-and-laminated websites, the student-produced timeline, and the conspicuously aged midcentury items of varying degrees of relevance.

Without question, the centerpiece of the museum was the timeline. Composed of ten poster boards affixed to an interior partitioning wall in a long, horizontal row, the timeline began with Till's birth in 1941 and ended with the 2003 death of Mamie Till-Mobley. According to Professor Barry Norwood of Prairie View A&M, the students spent "two good weeks" of research before producing their timeline.[54]

Two weeks was apparently not long enough, as the timeline was plagued with egregious historical errors. It stated that Till was born in Webb, Mississippi (he was born in Cook County Hospital in Chicago);[55] that Till's mother Mamie was married to "Lemorris Bradley" at the time of Till's death (there was no such person; Mamie married Lemorse Mallory on August 19, 1946, and Pink Bradley on May 5, 1951);[56] that Till arrived in Money on August 21, 1955 (he arrived on August 20);[57] that Milam and Bryant were arrested on August 29 (Bryant was arrested a day earlier, on August 28);[58] that Willie Reed and Moses Wright testified to the grand jury on November 9, 1955 (it was November 8);[59] that Rosa Parks refused to give up her seat on December 5, 1955 (it was December 1); and that Roy Bryant died in 1990 (he died on September 1, 1994).[60] Moreover, although the timeline correctly noted that *Jet* magazine famously printed pictures of Till's body on September 15, 1955, it incorrectly displayed the *Jet* cover from July 23, 1964, the issue that announced SNCC's Freedom Summer. Finally, the students marked the date of the Till trial with a picture of a crowd posed on what appears to be the front steps of a courthouse—presumably the Sumner courthouse where the Till trial was held. In fact, however, the picture is a famous photograph by Allen E. Cole of the 1929 annual session of the NAACP held at the storied Mount Zion Temple Church in Cleveland, Ohio—twenty-six years before the Till trial and eight hundred miles away![61] By including only the left third of the original panoramic photograph, the students eliminated the oversized banner that read "NAACP" and thereby made their fraud (a little bit) less obvious.

From the perspective of Glendora and Johnny B. Thomas, however, the most alarming fact about the timeline would not have been its litany of typos or fraudulent photographs. Rather, Thomas must have been vexed by the basic narrative of the murder advanced by the students. The timeline is clearly based on Huie's account of the murder as it was published in *Look* magazine. It claims that there were only two murderers, that Till was shot on the banks of the Tallahatchie River, and that his body was rolled—not dropped—into the river. In addition to being historically incorrect, this story eliminates the facets of the story dearest to Mayor Thomas: Henry Lee Loggins, King's Place, the Glendora Cotton Gin, and the Black Bayou Bridge. Without the inclusion of these sites in Till's story, the historical relevance of Glendora shrinks considerably. While the town could still claim to be the site of Milam's home, the house was removed years ago, and the overgrown field where it once stood offers little in the way of investment potential.

Thus, as odd as it may seem, Glendora's own museum advanced a story about Till's murder that worked against the town's long-term approach to economic development. That approach hinged on the relevance of the cotton gin and the bridge: two structures that, by retroactively routing the murder party through Glendora, could provide the historical leverage needed to secure grant funding. Yet these very structures had no role in the ETHIC museum. Unsurprisingly, then, from virtually the moment the museum was opened, Thomas has pursued funding to renovate it. Until 2010, when he finally secured funding for a renovation, these efforts took the form of three unsuccessful efforts to use the geography of Till's murder as financial leverage. While these efforts failed across the board, their failure casts in bold relief the dependence of Glendora's commemorative efforts on poverty and municipal services.

## THE INSUFFICIENCY OF TILL'S STORY

When Mayor Thomas talks about Till's murder, he talks about the Glendora Cotton Gin and the Black Bayou Bridge. If these two structures were legitimately part of the murder, Glendora would rival Sumner or Money as the most important site in the world of Till commemoration. Including the cotton gin would decisively route the murder party through Glendora and implicate Milam's neighbor Elmer Kimbell without, as Huie had done, letting Leslie Milam off the hook. Including the bridge would solve one of the most vexing mysteries in the entire range of Till lore. Ever since Huie's tale was discredited by Benson, Beauchamp, and the FBI in the early years of the century, there has never been a compelling, public theory of where, precisely, Till was dropped in the water.

Between 2005 and 2010, Mayor Thomas tried three times to commemorate these structures. Each of these efforts was grounded explicitly on Glendora's historical record. This is a marked shift in commemorative strategy. Unlike the ETHIC museum, which was founded with a grant designed to provide broadband service, and the Emmett Till Memorial Park, which was funded by a grant from the Mississippi Department of Wildlife Fisheries and Parks, these three efforts staked their validity on the historical question of what happened in Glendora in 1955. The failure of these initiatives demonstrates convincingly that the only possibility for Till commemoration in Glendora is linked to the poverty of its people. The historical record just won't do.

### The Glendora Welcome Center

Perhaps Thomas's most far-fetched economic scheme was his 2008 proposal to the ETMC to allow Glendora to serve as a "welcome center" for the commission's eight-site Tallahatchie Civil Rights Driving Tour. Unhindered by the logistical difficulties of charging to view roadside markers, on March 12, 2008, Thomas used an ETMC meeting to champion the creation of a "Glendora Tallahatchie Welcome Center." The proposed center was to be located in Glendora and charge a "fee of $15 to $18 per person" for a "tourism program" of 90–120 minutes.[62] Thomas proposed that welcome center profits be split between the ETMC (who created the tour) and the GECDCO, which would staff the center, give the tours, and provide long-range marketing plans. The first 20 percent of profits would go to the GECDCO for "administrative support," after which the remaining money would be split equally between the ETMC and the GECDCO.[63]

Thomas's proposal met stiff opposition. Some of the opposition was likely due to lingering animosities between Mayor Thomas and the commission stemming from the previous month's meeting. On February 13, 2008, when Thomas first mentioned his idea for a Glendora welcome center, the meeting devolved into accusations of racism. Commission grant writer Kitty Dumas had learned of Thomas's criminal background and was concerned that the commission would not be able to obtain grant money so long as Thomas, a "convicted felon," served as treasurer.[64] In 1988, Thomas had been sentenced to six months in prison for a variety of illegalities: reselling whiskey, serving as mayor and judge at the same time, and accepting kickbacks in exchange for allowing slot machines to operate in Glendora. One year later, he was sentenced to another eight months in prison for operating slot machines out of his café and taking bribes from the owners of the machines. Although the prison time did not cost him his job as mayor—a post he has held continually from 1982 to the present—it did cost him his ability to serve as treasurer of the Till commission.[65] Betty Pearson agreed with Dumas, and the commission asked Thomas for his resignation.

From the perspective of Mayor Thomas, the federal convictions were an example of racism. Slot machines were something of an open secret in Tallahatchie County. While they were illegal, Thomas estimates that there were fifty to sixty entrepreneurs running gambling operations in the county; even the sheriff ran slots at his country club. And, yet, Thomas "was considered a black radical who got out of his place" and, for this reason, was "busted because of racism."[66] While he may well have been correct, the ETMC was unswayed, and he was forced to resign his position as treasurer.

Undeterred by the loss of his official role, Thomas immediately requested that the commission allow Glendora to serve as a "Welcoming Center for Tourism." When this motion was tabled and added to the agenda for the subsequent meeting, Thomas accused the commission of racism—of using "affluent white people" to force his resignation. Robert Grayson, the African American cochair of the ETMC, tried in vain to convince Thomas that neither the request for his resignation nor the commission's refusal to immediately consider a Glendora welcome center were evidence of racism.[67]

A month later, tensions remained high. The commission was well aware that Thomas was not an objective advocate for the welcome center. With 60 percent of welcome center profits designated for the GECDCO—an organization that otherwise had no role in the driving tour—Thomas's proposal must have seemed gratuitously self-serving. He was, in effect, proposing that he be paid by charging people to visit roadside markers that were created and maintained by the commission. If this were not enough, Betty Pearson noted that the commission did not have the authority to create a welcome center and, even if they did, a more logical place would be in Sumner, a site of undisputed importance to both Till's legacy and the commission's official mission. This was likely the beginning of the long-running feud between Thomas and the ETMC about the proper place for a Till museum. By 2010, the tension was so stark that Mississippi Valley State University historian (and one-time ETMC consultant) Kathryn Green described the ETMC and ETHIC as "dueling museums."[68] At a meeting hosted by Green at Mississippi Valley State on June 30, 2010, an argument broke out between Mayor Thomas and Jerome Little about what, precisely, the commission considered as their "museum"—was it in Glendora, in Sumner, or in both? The argument grew so heated, and the competition between Thomas and Little so distasteful, that Reed Resneck (an original member of the ETMC) called Green to apologize for the behavior of the commission.[69]

Undeterred by the commission's antagonism to his Glendora museum, Mayor Thomas urged the commission to vote on his proposal for a welcome center immediately, "not months or years later."[70] When the motion died on the floor for want of a second, Thomas was angry once more. To his mind, the collective refusal to bring his motion to a vote signaled yet another slight against Glendora, its history, and its role in the Till murder. He responded to the slight with a misinformed accusation against the ETMC, as if they were systematically writing Glendora out of Till's history. He claimed that the driving tour snubbed Glendora. According to the minutes of the ETMC, Thomas "stated that there is only one site sign that mentions Glendora" and complained that even the sign that marks the location of J. W. Milam's home in the heart of town should "have Glendora mentioned on it." These accusations have no merit. If anything, the ETMC driving tour disproportionately features Glendora; six of the eight original signs, all of which were approved by the commission while Thomas was still treasurer, were in or around Glendora. The facts notwithstanding, Thomas accused the commission of racism. After objecting, incorrectly, that "the one thing that an African-American has brought to this commission was not passed," he walked out of the meeting.[71]

The depth of Thomas's frustration stems from a combination of factors. Among these are his intellectual commitments to Glendora's role in the murder, his sense that Till commemoration could be an economic lifeline for his impoverished village, and his deep disappointment at seeing grant after grant after grant invested in Sumner. His role on the ETMC afforded him a front-row seat as, year after year, commemorative money flowed into Sumner but never seemed to make it to Glendora. Over the years, the mayor has become increasingly critical of the commission on which he serves. He told me that the ETMC was motivated by the chance at a "free courthouse" (which has a measure of truth) while the ETHIC museum was trying to end racial hostility. By 2016, he was convinced that Sumner and the commission "stole" the idea of a Till museum from him.[72] If his anger could derail a meeting, as it did at Mississippi Valley State in 2010, it is not hard to understand why. He knew that Glendora was, historically speaking, a far more relevant site than Sumner, but his efforts to turn that relevance into financial commitments were stymied at every turn by the very commission that he helped to found.

While the idea of a Glendora welcome center for the ETMC was never mentioned after the spring of 2008, Thomas never gave up on the idea of charging for a guided tour of Till sites. To this day, Thomas offers the "Till Trail of Terror Tour." It is offered not through the ETMC, but rather through the office of the Glendora mayor. It costs $15 per person.[73]

## National Historical Register Nominations

In late 2009 or early 2010, Mayor Thomas asked Bill Gatlin to nominate his two cherished Glendora structures to the National Register of Historic Places: the cotton gin and the bridge (figures 22 and 23). As the National Register coordinator for the MDAH, Gatlin was happy to comply. On February 23, 2012, Gatlin informed Mayor Thomas that the bridge was successfully added to the National Register of Historic Places but he was unable to complete the nomination for the Glendora Cotton Gin.[74] Although Thomas did not respond to the letter, he must have been disappointed on both counts. For while Gatlin prepared both nominations at the mayor's request, the two men differed sharply in their opinions of *why* the buildings deserved to be on the National Register of Historic Places. Thomas argued that their historical significance stemmed from their association with Till's murder. He claimed that the gin was the site where the fan was obtained and the bridge was the site where Till's body was dropped in the water. Gatlin disagreed on both counts. After a remarkably thorough inquiry, which involved reading virtually everything that had been written on Till's

FIGURE 22. Glendora Cotton Gin and ETHIC Museum, Glendora, MS. Photo by Ashleigh Coleman. Used by permission.

FIGURE 23. Black Bayou Bridge, Glendora, MS. Photo by Ashleigh Coleman. Used by permission.

murder to date, Gatlin refused to nominate either structure based on its role in Till's murder. Instead he nominated the gin "for its association with Agriculture and Industry" and the bridge as a "good local example of an early 20th century Warren pony truss vehicular bridge."[75]

While Gatlin saw the history of agriculture and industry—and, by extension, the gin and the bridge—as worthy of preservation, Thomas was invested in these structures only insofar as they bore witness to Glendora's connection to the Till murder. If the ETMC would not grant him a welcome center and thus validate his town's role in the murder, perhaps the National Register of Historic Places could do so. After all, listing on the National Register was far more prestigious than the acknowledgment of a county commission, and it would allow Glendora to apply for a wider range of preservation grants.

When Thomas approached Gatlin about the National Register of Historic Places, he stressed the connections between the town of Glendora and Till's murder. He had, after all, just been advised by the MDA that a professional Till experience was the path to economic development. Moreover, there was local precedent for placing civil rights cotton gins on the National Register as a form of economic development. At virtually the same time Thomas was arguing to put the Glendora Cotton Gin on the National Register of Historic Places for its connection to the Till murder, the Vicksburg Foundation for Historic Preservation learned that their bid to place the Westbrook Cotton Gin in Liberty, Mississippi, on the National Register was successful. Like the Glendora gin, the Westbrook gin was a twentieth-century cotton gin with connections to the civil rights movement. In 1961, the gin was the site where Mississippi state representative E. H. Hurst murdered Herbert Lee—a civil rights worker who helped Bob Moses with voter registration in Amite County.[76] Much like Thomas, the citizens of Liberty were trying to marshal the civil rights history of their gin as a source of revenue—they refurbished the building as a restaurant called "The Cotton Gin." When the structure was added to the National Register of Historic Places in September 2010 because it was "the site of the murder of a black man by a white man during the Civil Rights era," the restaurant had a newfound appeal.[77]

Gatlin was well aware of the Westbrook Cotton Gin's recent election to the National Register of Historic Places. He even used the example of the Westbrook gin in his nomination of the Glendora gin. However, Gatlin maintained that the two gins were historic for different reasons. While Westbrook gin was of historic value in the categories of social history, ethnic history, and black history, Gatlin held that the Glendora gin was historic only because of its connection to the cotton economy. When he invoked the Westbrook gin in his nomination, he did not even mention Herbert Lee or the gin's civil rights history; from his perspective, the only reason the Westbrook gin served as example for the nomination of the Glendora gin was the common age of the facilities and their common role in the southern economy. For this reason, Gatlin left unchecked the box on the Glendora nomination form that indicates whether the "property is associated with the lives of persons significant in our past." It may have been, but from his point of view this was unrelated to its historical value.

Gatlin did not reach these decisions lightly. Upon Thomas's request to nominate the gin and the bridge, Gatlin conducted an extensive inquiry into the history of both structures. He first reached out to Luther Brown and Henry Outlaw—both of whom were locally recognized experts on the Till murder. At the time, both Brown and Outlaw were at Delta State University in Cleveland, Mississippi. Brown was the founding director of the Delta Center for Culture and Learning; Outlaw was both a professor of chemistry and a "program associate" in the Delta Center.[78] Together, Brown and Outlaw won a small grant from the Mississippi Humanities Council to record oral histories of local people sharing their memories of the Till murder. This was a remarkable project that bore long-term fruit. With the help of Delta State University archivist Emily Jones, Outlaw built a traveling exhibit on the Till murder based on his oral histories. The exhibit consisted of ten freestanding silk-screen panels, thirty-nine inches wide by seven feet tall. Since its creation in 2007, the exhibit has traveled to both coasts.

The success of the oral histories program also led to a recurring summer workshop for school teachers titled "The Most Southern Place on Earth." While the workshop considered the history and culture of the Mississippi Delta in general, an entire day was reserved for the Till murder. Created jointly by Brown and Outlaw and funded by the National Endowment for the Humanities, the workshop gave the teachers an immersive, on-site education in the history of Till's murder.[79] Since its inception in 2009, the workshop has spent a day at the Tallahatchie County Courthouse in Sumner, where participants interact with members of the Till family as well as Dale Killinger, the FBI special agent in charge of the Till investigation from 2004 to 2006.

Finally, in addition to his work for the Delta Center and the National Endowment for the Humanities, Brown led the fateful Mississippi Center for Justice tour to Bryant's Grocery and Meat Market in 2009 (chapter 4). It was that tour that led to the creation of the Mississippi Freedom Trail. In addition to serving as a formal advisor to the entire Freedom Trail initiative, Brown crafted the prose for the sign that was later erected between Bryant's Grocery and Ben Roy's Service Station.

In sum, although neither Brown nor Outlaw ever published on Till's murder, and for this reason are virtually unknown outside the Delta, they were without question the Delta's most prominent experts on the murder. In fact, in terms of a nuanced understanding of the murder, Brown and Outlaw were years ahead of the published accounts of the murder written by scholars from across the country. It was only after the publication of the FBI report in 2005 that the national community of scholars caught up to Brown and Outlaw in their knowledge of the murder. The only other figure in the Delta who could rival the team from Delta State (both in terms of inside information about the murder and obscurity outside the Delta) was Plater Robinson, the chosen expert of the ETMC. Unlike Robinson, however, whose trips to the Delta were sporadic and whose insight into the Till murder remains unvetted by any outside authority, Brown and Outlaw lived in the Delta, accumulated their wisdom over a number of years, and had their work vetted by the Mississippi Humanities Council and the National Endowment for the Humanities. By approaching Brown and Outlaw, Gatlin was approaching the two most reliable sources in Mississippi.

In separate emails of March 1, 2011, Outlaw and Brown both told

Gatlin that there was no historical evidence that the fan that weighted Till's body in the water was stolen from the Glendora gin. Brown was the most direct, "I know the Mayor believes the gin was historically linked to the case, but I don't have knowledge of that myself."[80] Brown encouraged Gatlin to read the massive, five-hundred-page report published in 2005 by the FBI.

He had already done so. In fact, Gatlin had read virtually everything that had been written on the Till case. He even wrote a "Summary of Research" for the MDAH that provided an overview of Till scholarship. He carefully reviewed the *Look* magazine account, considered the evidence of the Whitaker's 1963 MA thesis, Olive Arnold Adams's 1956 "Time Bomb" (the article built on T. R. M. Howard's research into Sunflower County), Whitfield's 1988 *Death in the Delta*, Beauchamp's 2005 documentary, Beito and Beito's 2009 *Black Maverick* (the best scholarly account then available of the Sunflower County version of the story), the Rhodes College honors thesis written by Ellen Whitten, and the FBI report. As he combed through this literature, he paid particular attention to the historical questions at stake in nominating the Glendora structures to the National Register of Historic Places: from where was gin fan stolen and where was Till's body dropped in the water. He remained agnostic on both questions.

Gatlin noted that the two historic options for the site from which the gin fan was stolen were the Progressive Ginning Company near Boyle, Mississippi, or a gin operated by a brother of J. W. Milam in Itta Bena, Mississippi. The story of the Boyle gin can be traced back to Huie, who used the out-of-the-way gin as part of his fabricated itinerary to keep the murderers away from Sunflower County. Gatlin properly concluded that Huie's account was "highly questionable." Although Gatlin was unaware of the fact, Roy Bryant himself admitted in 1985 that the murder party never went to the Progressive Ginning Company.[81] Likewise, the theory that the fan came from Itta Bena has never had much traction. Appearing only in Adams's "Time Bomb," the theory runs that the white authorities stopped by the Itta Bena gin during the recess in the trial occasioned by the introduction of witnesses from Sunflower County (see chapter 1). While this may be true, there is no record that any evidence was discovered, and the Itta Bena theory has all but disappeared from the historical record. The simple fact that Gatlin was aware of the Itta Bena theory is a testament to the quality and depth of his research.

At the end of Gatlin's "Summary," he reached the same conclusion as Brown and Outlaw, "Nothing establishes [that] the gin fan came from Glendora." On the question of where Till's body was dropped in the water, Gatlin remained similarly agnostic, simply (and accurately) noting that the literature does not address "the location where Till's body was placed in the river."[82] With support from neither local experts nor the scholarly literature, Gatlin refused to nominate either the Glendora Cotton Gin or the Black Bayou Bridge based on Thomas's claims that the structures were involved with Till's murder. Instead, he nominated the gin "for its association with Agriculture and Industry" and the bridge as a "good local example of an early 20th century Warren pony truss vehicular bridge."[83] The nomination for the bridge went smoothly, and, on March 21, 2011, the bridge was added to the National Register of Historic Places.

The nomination for the cotton gin did not go smoothly. To complete the nomination form, Gatlin needed help from Thomas to establish the historical facts of the building—when it was built, dates of operation, and a floor plan. But Thomas was not interested. Although Gatlin wrote at least four appeals between August of 2010 and February 2012, Thomas never provided the information Gatlin needed to complete the nomination for the Glendora Cotton Gin. In an undated 2011 memo to an associate, Gatlin complained that "Mayor Thomas sent a good floor plan, but no other useful information."[84] There was a good reason for Thomas's silence. He likely recognized Gatlin's nomination of the Glendora gin as a threat to his capacity to capitalize on Till's memory. To build the ETHIC museum, Thomas had renovated portions of the gin. However, if the gin was to be added to the National Register "for its association with Agriculture and Industry," these renovations may have to be undone. The nomination noted that the 2005 renovations "could be reversed" to return the gin to its original design and thereby better convey the agricultural significance of the building. Thus, while Thomas asked Gatlin to nominate the building to the National Register for its historical connections to Till's murder, at the end of Gatlin's research it appeared that the nomination might have the opposite effect: it would render the gin's connection to Till even more invisible than it already was. The nomination, if pursued further, could require Thomas to remove the ETHIC museum, and this was something he was not willing to do. His refusal to respond to Gatlin's repeated requests for information suggests that Thomas preferred that the building remain off the National Register if that meant he could retain the museum. Ironically, a listing by the National Register would actually run counter to the town's commemorative goals. Remembering the murder of Emmett Till was in a competition with remembering the agricultural history of Glendora. It was a zero-sum game in which only one thing—Till's murder or agricultural history—could be commemorated.

The failed nominations were a major setback for Mayor Thomas. They were his most direct effort to commemorate the two sites central to Glendora's claim on Till's memory. Moreover, they were an attempt to circumvent the control of the ETMC over Glendora's commemorative infrastructure. Finally, the nominations pursued Till's commemoration on its own terms, rather than bundling it with city services such as computer labs or public parks. Unfortunately for Glendora, Thomas's chosen sites would not receive the validation of the National Register, Glendora would not escape the control of the ETMC, and, perhaps most personally for Mayor Thomas, his bid to create a Glendora-centric narrative of Till's murder that could provide a foundation for economic development was blocked.

## An Unfunded Civil Rights Historical Sites Grant

On May 6, 2011, Thomas applied for a MCRHS grant from the MDAH— the same program that funded, among other projects, the restoration of Ben Roy's Service Station in Money, the creation of the Mississippi Freedom Trail, and portions of the courthouse renovation in Sumner. Thomas asked for $201,600 to restore and preserve "a 1938 cotton gin" and to "create an educational center and museum." The majority of the money was slotted to renovate the building itself: driveway repair, waterproofing, heating and air conditioning repair, roofing, insulation, repairing window casements, and refinishing the sign. An unspecified amount of money was also reserved for "museum displays."[85] The MCRHS grant was an attempt to professionalize the ETHIC museum.

Thomas was well aware that the museum needed help. After the MDA visited Glendora in 2010, their strongest recommendation centered on the professionalization of the ETHIC museum. One development specialist noted, the "Emmett Till Museum needs a 'B. B. King Museum' makeover"—a reference to the state-of-the-art, milliondollar blues museum recently built adjacent to a cotton gin in Indianola.[86] The relatively modest resources of the MCRHS grant could not have brought the ETHIC museum to this level, but it would have been a good start. In addition to providing the infrastructural attention required by the old building, Thomas argued that the resources of the MCRHS grant could help Glendora realize its potential as a tourist attraction. Along with the "Emmett Till trail" markers currently in Glendora (a reference to the ETMC driving tour), Thomas argued that the gin will "draw tourists and locals, and encourage the promotion of the civil rights movement."

Thomas grounded his application for MDAH money on two arguments: the connection of the Glendora Cotton Gin to the Till murder (and thus to the civil rights movement) and the connection of the gin to the history of agriculture. The first argument was essential. Because the grant required funded projects to bear a connection to the history of civil rights, the success of Thomas's application hinged on the history of the gin. Thus he wrote, "The 1938 gin was once one of the largest employers in the Glendora community, and is also believed to be the location the murderers of Emmett Till obtained the fan to tie around the neck of Emmett Till."[87]

The second argument must have been a response to his experience trying to place the building on the National Register. Thomas argued that the "gin is a classic example of the 'Machine Era' in farming."

Renovated, the building could "show the evolution of crops, workers, [and] equipment as well as the transfer and storage of the crop and where its thread, cloth, and fabric are improved and last longer or do a better job when blended."[88] While none of this was relevant for the grant, which was designed to fund civil rights sites, it does mirror rather precisely the convictions of Bill Gatlin, who was at that time preparing the nomination of the gin for the National Register of Historic Places. While Thomas would not allow Gatlin to pursue this nomination because it threatened the existence of the ETHIC museum, he was willing to use Gatlin's conclusions about the agricultural importance of the Glendora gin to give his own site additional historical value.

The MDAH was not convinced. They found the argument about machine-era farming irrelevant and the argument about the civil rights history of the gin unconvincing. In fact, the department was so unimpressed by Thomas's application, that the Glendora Cotton Gin was one of only three applications that were rejected—the MCRHS grant was never intended to be competitive. It is no secret why the MDAH rejected Thomas's application. The MDAH administered the grant through their Historic Preservation Division—the same division from which Bill Gatlin organized nominations for the National Register of Historic Places. Indeed, Gatlin's office is just downstairs from the office of the grants administrator, and it is quite likely that the review committee had access to the "Summary of Research" written by Gatlin.[89] The timing makes this all the more likely, as the Historic Preservation Division of the MDAH was simultaneously considering both the Historical Register nominations in Glendora and Thomas's application for a MCRHS grant. In one eight-day period during August 2011, the Historic Preservation Division sent three separate letters to Thomas, one each about the two historical register nominations and a third about the grant application. Although these letters came from different people—Mingo Tingle, Ken P'Pool, and Bill Gatlin— the entire staff works collaboratively and in close proximity inside the Capers Building in downtown Jackson. For this reason, when Gatlin concluded that "nothing establishes that the gin fan came from Glendora," this may well have undermined both projects. Whether or not these decisions were based on Gatlin's report, the MDAH has never agreed to Thomas's claims about the histories of the cotton gin or the Black Bayou Bridge. In October 2016, staff from the Historic Preservation Division put it to me plainly: Glendora did not receive state money because Thomas's claims about Glendora's connections to the civil rights movement are not true. There was no mention of Thomas's argument about the gin as an example of machine-era farming; from the perspective of the MCRHS grant, this was altogether irrelevant information.

The failure of Glendora's MCRHS grant application demonstrates once again Thomas's inability to secure grant money based on the town's connection to the Till murder. Although he did attempt to use his gin's agricultural history as source of leverage on the MDAH, it did not work. For the purposes of the MCRHS grant application, the MDAH was solely interested in the civil rights history of the property. At the end of the day, the department simply did not trust Thomas and did not believe that the Glendora Cotton Gin had any connection to the murder of Emmett Till.

### RENOVATING ETHIC

Collectively, the welcome center debacle, the failed attempt to place the gin and bridge on the National Register of Historic Places, and the town's inability to secure a noncompetitive MCRHS grant dramatized the fact that Thomas's claims about the centrality of Glendora to the Till murder could not survive on the open market. By 2011, Thomas had been pursuing Till commemoration for at least seven years. While he had managed to found the ETHIC museum and create a Till-themed walking trail, these projects were not funded by Till's memory. What Thomas understood as the simple facts of Till's murder regarding the theft of the fan and the disposal of the body were simply not sufficient to command commemorative resources. At least in Glendora, Till's murder needed to be packaged with a civic good and framed as poverty intervention before it could be a feasible—by which I mean fundable—project.

In 2011 ETHIC completed its last round of renovations. In some ways, the renovation marks the end of an era, as Thomas finally managed to commemorate Till's murder without bundling commemoration and poverty remediation. In another sense, however, the renovation still bears witness to the ties that have always bound Glendora, Till's story, and economic development.

The task of renovation presented Mayor Thomas with a sizeable challenge. Because his historical claims had always failed to win grant money, and because it was difficult to pitch the renovation of the museum as a form of welfare, the renovation of the museum required a noncompetitive funding source—a source that would invest in Till's memory without vetting his specific historical claims. For while his claims about the gin and the bridge were certainly plausible, it must have been painfully obvious to him that plausibility was not sufficient leverage to command competitive funding. Thankfully, Thomas had a long and close relationship with US representative Bennie Thompson. Thompson was a guest of honor at the 2006 grand opening of the ETHIC museum and the computer lab. In September 2008, the GECDCO-owned bed-and-breakfast in Glendora opened the "Bennie G. Thompson Congressional Suite."[90] In March 2011, Thompson wrote a strong letter of support for Thomas's MCRHS grant. In the letter, he noted that the ETHIC museum "fills a huge void that would most assuredly exist if it were not for [Thomas's] dedicated efforts."[91] Four months later, he wrote an open letter of support for the ETHIC museum, which hangs in its lobby to this day. Strangely, after lavishing praise on the museum, the letter is signed, "Bennie G. Thomas [sic], Member of Congress." The congressman apparently misspelled his own name, combining it with the mayor's. While this may be little more than an embarrassing typo, it is also a handy way to remember the closeness of the bond that joined Johnny B. Thomas and Bennie G. Thompson.

In March 2014, Thompson gave a speech in the US House of Representatives in honor of Thomas. The speech was pure hagiography, an unalloyed paean to Mayor Thomas and the ETHIC museum. Without a single note of criticism, Thompson cast Thomas as an unsullied public servant. The speech did not mention Thomas's stints in federal prison, his slot-machine history, his creative use of federal grant funds, the controversy that surrounds GECDCO and his thirty-five-year (and counting) tenure as mayor, or the ongoing poverty of Glendora. Most outlandish of all, however, was Thompson's characterization of the renovated ETHIC museum. In this regard, Thompson's speech is equally noteworthy for what he said and what he failed to say. First, Thompson called the ETHIC a "state-of-art museum."[92] While the museum had been significantly improved from the days (2005–10) when it's primary exhibit was a homemade, error-riddled timeline, it did not approach a state-of-the-art museum. Such a characterization is patently untrue. Second, Thompson did not acknowledge that it was his own, behind-the-scenes legislation that funded the renovation.

In 2010, Thompson secured a $400,000 earmark for the renovation of ETHIC.[93] Although the earmark was distributed through a congressionally directed grant from the Institute for Museum and Library Services (IMLS), the funding was not competitive.[94] The IMLS "grant" was simply an after-the-fact mechanism for distributing money that was provided by Thompson. This is an important point, because it means that the renovation of the ETHIC museum was not an exception from the pattern noted above. Thomas was not, at long last, able to compel a granting agency to fund Till commemoration in Glendora. Even after the renovation, it was (and remains to this day) the case that Thomas's convictions about the histories of the gin and bridge have *never* been sufficient leverage for commemorative funding. In Glendora, the memory of Till's murder required either creative packaging with city services or, in the case of the renovation, a friend in high places.

Because the IMLS grant was not competitive, agency records provide minimal insight into the specifics of how the money was spent. Unspecified "supplies and materials" accounted for $165,000 of the budget. The narrative portions of the application supplied answers in the most abbreviated form possible, and much of the application was left blank altogether. The usually critical "Project Description," for example, contained only a single sentence: "The proposed project consists of developing and implementing a development plan to strengthen the ability of the museum." Without plans or materials, the application dedicated just over half of the grant ($209,600) to salaries and consultant fees. The application specified that the museum would hire six positions for three years: three unspecified positions ($129,600), a museum consultant ($32,160), a curator ($27,840), and an administrator ($20,000). Because IMLS records contain no cancelled checks, invoices, quarterly status reports, or correspondence, it is difficult to know who was hired or how, precisely, the money was spent.[95]

Virtually the only thing known about the how the money was spent was that Temita S. Davis and Dr. Marvin Haire oversaw the renovation. With a graduate degree in political science from Clark University in Atlanta, Davis was the "development specialist" and the key figure in the renovation. She worked closely with Dr. Haire, her former graduate school advisor and a member of the founding board of her nonprofit. Davis and Haire were both enchanted by Glendora and, in particular, by the storied Black Bayou on the south side of town. Haire was part of the 2009 group sent to Glendora as part of the MDA's asset mapping program. He was the only one of the entire group who indicated a willingness to live in Glendora, although he was also the only one who failed to identify a single asset beyond the "intrepid spirit" of the citizens.[96] However, if Haire could find no material assets in the town, he was smitten with the beauty of the bayou. Using his website, he published a series of photographs of the bayou and its bridge, explaining that "oral history" established the bridge as the site from which Emmett Till was dropped in the water.[97]

For her part, Davis was equally enchanted by the slow-moving river on the south side of town. When, in 2007, she opened a nonprofit to help communities acknowledge their heritage, she named it Black Bayou Cultural Heritage Management Services. As the site where Till's body was disposed of, she could think of no more powerful namesake for an organization dedicated to fostering collective memory. For help with the nonprofit, she turned to her former professor, Dr. Haire, who had since moved to Mississippi Valley State University, become involved with the ETMC, and founded the Delta Research and Cultural Institute. Working in collaboration with the Delta Research and Cultural Institute and the town of Glendora, Davis's nonprofit and Haire's institute guided the renovation of the museum. Davis interviewed Till family members, oversaw community outreach, and was responsible for the conceptual design of the new museum. The institute was responsible for the historical research and media development.

All told, Davis and Haire did remarkable work for the ETHIC museum. If they did not turn it into a "state-of-the-art" museum, they vastly improved and professionalized the experience. Under the oversight of Davis and the labor of Haire, the museum charged less (now five dollars per person) and offered far more: a series of well-executed exhibits designed with input from the local community. The improvement to the museum is uncontested and extensive.

The renovated space features a small theater and an expanded exhibit hall. With the assistance of Charles Johnson, the same contractor who designed the ETMC signs, Davis turned the gin into an immersive experience in which visitors begin in the theater and, after viewing a short lo-fi video, move through a serpentine hallway along which exhibits are arranged chronologically. While some plans called for the computer lab—the last remaining relic of USDA involvement—to be moved to the second level of the gin, this never happened.[98] Davis's renovation marked the end of Ike Fowler's dream and the USDA-funded community center. It is unclear precisely when the lab folded, but it was not in the gin when the museum reopened in 2011. Moreover, when the Boston nonprofit Partners in Development arrived in February of 2014, they found a village with no electronic resources; one of their first tasks was to set up a community computer lab across the tracks from the gin.[99]

The exhibit hall begins with a tribute to the history of Glendora (originally a logging community) and a couple exhibits focused on the local history of the blues (here the influence of Haire is evident). Quickly, however, the emphasis shifts to the Till murder, with exhibits along the winding path recreating Till's journey from Bryant's Grocery in Money to the open-casket funeral in Chicago. Some of the exhibits are intricate recreations. The facade of Bryant's Grocery, for example, is recreated in elaborate detail, and the cutaway of King's Place features vintage Americana: a juke box, piano, records, and playing cards. The recreation of the casket is powerful enough that the museum requires parental permission before allowing students to walk its halls.[100] Other exhibits are little more than informational placards accessorized with midcentury paraphernalia. The abduction exhibit is half a rusted bed and a midcentury bureau (representing the Wright home); the courthouse exhibit is just four placards surrounding an old-fashioned scale (ironically, a symbol of justice); and the Sunflower County barn exhibit is a small, corrugated piece of metal jutting out from the wall (symbolizing the roof of a barn) under which an informational placard is posted.

Davis imagined the journey through the renovated space as a "truth tour," and her ultimate goal was to tell the story of Till's murder in simple and compelling terms.[101] Of course, Davis's "truth tour" was, from the perspective of the MDAH, a highly questionable affair. Davis presented as uncontested the very events that Gatlin and the MDAH refused to fund. Placards posted throughout the museum noted that the gin fan was stolen from the Glendora gin and that the body was dropped from the Black Bayou Bridge. The welcome video at one point featured the seldom-seen testimony of Robert Walker, a Glendora resident who told the FBI that he saw Milam's truck parked in front of the Glendora gin.[102] Although he never mentioned the gin fan to the FBI, in the ETHIC video, he claims that he saw the fan thrown into the back of Milam's truck while it was parked adjacent to the Glendora gin.[103]

The inclusion of the bridge and the cotton gin are, of course, the renovation's most important achievements. At long last, Thomas had managed to tell *his* version of Till's story without the obligation of providing municipal infrastructure. If it is difficult to know who the IMLS paid beyond Davis and Haire, we can say with certainty that the money was a substitute for the role traditionally played by sidewalks, apartments, and the internet: it was the cost of changing Till's story.

While Thomas must have been relieved by the blank check that came with no strings attached, Loggins and Kimbell would have been terrified. Although they did not live long enough to see it, Thompson's earmark would have served as a personal threat. Until Thompson's gift, the obligations of providing city services had held Thomas's efforts to rewrite Till's story in check. With these obligations gone, Thomas was free to write Loggins, Kimbell, the gin, and the bridge into Till's story.

In 2007, Marvin Haire joined forces with filmmaker Ed Silvera to create the Delta Media Project—an ambitious but short-lived attempt to create a "one-stop" "digital repository" of all Delta related media: photography, websites, and films.[104] With a mission of "Preserving Yesterday with Today's Technology," the story of the Delta Media Project is a fitting end point to the story of the ETHIC museum. In 2012, the Delta Media Project produced an eight-minute film titled "Mayor Thomas Shows the Black Bayou Bridge about Emmett Till Murder."[105] Although I do not know if the film ever ran in the ETHIC theater, it is similar in form, content, and length to the films that did.

The film opens with Mayor Thomas picking his way through dense brush, trees, and "razor wire" (ostensibly strung by "white folks intending to catch us") that had overtaken the road connecting the bridge to downtown Glendora. As he moved slowly through the thicket, Thomas explained that the closing of the bridge was a politically motivated attempt to "kill the community."[106] According to Thomas, the bridge was closed in the late 1980s, "three or four years" after he assumed the office of mayor. At the time, he explained, Glendora was "thriving pretty good." After the bridge was closed and the "main thoroughfare" into town eliminated, however, his own business suffered, and people from "Greenwood, Grenada, Cleveland, Ruleville, Minter City, Philipp, and Charleston" were cut off from Glendora's supposedly thriving business district. If the closure of the bridge could be blamed for his town's economic woes, he also believed that the thicket-covered bridge could now—twenty-five years later— rescue Glendora's economy. He noted that the community was going to "clean it up" and "open it up for tourism."

None of this is true. First, Glendora's economic downturn began in

1962, and, according to census figures, by 1990 the town's per capita income was under $4,000 per year—hardly a "thriving" economy.[107] Second, after Bill Gatlin researched the history of the bridge for its nomination to the National Register of Historic Places, he concluded that the bridge was closed "c. 1955." The closure was not political retribution; rather, Gatlin noted that the bridge was closed when a newer bridge was built just to the north of town.[108] Third, although it is true that Thomas's personal business enterprises suffered in the late 1980s, this was not because the Black Bayou Bridge was closed. More likely, it was because he spent two stints in jail for running his businesses illegally.[109] Fourth, no matter when the bridge was closed, its closure never would have kept people from accessing Glendora. The opposite is likely true. By 1955, the Black Bayou Bridge was repetitive. Highway 49E spanned the bayou less than a mile to the west and provided quick access to the town from the same direction as the bridge in question. Thus, when the Black Bayou Bridge was decommissioned, the town lost nothing but, if Gatlin is right, gained a bridge over the Tallahatchie River just north of town. If people were truly looking to access Glendora, they had more options than ever before.

Quite apart from the truthfulness of Thomas's tale, there is an unmistakable note of irony in his partisan history of the bridge. Until the renovation of the ETHIC museum, questions of economic development and municipal infrastructure had dominated the commemoration of Till's murder. The development of infrastructure led to the development of memory. In the video, Thomas essentially reversed the time-tested logic, suggesting that infrastructural developments (the decommissioning of the bridge) harmed the economy but could be reversed by commemoration. He was wrong. To this day, the old road to the bridge is choked with brush and inaccessible to all but the most determined, although there is no razor wire. Thomas's counterhistory of the bridge notwithstanding, it appears that, with the exception of Thompson's earmark, every effort to tell Till's story in Glendora is connected to infrastructural development. No infrastructure, no memory.

The mission of the Delta Media Project is a perfect way to remember the connection of memory and municipal infrastructure: "Preserving Yesterday with Today's Technology." While Haire and Silvera imagined that they would "preserve yesterday" by capturing oral histories in digital form, their mission statement has a broader application than they ever dreamed. It was precisely through "today's technology," that is, through high-speed broadband service provided by AbsoCom to the town of Glendora, that Till's story was preserved. Had Ike Fowler never ventured south on a mission to heal to the digital divide, the ETHIC museum never would have begun, and Loggins, Kimbell, the gin, and the bridge would never have been so securely written into Till's story.

# VANDALISM AND MEMORY
# AT GRABALL LANDING

On October 2, 2007, the ETMC announced a historical marker at Grab-all Landing to mark the spot on the Tallahatchie River where they believed Emmett Till's body was retrieved from the water. Members of the Till family had traveled from Chicago for the occasion and were gathered at the water's edge outside the village of Glendora, one hundred miles south of Memphis, in the heart of the Mississippi Delta. The riverside marker at Graball Landing was the final site on the Civil Rights Driving Tour, an eight-site pilgrimage intended by the commission to, among other things, symbolize the effort to forge a "new kind of bi-racial community." That, at least, was the vision of Betty Pearson, the eighty-four-year-old scion of one of the Delta's oldest white families and a battle-tested veteran of the Mississippi freedom movement.[1]

In the years that followed, Graball Landing would become a nationally recognized site of remembrance, but it would not, as Pearson dreamed, lead to a new biracial community. Indeed, once the ETMC placed the commemorative marker at Graball Landing, the site became the focal point of racial agitation and geographic uncertainty. For these reasons, the long history of Graball Landing makes the perfect conclusion to a book on the ecology of memory. In what follows, I consider the histories of violence, vandalism, and remembrance at

Graball Landing, stressing—as always—the sheer extent to which race, place, and commemoration shift in tandem.

## COMMEMORATION AND RACE

Betty Pearson's enthusiasm for the commemorative marker at Graball Landing was not widely shared. Six months after the commission installed the sign, it disappeared. Tire tracks leading from the site to the riverbank led Sheriff William Brewer to conclude that the sign had been tossed into the Tallahatchie River, just as Till's body once had—an irony not lost on the local black community. For Jessie Jaynes, public relations officer of the ETMC, the theft and disposal of the sign felt like a "reenactment" of the murder itself: "It seems they threw this sign in the river, just like the body of Emmett Till was thrown into the river." The commission replaced the Graball sign, but by the spring of 2013, vandals had riddled it with bullet holes (see figure 24). For ETMC founder and county supervisor Jerome Little, the vandalism was evidence of racially motivated hostility to the very idea of Till commemoration. He blamed white people.[2]

In October 2016, the local debate over the meaning of the vandalized sign exploded on the national scene. New York University film student Kevin Wilson Jr. was in the Delta creating a short film on the Till murder when he found the Graball Landing sign filled with bullet holes. Unaware of the eight-year history of vandalism at the site, or the politics involved in its placement, Wilson snapped a picture of the bullet-riddled sign and posted it to Facebook. The post claimed to be at the "exact site where Emmett Till's body was found" and was widely interpreted as the discovery of theretofore unknown racial violence.[3] Thousands of shares later, the entanglement of race and commemoration at Graball Landing was being covered by the *New York Times*, *Washington Post*, and a vast array of media outlets.[4] Disseminated by powerful media, the image of the bullet-riddled sign generated intense moral outrage and a widespread demand to replace the sign. When the big-hearted Brooklyn sign manufacturer Lite Brite Neon volunteered to fabricate, ship, and install a new marker free of charge,

FIGURE 24. The Emmett Till Memorial Commission "River Site" sign at Graball Landing, near Glendora, 2016. Photo by Maude Schuyler Clay. Used by permission.

the commission quickly cut down the old sign to make room for the new one (see figure 25).

And yet the fate of the old signs deserves our lingering consideration, not least because of the troubling parallels between the signs' fate and that of the victim they memorialized. Their fate also captures the ecology of memory—the powerful ways in which commemoration is bound up with questions of race and place. Intended to symbolize a "new kind of bi-racial community," the markers became visible signs of shamefully enduring racism. Standing on the site of the original sign, Jerome Little explained the tension. "One of the purposes of the Emmett Till Memorial Commission was to help have racial reconciliation, and I think we have, but I think there are some who still have ill feelings about Emmett Till and blacks. Things ain't changed that much."[5]

Not everyone in the Delta saw things as Little did. For some, the damage to the sign was evidence of nothing more than equal-opportunity vandalism: teenagers with access to guns and beer would shoot any rural sign.[6] From this perspective it was Jerome Little who

FIGURE 25. Graball Landing, location of the "River Site" sign, late fall 2016. Photo by Ashleigh Coleman. Used by permission.

was racist. One community member read Little's anger as evidence of a broad hatred for white people.[7] In a storm of letters to the editor, a wide range of citizens promptly called on Little to apologize for blaming the vandalism on white people (which he did) and to resign his post as county supervisor (which he did not).

The controversy between Little and the white readership of the *Sun-Sentinel* made one thing clear: the vandalism of the signs brought the ecology of memory to the foreground. The moment the signs were destroyed—thrown in the Tallahatchie River in the first case and disfigured by bullets in the second—their range of meaning was broadened. To be sure, the markers still gestured to the atrocities of Till's murder. Even the empty aluminum posts left behind by the thieves who stole the first sign still functioned in this manner. We know this because local community members gathered at the empty posts to comfort each other and reflect on the murder of Emmett Till. In addition to their backward glance, however, the vandalized signs now brought the racism of the twenty-first century into clearer view. The vandalism did not keep the signs from their primary commemorative function (locals still used the signposts for remembrance), but it did give them a broadened meaning. Vandalized, the Graball signs now gestured to racism past *and* present, to the murder of Emmett Till and to the ongoing racial fault lines between Little and his antagonists.

Little had no patience for the destruction of his signs and the racism it portended. He came of age "chopping cotton" on a plantation that kept the story of Emmett Till a well-guarded secret. Although Little did not learn of Till's murder until he left the Delta (see chapter 2), he made it his life mission to ensure that Till's story would circulate broadly. "Something was just in me," he explained, to ensure "that everybody in this county, everybody in this state, and everybody in this nation understands what happened [and] why it happened." With this background, Little would not tolerate a vandalized sign. After the original sign was stolen, he told the local paper, "I want to make sure that whoever did this knows that this sign is going back up. Every time it's taken down, it's going back up."[8]

Although he passed away in 2011, Little's commitment to unblemished signage has become the standard operating procedure of the commission. Had he lived to see it, Jerome Little would have loved the Lite Brite sign. It will be pristine — no more chipped magnolia flowers, stolen finials, dented aluminum posts, or bullet holes. In fact, the sign will *never again* be filled with holes; the Lite Brite sign is going to be bulletproof.[9]

My immense respect for the commission notwithstanding, their determination to erect a memorial that will bear no sign of those who oppose its meaning has come at a tremendous cultural cost. Each new sign the commission installs hides the ecology of memory, hides the entanglement of race and commemoration, and hides the power of the sign to testify to what persists from the distant tragedy that it commemorates. Each successively newer sign may capture the facts of 1955, but can't capture the ways that the memory of Till's murder continues to function in the Delta as an inspiration for both reconciliation and racism. A bulletproof sign might tell of the events of Till's murder, but it will obscure the racial legacy of the murder. In this sense, a pristine Lite Brite sign wrongly suggests that the past is entirely in the past, discreet and disconnected from the present. The bullet holes, by contrast, bear witness to the entanglement of race and memory; they are simple, eloquent, affectively charged reminders that the remembrance of Till's murder is, as it were, shot through with racial politics.

No one has captured the affective power of vandalized commemoration better than Ralph Ellison. Newly enrolled in a fictional college modeled on the Tuskegee Institute, the narrator of Ellison's *Invisible Man* is puzzled by a statue of the college founder. The statue employed the archetypal visual language of racial uplift and should not have been puzzling. A dignified likeness of Booker T. Washington, standing erect in a five-button vest, fitted with all the accouterments of genteel respectability, lifting the veil of ignorance from a coiled black body—there could hardly be a more commonplace figuring of liberation. And yet, despite the sheer banality of the symbolism, the narrator finds himself puzzled.

> In my mind's eye I see the bronze statue of the college Founder . . . his arms outstretched in the breathtaking gesture of lifting a veil that flutters in hard, metallic folds above the face of a kneeling slave; and I am standing puzzled, unable to decide whether the veil is really being lifted, or lowered more firmly in place; whether I am witnessing a revelation or a more efficient blinding. And as I gaze, there is a rustle of wings and I see a flock of starlings flighting before me and, when I look again, the bronze face, whose empty eyes look upon a world I have never seen, runs with liquid chalk—creating another ambiguity to puzzle my groping mind: Why is a bird-soiled statue more commanding than one that is clean?[10]

Here we witness the power of vandalized commemoration. While the undefiled statue equates education with liberation, the whitewashed, bird-soiled version suggested that the college was, at the same time, an instrument of the racist white establishment—a lesson the invisible man would learn all too well. Once soiled, the statue pointed in two directions at once: to the hope of liberation and the fact of oppression.

Ellison's narrator is puzzled not by one message or the other, but by the tension resulting from the simultaneous presence of competing claims. For Ellison the puzzled response is key, summoning the invisible man toward a fuller, more complex, more honest portrait of the past than an unsoiled statue could ever provide.

We have not learned Ellison's lesson. In the case of the disfigured sign at Graball Landing, the bullet holes have been either decried as evidence of racism or dismissed as the innocent by-product of thrill-deprived teenagers in rural America. While this controversy splits the ETMC down the middle, neither of these positions take Ellison seriously. On the one hand, black commissioners such as Little denounced the vandalism but suggested that commemorative work could be resumed with a new sign. On the other hand, some of the white commissioners held that the bullet holes were unrelated to the message of the sign. One party wants to get rid of the bullets holes; the other suggests that they are irrelevant. Neither entertains the possibility that Ellison was right, that the very defacement of the sign enlarges its commemorative power.

Regardless of whether or not the shooters were motivated by racism, the bullet-pierced historical marker was the perfect icon for a community still rent by the memory of Till's murder. For, as I have argued throughout this book, the work of remembering the murder in the twenty-first-century Delta has exposed long-dormant racial fault lines. Behind the smooth veneer of the commission and their high-profile memory work is a commission—and a region—deeply divided by the past and the work of remembrance. Moreover, as their preference for replacing vandalized signs suggests, it is a commission deeply uncomfortable with ecology of memory, the ways in which the Delta's habits of remembrance are, time and again, entangled with racial politics.

## COMMEMORATION AND PLACE

In 2007, when the Till family journeyed to the banks of the Tallahatchie River for a presentation by Plater Robinson and the announcement of the Graball sign, they may have gone to the wrong place. Graball Landing, an eighteenth-century steamboat landing at the confluence of the Tallahatchie River and the Black Bayou, is one of several possible options of where Till's body may have been pulled from the water. In the immediate aftermath of the murder, multiple newspapers suggested that the body was found near Pecan Point, 3.5 miles downstream from Graball Landing.[11] At the trial, the seventeen-year-old Robert Hodges, who found the body, and his landlord B. L. Mims both testified that the body was recovered north of Philipp on the portion of the river that divides Leflore County from Tallahatchie County, a minimum of six miles downstream from Graball Landing.[12] Huie's account is consistent with Hodges and Mims. He claims the body was dropped in the water 3.5 miles south of the Sharkey Bridge before floating downstream for eight miles.[13] This would put the recovery point just north of Philipp, significantly downstream from Graball Landing. Finally, as I indicated in chapter 3, after taking Hodges back to the spot in 2006, the FBI concluded that the body was recovered where the river dips briefly into Leflore County, nearly five miles downstream from Graball Landing.[14]

The plethora of options notwithstanding, Graball Landing remains a plausible site. Beyond a strong local tradition that Till's body was pulled from the water at the old steamboat landing, the site has strong advocates in Plater Robinson, the ETMC's long-standing guide to historical matters, and Johnny B. Thomas, the controversial mayor of Glendora. The support of Robinson and Thomas is complicated, however, because they have mutually exclusive theories of how the body arrived at Graball Landing—both of them cannot be correct. In the same letter in which Robinson implored the ETMC to put their sign at the landing, he also told them that the body was placed in the mud adjacent to the river as a warning to a local black community— a claim he later retracted when he learned his source had misled him. Thomas, for his part, claims that the body was dropped from the Black Bayou Bridge in Glendora and floated 1.3 miles through the bayou to the Tallahatchie River before being recovered adjacent to the landing.

Thomas's theory is plausible, but it is not without controversy. Depending on whom you ask, the sheer proximity of the Black Bayou Bridge in Glendora to Graball Landing (1.3 miles) either makes both sites more plausible or calls into question the objectivity of Thomas. At the time the ETMC chose the landing, Thomas was both a member of the commission and a grant writer pursuing state funding for the bridge (see chapter 5). When the ETMC chose Graball Landing, Thomas's pursuit of funding must have seemed all the more legitimate: if the body was recovered at Graball, the Black Bayou Bridge becomes a compelling disposal site.

For these reasons, the placement of the ETMC sign at Graball Landing implicated the commission in an ongoing controversy about the geography of the murder. The commission could not have followed the FBI's 2006 conclusion, for the simple reason that they were incorporated by Tallahatchie County and their commemorative authority stopped at the county line (see chapter 3). They could have chosen Pecan Point or the site indicated by the original testimony of Hodges and Mims. Had they done so, however, their sign would have undermined the pet project of one of their own officers. The further the recovery site is moved downstream, the less likely it is that Till's body was dropped from the Black Bayou Bridge. On this score, note that Huie has the body recovered over eleven miles south of Glendora.[15] This is further south than any other proposed site, and it is likely one more attempt by Huie to eliminate from the story the Glendora clan from whom he could not obtain release forms (Elmer Kimbell, Henry Loggins, and Levi Collins).

The fact that the extraction point is both uncertain and consequential speaks to the powerful entanglement of memory and geography. The further south the body was recovered, the smaller the murder party. Likewise, by commemorating the northernmost option, the ETMC was effectively rerouting the murder through Glendora and writing Elmer Kimbell, among others, into the plot. In other words, memory and geography shift in tandem; to move the extraction point north or south on the Tallahatchie River is to adjust the terms of Till's story.

## PLACE AND RACE

In 1840, 168 years before the ETMC erected their sign, Cullen McMullen (b. 1794) came to the Delta. He arrived with thirty-five enslaved persons via a Tallahatchie River steamboat and disembarked at Graball Landing near what we now know as Glendora. Although the names of the enslaved are not recorded, and although there is no photographic record, McMullen's great-grandson Joseph Albert May was still using African American labor to clear land near Graball in 1925 (see figure 26). Although the photograph of May's workforce was not taken at Graball Landing, the image of thirty-six laborers, axes in hand, is a good reminder of the complicity of racism and nature. Even the unbroken flatness of the Delta, the bioregion's most conspicuous "natural feature," is a product of black labor. The image of the ax-wielding laborers is also a powerful reminder that slavery and, later, sharecropping must not be understood as racial accommodations to a land whose flat, open spaces naturally required exploited labor to turn a profit. While it is true, as I noted in chapter 2, that the rich, flat land of the Delta molded racism into the form of paternalism, we must not therefore conclude that the flatness of the land preceded its investment by racism. Race was not a late addition to the natural landscape, a supplement added in order to extract profit from an already flat land. Racism came first, in the form of thirty-five ax-wielding slaves, and the very flatness of the land, the storied mineral-laden fields of the Delta, followed quickly behind them, reshaping the very racism that flattened the land in the first place. It is difficult to imagine a more intricate entwining of race and nature.

In the case of the McMullen Place Plantation, thirty-five black slaves entered the Delta at Graball Landing and cleared the land so that McMullen could farm it while one of his sons died carrying the Confederate flag at Shiloh. In 1894, a tornado wiped the land clean, eliminating the old steamboat landing and a nearby lake in one fell swoop. By the time 1955 arrived, all that was left of the landing was a clearing, a break in the otherwise impenetrable vegetation that lined

**FIGURE 26.** "Clearing Land." Photo courtesy of Maude Schuyler Clay. Used by permission.

the Tallahatchie River. In a sad, historical irony that stretches over generations, the same slave labor that made the cotton economy possible left behind a clearing that made it feasible for a body to be pulled from the water. Although they could not possibly have recognized the irony, the slaves who landed at Graball in the nineteenth century prepared the land for Emmett Till twice. They exposed the soil, flattened the horizon, and so made possible the brutal cotton economy from which Till would never emerge. And, by the same means (axes), they left a clearing where, 115 years later, Till's body may have been pulled from the water. If you visit Graball Landing today, even the clearing is gone. The only evidence of human activity you would see are tire tracks and two sawed-off aluminum posts marking the spot where the ETMC's shot-up sign once stood (see figure 25).[16]

At six generations remove, the *same family* that once cleared the land put up a sign. McMullen's great-great-great-granddaughter is Anna Booth Schuyler Clay Weems, whose mother is Maude Clay, the photographer who connected the ETMC to Plater Robinson, and whose husband is Patrick Weems, director of the ETMC's Interpretive Center.[17] From his post at the center, Weems takes tourists to Graball Landing, a site that for nearly two hundred years has borne silent witness to the violent entanglement of racism and the natural environment. When the Till family traveled to Graball Landing in October 2007, they were met by Robinson, who convinced the ETMC to put their sign at Graball in the first place. Although it boggles the mind, the same family cleared the land, exposed the soil, jump-started the cotton kingdom, left a clearing for body retrieval, and made the interpersonal connections that eventuated in a historical marker that would, in turn, be vandalized because of the racism set in motion by the flat land and fertile soil. Race, place, and commemoration can simply not be disentangled.

The photographs of the bullet-riddled sign and the ax-wielding laborers (figures 24 and 26) are reciprocal images of the same lesson. Both are images of violence, race, and place. As I've tried to suggest across *Remembering Emmett Till*, the flatness, soil, and cotton of the Delta landscape have intermingled with Till's murder and memory in more ways than we have ever acknowledged. The image of thirty-six black laborers, axes in hand, is a reminder that Delta land was racially charged long before Till arrived. The bullet holes in the shot-up sign suggest that the racial charge persists and finds expression in communal acts of remembrance. These acts of remembrance, in turn, shape the land itself. Graball Landing, after all, was turned into a tourist site through the ETMC's commemorative politics (their need for a northern extraction point). Together, the images speak to the ecology of memory: Graball Landing was made possible by the labor of thirty-five slaves and, generations later, the commemorative commitments of the ETMC. The labor worked racism into nature so intimately that the flatness of the land seems more a result of prejudice than a floodplain. Cleared, the land bore cotton and paternalism, which, together, cost Till his life and have controlled the terms of his commemoration.

The eight-year history of the sign erected at Graball Landing thus replays, in condensed form, the entanglements of race, place, and commemoration that have long structured Delta life. Erected, stolen, replaced, filled with bullet holes, cut down, replaced, and shot again, the cycles of signage at Graball Landing remain the Delta's most poignant marker of the ecology of memory.

# NOTES

## Introduction

1. The fact of the whistle may be the least controversial event of the entire episode at Bryant's Grocery. Although it is not uncontested, we know with virtual certainty that Till whistled at Carolyn Bryant after leaving the store. Anderson, *Emmett Till*, 363; Tyson, *The Blood of Emmett Till*, 54. Wheeler Parker, the last remaining eyewitness to the events at the store, has told me in no uncertain terms that the whistle happened.

2. "The Mississippi Freedom Trail: Civil Rights in Mississippi," proposal, Division of Tourism, Mississippi Development Authority, January 20, 2011 (hereafter cited as "The Mississippi Freedom Trail" proposal). In author's possession.

3. On the origin of the Freedom Trail, see Stephen A. King and Roger Davis Gatchet, "Marking the Past: Civil Rights Tourism and the Mississippi Freedom Trail"; and Jessica Taylor, "'We're on Fire': Oral History and the Preservation, Commemoration, and Re-birth of Mississippi's Civil Rights Sites."

4. Federal Bureau of Investigation (FBI), "Prosecutive Report of Investigation Concerning . . . Emmett Till, Deceased, Victim," Appendix A—Trial Transcript, February 9, 2006, 263–77 (hereafter cited as FBI, "Prosecutive Report").

5. For the "justifiable homicide" thesis, see Houck and Grindy, *Emmett Till and the Mississippi Press*, 96.

6. FBI, "Prosecutive Report," 262.

7. FBI, 274. For the details of the 2008 confession, see Tyson, *The Blood of Emmett Till*, 1–7.

8. Whitaker, "A Case Study in Southern Justice," 155; Tyson, *The Blood of Emmett Till*, 180.

9. "The Mississippi Freedom Trail" proposal.

10. There is some precedent for the term, although not as I use it here. In 2016, *Mem-*

*ory Studies* editor Andrew Hoskins wrote of the "new memory ecology": it sees the "material and cultural environment in consort with cognition and emotion availed through it to illuminate the emergence of remembering and forgetting." While Hoskins posits an "ecology of memory," *Remembering Emmett Till* gives flesh to the term, demonstrating the particular ways in which memory works in tandem with the "material and cultural environment." Hoskins, "Memory Ecologies," 354. See also Fivush and Merrill, "An Ecological Systems Approach to Family Narratives."

11. Morton, *The Ecological Thought*, 28.

12. Or, to take a different example, just as "queer ecologies" have demonstrated the reciprocal influence of nature and sexuality (ideas of nature influence ideas about sex and vice versa), so my memory ecology is dedicated to tracing the symbiotic relationships of memory with place and race. Mortimer-Sandilands and Erickson, *Queer Ecologies*.

13. As Elizabeth J. Stigler has written, "Rather than delineate the boundaries around memory making as an internal, individual act, an ecology of memory demands the inclusion of exterior, environmental factors as essential parts of memory making." "Cooking Up Resistance," 38.

14. Description has been dramatically undervalued as a critical methodology in the humanities. See Foucault, *The Archaeology of Knowledge*, 107–10; and Latour, *Reassembling the Social*, 110–12, 137, and 147. If description has occasionally registered as a noncritical or apolitical methodology, this just means that the method has never been descriptive enough.

15. On the historic linkages between memory and knowledge more generally, see Mary Carruthers, *The Book of Memory: A Study of Memory in Medieval Culture*.

16. Johnson, *Song and the Silence*, 195.

17. Dunbar, *Delta Time*, 5; Whitfield, *A Death in the Delta*, 13.

18. Cobb, *The Most Southern Place on Earth*, vii.

19. Cohn, *God Shakes Creation*, 14.

20. Cohn, 14; Yolande Robbins, "Despite What You May Have Heard, Vicksburg Doesn't Have a Catfish Row," *Vicksburg Post*, July 22, 2017, http://www.vicksburgpost .com/2017/07/22/despite-what-you-may-have-heard-vicksburg-doesnt-have-a -catfish-row/.

21. Cotton, of course, is the classic articulation point of nature and race. See Dattel, *Cotton and Race in the Making of America*, and Johnson, *River of Dark Dreams*. To cotton, I add rivers, hills, soils, and, in the conclusion, the flatness of the land as relay points between race and nature.

22. Cohn, *God Shakes Creation*, 60. As William Alexander Percy—chief of the Delta's aristocratic literati—put it, "For our soil, very dark brown, creamy and sweet-smelling, without substrata of rock or shale, was built up slowly, century after century, by the

sediment gathered by the river in its solemn task of cleansing the continent." Percy, *Lanterns on the Levee*, 3.

23. Faulkner, *Go Down, Moses*, 324.

24. I have never seen the curvature of the earth, but see Rubin, *Confederacy of Silence*, 47; Moye, *Let the People Decide*, 27.

25. Johnson, *The Song and the Silence*, xv.

26. Dattel, *Cotton and Race in the Making of America*, 40, 81.

27. Johnson, *River of Dark Dreams*, 5.

28. Dattel, *Cotton and Race in the Making of America*, 314–20.

29. Quoted in Dattell, *Cotton and Race in the Making of America*, 316.

30. Johnson, *The Song and the Silence*, xvi.

31. Dattel, *Cotton and Race in the Making of America*, 314.

32. Johnson, *River of Dark Dreams*, 5.

33. Dattel, *Cotton and Race in the Making of America*, 53; Johnson, *River of Dark Dreams*, 244.

34. Johnson, *The Song and the Silence*, 91.

35. Ralph McGill, editorial, *Atlanta Constitution*, October 22, 1952, 1. Quoted in Whitaker, "A Case Study in Southern Justice," 22.

36. "Sheriff Clarence Strider: The Murder of Emmett Till," *American Experience*, PBS, http://www.pbs.org/wgbh/americanexperience/features/emmett-biography-sheriff -clarence-strider/.

37. Dan Wakefield, "Justice in Sumner: Land of the Free," *The Nation*, October 1, 1955, 285.

38. Dattel, *Cotton and Race in the Making of America*, 29, 85–86; Johnson, *River of Dark Dreams*.

39. On the reactionary impulse to define places as internally sufficient, see Massey, *Space, Place, and Gender*, 157–73.

40. Dattel, *Cotton and Race in the Making of America*, 358.

41. Dattel, lx; Cobb, *Most Southern Place on Earth*, 204.

42. Grant, *Dispatches from Pluto*, 80; Johnson, *The Song and the Silence*, 113. The quotation is attributed to Neil Peirce.

43. Cobb, *Most Southern Place on Earth*, 331.

44. Crowe, *Getting Away with Murder*, 15; Wright, *Simeon's Story*, 54–55.

45. Wright, *Simeon's Story*, 6; Huie, "What's Happened the Emmett Till Killers?," 65.

46. Cobb, *The Most Southern Place on Earth*, 228.

47. Dattel, *Cotton and Race in the Making of America*, 357.

48. Cotton is still grown in the Delta to this day. By "postcotton Delta," I indicate the historical transition away from a time when cotton could adequately support the economy of the Delta.

49. Here I follow Samantha Senda-Cook, Michael K. Middleton, and Danielle Endres, who argue that place is not "simply [the] location, backdrop, or context" of action. Rather, a place "acts with, against, and alongside the rhetorical practices it hosts." Senda-Cook, Middleton, and Endres, "Interrogating the 'Field,'" 23–24.

50. Nora, "Reasons for the Current Upsurge in Memory," 437.

51. Huyssen, "Present Pasts: Media, Politics, Amnesia," 430; Olick and Robbins, "Social Memory Studies: From 'Collective Memory' to the Historical Sociology of Mnemonic Practices," 107.

52. Gillis, "Memory and Identity," 13; Young, *The Stages of Memory*, 2–3, 49–50.

53. Doss, *Memorial Mania*, 2.

54. "The more fragmented and heterogeneous societies become, it seems, the stronger their need to unify wholly disparate experiences and memories with the common meaning . . . created in common spaces." Young, "The Memorial's Arc," 329. See also Huyssen, "Present Pasts: Media, Politics, Amnesia"; Landsberg, *Prosthetic Memory*, 2; Massey, *Space, Place, and Gender*; Dickinson, *Suburban Dreams*.

55. Dattel, *Cotton and Race in the Making of America*, 29, 36; Johnson, *River of Dark Dreams*.

56. As Massey notes, the putatively destabilizing effects of postmodernism are experienced most acutely by the cultural elite—not a demographic in abundant supply in the Mississippi Delta.

57. See Pollack and Metress, *Emmett Till in Literary Memory and Imagination*.

58. Anderson, *Emmett Till*, 287–88.

59. Moody, *Coming of Age in Mississippi*, 123–24.

60. MacLean, *The Past Is Never Dead*, 88; Barton and Leonard, "Incorporating Social Justice in Tourism Planning," 315; Samuels, *The Murder and the Movement*; Little, *Oral History by the William Winter Institute*.

61. Anderson, *Emmett Till*, 344.

62. Anderson, 289.

63. *Eyes on the Prize* producer Jon Else called the Till story "our carnival barker, our noir tease, and our declaration of theme, purpose, and style." *True South*, 237.

64. Wilkerson, *The Warmth of Other Suns*, 191. Here I follow James C. Scott, who argues that it is sheer folly to think subversive discourse will appear openly on the public record. Scott, *Domination and the Arts of Resistance*. For more on the subversive politics of the *Defender* and the racial consequences of possessing it, see Anderson, *White Rage*, 50, and especially Grossman, *Land of Hope*, 78.

65. ETMC Minutes, Binder 1, June 20, 2006.

66. Upton, *What Can and Can't be Said*, 10.

67. Romano and Raiford, *The Civil Rights Movement in American Memory*, xii.

68. Whitaker, "A Case Study in Southern Justice," 16.

69. The Delta is "the distilled essence of the Deep South." Cobb, *The Most Southern Place on Earth*, vii.

70. See, for example, Mace on the town of Sumner, quoting the *New York Times*, "Sumner, Mississippi . . . the county seat of Tallahatchie County, is the epitome of the way of life, the mores, the racial attitudes and the racial tensions that are summoned up by the words 'deep south.'" Quoted in Mace, *In Remembrance of Emmett Till*, 104.

71. Cobb, *The Most Southern Place on Earth*, 112, 125, 162, and 228.

72. Percy, *Lanterns on the Levee*, 249–69.

73. On the issue of whether or not Till's murder qualified as a lynching, see Wood, *Lynching and Spectacle*, 265; Mace, *In Remembrance of Emmett Till*, 27; Anderson, *Emmett Till*, 63.

74. "Mississippi Freedom Trail Markers, Statewide" and "Narrative," MDAH, Jackson, MS, Folder: Mississippi Civil Rights Historical Sites (MCRHS) Grant #2011-002.

75. "The Mississippi Freedom Trail" proposal.

76. Payne, *I've Got the Light of Freedom*.

77. Strider pulled the body from the water, completed the death certificate (which indicated the body was "colored"), and sent the body to Greenwood's black undertaker. On the last day of the trial, however, he testified that the body was so decomposed its race could not be determined. Based on the exaggerated decomposition of the body, the defense argued that the body in the river could not be Till, who had been missing only three days and could not be decomposed.

78. Alexander, *The New Jim Crow*, 183–84.

79. On 1985 as a turning point in the Till literature, see Anderson, *Emmett Till*, 279–89.

80. Anderson, 315.

81. *Tallahatchie County Feasibility Study*, Appendix A, MDAH, Jackson, MS, Folder: Community Heritage Preservation Grant #2006-026.

82. Olick and Robbins, "Social Media Studies," 108.

83. Nora, "Between Memory and History," 8–9.

84. In this context, (the brilliant) historian David Blight's critiques of Ken Burns are representative. Blight, *Beyond the Battlefield*, 121.

85. Metress, *The Lynching of Emmett Till*, 9–10.

86. Emmett Till Interpretive Center, http://www.emmett-till.org/. Here credit goes to Patrick Weems, who has recognized and mobilized the power of historical narrative for purposes of social justice.

87. Soja, *Postmodern Geographies*, 10–42.

## Chapter One

1. FBI, "Prosecutive Report," 265.

2. The differential geographies were a key point of disagreement in the battle over whether or not the Till lynching could be framed by the defense as a "justifiable homicide." See Houck and Grindy, *Emmett Till and the Mississippi Press*, 96.

3. "State 2 Negroes Last Seen with Till Disappear," *Laurel Leader Call*, September 21, 1955, 2.

4. John Herbers, "Wolf Whistle Murder Case Goes to Jury in Sumner Circuit Court," *Delta Democrat Times*, September 23, 1955, 1,7.

5. Dittmer, *Local People*, 57.

6. James L. Hicks, "Hicks Says Key Witnesses in Jail During Till Case Hearing." *Atlanta Daily World*, October 4, 1955, 1.

7. Beito and Beito, *Black Maverick*, xi.

8. Anderson, *Emmett Till*, 103.

9. Beito and Beito, *Black Maverick*, 120.

10. Beito and Beito, 121.

11. Clark Porteous, "Jury Being Chosen in Till Trial," *Memphis Press-Scimitar*, September 19, 1955, 4; Clark Porteous, "New Till Evidence: Reporter Finds It," *Memphis Press-Scimitar*. September 21, 1955, 2.

12. Booker, "A Negro Reporter at the Till Trial," 136.

13. Quoted in "Wolf Whistle Jury Panel Will Be Selected Today," *Memphis Press-Scimitar*, September 12, 1955, 13.

14. Clark Porteous, "New Angle in Till Case Claimed," *Memphis Press-Scimitar*, September 20, 1955, 5.

15. The Sturdivant Plantation was widely misidentified as the Clint Shurden Plantation (or sometimes even the Sheridan Plantation). The Shurden and Sturdivant Plantations were adjacent to each other in Sunflower County. There is no such thing as the "Sheridan Plantation." On this confusion, see Anderson, *Emmett Till*, 128. Citing various newspaper articles, Anderson claims that the plantation was owned by M. P. Sturdivant of Glendora. A title dated December 22, 1952, retrieved from the Sunflower County chancery clerk's office indicates that Ben W. Sturdivant owned the land, but had sold a "one-half undivided interest" in the property to the Milams. Because the notes had not been paid at the time of the murder, it effectively remained the Sturdivant Plantation. "Contract and Agreement," Ben W. Sturdivant, L. F. Milam, Mrs. L. F. Milam, J. W. Milam, and Mrs. J. W. Milam, Sunflower County Chancery Clerk's Office, Indianola, MS. Copy in the author's possession.

16. "Contract and Agreement," Ben W. Sturdivant, L. F. Milam, Mrs. L. F. Milam, J. W. Milam, and Mrs. J. W. Milam, Sunflower County Chancery Clerk's Office, Indianola, MS. Copy in the author's possession.

17. Anderson, *Emmett Till*, 102; Clark Porteous, "Officers Work All Night on Searches," *Memphis-Press Scimitar*, September 21, 1955, 7.

18. Anderson, *Emmett Till*, 83.

19. FBI, "Prosecutive Report," 225.

20. Adams, *Time Bomb*, 20; Amos Dixon, "Till Case: Torture and Murder," *California Eagle*, February 9, 1956, 2.

21. FBI, "Prosecutive Report," 225.

22. Dixon, "Till Case," February 9, 1956, 2. "Dixon" may well be the pseudonym of Clark Porteous, who was one of the few white reporters to have access to the information disseminated by the *California Eagle*.

23. Hicks, "Hicks Says," 1, 4; James L. Hicks, "Sheriff Kept Key Witness Hid in Jail during Trial," *Cleveland Call and Post*, October 8, 1955, 8-C. Reprinted in Metress, *The Lynching of Emmett Till*, 155–61.

24. Hicks, "Sheriff Kept Key Witness." Reprinted in Metress, *The Lynching of Emmett Till*, 155–61.

25. Hicks, "Sheriff Kept Key Witness." Reprinted in Metress, *The Lynching of Emmett Till*, 155–61.

26. Anderson, *Emmett Till*, 83; Porteous, "Officers Work All Night," 7.

27. Amos Dixon, "Mrs. Bryant Didn't Even Hear Emmett Till Whistle," *California Eagle*, January 26, 1956, 2.

28. For the best guess on who the men were in the back of the truck, see Anderson, *Emmett Till*, 374. Even if Collins was not on the truck, "Amos Dixon" still placed him in Sunflower County, arguing that Milam had Collins clean his truck on site in Sunflower County. Dixon, "Till Case," February 16, 1956, 1, 2.

29. Loggins was in the back of the truck "holding Emmett as if to keep him from getting away." Adams, *Time Bomb*, 19.

30. Amos Dixon, "Milam Master-Minded Emmett Till Killing," *California Eagle*, February 2, 1956, 1, 2.

31. Hicks, "Hicks Says," 1.

32. Note that Hicks's professed desire to go public with the story immediately contradicts his earlier claim that he feared his life would be in danger if he published the story immediately.

33. Anderson, *Emmett Till*, 95.

34. Anderson, 104.

35. Anderson, 95.

36. James L. Hicks, "Hicks Arrested during Trial in Till Lynch-Murder Case," *Atlanta Daily World*, October 18, 1955, 1.

37. Booker, "A Negro Reporter," 137.

38. Anderson, *Emmett Till*, 105–6. The witnesses were Young, Willie Reed, Add Reed, Mandy Bradley, and Walter Billingsley, who had been near the barn milking cows.

39. Technically, the same is true for Add Reed and Mandy Bradley—but their testimony during the trial was brief and little more than a confirmation of what Willie Reed testified. Moreover, while Willie Reed lived on to play an important role in the commemoration, the same is not true of Add Reed or Mandy Bradley.

40. Anderson, *Emmett Till*, 152.

41. FBI, "Prosecutive Report," 289; James Featherstone and W. C. Shoemaker, "Verdict Awaited in Till Trial," *Jackson Daily News*, September 23, 1955, 9.

42. Anderson, *Emmett Till*, 231–32.

43. Tell, *Confessional Crises*, 67–72.

44. James L. Hicks, "Unbelievable! Inside Story of Miss. Trial," *Baltimore Afro-American*. October 29, 1955, 1.

45. Tell, *Confessional Crises*, 69.

46. Anderson, *Emmett Till*, 201.

47. Anderson, 271–72. Milam did eventually obtain a loan from a local bank with the help of his lawyer John Whitten.

48. The NAACP's *Crisis* used the murder of Emmett Till to attack "the state of Jungle fury" in Mississippi and argued (falsely) that no "highly-placed Mississippian denounces the crime." Whitfield, *A Death in the Delta*, 28.

49. Whitfield, *A Death in the Delta*, 27.

50. Whitfield, 30; Anderson, *Emmett Till*, 60.

51. David Halberstam, "Tallahatchie County Acquits a Peckerwood," *The Reporter*, April 19, 1956, http://users.soc.umn.edu/~samaha/cases/halberstam_peckerwood.html.

52. Tell, *Confessional Crises*, 64; Raines, *My Soul Is Rested*, 388–89.

53. William Bradford Huie to Basil Walters and Lee Hills, October 18, 1955, William Charvat Collection of American Fiction, Ohio State University Libraries, Box 39, Folder 353c (emphasis in original).

54. William Bradford Huie to Dan Mich, October 23, 1955, William Charvat Collection of American Fiction, Ohio State University Libraries, Box 39, Folder 353c.

55. Raines, *My Soul Is Rested*, 388.

56. Robinson and Williams, "The Murder of Emmett Till," minute 22.

57. Houck and Grindy, *Emmett Till and the Mississippi Press*, 150.

58. William Bradford Huie to John L. Whitten, October 30, 1956, William Charvat Collection of American Fiction, Ohio State University Libraries, Box 39, Folder 353b.

59. Houck and Grindy, *Emmett Till and the Mississippi Press*, 150.

60. William Bradford Huie to Roy Wilkins, October 12, 1955, William Charvat Collection of American Fiction, Ohio State University Libraries, Box 39, Folder 353c.

61. William Bradford Huie to Dan Mich, October 17, 1955, William Charvat Collection of American Fiction, Ohio State University Libraries, Box 39, Folder 353c.

62. William Bradford Huie to Basil Walters, October 18, 1955, William Charvat Collection of American Fiction, Ohio State University Libraries, Box 39, Folder 353c.

63. James L. Hicks, "Hicks Arrested," 1, 2.

64. Writing in 1988, Stephen Whitfield claimed that the identity of the white men "remained anonymous." Whitfield, *A Death in the Delta*, 56. This was not quite true. By the late 1980s, a handful of people knew the identities of the white men, but the circle of the knowledgeable was not big, and Whitfield was not part of it. See Anderson, *Emmett Till*, 333; Keith Beauchamp, "What Really Happened to Emmett Till: A Corrective to the 1956 *Look* Magazine Confession."

65. Huie to Mich, October 23, 1955.

66. Huie to Mich, October 23. 1955.

67. "According to J. W. Milam, the account of the lynching that he and Roy Bryant gave to William Bradford Huie was a lie." Blue, *Emmett Till's Secret Witness*, 408.

68. Wagner, "America's Civil Rights Revolution," 192.

69. Houck and Grindy, *Emmett Till and the Mississippi Press*, 151.

70. Monteith, "The Murder of Emmett Till," 39.

71. Wakefield, "Justice in Sumner," 284, 285.

72. Anderson, *Emmett Till*, 335.

73. Anderson, 333–34. The interviewer was actually Bonnie Blue. See Blue, *Emmett Till's Secret Witness*.

74. Anderson, *Emmett Till*, 234–35.

75. FBI, "Prosecutive Report," 91.

76. William Bradford Huie, "The Shocking Story of Approved Killing in Mississippi," 49.

77. Huie, 49.

78. Whitten, "Injustice Unearthed," 16.

79. Mamie Till-Mobley and Benson, *The Death of Innocence*, 212.

80. Huie, "The Shocking Story of Approved Killing in Mississippi," 49.

81. Whitfield, *A Death in the Delta*, 57.

82. Thomas and Durant, *A Stone of Hope*, 132.

83. Nelson, *The Murder of Emmett Till*. The testimony of Willie Reed and Warren Hampton cannot be squared. Both are Sunflower County witnesses who remember screams. But Reed testified that the screaming stopped by the time Till was loaded in the truck and placed under a tarp; Hampton remembers screaming from underneath the tarp.

84. Huie, "The Shocking Story of Approved Killing in Mississippi," 49.

85. Anderson, *Emmett Till*, 330; Beauchamp, "What Really Happened to Emmett Till."

86. William Winter Institute for Racial Reconciliation Collection, Box 3, Folder:

Emmett Till Historic Marker. Robinson confuses the Shurden Plantation, on which Willie Reed lived, with the Sturdivant Plantation, on which Milam worked and across which Willie Reed was walking when he heard screams from the barn. On the historic confusion of these two plantations, see Anderson, *Emmett Till*, 128.

87. Dozens of scholars—myself included—have suggested that, at least until 2005, the confessional account in *Look* held a virtual monopoly on the memory of Till's murder. Tell, *Confessional Crises*, 88. Huie's story has "dominated the discourse" surrounding Emmett Till and "pushed aside" competing accounts (Beito and Beito, "Why It's Unlikely"). "Huie's version assumed the status of the primary 'account' of Till's murder" (Monteith, "The Murder of Emmett Till," 40). "No other account of the case has had such a far-ranging influence on other retellings of the Emmett Till story" (Metress, "Truth Be Told," 50). Huie "defined nearly every account found in the print media" (Mace, *In Remembrance of Emmett Till*, 137).

88. Till-Mobley and Benson, *Death of Innocence*, 213.

89. Beauchamp, *The Untold Story of Emmett Louis Till*. This number was not verified by the FBI and, to my knowledge, the fourteen people have not been named by Beauchamp.

90. Wagner, "America's Civil Rights Revolution." 191.

91. Whitaker, "A Case Study," 112.

92. Whitaker, 111.

93. The theft of the fan was never a legal event.

94. Clayborne Carson, quoted in "Bleary Days for Eyes on the Prize," *Wired*, December 22, 2004, https://www.wired.com/2004/12/bleary-days-for-eyes-on-the-prize/.

95. Whitfield, *A Death in the Delta*, 55–58.

96. Whitfield.

97. Whitfield, 56.

98. Wagner, "America's Civil Rights Revolution," 194.

99. Nelson, *Murder of Emmett Till*.

100. FBI, "Prosecutive Report," 213–14.

101. See Wagner, "America's Civil Rights Revolution," 193.

102. Whitten, "Injustice Unearthed."

103. Whitten, 16.

104. FBI, "Prosecutive Report," 88.

105. Wagner, "America's Civil Rights Revolution: Three Documentaries about Emmett Till's Murder in Mississippi (1955)," 191.

106. FBI, "Prosecutive Report," 89. Loggins's name is redacted because he was still alive in 2006.

107. FBI, 91.

## Chapter Two

1. Saikku, *This Delta, This Land*, 96, 139.

2. Cohn, *God Shakes Creation*, 60. "The drainage area of the greater Mississippi covers some 1.2 million square miles, or more than 40 percent of the coterminous United States, from New York to Wyoming." Saikku, *This Delta, This Land*, 27.

3. Percy, *Lanterns on the Levee*, 3.

4. Saikku, *This Delta, This Land*, 143.

5. Saikku, 157. I am unsure if love is included as a "natural phenomenon."

6. Saikku, 147.

7. Shaila Dewan, "How Photos Became Icon of Civil Rights Movement," *New York Times*, August 28, 2005, http://www.nytimes.com/2005/08/28/us/how-photos-became-icon-of-civil-rights-movement.html.

8. "Project Completion Report (Appendix F)," Folder: Mississippi Civil Rights Historical Site Grant #2011-012, MDAH, Jackson, MS; Lawrence J. Pijeaux Jr., "Site Visit Assessment and Recommendations for the Emmett Till Memorial Complex," December 2, 2009, Minutes of the ETMC, Binder 2.

9. "Public monuments do not arise as by natural law to celebrate the deserving; they are built by people with sufficient power to marshal (or impose) public consent for their creation." Savage, "The Politics of Memory," 135.

10. Young, *At Memory's Edge*, 95; Young, *The Texture of Memory*, 2.

11. Cobb, *The Most Southern Place on Earth*, 124.

12. "While Mississippi has always been poor, the Delta since its development as a major agricultural center has been an enclave of prosperity for some." Dunbar, *Delta Time*, 15.

13. Brandfon, *Cotton Kingdom of the New South*, 74 (emphasis mine).

14. Saikku, *This Delta, This Land*, 88.

15. Dittmer, *Local People*, 11.

16. Cobb, *The Most Southern Place on Earth*, 131.

17. Cobb, 142, 141. See also Payne, *I've Got the Light of Freedom*, 112.

18. Faulkner, *Dollar Cotton*, 135.

19. Cobb, *The Most Southern Place on Earth*, 316.

20. Cobb, 146.

21. "Race relations differed in the two contexts. In the hills, Blacks and whites were more likely to find themselves in economic competition, and among hill country whites there was little of the Delta's pretense about an aristocratic tradition of race relations. Hill counties were plain mean, and they didn't try to dress it up. Rabid racists like Bilbo tended to be champions of the hills; their crudity was considered an embarrassment in the Delta." Payne, *I've Got the Light of Freedom*, 112.

22. Watts, "On the Levee," 116; Cobb, *The Most Southern Place on Earth*, 67.

23. Cohn, *God Shakes Creation*, 199.

24. Cohn, 287.

25. Cohn, 286.

26. Cohn, 199–200, 201.

27. Cobb, *The Mississippi Delta and the World*, 190; Watts, "On the Levee," 116.

28. Cohn, *God Shakes Creation*, 223.

29. Cohn, 286, 287.

30. Cohn, 280.

31. Cobb, *The Most Southern Place on Earth*, 162.

32. Percy, *Lanterns on the Levee*, 249–69.

33. Percy, 257–58.

34. Percy, 258.

35. Cohn, *God Shakes Creation*, 287.

36. Powdermaker, *After Freedom*, 23–24; Dollard, *Caste and Class in a Southern Town*, 69.

37. Payne, *I've Got the Light of Freedom*, 112.

38. Cohn, *God Shakes Creation*, 201.

39. Powdermaker, *After Freedom*, 29.

40. Percy, *Lanterns on the Levee*, 229–41; Cohn, *God Shakes Creation*, 286.

41. Cobb, *The Most Southern Place on Earth*, 148.

42. Brandfon, *The Mississippi Delta and the World*, 133.

43. Cobb, *The Most Southern Place on Earth*, 62.

44. Payne, *I've Got the Light of Freedom*, 20.

45. Payne, 16.

46. In Payne, 16.

47. Whitaker, "A Case Study in Southern Justice," 13.

48. Cohn, *Where I Was Born and Raised*, 228.

49. Halberstam, "Tallahatchie County Acquits a Peckerwood."

50. Vivian, *Public Forgetting*, 19–38.

51. Faulkner, *Go Down Moses*, 324.

52. Moody, *Coming of Age in Mississippi*, 121, 128.

53. Tyson, *The Blood of Emmett Till*, 58.

54. Till-Mobley and Benson, *Death of Innocence*, 164; see also "Son of Hernando Attorney Recalls 1955 Till Murder Trial," *Greenwood Commonwealth*, May 30, 2005, 12.

55. Whitfield, *A Death in the Delta*, 34.

56. Cobb, *The Most Southern Place on Earth*, 221; see also, Whitfield, *A Death in the Delta*, 34.

57. Arthur Everett, "Hint New Witnesses May Shed More Light on Till Killing," *Jackson Clarion-Ledger*, September 21, 1955, 5.

58. Whitaker, "A Case Study in Southern Justice," 146; Anderson, *Emmett Till*, 92, 100.

59. Whitaker, "A Case Study in Southern Justice," 144; Anderson, *Emmett Till*, 92.

60. Beito and Beito, *Black Maverick*, 127.

61. Huie, *Wolf Whistle*, 28.

62. Whitaker, "A Case Study in Southern Justice," 146.

63. Whitaker, 146.

64. Whitfield, *A Death in the Delta*, 44.

65. Hailman, *From Midnight to Guntown*, 234.

66. Beito and Beito, *Black Maverick*, 127.

67. Beito and Beito, 45.

68. Houck and Grindy, *Emmett Till and the Mississippi Press*, 28–31; Whitaker, "A Case Study in Southern Justice," 122; Whitfield, *A Death in the Delta*, 28; Hailman, *Midnight to Guntown*, 234; Anderson, *Emmett Till*, 60–68.

69. Beito and Beito, *Black Maverick*, 128.

70. Whitten, "Injustice Unearthed," 24.

71. Whitten, 48.

72. Whitten, 25.

73. Anderson, *Emmett Till*, 92.

74. Whitaker, "A Case Study in Southern Justice," 144.

75. Anderson also cites two newspaper accounts of the jury composition. Although these accounts do specify the hometown of each jury member, they are silent on the hills/Delta schism. This leaves Whitaker as the only source for the ideology of the paternalistic Deltan. Anderson, *Emmett Till*, 416n44.

76. Till-Mobley and Benson, *Death of Innocence*, 160, 166.

77. Till-Mobley and Benson, 161.

78. Till-Mobley and Benson, 100.

79. Nelson, *The Murder of Emmett Till*.

80. Beauchamp, *The Untold Story of Emmett Louis Till*.

81. Clotye Murdock, "Land of the Till Murder," *Ebony* 11, no. 6 (April 1956): 91–96.

82. Gurney, *Mississippi Courthouses*, 145–47; Clark Porteous, "Jury Being Chosen in Till Trial," *Memphis Press-Scimitar*, September 19, 1955, 1.

83. In 1902, Sumner beat out the town of Webb as the site of the county's second courthouse. Gurney, *Mississippi Courthouses*, 145.

84. MacLean, *The Past Is Never Dead*, 88.

85. Porteous, "Jury Being Chosen in Till Trial," 1, 4.

86. MacLean *The Past Is Never Dead*, 91; Barton and Leonard, "Incorporating Social Justice," 308.

87. Betty Pearson, telephone conversation with author, October 19, 2015.

88. Clay McFerrin, "Sumner Courthouse Needs Saving," *Sumner Sentinel*, March 8, 2007, 2.

89. Grand Jury Report," Tallahatchie County, Second Judicial District, April 2004, Folder: Community Heritage Preservation Grant #2002-029, MDAH, Jackson, MS.

90. Belinda Stewart Architects, *Tallahatchie County Feasibility Study*, Folder: Community Heritage Preservation Grant #2006-026, MDAH, Jackson, MS (hereafter cited as *Feasibility Study*).

91. Mace, *In Remembrance of Emmett Till*, 73; Barton and Leonard, "Incorporating Social Justice," 308.

92. Barton and Leonard, "Incorporating Social Justice," 308.

93. Jerome Little to Senator Thad Cochran, January 7, 2008, Folder: Community Heritage Preservation Grant #2006-026, MDAH, Jackson, MS (hereafter cited as Little to Cochran).

94. Little understood the purpose of the ETMC was to "keep the taxpayers and the county from bearing the costs to repair the courthouse." Minutes of the ETMC, Binder 1.

95. Clay McFerrin, "Till Commission Ponders Courthouse Plans," *Sun-Sentinel*, September 21, 2006, 1, included in Folder: Community Heritage Preservation Grant #2007-015, MDAH, Jackson, MS.

96. Little to Cochran.

97. Michael Fazio, "Historic Structure Report for the Tallahatchie County Courthouse, Sumner, MS," in Stewart, *Feasibility Study*, in Folder: Community Heritage Preservation Grant #2006-026, MDAH, Jackson, MS.

98. Clark, "Legacy of an Architect," 23, 25.

99. Minutes of the Tallahatchie County Board of Supervisors, book 17, 1971–72, meeting of May 8, 1972; Minutes of the Tallahatchie County Board of Supervisors, book 18, 1972–73, meeting of June 9, 1972.

100. On the square footage, see Richard Dickson, "Area Analysis," in Folder: Community Heritage Preservation Grant #2002-029, MDAH, Jackson, MS.

101. "The Emmett Till Memorial International Site Fact Summary," in Folder: MCRHS Grant #2011-012, MDAH, Jackson, MS.

102. Richard Dickson, conversation with author, Clarksdale, MS, October 5, 2016.

103. Tim Kalich, "What Happened to the Transcript from the Trial of Emmett Till?," *Sun-Sentinel*, February, 24, 2005, 12.

104. Richard M. Dickson to Marvin Doss, Tallahatchie Board of Supervisors, January 25, 2007. Letter in author's possession.

105. Richard M. Dickson, "Historical Restoration and Addition, Tallahatchie County Courthouse, Sumner, Mississippi," January 4, 2006, in Folder: Community Heritage Preservation Grant #2002-029, MDAH, Jackson, MS (hereafter cited as "Historical Restoration and Addition").

106. Richard M. Dickson, "Historical Restoration and Addition."

107. Dickson to Doss, "Acceptance of Payment in Full," February 1, 2007. Release in possession of author. A few years earlier, Dickson was paid $14,444.30 by the MDAH for weatherization work on the exterior of the courthouse. This payment, however, stemmed from a 2002 grant that preceded the earliest thoughts of combining courthouse repair with Till commemoration.

108. Community Heritage Preservation Grant #2006-026, MDAH, Jackson, MS. The final payment to Belinda Stewart Architects was on August 10, 2007.

109. Stewart, *Feasibility Study*, 1.

110. Dickson, conversation with author.

111. Dickson, conversation with author.

112. The *Sun-Sentinel* reports that this was the first meeting of the ETMC. Clay McFerrin, "Supervisors Seek Funds for Sumner Courthouse Work," *Sun-Sentinel*, February 23, 2006. Moreover, this is the first meeting for which formal minutes exist. However, Susan Glisson reports that the commission began in October 2005 with an unrecorded meeting in Charleston.

113. Minutes of the ETMC, Binder 1.

114. Jonathan Tilove, "Murder of Black Teen Still Haunts Miss. Town: Apology May Be Step toward Healing," *Newhouse News Service*, September 30, 2007.

115. Little, oral history interview 1.

116. Little, oral history interviews 1, 12, and 9.

117. Minutes of the ETMC, Binder 1, August, 22, 2007.

118. Jerome G. Little, "Jerome 'G.' Little," William Winter Institute for Racial Reconciliation Collection, Box 3, Folder: Tallahatchie County Historical Marker.

119. MacLean, *The Past Is Never Dead*, 89.

120. Thomason, *Delta Rainbow*, 178.

121. Thomason, 42.

122. Thomason, 44–46.

123. Thomason, 104, 108; Betty Pearson, telephone conversation with author, October 19, 2015; see also the draft of her brief, untitled autobiography. William Winter Institute for Racial Reconciliation Collection, Box 1, Folder: ETMC 2 of 2. Much of the autobiography was later published in Pearson, "Pearson."

124. William Winter Institute for Racial Reconciliation Collection, Box 3, Folder: Tallahatchie County.

125. MacLean, *The Past Is Never Dead*, 89.

126. William Winter Institute for Racial Reconciliation Collection, Box 3, Folder: Tallahatchie County.

127. Barton and Leonard, "Incorporating Social Justice," 315, 314.

128. Quoted In Jubera Drew, "Decades Later, an Apology," *Atlanta-Journal Constitution*, October 2, 2007.

129. Anderson, *Emmett Till*, 351.

130. Minutes of the ETMC, "Notes" Binder; also William Winter Institute for Racial Reconciliation Collection, Box 3, Folder: Tallahatchie County Meeting Minutes.

131. For an up-close account of this conflict, see Thomas and Durant, *Stone of Hope*, 112.

132. Grayson grew up on the Pearson Plantation; Little grew up on the Mitchener Plantation.

133. MacLean, *The Past Is Never Dead*, 149.

134. MacLean speaks to the importance of maintaining the original footprint. *The Past Is Never Dead*, 238.

135. *Feasibility Study*, 47–48. The space now houses the Emmett Till Interpretive Center, the outreach wing of the ETMC.

136. Minutes of the ETMC, Binder 1, May 3, 2010.

137. For a partial list of grant funding, see Minutes of the ETMC, Binder 1, June 9, 2009.

138. MCRHS Grant, #2011-012, MDAH, Jackson, MS.

139. Minutes of the ETMC, Binder 1; *Feasibility Study*, 43.

140. William Winter Institute for Racial Reconciliation Collection, Box 1, Folder: ETMC Bylaws.

141. Minutes of the ETMC, Binder 3, November 29, 2006. See also MacLean, *The Past Is Never Dead*, 150.

142. Minutes of the ETMC, Binder 1, August 22, 2007.

143. Minutes of the ETMC, Binder 1, May 15, 2007.

144. Minutes of the ETMC, Binder 3, November 29, 2006.

145. MacLean, *The Past Is Never Dead*, 150.

146. William Winter Institute for Racial Reconciliation Collection, Box 3, Folder: Tallahatchie County Meeting Minutes. "Text of the Emmett Till Commission's Resolution," *Sun Sentinel*, October 4, 2007, 6.

147. Thomason, *Delta Rainbow*, 179.

148. Anderson, *Emmett Till*, 351.

149. Ron Maxey, "Pain Relief: Sumner Put Aside Resentment to Embrace Civil Rights History," *Memphis Commercial Appeal*, March 20, 2015, 2.

150. MacLean, *The Past Is Never Dead*, 224.

151. Anderson, *Emmett Till*, 351.

152. Little, oral history interview 4.

153. Cobb, *The Most Southern Place on Earth*, 162.

154. This was done by April 4, 2007, on which date he told the ETMC he had revised the document and was now willing to sign. Minutes of the ETMC, Binder 1, April 4, 2007.

155. MacLean, *The Past Is Never Dead*, 235.

156. Audie Cornish, "County Apologizes to Emmett Till Family," *All Things Considered*, National Public Radio, October 2, 2007; quoted in MacLean, *The Past Is Never Dead*, 231.

157. Jordan, *David L. Jordan*, 199. For Freeman info, see Minutes of the ETMC, Binder 1, August 28, 2007.

158. Quoted in Audie Cornish, "County Apologizes to Emmett Till's Family," *All Things Considered*, National Public Radio, October 2, 2007.

159. Worster, *Rivers of Empire*, 5.

160. On hybrids, see Latour, *We Have Never Been Modern*. For a fascinating study of hybrid politics, see Graham, "Steam-Powered Rhetoric."

161. Haraway, *Primate Visions*, 1.

## Chapter Three

1. Richard M. Dickson, "Historical Restoration and Addition," Folder: Community Heritage Preservation Grant #2002-029, MDAH, Jackson, MS (hereafter "Historical Restoration and Addition"). In 2017, the PBS *American Experience* website was completely remade. The pages that Dickson copied are no longer available.

2. Quoted in Harris, "It Takes a Tragedy to Arouse Them," 36.

3. Metress, *The Lynching of Emmett Till*, 3.

4. For examples of cautious (Whitfield) and unchecked (Hudson) versions of the argument, see two works from 1988. Whitfield, *A Death in the Delta*, 85–107; Hudson, "Emmett Till: The Impetus for the Modern Civil Rights Movement."

5. See, for example, Dittmer, *Local People*, 57; Payne, *I've Got the Light of Freedom*, 54; and Mace, *In Remembrance of Emmett Till*, 49.

6. Dickson, "Historical Restoration and Addition."

7. See Mingo Tingle to Richard Dickson, "Plans for the Grant," Folder: Community Heritage Preservation Grant #2002-029, MDAH, Jackson, MS (hereafter "Tingle to Dickson"). See also Richard M. Dickson to Roderick Gordon, September 29, 2006, Folder: Community Heritage Preservation Grant #2007-015, MDAH, Jackson, MS (hereafter "Dickson to Gordon").

8. The application is misfiled. See "Community Heritage Preservation Grant Application Round V," Folder: Community Heritage Preservation Grant #2006-026, MDAH Jackson, MS.

9. Fourteen of seventeen applications were funded in this program. Aileen de la Torre, conversation with author, Jackson, MS, October 3, 2016.

10. Bill Gatlin, "Glendora Cotton Gin, Black Bayou Bridge," September 17, 2010, Folder: "135-GLN-0003, Glendora Gin (Emmett Till Historic Intrepid Center)," Historic Preservation, MDAH, Jackson, MS.

11. Patrick Weems, "Tallahatchie Co. Courthouse Restoration and Implementation of Emmett Till Related Exhibits," October 21, 2016, 23. This is a grant application to the National Park Service; it is in author's possession.

12. David Halberstam called the trial "the first great media event of the civil rights movement." Quoted in Metress, *The Lynching of Emmett Till*, 3.

13. Payne, *I've Got the Light of Freedom*, 152, 155, viii.

14. Dittmer, *Local People*, 130.

15. Anderson, *Emmett Till*, 255; Mace, *In Remembrance of Emmett Till*, 146.

16. Anderson, *Emmett Till*, 255.

17. On the up-again, down-again life of the statue, see Anderson, *Emmett Till*, 255, 453n14. Since Anderson published his book in 2015, the statue has been taken down and erected yet another time. As of November 2017, it stands in Pueblo, Colorado. Jon Pompia, "Statue of King, Till Returns to Site of Former Pueblo Museum," *Pueblo Chieftain*, January 10, 2017, http://www.chieftain.com/news/pueblo/statue-of-king-till-returns-to-site-of-former-pueblo/article_0ac6f1d2-8b43-5088-972b-43264130c161.html.

18. On Till's importance in *Eyes on the Prize*, see, Metress, *The Lynching of Emmett Till*, 3.

19. Hudson, "Emmett Till." 50. Over the years Hudson (now writing as Hudson-Weems) has become increasingly defensive about this claim, insisting wrongly that she alone was responsible for this insight. In 2007, she even claimed to hold the "research rights to Emmett Till." "Civil Rights Speaker Deals Dose of Reality to Community." For further examples, see Hudson-Weems, "Resurrecting Emmett Till," and Hudson-Weems, *Plagiarism*. See also Devery Anderson, *Emmett Till*, 462n17.

20. "Civil Rights Speaker Deals Dose of Reality To Community," 26.

21. Hudson-Weems, *The Definitive Emmett Till*, 179; see also Hudson-Weems, *Plagiarism*, 6.

22. Anderson, *Emmett Till*, 462n17.

23. "Nation Horrified by Murder of Kidnapped Chicago Youth," 9.

24. Wideman, "Looking at Emmett," 24.

25. Wideman, *Writing to Save a Life*, 69.

26. Till-Mobley and Benson, *Death of Innocence*, 139.

27. Robin D. G. Kelley, "Mike Brown's Body: A Meditation on War, Race, and Democracy," April 14, 2016, Lawrence, KS.

28. Roberta Smith, "Should Art That Infuriates Be Removed?," *New York Times*, March 27, 2017, https://www.nytimes.com/2017/03/27/arts/design/emmett-till-whitney-biennial-schutz.html.

29. From the perspective of the ETMC, the controversy has been happily settled. Schutz has traveled to Mississippi, visited with the Till family and local invested parties, and become a supporter of the ETMC's efforts.

30. Harris, "It Takes a Tragedy to Arouse Them," 35.

31. Berger, *For All the World to See*, 108.

32. Quoted in Harris, "It Takes a Tragedy to Arouse Them," 36.

33. Quoted in Wood, *Lynching and Spectacle*, 266.

34. Harold and DeLuca, "Behold the Corpse," 274, 265 (emphasis mine).

35. It would be impossible to document everyone who has made this claim. But, for starters, Hampton, *Eyes on the Prize*; Dittmer, *Local People*, 58; Nelson, *The Murder of Emmett Till*; Wood, *Lynching and Spectacle*; Maurice Berger, *For All the World to See*.

36. "When One Mother Defied America: The Photo That Changed the Civil Rights Movement," *Time*, July 10, 2016, http://time.com/4399793/emmett-till-civil-rights -photography/.

37. Harold and DeLuca, "Behold the Corpse," 276.

38. Quoted in Harold and DeLuca, "Behold the Corpse," 273.

39. Quoted in Williams, *Eyes on the Prize*, 57.

40. Quoted in Harold and DeLuca, "Behold the Corpse," 276.

41. "Suggested Text for One MS Dept. of Archives & History Marker at the Sumner Courthouse," William Winter Institute for Racial Reconciliation Collection, Box 3, Folder: Tallahatchie County—Emmett Till Historic Marker, University of Mississippi, Oxford (hereafter: "Suggested Text").

42. "Suggested Text."

43. Dickson, "Historical Restoration and Addition."

44. Quoted in Clay McFerrin, "Till Commission Ponders Courthouse Plans," *Sun-Sentinel*, September 21, 2006, 1. Included in Community Heritage Preservation Grant #2007-015, MDAH, Jackson, MS.

45. "Grand Jury Report," Tallahatchie County, Second Judicial District, April 2004, Community Heritage Preservation Grant #2002-029, MDAH, Jackson, MS.

46. Memorandum of Agreement, June 6, 2003, Community Heritage Preservation Grant #2002-029, MDAH, Jackson, MS.

47. This trend began with Community Heritage Preservation Grant #2009-016, MDAH, Jackson, MS.

48. "Historical Significance," Community Heritage Preservation Grant #2009-016, MDAH, Jackson, MS.

49. Weems, "Tallahatchie Co. Courthouse Restoration and Implementation of Emmett Till Related Exhibits," 23.

50. "Project Description," Jerome Little to Thad Cochran, January 7, 2008, Community Heritage Preservation Grant #2006-026, MDAH, Jackson, MS.

51. Little, oral history interview 9.

52. T. R. M. Howard, "Terror Reigns in Mississippi: Address of T. R. M. Howard," *Baltimore Afro-American*, October 8, 1955, 6. See also the Howard-informed booklet by Olive Arnold Adams, *Time Bomb*.

53. Beito and Beito, *Black Maverick*, 139.

54. Anderson, *Emmett Till*, 218, 446n75; Till-Mobley and Benson, *Death of Innocence*, xii.

55. Clay McFerrin, "Till Commission Ponders Courthouse Plans," *Sun-Sentinel*, September 21, 2006.

56. Jordan, *David L. Jordan*, 18.

57. Anderson, *Emmett Till*, 446n75.

58. "The Mississippi Freedom Trail" proposal.

59. "MDA Tourism Announces Mississippi Freedom Trail," May 5, 2011. In possession of author.

60. For example, Howard Hollins to Mingo Tingle, October 2, 2009, Community Heritage Preservation Grant #2009-016, MDAH, Jackson, MS.

61. Community Heritage Preservation Grant #2009-016, MDAH, Jackson, MS.

62. "Emmett Till National Site Development," Community Heritage Preservation Grant #2009-016, MDAH, Jackson, MS.

63. William Winter Institute for Racial Reconciliation Collection, Box 3, Folder: Tallahatchie County Meeting Minutes, University of Mississippi, Oxford.

64. Minutes of the ETMC, Binder 1, November 29, 2006.

65. MacLean, *The Past Is Never Dead*, 234.

66. Robinson, conversation with author, November 15, 2016. Quotations from Robinson, "The Murder of Emmett Till."

67. Clay, *Delta Land*, 9.

68. Robinson, conversation with author, November 15, 2016. Maude Schuyler Clay, conversation with author, November 4, 2016. See also Kimberly Krupa, "Black Teen's Death Still Offer's Lesson," *The Courier*, April 18, 2002, http://www.houmatoday.com /news/20020418/black-teens-death-still-offers-lesson.

69. Minutes of the ETMC, undated, Binder: "Notes, Any info that is not a part of the minutes."

70. William Winter Institute for Racial Reconciliation Collection, Box 3, Folder: Tallahatchie County—Emmett Till Historical Marker, University of Mississippi, Oxford.

71. For the mission statement, see Minutes of the ETMC, September 27, 2011, Binder 1. For the bylaws, Minutes of the ETMC, undated, Binder 1.

72. The documentation for the signs in front of Milam's home and the Glendora gin both cite Huie. The signs in front of the Delta Inn, the Sumner courthouse, the Melton murder site, and the Tutwiler Funeral Home cite Whitaker. William Winter Institute for Racial Reconciliation Collection, Box 3, Folder: Tallahatchie County—Emmett Till Historical Marker, University of Mississippi, Oxford.

73. William Winter Institute for Racial Reconciliation Collection, Box 3, Folder: Tallahatchie County—Emmett Till Historical Marker, University of Mississippi, Oxford.

74. Minutes of the ETMC, undated, Binder: "Notes, Any info that is not a part of the minutes."

75. William Winter Institute for Racial Reconciliation Collection, Box 3, Folder: Tallahatchie County—Emmett Till Historical Marker, University of Mississippi, Oxford.

76. William Winter Institute for Racial Reconciliation Collection, Box 3, Folder: Tallahatchie County—Emmett Till Historical Marker, University of Mississippi, Oxford.

77. James Hicks, "Sheriff Kept Key Witness Hid in Jail During Trial," *Cleveland Call and Post*, October 8, 1955.

78. The sign also states, erroneously, that Hicks was "the only reporter to go into the black community to research evidence in the Till case." Robinson told the ETMC this was incorrect, and provided the example of Simeon Booker as evidence.

79. Metress, *The Lynching of Emmett Till*, 154.

80. Minutes of the ETMC, October 24, 2007, Binder 1.

81. Minutes of the ETMC, March 23, 2006, Binder 1.

82. FBI, "Prosecutive Report," 309–11. See Anderson, *Emmett Till*, 427–28; Hendrickson, *Sons of Mississippi*, 310–11.

83. James Featherstone and W. C. Shoemaker, "Verdict Awaited in Till Trial," *Jackson Daily News*, September 23, 1955, 1. On Kellum's long refusal to acknowledge the injustice of the verdict, see Rubin, "The Ghosts of Emmett Till."

84. Brooks, "A Chronicle of Civil Rights Events," n.p.

85. William Winter Institute for Racial Reconciliation Collection, Box 1, Folder: ETMC 1 of 2, University of Mississippi, Oxford.

86. Minutes of the ETMC, June 27, 2006, Binder 1.

87. "Suggested Text."

88. William Winter Institute for Racial Reconciliation Collection, Box 3, Folder: Tallahatchie County—Emmett Till Historical Marker, University of Mississippi, Oxford.

89. Hendrickson, *Sons of Mississippi*, 310–11.

90. William Winter Institute for Racial Reconciliation Collection, Box 3, Folder: Tallahatchie County—Emmett Till Historical Marker, University of Mississippi, Oxford.

91. For a detailed itinerary of the body's movement, see Anderson, *Emmett Till*, 45–49.

92. The uncertainty of placement is recorded in the marginalia of a draft of the sign. The word "location" is surrounded by two question marks next to the draft of the river site sign. William Winter Institute for Racial Reconciliation Collection, Box 3, Folder: Tallahatchie County—Emmett Till Historical Marker, University of Mississippi, Oxford.

93. William Winter Institute for Racial Reconciliation Collection, Box 3, Folder: Tallahatchie County—Emmett Till Historical Marker, University of Mississippi, Oxford.

94. FBI, "Prosecutive Report,", 71.

95. John Herbers, "Cross-Burning at Sumner Went Almost Un-Noticed Yesterday," *Delta Democrat Times*, September 22, 1955, 1. Plater Robinson mailed this article to Susan Glisson.

96. Maude Schuyler Clay, "The Delta Inn," William Winter Institute for Racial Rec-

onciliation Collection, Box 3, Folder: Tallahatchie County—Emmett Till Historical Marker, University of Mississippi.

97. Anderson, *Emmett Till*, 267.

98. Whitten is a collector of war memorabilia. Ward Schafer, "A Sordid History: Manhunt Leader Has History of Violence," *Jackson Free Press*, September 9, 2009, http://www.jacksonfreepress.com/news/2009/sep/09/a-sordid-history-manhunt-leader-has-history-of/.

99. Clay McFerrin, "Sumner's Delta Inn to Disappear," *Sun-Sentinel*, June 16, 2005, 1.

100. "6 Decades Later, Acquittal of Emmett Till's Killers Still Troubles Town," *Morning Edition*, NPR, September 25, 2015, http://www.npr.org/player/v2/mediaPlayer.html?action=1&t=1&islist=false&id=443205842&m=443334582&live=1.

## Chapter Four

1. Ray Tribble has consistently affirmed the jury's decision to acquit the murderers. In 1980, he told documentary filmmaker Rich Samuels that the "jury was right." Samuels, *The Murder and the Movement*. In 1986, he claimed that the body pulled from the river could not be Till's: "The body they displayed was in excess of six feet and Emmett Till was less than five feet tall." Steve Saltzman, "County Candidates Address Voters League," *Greenwood Commonwealth*, March 27, 1986, 2. As recently as 2005, Tribble told the *New York Times Magazine* that the body had hair on its chest, "and everybody knows . . . that blacks don't grow hair on their chest until they get to be about 30." Richard Rubin, "The Ghosts of Emmett Till," *New York Times Magazine*, July 31, 2005, http://www.nytimes.com/2005/07/31/magazine/the-ghosts-of-emmett-till.html?_r=0.

2. Kyle Martin and Genie Alice Via, "Bryant's Grocery: What's in Store?," *Greenwood Commonwealth*, August 29, 2005, 12. On Tribble ownership of Bryant's Grocery, see also Sherri Williams, "Haunted by Murder," *Columbus Dispatch*, August 28, 2005, C2; Bob Darden, "Restoring History," *Leflore Illustrated*, Fall 2013, 22–23. These sources are inconsistent on precisely which siblings own the store.

3. This chapter is not an inquiry into the racial politics of the Tribble family. While the family has owned both buildings since 2002, and for this reason is featured extensively herein, I have neither the ability nor the desire to gauge their racial convictions or their beliefs about the Till murder. On the one hand, it is tempting to assume that, as owners of the property and descendants of an unrepentant juror, the family aims to minimize the bigotry of their patriarch and maximize their profits. Such impressions have been cultivated by rumors of seven-figure price tags circulated by the mainstream media. The family insists that these rumors have no basis. On the other hand, the Tribble family has long expressed willingness to use their property to commemorate Till's murder. In 2004, for example Harry Tribble told the Associated Press that he

wants to turn Bryant's Grocery into a civil rights museum. Lynda Edwards, "Residents of Mississippi Town Say Till Killing Not Often Discussed," *Northwest Indiana Times*, May 17, 2004, http://www.nwitimes.com/news/local/residents-of-mississippi-town-say-till -killing-not-often-discussed/article_1720b867-8062-56eb-b8e2-2ae147616aba.html. Likewise, in 2005, Martin Tribble spoke out against those who would level the ruins. "Some people want me to take a bulldozer to it. I can't do that. It's too important. I respect history." Williams, "Haunted by Murder," C2. After Hurricane Katrina, which inflicted extensive damage on the grocery, the family expressed a desire to stabilize it before more damage was done. Kyle Martin, "Bryant's Grocery Takes a Hit," *Green-wood Commonwealth*, September 9, 2005, 1. Finally, after the once-stolen front doors to Bryant's Grocery were recovered, the family donated them to the MDAH. This chapter, then, will make no comment on the political or racial convictions of the Tribbles. The family appears herein in the role once reserved for the buildings themselves in the forensic tradition: as background to an inquiry whose aims lie elsewhere.

4. A nomination form to include Bryant's Grocery on the Mississippi Heritage Trust's "10 Most Endangered Historic Places 2005" list notes that there is "opposition to the site's preservation": "The opposition comes in the form of the owners [of] the property not willing to restore it or to sell it to some[one] who is interested in restoring it." "Mississippi's 10 Most Endangered Historic Places 2005 Nomination Form," Folder: 083-MNY-002 thru 2008, MDAH, Jackson, MS.

5. James E. Young notes that sites of historical destruction often assume "lives of their own." This has certainly been the case with Bryant's Grocery and Meat Market. Young, *The Texture of Memory*, 120.

6. "Civil rights devotees from all over the world make pilgrimage to Leflore county to see the ramshackle remains of the grocery store where Till let out his fatal wolf whistle." Tim Kalich, "Till Trial about Drama, Not Justice," *Sun Sentinel*, March 23, 2006, 2. As Hariman and Lucaites write in the discussion of ruins, "The ruin is a fragment, a trace, a sign of time's corrosiveness . . . a call to memory." Hariman and Lucaites, *The Public Image*, 127.

7. "Money, Mississippi Historic Storefront Restoration, Phase 1," MCRHS Grant #2011-11, MDAH, Jackson, MS.

8. "Goals and Expectations," "Money, Mississippi Historic Storefront Restoration, Phase 1," MCRHS Grant #2011-11, MDAH, Jackson, MS (hereafter cited as "Goals and Expectations").

9. This is a cumulative figure. On July 22, 2011, the MDAH awarded the project $152,004.80. On January 17, 2014, they increased the amount by $54,536. Both amounts required a 20 percent match.

10. Harry Tribble claimed that it was only his respect for history keeping him from razing the entire building. Williams, "Haunted by Murder," C2.

11. Anderson, *Emmett Till*, 201.

12. For a powerful account of the symbolic and affective complexity of ruins, see Young, *The Texture of Memory*, 119–54.

13. Houck and Grindy, *Emmett Till and the Mississippi Press*, 80, 87.

14. Quoted in Houck and Grindy, 87.

15. Houck and Grindy, 81, 96. See also Houck, Davis, "Unique Defense helped Emmett Till's Killers Get Away With Murder." *Jackson Clarion Ledger*, August 29, 2018.

16. FBI, "Prosecutive Report," 265.

17. Metress, *The Lynching of Emmett Till*, 295.

18. Anderson, "A Wallet, a White Woman, and a Whistle."

19. Anderson, *Emmett Till*, 361–80.

20. Tyson, *The Blood of Emmett Till*, 6. In August of 2018, as this book is going to print, the veracity of the confession is now being questioned. Jerry Mitchell, "Bombshell Quote Missing from Emmett Till Tape. So Did Carolyn Bryant Donham Really Recant?," *USA Today*, August 21, 2018, https://www.usatoday.com/story/news/nation-now/2018/08/21/emmett-till-carolyn-bryant-donham-no-recant-maybe/1057017002/.

21. Samuels, *The Murder and the Movement*.

22. Murdock, "Land of the Till Murder," 91–96.

23. Murdock Larsson, "Land of the Till Murder Revisited," 53–58.

24. Rubin, *Confederacy of Silence*, 11.

25. See a litany of critical review in the *Greenwood Commonwealth*, Rubin's former place of employment. E.g., Tim Kalich, "Memoir Compelling, If Partly Make-Believe," *Greenwood Commonwealth*, July 17, 2002, 1, 12; Tim Kalich, "Nonfiction Supposed to Be Just That," *Greenwood Commonwealth*, July 21, 2002, 4; Susan Montgomery, "Writing of 'a True Tale,'" *Greenwood Commonwealth*, July 17, 2002, 1, 12.

26. Rubin, *Confederacy of Silence*, 179.

27. Rubin, 2.

28. Rubin, 179–80, 9. He moved in the summer of 1988, and visited regularly during the first six months of his stay.

29. Rubin, 179–80.

30. Martin and Via, "Bryant's Grocery: What's in Store?"

31. I reached out to Rubin multiple times by email. Although he once responded and volunteered to speak at the University of Kansas (where I work), he ignored my questions about Bryant's Grocery and quickly stopped responding to my emails.

32. Rubin, *Confederacy of Silence*, 179.

33. Rubin, 179.

34. For this reason, *Remembering Emmett Till* is, in terms of its arrangement, the precise opposite of Anderson's *Emmett Till*. While Anderson refused to allow secondary sources to sully the story of his primary sources, my project is an experiment in what

we can learn when the events of 1955 are placed in the perspective of what has always been considered secondary: the enduring materiality of the Delta.

35. Martin and Via, "Bryant's Grocery: What's in Store?," 1, 12.

36. Carruthers, *The Craft of Thought*, 53.

37. Paul Hendrickson, "Mississippi Haunting," *Washington Post*, February 27, 2000, 6.

38. Hendrickson.

39. In distinction to the forensic tradition, Hendrickson's rhetoric is characterized by an insistent ecomimesis, Timothy Morton's term for a rhetorical style by which an author relentlessly situates his or her story within a surrounding environment. Following Morton still further, *Remembering Emmett Till* might be characterized as a project of ambient poetics, a term Morton uses to describe a "way of reading texts with a view to how they encode the literal space of their inscription." Adapted to memory studies, such an approach asks of every memory practice how it encodes the space of commemoration. Morton, *Ecology without Nature*, 3, 32, 47.

40. Martin and Via, "Bryant's Grocery: What's in Store?," 12.

41. Hendrickson, *Sons of Mississippi*, 12.

42. Else, *True South*, 237–38.

43. Hariman and Lucaites, *The Public Image*, 125.

44. On the affective power of ruins, see Young, *Texture of Memory*, 132, and Hariman and Lucaites, *The Public Image*, 124–29.

45. Richard Rubin, "The Ghosts of Emmett Till," *New York Times Magazine*, July 31, 2005.

46. Robert Jenkins, conversation with author, March 20, 2017.

47. Jerry Mitchell, "Civil Rights-Era Landmark Eyed for Restoration," *Jackson Clarion Ledger*, August 17, 2008, 1A, 9A.

48. Neil Padden, conversation with author, October 30, 2017.

49. Quoted in Jerry Mitchell, "'They just want history to die': Owners Demand $4 million for Crumbling Emmett Till Store," *Jackson Clarion Ledger*, August 29, 2018.

50. Jerry Mitchell, "'Symbol of the Movement' Sits in Ruin; Family Looking for Buyer," *Jackson Clarion Ledger*, February 11, 2007.

51. J'na Jefferson, "Vandals Destroy Sign for Emmett Till on Mississippi Freedom Trail," *Vibe*, June 27, 2017, https://www.vibe.com/2017/06/emmett-till-sign-vandalized/.

52. House Bill 1701 (as Sent to Governor), *Laws of Mississippi* (2010).

53. "Tourism Benefit," "Money, Mississippi Historic Storefront Restoration, Phase 1," MCRHS Grant #2011-11, MDAH, Jackson, MS.

54. "Goals and Expectations."

55. "Project Description," "Money, Mississippi Historic Storefront Restoration, Phase 1," MCRHS Grant #2011-11, MDAH, Jackson, MS.

56. "Existing Conditions," "Money, Mississippi Historic Storefront Restoration, Phase 1," MCRHS Grant #2011-11, MDAH, Jackson, MS (emphasis mine).

57. Darden, "Restoring History," 23.

58. See "In Kind Services," "Money, Mississippi Historic Storefront Restoration, Phase 1," MCRHS Grant #2011-11, MDAH, Jackson, MS.

59. "Money, Mississippi Historic Storefront Restoration, Phase 1," MCRHS Grant #2011-11, MDAH, Jackson, MS.

60. "Goals and Expectations."

61. "Project Narrative," "Money, Mississippi Historic Storefront Restoration, Phase 1," MCRHS Grant #2011-11, MDAH, Jackson, MS.

62. "Goals and Expectations."

63. Beito and Beito, *Black Maverick*, 80; Tyson, *The Blood of Emmett Till*, 87; Payne, *I've Got the Light of Freedom*, 32.

64. Beito and Beito, *Black Maverick*, 80–81.

65. Richard Rubin, *Confederacy of Silence*, 90.

66. Wright, *Simeon's Story*, 84.

67. Wright, 54–55.

## Chapter Five

1. There is some uncertainty as to when the museum and computer lab opened. Some sources indicated 2005. "Emmett Till Historical Center in Glendora Reopens Saturday," *Mississippi Link*, September 23, 2011. I use the 2006 date, as this is the date that hangs in the lobby of the museum.

2. On internet technology in the Delta, see W. Ralph Eubanks, "The Land That the Internet Era Forgot: Equality in the Digital Age," *Wired*, November 17, 2015, https://www.wired.com/2015/11/the-land-that-the-internet-forgot/.

3. "In 2005, the facility became the Thomas Technology Center and Emmett Till Historic Intrepid Center (ETHIC), with a grant from the USDA Broadband Initiative." "Project Narrative," MCRHS grant [unfunded application], Folder: 135-GLN-003, Glendora Gin, ETHIC, May 6, 2011 (hereafter Project Narrative, MCRHS grant), MDAH, Jackson, MS. Thomas confirmed this in personal conversation, December 19, 2016.

4. Eubanks, "The Land That the Internet Era Forgot."

5. "Award summaries for Community Connect Broadband Grant Program 2005," US Department of (USDA), Rural Development, 4, https://www.rd.usda.gov/files/UTP-CCProjectSummaries2005.pdf.

6. Savage, "The Politics of Memory," 135.

7. Kimbell has been a long-rumored part of the murder party. Carolyn Bryant has even suggested that he was involved. See Anderson, *Emmett Till*, 330.

8. Sértő-Radics and Strong, "Empowerment and Ethnic Relations," 17, 61.

9. "Glendora, Mississippi Asset Mapping," Mississippi Development Authority, May 5, 2010 (hereafter cited as "Glendora, Mississippi Asset Mapping").

10. "Executive Summary," Application for Federal Assistance, USDA, May 31, 2005, 1–3, Freedom of Information Act Case No. 2016-RD-04747-F (hereafter "Executive Summary," Application for Federal Assistance, USDA); Thomas and Durant, *Stone of Hope*, 9.

11. "Glendora, Mississippi Asset Mapping."

12. See, for example, Grant, *Dispatches from Pluto*, 4; MacLean, *The Past Is Never Dead*, 18.

13. Patrick Magennis, "Update from Mississippi," *PID Post*, Fall 2014, http://www.pidonline.org/wp-content/uploads/PID-post-fall-20141.pdf.

14. FBI, "Prosecutive Report," 49; Keith Beauchamp, "What Really Happened to Emmett Till?," 4.

15. Mayor Johnny B. Thomas of Glendora, MS, undated, https://www.youtube.com/watch?v=eLkx4ZyatfQ.

16. Thomas and Durant, *Stone of Hope*, 32.

17. Radutzky, "The Murder of Emmett Till"; see also the Linda Beito, unpublished interview with Henry Lee Loggins, July 21, 2005. In author's possession.

18. Thomas and Durant, *Stone of Hope*, 47.

19. "Loggins Seeks Immunity," *Greenwood Commonwealth*, July 9, 2005, 1.

20. On the "stepson" comment, see Beito, unpublished interview with Henry Lee Loggins.

21. "My Father Helped Kill Emmett Till," part 1, interview with Johnny B. Thomas, WeAllBeTV, March 2012, https://www.youtube.com/watch?v=XkthhlDJP5Y; "My Father Helped Kill Emmett Till," part 2, interview with Johnny B. Thomas, WeAllBeTV, December 31, 2012, https://www.youtube.com/watch?v=EqjGHtdDrP8.

22. Thomas and Durant, *Stone of Hope*, 112.

23. Representative Bennie G. Thompson, "Honoring Johnny B. Thomas," speech, US House of Representatives, March 4, 2014, https://the-constituent.com/honoring-johnny-b-thomas-by-representative-bennie-g-thompson/speech/24645.

24. Thomas and Durant, *Stone of Hope*, 46, 129.

25. Huie suggests the body was deposited directly in the Tallahatchie River, 3.5 miles south of the Sharkey Bridge near Glendora. Huie, "Shocking Story of Approved Killing in Mississippi," 49.

26. Beauchamp, "What Really Happened to Emmett Till?"

27. Despite claims of noninvolvement, Thomas did insist publicly that the body was thrown into the bayou, not the river. Radutzky, "The Murder of Emmett Till."

28. Charles "Bubba" Weir, "In Memory of Ike Fowler," eulogy, March 2011. In author's possession.

29. "Connecting Clarksdale to the World: Pilot Program Expands Broadband Internet Access across Coahoma County," *Innovate Mississippi*, 2010.

30. Curtis Anderson (USDA) to Johnny B. Thomas, September 27, 2005, Freedom of Information Act Case No. 2016-RD-04747-F.

31. "Executive Summary," Application for Federal Assistance, USDA.

32. Pat McDonough, then the business development specialist at AbsoCom, doesn't remember anything related to Till. Pat McDonough, conversation with author, August 2, 2017.

33. Charles "Bubba" Weir, conversation with author, June 29, 2017.

34. For the internet predictions, see "Financial Information and Stability," Application for Federal Assistance, USDA, May 31, 2005, 2, Freedom of Information Act Case No. 2016-RD-04747-F. For population decline, see "Glendora, Mississippi Asset Mapping."

35. Kenneth Kuchno (USDA) to the Honorable Johnny B. Thomas, October 3, 2008, Freedom of Information Act Case No. 2016-RD-04747-F. Thomas blames the failures of AbsoCom for the failure of the project. Thomas and Durant, *Stone of Hope*, 118.

36. "Glendora, MS Broadband Budget," Application for Federal Assistance, USDA, May 31, 2005, Freedom of Information Act Case No. 2016-RD-04747-F.

37. Project Narrative, MCRHS grant.

38. Thomas and Durant, *Stone of Hope*, 50.

39. For details on the purchase, forfeiture, and conveyance of the property, see "Local Match, $8,500," October 15, 1999, Freedom of Information Act Case No. 2016-RD-04747-F. For the sweet potato operation, see Sértő-Radics and Strong, "Empowerment and Ethnic Relations."

40. Glendora was required to provide a 15 percent match. Application for Federal Assistance, USDA, May 31, 2005, Freedom of Information Act Case No. 2016-RD-04747-F.

41. Thomas claimed that this figure was "based on comparable value of full-service rental." Johnny B. Thomas to Director ASD, Rural Utilities Service, May 27, 2005, Freedom of Information Act Case No. 2016-RD-04747-F.

42. It is hard to judge whether this was a legitimate complaint or not. According to the timeline submitted by Mayor Thomas to the USDA, the renovation was already months behind schedule when the original contract with Butler was signed. "Scope of Work," Application for Federal Assistance, USDA, May 31, 2005, Section E, Freedom of Information Act Case No. 2016-RD-04747-F.

43. Johnny B. Thomas to Mr. Scott Steiner (USDA), June 23, 2006, Freedom of Information Act Case No. 2016-RD-04747-F; Johnny B. Thomas to Mr. Kenneth Kuchno (USDA), July 3, 2006, Freedom of Information Act Case No. 2016-RD-04747-F.

44. Johnny B. Thomas to Mr. Peter Aimable, Coordinator of Southern Technical Services (USDA), undated, Freedom of Information Act Case No. 2016-RD-04747-F.

45. Blackmon, *Slavery by Another Name*; Alexander, *The New Jim Crow*.

46. "Contract Invoice Number 2," Glendora Economic and Community Development Corporation, undated, Freedom of Information Act Case No. 2016-RD-04747-F.

For Brown as "Glendora librarian," see Patricia Brown to Mayor Thomas, May 27, 2005, Freedom of Information Act Case No. 2016-RD-04747-F. For the admission that the town has no library, see "Extent to Which the Community Center Will Be Used for Educational or Instructional Purposes," Application for Federal Assistance, USDA, May 31, 2005, Freedom of Information Act Case No. 2016-RD-04747-F.

47. Thomas to Kuchno, July 3, 2006.

48. "The town tax base was next to none with the town collecting approximately $220.00 per year in taxes, as a result GECDCO was born." Thomas to Kuchno, July 3, 2006.

49. Thomas and Durant, *Stone of Hope*, 120–21.

50. GECDCO's 2014 990 IRS filing lists $133,614 in revenue, http://www.guidestar .org/. This income came from the Flautt apartments. Johnny B. Thomas, conversation with author, December 20, 2016.

51. Gale Hull, president of Partners in Development, conversation with author, May 24, 2016. The two independent sources on the amount of the contracts are two different employees with Partners in Development. The fact of subminimum wage contracts was confirmed independently by a former museum worker (unconnected to Partners in Development) who wishes to remain anonymous and by the mayor himself. Johnny B. Thomas, conversation with author, December 20, 2016.

52. GECDCO's 2013 and 2014 990 IRS releases list Thomas's income at $20,250. Freedom of Information Act Case No. 2016-RD-04747-F. For average per capita income, see "Glendora, Mississippi Asset Mapping."

53. Photographs of the original museum were archived as part of the MDA Asset Mapping project. "Glendora, Mississippi Asset Mapping."

54. Clay McFerrin, "College Students Join Hands in Glendora," August 14, 2008.

55. Anderson, *Emmett Till*, 10; Till-Mobley and Benson, *The Death of Innocence*, 3.

56. Anderson, *Emmett Till*, 12, 16, and 253.

57. Crowe, *Getting Away with Murder*, 47.

58. Anderson, *Emmett Till*, 42.

59. Anderson, 205.

60. Anderson, 281.

61. On the history of this photograph, see Black and Williams, *Through the Lens of Allen E. Cole*, 58–59.

62. It is unclear what, if anything, was involved in the "tourism program" beyond visiting the ETMC's eight sites. Even with minimal amounts of time spent at each site, driving to all eight would take 90–120 minutes.

63. "Visitors Welcome Center," William Winter Institute for Racial Reconciliation Collection, Box 3, Folder: Tallahatchie County Meeting Minutes, University of Mississippi, Oxford.

64. Minutes of the ETMC, Binder 1, February 13, 2008.

65. For Mayor Thomas's criminal history, see Brooks, "A Chronicle of Civil Rights Events," n.p.

66. Thomas and Durant, *Stone of Hope*, 113.

67. Minutes of the ETMC, February 13, 2008.

68. Kathryn Green, conversation with author, July 31, 2017. For background on the dissension, see Kathryn Green, notes on a June 30, 2010, meeting of the ETMC at Mississippi Valley State University. In the author's possession.

69. Kathryn Green to Tazinski Lee, July 1, 2010. In author's possession.

70. Minutes of the ETMC, Binder 1, March 12, 2008.

71. Formal Proposal and Minutes, March 12, 2007, William Winter Institute for Racial Reconciliation Collection, Box 3, Folder: Tallahatchie County Meeting Minutes, University of Mississippi, Oxford.

72. Johnny B. Thomas, conversation with author, December 20, 2016.

73. Village of Glendora, MS, http://www.glendorams.com/.

74. Bill Gatlin to Johnny B. Thomas, February 23, 2012, Folder: 135-GLN-001-NR, Department of Historic Preservation, MDAH, Jackson, MS.

75. For the gin, see "National Registration of Historic Places Registration Form," Folder: Glendora Cotton Gin, Tallahatchie County, Department of Historic Preservation, MDAH, Jackson, MS (hereafter cited Glendora Cotton Gin, National Register Registration). On the bridge, see "National Register of Historic Places Registration Form," January 25, 2011, Folder 135-GLN-001-NR, Department of Historic Preservation, MDAH, Jackson, MS (hereafter cited as Black Bayou Bridge, National Register Registration).

76. Payne, *I've Got the Light of Freedom*, 122.

77. Westbrook Cotton Gin, National Register of Historic Places, Registration Form, September 21, 2010, https://www.apps.mdah.ms.gov/nom/prop/103097.pdf.

78. "University Mourns the Loss of Dr. Henry Outlaw," Delta State University, February 21, 2015, http://www.deltastate.edu/news-and-events/2015/02/university-mourns-loss-of-dr-henry-outlaw/.

79. Federal/State Partnership Staff, "Remembering Emmett Till and the Spark That Lit the Civil Rights Movement," National Endowment for the Humanities, March 19, 2012, https://www.neh.gov/divisions/fedstate/featured-project/remembering-emmett-till-and-the-spark-lit-the-civil-rights.

80. Luther Brown to Bill Gatlin, email, March 1, 2011, Folder: ETHIC Gin Restoration, Department of Historic Preservation, MDAH, Jackson, MS.

81. Anderson, *Emmett Till*, 377.

82. Bill Gatlin, "Summary of Research," September 17, 2010, Folder: Glendora Cotton Gin, Tallahatchie County, Department of Historic Preservation, MDAH, Jackson, MS.

83. Glendora Cotton Gin, National Register Registration; Black Bayou Bridge, National Register Registration.

84. Bill Gatlin to Jennifer Baughn, addendum, March 1, 2011, Folder: "Emmett Till Historic Intrepid Center Gin Restoration, Town of Glendora, Glendora, Tallahatchie County," Department of Historic Preservation, MDAH, Jackson, MS.

85. "Emmett Till Historic Intrepid Center Gin Restoration," Folder: "Emmett Till Historic Gin Restoration, Town of Glendora," Department of Historic Preservation, MDAH, Jackson, MS.

86. "Glendora, Mississippi Asset Mapping."

87. "Emmett Till Historic Intrepid Center Gin Restoration," Folder: "135-GLN-003, Glendora Gin, Emmett Till Historic Intrepid Center," Department of Historic Preservation, MDAH, Jackson, MS.

88. "Emmett Till Historic Intrepid Center Gin Restoration," Folder: "135-GLN-003, Glendora Gin, Emmett Till Historic Intrepid Center," Department of Historic Preservation, MDAH, Jackson, MS.

89. When Aileen de la Torre resigned her position as grants administrator in December 2016, the MDAH did not fill her position. There is no longer an office dedicated to grant administration.

90. "Glendora to Dedicate New Till Park," *Sun Sentinel*, September 18, 2008.

91. "Emmett Till Historic Intrepid Center Gin Restoration," Folder: "135-GLN-003, Glendora Gin, Emmett Till Historic Intrepid Center," Department of Historic Preservation, MDAH, Jackson, MS.

92. Thompson, "Honoring Johnny B. Thomas."

93. Rep. Bennie G. Thompson—Mississippi District 02, Earmarks, Fiscal Year 2010, https://www.opensecrets.org/politicians/earmarks.php?cid=N00003288.

94. "Emmett Till's Center Re-Opens: The Healing Begins," *The Mississippi Link*, September 29, 2011, http://themississippilink.com/2011/09/29/emmett-tills-center-re-opens-the-healing-begins/.

95. "Town of Glendora," Application for Federal Domestic Assistance, Institute of Museum and Library Sciences, April 1, 2010, Freedom of Information Act Case no. 16-36.

96. "Glendora, Mississippi Asset Mapping."

97. The Delta Media Project, http://thedeltamediaproject.homestead.com/drhaire1.html.

98. "Emmett Till's Center Re-Opens." Davis told me that the computer lab was not part of the renovated space. Davis, email with author, August 25, 2017.

99. Magennis, "Update from Mississippi."

100. Davis, conversation with author, August 25, 2017.

101. Davis, conversation with author, August 25, 2017.

102. FBI, "Prosecutive Report," 64; see also Gatlin, "Summary of Research," 2.

103. Anderson, *Emmett Till*, 377, 482n63.

104. "Prospectus," Delta Media Project, January 2008, 2. In author's possession.

105. Ed Silvera, "Mayor Thomas Shows the Black Bayou Bridge about Emmett Till Murder," Delta Media Project, 2007, https://www.youtube.com/watch?v=FmNum6ZDdyA.

106. See also Thomas and Durant, *Stone of Hope*, 147.

107. Sértő-Radics and Strong, "Empowerment and Ethnic Relations," 20; "Glendora, Mississippi Asset Mapping."

108. "Narrative Statement of Significance," Black Bayou Bridge, National Register Documentation, January 25, 2011, Folder: "135-GLN-001-NR," Department of Historic Preservation, MDAH, Jackson, MS.

109. Brooks, "A Chronicle of Civil Rights Events."

## Conclusion

1. William Winter Institute for Racial Reconciliation Collection, Box 3, Folder: "Tallahatchie County Courthouse," University of Mississippi, Oxford.

2. Clay McFerrin, "Historical Marker Taken from Till Memorial Site," *Sun-Sentinel*, October 30, 2008, 1.

3. Tell, "A Brief Visual History of the Bullet-Riddled Emmett Till Memorial Sign." See also Eubanks and Tell, "For Better or Worse, How Mississippi Remembers Emmett Till"; and "Kevin Wilson Jr. Discovers Bullet-Riddled Emmett Till Sign, Raises Awareness of Racial Injustice," *TISCH* news, October 25, 2016, https://tisch.nyu.edu/grad-film/news/kevin-wilson-jr-discovers-bullet-riddled-emmett-till-sign.

4. Katie Rogers, "Struggling for an Emmett Till Memorial That Withstands Gunshots," *New York Times*, October 24, 2016, http://www.nytimes.com/2016/10/25/us/in-mississippi-struggling-for-an-emmett-till-memorial-that-withstands-gunshots.html; Derek Hawkins, "Emmett Till Was Brutally Slain in 1955. Now, a Sign Marking Where His Body Was Found Is Riddled with Bullet Holes," *Washington Post*, October 24, 2016, https://www.washingtonpost.com/news/morning-mix/wp/2016/10/24/emmett-till-was-brutally-slain-in-1955-now-a-sign-marking-where-his-body-was-found-is-riddled-with-bullet-holes/?hpid=hp_hp-morning-mix_mm-till%3Ahomepage%2Fstory.

5. McFerrin, "Historical Marker Taken from Till Memorial Site," 1.

6. I have heard this argument a number of times, but see Clay McFerrin, "Leaders Should Talk Carefully," *Sun Sentinel*, November 13, 2008, 2.

7. Leon Tubbs, "Supervisor's Words Spoken without Much Forethought about Consequences," *Sun-Sentinel*, November 13, 2008.

8. "Tallahatchie County—Interview with Jerome Little," Interviews 1, 12, and 9, William Winter Institute for Racial Reconciliation, Oxford, MS; McFerrin, "Historical Marker Taken from Till Memorial Site," 1.

9. A bulletproof sign was the original offer made by Lite Brite Neon and accepted by the ETMC in October 2016. At the time of this writing, May 2017, negotiations are

ongoing. A bulletproof sign remains a possibility, although other options are being considered.

10. Ralph Ellison, *Invisible Man*, 36.

11. "NAACP Officials Launch Bitter Attack on State," *Jackson Clarion Ledger*, September 1, 1955, 5; "Find Kidnapped Chicago Boy's Body in River," *Chicago Tribune*, September 1, 1955, 1.

12. FBI, "Prosecutive Report," 118.

13. Huie, "Shocking Story of Approved Killing," 49.

14. FBI, "Prosecutive Report," 71.

15. Huie, "The Shocking Story of Approved Killing in Mississippi," 49.

16. Between the final submission of this manuscript and its copyediting, the ETMC replaced the Graball sign. It stood pristine for thirty-five days before it too was disfigured bullets. Plans are already afoot to replace it again. See Dave Tell, "Till Marker Was Just 35 Days Unshot," *Tallahatchie Sun-Sentinel*, August 9, 2018, 5.

17. For the long history of Graball Landing, I am deeply indebted to Maude Schuyler Clay. See Schuyler Clay, *Delta Land*, 85–93.

# BIBLIOGRAPHY

## Archival Collections

"Glendora, Mississippi Asset Mapping," Mississippi Development Authority, Jackson.

Minutes of the Emmett Till Memorial Commission (ETMC), Glendora, Mississippi.

Minutes of the Tallahatchie County Board of Supervisors, Tallahatchie County Courthouse, Charleston, Mississippi.

Office of Grants Administration, Mississippi Department of Archives and History (MDAH), Charlotte Capers Building, Jackson.

Office of Historic Preservation, Mississippi Department of Archives and History (MDAH), Charlotte Capers Building, Jackson.

Papers of William Bradford Huie, William Charvat Collection of American Fiction, Ohio State University Library, Columbus.

William Winter Institute for Racial Reconciliation Collection, University of Mississippi Archives and Special Collections, Oxford.

## Freedom of Information Act Requests

Case No. 16-36, Institute of Museum and Library Sciences.

Case No. 2016-RD-04747-F, US Department of Agriculture.

## Sources

Adams, Olive Arnold. *Time Bomb: Mississippi Exposed and the Full Story of Emmett Till.* Mound Bayou: Mississippi Regional Council of Negro Leadership, 1956.

Alexander, Michelle. *The New Jim Crowe: Mass Incarceration in the Age of Colorblindness.* New York: New Press, 2012.

Anderson, Carol. *White Rage: The Unspoken Truth of our Racial Divide*. New York: Blooms-
　bury, 2017.

Anderson, Devery S. *Emmett Till: The Murder That Shocked the World and Propelled the
　Civil Rights Movement*. Jackson: University Press of Mississippi, 2015.

———. "A Wallet, a White Woman, and a Whistle: Fact and Fiction in Emmett Till's En-
　counter in Money, Mississippi." *Southern Quarterly* 45, no. 4 (2008): 10–21.

Baldwin, James. *Blues for Mister Charlie*. New York: Dial, 1964.

Barton, Alan W., and Sarah J. Leonard. "Incorporating Social Justice in Tourism Plan-
　ning: Racial Reconciliation and Sustainable Development in the Deep South." *Com-
　munity Development* 41, no. 3 (2010): 298–332.

Beauchamp, Keith A., prod. *The Untold Story of Emmett Louis Till*. Till Freedom Come
　Productions, 2005.

———. "What Really Happened to Emmett Till: A Corrective to the 1956 *Look* Confes-
　sion." Privately circulated paper. Copy in author's possession.

Beito, David T., and Linda Royster Beito. *Black Maverick: T. R. M. Howard's Fight for Civil
　Rights and Economic Power*. Urbana: University of Illinois Press, 2009.

———. "Why It's Unlikely the Emmett Till Murder Mystery Will Ever Be Solved." *His-
　tory News Network*, April 26, 2004. http://hnn.us/articles/4853.html.

Berger, Maurice. *For All the World to See: Visual Culture and the Struggle for Civil Rights*.
　New Haven, CT: Yale University Press, 2010.

Black, Samuel W., and Regennia N. Williams. *Through the Lens of Allen E. Cole: A History
　of African Americans in Cleveland, Ohio*. Kent, OH: Kent State University Press, 2012.

Blackmon, Douglas. *Slavery by Another Name: The Re-Enslavement of Black Americans
　from the Civil War to World War II*. New York: Anchor, 2009.

Blight, David W. *Beyond the Battlefield: Race, Memory, and the American Civil War*. Am-
　herst: University of Massachusetts Press, 2002.

Blue, Bonnie. *Emmett Till's Secret Witness: FBI Confidential Source Speaks*. Park Forest, IL:
　BL Richey Publishing, 2013.

Booker, Simeon. "A Negro Reporter at the Till Trial." *Nieman Reports* 54/55 (Winter
　1999–Spring 2000): 136–37.

Brandfon, Robert L. *Cotton Kingdom of the New South: A History of the Yazoo Mississippi
　Delta from Reconstruction to the Twentieth Century*. Cambridge, MA: Harvard Uni-
　versity Press, 1967.

Brooks, Gwendolyn. "A Bronzeville Mother Loiters in Mississippi. Meanwhile a Mis-
　sissippi Mother Burns Bacon." In *Blacks*, 333–39. Chicago: Third World Press, 1987.

Brooks, S. Anne. "A Chronicle of Civil Rights Events." Unpublished manuscript.

Carruthers, Mary. *The Book of Memory: A Study of Memory in Medieval Culture*. Cam-
　bridge: Cambridge University Press, 2008.

Clark, Janet. "Legacy of an Architect." *Mississippi Magazine*, March/April 1987, 22–26.

Clay, Maude Schuyler. *Delta Land*. Jackson: University Press of Mississippi, 1999.

Cobb, James C. *The Mississippi Delta and the World: The Memoirs of David L. Cohn*. Baton Rouge: Louisiana State University Press, 1995.

———. *The Most Southern Place on Earth: The Mississippi Delta and the Roots of Regional Identity*. New York: Oxford University Press, 1992.

Cohn, David L. *God Shakes Creation*. New York: Harper and Brothers, 1935.

———. *Where I Was Born and Raised*. South Bend: University of Notre Dame Press, 1967.

Crowe, Chris. *Getting Away with Murder: The True Story of the Emmett Till Case*. New York: Dial Books for Young Readers, 2003.

Dattel, Gene. *Cotton and Race in the Making of America: The Human Costs of Economic Power*. Lanham, MD: Ivan R. Dee, 2011.

Dickinson, Greg. *Suburban Dreams: Imagining and Building the Good Life*. Tuscaloosa: University of Alabama Press, 2015.

Dittmer, John. *Local People: The Struggle for Civil Rights in Mississippi*. Urbana: University of Illinois Press, 1994.

Dollard, John. *Caste and Class in a Southern Town*. Madison: University of Wisconsin Press, 1988.

Doss, Erika. *Memorial Mania: Public Feeling in America*. Chicago: University of Chicago Press, 2010.

Dunbar, Tony. *Delta Time: A Journey through Mississippi*. New York: Pantheon Books, 1990.

Dylan, Bob. "The Death of Emmett Till." Recorded July 2, 1962. Lyrics in *Writings and Drawings*, 19. New York: Knopf, 1973.

Ellison, Ralph. *Invisible Man*. New York: Vintage, 1995.

Else, Jon. *True South: Henry Hampton and Eyes on the Prize, the Landmark Television Series That Reframed the Civil Rights Movement*. New York: Viking, 2017.

Eubanks, Ralph W., and Dave Tell, "For Better or Worse, How Mississippi Remembers Emmett Till." *LitHub*, November 2, 2016, http://lithub.com/for-better-or-worse -how-mississippi-remembers-emmett-till/.

Faulkner, John. *Dollar Cotton*. New York: Bantam, 1951.

Faulkner, William. *Go Down Moses*. New York: Random House, 1990.

Federal Bureau of Investigation (FBI). "Prosecutive Report of Investigation Concerning ... Emmett Till, Deceased, Victim." February 9, 2006. www.fbi.gov.

Fivush, Robyn, and Natalie Merrill. "An Ecological Systems Approach to Family Narratives." *Memory Studies* 9, no. 3 (2016): 305–14.

Foucault, Michel. *The Archaeology of Knowledge*. New York: Vintage Books, 2010.

Gillis, John R. "Memory and Identity: The History of a Relationship. In *Commemoration: The Politics of National Identity*, edited by John R. Gillis, 3–24. Princeton, NJ: Princeton University Press, 1994.

Graham, Chelsea. "Steam-Powered Rhetoric." PhD dissertation, University of Kansas, 2016.

Grant, Richard. *Dispatches from Pluto: Lost and Found in the Mississippi Delta*. New York: Simon and Schuster, 2015.

Grossman, James R. *Land of Hope: Chicago, Black Southerners, and the Great Migration*. Chicago: University of Chicago Press, 1989.

Gurney, Bill. *Mississippi Courthouses: Then and Now*. Ripley, MS: Old Timer Press, 1987.

Hailman, John. *From Midnight to Guntown: True Crime Stories from a Federal Prosecutor in Mississippi*. Jackson: University Press of Mississippi, 2013.

Halberstam, David. "Tallahatchie County Acquits a Peckerwood." *The Reporter*, April 19, 1956.

Haraway, Donna. *Primate Visions: Gender, Race, and Nature in the World of Modern Science*. New York: Routledge, 1989.

Hariman, Robert, and John Louis Lucaites. *The Public Image*. Chicago: University of Chicago Press, 2016.

Harold, Christine, and Kevin Michael DeLuca. "Behold the Corpse: Violent Images and the Case of Emmett Till." *Rhetoric and Public Affairs* 8, no. 2 (2005): 263–86.

Harris, Frederick C. "It Takes a Tragedy to Arouse Them: Collective Memory and Collective Action during the Civil Rights Movement." *Social Movement Studies* 5, no. 1 (2006): 19–43.

Hendrickson, Paul. *Sons of Mississippi: A Story of Race and Its Legacy*. New York: Alfred A. Knopf, 2003.

Hoskins, Andrew. "Memory Ecologies." *Memory Studies* 9, no. 3 (2016): 348–57.

Houck, Davis, and Matthew Grindy. *Emmett Till and the Mississippi Press*. Jackson: University Press of Mississippi, 2008.

Hudson, Clenora Frances. "Emmett Till: The Impetus for the Modern Civil Rights Movement." PhD dissertation, University of Iowa, 1988.

Hudson-Weems, Clenora. *The Definitive Emmett Till: Passion and Battle of a Woman for Truth and Intellectual Justice*. Bloomington, IN: AuthorHouse, 2007.

———. *Plagiarism: Physical and Intellectual Lynchings; An Emmett Till Continuum*. Bloomington, IN: AuthorHouse, 2007.

———. "Resurrecting Emmett Till: The Catalyst of the Modern Civil Rights Movement." *Journal of Black Studies* 29, no. 2 (1988): 177–88.

Hughes, Langston. "The Money, Mississippi Blues." In *The Lynching of Emmett Till: A Documentary Narrative*, edited by Christopher Metress, 296–98. Charlottesville: University of Virginia Press, 2002.

Huie, William Bradford. "The Shocking Story of Approved Killing in Mississippi." *Look*, January 24, 1956.

———. "What's Happened to Emmett Till's Killers?" *Look*, January 22, 1957.

———. *Wolf Whistle and Other Stories*. New York: Signet Books, 1959.

Huyssen, Andreas. "Present Pasts: Media, Politics, Amnesia." In *The Collective Memory*

*Reader*, edited by Jeffrey K. Olick, Vered Vinitzky-Seroussi, and Daniel Levy, 430–36. New York: Oxford University Press, 2011.

Johnson, Walter. *River of Dark Dreams: Slavery and Empire in the Cotton Kingdom*. Cambridge, MA: Harvard University Press, 2013.

Johnson, Yvette. *The Song and the Silence: A Story about Family, Race, and What Was Revealed in a Small Town in the Mississippi Delta While Searching for Booker Wright*. New York: Atria Books, 2017.

Jordan, David L. *David L. Jordan: From the Mississippi Cotton Fields to the State Senate, A Memoir*. With Robert L. Jenkins. Jackson: University Press of Mississippi, 2014.

King, Stephen A., and Roger Davis Gatchet. "Marking the Past: Civil Rights Tourism and the Mississippi Freedom Trail." *Southern Communication Journal* 83, no. 2 (2018): 103–18.

Landsberg, Alison. *Prosthetic Memory: The Transformation of American Remembrance in the Age of Mass Culture*. New York: Columbia University Press, 2004.

Latour, Bruno. *Reassembling the Social: An Introduction to Actor-Network-Theory*. New York: Oxford University Press, 2007.

———. *We Have Never Been Modern*. Translated by Catherine Porter. Cambridge, MA: Harvard University Press, 1993.

Little, Jerome G. Twenty-four oral history interviews. William Winter Institute for Racial Reconciliation, August 2006. https://vimeo.com/album/1669654/.

Lorde, Audre. "Afterimages." *Cream City Review* 17, no. 2 (Fall 1981): 119–23.

Mace, Darryl. *In Remembrance of Emmett Till: Regional Stories and Media Responses to the Black Freedom Struggle*. Lexington: University of Kentucky Press, 2014.

MacLean, Harry N. *The Past Is Never Dead: The Trial of James Ford Seale and Mississippi's Struggle for Redemption*. New York: Basic Civitas Books, 2009.

Massey, Doreen. *Space, Place and Gender*. Minneapolis: University of Minnesota Press, 1994.

Metress, Christopher, *The Lynching of Emmett Till: A Documentary Narrative*. Charlottesville: University of Virginia Press, 2002.

———. "Truth Be Told: William Bradford Huie's Emmett Till Cycle." *Southern Quarterly* 45, no. 4 (2008): 48–75.

Monteith, Sharon. "The Murder of Emmett Till in the Melodramatic Imagination: William Bradford Huie and Vin Packer in the 1950s." In *Emmett Till in Literary Memory and Imagination*, edited by Harriet Pollack and Christopher Metress, 31–52. Baton Rouge: Louisiana State University Press, 2008.

Moody, Anne. *Coming of Age in Mississippi*. New York: A Laurel Book, 1976.

Morris, Willie, and David Rae Morris. *My Mississippi*. Jackson: University Press of Mississippi, 2000.

Morrison, Toni. "Dreaming Emmett." Premiere at Marketplace Theatre, Albany, New York, January 4, 1986.

Mortimer-Sandilands, Catriona, and Bruce Erickson, eds. *Queer Ecologies: Sex, Nature, Politics, Desire*. Bloomington: Indiana University Press, 2010.

Morton, Timothy. *The Ecological Thought*. Cambridge, MA: Harvard University Press, 2012.

———. *Ecology without Nature: Rethinking Environmental Aesthetics*. Cambridge, MA: Harvard University Press, 2009.

Moye, Todd. *Let the People Decide: Black Freedom and White Resistance Movements in Sunflower County, 1945–1986*. Chapel Hill: University of North Carolina Press, 2004.

Nelson, Stanley, prod. *The Murder of Emmett Till: The Brutal Killing That Mobilized the Civil Rights Movement*. Firelight Media, 2002.

Nora, Pierre. "Between Memory and History: *Les Liexu de Memorie*." *Representations* 26 (1989): 7–24.

———. "Reasons for the Current Upsurge in Memory." In *The Collective Memory Reader*, edited by Jeffrey K. Olick, Vered Vinitzky-Seroussi, and Daniel Levy, 437–41. New York: Oxford University Press, 2011.

Nordan, Lewis. *Wolf Whistle*. Chapel Hill, NC: Algonquin Books, 1993.

Olick, Jeffrey K., and Joyce Robbins. "Social Memory Studies: From 'Collective Memory' to the Historical Sociology of Mnemonic Practices." *Annual Review of Sociology* 24 (1998): 105–40.

Payne, Charles M. *I've Got the Light of Freedom: The Organizing Tradition and the Mississippi Freedom Movement*. Berkeley and Los Angeles: University of California Press, 2007.

Pearson, Betty. "Betty Pearson." In *Pieces of the Past: Voices of Heroic Women in Civil Rights*, edited by Joan H. Saddoff, 17–34. New York: Tasora Books, 2011.

Percy, William Alexander. *Lanterns on the Levee: Recollections of a Planter's Son*. Baton Rouge: Louisiana State University Press, 2013.

Pollack, Harriet, and Christopher Metress, eds. *Emmett Till in Literary Memory and Imagination*. Baton Rouge: Louisiana State University Press, 2008.

Powdermaker, Hortense. *After Freedom: A Cultural Study in the Deep South*. New York: Athenaeum, 1968.

Radutzky, Michael, prod. "The Murder of Emmett Till." *60 Minutes*. CBS, October 24, 2004.

Raines, Howell. *My Soul Is Rested: Movement Days in the Deep South Remembered*. New York: Penguin Books, 1983.

Robinson, Plater, and Loretta Williams. "The Murder of Emmett Till." Laurel, MD: Soundprint Media, 1996.

Romano, Renee C., and Leigh Raiford, eds. *The Civil Rights Movement in American Memory*. Athens: University of Georgia Press, 2002.

Rubin, Richard. *Confederacy of Silence: A True Tale of the New Old South*. New York: Atria Books, 2002.

Saikku, Mikko. *This Delta, This Land: An Environmental History of the Yazoo-Mississippi Floodplain*. Athens: University of Georgia Press, 2005.

Samuels, Rich, writer. *The Murder and the Movement*. WMAQ-Channel 5, Chicago, 1985.

Savage, Kirk. "The Politics of Memory." In *Commemorations: The Politics of National Identity*, edited by John R. Gillis, 127–49. Princeton, NJ: Princeton University Press, 1994.

———. *Standing Soldiers, Kneeling Slaves: Race, War, and Monument in Nineteenth-Century America*. Princeton, NJ: Princeton University Press, 1997.

Scott, James C. *Domination and the Arts of Resistance: Hidden Transcripts*. New Haven, CT: Yale University Press, 1992.

Senda-Cook, Samantha, Michael K. Middleton, and Danielle Endres. "Interrogating the Field." In *Text + Field: Innovations in Rhetorical Method*, edited by Sara L. McKinnon, Robert Asen, Karma R. Chavez, and Robert Glenn Howard, 1–21. University Park: Pennsylvania State University Press, 2016.

Sértő-Radics, István, and John Strong. "Empowerment and Ethnic Relations: A Comparative Study of Hungarian Roma and African Americans in Selected Rural Communities." Unpublished manuscript, 2004.

Soja, Edward W. *Postmodern Geographies: The Reassertion of Space in Critical Social Theory*. Brooklyn, NY: Verso, 1989.

Stigler, Elizabeth J. "Cooking Up Resistance: Exploring Czech Identity in Cook County through Co-Culinary Oral Histories." PhD dissertation, University of Kansas, 2018.

Taylor, Jessica, "'We're on Fire': Oral History and the Preservation, Commemoration, and Rebirth of Mississippi's Civil Rights Sites." *Oral History Review* 42, no. 2 (September 2015): 2311–54.

Tell, Dave. "A Brief Visual History of the Bullet-Riddled Emmett Till Memorial Sign." *Reading the Pictures*, November 15, 2016, https://www.readingthepictures.org/2016 /11/emmett-till-bullet-riddled-memorial-sign/.

———. "Can a Gas Station Remember a Murder?" *Southern Cultures* 23, no. 3 (Fall 2017): 54–61.

———. *Confessional Crises and Cultural Political in Twentieth-Century America*. University Park: Penn State University Press, 2013.

Till-Mobley, Mamie, and Christopher Benson. *The Death of Innocence: The Story of the Hate Crime That Changed America*. New York: Random House, 2003.

Thomas, Johnny B., and Thomas J. Durant Jr. *Stone of Hope: Rising above Slavery, Jim Crow, and Poverty in Glendora, Mississippi*. Lexington, KY: Durant Publishing Company, 2017.

Thomason, Sally Palmer, with Jean Carter Fisher. *Delta Rainbow: The Irrepressible Betty Pearson*. Jackson: University Press of Mississippi, 2016.

Tyson, Timothy B. *The Blood of Emmett Till*. New York: Simon and Schuster, 2017.

Upton, Dell. *What Can and Can't Be Said: Race, Uplift, and Monument Building in the Contemporary South*. New Haven, CT: Yale University Press, 2015.

Vivian, Bradford. *Public Forgetting: The Rhetoric and Politics of Beginning Again*. University Park: Pennsylvania State University Press, 2010.

Wagner, Terry. "America's Civil Rights Revolution: Three Documentaries about Emmett Till's Murder in Mississippi (1955)." *Historical Journal of Film, Radio and Television* 30, no. 2 (2010): 187–201.

Wakefield, Dan. "Justice in Sumner: Land of the Free." *The Nation* 181, no. 14 (October 1, 1955): 284–85.

Watts, Rhonda Lee Mullen. "On the Levee: The Literary Legacy of William Alexander Percy." PhD dissertation, Georgia State University, 1996.

Whitaker, Hugh Stephen. "A Case Study in Southern Justice: The Emmett Till Case." Master's thesis, Florida State University, 1963.

Whitfield, Stephen J. *A Death in the Delta: The Story of Emmett Till*. New York: Free Press, 1988.

Whitten, Ellen. "Injustice Unearthed: Revisiting the Murder of Emmett Till." Undergraduate honors thesis, Rhodes College, 2005.

Wideman, John Edgar. "Looking at Emmett." In *In Fact: The Best of Creative Nonfiction*, edited by Lee Gutkind, 24–48. New York: W. W. Norton, 2004.

———. *Writing to Save a Life: The Louis Till File*. New York: Scribner, 2016.

Wilkerson, Isabel. *The Warmth of Other Suns: The Epic Story of America's Great Migration*. New York: Vintage Books, 2011.

Williams, Juan. *Eyes on the Prize: America's Civil Rights Year, 1954–1965*. New York: Viking Press, 1987.

Wood, Amy Louise. *Lynching and Spectacle: Witnessing Racial Violence in America, 1890–1940*. Chapel Hill: University of North Carolina Press, 2009.

Worster, Donald. *Rivers of Empire: Water, Aridity, and the Growth of the American West*. New York: Oxford University Press, 1985.

Wright, Simeon, with Herb Boyd. *Simeon's Story: An Eyewitness Account of the Kidnapping of Emmett Till*. Chicago: Lawrence Hill Books, 2010.

Young, James. *At Memory's Edge: After-Images of the Holocaust in Contemporary Art and Architecture*. New Haven, CT: Yale University Press, 2000.

———. "The Memorial's Arc: Between Berlin's *Denkmal* and New York City's 9/11 Memorial." *Memory Studies* 9, no. 3 (2016): 325–31.

———. *The Stages of Memory: Reflections on Memorial Art, Loss, and the Spaces Between*. Amherst: University of Massachusetts Press, 2016.

———. *The Texture of Memory: Holocaust Memorials and Meaning*. New Haven, CT: Yale University Press, 1994.

# INDEX

*Pages in italics refer to illustrations.*

# ALBANY

# ALBANY

by

# Laura Black

III

cop. I

St. Martin's Press
New York

Library of Congress Cataloging in Publication Data

Black, Laura.
  Albany.

  I. Title.
PR6052.L32A79   1984        823'.914        84-11729
ISBN 0-312-01708-1

First published in Great Britain by Hamish Hamilton Ltd.


10 9 8 7 6 5 4 3 2

# ALBANY

# 1

I said goodbye to my Aunt Sophia, in the doorway of the modest house where I had lived all my life. I was going away, for almost the first time; I was going, it seemed, to no modest house but an immodest castle. I was going from Millstounburn, near Dalkeith in East Lothian, in the Lowlands of Scotland, to a place much further away than I had ever travelled, in the high bare country of West Perthshire, more unfamiliar to me than the landscape of the moon, which I had at least seen.

Aunt Sophia would have come with me – she had been most cordially invited – but all manner of local obligations, of a tiny kind, seemed to her tender conscience to keep her at home. Old Eppie Tainsh, now quite blind, had to be read to, from the Old Testament or from the sermons of the Covenanting Saints, twice a week; and she could tolerate no voice except Aunt Sophia's. The feckless Johnston family, said to be settled tinkers, had to be visited, and their running-nosed swarms of children inspected for signs of infectious disease. Such was a large part of Aunt Sophia's life; most of the rest, for most of my life, had been me. Consequently it was a difficult parting for us both. My gentle aunt fought to hold back her tears, and looked for a time to be succeeding. I wept also, not at our separation, which was temporary, but at her weeping. Tears were to me as infectious as yawns – as infectious as the many diseases which Aunt Sophia detected among the Johnston children.

There was a deferential cough in the middle distance, bringing to an end farewells which might otherwise have gone on until night.

The cough came from Miss Grizelda Hamilton, the stately and gorgeous elderly lady who was to be my companion on

1

the journey. Lady Lochinver, my shortly-to-be hostess, would have come herself, Miss Hamilton said, but could not, for domestic reasons. Miss Hamilton was her ladyship's companion and confidante. Miss Hamilton sent her ladyship's most profound regrets and apologies; Miss Hamilton herself apologized, in florid language and at length, for subjecting me to so humble and inadequate a substitute. This was so ridiculous, and so astonishing, that I think my mouth inelegantly gaped open. I did not, fortunately, laugh, which would have been still more inelegant, and horridly rude to Miss Hamilton.

Miss Hamilton stood by the travelling-carriage which Lady Lochinver had sent for me. Its door was open and its steps down. The coachman was on his box; one footman stood by the horses' heads, and one by the carriage door. The varnish and brass of the carriage blazed in the moderate spring sunshine so as to hurt the eye, and so did all the buttons and buckles on the liveries of the men, and so did the pendants and lockets with which Miss Hamilton was hung about (in that year of 1865 it was not fashionable to be austere in personal decoration).

'At your convenience, Ma'am,' said Miss Hamilton, in a tone which marvellously combined humility with impatience.

Ma'am? Me?

I was not Ma'am to anybody. I was Leonora Albany, almost penniless, not quite eighteen years old. I was Leo to my friends, and Nora to Aunt Sophia. I was nobody. I did not particularly like being a nobody, but I had been one all my life, and I was used to it. I had expected to remain a nobody. I had been, for nearly eighteen years, quite, quite sure that I should die as much a nobody as I had lived. So to be addressed as 'Ma'am' by a fashionable silken lady – to be curtseyed to so reverently that the lady's forehead almost brushed the ground, like that of an Arab at his prayers . . .

By the front door of Millstounburn House, there was a tall window, giving on to the dark little hallway. In it, on a bright day, one could see oneself vividly reflected. Whenever I left the house (whenever, that is to say, I remembered) I glanced at myself in this convenient mirror, not altogether out of vanity, but also to make sure that my hat was straight, and that I was not wearing odd gloves. Out of habit I did so now,

2

and saw the familiar reflection which was so far from deserving to be called 'Ma'am'. I was, for a start, too small to be addressed so worshipfully – a full six inches shorter than dear beanpole Aunt Sophia (which made our parting · embraces awkward) and shorter by still more inches than the stately Miss Hamilton. I had been told, recently and often, that my face and figure passed muster, to put it most mildly: probably this was bad for a very ignorant seventeen-year-old, but I cannot pretend I found it disagreeable. Also I was obliged to agree.

There was, to be sure, an oddity about my face, besides its reported capacity to pass muster: it was one which people were often in the way of supposing they had seen before. Perfect strangers fancied that they recognized me, when there was no possibility that they had ever clapped eyes on me. In the middle of Edinburgh, in Prince's Street, only a fortnight previously, a middle-aged gentleman in important clothes had raised his hat to me, in a curious uncertain way, as though he was sure he knew me, and must therefore out of politeness salute me, although he had no idea who I was. I was by this time no longer surprised by this oddity; by this time I knew why my face was so familiar to so many. I had been familiar to Lady Lochinver, and Edgar Smith, and Simon Donaldson, and the Barone Lodovico di Vigliano, all the strange persons who had entered my life and were about to transform it; it had been instantly familiar to Miss Grizelda Hamilton, and caused her to perform a curtsey which would have done credit to an acrobat.

My clothes were respectable – they were the very best I had – but in terms of Miss Hamilton and of the glittering carriage they did *not* pass muster. I had been told that all that would be put right. Lady Lochinver would equip me for my new station in life; dressmakers would fight to adorn me, as an advertisement for their skill and taste. This not because of what I looked like, but because of what I was.

I was far from having grown used to it all. I was far from grasping what was happening to me.

By dint of further coughs, Miss Hamilton levered me away from Aunt Sophia's renewed embraces, and I was at length handed up into the carriage. Miss Hamilton followed me in; the steps were raised and the door closed. Miss Hamilton

3

seemed almost reluctant to sit, as though it was taking an outrageous liberty to sit herself in my presence. Everything was topsy-turvy.

Our journey was something over eighty miles, as the roads looped, going by Edinburgh, Stirling, Callander and Lochgrannomhead. We spent a night on the way in the tall, dismal house of persons I did not meet. It seemed they were away from home, but their servants were charged to treat us (me, at least) like royalty. I found this arrangement extraordinary, but Miss Hamilton said that it was Lady Lochinver's decision, and that it was wisest and safest.

Safest? Why should I not be safe?

Well, there came indeed a moment when I was not very safe, and not at all dignified, and by an irony it came about as a consequence of the strange precautions Lady Lochinver had taken. For if I had not been in that tall, depressing, silent house, among tall, depressing, silent servants, I would probably not have felt impelled to go in the early morning for a solitary walk in the park: and so I would not have seen a man who, with quite a small pony, was trying to drag a tree-root out of the ground. He was a wizened little man with a fringe of red beard, and one of his eyes was bloodshot. The task was very evidently beyond the pony's strength, and the man sought to give the poor beast extra power by whipping it mercilessly with a long plaited leather whip, tipped, as I saw in the early sunshine, with inches of metal. The man was in a blind rage, with the pony, and with the tree-stump, and with the task he had been set.

Dear Aunt Sophia used to lament my headstrong impetuosity, which had got me into numberless scrapes and even, when I was small, a good many fights. I did not mean to do rash and ill-judged things, but found myself carried forward by my own fury, as though by a bolting horse.

So it was this time.

I screeched at the man, not at all in the manner of a female addressed as 'Ma'am': I screeched that he was cruel and stupid, and that he was punishing his beast for his own stupidity, which was quite true, but imprudent.

What happened next would not have happened, except that he was senseless with rage. He turned, and raised the whip, to use it on me. But I was very nimble on my feet, and dodged

4

behind the poor pony, so that the wretched beast received yet another blow. By instinct, and not thinking of the horrid possible consequences, I caught hold of the whiplash, and tugged at it, just at a moment when the man's grip had slackened with the completion of his blow. I twitched the whip out of his fingers, and in a second had the handle in my own hand. And then I did what I should not have done – I raised the whip to strike him: and he wailed and fled, which I had not expected. I had heard that all bullies were cowards; this one was only a little man, but he was a great bully and a great coward.

So I untied the pony's traces from the tree-stump, and using them as reins I rode the little beast most of the way back to the house. I found that I could not stay on, riding side-saddle without a saddle, so I rode astride, which I had never done before, and which was gravely indecorous, because my skirt was about my waist. But I was sure that, at so early an hour, there was nobody to see me; and, having been made a present of a pony, I could not resist riding it.

When I walked, scarlet-faced and dishevelled, into the house, I found that I was still holding the villainous whip. This was not the least of my mistakes. I walked into a dreadful silence of waiting servants, and a volley of horrified coughs from Miss Grizelda Hamilton. Nothing was said about my escapade, and I said nothing. I thought that, most likely, the folk in the house would never hear of it; the man would keep quiet about his cruelty and cowardice, and his master would find him another whip, and the pony would trot home. I did not guess what frightful consequences my rashness would have.

By and by we resumed our journey, and the country changed from Lowland to Highland, and I looked with awe and delight at bigger hills than I had ever seen; and we came at last into a great glen, which was Glen Alban; and in its midst, high above a river, to a great castle, which was Glenalban Castle. And it was no coincidence that the obscure Miss Leonora Albany, scarce out of the schoolroom, should be come to a place almost of her own name: for glen and castle and girl came all by their names from the same source, and that was why I was there (though, after the events of the morning, I was very nearly not there).

5

The glen was so grandly beautiful that it made my heart leap. The castle was so ancient and enormous that it made my heart sink into my boots. It was not a house but a medieval walled city, set on a crag for defence, towered and moated, so that one looked for regiments of archers on the battlements, and listened for the sound of drums and trumpets.

The carriage rattled over the drawbridge (which Miss Hamilton told me, to my disappointment, could no longer be raised and lowered) into a great courtyard, from which rose a flight of broad stone steps to an enormous door. At the foot of the steps I saw to my delight my friend and benefactress, the cheerful Lady Lochinver. I jumped down from the carriage the moment the steps were lowered, and hurried across the courtyard to greet and to thank her.

Her curtsey was as low as Miss Hamilton's.

By the steps stood a piper, in full Highland dress. His plaid I recognized as the Royal Stuart tartan, which I had seen in ceremonies in Edinburgh. He began to play, as I reached the foot of the steps, and his tune was that great Jacobite air *Charlie is my Darling*.

And a magnificent person in livery, bearing a staff, led me up the steps and through the door. And in a hall as large as a church a squadron of servants stood, and the men bowed so that they were bent double, and the women curtseyed so that they were all, like Miss Hamilton, Arabs at their prayers.

All this, for me.

It was as though I owned the castle: as though I were queen.

I did. I was.


My father never had any money to speak of. He never owned Millstounburn, but was tenant of some benevolent cousins in Australia, who did not need it, nor wish to sell it, nor desire to make any money out of it, and so let it to their impoverished kinsman at a peppercorn rent. The obligation on our side was to maintain the property decently: which, because it was small and solid, was seldom a heavy imposition.

My parents were wildly mismatched, but, as often happens, deeply devoted – either in spite of the differences between them, or because of them. My father was by all accounts a man strong in courage and gaiety, and weak in prudence; but my knowledge of him was all hearsay, for he fell from his horse and broke his neck when I was only two years old. I understood that the manner of his death was typical of his life: he was attempting an impossible leap, over the iron fence of a railway crossing, for a wager.

It seemed that my mother was, in total contrast, a good and frugal manager, but timorous both physically and socially. She was also an invalid, confined to sofa or bed as far back as I can remember.

It would have been good if I had inherited my mother's prudence with my father's courage; but it seemed I had not.

After my father's death, my mother's unmarried sister, Sophia Grant, came to live at Millstounburn, to keep house, to cherish the invalid, and to bring me up. Poor Aunt Sophia! As gentle and frugal as my mother, but without her competence; as enthusiastic as my father, but without any of his courage – I loved her deeply and dearly, and my gratitude to her was bottomless, but she was not the ideal custodian of a child prone to whim and wildness.

When I was seven, my mother fell seriously ill; and soon after my eighth birthday she died. Aunt Sophia and I were both heartbroken: but Mamma's death released Aunt Sophia to the charitable works in which she was thereafter indefatigable; and it released me to run wilder even than before.

We were oddly placed. We were of a class with the neighbouring lairds, and we were considered by the country folk – and considered ourselves – a class above the rich Edinburgh tradesmen who had bought places in the countryside. Yet we hardly mixed with the families of the lairds, nor yet with those of the tradesmen, because we could not afford to return their hospitality. It was a simple matter of money. Our neighbours were a purse-proud lot (it was a purse-proud age) and Aunt Sophia and I could not compete with them. She, to be sure, did not want to. I would dearly have loved to. I would dearly have loved silk gowns and jewels and parties, and I had none of these things. I did have a sound roof over my head, and a sufficiency of food. (That was highly important. I could have suffered without any qualm a bucket in my bedroom, to catch drips from a hole in the roof: but, active as I was, I could never have survived without enough to eat. My appetite

7

amazed Aunt Sophia, and even myself, because I ate like an elephant, yet I was always as slim as a little boy; approaching my eighteenth birthday, my body had belatedly developed into a woman's, in all particulars, but I was still very slim, with small bones, and a waist about which I could almost put my spread hands.)

A consequence of our embarrassment was that I made friends where I found them. They were a raggle-taggle lot, and I was and remain grateful for the high times I had with them. Benjie Balfour the poacher's son taught me most, and got me into deepest trouble. And it was the daughter of the Wee Free Minister in Dalkeith who taught me, long before I should have known, about men, and women, and the making of babies, and the joys and perils thereof. I wondered then how she knew so much, and I wonder still . . .

Though we had only a very small income, paid quarterly by Trustees in Edinburgh, we did have some choice possessions, relics of my father and of his forbears. There were swords with gilded hilts, pictures, pieces of old furniture. There were in the attic trunks of papers, well-preserved but as far as we could see without interest or value. At times of crisis – they occurred once a year or so – things were sold. In this connection, we had the good fortune that Aunt Sophia was acquainted with a Mr David Maitland, an antiquarian of Edinburgh, a man of scholarship and scrupulous honesty, who maintained a cele-brated shop in Prince's Street. He had been out to Millstoun-burn to appraise some of the contents of the place. He said that, when the time came for him to retire from his shop, he should make a serious search amongst the papers in the trunks in our attic, for there might be matter there of historical value. When we were obliged to sell something, it was he who sold it for us, and I believe that he did not withhold his usual commission.

On a November day (which turned out, in ultimate con-sequence, so very fateful) the roof did suddenly begin to leak, so that plaster came down from a bedroom ceiling, and buckets were all over the floor. It seemed that, in a gale, a branch had broken slates and the battens on which they rested, and that the necessary repairs would be more consider-able than we had at first supposed. It was not a thing which could be ignored, nor yet postponed, because of the further

8

expensive damage that would be done. A price for the work was given to us. Aunt Sophia almost swooned, and I was solemn. From our regular income the cost could not possibly be met, and we did not receive another instalment until the New Year, and the Trustees could not or would not give us any sums in advance.

Another sale, then, to or through Mr David Maitland. So much had already gone! There were darker oblongs on the walls, where pictures had hung, and gaps in the furnishings of rooms, where tables or chests or chairs had stood. All that remained was the more beloved, and losing more household gods would have been like losing teeth or limbs.

And then I remembered the sword, which had lain for some forgotten reason always in a cowhide trunk in the attic, with the dustiest and most repellent of the hoarded papers. It had a silver scabbard – surely not valueless, we thought – and a hilt of unusual design, and the blade was engraved with indecipherable words in what seemed a foreign tongue. The sword had been handed down through the generations, and with it a scrap of its history, which my mother had had from my father, and Aunt Sophia from my mother, and I from Aunt Sophia: my great-grandmother had brought the sword back with her from France in 1770, because it had meant something of importance to her. It meant something of importance to us, too – it would pay for mending the hole in the roof, and replastering the ceiling of the ruined bedroom. Off it went accordingly to Mr David Maitland, and he acknowledged receipt by return of post, and undertook to find a purchaser at an equitable price.

Scarcely had the sword gone on display in Mr Maitland's shop, than it produced for us a visitor. Visitors of any sort were rare at Millstounburn, and threw Aunt Sophia into a flutter, so that she bleated of refreshments, and looked as though she wanted to run away. This one was not like any we had ever entertained – not at all like the doctor, or the representative of the Edinburgh Trustees, or the Episcopalian Minister, or any of the charitable ladies with whom Aunt Sophia was in league or in rivalry. He was a big, plump man, approaching the middle of his middle age (I could not be more exact than that), smooth-shaven and with a glossy look, as

9

though polished with a leather by a servant; his manner was gentlemanly – Aunt Sophia described him afterwards as 'urbane', which I thought a good word, and one I had never before heard her use, and did not know she knew. Our visitor's face, which was somewhat moonlike, was not unhandsome, and not at all displeasing, except that it was disfigured by a purple birthmark beside his left ear: not large, but impossible not to notice, being livid in colour, and resembling in outline the silhouette of a flying bird.

It was one of those things which you do not know whether to look at, or look away from – to pretend not to see, or to show that you have seen and do not mind. At least I, not so very long past my seventeenth birthday, did not know how to react to the birthmark, and it was very evident that poor Aunt Sophia did not know either. I was in a terror lest she should say 'birthmark' instead of some quite other word; I was in some fright lest I should do so. Our visitor's affability of manner showed that he, at any rate, rose quite above his disfigurement. If he had been worried by it, he could have covered it with whiskers. That he did not deign to, I thought did him credit, and I strove to be as unembarrassed as he was.

He did not have a card about him, owing to the incompetence of his servant, but he announced himself as Doctor Colin Nicol. He was not a medical doctor, as he hastened to explain, but held some other superior academic degree; he was an historian and an antiquarian, like our friend Mr David Maitland; but instead of keeping a shop he was a teacher, scholar and writer. He was at the time engaged on research towards a new biography of Prince Charles Edward Stuart, the Young Pretender, Bonnie Prince Charlie. He explained that much new material had come to light about the Prince's life, and more was expected yet to come, which required reappraisals of this or that aspect of his career, and that this justified and even demanded a new study of a man already often studied. He was at pains, it seemed to me, to justify his project to us, and to make us agree that his labours were timely and meritorious.

We listened, puzzled, in the parlour of Millstounburn. We did not know why he thought it necessary to explain himself to us; we did not know why he had come.

He said that, whenever he was in sufficient funds, he was a

10

client of Mr David Maitland in Prince's Street, and had there formed the basis of a collection of memorabilia of Prince Charles Edward. He had acquainted himself with the various devices, heraldic and decorative, used by the Prince at different times of his confused life; he was thus able to recognize and identify, with fair certainty, objects associated with His Royal Highness.

In Mr Maitland's shop, a day or two previously, Doctor Nicol had seen a sword. He saw at once – and Mr Maitland agreed with him – that it was not of Scottish or English craftsmanship, for the design of the hilt was of another school of swordsmiths. Doctor Nicol believed it to be French, though Mr Maitland was inclined to give an Italian ascription. Closer examination, with a glass, and after some careful polishing, revealed a badge engraved on the hilt, of a crowned leopard running; further search, of the blade, revealed part of a French inscription engraved on the steel, which suggested that the sword had been given to some great person by the citizens of a town. In sum, the evidence pointed with some certainty to the sword having been the property of Prince Charles Edward.

Doctor Nicol had been and remained greatly excited by this identification, owing to his passion for objects associated with the ill-fated Prince. He had prevailed on Mr Maitland to reveal the provenance of the sword. Mr Maitland would not normally have given Aunt Sophia's name and direction to a stranger: but Doctor Nicol was not to him a stranger, and he was a scholar of repute. Mr Maitland, it seemed, after some initial reluctance, saw no harm in naming Millstounburn and Miss Sophia Grant; we saw no harm in it, either. Doctor Nicol's enthusiasm was infectious, and his manners were excellent, and he was outspokenly grateful for our kind reception of him; we could not regret that he had come.

As to the sword, we could only tell him that it had been brought back from France, as we believed, by my great-grandmother in the year 1770. We did not know how she had come by it, nor why she esteemed it so high. He wanted to know more, much more; but we were no use to him.

I had been made known to him by Aunt Sophia, at his first arrival; but at that point she was flustered and ill at ease, by the mere fact of an unexpected visitor, and mumbled my

11

name, so that he did not catch it. Now he learned that my great-grandmother's married name had been Albany: and that her son and grandson and great-granddaughter were surnamed Albany. This unimportant fact threw him into a state of almost frightening excitement.

'Not a usual name,' he said. 'Far from a usual name, if I may be permitted to be personal. *Then felt I like some watcher of the skies* . . . You say, Ma'am,' he turned to Aunt Sophia, 'that the sword has reposed, time out of mind, in a box with a collection of ancient papers? Dare I request the privilege of examining those papers? Should I discommode or offend you, if I made so bold? Nothing will be removed, nor shuffled out of sequence – but *may* I look at the contents of that box?'

Of course he might. We had both rather that he suffocated himself with century-old dust, than that we did. We had kept the papers against the eventual leisure of Mr Maitland; there was no reason in the world why Doctor Nicol should not examine them first.

I showed him to the attic, and to the cowhide trunk where the sword had lain. Politeness obliged me to offer to remain with him, but to my relief he said that he would do very well on his own, and would not inconvenience me further. I came downstairs wondering why an unusual patronym should throw an eminent scholar into such a storm; wondering also at a taste which led a healthy man to prefer dusty attics to the clean bright air of the countryside. I hardly went into our attics from year's end to year's end; they were full not only of dust, but also of spiders and scuttling things, and I suspected bats. Not all the temerity I had inherited from my father equipped me to face the notion of a bat caught in my hair. (My hair was fair – it was commonly called 'bright', which was a nice word – though, unusually in the Scottish Lowlands, my eyes were brown. To get drifts of dust in my brown eyes was almost as disagreeable an aspect of the attic, as to get a bat entangled in my bright hair.)

No sooner was I downstairs, than Aunt Sophia and I were astonished by another visitor. It was good Mr David Maitland, come galloping up in a hired carriage. With him were two sturdy men in long coats and billycock hats, whom he introduced to us as Police officers.

Police officers! Aunt Sophia put a hand to her breast, and

12

began to make a moaning noise, like a poor cow I had once seen, on the point of death after eating a branch of yew.

'You have a stranger within your gates, Miss Grant?' said Mr Maitland.

I replied, since Aunt Sophia was plainly incapable of doing so, 'Yes. He is Doctor Nicol. He is in the attic, sneezing.'

'Sneezing?'

'He is certain to be sneezing, on account of the dust.'

'The attic. As I thought. Ha. So, gentlemen,' said Mr Maitland to the Police officers, 'our fellow is caught like a rat in a trap, and we can take our time.'

They nodded. They were like wooden men, showing nothing in their faces; but I was glad I was not a fugitive criminal.

Mr Maitland turned to Aunt Sophia. But she was still pressing a hand to her breast, and making the noise of a poisoned cow; so he turned back to me.

'Doctor Nicol, did he call himself?'

'Yes.'

'A big man, with a wee birthmark here?' He indicated the side of his face, by his left ear.

'It looks like a bird.'

'Ay, and a kind of bird he is, too. A hoodie-crow, maybe, or a thieving magpie. Your precious Doctor Nicol, Miss Leo, is a villain named Edgar Smith, who presented himself to me two weeks syne, seeking employment in the shop, and carrying letters of testimonial that made him out all kinds of a scholar and gentleman. No doubt they were forged. That's one of the matters my friends of the Police will be investigating. Well, he left my employ this morning, a mite suddenly, when I found his fingers in the cash-box. And when he left, as I discovered two minutes later, his pockets contained a gold snuff-box, said to have been the property of the great Duke of Montrose, and a set of miniature paintings of the Blair family.'

I goggled. At least, that is what I think I must have done; for my face felt as though I were goggling.

'He was in my shop when your sword arrived,' said Mr Maitland. 'He knew where it came from. He knew nothing about it, I think, because he knew nothing about anything. Fool that I was, I told him. Maybe it was vainglory, the old man showing off his knowledge; I hope it was in part a kind of charity, to educate a poor body I still trusted. I showed him

13

the badge on the hilt, and the line of French engraved on the blade, and I said it had likely been the property of Prince Charles Edward, who in his lifetime owned a muckle lot of swords. I said that there were more old papers in the place whence the sword had come, than in the library of the University of Edinburgh, and that, if the sword was in truth Prince Charlie's, then some of the papers were maybe his also. I said I was proposing to devote a part of my retirement to a thorough examination of them. All that I said to the villain, for which I should throw dust on my head.'

Though almost speechless with astonishment, I somehow said, 'How did you know he was coming here today?'

'We did not know, for certain, but it seemed a likely guess. He was bent on coming here, because I had told him what treasures I thought might lie in your attic (*I* told him! Idiot that I was, *I* told him!) and he knew that if he did not come here quick, he would not come at all, because I would have warned you against him. I thought he would come at once, today, and my friends of the Police agreed. Ha, my mannie! We'll have the Duke's snuffbox back, and the Blair miniatures, and your wrists in a pair of handcuffs.'

Mr Maitland was fairly dancing with satisfaction. The constables remained wooden. One of them said that he would go round to the back of the house, to prevent Edgar Smith's escape by the back door.

Aunt Sophia had stopped moaning, but still she clutched her breast.

There was a man's shout. There was a scream, which I recognized as that of Morag the little housemaid. I sped round the house, followed by Mr Maitland at almost equal speed, the second constable more slowly, and Aunt Sophia more slowly still. I was in time to see 'Doctor Nicol', no longer so glossy in appearance, hitting the first constable a tremendous blow in the face, which knocked the man flat. 'Doctor Nicol' had a bundle of papers under his left arm. He had stolen them, from the attic. He jumped over the fence which divided the kitchen garden from the little paddock; he jumped without dropping any of the papers. He ran to our old horse Virgil. Pulling him by the mane, he led Virgil to the gate out of the paddock. Mr Maitland and I and the second Police officer ran to catch him, but he was far ahead of us; and none of us

14

jumped the fence as nimbly as he had done, for all he was a big fat man. He opened the gate, and jumped on Virgil's back; holding the mane with both hands, he kicked the old horse into a canter. This he could not do, while still holding the bundle of papers under his arm – the papers flew away in a cloud, drifting behind him like the leaves of a plane-tree in a gale.

The constable and I ran after Virgil, quite fruitlessly. Mr Maitland ran after the swirling papers, with more success. Aunt Sophia subsided against the fence, which she did not try to climb.

Mr Maitland was more than ever anxious to examine the papers, but had less than ever time to do so. We returned them to the trunk from which the sword had come. We locked the trunk; but we were sure that we would not see Edgar Smith again, the urbane 'Doctor Nicol' of the unmistakable birthmark.

Virgil was found by the Dalkeith railway station. Edgar Smith was not found.

These melodramatic events put our little household most strenuously on its guard. Never again would we be hood-winked by a plausible rogue, especially one pretending to be a student of history, and most especially one pretending to be preparing a life of Prince Charles Edward.

Consequently, our reception of poor Simon Donaldson was suspicious and hostile in the last degree.

The first we knew of him was a rattle of hooves and a rumble of wheels, as a dog-cart turned the corner of the road. John Anderson, the gardener, straightened from his digging, to watch the dog-cart go by on the road – like all the rest of the household, old John was alert to identify and repel marauders. The dog-cart drew up at our gate, which was nowadays kept closed, though it had always before stood open. John Anderson picked up his fork, and advanced to guard the gate. He carried his fork before him, as though it had been a partisan; he was a big man; watching from an upstairs window, I did not think any stranger would care to dismount from his vehicle and enter.

15

It chanced that David Laurie, the nearest farmer, went by at this moment in a trap, on his way home from market. He was a good friend of ours (though he had been no friend of mine, in my lawless childhood) and of course he knew all about Edgar Smith. Seeing the stranger, seeing John Anderson with his warlike garden fork, he pulled up, jumped out, and approached the dog-cart from the other side. He was a big man, too, and he carried a stick as gnarled and heavy as a cudgel.

Through the upstairs window, and divided from the scene by the front garden, I did not hear what was said. But the progress of the scene was plain enough, in dumb-show. The two big old men with their weapons were telling the stranger to get himself away and to stay away. And he was expostulating, and showing them pieces of paper; and they were unimpressed by his expostulations and his papers; and John Anderson brandished his fork, and David Laurie brandished his cudgel; and I was glad that we were protected from robbers.

This robber, still perched unhappily on the box of his dog-cart, was much unlike Edgar Smith. He was a young man – in his middle twenties, I thought – and at a distance he looked like a gentleman. (So, to be sure, had Edgar Smith; but this one looked like a gentle man, as well as a person of breeding.) He wore an ulster over tweed knickerbockers, and looked like a laird on his way to a superior shooting party, instead of a robber on his way to our attic.

I continued to watch this scene being played, in silence and at a distance; perhaps I should have run at once out to intervene, but the weather was raw, and the house was warmer than the garden, and I did not want chapped lips or a purple nose.

It seemed, after a time, that John Anderson and David Laurie were impressed by what the stranger said – when at last they allowed him to say anything – or by the way he said it, at least so far as to allow him the benefit of the doubt; for John Anderson opened the gate for the dog-cart. But still he held his garden fork at a threatening angle, and David Laurie came into the garden, with his cudgel on his shoulder like a musket.

When the stranger jumped out of his dog-cart, I saw that he

16

was much taller than I had supposed; and, when he removed his hat before ringing our doorbell, I saw that he was much fairer than I had supposed. His hair was thick, of the sort that can never be made to look perfectly tidy, and buttercup-yellow. Since I was standing in a window directly over the front door, all I could see of the newcomer was this hair. I liked it. A doubt entered my mind, provoked entirely by unruly buttercup hair, about whether he was in truth a criminal.

Little Morag answered the front door (for we kept no manservant within doors), and there was at once a very Babel of voices: John Anderson, whose voice was a deep bass, was thundering out warnings and suspicions; and David Laurie, who for all his bulk had a high tenor voice, was calling out his own fears and doubts, in a kind of musical counterpoint; and the stranger, whose voice was a light baritone, was trying to announce himself, and to ask for Miss Sophia Grant; and Morag, whose voice when excited was a peahen shriek, was saying that her mistress would admit no stranger at all, and at the same time telling John Anderson and David Laurie the story of Edgar Smith's assault on the constable, every detail of which they already knew. And then a moaning noise joined the chorus, by which I knew that Aunt Sophia had entered the hall: and I concluded that it was time I descended.

Well, he was called Simon Donaldson, and he had documents to prove it. And he had a letter, addressed to Aunt Sophia, from no less a person than Mr David Maitland, that established him as a *bona fide* scholar, and introduced him to Millstounburn as a person to be welcomed and trusted; and another letter, addressed 'to whom it may concern', from a Professor of the University of Aberdeen, that established Mr Donaldson not only as a scholar but as a gentleman of irreproachable character.

I was the first to be convinced, by his face and hair and manner and voice and clothes, and by these letters, that he was an honest man on an honest errand. David Laurie was next to be convinced, perhaps because he wanted to get away home to his dinner. Aunt Sophia was slower to be convinced, because she could not at once find her spectacles to read the letters, and there was too much disputation for my reading

17

of them to be audible. John Anderson was reluctant to be convinced, and cross when he was obliged to admit himself convinced, because he admired himself in the role of soldier, and wanted to save helpless ladies from a footpad. Morag was never convinced, then or later.

It was almost unbelievable. Simon Donaldson's story was word for word identical to that of 'Doctor Nicol'. He was a scholar and an antiquarian. He was a customer, when he could afford it, of Mr Maitland's shop. He was engaged on a study of Prince Charles Edward Stuart, which he believed justified by the new facts which were continually coming to light. He was keenly interested in any objects or papers associated with the Prince. He had seen our sword in Mr Maitland's shop.

It seemed a coincidence too gigantic to swallow. But, of course, it was no coincidence at all. In Mr Maitland's shop, Simon Donaldson had met Edgar Smith, who was still at the time employed there as an assistant. Simon Donaldson had talked to Mr Maitland, in Edgar Smith's hearing. They talked about the sword, and about Simon Donaldson's researches into the life of Bonnie Prince Charlie. Edgar Smith then invented a name and a doctorate for himself, and otherwise came to us and performed an imitation of Simon Donaldson. So it was that Simon Donaldson's account of himself so closely echoed its own pre-echo; and so it was that Simon Donaldson was nearly impaled on John Anderson's fork, and cudgelled with David Laurie's walking-stick.

It was some time before we could fully grasp that Simon Donaldson was in reality exactly what Edgar Smith had pretended to be. I spent that time inspecting him, as well as listening to him. He was tall and slim, not with the scholar's scrawniness, but with the athlete's wiriness. His face was open and pleasing; he had wide-set grey eyes, an aquiline nose, and a cleft chin. His voice was educated; he was indeed a gentleman. His manner was a little hesitant and shy, far from the confident ebullience of 'Doctor Nicol'. I liked what I saw, and what I heard.

More covertly, he was inspecting me, which is something of which it is impossible not to be aware. He looked at me with a kind of astonishment. I understood, in part. It was this face of mine, which people fancied they had seen before. Perhaps it

18

was more than that (I hoped it was more than that) but it was certainly that.

Once again, Aunt Sophia's social embarrassment caused her to mumble when she told him my name. It came into the conversation, as it was bound to do, in connection with my great-grandmother, who had brought back from France the sword which was the reason for his visit.

He seemed staggered.

'A family called Albany,' he said, 'have lived in this house since 1770, and the first who came here of that name, came here from France? Is that right? Do I understand you perfectly correctly?'

We assured him that he did.

He seemed to forget Prince Charles Edward, and to embark on a new line of research, of lesser importance. He wanted to know about my family.

I said that, on my mother's side, I had numerous Grant relatives; that on my great-grandmother's father's side, I had numerous, but remoter, Bruce relatives; that it was a descendant of the Bruce connection who owned Millstounburn, and allowed us to live in it.

'But Albany!' he said. 'Albany! What of Albany cousins?'

'There are none,' I said. 'It is odd, but my grandfather was an only child, and my father was an only child, and I am an only child.'

'You are therefore the single living descendant of your great-grandfather, who was named Albany?'

'Yes,' I said, greatly surprised by his excitement. 'But we do not know anything about him. We suppose he died abroad, and so my great-grandmother came back to Scotland with her baby son. She lived here with her brother. He was John Bruce. Whyever is that interesting, Mr Donaldson?'

He took a great shuddering breath. His eyes burned and his hands trembled. 'This,' he said softly, 'is going to rock the stones of castles. To humble the mighty and elevate the humble. I have believed for a long time, and my patron too, that there was an earlier marriage, perhaps with issue, but it has been impossible to prove . . . Great heaven, Miss Albany, do you not know who you are? Do you not know why your face is recognized? Do you not know who your great-grandfather was? Of course you do not. And we are running ahead of

19

ourselves. That trunk of papers in the attic, which we suppose came back from France with the sword – that should, that surely must, include documents which will prove that you are . . .'

'What am I?' I asked nervously, not knowing in the least what he was talking about.

'I think,' he said, 'that you are Queen of Scotland.'

# 2

The only sound in the parlour was the fluttering of a baby flame in the grate. The ticking of the grandfather clock would have been deafening, but the clock had not worked in my lifetime. We were struck dumb.

My brain began to recover from the shock it had been dealt, and began to work normally. And, as soon as it did so, I was immediately convinced that our visitor was either a lunatic or a prankster.

Simon Donaldson was looking at me intently: and I suppose that my feelings showed on my face, as they always unfortunately did.

He said, 'You are thinking, Miss Albany, that these are either the ravings of a maniac, or a cruel practical joke. With God's help, I shall prove to you that they are not. I shall prove to you and to the world that this is sober truth.'

Still his words held no meaning for me.

I was an obscure little creature, who dwelt in a modest house in an unimportant corner of Scotland. I was used to being so. I contrived, on the whole, to be resigned to being so.

Queen?

Simon Donaldson and I rushed at once to the attic. But the men who were mending the hole in the roof occupied all the attic with their tools and materials, and had buried the cowhide trunk under all manner of rubble. It did not do to interrupt their work, because even queens need mended roofs over their heads. They said that, by noon the next day, the rubble would be removed, and we could get at the trunk.

I was close to screaming with impatience, and Simon Donaldson looked close to screaming too. Aunt Sophia moaned at the unholy disorder the builder's men were making.

Of course, we asked Simon Donaldson to stay in the house, for the night and for as many nights as his researches would take. He thanked us warmly, but said that he would not stay. He had established himself at an inn in Dalkeith, and his razors and changes of clothes were in a chamber there, and he was expected back. He did, however, accept our invitation to dine: and over dinner, and afterwards, he told us an extraordinary story.

'You must know,' he said, 'that Albany is the ancient name for the major part of Scotland, that occupied by the Pictish folk, the Scots from Ireland, and by numbers of invading Angles. Albany, Albania, Alban – the name comes in many forms. In the fourth century, Albany was taken to be all of Scotland east of Drumalban, which was the name they gave to the mountain barrier which reaches from Loch Lomond in the south to Cape Wrath in the north. West of Drumalban the Norsemen came, as they came to Orkney and the Hebrides.

'Now the Norsemen were always rebellious and turbulent, so that the boundary was held by castles in which the Kings of Scotland put their most loyal feudatories. I speak of King David I, and Alexander II and III, and I speak of the thirteenth century. Those castles, at that period, were built for the first time of stone. They were very massive. They were entirely military in design and function; we believe they must have been odious to live in, most squalid and uncomfortable.

'Am I tiring you? Is this history lecture as odious as a thirteenth-century castle?'

We said that he was not; that it was not.

'The first great leader who aspired to a truly united Scotland was Robert the Bruce,' Simon Donaldson went on, almost dreamily, reliving history that was to him evidently as vivid as the events of yesterday. 'He fought the Comyns and the Balliols, the autonomous and turbulent lords of the North and West. His son-in-law, who married Bruce's daughter Margery, was Walter Fitzalan, hereditary steward of Scotland. Steward became Stuart, and Stuart became king.

'And then a younger branch of the royal house became Dukes of Albany, in the late fourteenth century. They rebelled, and were captured and executed, and their lands and titles reverted to the crown. Albany became as royal a name as Stuart.

22

'Another remarkable man came to the throne, which was King James IV of Scotland, who married the daughter of Henry VII of England. In the earliest years of the sixteenth century he travelled everywhere, making and keeping the peace. He built far finer and more comfortable castles than any Scotland had seen before, on a French plan. One of these was in Glen Alban, renamed so, by the king, as a symbol of the extension of his power. In the Castle of Glenalban he installed a grieve, as you would say a factor or agent. Then he was killed on Flodden Field, in 1513, and the nobles waxed fat and rebellious, and chaos descended again on Scotland. And the grieve of Glenalban had a son, who succeeded him in the appointment, and they became the family of Grieve of Glenalban, and nobody remembered that they were only royal servants. But the Grieves were not the rightful owners of Glenalban then, or at any time, and they are not its rightful owners now. They are Earls of Glenalban by one royal patent; and they are the tenants of Glenalban by another.'

'How can you know this?' I asked.

'Because I lived and worked there for months. Three years ago I graduated from the university, somewhat qualified to handle and assess ancient documents, and, through the good offices of one of my professors, I was engaged by the present Earl of Glenalban, descendant of the original grieve who became Grieve. I was engaged to explore and catalogue centuries' worth of documents, deeds, charters, account-books and the like, which had piled up in the muniment-room in the castle. It seemed likely to my professors that there might be much valuable historical material in those oaken chests.

'They were right.

'King James VI of Scotland, who became King James I of England, was a canny and cantankerous kind of man, not at all inclined to let anything go that was his. He confirmed the Grieves in their stewardship of Glenalban, but he also confirmed his own ownership of it. The documents are in the castle, of course, where they belong; I have copies of them. James I's son had his head chopped off by the Roundheads; his son in turn was the Merry Monarch, who did not have time for remote Scottish castles; and his younger brother was James II, who tried to turn England Catholic, and was packed

23

away abroad for his pains. Now I am not pleading a Tory or Jacobite case, but I am saying that on a strict reading of the law the 'Glorious Revolution' of William and Mary was a piece of the most barefaced usurpation. It saved the Church of England and the Kirk in Scotland from the Romans, but it was not lawful. It was arguably good and necessary, as we have all been taught all our lives, but there was no shred of legality about it. James II was rightful King of England and Scotland, to the day of his death, though he lived out his days an exile in France.

'In that exile, he was visited by many well-wishers and some ill-wishers, especially from Scotland. One of his visitors was Duncan Grieve of Glenalban, whose motives were probably mixed. We may guess that Duncan Grieve swore fealty to his rightful sovereign, and touched the hilt of his sword in homage, and so forth, and that he was as two-faced and treacherous as his family have been before and since. Anyhow, James II, from his exile, once again confirmed the Grieves in Glenalban, but with the qualification that if any descendant of his own body had need of the castle, then castle and estate were his, and the Grieves no more than caretakers – never more than caretakers – for the royal house of Scotland. This document, too, is in the muniment-room of the castle, and I have a copy of it.

'James II's son was James Edward, known as James III to his friends and as the Old Pretender to his enemies. The Earl of Mar raised his standard in Scotland in the winter of 1715, and James Edward arrived himself for a couple of months. Nothing came of it. By all the rules of chivalry and loyalty, the Grieves should have been among the first to rally to that standard. They did not. They sat tight in Glenalban, as greedy and cowardly as ever.

'So we come to James Edward's son, Charles Edward, whose mother was Maria Clementina Sobieska. He was born in Rome in 1720, to a diligent, dullish, bookish father, and a pious termagant of a mother. He was a skilful sportsman, a linguist, a musician. He had light brown hair that was called 'bright', and he inherited brown eyes from his mother. He was slender. His nose was high-bridged and his chin pointed. Yes, Miss Albany. There are many paintings of him, and from those paintings very many engravings, and the people of

Scotland know these features well, as part of their national inheritance. Of course you are recognized!'

'But I . . .' I began: but I choked, and ceased.

'Charles Edward was not much educated and not much disciplined. He was spoiled and wilful. He was highly attractive to women, but not apparently, in his youth, much interested in them. He travelled extensively. As early as his seventeenth year, he travelled with a guardian. He adopted, when he travelled, the style of Count of Albany. He continued to do so, off and on, all his life.'

'Oh,' I said.

'Conte d'Albani, Comte d'Alban, and other variations.'

'Oh.'

'He came to Scotland in 1745, and declared his father king; and the little people rallied, and some of the great; and most of the great played as safe as they knew how, being concerned with saving themselves, and enriching themselves, and paying off a few scores; and, if the Grieves were no worse than most others, they were certainly no better. Charles Edward went to Glenalban about the middle of August of 1745, on his way to Blair Atholl, knowing full well from his father that the place was his, and the people his tenants and servants. No doubt every kind of protestation of loyalty was made to him, and every kind of treachery afterwards committed.

'Well, you know the end of that story – the Prince escaped to the Isle of Skye in a little boat with Flora Macdonald, and spent the rest of his life doing nothing in particular. He was involved with various ladies, quite aside from which he tried to marry various princesses. He began to drink heavily about 1750. He had an English lady-friend thenabouts, a passionate High Tory Catholic called Clementina Walkenshaw. She bore his daughter Charlotte, in 1752 or '53.'

'Who rightly owned Glenalban?'

'No, because she was illegitimate. Clementina ran away a few years later, taking the child. They were protected against Charles Edward by King Louis of France himself, which suggests that he was given to violence . . . He was all over the place in those years, drifting round France and Italy, sometimes in much better health, but often drinking heavily. In 1766 his father died. Thereafter he was rightfully King Charles III of England and Scotland. Yes, he was. Make no

25

mistake about that. But nobody took him seriously, except some romantical Scots. He was an embarrassment to every government. He was a hopeless case. But he was King Charles III.

'People came across him from time to time, travelling obscurely, begging and borrowing money, calling himself usually Count of Albany. And those people wrote letters, and some of those letters are preserved, and there is in them a persistent rumour, round about 1768, that he had married at last. There is mention of a countess of Albany, and elsewhere of a Contessa d'Albani. This is not conclusive, you understand, because a lady with whom his union was not regularised might have adopted that style. But it has led my patron and myself to believe that there was a secret marriage. We have assumed that his wife died, and without issue, because he did undoubtedly marry in 1772. Either he was a widower, or this second marriage was bigamous. In any case, it ended in divorce ten years later. After which his natural daughter Charlotte was legitimized and made his heir.'

'Oh,' I said.

'She never married.'

'Oh.'

'So the search continues.'

'For . . . ?'

'For evidence of that previous marriage, about which there were so many rumours. For evidence of living and legitimate descendants of that marriage. For evidence which will return Glenalban to its owner, and take it away from the proud and cruel and treacherous usurper who sits there now.'

We had the trunk brought down out of the attic by the builder's men. Morag swept a bucketful of dust off the outside, and another off the papers inside. They were all in a muddle after Edgar Smith's piracy, and it was three full days before Simon Donaldson had put all in order.

Much of it was valueless. Some was of only specialized interest, old household accounts, and the like. And mounds of it were the intimate journal of a young girl who left Millstounburn in 1766 as Leonora Bruce, and returned four years later with another name and with an infant son.

The hand was spidery and strange. Simon Donaldson was trained to decipher it, and did so with ease.

'3rd of March 1766. Calamity! I was never so distracted! Brother J. saw me in the Larch Plantation with my Beloved, embracing as wee cannot forbear to doe whenever wee meet in Secret, and told Papa, who has forbid me to see or meet my Ralph, on pain of my being sent Away to Cousin Henrietta in that Detestable City, and of Dearest Ralph being deprived of his Position on the Estate. Papa and J. were to be gone on a Great Journey about the Nations of Europe, J. to complete his Education and Papa to commence his, not having had the Opportunity of Voyaging when he was young, and now the plann is that I am to go with them, so that I may be Saved from the Contagioun (as they call it) of my Ralph. So to one distraction is added this Other, because I shall need a Host of Gowns and Cloakes and Shifts and I do not know what, and where are they to be hadd in this desert at a few Weekes Notice?'

The next many pages were devoted to preparations for the journey, and visits to dressmakers, and the packing of cloak-bags; and to lamentations about Leonora's separation from her unsuitable lover (Ralph was apparently a clerk employed by her father on the farm). These passages were full of underlinings and marks of exclamation; certainly the writer convinced herself she was passionately in love with her Ralph. The breaking of her heart, I thought, was losing nothing in the telling.

'I think she was a conventionally romantical girl,' said Simon Donaldson, after we had subjected ourselves to some pages of miserable outpourings, 'with a clear idea of how she ought to feel in such cruel circumstances, derived from works of fiction.'

'You mean, you think she was not truly in love with Ralph?' I said.

'She was very young.'

'She was older than I am now.'

He smiled. His smile was most warm and friendly. He had overcome the shyness with which he had first made our acquaintance: but still his manner was gentle and unassertive. His smile said that I too, like my namesake, was too young to know my heart, but that he was not going to risk my wrath by saying so.

27

Leonora Bruce showed the passionate enthusiasm of her nature, in a new and surprising way, amongst her outpourings about gowns and about Ralph. She recorded in her journal the news, which was come from Rome, of the Death of James Edward Stuart, called James III, called also the Old Pretender. 'Ah Black Day!' she wrote with frenzied strokes of her pen. 'My Rightful Soverain is extinguished, in Lamentable Exile, far from the Purple Heather of his beloved Land!'

There was much more in the same strain. It appeared that Leonora was a romantic Jacobite; the effect of these effusions was to make her seem younger – a silly schoolgirl, in fact, with a head full of maggots.

From the dead father, her romantical ramblings went to the living son. To her, he was a kind of god, a paragon of beauty and courage, a living legend. I knew from Simon Donaldson that Prince Charles Edward was in fact, by this time, a drunken ruin, a beggar and a sponger: but to Leonora Bruce he wore shining armour, and was her Champion and her King.

I think there were a lot of young ladies in Scotland then who felt the same girlish loyalty to the 'Young Chevalier'. But most of them, fortunately, did not go to Southern Europe with their brothers and Papas.

Leonora in due course did so, and the next piles of her journal were a record of coaches, postillions, inns, sinister travellers, beautiful and mysterious travellers, flies and cockroaches, unfamiliar dishes which affected her digestion, and descriptions of scenic and artistic beauty which had an air of being written from a sense of obligation. She was more interested in clothes than in cathedrals, in mantillas than in mountains; she *was* a silly schoolgirl, though, when she wrote what we read, she was older than I.

It was difficult to keep remembering that all this girlish stuff had been written down almost exactly one hundred years before.

We skipped rapidly through pounds of material, some of which made us laugh but much of which made us yawn: and so followed the family and their servants down through France to Avignon, where Leonora dutifully described the famous bridge, the Palace of the Popes, and the fine eyes of an ostler at the inn.

28

'August the Third. It is vexatious beyond anything, but our coach is broke down on the road between Avignon and Nîmes, and we are to be Obliged to shelter in an Humble house by the side of the road, where I am writing this in a Bed Chamber no bigger than a Privvy, and no Cleaner. The House is indeed a kind of Inn, but has an Insufficiency of Chambers, and those too small, so that my poor Wench Sarah is Obliged to lie in a kind of Attick, with the serving girls of the House, and I must make shift to Dress and Disrobe myself . . .'

These complaints continued for a page or two, the worst aspect being that no blacksmith was immediately available to mend whatever part of the coach had broken (on mechanical details Leonora was silent).

'August the Fourth. Exploring this place, for want of any other Employment, I saw that the Building is larger than we had supposed, having a sort of Wing extending out at the back, in which there is a much Larger and Finer Bed Chamber. Papa tried to engage this Chamber for himself, but it is Bespoke by a Traveller who is expected, Whos Servant is all ready here, making preparations against his Master's coming. The Inn Keeper speaks of "Milor", but I cannot determine from him, what Lord is expected, of even of what country, from the fact that in this Region of France, they speak all through their noses, so that it is nigh impossible to understand a Word. The Servant is a Strange and Gaunt old man, with a grey Beard. I heard him speaking in a kind of French to the People of the House, but I think he is not French, and he and the Women did not at all understand One Another.

'Evening. We have just eat Dinner, which was Ill, as the Host and his Wife and all the Folk of the Inn are devoted entirely to the new Arrival, who came quietly in, so that Wee did not see him, and they say that he will keep to his Chamber, which makes me suppose that he is a person of High Importance, on an Embassy, or Secret Mission.

'August the 5th. The most mad and Freakish night just past, which has left me Dropping for want of Sleep. Long after Dinner, when we were all abed, but I do not know what o'clock, there rose up from the Yard behind the house, a Dreadful Droning, and Groaning, and Shreaking, which Presently Resolved itself into a kind of Rough Musicke, and to my Compleat Amazement, I understood that I was listening to a Scotch Bagpipes! Nothing could be, that could Astound me more, than to hear this of all Noises here! I threw on a Dressing Robe, and ran downstairs, to see a thing that could not be Believed. The secret Milor's Servant was Marching up and down, as Pipers do, beneath the window of the Milor's Chamber. On his Head was a Scotch Bonnet. And the Yard Filled up with people, Papa and Brother J and the Host and Hostess and Servants, all in dressing Robes and Night Caps, calling on the old man to stop his Noise, but he would not, and Marched on, Playing on his Pipes. Papa called out to him in English, Forgetting in his Rage where we were, to let Decent People sleep, and the servant stopped his Piping long enough to reply, in a thick and broad Scotch Voice, Syne ma Maister canna sleep, he'll hae the soond o' the Pipes. And indeed there was a candle in the window of the great Bed Chamber, and a face beside it, but we could not well see the face.

'Later. Papa has spoke to the Servant, who is in Truth a Scotchman, but he has followed his Master for twenty years, travelling the cities and Villages of Europe, and Papa says the old Man was Moved almost to tears, to heare a Scotch voice, and see a Scotch Face.

'The Servant called his Master "His Highness", but he would not say more who he was.

'Later. There has been a Battle about the Inn, going from the Kitchen to the Hall, and so to the Yard, and backe again, between the Scotch Servant and the Host and Hostess. Papa, thinking to go to the Aid of a Distressed Fellow Countryman, discovered Milor cannot pay his Reckoning. It is not a great sum. At last, upon his knees, the old man begged Papa to assist his Master, and all would one day be repaid, when his Master came into his own, which he would Surely Do. Papa said that he would Assist any Creature in Need (which is not entirely True) but that he must know who he was Helping. In sum, he would not part with any Gold, until he knew who "His Highness" was. The Servant whispered to him, looking round as though for fear of Eavesdroppers. Papa said "That is just as I thought," and gave the Servant more than he asked him for.

'Later. Papa has told Brother J and me, in the Greatest Confidence, what we will remember all our Lives. I can scarce

30

hold the penn, for Agitation, for "Milor" is no other than the King Over the Water, to whom I have in my Secret Heart, and in the Hidden pages of this Journal, vowed *Lifelong devotion*, and in whose Cause, I would *sacrifice all!*

'August 9th. Three Days have past, when I have not known if I was on my head or my heels, my Mind and Heart being in such a Whirl, that I could not find Time or Strength to take up my Penn. but now my Beloved Lord sleeps, and in Tranquilitie I sett down the Strangest Events that ever Overtook a Young Female.

'I was making myself ready for my bed, though was still for the most part dressed, when came a knock on the door, which I thought must be my wench Sarah, or one of the Maids of the House. I went to the door, and to my great amazement there stood the old Scotch Servant, whom I now knew to be named Wedderburn. He bowed to me, holding his bonnet in his hands. He said that his Master had seen me from the window of his Chamber, as I crossed the Yard, or was about some business behind the House, and desired that I should Present myself to him, for that he wished to make my Acquaintance, and to hear news of Scotland, and how it went with those that had Followed him twenty years before.

'I trembled at the Thought of making my Reverence to a Prince, that should have been a King, and was almost too alarmed to have followed Wedderburn, but A request from this Prince, was to me the most Absolute and Binding Command, so I summoned my Feeble Courage, and followed the old man through back passages, to the Door of the Princely Apartment.

'Of my Graceful Reception by His Royal Highness I can not write without a flood of grateful Emotion. He rose as I entered the Chamber, and by the Light of his Candles I saw him to be moderate tall, no longer perhaps as Slender as I had seen him Pictured in his hot Youth, but still elegant, and Well Formed in all Particulars, with Features sufficiently pleasing, though shewing Signs of the Manifold Hardships and Deprivations which it had been his Lott to bear. I curtseyed deep, but he took my hand, and raised me, and with the Greatest Affability, conducted me to a chair, desiring me to sit, and take my Ease, and then with his own hands (for Wedderburn had left the Chamber) poured out for me a glass

31

of Wine, which I knew I should not take, but which from the Royal hand I must accept. His condescension then, as he sate near to me, is what I despair of being able to Express. He pressed me for Details of the Situation in Scotland and in England, of which alas! I shewed a wofull ignorance; and was so obliging as to express a lively interest in Myself, and in my family and life, and whether I were in Love, and whether Betrothed. He pressed more Wine upon me, which I knew I should not take, for fear of Inflammation of the Nerves, and of becoming too Free with my Speech. And after some Glasses of Wine, I told him about Ralph. Answering his Questions, I admitted that Ralph had kissed me with Ardour, and that I had felt his hands on my Bosom, but not quite inside my Clothes. Then, to my Stupefaction, I found that he was upon his Knees before my chair, Speaking very rapidly and Hoarsely, praising what he called my Beauty of face and figure. And then he said, Did your Ralph touch you so? And so? And placed his Royal Hands upon my bosom, and kissed me! And then he asked me in a low Tone, about my Sympathies, and whether I were Loyal to the Hanover Rats of England, and I cried out that I was His Loyal subject and servant, at which he gave me more wine, which I knew I should not have taken. I made so bold as to kiss his hands, as Token of the Reverent Loyalty I felt for Him, but he raised my head, and kissed my lips, and Embraced me with a mounting Passion, to which my Loyal Fervour inspired me to respond, as also did the Wine, so that he carried me, overcome by my emotions, to the bed, and there undressed me, and had his Will of me, and I could not resist, and would not if I could, for I was Honoured above all Females.

'So he fell at last asleep beside me, and I watched over him with Adoration, and slept at length also. In the dawn I woke, my head thick with sleep and with Wine, but he slept on, breathing with a great Noise.

'Then suddenly below there was a Hubb-Bubb, and in dismay I heard Papa's voice, and old Wedderburn's, and I thought blows struck, and Brother J's voice raised up very high and Furious. In a moment there was a great pounding on the door, which burst open, and Papa was within, shouting of Disgrace, Treachery, Fornication, and such stuff, which was an Ill way to speak to a Prince, and Brother J had drawn his sword, and was shouting also. The Chamber was quite full of People, all shouting, and all saw my Lord in his Bed, and me with him unclothed. Papa said something behind his hand to my Brother J, who nodded, and rann off, still carrying his Sword.

'I thought nothing would have woken my Beloved Lord, so profound was his sleep, but at last he Stirred, and groaned, and looked with the greatest astonishment at the Croud which had gathered in his Chamber. He sate up in the bedd, and commanded silence, and that all those present should at once depart, but Papa would not, and with his sword prevented Wedderburn and the Host from removing him, at which I screamed.

'So matters rested for a time, during which I began to feel increasingly Ridiculous, and then at last Brother J returned, from the next village, with a Priest. And Papa said that the Priest should immediately Marry us, and if he did not, there would be Breasts spit on his Sword.

'So there was at once a Ceremony, of which I understood Nothing, for it was conducted part in Latin, and part in French. And at the end of the Ceremony, I was the Lawfull Wedded wife of His Royal Highness Prince Charles Edward Stuart, rightfully King Charles III of England and Scotland. But he was not married under that name, but under another style he used, which was Count of Albany.

'There was a Paper give me by the Priest, which sets forth that we were Wedd, and shews if ever I am challenged in the matter that I am indissolubly the Wife of the Prince.'

'This is the paper, I fancy,' said Simon Donaldson, drawing a yellowed document from between the pages of the journal. 'Oh yes. I have seen just such certificates before. That marriage was entirely legal and valid.'

'Let us get on,' I said, choking.

'This must have been a shock to you, Miss Albany. I am sorry you should learn so – so brutally about your great-grandmother's . . .'

'Immorality? You have not been brutal. Did the, hum, improper events of that night take place because she was drunk, or because she was a Jacobite and he her king, or because she fell in love with him?'

'I would say equal parts of all three,' said Simon Donaldson

33

slowly. 'He was an experienced man of nearly fifty, who had had a number of mistresses, and who had been, if he no longer was, highly attractive to women; and she was a very green girl. He was a royal prince, and her greatest hero. He filled her with wine, to which she was unused. It was all very easy for him. It does him no credit. I wonder if it does her father credit, that he forced them into instant marriage at the point of his sword?'

'Let us see how they fared, and then we can tell.'

Well, the new Countess of Albany's Papa and brother John stayed on a few days at the same inn, and then resumed their travels. Leonora, of course, stayed with her husband, and began to share with him the obscure and purposeless travellings which had been his life since the defeat of his rebellion.

The journal became scrappy and allusive. It seemed to us that, after a sober period, the Prince began to drink heavily again. Money was a constant and degrading worry; mostly, this extraordinary royal couple lived on what the old sevant Wedderburn begged on their behalf.

It seemed, to Simon Donaldson and me, that Leonora sometimes begged on her husband's behalf; but this was reading between the lines. She remained steadfastly loyal to him, even in the secrecy of these pages.

A son was born to them, in an Italian city; and this, as the diarist wrote, at once changed everything.

'The Course of Life, which my Royal Husband has adopted, is one which I have been able to Stomach, tho often it has been hard, and often laid me open to Humiliation and Despaire. But an Infant cannot travel Europe like a Parcel, nor be exposed to the Dirt and Fatigues of everlasting coaches and inns. I have writ to Brother J, Papa being dead, for a Draft to pay for my journey home.'

Home was Millstounburn, where her brother John now reigned.

Of her parting with Prince Charles Edward, Leonora wrote pages of script that seemed to us to be shaking with emotion. But we read that she was writing them in the coach that carried her north from Genoa, and the rattling of the coach was what caused the waywardness of her pen. She was not so very grieved; all too clearly, this was because the Prince had become a hopeless case. Her feelings, as she revealed them, were very much the mixture that might have been expected – part of her still revered the Prince, part could no longer tolerate the man. And it was no life for a baby.

Of course she wanted something to remember him by. He had almost nothing: everything, even to his pistols, had been sold to pay for wine. He gave her a sword, presented to him by the citizens of Carcassonne, on the occasion of his birthday.

We read of her homecoming with the infant James Edward. She resolved to say nothing to anybody, then or ever, about her husband, but to let it be assumed that he was a foreigner, now dead. This was out of loyalty. Out of loyalty also, she retained the name Albany, but abandoned the title of Countess, although she was perfectly entitled to have used it.

James Edward Albany was baptised only after his return, in the Episcopalian church in Dalkeith. His mother had not become a Roman Catholic on her marriage, and did not wish her son to be so.

'That baptism will be recorded in the church register,' said Simon Donaldson. 'Put beside these pages, it will absolutely confirm that your grandfather was the son of Prince Charles Edward.'

Well, we read the rest of Leonora's journal, Simon Donaldson and Aunt Sophia and I, during those thin midwinter days, in the search for anything else that would throw more light on our discovery. There was nothing. James Edward grew up, married, and had a son. John Bruce died; his son went out to Australia, like many Scotsmen at that time, and James Edward became his tenant at Millstounburn. Leonora lived on obscurely until her death in 1818, keeping up her journal until her final illness. She became increasingly devoted to religion, and the later parts of the journal contained many long extracts from sermons and from the Scriptures.

There was a final note, in what Aunt Sophia said was my father's hand, recording Leonora's death. It was evident that neither he nor my grandfather had ever read any of the journal, or knew anything of its contents. This may have been because they thought they would have been guilty of prying; or because they were not much given to reading.

Simon Donaldson made copies of the relevant pages of the journal, and of the marriage certificate; he also went to the church in Dalkeith, and copied the entry in its Register recording my grandfather's baptism. With these copies, he went away to Edinburgh, promising to return.

And, when he had gone, I found that I missed him dreadfully. He had almost lived at Millstounburn, all during the time of our reading, often arriving early and leaving late, often sharing our dinner, more and more becoming a member of the household. To Aunt Sophia he was always gentle and considerate, so that she was at ease with him as with almost no one else, and she talked freely with him, and even laughed. To me he was also gentle and considerate, but bit by bit he was more – much more. He became my intimate companion and confidant. He became my closest friend. He became more – much more. By looks as much as by words, he declared the warmth of his feelings for me. And by my looks I, no doubt, declared that I returned those feelings.

It had never happened to me before. I felt as drunk, on those warm looks of Simon's, as Leonora Bruce on Prince Charles Edward's wine.

In those dragging days either side of Christmas, my mind was in a rare muddle. I could not begin to guess what the implications were, of what we had discovered. That was muddle enough: and there was the memory of Simon himself, to muddle me further.

And, to muddle me further still, Simon reappeared in the middle of January, far sooner than he had given us to expect.

'This is a fleeting visit,' he said. 'There are some more pages the lawyers want to see, so I must copy them.'

I thought he was glad to have an excuse to come to Millstounburn. In my vanity, I thought he was joyful to see me again. He looked joyful, as he took my hand. I am very sure I looked joyful.

His copying was done quick – so quick, that I wondered if there was truly any to do. Aunt Sophia had asked him to stay for dinner, and it came about that Simon and I had some time together in front of the parlour fire.

He said, very quietly, looking into the fire, that he was in a daze of happiness to see me again, and to be with me.

'I am happy too,' I said.

'But for two reasons I cannot speak my heart to you, Leo. The first is, that I gave my word to your aunt that I would not

36

speak until after your eighteenth birthday. I suppose she was right, to extract that promise from me. Think of what befell your great-grandmother! As you yourself said, she was older when she went off to France than you are now. But soon you will be older than she was then . . .'

'It is bad enough that there is one reason why you cannot – speak your mind,' I said. 'I do not want another reason.'

'But you must have it. At the moment, I am hardly able to support myself. I am living on charity. My patron would not put it like that, but honesty obliges me to. You must see that, even if I had not given my word to Miss Grant, I must altogether change my circumstances before I say – anything to you.'

'You could perhaps,' I said anxiously, 'give me an idea of what you are going to say, when you come to say it, so that it will not come as a shock to me. Shocks are bad for people, you know, and lead to disordered nerves . . .'

He smiled. In the firelight, his smile seemed to me enchanting. There was something of a renewed shyness in his smile, because he was talking about his feelings for me.

He said, looking away, with a choke in his voice, 'You know very well what I shall say, dearest Leo.'

'And you know very well what I shall reply,' I said.

'I am in imminent danger of breaking my word to your aunt,' said Simon. 'And of acting dishonourably in that other sense, too. I can earn a living, you know. I have done so, and will do so again, when this project of ours is complete.'

'Yes, of course. I do not doubt that.'

'Things have gone strangely for me.'

'Tell me.'

'There are more interesting things to discuss than my poor affairs.'

'Not to me,' I said.

'Well, if you must subject yourself to my story, at least it is quite brief. As you know, I went from the university almost directly into that position as archivist at Glenalban. I believed then, and I believe still, that I was doing competent and valuable work in that muniment room, and I had and have reason to think that my labours were appreciated by my employer's aunt, the Dowager Lady Lochinver, who has lived at Glenalban since her husband's death. She was unfortunately away, visiting her married daughter, when the Earl of Glenalban suddenly and summarily dismissed me.'

'Why did he?'

'For no reason. A man like that needs no reason for what he does. In that place he is an autocrat, a whimsical tyrant, a Tiberius, a Borgia, a Napoleon. Perhaps he resented my being younger than he, and – dare I say it? – cleverer and better read than he. It is repugnant to his philosophy that anyone should be better at anything than he. All his life, I think, his family and friends have allowed him to win games, because he has made life so disagreeable if he was defeated. I was – I am – demonstrably better at matters historical and archival than he. I was a daily reminder of his own ignorance and stupidity. Thus I became first an irritant, and then a reason for fury.'

'But that is ridiculous,' I said.

'Many of the things the Earl of Glenalban does are ridiculous. His reasons are childish, laughable. But the results are often tragic. I do not mean in my case – I am alive and well and happily occupied: I am not swimming in a soup of self pity. But in the case of the tenant farmers suddenly evicted, without justice or humanity – men barely able at the best of times to feed their children . . .'

'He does that?' I said, appalled: for, like everybody else who ever saw a newspaper, I knew of the frightful sufferings of crofters evicted by cynical landlords, who wanted the land for deer-forest, or grouse-moor, or sheep-walk, from which more money could be made.

'He has come near to doing it countless times,' said Simon. 'He has, mercifully, often been restrained by his own family from acts of arbitrary barbarity.'

'Is he mad?'

'No. Not in a medical sense. But the effect of almost unlimited domestic and local power, on an indifferent intellect, produces results which look like the work of a wicked madman.'

'Can nothing be done to curb him?'

'All that is possible is continuously done, by many decent people. But they are not Earls of Glenalban.'

'Did he give any reason for dismissing you?'

'He said that I was incompetent, which I believe was not true. It was a point, moreover, on which he was himself incompetent to judge. He said that I was dishonest.'

38

'But that is absurd!'

'I am glad you think so, Leo. You have the benefit, if it is one, of knowing me moderately well. The people to whom the Earl wrote, when I was seeking other employment, did not know me. Consequently, they believed the Earl.'

'But that is vicious!'

'The mildest of the words I have used about it myself,' said Simon. 'I felt physically sick, when I was shown one letter he wrote about me, in response to an enquiry. The gentleman who showed me the letter did not quite believe it himself. But he could not take the risk of engaging me as tutor to his sons – a man branded by his only previous employer as a scoundrel. Of course, he was right. He could *not* take that risk. I do not blame him at all. The whole fault lies elsewhere.'

'I did not think such things happened.'

'Nor did I. I have always been optimistic. I have – I had – always believed in the essential goodness of humankind, which is the working of the Holy Spirit. An episode like that shakes one's faith in God and man.'

'Perhaps I can help to restore it.'

'Yes. You, your aunt, my patron, Mr David Maitland, the eminent people I have been seeing in Edinburgh – I have been more fortunate recently.'

'I do not understand about this patron.'

'Ah. He is a fascinating man. An Italian aristocrat, the Baron Vigliano – il Barone Lodovico di Vigliano. Highly educated, highly civilized, himself a scholar, much travelled. The point is that he is descended on his mother's side from Princess Louise de Stolberg.'

I looked blank.

'The wife, whom we now know to have been bigamously married, of Prince Charles Edward Stuart.'

'My great-grandfather.'

'Just so. This relationship inspired the Baron to focus his abundant energies and his formidable scholarship on the Europe of the late eighteenth century, and in particular on its various royal families, and most particularly on the sad outcast among them whom his ancestress had married.'

'Good gracious. Is he producing a book to be a rival to yours?'

39

'On the contrary, he is assisting in and financing mine. By a staggeringly lucky chance, he wrote to a professor at Aberdeen, with whom he had been corresponding for years, asking to be recommended a person who could conduct research in Scotland, while he conducted it in France and Italy – and the professor received this letter not long after my dismissal from Glenalban. Very kindly, the professor submitted my name, not being in the way of believing slanders about his former students. The Barone wrote that he must meet me, before any firm arrangement was made. He could not at that time come to Britain, owing to pressure of business, so I must go to Turin. My fare and all expenses were paid – fortunately, for I could not have paid for them myself. I was enchanted by him. You will be, too.'

'How will I be?'

'Did I not tell you? He is coming here, for the first time in his life. He speaks good English, but he has never used it in England or Scotland. He is coming because he is fascinated by what I have already been able to tell him, about our discoveries.'

'Yours.'

'Without you, none of this would have come to light.'

'Without your having seen that sword . . . Which was only in Mr Maitland's shop, because we needed money, because of a hole in the roof . . . How oddly things turn out. When is your Baron coming?'

'He writes that it will be as soon as possible. He himself does not know when he can get away. I warned him of the Scottish winter, but I do not think ice or fog will deter him, especially in view of another reason that he has for coming. He is avid to meet the single living legitimate descendant of Charles Edward.'

'Oh.'

'Of course he knows exactly what the Prince looked like, from engravings. So that, although he has never seen you, he will recognize you at once, and would do so from a thousand girls. In fact, he would not need to be aware of your uncanny resemblance to your great-grandsire, to recognize you straight away. I told him you were the most beautiful girl in Scotland, so he would pick you out from any crowd, with no difficulty, from that description.'

40

'Um,' I said, deeply pleased, but not having had any experience of making a proper reply to such a remark.

'I am forgetting myself again,' said Simon. 'I wonder if, after all, you have an immoral influence on me?'

'We are not allowed immoral influences on one another yet,' I said. 'But when I am eighteen . . .'

The conversation was taking a lovely but disquieting turn; perhaps it was as well that Aunt Sophia returned from a charitable errand, to interrupt it.

'I do not think,' said Simon at dinner, 'that there would be any profit in your pursuing claims to the crowns of England or Scotland.'

'Mercy,' said Aunt Sophia, rattling her knife against her plate in agitation at the thought.

'We are all loyal subjects of Her Majesty Queen Victoria,' said Simon. 'We had better remain so, I think.'

'Yes,' I said: for I was not going to admit to some of the wild dreams I had had.

'What, then, does all this mean to you, Leo?'

'Well, what does it mean to me?'

'The Lord Lyon King of Arms, in Edinburgh, accepts the probability, which can shortly be turned into certainty, that you are Countess of Albany in your own right. It was a legitimate title, legitimately used by Charles Edward, and it can descend in the female line if there are no male heirs.'

I pondered this. I thought I would like to be a Countess, but there were difficulties.

'To make any sense of being a Countess,' I said, 'you need all kinds of things. Things I have not got, and cannot get. How can I be a sensible Countess, living here, and wearing what I wear, and eating boiled mutton twice a week? To make any sense of being a Countess, you need a castle and a lot of money.'

'You have those things.'

'What?'

'You are the owner of Glenalban, castle and estate. You are one of the richest individuals in Scotland. The lawyers have examined the evidence, and your claim is as solid as the Palace of Holyroodhouse.'

'Mercy,' said Aunt Sophia.

41

# 3

Simon came again, two weeks later, with a little shrivelled man who was some important kind of lawyer. What the lawyer had to do, was to confirm that Simon had accurately transcribed my great-grandmother's journal and marriage certificate; the courts would then accept the documents as genuine, without having to inspect the originals.

We were moving gradually closer to my claiming the abeyant Earldom of Albany. I could not yet picture claiming the castle and estate of Glenalban.

The lawyer was always with Simon, during that visit. There was no chance of another lovely and disquieting conversation. My feelings towards the lawyer were consequently mixed, resentment of his presence striving against gratitude for his labours. My feelings towards Simon were not mixed at all. I know now that I was not yet truly in love with him, but I thought then that I was.

Aunt Sophia was right. I was far too young for all this. The hole should have been made in the roof a year later, so that the sword would have gone to Edinburgh to pay for the repairs a year later, so that Simon Donaldson and his dis-coveries would have come into my life when I was well into my nineteenth year. Then I would have brought at least a smattering of experience to bear on these new problems – at least a wisp of maturity, to keep cool and calm. But I had no experience and no maturity, and I did not keep very cool or calm.

Of all the seventeen-year-old girls in Scotland, I was the least qualified for greatness of position, or for emotional storms. But, of all the young girls in Scotland, I was the one who would shortly be Countess of Albany.

The lawyer confirmed this, when he left with Simon. He

was the first one who called me 'Ma'am'. I was completely startled, because seventeen-year-old-girls are not called 'Ma'am'. But ladies of royal blood are.

They left; and life at Millstounburn returned, to all appearance, to normal. But it was not normal. Nothing would ever again be as it was.

Presently word came from Simon that dates had been fixed for my formal petitions to the courts. They were not in the very near future. This was fortunate, for the legal processes of pursuing gigantic claims like mine would be hideously expensive, especially the fees for the leading advocates we would require.

Hearing of these, from our own solicitor in Dalkeith, made Aunt Sophia moan and myself goggle. We concluded that we must at once abandon the entire project, and forever.

But Simon wrote that, long before my petitions were presented, the Barone Lodovico di Vigliano would be in Scotland, and that he could and would pay every penny involved. He would be delighted to do so – proud to do so – said Simon. And we should not worry about accepting money from him, because he had a very great deal of it; and, by and by, I would have a very great deal of it too, and could pay him back.

Simon wrote again, in excited and delighted terms, that he was expecting the Barone before the end of February, and that, the minute he arrived, Simon would bring him to see us.

He came to Millstounburn, with Simon, in a fine hired carriage – a big, ebullient man between forty and fifty, with long glossy black hair touched at the temples with grey, and with a beard of such magnificence that it could only have belonged to an Italian aristocrat or a French poet. He was dressed in a frock coat, with pale coloured trousers, and button boots, and a prodigious cravat of silvery material with a large jewelled pin in its midst. He wore the tallest top hat I had ever seen, and he carried an ebony cane with an ivory knob bigger than a cricket ball.

He was in the most total contrast to Simon, who was quietly dressed in his usual tweeds, and looked like a laird of serious tastes. Yet, although the Barone was exotic, his appearance was no more incongruous (after the first moment of shock) than Simon's was, because his clothes suited him, and he them. Like Simon, he was dressed as himself; he was not pretending to be in any particle different from what he was.

He jumped down from the carriage, very active for such a big, plump man: and I thought he would bounce as he met the ground, as high as the carriage roof. Indeed he had the appearance of bouncing, as he walked with Simon towards the house.

He bowed over Aunt Sophia's hand, and kissed it. She was too amazed to speak. Hands were not commonly kissed in East Lothian. Probably Aunt Sophia's hand had never been kissed before.

Nor had mine; but it was kissed now.

'It is not correct, Contessa,' said the Barone, 'to kiss the hand of a young lady not *sposata*. But it is most correct to kiss the hand of a royal princess.'

He spoke English very rapidly, and somewhat loudly, in a strong accent that was not at all displeasing; this was because, like his clothes, it suited him; beard, button boots, tiepin and accent all fitted together; for such a gorgeous exotic to have spoken normal English would have been the incongruous thing.

He straightened from a bow lower than I would have supposed such a portly man could make. He stared down at me, from an impressive height. (He was a little taller than Simon, and Simon was tall.) He stared at my face, with a frown that held no hint of anger or disapproval.

'My friend Simon is right,' he said at last, more softly. '*A ragione, come sempre.* Your face, *piccola Contessa*, is the face of that great man who was a king and not ever a king. Simon is right, that I should know your face among a thousand. I do not know if he is right that you are the most beautiful of all the *signorine* of Scotland, because I have not seen every one of the young girls of Scotland, but I guess that he is right, yes. *Indovino cosi.* Of the Prince you have the *capelli chiari*, the bright hairs described by people of his time, the brown eyes from his mother, the chin with a kind of point. Now – haha! – we have another *revoluzione*, my little Simon. We shall gather up all the clans! We shall march ourselves upon Edimburgo, with our *piccola Contessa* riding in the frontal on a white horse, and you and I, little Simon, shall ride close behind on other horses, and all the clans will march behind, full of *valore* and love of their true Queen . . . There will be horrible noises, which you call music, from those goatskin bags which you call *pipi*, which I have heard once in Mentone, but all revolutionaries must suffer hardships with courage, and I shall suffer the music of your bagpipes . . .'

Simon began to laugh – the infectious, husky laughter which, when he had overcome his shyness, we had heard so often at Millstounburn. I began to laugh. The Barone, after a moment of pretended anger, laughed loud and long at his own fooleries, a rich baritone trumpet-call of laughter, which threatened to shiver the windows of the house.

Even Aunt Sophia, overwhelmed by the Barone, managed a little strangled giggle.

We conducted the Barone to the unoccupied bedchamber where my great-grandmother's trunk had been put. We showed him the journal. He did not attempt to read it, because Simon had, weeks previously, sent him copies of the pages that concerned us. But he was most anxious to see and handle the original strange document, and did so with a kind of reverence.

Even while he turned the pages of Leonora's spidery handwriting, he continued his fanciful and ludicrous account of the new Jacobite rebellion we were to lead. He had us fortified in Edinburgh Castle, then throwing an army down into the Borders. He had flying columns of cavalry striking deep into Northumberland, and at last myself being crowned in Westminster Abbey, with poor Queen Victoria going off into exile in Holland.

Turning suddenly serious, he said, '*Signorina Principessa*, I think you will not wear a crown in London. But I think you will wear a coronet in the *Castello di Glenalbani*. I think we shall make it so.'

'Why?' I said. 'I mean, why are you helping me?'

'Because I am poet. I am lover of art and of justice. I am lover of Carlo Eduardo and his Highlanders. Poetry and art and justice and politics and history, all these things say to me that a wrong must be made right, and a fairy story must have the happy endings.'

I thought that really was what he meant. He wanted to be

45

the one to turn, if not a frog into a prince, then a mouse into a Countess. It seemed to me a good reason, a nice reason for helping me; and I thought that a man who spent a lot of money for such a reason, was a nice man.

Besides, as Simon had said, I would one day be able to pay him back.

Of course, they both stayed for dinner. The Barone was extravagant in his praise of the beef, of which he ate many slices. He said that Scotland was to be admired above all nations for the beauty of its women and the succulence of its cattle. He insisted on meeting Mrs Murray the cook, and gave her a gold coin; she tucked it away so rapidly, that I did not see of what country it was. Morag shrank away from him, in horrified astonishment, but Mrs Murray was a-flutter with delight.

It was just at this moment that I had the silly idea that I had seen the Barone before. I knew I could not have done, because he had never been across the English Channel. But the notion persisted. I said to Simon that, as the Barone recognized me from pictures of Charles Edward, so I thought I recognized him from something.

'Many people do,' said Simon. 'There is a sort of similarity to your own case. The Barone bears a certain likeness to Garibaldi, of whom you are bound to have seen pictures. To tell you the truth, I think his beard is deliberately modelled on Garibaldi's, to increase the resemblance.'

This seemed eminently probable. The Barone was nothing if not theatrical. That great swashbuckling patriot would have appealed immensely to his romantic notions, as my own royal great-grandfather did. And this fitted, too, with his ambition to manage a happy ending for our fairy tale, and turn the country mouse into a castellated Countess.

It was all very endearing, as well as being very convenient.

And, because I was thinking on these lines, I said, as they were gathering up their things to leave, 'Is that a swordstick?'

With his face comically solemn, the Barone twisted the great ivory knob of his cane, and pulled it out, revealing a few inches of narrow, highly polished steel.

'There are many *banditti* in my country, small Contessa. A wise man goes armed.'

'Have you ever used it?'

46

'Yes! Surely! There was one time when I had deep need of my sword, and I was thankful that I had it.'

'You were attacked by bandits?'

'I was by the *Lago di Como*, far from help, far from any houses or any person. I was in despair.'

'How many bandits?'

'There were no bandits there. I had a melon, which I wished to slice. It was a very good melon.'

He burst out into his trumpet-call of laughter. I thought he carried a swordstick simply as part of his play-acting. I thought it was not exactly childish, but child-like. It was odd to find this trait, in a man so clever and learned; it was all of a piece with the other things I had learned about him. It was, as Simon said, rather enchanting.

Simon's letters were written on such odd scraps of paper as he had by him, I suppose, when he was working. They were addressed jointly to Aunt Sophia and myself. I would have liked a private letter, directed only to myself; but I accepted that this would have been a breach of Simon's vexatious promise to Aunt Sophia.

Now a letter came which was addressed to me only; and it was not written on an odd scrap of paper. In the envelope, it was so heavy, that I was surprised it could be carried by the penny post.

I could not think who in the world would write to me, that would use such paper. My surprise at receiving it was nothing to my astonishment at reading it.

Glenalban Castle
February 8th, 1865

My Dear Miss Albany,

Next week I shall be making one of my rare visits to Edinburgh, after which I am to go for two nights to Dalhousie. I understand that you live only a few miles from that place. I am anxious to meet you, and believe that we have much to discuss. May I propose to call on Miss Grant and yourself on Wednesday next, in the early afternoon?

If this is *not* convenient, perhaps you would be so kind as to convey a message to Dalhousie Castle, in time to stop me

47

making a fruitless journey. If I do not hear from you, I will take it that my arrival with you is expected.

I am greatly curious to meet you and, from what I have heard, shall greatly enjoy doing so.

Until Wednesday next I remain, dear Miss Albany,

    Yours very truly,

      Rosanna Lochinver.

It was another moment for goggling.

Aunt Sophia was watching me, with what was clearly unbearable curiosity. I handed her the letter, and presently she found her spectacles.

She moaned as she read.

'Rosanna Lochinver,' she said. 'Who can she be?'

'Let me think,' I said. 'Simon has mentioned her. She is the aunt of the Earl. She is a widow. She lives at Glenalban. When Simon was there, she knew he was giving good service. I think he liked her. Yes, he spoke as though he liked her, as though she was kind to him.'

'Lady Lochinver!' wailed Aunt Sophia. 'Straight from Glenalban! I cannot entertain such a person here! What will she think of us?'

I wondered, too. I wondered what on earth she wanted with me. The tone of her letter was formal, but affable enough.

She had befriended Simon. That suggested that she was a civilized person. It also raised the possibility that they had kept in touch – that she knew something of what had been engaging Simon these past weeks.

From this possibility, a thousand possibilities sprouted. She might know what we were about, the Barone and Simon and I. She might most bitterly oppose it, on her nephew's behalf. In spite of the friendliness of her letter – which might have been deliberately adopted so that we would be disarmed, and receive her – she might be bent on threatening or terrifying me out of the course to which I was now committed. She might be intending to buy me off, to bribe me into silence. She might be simply curious. She might be favourable to my claims, though this seemed the remotest possibility. She might know nothing of Leonora's journal, nothing of the true ownership of Glenalban, but merely be curious to see the person of whom

Simon had written – whatever he had written. If, indeed, he had written.

It was barely possible, I supposed, that she was curious to inspect me for some quite other, unguessable reason, having heard something about me from some quite other, unguessable source.

The following Wednesday afternoon was perfectly convenient. I was prepared to abandon, for as long as Lady Lochinver honoured us, the course of reading which Aunt Sophia had set me. Aunt Sophia could postpone (she would never abandon) the charitable errands for which those hours had been earmarked. No message therefore went to Dalhousie. We steeled ourselves to receive a lady as august and frightening as Boadicea.

Anyone less august, anyone less frightening than Lady Lochinver could not be imagined. She was the kind of person whom one likes from a distance, and who makes one smile before a word is said.

I put her age at fifty. In person she was plump, in height moderate, in dress untidy. Her clothes were doubtless expensive and certainly fashionable, but she had the air of wearing them as a joke. Her face was round, with a high fresh colour like a Ribston pippin. Her hair, which was a thick bundle of pepper-and-salt, looked on the verge of tumbling down from under a hat which looked on the verge of falling off.

Where the Barone had seemed to bounce on his way from his carriage to the house, Lady Lochinver seemed to hop. I do not mean that she literally proceeded across the gravel on one leg, but she advanced with the perky eagerness of a bird, of a plump redbreast certain of a welcome.

I curtseyed to her. She stretched out both her hands, and took mine. She smiled, very broad and warm.

She said, 'They were right. You are the image of the Young Chevalier. And you are the most beautiful girl in Scotland.'

I challenge anyone to make a reply, unrehearsed and on the instant, to such an opening from a total stranger.

She drank tea, and ate an astonishing quantity of Dundee cake; she chatted to Aunt Sophia about household expenses, and whether vegetables grown in the garden were in truth an economy, considering the wages of gardeners.

Aunt Sophia was put at her ease by Lady Lochinver even more quickly than by Simon Donaldson. One would have said that they were friends of thirty years' standing, as they discussed the respective merits of wood and coke in a kitchen range, the scandalous cost of feeding servants, and the dangerously advanced views of a certain Episcopalian bishop. Lady Lochinver was garrulous, kind, and I thought essentially simple in the nicest way. She was like a country neighbour of our own station of life, if we had been lucky enough to have any such neighbour.

She finished the last crumbs of cake on her plate; she finished her third cup of tea. She turned to me and said, 'You must have guessed that I have had word from Simon Donaldson.'

'I thought it might be that,' I said.

'I have remained in his confidence, and he in mine, since that horrid business with my nephew.'

'What did happen?'

'I scarcely know. I was away at the time, which was so unlucky. Simon wrote to me that he did not really know why Glenalban turned against him. Glenalban said Simon was incompetent and dishonest. I know quite well that he was neither. You do too, I think. So, to answer your question, what happened is simply that Glenalban behaved as he is apt to behave, when I am not there to stop him. Reason doesn't come into it. Justice certainly doesn't come into it.'

'Why do you live there, Ma'am?'

'I do so reluctantly. I do so out of duty. I was brought up, as I can tell that dear Miss Grant was brought up, to very strict religious and moral principles, which I pray God I have not lost. Glenalban Castle has hundreds of tenants and servants, every single one at the mercy of a . . . common bully. You will think it more than odd that an aunt should talk so of her nephew, of my own sister's son. He does not inherit his qualities from that unfortunate creature, who I think died of misery. It is the damnable Grieve inheritance of cruelty and stupidity. Like father, like son. That is why I do not like living there, but why I am bound to live there. It is why I have come to see you.'

I looked at her, puzzled, not understanding this new turn.

50

'What Glenalban needs,' said Lady Lochinver, 'is a new owner.'

'That is what it has,' said Aunt Sophia, most unexpectedly.

'That,' said Lady Lochinver, 'is what it will have, God willing, thanks to a secret wedding near Avignon in 1766, and to Simon Donaldson and his Italian colleague – who is delightful, I am told, and whom I am most anxious to meet. It will be a very pretty turn-up, my dears, and I shall be standing by applauding.'

Lady Lochinver sat back beaming, after this amazing speech. It came to me that the word for her was 'motherly'.

She went on to say that there was no conflict or confusion in her mind, in the way she reacted to the explosive news Simon Donaldson had confided to her. She scarcely felt any kinship with the Earl, although he was her nephew, and so was unmoved at the thought of his expulsion from Glenalban. She violently deplored his character and actions, and so, from this point of view, actively welcomed the prospect of his expulsion. She knew me to be the rightful owner of Glenalban, so the strict moral principles of which she had spoken drove her to champion my claim to my inheritance. And although she was perfectly realistic, and perfectly loyal to the Queen, she was a romantic Jacobite almost in the mode of my earnest, silly great-grandmoter.

'You are the legitimate heiress of the Bonnie Stuarts, Leonora,' said Lady Lochinver. 'You cannot have the crown that is yours, more's the pity, but you can and shall have the castle that is yours. That will serve the Grieves right, for their treachery to our Prince in the Forty-Five.'

I understood that she was well read in the Waverley novels of Sir Walter Scott, and they had heavily influenced her view of history. Rob Roy came into her conversation more than once. This was, for me, yet another prodigious stroke of luck, and made Lady Lochinver my ally from every possible point of view.

Because she was garrulous, her own history came tumbling out, as I thought it probably did to everbody she met. She was one of three sisters, daughters of General Sir George Frith. They were widely spaced in age, because of her father's prolonged absences on military duty. She had married moderately well in a worldly sense, and brilliantly well in the way of personal happiness. Her much older sister had married brilliantly well in a worldly sense, becoming Countess of Glenalban and mistress of its Castle, but miserably in every other way. In contemplation of that marriage, Lady Lochinver thought, her youngest sister Louisa had never married.

'Although,' she said, 'Louisa was a beautiful girl, and is still a very handsome woman, as I was not and am not. And she is one of the people who achieve perfection in their dress, which is a trick I have never mastered, how ever much money I spend . . . She has lived at Glenalban since our older sister's calamitous marriage, I only since my dear Lord died.'

Lady Lochinver's son had inherited their property, in Sutherland in the far north-west of Scotland; her daughter was married, and lived near Perth. We heard a good deal about their childish ailments, their beauty, their astonishing precocity. Lady Lochinver was clearly one of those mothers, round the shoulders of whose children the sun rises and sets. She was a creature of the greatest goodness of heart. I thought I was supremely lucky in all my allies.

As though divining my thoughts (or perhaps they showed once again plainly on my face) Lady Lochinver turned from Aunt Sophia to me. She said, 'In the courts of law, my dear, I shall stand your friend. But in my heart I am something quite different. I am your subject.'

This was graciously said. But I thought it was carrying romantic Jacobitism a shade far. It verged on the ridiculous. The Barone had talked in such terms – and then roared with laughter, because he was exaggerating my importance in order to construct a comic fantasy. Lady Lochinver looked completely serious, her broad smile for once quite wiped away by solemnity.

Glenalban would have a new owner, who would be just and humane. That was one thing. It was an awe-inspiring prospect, but it was more and more evidently within the realm of the possible. We were talking of stones and mortar, of tenants and servants, practical matters, susceptible of a practical resolution. But that the widow of a Peer of the Realm should describe herself as my 'subject' – that was bordering on the bizarre.

I did not even like it very much. I wanted Lady Lochinver

to be my friend, not my subject. In my life, I wanted friends rather than subjects. I did not feel myself of an age, of a size, of a character, to have people thinking themselves my subjects.

Of course there was something intoxicating about it. How could there not be? But I was wary of intoxication, remembering the awful example of my great-grandmother.

When presently Lady Lochinver took her leave, I curtseyed to her – and she curtseyed to me. Her curtsey was deeper than mine, which was an ordinary little curtsey, in which I descended a few inches. She descended most of her height. She was more graceful than one would have supposed such a dumpy person could have been. On her face was a kind of radiance. She made me feel like a queen. She made me feel a part of the Barone's wildest comic fantasies.

Yes, it was intoxicating, and I fought with uncertain success against the intoxication.

'Do you mind very much, dear,' said Aunt Sophia, with an unusual touch of dryness in her voice, 'if I do *not* curtsey to you?'

I burst out laughing; and she smiled.

And so she gently and wisely reminded me that I was still an obscure nobody, whatever I might become; and she stopped me getting a swelled head, and a silly notion of my own importance.

Two crawling weeks later, another letter came to me from Lady Lochinver, which made me wonder if she were entirely sane.

Glenalban Castle
March 1st 1865

May it please your Royal Highness,
(For so I regard you privately, and so in a private letter I address you.)

My nephew Glenalban will be in London next month, for Parliament is sitting and he will be attending the House of Lords. His sister will be with him. It is an opportune time for your Highness to claim her own!

In all humility, I deplore that I should find myself in

53

the false and invidious position of inviting your Royal Highness to your own castle; but that will be put right on your arrival.

I venture to suggest that your wardrobe can also be put right, if I may venture the audacity of the observation. I beg you will allow me the honour of introducing to you some dressmakers and milliners that I believe to be not without merit; and I beg that you will do me the honour to allow the reckoning to my affair.

The lawyers are busy, and matters march.

My grief is that I dare not invite our friend Simon Donaldson to share your triumph, which would be only just; Glenalban's servants, on Glenalban's orders, would do him harm, even to serious injury. No doubt the time will come, when your Royal Highness will honour him with a summons; but it is not yet.

My sister and I pray that you will honour your own house with your gracious presence about the beginning of April. Of course we trust that the estimable Miss Grant will also give us the keen pleasure of her company.

Presenting my humble duty to your Royal Highness,

I remain, yours most obediently to command,

Rosanna Lochinver.

'She is two different people,' I said to Aunt Sophia. 'And only one of the two is sane.'

'You should not mock such kindness, dear.'

'No, I do not mock it, exactly, but you yourself have told me not to take all of it seriously.'

'Take the kindness *very* seriously, Nora. Take the reverence with a pinch of salt.'

Well, I did, and I did not. I was still a distance short of my eighteenth birthday.

Aunt Sophia would not, as it happened, give Lady Lochinver and her sister the pleasure of her company. Once we got to Glenalban, there was no knowing how long we would stay. I, perhaps, forever. Aunt Sophia felt that she could not be spared about Millstounburn. Her conscience was indeed as lively as Lady Lochinver's.

I thought that she did not altogether want to go to

54

Glenalban. She did not want to see me treated as royalty, because she thought it would be thoroughly bad for me. (As it is apt to be, no doubt, for other royalty: as it certainly was for my hapless great-grandfather.)

She was frightened of the size of Glenalban, and its rules and protocol; she was frightened of making herself ridiculous, by losing her way between one room and another; she was frightened of using the wrong fork, and of curtseying to an upper servant in the belief that she was a visiting duchess.

So was I. But I was going.

So, on the 31st of March, came Miss Grizelda Hamilton, humbly representing Lady Lochinver; and Aunt Sophia and I made our ill-matched farewells.

And, on the journey, I brooded about what had happened, and what was to happen.

I rejoiced in the friendship of the Barone Lodovico di Vigliano; and in the much-more-than-friendship of Simon Donaldson. I rejoiced in the goodwill of Lady Lochinver, although I thought she had a streak which was silly to the point of embarrassment.

Remembering, I thought for the first time in weeks of Edgar Smith, 'Doctor Nicol' of the birdlike birthmark, that greedy and violent man. I wondered what had become of him, and whom he had been robbing. I thought we would not hear of him again – that he would attempt his crimes in another place, under yet another name.

We came to the gaunt house with the gaunt servants, and my indiscretion with the whip.

We came to Glenalban – to Lady Lochinver's reverential curtsey, and the Jacobite screaming of the piper, and the obeisances of the army of servants.

All Aunt Sophia's fears were realized. It was very bad for me. How could I not feel somewhat glorious, when the whole visible world was treating me like an empress?

The liveried grandee with the wand of office, who had led me up the steps into the hall, now presented to me, in a graveyard voice, the housekeeper. It seemed she was Mrs McKim. She kept her face averted from me, first by the depth of her curtsey, and then by what I took to be awe. An awestruck housekeeper was something new to me – all those I

55

had encountered inspired terror, rather than felt it. To strike awe was also new to me, and not altogether agreeable.

Mrs McKim said, in a strangled voice, 'Will her Highness be pleased to follow me upstairs?'

It seemed they were all romantic Jacobites in this place. I thought life would be simpler, if they accepted me as their mistress, without raising me up on to a throne.

I looked round for Lady Lochinver, with whom I had hardly yet exchanged a word. She was not to be seen. Evidently I was, now, a royal parcel, given into the charge of Major Domo and Housekeeper.

'Your Highness wull occupy the King's Room,' said Mrs McKim, still in a strangled voice. 'It will no' hae been slept in, syne the last veesit o' King James the Sixth o' Scotland.'

'Prince Charles Edward came here,' I said, suddenly remembering Simon's history lesson.

'He didna bide the nicht, your Highness.'

I was startled at the notion of a bedchamber, doubtless the finest in the castle, unused for more than two and a half centuries, because it was reserved for the exclusive use of royalty. To be sure, there was a sufficiency of other rooms.

The very fact of there being a 'King's Room' bore out what Simon had discovered. It was kept for the use of the owner, as might be a room in a laird's outlying farm.

It was a great climb to the King's Room, and after the great climb a long walk, down a corridor as wide as a church, carpeted in tartan, and hung with old pictures. I made an effort to remember the turns we took, and the landmarks we passed, so that I should be able to find my way back without a guide.

We went very slowly, as though it had been a royal progress. To those old upper servants, I supposed that that was what it was.

As we reached another flight of stairs, which rose from a great archway, a pale young man in black came hurrying along the corridor after us. He was not dressed as a servant; I took him for a kind of secretary.

'Ma'am,' he panted, bowing, 'Lady Lochinver sends infinite regrets, but she has just been summoned post-haste to the bedside of her daughter.'

56

'Is her daughter ill?'

'She is, er, in an interesting condition, Ma'am, and we understand that there are complications affecting the imminent confinement. It is to be her Ladyship's first grandchild, and she humbly begs –'

'Of course she must go!' I cried. 'Of course her place is with her daughter at such a time!'

'So she feels, Ma'am. In fact she has already gone. Her Ladyship's sister, Miss Louisa Frith, will venture to entertain your Highness, when you are pleased to descend to the drawing room.'

'That is kind of Miss Frith. But I hope mother and child will be safe.'

'They will be better for Lady Lochinver's presence, Ma'am.'

'That is certainly true.'

He bowed. He murmured something to Mrs McKim, who glanced at me and nodded. He bowed to me again, and hurried away. From his way of addressing me, he was yet another Jacobite. I had not supposed there were so many, in all Scotland. In fact, I had not supposed there were any.

I wondered if the air of the glen, or perhaps the drinking water, caused a mild form of hereditary insanity. Well, it did not do any harm; least of all, did it do me any harm.

We reached the King's Room at last, and it was superb.

It must have been new, when James VI used it, for the windows were great expanses of leaded glass, in the Tudor style, not medieval slits in the stone; and it must have been newly furnished and fitted then, for even to my ignorant eye the great bed and the hangings and chairs were of the Elizabethan period.

A thin, dark-haired woman with a sallow face curtseyed as I came in. I understood that she was Mary MacAndrew, and that, if I pleased, she was to be my personal maid.

I had never had such a thing. It was an aspect of my new situation which I had not considered. Aunt Sophia and I had always done all our own sewing, and much of our own ironing. And dressing and undressing myself, and arranging my own hair, had never seemed to offer any problems. I thought Mary MacAndrew would have an idle time of it.

I walked over to the windows, and looked out. The prospect

57

took my breath away – it was magnificent. I had been seeing great hills for much of the latter part of the journey to this place, but from ground level. To look at them from an eminence was splendid, and to look far down to the descending sequence of terraces – some paved, some grassed and close-mown, some with intricate geometrical parterres – which merged into parkland, still descending, and so to the silver rapids of the river far below.

I looked across the glen at the high tops opposite, still covered in snow, though it had melted on the lower ground. The air was clear; the distances I could see were huge. I caught myself wondering how much of what I could see was mine.

A door opened in the side of the enormous room, which gave to another and much smaller room. Through it came, bowing, a burly young man in livery. I understood that he was Kenneth Doig, and that, if I pleased, he was to be my personal footman.

This was becoming too much for me. To what possible use could I put a personal footman? Was he to run with messages? To whom? Was he to fetch books, or embroidery? Move my footstool? Shade me from the sun?

It occurred to me that the very rich made their lives needlessly complicated; and that when I became very rich I would simplify things. I would not dismiss such as Mary MacAndrew and Kenneth Doig, because that would be just the kind of cruelty which Lady Lochinver trusted me not to commit; but I would find them more useful things to do than dogging my footsteps and picking up things I dropped.

I smiled at the maid and at the footman. The maid did not return my smile. Her face remained completely solemn. She bowed her head. I thought that, if I must have a personal maid, I should prefer one with a more cheerful air. Perhaps in Glenalban no one wore a cheerful air, on account of the Earl; perhaps even Lady Lochinver, when she was here, lost her blithe garrulity.

That too I would change.

The man Kenneth Doig did begin to smile to answer mine: but he wiped it off his face almost before it had started. He composed his features, so that he looked as wooden as the police officers who had come to catch Edgar Smith.

Mrs McKim said that, if it pleased me, I should look at the wardrobe. I was surprised. I was not much interested in inspecting any wardrobe, until it contained the fine new clothes I had been promised. But, in order not to offend her, I looked about for a wardrobe. There was none. The small room from which the footman had come was the wardrobe. The clothes of kings would not fit, I supposed, into a piece of furniture; nor would my new clothes.

I went obediently into the little room, out of consideration for Mrs McKim's feelings. In fact, I saw that it was furnished as a bedchamber, though barely. There was a small cot, low to the floor, with a thin mattress and a single blanket. There was a wooden chair and a small wooden table. There was an enamel washbowl on a wooden stand in the corner, and under it a bucket. That was all. There was one small high window.

I looked round this dreary little cell, pretending interest, out of politeness. I did not understand why such a point had been made that I should see it. Surely Mary MacAndrew was not going to sleep in it, so that she could look after me twenty-four hours of the day? I did not think any servant would be subjected to such discomfort.

I turned to leave the 'wardrobe', having, I thought, done all that politeness required.

At that moment, the door slammed shut. I heard a key turn in the lock.

I twisted the doorknob, and rattled it. I knew it was useless. I shouted out. I knew that was useless too.

It was not Mary MacAndrew who was going to sleep in the cell.

# 4

It was a long time before I could quieten the turbulence in my head, and make any sense of what was happening to me.

When I was a child, the punishment I most detested was being shut in. I had a horror of confined spaces – of being accidentally imprisoned by the latch of a cupboard or the bolt of a shed. It was not so much that I was frightened of the dark, or of suffocation – I had no morbid fears, of the kind to which the Faculty gives long names – as that I needed to be forever free to move, to dart about, to go in and out and about and up and down. Of course I could sit still to my sewing or my book, when I was obliged to, but I needed to feel that I *could* get up and dash out of the house.

This was one reason for my extreme dismay at being locked in the wardrobe.

The other was that I had, simply and stupidly, walked into a trap.

I tried to understand, and by and by I thought I did. All those servants I had seen – at least those I had met – were the creatures of the Earl of Glenalban, and loyal to him. From what I had heard of him, they were either bribed into being so, or frightened into being so. Thus, as soon as Lady Lochinver was called away to her daughter's bedside, and her benevolent influence removed, I was tricked into my prison. That was what the young black-suited secretary was about. That was what the Major Domo, and the Housekeeper, and the lady's maid, and the footman were about.

I thought it highly probable that Miss Louisa Frith had been kept in complete ignorance of the doings of her nephew's servants. I thought she would be told some story that I had run away, too awed by the size of the castle and the numbers of its servants to stay. Something like that. And so she would raise the alarm, and there would be a search for me up and down the glen, and perhaps the river would be dragged; and it would all be pretence, because there would be those who knew that I was fast in the wardrobe of the King's Room.

Of course I might not be here long. I might be kept to await the punishment of the Earl for my temerity; or I might not be kept at all, but knocked on the head and sunk in a peat-hag.

I was very angry, and I was very frightened.

Obviously, Lady Lochinver would not have breathed a word to the Earl her nephew about me – about my claims, or about my coming. But, as soon as the Earl was away, she had told those servants, who had pretended to agree with her, so that they should greet and treat me as she thought proper. And most gloriously they play-acted, for her and for myself!

As soon as they knew about me – it might have been only that very day – word would have been sent to the Earl. No doubt the secretary had seen to that. I imagined a courier had galloped to the nearest railway station, wherever that might be, and a special packet had been handed to the guard of the London train, for urgent delivery into the Earl's hands.

The Earl's sister was with him in London. I had no mental picture of her – Lady Lochinver had hardly spoken of her. That suggested that she was cut from the Earl's cloth. Presumably she was entertaining for her brother, at his London house. That meant that he had no wife. Either he was not married, or he had driven his wife in misery to the grave, as his father had driven Lady Lochinver's sister.

What would the Earl's sister make of these events? What would she make of me? Quite likely, I thought, she would never see me. Nobody would see me, except my guards and executioner.

For, trying hard to bring logic to my predicament, I did not see that the Grieves would have much choice. If I remained alive, my friends would still press my claims on my behalf, amply financed by the Barone. What mattered was the proof of my ancestry, and the title to Glenalban; my face was not needed in the courts. But if I were dead there was no case,

61

because there was no claimant; there was no legitimate descendant of King James II's body. The Grieves were safe in Glenalban for ever.

And they would be spared the cost of defending their title in the courts.

The one other thing they could do was to keep me prisoner for ever, in this little cell, or some other little cell. In a place as big as Glenalban, that would be perfectly possible. But it would be cheaper and safer to kill me. It was their prudent course. There was nothing whatever I could do about it. Being forewarned was not being forearmed.

I examined my cell minutely. It did not take long. I did not know what I was looking for. I did not find it.

I thought the wooden chair might have a loose leg, that I could pull away and use for a club. It did not. All the furniture was simple, even rough, but extremely solid.

I stood on the table, to look out of the window. I leaned far out. I thought I could have wriggled through, with a squeeze, though I think not many persons could have done so. But below the window the wall fell sheer to the stones of the highest of the terraces, a very long way down; and it rose sheer above to the battlements; and it stretched smooth and unbroken by any projection to a corner on my right, and to the great windows of the King's Room on my left.

I had never felt unnerved by heights. As a child, I spent much time in the tops of trees, frightening Aunt Sophia half to death, and I wished I was a poor working boy, so that I could have become a steeplejack. But the thought of climbing out of the window of the wardrobe made my head spin. It was certain death. There was no escape that way. There was no escape any way.

I stayed hanging out over the window-ledge, my toes just touching the table-top; because, although it was alarming to look straight downwards, it was better to look at hills and glens than at the white-painted walls of my cell. I could see nobody. It was as though the world were suddenly deserted; although I knew that the castle below and about me teemed with people.

Then, as darkness gradually fell, pinpricks of light appeared here and there in the distance, as folk lit their lamps; and below me some light washed out from the castle windows on to the stones of the terrace.

My little room grew very dark, even while the sky outside was still pale, because the window was so high and small. It grew cold. Reluctantly, I shut the window. I nearly tumbled, climbing down from the table in the dark.

I was frightened and angry, and I was cold and hungry.

Two people who wished me well knew where I was. Aunt Sophia would not expect to hear from me for some days; she would be happy to think that I was under the protection of Lady Lochinver. Lady Lochinver herself would be preoccupied with her daughter; she would be happy to think that I was under the protection of her sister.

It was conceivable that Simon Donaldson knew where I was, from Lady Lochinver, or would know, from Aunt Sophia. But he would not show his face within miles of Glenalban; and he would think me perfectly safe, with the Earl away.

It was conceivable that the Barone Lodovico di Vigliano knew where I was, from Simon. He would expect one day to come to Glenalban, but not for many weeks yet.

There was no help to be hoped for, from any of those well-wishers. The only help was to be prayed for. I prayed for it, there in the dark by the cot. I hoped my prayers were strong enough to pierce the massive granite above me.

After a long time – I could not guess how long – I heard the key in the lock of my door. Light flooded into my cell. Mary MacAndrew the sallow maid came in quickly, carrying a tray which she put on the table. Behind her, blocking the door, stood Kenneth Doig the sturdy footman.

Well, they had been described as my personal attendants. In their fashion, they were attending to me.

I said, with what must have been some violence, 'Why am I being treated like this? Will you please give me a reason?'

The maid made no reply, nor showed any emotion. The footman, who had started to smile when I first saw him, maintained his face of wood.

They had been told to say nothing. They were frightened to disobey. They were not frightened of me.

On the tray was a bowl of meat stew, a piece of dry bread,

and a burning candle in a short brass candlestick. There was only an inch of candle. It would do for me to see to eat my supper, but it would not last long after that.

I thought there was deliberate cruelty in these arrangements.

I was locked in again. I did not hear their retreating footsteps, because of the depth of the carpet in the King's Room. There was no carpet in the wardrobe.

I sat to the table, and ate my stew greedily. It was good, but there was not enough. To be sure, that might not be deliberate cruelty. Nobody in this place had had a chance to study my appetite.

The maid came back, with the footman always behind and blocking the door. She put a jug of water by the washstand, with a towel. She put another blanket on the cot. She put a white cotton nightdress on the cot. She put a comb and a toothbrush on the table. I recognized them as mine. My scanty luggage had been opened and examined, then. The nightdress was not mine.

'Do you know that what you are doing is a crime?' I said. 'I suppose you have been ordered to do it, but still you are committing a crime. Do you understand? You will go to prison, when I tell the police what you have done to me.'

They were silent. Their faces were as impassive as before. They did not think they would go to prison.

They left me alone, in the dark.

I thought I had not been sensible, telling them they would go to prison when I had reported them. They would make sure I never did report them.

I think I had never prayed so hard as I did that night. Aunt Sophia was used to say that one's prayers should be for other people, not for oneself. Mine, that night, were for myself.

My great concern was not to weep. It would not have mattered – God knew, nobody was there to see me. But as a point of pride, I was determined not to weep, and I did not.

I did not sleep, either, although I found I was deeply exhausted. For one thing, I was cold, although I spread my clothes as well as the blankets over myself on the cot. For another, unanswerable questions screamed at me from the black corners of the room; and I wondered where I would be the next night, and whether sleeplessness would ever again be a problem for me.

I thought not. In my more rational moments in that dreadful and endless night, I thought that whoever had been left in charge by the Earl – bailiff, factor, housekeeper, steward, secretary – would think it best to solve the problem posed by my existence, and permanently, while the Earl was far away. Then he need never even know the squalid details, and never be implicated at all. If all bullies were in truth cowards, then he would not wish his hands dirtied. His creatures would earn his gratitude, if he came home and found the nuisance removed.

Drably, in the small hours, I wondered who they would pick. I thought either a forester, with an axe, or a game-keeper, with a sporting rifle. I prayed that I would face either with courage and without tears. But I was frightened that I would break down, and shriek, and weep, and beg for mercy. I think I was as frightened of that humiliation, as of axe or rifle.

I wondered what they would have done, if Lady Lochinver had not been called away. I wondered what they would do, when at last she came back. They could explain my absence by all sorts of stories, if I was not there. How could they explain my presence, and in a cell, if I was there? This seemed, in the small hours, a remote possibility.

The little high oblong of the window paled, at long, long last. Presently, a-tiptoe on the table, I saw the big hills take shape in the pearly air, and then the rim of a chilly sun behind them.

As well as I could with cold water and without a looking-glass, I washed and dressed and made myself tidy. Whatever was coming to me next, I wanted to meet it with dignity.

What came next, to my relief, was breakfast. The same servants, in the same silence. The maid emptied the wash-bowl, and gave me a ewer of fresh water. She gave me a bowl of porridge, and a cup of tea. She looked as though she did not enjoy giving me even so much. The footman looked as though playing prison warder came naturally to him.

I tried to talk to them, with the same success as before. They might have been deaf mutes.

An hour passed. The sun climbed higher, but there was no other change at all. I spent most of the time tiptoe on the table, looking at the profiles of hills which were becoming terribly familiar. My thoughts spun round in my head, like peas in a tambourine, and of no more use.

Sometimes I was enraged almost to screaming, sometimes frightened to prayer. I did not weep.

Almost worst, was the contrast between the enormous and glorious landscape spread before my window, and my world of twelve feet by ten feet – between terraces, park, river and snowcapped hills, and a table and chair and cot and washstand.

It was too early in the year for flowers to be bedded out in the parterres, but I thought they had already been dug and made ready, and the shrubs pruned. So there was nothing for the gardeners to do on the terraces below me, and I still saw no one.

Then I saw a man far away in the park, crossing in front of the castle, with a dog at his heels. He was surely part of the Glenalban estabishment, but, as an outside man, he might not be part of the conspiracy which had imprisoned me. At least it was a chance worth taking, and I had nothing to lose.

I waved and shrieked. If he saw and heard, he would at least know that there was someone in distress in the great tower of Glenalban. Very likely he knew already; there was a possibility that he did not.

The wind was blowing gustily from the river towards the castle. If the man I saw had shouted loud, I would have heard his voice carried downwind to my window. But my shrieks were puffed back into my own face.

He saw me, though. He waved back. He was too far away for me to see his face, but it seemed a cheery wave, a friendly gesture of 'good morning'.

He thought I was a saucy maidservant. He went about his business with his dog, and I was alone in the world again.

How the time dragged! How my thoughts whirled!

I heard the key in the lock, and scrambled down from the table.

In the doorway, with the footman on guard behind her, stood a lady I had not before seen. But I knew at once who she was. My heart leaped – and then sank again, because immediately one of my tiny sparks of hope was snuffed out.

Miss Louisa Frith had that certain, small resemblance to her sister which is usual among sisters; but she was a creature of a different kind.

She was much younger than Lady Lochinver – hardly turned forty, I thought. She was still beautiful, with the kind of strong and well-boned face which the years are most kind to, and which even increases in handsomeness with age. She was slim and elegant. As Lady Lochinver had described her, she was superbly dressed, and carried her clothes superbly. I had seen enough grand ladies in Edinburgh to realize that Miss Frith was very grand indeed.

But the greatest difference between the sisters lay in the manner in which they regarded me. Miss Frith looked at me with unmistakable disgust. To her, I was a cockroach, or a rat, unclean vermin to be despatched by someone wearing gloves.

She stared at me long and intently, frowning.

I stared back. I attemped dignity.

I said, rashly, 'I have been subjected to an outrage.'

'No, not you,' said Miss Louisa Frith. 'An outrage has been attempted, by you and your confederate. He chose ingeniously, when he picked you as his candidate. He has throughout been ingenious. He forged old documents purporting to relate to the ownership of this property. He forged pages of a spurious journal, and planted them where they would be found. He searched Scotland for a young woman who combined brazen audacity with a need for money, and a fleeting resemblance to Prince Charles Edward. One might say another forgery, a false Stuart, an impersonation. No, Miss Albany – your real name, whatever it is, is of interest to the police rather than to us – you have been subjected to no outrage.'

'You have got everything completely wrong!' I cried. 'Simon Donaldson –'

'Was dismissed from this place for most dastardly and cruel behaviour, by which he had hoped to enrich himself.

67

Unfortunately, the folly of a person here very nearly allowed him to succeed, and in order to protect the reputation of that person, we have not broadcast the whole truth about your friend. The folly of another person here has given you grounds to hope that Donaldson's new piracy would succeed. It will not.'

'Simon Donaldson is a learned man!'

'Yes. He could not have attempted this fraud if he were not.'

'He has testimonials from his professors!'

'Whose noses are so deep in their books that they do not observe the devices of confidence tricksters.'

'Lady Lochinver says of him that —'

'My sister is good-hearted and infinitely gullible. Because Simon Donaldson is a pretty young man with cajoling manners, and a most adroit pretence of bashfulness, she will not be shaken in her faith in him as a pure knight. The evidence of his treachery here, where he had been shown nothing but kindness, would convince a blind lunatic. It will not convince my sister. She is a goose. She took one look at your face, I imagine, and was instantly convinced that you were of royal blood. She stuffs her head with romantical claptrap from cheap novels, and thinks life imitates them. It does not, Miss, er, Albany —'

'My name is Leonora Albany,' I said.

'We will indulge that fiction, if you wish. It is the only wish of yours which is likely to be indulged. Even from your point of view, perhaps, it was providential that my sister was suddenly called away. The sentence of the judge will be less, I imagine, because your scheme was stifled almost at birth. I shall make myself responsible for you, until my nephew's return from London. It will be up to him, then, to decide what to do with you. You will find him just, but I do not think, in a case like this, you will find him indulgent. The fact that you are the confederate of Simon Donaldson is of itself enough to brand you.'

'This is all lies! The Earl —'

'Acted, in the matter of Donaldson, with what seemed to me excessive tolerance. Donaldson did not go to prison. Subsequent events have confirmed that he belonged there.'

68

'The letters the Earl wrote, poisoning people's minds against Simon –'

'Were written with distaste, and from a sense of duty. Great Heavens, girl, would even you have permitted such a man to enter other households, to take charge of young children, to cheat the unsuspecting and rob the preoccupied?'

'The Barone di Vigliano –'

'Is either another imposter or another dupe. I suspect the latter, but we shall know better when enquiries have been completed. If he has been duped, it is by you as well as by the man Donaldson. Knowing the explosive Italian temperament, I imagine the Barone will be angrier than the Earl of Glenalban.'

'If you are making enquiries,' I said angrily, 'you will come to learn the truth. You will not wish to admit it, but the courts will make you do so. Then you will apologize to me, and when you have done that you will pack your bags and go.'

'A creditable performance, Miss. Righteous indignation almost convincingly played. Bah. Your bluff has been called, and your histrionics are wasted. And so has a sufficiency of my time. I shall leave you to your thoughts. I should, if I were you, direct them to methods by which you may reduce the term of your prison sentence.'

I opened my mouth to make a defiant reply, with no clear idea of what I was going to say; but before any words came she was gone, and the key turning again in the lock.

Then nothing happened, nothing at all, until they brought me luncheon. Again it was quite good, and again not enough. But I would not humiliate myself by asking for more.

Miss Louisa Frith was wholly in the Earl's camp, then. I wondered at Lady Lochinver's sister being so. Then I thought that, as a dependant spinster, she knew on which side her bread was buttered. By following the Earl, and working for the Earl, she assured herself a life of elegance and luxury. To have flouted the Earl – to have taken an honest and independent line – might have threatened her with life in an Edinburgh lodging house, without any of those silks and jewels she wore. Perhaps she had contrived to convince herself that the Earl was in the right, in all things. If not, she must have woken up in the middle of many nights, and lain in the dark sickened by self-disgust.

I thought it was a kind of prostitution, to live as she lived.

I thought it was a kind of purgatory, to live as I was living and to look out on the great hills.

In the afternoon, some people came out of the castle, to stroll upon the terraces. They too had had their luncheons – more than I had had, I supposed – and they were enjoying the clear April sunshine. They were free. They were Miss Louisa Frith's guests; they were not in the pay of the Earl.

So I screamed and waved from my window. I screamed that I was a prisoner, that I was blameless, that I must at once be released.

The people looked up, far up to where I hung out of my window. The dark of hats turned, below me, to the white of questioning faces. I seemed to see an air of sympathy. I screamed again, begging to be helped. They looked down and away, and strolled on. I seemed to see that they shrugged, with pity, or with indifference.

'Your demonstration to my guests,' said Miss Louisa Frith the following morning, 'was purposeless. They had been told that a young maidservant is crazed with grief, after the death by drowning of her lover in the river, that we consider it more merciful to keep her here, locked up but well cared for, than to throw her into the public lunatic asylum. She is an orphan, you understand, with no family to go to.'

'And so you earn a reputation for charity,' I said bitterly.

She looked at me coldly, gave a quick cold smile, and left me.

I asked for pen and ink. They were brought, though not until the following day. The writing paper I was given, was of the sort on which Lady Lochinver had written to me.

At least they did not stint me, as to the quality of the paper they gave me.

I wrote to Aunt Sophia, saying that there had been a horrible misunderstanding, and that I was being held prisoner on suspicion of my claims being fraudulent. I begged her to get in touch with Simon Donaldson and the Barone di Vigliano, so that something could be done to free me, and to establish as soon as possible that I was no imposter, and that my claims were at least sincere.

I had no real hope that this letter would reach Millstoun-burn. But there was a tiny chance that it might find itself in a pile of others, and be stamped and sent off with them by a servant to whom 'Miss Sophia Grant' meant nothing.

There was also a chance that Miss Louisa Frith, reading my letter as I was sure she would, might be given a jolt by the truth, and reconsider her course of action. I thought this a much smaller chance, than that of the letter being sent off.

Days passed. I did not know how many days. I became muddled, and lost track, because every day was exactly like every other. The weather outside continued glorious. Into my cell crept a little morning sun, but only a little, and that not for long.

I began to feel like a plant that sprouts in a cellar, and grows white and weak.

'The servants have reported to me that you seem in indifferent health,' said Miss Louisa Frith. 'I suppose you are accustomed to vigorous exercise, running about the streets of a city and picking pockets. Or perhaps you are already a member of a still older and more dishonourable profession.'

I did not realize, until I thought about it later, what she meant by this observation. This was probably lucky. I would have lost my temper completely, with grievous results.

'You will be given thirty minutes' exercise on the battlements, guarded, at dawn and dusk,' said Miss Louisa Frith. 'If you attempt to abuse this privilege in any way, it will be withdrawn. I have made myself responsible for your health and safety, as well as for the restriction of your movements. I am not in the way of shirking my responsibilities, and I shall not do so now. I am not acting out of kindness. I feel no kindness towards such as you.'

So, that evening and thereafter, I promenaded up and down a kind of avenue of stone, behind the battlements, and dividing them from a steep-pitched roof made of mossy stone slabs. A few paces behind me came sallow Mary MacAndrew. At each end of my promenade, which was some forty paces long, stood a footman, Kenneth Doig and another. None of

71

the three ever said a word to me. So, after a time, I never said a word to them.

As far as possible, I made sure that I took the exercise which I so desperately needed. I fairly sprinted along my promenade, with Mary MacAndrew panting behind. Or I strode; or I strolled, breathing in deeply, thankful to have the heavens above me.

The dawn was the better time. Sometimes it was very cold, but the air was as sweet as a nut.

What was miserable was that the battlements were too high for me to see over. A man of normal height could have done so, which I suppose is why they were built as they were built. I could have jumped, and caught a split-second glimpse of hills; but that would have brought my guards on to my head.

My footsteps were dogged, and each end of my walk was guarded. But they did not post a guard on the ridge of the roof. They did not think I could climb the roof. I thought I could. But I did not know what I would find, when I looked down from the top on the other side. I risked fresh air and exercise, if I uselessly went like a spider up to the ridge, and then sat there helplessly waiting to be caught.

The roof remained a faint possibility of escape; the only possibility.

I did speak to one person, who listened to me, and replied at length, and preached to me, and prayed at me. He was the castle Chaplain. He was the Reverend Joseph Cardew, a skinny little man of about thirty, with amazing white hands, which he flapped as he spoke, as though trying to fly.

He would have come on a pastoral visit to see me before, he said, but he had been away on leave of absence, visiting his widowed mother in Glasgow, by gracious permission of his Lordship, who was always so liberal to those who worked for him.

It was easy to see to which camp the Chaplain belonged.

'I beg and implore you, my child, to consider your conscience.'

'There is nothing on my conscience,' I said.

'Ah, contumaciousness! To persist in this scandalous and audacious folly will bring the vials of wrath upon your head!

72

You are too young and too comely, my child, to consort with notorious evil-doers –'

'Comely' was a word I had never been called. Indeed, I think I had never before heard it used. I was interested to be termed 'comely', but I did not want compliments from this sanctimonious little man. And I did not care to listen to yet more slanders on Simon Donaldson.

'The first evil-doers I have met in my life,' I said, 'have been here.'

Even as I spoke, I remembered Edgar Smith, who smote the policeman and tried to steal the journal. But I thought it would be better not to bother with qualifying my statement.

'Deny, before me and before God,' cried Mr Cardew, 'your insolent and mendacious claims! Confess, to me and to God, that you are not what you have audaciously claimed yourself to be, and that you do not have a title of right to the property that you claim to own! Make humble confession, meekly kneeling upon your knees! Then I will attempt to intercede with his Lordship, as we are assured that Jesus Christ will intercede with God the Father. Admit, my child! All will go better for you, in body and in spirit, if you make a full confession now!'

'I will tell you the truth,' I said.

'Blessed be the name of the Lord, that the lost sheep is returned to the fold!'

'I am the great-granddaughter of Prince Charles Edward Stuart. I am Countess of Albany. I am the rightful owner of Glenalban Castle, being the single legitimate descendant of King James II.'

'Alas!'

'I am,' I said incautiously, having worked myself into a passion of rage, 'rightful Queen of England and Scotland, and would be so in fact as well as in law but for the usurpation of William and Mary.'

'Alas, alas!' Mr Cardew flapped his hands, like a nestling trying to fly. That was when he began to pray at me. He prayed that my obduracy might be softened by the Holy Spirit, my proud head humbled, my wild folly disciplined by reason, my maniacal ravings forgiven.

His prayers were not answered.

73

I thought the Chaplain's position in the castle was even worse than Miss Louisa Frith's; because a dependent spinster could more readily be forgiven for hypocrisy than a man of God. But after some time of thinking about this (it may not have been truly worth thinking about, but I had nothing else to do) I concluded that Miss Frith was worse. The Reverend Joseph Cardew was stupid. Miss Frith was many unutterable things, but she was not stupid.

I had no means of discovering what lay beyond the ridge of roof behind the battlements where I walked. There was no one I could ask who would answer. And there was no one I could ask who would not at once realize, from my question what was in my mind.

I did not know how the tower in which I was lodged joined on to the rest of the castle. I tried to remember the complicated route by which we had reached the King's Room, but my confused memory of the interior gave me no picture of the exterior. There might be a slope of roof, then a sheer drop to a courtyard. There might be battlements; if so, a way out, for the ancient defenders of the castle must have been able to come and go. Those ways might be locked or guarded. If they were not, I would find myself in a warren of upstairs passages, and would most likely run into a squadron of servants. In all these eventualities, my last state would be worse than my first. Any attempt I made to escape must be less hit and miss.

I needed guile. I thought I was not gifted with guile. I was better at running than at thinking.

Then I had an idea of the purest genius, and it made me gulp with terror. I did not know how the idea had come to me; at the same time, I could not understand why it had not come to me days before.

I considered the materials I had at hand. The towel I had been given was only a yard long – too short by far. The curtains over the window were no larger; and I needed those curtains. I would have cut a blanket into strips, but I had no knife or scissors, and there was no sharp projection in my cell by means of which I could cut anything. The mattress had no loose cover over it. All that remained of fabric were my clothes. I wondered if they were strong enough. There was only one way to find out. I undressed myself. I tried my stockings for strength, for they would have been ideal. They would not take my weight. My shift I did not at all trust, for I had sewn it myself. The only thing that would bear my weight, and that was long enough, was my dress. It was not such very heavy material; but I was not so very heavy either.

I climbed on to the table, and hooked the back of the dress over the catch of the window. Then I took hold of the dress, and hung by it over the floor. I found that if I tucked up my shift, I could grip with my legs as well as with my hands, and it was no great effort to hang so. The good Scottish wool held me. It might stretch a little, and so be baggy when I put it on again. That was not one of my major worries.

This must be done in the dark. I might not be so frightened, if I could not see the ground. And they were far less likely to see me, where I should be. And nobody outside the castle would see me. And I was more likely to get through the castle, and clear of the castle, when there were more shadows in the corridors, and fewer folk in them.

The two servants had to react exactly as I planned for them to react. This was the weakest part of a plan none of which, on examination, was so very strong. People behave in unexpected ways, and when you think they will run away shouting, they stand and stare, and when you think they will leave doors open, they lock them . . .

I had the impression that the servants came with my meals like clockwork. But I could not be sure, as I had no clock. I thought my supper would arrive about an hour after it was full dark. I was lucky it was only April, with the evenings still falling early, and not June, when it would be light until very late, and in the north not so very dark even when it was full night.

I waited with a tearing impatience for the sun to go down. At the same time, a part of me, which grew an increasingly large part, wanted the sun to remain as long as possible in the sky, because I was frightened of what I faced.

The nearer the moment for action came, the less I relished it.

But I could not stomach any more of this dim half-life in the wardrobe; and I think the Reverend Joseph Cardew's prayers had been the last straw.

I had my evening promenade on the battlements. No word was said. I was locked up again.

I watched the last of the sun on the snow on the hilltops. They turned from gold to blue to purple. Sparks of light showed from crofts up and down the glen; and the nightly wash of light spilled out from the castle windows on to the terraces.

I would have moved at once; but my shift was white, and would show against the stones of the tower like a moth on a gravestone. I made myself wait. And, when the time came, I had to make a very great effort to make myself stop waiting.

I thought the servants would come with my supper in a quarter of an hour.

I did not want to hang from my dress a moment longer than I needed to, for the sake of the dress as well as for my own muscles and safety. But I must be ready before the servants actually came into the room. With a great effort, I heaved the heavy metal cot across the room, and against the door. It would not delay Kenneth Doig long, but I thought it would take him long enough to push it out of the way with the opening door.

I fixed the collar of my dress again to the catch in the window-frame. I lowered the dress out of the window, so that it hung behind the curtain, and then out of sight down the wall.

I wanted to go out of the window feet first; but I could not. I put the chair on the table, and climbed on the chair. I pushed my head and my shoulders through the window, and held fast on to my dress, hanging beside the window. I kicked away the chair, so that it fell off the table on to the floor. Nearly all my weight was on the windowsill; I could safely stay where I was for ever, or until I died of cold. The thought of my next movement made my heart jump in my throat; and the thought of the flagstones far below me.

I waited for the sound of the key in the lock.

It seemed to me that the servants were much, much later that evening, and that I hung on the windowsill for hours. Probably they were no later, and I was just there for five minutes. I gulped at the prospect of the immediate future. I prayed. I found myself bitterly blaming the Reverend Joseph

Cardew, for driving me to risking my neck. Even at the time, it occurred to me that this was scarcely fair, as neither he nor anyone else could have predicted that a few prayers would have such a desperate effect.

I heard the key.

I wriggled through the window like a rabbit, clutching my dress, so that I hung in a void. I heard an exclamation outside the door, and a man's gruff reply. I heard a violent screeching, as the cot was pushed inch by inch across the floor. By this time I was completely out of the window. I lowered myself so that I was below it. I gripped with legs as well as with hands. Holding with one hand, I reached up and closed the window. I could not close it completely, because of the fold of my dress on the catch. But nobody would think, it seemed to me, that anybody would have thrown themselves out of a closed window. I was thankful to grasp the dress with both hands again. I prayed that the curtain hid the part of my dress which was still inside the room; and that the dress was strong enough; and that I was strong enough.

There was a final shriek of the iron feet of the cot on the floor, and the servants, furious, were in the room. I saw the flare of the candle through the window above me, and heard the jabber of voices.

'She didna lep,' said Kenneth Doig. 'Yon windie's closit.'

'She had nae rope.'

'A cateran wi' a key hae let her oot.'

'Ay.'

They poked about, searching. To search that room took two seconds. They ran away, to report to their mistress. I did not hear them lock the door. They had reacted as I had planned. Neither stayed to guard the room, since the horse had evidently bolted.

They took the candle with them, but left my supper on the table, as I discovered when I hauled myself in again, and put my foot in a bowl of soup.

I unhitched my dress from the window-catch, and struggled into it. I would have liked to take my comb; but I could not spend time groping for it in the dark.

I slipped into the King's Room, and wondered where to go next. The castle would be searched from top to bottom. Probably every one of the indoor servants had seen me, when

77

they were drawn up in the hall at my first arrival, and acting that cruel play. I could not pass myself off as a visitor, or a new maidservant, or a milliner come with a hamper of hats.

I peeped out into the corridor. There was no one, yet. To the right were the stairs by which we had come up, which led by stages into the public part of the castle, the great corridors and rooms and grand staircases. To the left, what? Back stairs? With servants already pounding up them?

Either way might be safe, or perilous.

They must think I had left the room by the door. I wondered how many keys there were to that door. Suppose Mary MacAndrew had the only one, or the housekeeper the one other? They must think an accomplice had somehow crept into the castle, and secured the right key; or that I had bribed or persuaded a servant.

They could not know when I had left the room. It might have been at any moment after my evening promenade. Therefore I might by now be miles from the castle, from the glen, going in a fast carriage in any direction. But equally, in their minds, I might be exactly where I was, dithering in the door of the King's Room, and wondering which way to go.

I turned right, because I had at least been that way, when I still thought I was a Queen.

I turned the first corner, and ran straight into the arms of Miss Louisa Frith.

She said nothing. I said nothing. Nobody said anything. She inspected the collar of my dress, which was pulled out of shape where I had hung from it. A servant took my arm, and I was led back to my cell. Mary MacAndrew came in with me, and Kenneth Doig stood in the doorway. Mary MacAndrew took my untasted supper away.

Almost at once, two men in leather aprons came. One had two heavy iron bars, of a little over a yard long; the other tools and a trowel and a bucket of mortar. They put the bars in my window.

Next morning, and next evening, I did not have my exercise on the battlements.

I heard the boom of a cannon.

I wondered dizzily if civil war had begun, and the Barone Lodovico di Vigliano were leading the clansmen to Glenalban to free me and proclaim me, as in his fantastical jokes.

On tiptoe on the table, peering through the bars, I saw far to my left, where the carriage-drive curved into the outer courtyard beyond the terraces, a carriage arriving, surrounded by outriders.

The Earl?

A little later, craning my neck, I saw below me people coming out of the castle on to the terrace; and one was a tall man, hatless, with black hair and broad shoulders. That was all I could see of him, for I was directly above.

The Earl?

He did not come to me. I was taken to him. I was expecting an arrogant bully, and that is just what I saw and heard.

He was undeniably handsome, if you liked that style of masculine beauty, which I did not. I supposed he was something over six feet tall, slim but with broad shoulders. He looked hard and much exercised; how would he not, since he was usurping so many of my acres? His hair was thick and black and sleek; many people perhaps admired it, but I did not, for I preferred unruly fair hair. His mouth was quite broad, which might have been considered an attractive feature, bespeaking humour and generosity; but his lips were thin, bespeaking cruelty and coldness. His eyes were grey and set wide apart, which was conventionally a good way for eyes to be; but they contained an expression of chilly disdain, which made them repulsive. He was about thirty years old; he bore himself with the ponderous gravity of a man three times his age, which I thought ridiculous.

He was in a kind of study, behind an enormous desk. The room was lined with books, and the desk covered in papers. He gave himself an air of busy importance. As I was thrust into his presence by the footmen who had brought me, the black-suited young secretary disappeared through another door.

I stood in front of the desk, my chin at what I intended to be a defiant angle.

He said, in a voice which would have been a pleasant baritone, if it had not been marred by a sneering harshness,

'Do you not curtsey, Miss Albany, when you are presented to the Earl of Glenalban?'

As an opening speech to a new acquaintance, I thought these words intolerable. I therefore incautiously replied, 'Do you not rise and bow, Lord Glenalban, when you come face to face with the Countess of Albany?'

He gave a sigh, and shrugged.

He said, 'Let us recommence. Under circumstances which I am beginning to understand, my remark was ill chosen.'

I nodded. It seemed to me the most dignified thing to do; and I did not trust myself not to say something unfortunate, if I opened my mouth just then.

He said, 'I must say first that I regret the necessity of the treatment you have been accorded. It is not our habit here to incarcerate strangers, and the thought of a young girl being shut up is as repugnant to us as it has been, no doubt, to you. I must however add that my aunt Miss Frith acted according to her conscience, and I cannot think that she could have acted differently. She has been, as always, correct in all things. I should welcome the opportunity to set you free, or to lodge you differently, but that opportunity can only be provided by yourself.'

I looked at him with raised eyebrows. I wondered how I was to provide the opportunity for my being let out.

He said, 'You know, as I know, that your pretensions are fraudulent. You have only to say so, and you will be taken home. You know, as I know, that your confederate Donaldson is a criminal. He was dismissed from his position here for evil, immoral and greedy behaviour which was not, in strict point of law, illegal; what he is now attempting, with you as cat's-paw, is illegal and is punishable by condign sentence of imprisonment. You also are in danger of such a sentence. You will escape all danger of it, if you sign a statement setting out the truth. I cannot be fairer than that, Miss Albany, so to continue to call you. I cannot be more merciful. Write and sign, in the presence of my Chaplain, a full and frank account of the inception and development of this ingenious attempt at gigantic fraud, and you are free as air. You will not subsequently be pursued or troubled. You have my word of honour on that score.'

My face probably revealed how I regarded his word of honour.

I said, very slowly, and in almost total control of myself, 'You are asking me to perjure myself, in order to save my own skin, and send an innocent man to prison. You are asking me to abandon a claim which I think you know is just. I am not used to lying, my Lord, nor to lying down. Do your worst.'

'I shall not do my worst, Miss Albany, to a girl I judge barely eighteen years old. You shall be exactly as you have been, until we persuade you to abandon this criminal folly. You will be adequately fed. You will resume your periods of exercise. If you fall ill, you will receive the best attention from my own doctor. I can think of nothing else at this moment. You will return to your chamber.'

And so I returned. And that was it. And there seemed no end to any of it.

# 5

The Earl had been fully informed about my claims, the moment they were known to his creatures in the castle. He had no doubt consulted lawyers, probably in London and Edinburgh. He must know that my claim was good. He was simply trying – as he would have been expected to try – to bludgeon me into surrender. And into betraying Simon Donaldson, with perjured evidence.

It was lucky that I had met Lady Lochinver, to have been given confirmation of what Simon had said about the Earl. But that was the only lucky thing in the whole situation.

I was not long back in my cell, when I had another visitor, another lady – another whom I had not seen before, but whose identity I knew at once.

The Earl's sister was very like her brother, in a gentler way, with the same dark hair and the same wide-set grey eyes. She was much taller than I, though almost as slender. I thought she was two years older than I was. She was very, very much better dressed.

'I have been talking to my brother,' she said. 'He did say you were beautiful, but I had not expected you to be quite so lovely.'

'He said that?' I said, startled.

'Yes, of course. That is why he has not sent for the police, to hand you over.'

'I am only out of prison,' I said slowly, trying to digest this extraordinary new morsel, 'because your brother thinks I am beautiful?'

'He hopes he can persuade you to admit that what you are doing is wrong and deceitful. And, oh, I hope so too! It is dreadful that a girl like you should be shut up!'

'I think so too,' I said.

'But it is better than prison.'

'Is it so different?'

'Oh, Leonora, have you ever seen the inside of a women's prison? And the kind of women there? You are a lady, and I doubt if you are quite eighteen.'

'Not quite eighteen.'

'Oh dear, the younger you are, the worse it makes everything. Won't you please, please, do as my brother asks?'

I thought Lady Flora Grieve was genuine. She was ten or more years younger than her brother, and she was a gentle creature; of course she immediately and blindly accepted everything that he said. But I thought she was the one person – with Lady Lochinver far off – whom I might convince.

'What is so odd about this situation,' I said, 'is that my story is true and my claim is genuine. The lawyers have said so.'

'Tell what lies you like to everybody else, but could you not, please, tell me the truth?'

'How can I convince you that I am telling the truth?'

She pleaded with me, begged me, to free myself by saying that it was all a fraud.

'Yes, and send an innocent man to prison?' I said.

'You mean Simon Donaldson? Innocent? that man?'

She believed her brother about that, then, too.

We stared at one another, she on the wooden chair, and I on the edge of the cot. We were scarce a yard apart, but we seemed to be divided by the breadth of the glen I could see from my window.

'You will not be helped,' she said at last, with a sort of desperate pity in her voice.

'Not in your way,' I said.

That night, Mary MacAndrew took my supper away as usual, but left behind a candle of decent length. I saw the hand of Lady Flora Grieve. She wanted me to have light by which to contemplate my sinful folly.

Some time after the door was once again locked on me, and I was thinking of preparing for bed, I heard the key again. And after it had turned I heard, with astonishment, a knock. You do not knock on the doors of prisoners' cells; at least, no one had knocked on mine.

I said, 'Come in.'

I blinked at the new arrival, and he at me.

He was a man of the Earl's age, not as tall but broader, with a pleasant, weather-beaten face. His hair was sandy and his eyes green. He was in full evening dress, but he looked as though his favourite clothes were those for shooting and fishing.

'Miss Albany?'

'There is nobody else in prison here.'

'My name is Avington. Jack Avington. Lord Avington, to put you fully in command of the facts. I am staying here for the salmon fishing. I mention that to reassure you that there is nothing strange or sinister about my being here.'

'How did you get the key?' I asked.

'From the place where keys are hung. I shall have it back there, before anybody notices it has gone. I have been talking to Lady Flora about you, and she filled me with the most burning curiosity to see this beautiful, miniature visitant that they are all convinced is a cunning criminal. Are you?'

'As Lord Glenalban's guest, you had better follow his line,' I said.

'I don't take anybody's line. I think as I find. And I find it hard to believe all that they say of you. People say the eyes are the window of the soul. What do yours reveal, I wonder?'

He stepped closer to me, and stared down into my eyes in the candlelight.

'No serpents there, that I can see,' he said. 'I begin to be prepared to believe that a dreadful mistake has been made. Tell me your side of the story.'

His manner was commanding, but not in a way I could resent. What he said was beautiful music.

I told him all my story, by the end of which the candle was guttering. He lit another from it. I probably allowed a good deal of passion and outrage into my voice.

'Hm,' said Lord Avington, when I had brought matters up to date, including my visit from Lady Flora. 'We have here what the lawyers call a diametrical conflict of evidence, on every single point. Simon Donaldson. That is a new name to me. He was not here any of the times when I have been here, and nobody has mentioned him. I am unable to judge between your opinion and Lady Lochinver's and your Italian

84

friend's, on the one hand, and the accepted Glenalban view, on the other. As to Duncan Glenalban himself, I have known him since we were lower boys at Eton together. But never very well. I always admired him as a sportsman, and still do. I find it difficult to think ill of a man who rides a wild horse as he does, and throws a salmon fly as he does, though I know my attitude is short of logic . . . Your Barone sounds a delightful soul. What a tangled story! Edgar Smith's birthmark, your great-grandmother's indiscretion, all the ingredients of something from Mrs Radcliffe. I am English, you know. I only come to Scotland on occasional visits. They are good long visits, to make the journey worth while, but I cannot pretend to know the country very well. I realize now that I do not know it at all – I had no idea that such desperate events took place.'

'Nor had I.'

'Oh God, what am I to believe?'

It was as though these words released a champagne cork, after the bottle had been violently shaken. An impassioned appeal spouted out of me, unstoppable. It contained no logic, I think, and not much coherence. But it must have carried conviction.

'By heaven, I believe you,' said Lord Avington, after a long pause, during which I wondered with anguish what his verdict would be.

'Then help me to get out of here.'

'Yes. Not now, because I must make a number of preparations. Tomorrow night.'

'Oh God,' I said. 'That will give you twenty-four hours in which to change your mind. You will talk to Lady Flora and the Earl and Miss Frith and the Chaplain –'

'I don't see why I should be obliged to talk to Glenalban's domestic parson.'

'Get me out tonight!'

But he would not. Of course he was right. A carriage had to be engaged, and a hiding place found for it, and a way out of the castle made passable.

'I swear I will come,' he said. 'No one will change my mind. No one ever does, once it is made up. You have made it up for me, and it will not be unmade. Not so much your words, my dear, but the fury in your face and voice. It was genuine. It

85

could not have been assumed. Whether everything you have said to me is quite exact I do not know, but I am very sure you think it is. I am at your service. I am in your service. I am your new Jacobite. I claim kinship with Flora Macdonald, who saved your great-grandfather.'

He kissed my hand when he left. There was a look in his eyes which reminded me of something. Of the look in Simon Donaldson's eyes, when he did not kiss my hand because of his promise to Aunt Sophia.

I do not know how I lived through the next twenty-four hours, without betraying the suffocating excitement that I felt. As far as I could, I kept my face averted from Mary MacAndrew and Kenneth Doig, for fear that they would read in it suspense and hope and joy. That is the worst of a face that reveals feelings.

Lord Avington's was such a face. *His* eyes were the windows to his soul. I was deeply flattered, and touched, and proud. I did not know how I felt in return. Ignorant as I was, I knew that gratitude was not to be confused with love. And I still thought often, often about Simon Donaldson.

I wondered where I would go, when Avington had got me out. It was a problem for later. The thing was to get out. He might have ideas. I thought they would be sensible and kind ideas, because he was sensible and kind.

I had another generous candle with my supper. But it burned completely out while I waited for deliverance. I sat on in the dark. Presently, exhausted by excitement, and by the effort of pretending that I felt no excitement, I lay on my cot.

And my shoulder was being gently shaken. I started up, puzzled, confused, frightened, with a stifled scream.

'Hush,' said Lord Avington. 'What a cool customer you are, to be able to sleep at such a moment.'

'It is the last thing I expected to do,' I said, rubbing the sleep out of my eyes, and yawning enormously.

He had a dark-lantern, and a travelling cloak for me.

We locked my cell behind us when we left it, to puzzle my gaolers; and we put the key back on its hook in the basement passage outside the housekeeper's room.

86

There were night-watchmen patrolling the castle in the hours of darkness; but they were not coy or secretive; they clashed about with keys and lanterns, and were easily avoided. I was immediately lost, but Lord Avington knew his way. He took me by the hand, and led me at last to a little door through which, he told me, vegetables were brought in from the kitchen gardens. He uncovered the beam of his lantern briefly, and seldom.

It was glorious to be outside those walls. I drew huge breaths. I danced where I stood. I wanted to shout in triumph. But I followed Lord Avington, like a mouse, through walled gardens and so across the park. There was a brisk breeze, to hide any small sound we made; clouds hurried across the moon. The carriage-drive showed white when the moon came out from a cloud. It went black, when it curved into a small wood. There, hidden under the trees, a carriage was waiting for us.

'Hired from Lochgrannomhead,' said Lord Avington. 'The owner wanted a reason, but he didn't get one. Have you considered where to go?'

'Home,' I said. 'Millstounburn.'

'If you insist. But I wouldn't advise it. It's the first place Glenalban will look for you.'

'Oh. But it is the only place I have to go to. I can go nowhere else. I know no one else.'

'I suggest Lady Lochinver.'

'Yes! . . . But her daughter is in some trouble, and she will not want to be bothered with me.'

'She cannot leave her daughter, I daresay. But, from what you told me, she will indeed want to be bothered with you. She believes in you as warmly as I do. And she will want to make amends, surely, for what her family have been doing to you.'

I thought that was true. Still I was dubious, to trouble Lady Lochinver at such a time.

'I don't think I can take you to my house in Berkshire,' said Lord Avington. 'A pretty scandal that would make, doing your cause no good, and not doing me much good. Besides, the house is being painted inside, and everything is under dust-sheets. In any case, you must be here, to fight your battles. I could take you to my sister, but she lives in Somerset, and her two youngest children have measles.'

'I think I have no choice,' I said slowly.

'I think not much. And I think you need not be a great trouble to Lady Lochinver. All she has to do is keep you hidden, until we have worked out the next step.'

'We?'

'Your friends and yourself. A council of war is the first need, I think – you and I, Lady Lochinver, this fellow Donaldson, and the Italian gentleman. They will know how things are going with the lawyers. With that knowledge, we can plan what to do and when to do it.'

'Are you coming with me now?'

'Of course. Young Countesses cannot cross Scotland alone in the middle of the night.'

'Then Glenalban and the rest will know you let me out.'

'Glenalban and the rest can do nothing about it whatever, except deny me hospitality in the future. That is a pity, because the fishing in the Alban Water is excellent –'

'Oh, you are sacrificing your sport for me!'

'I would sacrifice much more than that, my dear.'

And, in the carriage, he embroidered this theme. There was nothing he would not do for me, because he believed in me and admired me.

'But on that subject,' he said, 'I believe that honour obliges me to remain silent until your eighteenth birthday.'

It was as though he had been talking to Aunt Sophia. I did not know whether to be relieved or disappointed. My eighteenth birthday was going to be a busy time.

It was only my second meeting with him, yet already we were on most friendly and unembarrassed terms. It might have been embarrassing for him to say, and for me to hear, how much he admired me; but he was so frank and simple – without being in any way stupid – that there was no constraint or difficulty.

It was far too early for me to judge my feelings about him. I felt overwhelming gratitude, of course; and I thought it would be most easy to feel much more. But Simon's face was in a corner of my mind, and it would not go away.

We broke our journey for breakfast at an inn. The folk there thought we were eloping, and they treated us frostily. I called

Lord Avington 'Uncle', for the sake of respectability, which made him angry, and made him laugh, so that he choked over his kipper.

We reached the house of Lady Lochinver's son-in-law in the later morning. He was Sir George Stevens, known a little to Lord Avington, at the time away in London on urgent affairs. His absence was one of the reasons, it seemed, why Lady Lochinver had to be there. The house was a few miles west of Perth. It was long and low and white, and had a most welcoming and friendly look.

It was nothing like as welcoming and friendly as Lady Lochinver. We were ushered into a sunny morning-room, where she was writing letters with Miss Grizelda Hamilton; and she treated Lord Avington as an old friend, and she treated me as a queen.

She was speechless when she heard what they had done to me. It was what she might have expected from her nephew; it was astonishing in her sister; Lady Flora had no mind of her own, and followed her brother blindly; the Chaplain was a time-serving nothing; the upper servants and those guarding me were all terrified into doing exactly as they were ordered.

Avington was a hero and a saviour, a rescuer of damsels from dragons. I was boundlessly grateful for what he had done for me, but I thought Lady Lochinver overstated the dangers he had run and the sacrifices he had made. As he himself said, he had run no danger except falling downstairs in the dark; and there were other salmon rivers in Scotland.

Lady Lochinver's daughter, Lady Stevens, was confined to her room, and could not receive strangers. Through her mother, she asked to be forgiven, and sent her duty.

Her duty! This exaggeration – gratifying if a little silly – had been caught by daughter from mother.

I was to stay in the house as long as necessary. The time I was there would, of course, depend on the lawyers. I would be hidden, but I would be free. The servants were completely to be trusted. Lord Glenalban would not know I was there. My lodging would not be as grand as the King's Room, but it would be much more comfortable than its wardrobe.

Lady Lochinver was as garrulous and motherly as I remembered, and – when she remembered – as solemnly

89

reverent to me. I preferred the moments when she forgot, and treated me as a young girl whom she liked.

Lord Avington could not stay in the house, owing to the demands of the sickroom. Lady Lochinver was distressed at having to send him away, when he had acted so magnificently; but he understood, and had not expected to be asked. He said he would stay somewhere nearby, and would keep in close touch with us.

When he left, I tried to express my gratitude. He brushed it aside. He tried to express his admiration, without putting it into words. He entirely succeeded. I did not brush it aside, but lapped it up. The picture of Simon Donaldson I carried in the side of my mind wore a reproachful look. Simon had not saved me from a dungeon.

I stayed hidden in the house for a week – hidden, but free as air. In the dawn and at dusk I made up for my imprisonment, by taking gigantic walks, revelling in the mere fact of putting one foot in front of another on the open road.

I wrote a long letter to Aunt Sophia. This one would reach her. I asked her to make urgent contact with Simon and the Barone, and to tell them what had happened and where I was.

I did not see much of Lady Lochinver, and nothing of her daughter. Once again, Miss Grizelda Hamilton was an apologetic substitute.

It was as though my time at Glenalban had never been.

I found that I missed Lord Avington as much as I had missed Simon Donaldson – as much as I still missed him. Utterly ignorant of all these things, I wondered if it were possible to be in love with two people at once; and, for the first time, I had the sense to wonder if I were really in love with either.

'I have had a letter from your friend the Barone,' said Lady Lochinver.

'Oh, good! What news is there? May I see it?'

'I think I cannot show it to you, dear. It contains highly confidential material – in plain terms, some grossly slanderous material which he probably should not have written, and which I certainly should not share, even with you.'

I understood that the Barone, his exuberant Italian spirit

90

having been roused, had written intemperately about the Earl of Glenalban. I would have liked to see his outpourings on the subject; but I had to respect Lady Lochinver's discretion.

The important thing was, that we were to go to Crieff to meet two lawyers who were deeply involved in my affairs, and who wanted to hear my own story from myself. The Barone and Simon hoped to attend this meeting also, but might not be able to get away from Edinburgh.

I was excited. Matters were marching.

The office was dark, and a little musty. There was a shelf of dark books, behind glass. Behind a desk sat two clean-shaven men in black coats. I was surprised that they were so young – neither as much as thirty, I thought – having expected grey-beards. They were serious. Their voices were low and their faces grave. They asked me all manner of questions, and watched me closely as I answered. One took extensive notes of all I said. Lady Lochinver listened in silence. It appeared that Simon and the Barone had not, after all, been able to get away from Edinburgh.

They asked me how I knew that I was Countess of Albany. They suggested that I was, or should have been, Queen of England and Scotland. I agreed. They asked me probing questions, as though to test my sincerity and certainty. They covered ground I had covered so often, with Simon and the Barone and Lady Lochinver and Lord Avington.

At last one turned to Lady Lochinver, and said, 'What we have heard today amply confirms the deposition you have made to us. You did right to bring this unfortunate young woman to this place. Goodwill is no substitute for correct treatment. A simple delusion is sometimes susceptible to drugs and other techniques, but there are worrying aspects to the case. This Italian Barone, who is evidently the purest figment of a disordered imagination. His resemblance to Garibaldi confirms that he is a wish imaginatively fulfilled, a hero and deliverer to a kind that is the product of day-dreams. Then there is the equally fictitious aunt, a kindly relative longed for and so supplied by the brain to the brain. We understand that you heard an apparently lucid account of such a person, at a place called Millstounburn, and with relief sought to transfer the waif you had found, wandering and

91

raving, back into the care of her own family; but that Millstounburn is in fact the property of a Mr Bruce, and there is no such person as the supposed aunt.

'Still more worrying is the violence, and the attendant unseemly display. We have a sworn statement from a woodman, brought here by your friend Miss Hamilton, that the patient threatened him with a whip, utterly without reason or provocation – a phenomenon of sudden, mindless violence which is all too likely to be repeated. Miss Hamilton herself was approached by the patient who was still carrying the whip; she was obliged to take to her heels. We have a statement from a servant who saw the patient riding a pony in a grossly unseemly and exhibitionist way – a form of revolt, of a patient drawing attention to herself, which is, again, in nearly all recorded cases repeated.'

'Are you saying that I'm mad?' I asked, hardly able to speak.

'It is a kind of illness, child,' said Lady Lochinver.

They were not lawyers. They were doctors. They were the two doctors who, by law, had to sign the paper certifying a person a lunatic, and committing her to an asylum.

'Give me any test!' I shouted.

The doctors glanced at one another. It seemed to me that they edged further round the desk, for safety.

'You say, your Ladyship, that the unfortunate girl is virtually a pauper. She appears to have no family. Her real name is unknown, since her delusion leads her to claim the name she uses. You yourself cannot undertake the charges of private institution, and you do not feel able to ask your nephew to do so. We regret this decision, but of course we are obliged to accept it. As you may know, by law admission to a public asylum can only be made from a workhouse, at which a patient must have spent at least one token night. It is usually more, depending on the availability of beds in the local institutions. The patient must accordingly be taken to the workhouse today, and kept there under restraint until we have arranged for her admission. She had better have a name. It had better not be the one she has been using, as that will only foster the delusions of which it is to be hoped that she will eventually be cured. Can you make a suggestion, your Ladyship?'

'Smith,' said Lady Lochinver, shrugging. 'Mary Smith.'

Mary, the name of my gaoler at Glenalban. Smith, the man with the birthmark, who tried to steal my great-grand-mother's journal.

'I will not be Mary Smith,' I said.

'You will be what you are told to be,' said one of the doctors, with a new sternness. His face softened. He looked at me with pity. 'If you do exactly as you are bid, we may be able to make you quite better. But you must want to be better. You do want that, do not you? You will try, will not you?'

I could not answer.

Lady Lochinver rose and left, without a backward glance at me.

I was taken to a small, bare room, and left there in the charge of a nurse. She was a powerful woman. Her job was to subdue dangerous female lunatics. She could have subdued me with one hand.

Lady Lochinver had duped me from the very beginning. She had duped Simon Donaldson. She was as completely the creature of the Earl of Glenalban as her sister, and his sister.

Because he trusted her, Simon had committed the appalling blunder of confiding in her. She came to Edinburgh to see lawyers, as she wrote to me in her first letter. Indeed she was seeing laywers, on her nephew's behalf; she was finding out whether I had a case. She found out that I had a complete case, and that she and hers were likely to be expelled from Glenalban. Armed with this knowledge, she came to inspect me. She disarmed me in all ways – by her manner, by her motherliness, by her pretended regard for Simon, by her pretended determination to help me, by her pretended disapproval of the Earl – and, now that I thought about it, by the silly exaggeration of her pretended romantic Jacobitism. She overdid that part of her performance. And I rose to the fly like the stupidest trout in the river.

The affair of the whip; my bare-legged ride. She had done some sleuth-hound work there. That, no doubt, was why I had spent a week in her daughter's house, to give her time to collect all the evidence for the doctors.

My second letter to Aunt Sophia had not been sent, any more than my first.

There had been no letter from the Barone. Neither he nor anyone else would ever know what had become of me, or even under what name I went.

No doubt those servants had been told that I was a lunatic suffering from delusions of grandeur, and that I must be locked up for my own safety.

I made another discovery. Lady Lochinver, I thought, had not been called away at all. She had simply kept out of my sight. That was so that I would continue to trust her, which might be useful to their side.

It had been. I had continued to trust her, and I had led Lord Avington to trust her.

A new and dreadful thought struck me. Was Avington in the conspiracy too? But why should he bother to rescue me, simply in order to betray me? Why not leave me where I was? So that I would trust him, too, in case they needed that ploy?

But I remembered the look in his eyes, and I did not think it was counterfeit.

And now Lady Lochinver, the falsest friend anyone ever had, was subjecting me to the workhouse, and to the public asylum for pauper lunatics.

Lady Flora had said to me that women's prisons were terrible, and the women in them terrible. I thought the places I was going to would be worse.

In the workhouse I was stripped and scrubbed, and my hair inspected for lice. I protested that I was clean, but so the rules were, and those grim women were not in the way of listening to lunatics. My clothes were taken away, and I was given a coarse shift, and a woollen dress that had the look of a uniform. Both garments were faded and thin with a hundred launderings. For my feet I was given wooden clogs, the soles worn thin by generations of pauper feet.

I was Mary Smith. I had to answer to this name. If I had not, I would not have been fed.

I was taken to the 'Infirmary Ward' of the workhouse, where the inmates were watched over. There were fifteen beds, all but one occupied. They were close together. There were no cupboards between them. Apart from the beds, there was no furniture at all. There were no carpets on the floor, or curtains in the little high barred window.

94

On thirteen of the beds, old women crouched or sat or lay. One clutched her knees and moaned incessantly. Another, in a high sing-song whine, uttered a stream of gibberish, in which the only clear words were obscenities. Most stared in front of them, not moving or speaking, as good as dead. I wondered if they were all going to the public asylum, and if so, whether they were going to the same one where I would be. (But I later learned that, as these pathetic creatures were incurable, it was judged pointless for them to occupy beds in a place where cures were attempted. It was cheaper to keep them in the workhouse.)

The one other inmate of the Infirmary Ward was an emaciated young girl, who twitched and dribbled. She looked very mad. She was even more pitiable and horrifying, because her life was before her, and that was the life it was.

How could doctors, trained professional men, have confused me with such as these? Even if I told a story which was nearly incredible? I thought one answer was that they were very young, and so largely inexperienced, and had been chosen by Lady Lochinver on this account. I thought another reason was the power and influence of the Earl of Glenalban, who was doubtless Chairman of Hospital Boards and such-like, and could help the career of any doctor who pleased him.

The ward was cleaned by inmates of the workhouse who were not sick or insane. They were sluts, foul-mouthed and dirty. They made no attempt to clean the room properly, so that, because of the helplessness of the crazy old women, it stank abominably. The sluts were casually cruel to the old women. They jeered at them for their incontinence and helplessness, which made my blood boil. But I controlled my anger, because I was frightened for myself.

I am not proud of that. But, given everything, I am not so very ashamed.

Food was brought to us, nearly all turnips and potatoes. I never saw meat, or any green stuff, or even bread. Many of the old women could not eat. They could not hold their spoons. They dropped their bowls in their laps, and stared apathetically at the mess. Some I tried to feed, spoonful by spoonful, but it was slow work, and all the food was quickly taken away. So, while I was there, I went round the ward, hoping that

95

I could get some nourishment into each one of them. The only one I entirely failed to feed was the young girl, who pushed away the spoon, making the only sign of activity I ever saw from her.

My own mental state was odd. It seemed to me that this could not be happening. It was too terrible, too grotesque, to be true. It was a bad dream. I was numb. I came to let everything bounce off me, the jeers of the sluts and the brisk indifference of the attendants.

I could not escape. Knowing that, I knew I was wise not to try.

I was not precisely ill treated. I was not treated at all, as anything. I was a vegetable, to be moved to another place at some future moment, and for the time being ignored.

Leonora Albany no longer existed. Mary Smith was a friendless waif swallowed up into a foreign world, where she would never be seen by anybody, or heard of again.

Time lost all meaning. A day was not 'Tuesday', but the day on which I tried to shovel some turnips down the mouth of the old woman whose turn it was. An hour was not 'five', but that at which we were fed.

Place lost all meaning. I might have been in Timbuctoo, for all it mattered where I was.

I began to wonder if being treated as mad would send me mad.

Years later, because of my experiences, I was shown two fat volumes called *Care and Cure of the Insane*, written by Doctor J. Mortimer Granville, and published by Messrs Hardwicke and Bogue for the Royal College of Surgeons. The author had visited a large number of lunatic asylums, and described them in the minutest detail, in a series of articles in *The Lancet*; and then put them all together, and made them into this extraordinary book.

I could scarcely believe what I read.

Wise and kindly men had succeeded incompetent and cruel ones, in the management of public asylums for the insane paupers. They had fine new buildings, in healthy places, with extensive gardens and farms. The wards and dormitories were healthy and airy, with much space for each patient, and with bright and cheerful furnishings. The day-rooms were also airy and cheerful, sunny in summer and warmed by open fires in winter, with charming wallpapers, curtains, pictures, aviaries, and pianos and other musical instruments. The attendants were superior people, and under the strictest discipline. The diet was carefully arranged to be both nutritious and attractive, and it was often varied. The 'restraints' of the bad old days had been, almost everywhere, almost completely abandoned – padded cells, strait-waistcoats, leg-irons and the like – in favour of kindly persuasion. Certainly these things were never used as punishment, and never simply to save the attendants trouble. Opiate drugs were hardly ever used, and when they were it was for good medical reasons, and not, again, to save trouble for the staff. The patients were not dressed in clothes like prison uniform, nor the attendants dressed like prison warders.

They believed in giving the patients fresh air and exercise, and the 'airing courts' were planted with flowers, and the people could play bowls and croquet, and those that could worked in the gardens and farms, and it was very good for them.

And the centre of it all, was the idea that lunatics were ill, and many of them could be cured. And many of them were cured.

This was because the Medical Superintendent examined each lunatic as he arrived, and studied his behaviour and what he said, and gave special treatment to each case. And this was possible because there were not too many patients for one man; and because curable cases were kept separate from poor old incurables, and from criminal lunatics.

It all sounds so very obvious. It made me think that what the very wisest and best people have is common-sense.

There were still things wrong, said Dr Mortimer Granville. And the two worst things were these: the way people were certified as mad; and the fact that there were still some asylums as bad as the worst of the past.

'Not one in twenty of the average practitioners one meets is either qualified to form an opinion on a case of insanity, or justified in filling up a certificate ... On this malady, whereof he knows nothing – can know nothing, and in regard to which he may so readily make a mistake, perhaps worse than fatal – he is positively required to form and pronounce an

97

irrevocable judgement off hand, without either time for thought or opportunity for reference.

'Certificates of insanity are legal instruments of civil disability. They deprive the person named in them of the power to control himself and his property. They have proved worse than a death-warrant to many a poor wretch.'

There was an irony about the other thing. Again and again, to my amazement, I read that Scotland was in advance of England, in all these reforms. But the Scottish Board of Commissioners in Lunacy was separate from England's, and different. The difference was, that the people in charge were not doctors. And they could only advise, not enforce. So that, although Scotland may have had the best lunatic asylums, it also had the worst.

I cannot believe that any was worse than the Lochgrannomhead Burgh Asylum for Pauper Lunatics.

I do not remember life in that place as a continuous rope, or road, but as a series of pictures, like magic-lantern slides thrown on to a whitewashed wall.

I am collected from the workhouse by two men in billycock hats, like those of the police officers who came to arrest Edgar Smith. My memory is frozen at the moment when, gripped between them, I leave the Infirmary Ward. None of the old women I have tried to feed looks up. They have not noticed that anyone has come into the room or is leaving it. They are looking inwards, at nothing. The young girl twitches and dribbles, staring sightlessly at nothing.

If they look at me, they are still looking at nothing, because I am nobody.

The drive. I sit between them. I do not know where we are going, and they do not answer when I ask. I am not worth wasting words on, because I do not exist.

We are approaching the Burgh Asylum, on the edge of a town I recognize as Lochgrannomhead. There is a high, high, black stone wall. There is a great door in the wall, guarded by a man in what looks like the uniform of a prison warder.

We are inside the wall, in a dreary, treeless, featureless park of uncut grass and scrub. We are approaching a range of gaunt grey buildings, three stories high, with little narrow windows, all barred. The main door is closed, and guarded by a man in the uniform of a prison warder.

I am in the office of the Medical Superintendent, with some others being admitted, men and women.

He sits behind a table, a tall, thin, elderly man. His face is kindly, but harassed. There are great piles of papers on his desk. He picks nervously at the papers and at his thin beard.

He deals with each of the new arrivals in a few seconds, after reading documents among his pile of papers. He has difficulty finding the documents. He reads certificates about the wrong person, until an assistant points out his mistake. The assistant's voice is deferential, but his face is impatient and contemptuous.

I am standing in front of the desk, in the clothes the workhouse gave me. He hardly glances up at me. He reads the certificate issued by the very young doctors in Crieff.

'Maniacal delusions. Violent. Violence associated with exhibitionism.' To an attendant he says, 'Ward Seven. Strong dress.'

There is a brief picture as I leave the Medical Superintendent's office. It is of him taking a dark, square bottle out of the drawer of his desk.

All the attendants are dressed as prison warders. I see many inmates, who are doing nothing. They are dressed in a sort of prison uniform, dark grey, and all exactly the same.

My first impression of Ward Seven remains the total impression I had of it. It is as large as a cathedral. The little windows are ten feet above the floor. The beds are eighteen inches apart. There is no other furniture. The walls are of unfaced stone. Once they were whitewashed, but that was a long time ago. There are gas-jets high in the walls. The beds are of iron, with straw mattresses. Many have no mattresses, but only loose straw. The straw smells. The ward smells. It seems to be filled with a rancid fog. Attached to the iron

99

frames of many of the beds are straps and chains, placed to go over the ankles, wrists, waists, breasts or necks of the people in the beds.

They are putting me in my 'strong dress', so that I cannot undress myself to indulge my morbid exhibitionism. It is made of some very stiff and heavy material like canvas. The sleeves end not in cuffs but in bags, into which my hands go. I cannot use my hands. There is a heavy leather belt securing my dress round the waist. It is secured not with a buckle but with a padlock.

I have difficulty moving, because of the weight and stiffness of the dress.

I am taken to the day-room. My first impression of it remains my total impression; there is nothing to add. It is the twin of Ward Seven, except that there are wooden benches instead of iron beds. It is crammed with women, all dressed exactly alike in prison grey. None of them is doing anything, anything at all. Suddenly a fight breaks out between two women. They scream and punch and pull one another's hair. Attendants fall on them, dragging them apart, dragging them away to be chained up, for their own safety, for the safety of others, for the convenience of the attendants.

I am taken to the airing court which is reserved for the more violent women inmates. It is a bare expanse of gravel within high walls. There is nothing in it except the gravel, and a dense pack of women who are doing nothing. Since there is nothing for them to look at, they look inwards. I look at them, but that is worse than looking at nothing.

I am attacked in the airing court. I have never before seen the woman who attacks me. She might be forty or sixty. She is skinny but powerful. I do not know why she attacks me. There is no reason. For no reason, I am the cause of her misery, and the focus of her bitterness. She makes high noises like an animal, like a vixen in the spring. I try to defend myself from her fingernails, but with my hands inside canvas bags it is difficult. Attendants jump on us. She is pulled

100

off me. I am held also, with a force that hurts my arms and breast. I am equally responsible for the fight. It takes two to make a quarrel. I am known to be violent, because I raised a whip against a harmless passer-by. I am to be put in a strait-jacket, until I have worked off my fit of maniac aggression. This will be good for me. It will stop me injuring myself or others. It will save the attendants the bother of supervising me.

I have no clear memory of the strait-jacket, and cannot describe it. I was in the deepest pit of misery and despair, and memory has been merciful. But, in the book I was given, it is described by Sir William Ellis, who was in charge of a great asylum near London, and used the strait-jacket often; he is quoted with violent disapproval by Dr Mortimer Granville, the author of the book:

'The most simple and least objectionable mode of confinement, is that of a pair of wide canvas sleeves, connected by a broad canvas shoulder-strap ... They ought to come up well on the shoulders and to extend about an inch beyond the ends of the fingers; the part covering the hand should be made of tolerably stiff leather, to prevent the hand grasping anything. They are fastened at the back by two straps, one going from one sleeve a little above the elbow, across the loins to a similar position in the other sleeve; a second lower down, and by three similar straps in the front; the latter being secured by buckles, which, in large establishments where there are many patients to be attended to by one keeper, ought to be locked.'

Mine are locked.

'It is sometimes also requisite to secure the feet. For this purpose we find that a couple of leathern straps, well lined with wool, placed round the ankles and secured to the bed by staples, is all that is necessary.'

In my case, it is requisite to secure the feet. The woollen lining of the straps is not requisite.

Because I have been violent once, I shall be violent again. I am secured at night, by straps about my wrists and ankles.

I do not much notice, because I am drugged. The attendants are empowered to administer the 'House Mixture' to any inmate they think liable to create noise and disturbance at night. It is opium. It is for my own good, and for that of the other inmates of the ward. It is convenient for the attendants, who can sleep or play cards.

A picture I do not have, is that of being seen by any doctor, at any time.

# 6

After three or four nights (who counts days or nights in such a place?) I found that I had a violent dislike of being drugged. I spat out my cup of 'House Mixture', when the Attendant's back was turned. I said to myself that I would be my own mistress, in any way I could. Actually this was the only way.

I could not spit out the shackles on my ankles and wrists.

I never after that swallowed any of the pernicious 'Mixture'. I did not sleep so sound, among the moans and snores and twitchings all about me, and in the miserable discomfort of my shackles; but that was something of my own choosing.

I came through the period of apathy, which had been my defence against the intolerable. I became angry and rebellious and watchful. But I hid these things. I imitated the inward-looking passive misery of most of the rest. I play-acted like Edgar Smith when he was 'Doctor Nicol'; like Lady Lochinver when she was being my devoted subject.

I could see that, if this went on too long, the role would become the reality. I would slip back into apathy, and be one with my most pathetic companions. It became quite necessary that I should escape.

Necessary, and impossible.

As soon as I found myself in this mood, I was watchful all the time, looking for ground-floor windows left open, doors not always locked, back-stairs to kitchens, skylights, trap-doors, anything. I was even slimmer than before, because of the diet of the place; I could have crawled through a large keyhole.

But all the keyholes had keys in them, and all the locks were locked. The ward and the day-room had one door each, and the airing court was completely enclosed by its high black

103

walls. Worst, we were watched. Somebody's eyes were on us all, all the time, except when we were locked up.

I tried to make a plan, and came up against blank impossibility. I needed a distraction, to send all the Attendants rushing away; I needed a bunch of keys; I needed a ladder for the outside wall; I needed other clothes than my 'strong dress'; I needed, for those other clothes, an invisible cloak. Lack of any of these destroyed any chance of escape.

There was a matron, second-in-command to the Medical Superintendent, whom we saw as seldom as we saw him. I did not know what either of them did with their time; perhaps she, as well as he, kept a square black bottle in the drawer of a desk.

One day there was a great screaming and commotion, and a pounding of Attendants' feet towards the centre of the storm; and afterwards I heard two Attendants talking, and what had happened was that a violent lunatic had attacked the Matron, and nearly killed her.

So there was at once a new Matron. She seemed to me to share the old notions of madness, and to believe that we were all possessed by devils, or by the Devil. There were more purges, and cold douches, and restraints, and doses of 'House Mixture', by all of which our devils should have been exorcised. She was a big, grim woman. I thought she was not deliberately cruel; but I was not always certain about that. I never knew her name. She had a voice as hard and ringing as that of a Sergeant-Major I had heard drilling a company of soldiers in front of Edinburgh Castle – a voice heard everywhere in the Asylum, rasping down the corridors, and invading the remotest corners of day rooms and wards and airing courts. She had a moderately strong Scottish tone, as though she came from a family of prosperous shopkeepers. I imitated her voice, softly, to myself, as a way of occupying my mind. I almost amused myself. Not to the point of smiling; I did not expect ever again to smile.

It was in the small hours of the morning. Ward Seven sounded like some great cage in the Zoological Gardens, all snorts and whimpers and little, high, heartbreaking cries. The gas-jets were turned low, but there was enough light so that we could still be watched. But, because those of us who were violent were shackled, the Attendant could safely doze in a chair by the door.

Undrugged, I was wide awake, and jumbled, useless thoughts were spinning round in my head. My straw mattress was hard and full of lumps. It rustled when I moved. I could move very little. The blanket they had thrown over me tickled my bare feet and my chin.

The air felt thick as stagnant water, as fetid as a drain. It was very stuffy. For the first time in my whole life I felt ill, weak, wasted. I was frightened of weakness, because if by a miracle a chance of escape did occur, I would not be able to take it.

A bell began to ring, one I had not heard before, a clamorous and urgent bell. Other bells rang, deeper, from all parts of the range of buildings.

It came to me, after a moment of puzzlement, that they must be alarm bells. There was an attempt at a mass escape, or the assassination of the Attendants. Many of the poor women in the Ward screamed and whimpered at the frightening sound of bells in the darkness. Twisting my head, I could just see our Attendant poke her head out of the doorway into the passage.

I heard a man's voice, from a great distance, shout, 'Fire!'

I was shackled to my bed.

There was no sound of fire, or smell of smoke, or glow of flames in the little high windows.

The Attendant ran out into the corridor. The door was slammed. Obviously the key was turned in the lock, but I did not hear it for the clamour of the alarm-bells.

I thought: there is a rule here, that when there is a cry of 'Fire', every Attendant must go at once to help to put it out. I thought: there must be a rule, even here, that if the inmates are in danger, they are to be got safely out of the building; even here, even violent and incurable lunatics would not be left shackled to their beds, to be burned alive. So, I thought, the fire does not immediately threaten us here.

This was the kind of diversion I had been waiting for. And I could take no advantage of it, because of the shackles on my limbs, and because of the key in the lock.

The bells still rang.

105

After a little, to my surprise, the gas-jets were turned up to their highest, by someone outside in the corridor. The door of the Ward opened. Two male Attendants, in their uniforms like those of prison warders, hurried in. One was a big man, with a full black beard. I had never seen him. Confused, I thought he must spend all his time in some part of the Asylum I did not visit.

Except at times of crisis, or to deal with violence, male Attendants did not enter the female wards. I thought these two had come to release us, and to herd us to safety.

The smaller and slighter of them, whose face I could not see, took the key from the outside of the door, and put it into the lock on the inside. I saw him turn the key. This seemed to me absolutely extraordinary. Fifty female lunatics, about a third shackled to their beds, were now locked into a room with two men, in a building which was at least somewhere near a fire. Awful theories raced into my head.

The smaller Attendant called out, to my utter astonishment, 'Leo!'

'Here,' I cried.

They hurried over to my bed. I saw their faces. I knew them. My heart leapt. They were Simon Donaldson, and the Barone Lodovico di Vigliano.

'Talk later,' said Simon. 'My precious Leo, are you all right?'

'I am now,' I said. 'But how –'

'*Piu tarde*,' said the Barone.

From his pockets the Barone drew a hammer and a cold-chisel, which I knew from the peculiar gleam of the metal in the gas-light. At once he attacked the first of the metal shackles which chained me down. He was a big, powerful man, and accurate with hammer and chisel.

'Quick!' I said, sick with fear that the real Attendants would come back.

'*Prestissimo*,' said the Barone, and even as he spoke the first of the shackles fell away from my left ankle.

I gave way then to a weakness I had so far managed to resist; I burst into tears. I felt Simon's hand on my brow and cheek, and he murmured words of comfort and of love.

The alarm-bells had stopped their agitated pealing. The crash of the hammer on the chisel rang out like an act of murder. Many of the lunatic women were sitting up in their beds, and some were standing, and stumbling about in the garish light of the gas-jets. It was a scene from Hogarth or from Hell. The hammer cracked urgently on the chisel, and the chisel bit into the steel that held me. I wanted to speak, but I could not, for my sobs. Still Simon stroked my face, and my shoulder and breast, and whispered loving and lovely words.

And the Barone smote, and the second shackle parted; and those that held my wrists were not so massive.

As the Barone attacked the shackle on my left wrist, I was every second in a worse agony of suspense. If they had stopped ringing the alarm-bells, they had the fire under control. The Attendants would disperse, all running back to their normal duties. Simon and the Barone would be caught, and sent to prison for trying to abduct a dangerous lunatic. And I . . . And I . . . The thought of my own future was worse than ever before, because I was being given hope of freedom.

My left wrist was free. I found that my hand was pressed against Simon's cheek. I thought there were tears on his cheek, but perhaps they were my tears.

The madwomen in the Ward were exciting one another by howling and moving about, and they were agitated and puzzled by the unfamiliar sound of the cold-chisel crashing into my shackles. I remembered, idiotically, that in the old days 'Bedlam' had been the name for a Lunatic Asylum. It fitted Ward Seven that night.

My right wrist was suddenly free. I was unshackled. I sat up on the straw of the bed. I seized and kissed the Barone's hand, which was still holding the blessed hammer. Shameless, I threw my arms about Simon's neck. We kissed one another. I was very certain at last that I loved him. I was still sobbing.

'Now that I have got you back, my very dearest, I will never let you go,' said Simon into my hair.

I embraced him fiercely. I would never let him go, either.

'Come now,' said the Barone. *'Prest' andiam.'*

I saw, through tear-dimmed eyes, that he was smiling through his beard. He wished us well.

I stood. I stumbled, weakened by the half-life I had been half-living, and stiff from the shackles. Simon gave a cry of dismay, and supported me with an arm about my waist.

107

I had never before had a man's arm about my waist. It was comforting.

We hurried as best we could between the crowded beds to the door, the poor lunatics plucking at us, and crying out. The Barone put his ear to the door, to listen for approaching footsteps. We were not out of the wood yet, by a very long way. He shook his head. He could hear nothing, because of the shrieking and gibbering of the poor women.

He unlocked the door, and took the key from it. He opened the door a crack, and peeped out. He turned and beckoned. We slipped into the dim-lit corridor. The Barone locked the door again, from the outside. I saw that this was right. No one would know that anyone had been in, and no one would notice until morning that one violent lunatic was missing. For the same reason, the Barone turned down the gas-jets which lit the ward.

We hurried along the corridor. They knew their way, because they were retracing the route they had taken. I felt strength returning with each step, from the fact that I was on my way to liberty; but my legs did not quite agree, and Simon and the Barone were half carrying me between them.

I was no longer sobbing. I was giving thanks to God for such friends.

We passed the doors of two other wards, locked, unguarded. There was babbling and whimpering from both, as the women had been roused and frightened by the bells. We came to the end of the corridor, where there were iron stairs going both up and down. There should have been a gas-light at the head of the downward stairs, but it did not work, and things were not mended in that place.

We started down the stairs. The Barone's boot-soles rang very loud on the iron steps.

He said, '*Dio!*' and stopped dead.

For a rattle of many feet had started up the stairs. The Attendants were returning. They would be everywhere, in this corridor and the one above. We were trapped.

Suddenly, to my own astonishment, I took charge. I pulled Simon and the Barone up the stairs, and across the corridor to the foot of the other stairs. I hid myself behind the great bulk of the Barone. As the Attendants – I thought eight or ten of them – came to the top of the stairs and into the dark corridor, they would dimly see no more than two men in uniforms like their own.

I called out, very loud and ringing, in the voice of the new Matron, which I had imitated to myself to pass the time, 'Luk sharp, all o'ye – there's fechtin' in Ward Six!'

'Ma Goad,' said an Attendant in a weary voice.

It was probable enough that there would be fighting.

And they all ran away along the corridor, far along to the Ward at the furthest end.

'You've done it,' said Simon, triumph in his whisper, his arm tight round my waist.

'It was lucky the Matron was not with them,' I said shakily, the possibility that she might be there having only just struck me.

'*Andiam*,' said the Barone.

Unchallenged, we went down the stairs and out under the stars. As when I was rescued from Glenalban, I wanted to dance where I stood; but my legs would not have consented to dance.

We crossed the park, myself supported by my beloved friends. Dry grass crackled under my bare feet. If we were seen, we were a patient with two Attendants. No other Attendant would court extra fatigue, on such a night of labour, by interfering with his colleagues.

As we rounded a corner, an acrid smell struck my nostrils: burning: a fire that had been put out with water.

'You started a fire,' I said, this supremely obvious thought having only just struck me.

'In a sort of store-house,' said Simon. 'Piles of straw and blankets and broken furniture. No risk to anybody.'

'Except to ourselves,' grumbled the Barone. 'She go *pouf*, like a *lampa d'olio*.'

'Soon I shall begin to thank you,' I said, with difficulty. 'Soon I shall have words.'

'Later,' said Simon. 'You will need all your strength for the next step.'

And, indeed, I cannot think how they got me up the ladder and down it again on the other side. Simon going ahead and the Barone behind, they somehow got me to the top of the high black wall; there Simon held me, as I would surely have fallen, so weak was I, and trembling so uncontrollably. They had spread a heavy tarpaulin over the top of the wall when they had come in; through it, I could feel the sharp projections of the broken glass built into the coping. I blessed their forethought; without the tarpaulin we should have been cut to ribbons. While Simon held me, the Barone, astride the wall, exerted his great strength, and pulled the ladder up and over the top.

Going down the ladder was worse than going up it, for me and for them.

We went down into complete blackness, which was an unlit alleyway behind a warehouse. The Barone pulled the ladder down, and hid it somewhere. And then, with hardly any words spoken, we were in some kind of gig or trap, which the Barone drove; and Simon supported me still with his arm about me, and my head rested on his shoulder.

'The whole story, when you have rested,' he said. 'I have that to tell you, and other things to tell you. I am going to break my word to your Aunt. I should not do it, but I can no longer help myself.'

'Oh good,' I said dizzily.

'You know, of course, that we must have failed miserably, but for you. But for your courage and initiative, sending those fellows scampering away. It is impossible to believe that a girl who has been living as you have been living, should show such speed of thought, such brilliant intelligence. If anything had been needed to make you irresistible, dearest Leo . . .'

I did not feel irresistible. I felt like a bundle of old laundry. It shows how weakened I was, that a walk of a few hundred yards and the climbing of a ladder should have so collapsed me. Perhaps also it was the violence of the emotion of being free. Perhaps also it was another violent emotion, which I seemed to be feeling in its fullest strength for the very first time. At all events, collapsed I was, and sat helpless as a rag-doll. I would have fallen out of the gig, but for the blessed strength of Simon's arm.

We left the town, and rattled along a country road to a remote house. And then there were lights, and kindness, and a motherly woman; there was a great bowl of bread and milk, and I fell asleep repeatedly while I was eating it; and Simon kissed me goodnight, when the others' backs were turned . . .

'It looked impossible,' said Simon, 'but in the event it was easy. It took time, which I bitterly regret, because it condemned you to spend longer in that hellish place; and it took money, which the Barone seemed not to regret at all.'

We were sitting in a new-mown hayfield behind the little farmhouse, where the Barone had rented a couple of rooms. I was wearing my own clothes, fetched from Millstounburn some time before, against the day of my escape. The Barone was away about business – my business. Simon and I were alone together, out of sight of the world as completely as I had been in the lunatic asylum. So his arm could be about my waist, and my hand in his, and my head sometimes resting on his shoulder, and sometimes pressed against his cheek.

No, there could no longer be any doubt in my mind or heart.

'Now,' said Simon, 'we first knew something was strange or wrong from your Aunt Sophia. The fact that you had not written. It was inconceivable that you should not have written, to tell her you had arrived safely, to give her an account of Glenalban, to tell her what your plans might be. She was beginning to be seriously worried, and wrote to tell us so. We knew, of course, that it was Lady Lochinver who had brought you to Glenalban. We tried to make contact with her – for, as you know, she and I had remained in touch. We found out that she had left Glenalban, but we could not find out all at once where she had gone. Well, I knew who some of her friends were, from my days in the Muniment Room. It was a matter of proceeding by a process of elimination. We began, for no particular reason, with her daughter Lady Stevens. We guessed right first time.

'I had never been there, and was unknown to any servants or local people. So I was able to buy a footman a few drinks, at a modest cost to the Barone, and I learned that a beautiful and very young lady had been brought there by a person called Lord Avington, an Englishman unknown to me, and of whom, in fact, I had never heard. It seemed to us highly unlikely that he had delivered you to Lady Lochinver, being himself part of the conspiracy against you. Why should they involve any outsider in such a ploy? It was obvious that, on the contrary, he had rescued you from some threat at

111

Glenalban – that he was your friend. He would have learned from you that Lady Lochinver was also your friend, as you and I believed. We made a careful note of that name Avington. We thought we might need his help.

'Then what? My drunken footman told me that, after a week in Lady Stevens's house, you were taken off in a carriage to Crieff, and that Lady Lochinver had returned without you. That was all within the footman's observation. It made no sense. Why Crieff? What purpose had you there, and where had you gone from there?

'Getting Lady Stevens's coachman drunk took much longer, and cost much more. But I learned in the end where in Crieff you had gone. It was not so very disloyal of the coachman to tell me, because as far as he knew the errand was entirely innocent. The house of a Doctor Harold Fraser, a General Practitioner of the town. How could this be? You were not visibly ill, as coachman and footman reported it. You took long walks. You ate well. But you went on a visit to a doctor, and did not return. We were two full days speculating on this mystery, and trying and failing to bribe an apothecary and a nurse. And then a dreadful possibility struck us – the one way in which you could be made simply to disappear, and quite legally. You might have been murdered, but not, surely, by a doctor. You might have been abducted, and put on a ship to Brazil. But not by a doctor. No crime was committed by anybody. At worst, if this theory was right, a hint was given to a doctor to act a little unprofessionally.

'Now we were hampered by absence of rank, of official position. The Barone's title did not help us with Scottish petty officialdom. We needed a powerful friend. We remembered Lord Avington. The *Peerage* gave us his address. His household in England gave us, by the penny post, his present whereabouts. We went to find him, and found him. He had not revisited Glenalban, because he had defied Glenalban. He was an ally. He is one. I think I have never seen a man so angry, as he was at Lady Lochinver's treachery. He immediately enlisted himself to help us, and enlisted some formidable local dignitaries to help him, as they would never have helped us. He found out the workhouse you were locked up in – you, dearest and loveliest Leo, in a workhouse! God in Heaven, how could the woman do that to you? – and with

112

more difficulty he found out which asylum you had been put in, and under what name you went there.

'That was the limit of Avington's immediate usefulness, as he admitted and we recognized. You had been certified insane by properly qualified doctors, entirely according to the letter of the law. Only doctors could declare you cured. You were legally committed to the asylum, by a bestial weakness in the law, and it was illegal to get you out of it. A serious crime. I did not in the least object to committing a serious crime for you. The Barone did not regard it as a crime at all. Indeed, as soon as he realized what was involved, he was as excited as a schoolboy. But a man in Avington's position is differently placed – a Deputy Lieutenant of his own county, and so forth. He wished us luck, and pretended not to know what we were proposing.

'Once we had the asylum identified, it was simply the same again. We found the public-house closest to the asylum, on the theory that the Attendants would frequent it. They do. Some of them are shamefully drunken. We thus discovered five important facts, none of which was really in any way a great secret. One, Mary Smith was in Ward Seven. Two, the exact whereabouts of Ward Seven. Three, that Mary Smith was considered violent, and was shackled to her bed at night. Four, the obvious rule that, at a fire alarm, the Attendants are to lock in any patients not threatened by the fire, and are to help to put it out, in case the Municipal Fire Brigade is late or otherwise engaged. And five that, in an isolated part of the grounds of the asylum, a quantity of straw for bedding is stored. The ladder cost a few shillings. The hammer and chisel a little less. The hire of the gig and its horse cost a few pounds –'

'They can trace that to you, perhaps,' I said.

'No. It was hired by a Mr Edgar Smith, of Edinburgh.'

'What?' I said, much startled. 'Why that name?'

'No reason. It was a name that jumped into my head, in connection with you. A pretty safe name, I think, because we suppose it was a pseudonym anyway, and you cannot easily trace a man who does not exist.'

'How did you come by those horrid uniforms?'

'Once again drink. I shall never again approve temperance. Ardent spirits have oiled the wheels of our venture from first

113

to last. We spotted a large Attendant and one of moderate size. We reduced them to insensibility with whisky-and-beer, mixed with an unusual preponderance of whisky. We helped them away from the pot-house, acting their good friends and benefactors. We removed their outer garments. They were not, we thought, in this weather, in danger of catching cold. No doubt they reported that they had been robbed, but they would have suspected passing tinkers rather than ourselves of the robbery. Why should well-spoken gentlemen want the uniforms of Asylum Attendants? They have probably been obliged to replace their uniforms out of their own pockets, but I cannot feel as guilty about that as I should.'

'You make it all sound easy,' I said.

'It was easy.'

'It is not easy to thank you.'

'Oh yes it is,' said Simon, and he kissed me; and I drowned in his gentle, passionate kisses.

I had thoroughly examined myself in a looking-glass, before breakfast, for the first time in I did not know how long. I was dismayed at the pale waif I saw, with lustreless hair and a pinched face, and a kind of dullness, as though there were no life behind the skin of cheek and brow.

I looked at myself again, after a morning in the sunshine – after a morning of hearing all Simon's story, and after a morning of happy courtship, of kisses without number, of hearing and speaking words of love.

One morning. Hardly three hours. A different creature looked back at me from the murky glass. The colour had returned to my cheeks and the brightness to my hair. I saw a face so full of joy and thankfulness and love, that I could truly believe what they said. I could believe I was the most beautiful girl in Scotland.

The Barone came back in the early evening from his business – my business. He exclaimed at the change in my appearance. He said that the sunshine was good for me, and that Simon was good for me.

He had sent a message, highly confidential, by hand, to Aunt Sophia, saying that I was free and safe and well and with my friends.

He had seen the lawyers, telling them that I was back in the world after my disappearance, and that my claim could be proceeded with.

And he had seen a description of me, a hand-bill being circulated everywhere. I was a lunatic with a record of violence. I was very small, and could be overpowered by one or two strong men. I had bright hair and brown eyes, a combination which made me highly distinctive in my own country. There was a reward offered for information leading to my capture. It was, meanwhile, a criminal offence to harbour me, to assist me in any way, or to withhold information about me.

In fact, the Barone's news was a mixture of the best and the worst.

'I am safe here, for a time,' I said.

'But you cannot stay here for ever,' said Simon. 'And you will not be safe here for ever. Our hostess is trustworthy, but she is not a hermit. Her friends come in, for a crack and a dish of tea. It is only a question of time before one of them . . .'

'I can hide, when anyone comes.'

'You cannot spend your life hiding when anyone comes. I have a plan to make you safe.'

'What?'

'I will tell you when it is ready.'

'Your plans so far have been very good. I like your plans.'

'This is my best plan yet.'

He would say no more, but laughed his gentle laugh; and I was sure his plan would be a good one, and I would be safe.

He went out in the morning, on a mysterious errand. He would not tell me what he was about, but he looked hugely pleased with himself. His plan was going forward. I would be safe.

We went out into the little patch of flower-garden in front of the farmhouse, after dinner, in the thin darkness of the northern midsummer. There was no moon, but a great scattering of stars. The sweet-scented cottage-garden flowers, wet with the dew, filled the air with fragrance.

Simon said, with a catch in his voice, 'Dearest Leo, do you know the poems of Robert Herrick? He died two hundred

115

years ago, but he says what I want to say to you, now, before we kiss one another good-night. There is a poem called *The Night-Piece*. It is one of the few I know by heart. I shall recite it to you, changing one word.'

I did not think I wanted to hear a poem. But I changed my mind when I heard this poem, in his caressing voice:

'Her eyes the glow-worm lend thee,
The shooting stars attend thee;
    And the elves also,
    Whose little eyes glow,
Like the sparks of fire, befriend thee.

No Will-o'-the-wisp mislight thee;
Nor snake or slow-worm bite thee:
    But, on thy way
    Not making a stay,
Since ghost there's none to affright thee.

Let not the dark thee cumber;
What though the moon does slumber?
    The stars of the night
    Will lend thee their light,
Like tapers clear without number.

Then Leo let me woo thee,
Thus, thus to come unto me:
    And when I shall meet
    Thy silvery feet,
My soul I'll pour into thee.'

He came to an end. He repeated softly, ' "My soul I'll pour into thee." I love you more than I thought possible. I yearn and burn for you. Will you marry me?'

'Yes,' I said into his shoulder. 'Of course I will.'

'That is my plan.'

'You did say it was the best of all your plans. You are quite right. I like your plan.'

'It makes you safe. Safe from anybody. Safe for ever.'

'I feel safe.'

'As your husband, I shall be legally responsible for you.

Nobody can touch you. A hundred doctors can sign their horrible certificates, and we can laugh at them.'

'Oh. Is that the law? Your plan is even better than I realized.'

'There is a Minister a mile away. I went to see him this morning. He is a nice old man, and I told him a very little of our story. Enough so that he understands the need for speed and for secrecy. It is lucky we are in Scotland, and there is no law to prevent the marriage because you are under age.'

'Oh yes. That is why all those English couples run away to Gretna Green, to marry without people's consent . . . Aunt Sophia will be cross with us.'

'Perhaps not so very cross. I am distressed to break my word to her. But, when I gave it, you were not a fugitive from the law. I think that changes things.'

'I think it does,' I said, and raised my face to be kissed in the starlight.

'Tomorrow,' he said, after kissing me.

'What?' I cried; because although I wanted to marry him, I was stunned that it should be so soon.

'I think we dare not wait,' he said. 'The whole countryside will be looking for you. People like earning rewards. Bright hair and brown eyes are a rare combination. Think, dearest Leo. You will be able to go freely out, to see and be seen. You can go to Millstounburn, and to Glenalban to beard the Grieves in their lair, and to all the lawyers in Edinburgh. Until you marry me, your chin will be forever on your shoulder, and the risk you run continually will be shocking. And if they catch you, and you are not married, no power on earth will keep you out of the Pauper Asylum. But I do not urge this plan only for the sake of your safety. I urge it for the sake of my happiness.

> 'And when I shall meet
> Thy silvery feet,
> My soul I'll pour into thee.'

'All right,' I said huskily. 'Tomorrow.'

We went to the Kirk in the gig the Barone had rented, bizarrely using the name Edgar Smith. The Barone drove; he was to be our only witness. We were not dressed for a wedding; but the Barone made up in his usual magnificence for my shabbiness and Simon's informal tweeds.

A horseman, some distance behind, took the same road as we did. I felt a twitch of uneasiness. As things stood, there was a reward offered for information that would lead to my recapture.

But, in a few minutes, the whole legal position would be altered. My husband would be responsible for me – for my safety, and for my good behaviour. If he chose to keep me out of the asylum, though I was as mad as a bird, he could do so.

I would be safe. No solitary following horseman could lift a finger to harm me.

We went first to the Manse, to meet the Minister. He had insisted on that. Because I was so young, he had to satisfy himself that I was acting of my own free will, and that I understood what I was about, and truly wanted to marry Simon. He was anxious. He was troubled by the hurry we were in. He had never performed a ceremony of marriage in such a hole-and-corner way; all his other couples had been surrounded by their families and friends, and weeks of preparation had gone before.

The Barone made a contribution to the Kirk's Charitable Fund. I did not know how far this, of itself, laid the Minister's doubts. I thought his reluctance was genuine, a matter of conscience; I thought that my manner and words had more to do with his consent, than the contents of the Barone's purse. Now I am not so sure.

Well, consent he did; and the four of us crossed the strip of grass to the Kirk, which was a little grey unadorned box, some hundreds of yards from the huddle of crofts which made the village.

A horse was tied up near the Kirk. I thought it was the same horse that had been following us. There was no sign of the rider. Simon looked sharply at the horse. The same thought, I was sure, was going through his mind, as had gone through mine. He did not say anything. I was not yet safe, but in a few minutes I would be safe.

The horse's rider was in the Kirk before us. It was Lord Avington.

The expressions of astonishment on Simon's face and the

118

Barone's were so extreme, and so sudden, that they were almost comical. I was sure that the same expression made my face equally comical. The Minister could not understand what had stopped us in our tracks, and caused our eyes to stretch and our mouths to gape.

Lord Avington wore riding boots, and a long cotton coat against the dust of the road. His face had taken the sun; he looked more weather-beaten than before, and even more healthy. He carried his riding whip, and a broad brimmed hat. I could not read his expression. Whatever he was feeling he was hiding.

Until he glanced from Simon's face to mine. And then I saw in his eyes the expression I had seen there before. I had not forgotten that he said he loved me. I had not forgotten the gratitude I owed him. But I had, somehow, in the misery and the turmoil of my life since I had seen him, forgotten the flicker of response which his loving eyes kindled in me.

Well, it was too late. I would be a loving, faithful and dutiful wife. I was about to swear to those things, and I meant to keep my sworn word. I would not, ever again, allow myself a warm response to the love in any other man's eyes.

'What goes forward?' he said, in a voice without expression.

'I am to be safe,' I said. 'I am to be married.'

'I thought it would come to this. He wants what will be yours. He has tried to get it all before, you know. No, Leonora. You will not be married to anybody today, and you will not be married to Simon Donaldson on any day.'

'The Minister is here,' I said. 'The Minister will tell you differently.'

'I will convince you, Reverend Sir,' said Lord Avington to the Minister, 'that you must not perform this ceremony. That, in doing so, you would be inflicting the most dreadful misery on this young girl.'

'He is raving,' said Simon. 'He is jealous. I saw his face when he looked at you, Leo. He wants you. I do not blame him for that. But he shall not have you. I love you, and I have been giving thanks to God that you return my love.'

'Other people have returned what you have called your love,' said Avington, with a new touch of steel in his voice. 'The Minister, and Miss Albany, and the Signore Barone, should hear about these others.'

119

My mind was racing, and I saw that Simon was right. Lord Avington had told me that he loved me; and I knew – God knows how I knew, in my utter inexperience – that he was telling the truth. He loved and wanted me, not for the great noblewoman I might become, but for the girl I was.

Well – still my thoughts were racing – did I truly know that last part? His estates might be encumbered with mortgages, for all I knew. He might be on the verge of bankruptcy. He might be desperate for a rich wife, whose fortune he would absolutely control.

Whatever his motive, he wanted me; and he was announcing scandalous rubbish in order to discredit Simon.

It was not that he had come to believe the lies of the Grieves about Simon. It was that he wanted me to believe them. I thought this was a despicable way for him to be playing his game. I said so.

The Minister said, 'We'll no' hae this unseemly disputation in the Hoose of God.'

So we trooped out into the sunshine, and I thought it was the most extraordinary party I ever was a member of.

I thought that, after a little, the Minister and the Barone between them would get rid of Avington, and we could proceed. It could not be too soon for me. But Avington thought otherwise. He was not going to budge, and he was not going to be silent. He spoke reasonably, without heat, but with a note of conviction which the Minister could not have bettered in a sermon.

What he said might have been absolutely true, or absolutely false. It was not obvious which of the two it was.

He said, 'I cannot give you details of the one episode in this young man's history of which I have been made fully aware. To do so would be to breach the most absolute confidence, to break my word to a lady who has done me the honour to confide in me. But you may take my word – you, Reverend Sir, – you, Signore Barone – you, Miss Leonora Albany – my word, as a servant of the Crown and as a man of honour, that the episode brands Simon Donaldson as a cynical, heartless and greedy adventurer.'

'This is slander,' said Simon angrily. He had a right to be angry. He had a duty to be angry. 'I bear you to witness, gentlemen, that Lord Avington is falsely vilifying me in

120

public; I ask you to remember his words, and in due course to repeat them in a court of law.'

'Not so,' said Avington. 'In an action for libel or slander, truth is a perfect defence.'

The Minister looked troubled. I thought he was impressed by Avington's rank and by his apparent sincerity. I thought he was wondering where his duty lay. I thought he was, inwardly, praying for guidance.

I was, too.

The Barone looked wretched. He had been trusting Simon for months, working, spending. He had believed completely in Simon. But it was very difficult to disbelieve Avington.

'It is convenient,' said Simon, struggling to control his anger, 'to make these slanderous allegations, and to be unable to confirm them with even the smallest detail. Your position is adroitly taken, Lord Avington. You pretend that honour prevents you from providing proof of what you say. But I think my friends will demand facts. I think judge and jury will demand facts.'

This was a telling point. The Minister and the Barone were both too intelligent not to appreciate it. If Avington was lying, he was doing so most adroitly; and he was giving himself a beautiful excuse to tell us no facts to justify his charges.

The Minister and the Barone looked as though they were, after all, inclined to disbelieve Avington.

It was the oddest debate anybody ever witnessed. 'This House brands Simon Donaldson as a rogue, and will not countenance his forthcoming marriage to Leonora Albany, spinster.' And we were to vote on this motion, the Minister and the Barone and I; and my whole future rested on the way we voted.

Avington spoke again; and Simon. And they were both, when they spoke, utterly convincing.

Avington said, 'I put it to you, Reverend Sir, that you have known Simon Donaldson for no more than – what? – twenty-four hours. You can know nothing about him except that he is plausible. I grant him the appearance of sincerity. You must grant me that it is, as far as you can know, no more than an appearance. You, Signore Barone, are a man of great generosity and kindness. That has been evident to me in all our dealings. Your instinct is to trust and to believe. Simon

121

Donaldson was recommended to you in good faith, and in good faith you welcomed the recommendation. But, apart from one brief letter from an elderly and unworldly professor, do you know anything about Donaldson which he has not told you? I understand that you saw no need to confirm anything that he told you about himself, and you did not do so. You could not have done so, or you would not be here. I put it to you – on the hypothesis that he is a liar, you know nothing about him except that he is a good liar. Leonora, you are about to become massively rich, I think. You are not the first rich woman Simon Donaldson has made love to. I know that is true. You do not know it is untrue. I think you are too honest not to recognize the necessity of a doubt. I think you are too sensible, in a matter with such gigantic implications for yourself, for your whole future, to let your head be ruled by your heart.'

There was a long pause. It seemed that Simon, for the first time, had nothing at once ready to say, to rebut these shrewd blows of Avington's. And the rest of us were digesting Avington's words.

'Ye hae planted a wee doot, ma Lord,' said the Minister. 'I'll no' pairform the ceremony the day.'

'I am surprised that a Minister of Religion should break his given word,' said Simon.

But the Minister turned away and left us, and went across the grass to the Manse. He walked like a man who had aged thirty years in thirty minutes.

The Barone looked crumpled. All his usual ebullience was gone. It was as though gas had been let out of a balloon, so that it sagged and wrinkled. Avington had not proved a single thing he had said; but he had sown a doubt. Oh yes, in the Barone's mind he had sown a doubt; and in my mind.

Avington said, 'I am very sorry, Leonora. I am sorry you are hurt. I am sorry that I have been the instrument of hurting you. You need not completely believe me, as long as you do not completely disbelieve me. I think my duty now is to try to prove to you, once and for all, that you must have no dealings with this man.'

'You said you cannot prove it, without breaking your word. Where has your honour gone?'

'Where indeed?' said Simon.

122

'Come with me to Glenalban.'

'That is madness!' cried Simon. 'Dearest girl, would you run your neck into a noose?'

'*Sarebbe la follia,*' said the Barone, looking very puzzled at Avington.

Lord Avington ignored them. To me he said, 'We will not go to the castle, of course, but to a secret rendezvous. You will there get proof of what I say. In my company, in my care, you run no risk. I think you know you can trust me. Come. Good God, child, you must *want* to know the truth?'

'I want to know the truth,' I said miserably; because I was beginning to face the truth.

'You will be fed more lies,' said Simon.

But there was less confidence in his voice. There was the beginning of fear in his voice.

Misery must have shown in my face; doubt; indecision; fear.

Avington said, 'I will tell you this much. And you, Donaldson, will know that your case is ruined. I will take you, Leonora, to meet Lady Flora Grieve.'

'I have met her,' I said. 'I heard her out. I did not believe her then. Why should I believe her now?'

'You did not hear her out, because she did not speak out. She told me what she told you, and it was not enough. She will not want to tell you more, but when she knows the reason I think she will tell you all. Come.'

'I will come,' I said, 'because you are right. I must know the truth.'

Though it would break my heart, yes, I must know the truth.

Simon saw that I was decided to go with Avington. Suddenly he reached into his pocket, and pulled out a small pistol.

I screamed. I had never before seen a pistol held threateningly in a man's hand. I had had no notion that Simon had a pistol.

The Barone, with his heavy stick, knocked the pistol from Simon's hand. It went off as it hit the ground, with a shocking explosion. The bullet sped away somewhere. Avington hit Simon on the jaw, a tremendous blow. I screamed again. Simon crumpled. The Barone caught him as he fell, and laid him on the grass.

'Thank you, Signore,' said Avington.

'I do not know if I thank you,' said the Barone. '*Piccola Contessa*, you will tell me, not what you hear, but whether you believe what you hear. If you believe, I will believe. Ho – this is my pistol. I carry it because my country is full of *ladroni*, bandits. I did not know Simon had it. He took it from my case. He is *ladrone*. Already I begin to believe more and more. I begin to feel myself a very great fool.'

'So do I,' I said.

'Look after *la mia Contessina*, Milor'.'

'Can you doubt it?'

The Barone could not; and nor could I.

# 7

The Barone lent Lord Avington his hired gig, and himself took Avington's hired horse. We left Simon stretched on the grass by the Kirk; and before we were out of sight we saw a woman come out of the Manse to look after him.

Innocent or guilty, he was neither dead nor in danger.

I felt my heart crack, as I went away in the gig with Avington. I felt a volcano of anger inside me; but I did not know at whom it was to be directed. Simon? Avington?

We went into Lochgrannomhead. I shuddered as we approached the dismal town. Avington said I would not be recognized as a dangerous escaped lunatic, in spite of bright hair and brown eyes; it was plain to see, he said, that I was a demure and well-behaved young lady of perfect sanity.

We returned the gig to the livery-stable, and hired instead a travelling carriage. And it was after we had started our twenty-mile journey to Glenalban that Avington told me his story.

'It may have seemed bewildering coincidence that I was in the Kirk this morning,' he said. 'Of course, it was no coincidence at all. After I left you with Lady Lochinver, I quartered myself with other friends, sure that you were safe. I told my household in Berkshire where I was, because I am not in a position to allow myself to drop out of sight. My estates are considerable, my affairs complex, and my duties exacting; I live at the end of the electric telegraph. I am sorry if I sound self-important; the point is that it was perfectly easy for Donaldson and your Italian friend – I think a very good friend, by the by – to locate me.

'They had gone so far in finding you, which was hardly more difficult for them than finding me. Then they stuck. The task they accordingly gave me was beyond them, but

125

perfectly easy for me. A friend of a friend of mine is a Commissioner in Lunacy in Scotland, one of the lay members of the Commission. He could not intervene in any way once you had been certified insane by those ignorant young doctors. But he could put me in the way of finding out what had become of you. It was no secret, you see. There was no official reason why it should be confidential. There was no official reason why I should not be told that you were in such-and-such a place, having been given such-and-such a name.

'I told my friends what I knew, and turned my back on the matter. I had to. On a strict reading, I was already an accessory before the act of a felony. That I warmly approved of the proposed felony was nothing to the point. I could help you most by knowing least.

'Now a new element enters my story, which I speak of with reluctance and embarrassment.

'I saw Duncan Glenalban in London in the spring, and with him his sister Flora. As you know, she is a beautiful and gentle creature, not brilliantly clever – as I believe her brother is – but talented and artistic. I took to calling, quite often, too often. I liked and admired her. I was deeply gratified to realize that my growing admiration was reciprocated. Our acquaintance was only of a few weeks. She had never been south before, and when I had been to Glenalban, she was either invisible in the schoolroom, or, latterly, away with friends. A declaration would have been premature. In any case, I had first to declare myself to her brother; that also would have been premature, a point he would certainly have made. But I contrived an invitation to Glenalban, ostensibly for the salmon fishing. Flora contrived it for me, to be exact; and she knew as well as I did that it was not for the salmon fishing that I was coming.

'Almost as soon as I arrived for my visit to Glenalban, I heard about you. Naturally – you were the first topic on everybody's tongue. So very beautiful. So very young. So very shameless and audacious.

'The next chapter you know. And you know the effect you had on me. You know because I told you. You would have known, I think, even if I had not told you.

'As I said, I went off to Nairn, and quartered myself in a

126

fishing lodge. I flogged the Findhorn with my Silver Doctors and my Durham Rangers, and I was afflicted by conscience. I had led Flora to believe that I was emotionally, ah, committed to her. And I had been. There was no dishonesty or frivolity in my attitude, in any of my actions. I acquit myself of philandering. But my attachment cannot have been very deep. Because, Leonora, it dried up like dew in the sunshine. Your sunshine.'

'That is flattering. But it is sad and bad.'

'It was both those things, and there was nothing whatever I could do about it, except to behave as decently and honourably and kindly as I could. I concluded, consulting with my conscience and my salmon flies, that honesty was the best policy. It isn't always, you know. Kindness sometimes demands – prevarication, white lies. But Flora – she had to be told that – things were not on the footing we had both supposed. I owed it to her to tell her that, and I owed it to her to tell her why. She wrote in reply to my letter, consenting to meet me, and to do so secretly, because I had not obeyed, in her brother's house, the rules relating to the conduct of guests.

'Well, it was a deeply disagreeable scene. I do dislike hurting people, and I hurt her. I know I hurt you today, and I am sorry for that; but I think you are made of sterner stuff than Flora.

'She said, "But that girl is involved with Simon Donaldson."

'I said, "We have all always known that."

'She said, "If she is his accomplice, you should be as wary of her as I am of him. If she is his victim, you should rescue her from him. You have been frank with me, Jack," she said, "and, to make you understand, I shall be frank with you." She swore me to secrecy, and told me an awful story. It is the one I expect her to tell you. I believed it. You will.

'Well, this put a different and a dismal complexion on everything. I had told Simon Donaldson and the Italian where you were. I knew they were planning to remove you from the place. I knew the Barone was as completely duped as you were – as I had been, by the most plausible villain I have ever met. I feared very much for you. Not for your physical safety. That good Italian could be trusted to guard you – and, in any case, as Simon Donaldson's pawn you had to be alive and well. What I feared was something like today's abortive ceremony.

'So I watched them, while they planned and carried out their abduction of you. They did it very well, I must say – with dash and intelligence and a good deal of courage. Donaldson doesn't lack pluck. At any rate, after you were out, you were always under my hand.'

'Why did you not come to me sooner,' I said, 'with your story which I do not yet know whether to believe?'

'Because I did not know what Donaldson proposed. I could scarcely ask him. I could not ask you. You were never alone, and in any case hardly likely to know. I could not ask the Barone. He went away all day, your first day of liberty, and I could not follow him and keep an eye on you. Which I was determined at all costs to do, after what Flora had told me. My fear was . . . I cannot say this and look you in the eye. My fear was, that Donaldson would force you into marriage, by seducing you last night, which I thought he might have done, because of your gratitude to him.'

'He had no need to force me. He asked me, and I accepted.'

'Because of your gratitude?'

'It did not seem so. I am still not sure that I believe you. I am still not sure that I do not believe him.'

'The man who drew a pistol, to stop me taking you to hear Flora's story?'

'I shall know better what to believe,' I said, 'when I do hear it.'

I did know better what to believe.

The meeting-place was a deserted croft, on a hillside three miles from Glenalban. We approached it by a roundabout way, so that we went nowhere near the castle, and saw none of its people. This remained very necessary.

Lady Flora was already there when we arrived. I did not at once understand how Avington had got a message to her to come, so quickly after the events of the morning. The answer was, that they had made an arrangement, at their previous meeting, that she would come every third day to this place, for news of Simon Donaldson and of me; and this was one of the days.

Lady Flora wore a riding habit. Far away along the hillside

128

I saw a groom with two horses. She was still more beautiful than when I had last seen her, in my prison-cell, because the sun had turned her fair skin to a pink-gold; and because she seemed in her natural element on this wild hill.

When she saw Avington, she reached out a hand towards him, and then pulled it back.

When she saw me, she put a hand to her mouth. I thought she knew immediately why Avington had brought me.

Briefly, Avington told her that I had been rescued from a dreadful lunatic asylum, and then a still more dreadful marriage.

Lady Flora said to me, the words dragged out of her, 'Did you love Simon Donaldson? Do you?'

'This morning I was very certain that I did,' I said. 'Now I am not certain I do not.'

'I was very certain I did, too.'

I suppose I had understood for hours that this was what I should hear. It was the reason Avington could not betray Lady Flora's confidence. It was the reason Simon threatened to shoot Avington, rather than let him take me to hear the story. I had not quite faced the obviousness of it, because I had not wanted to.

'I was only sixteen,' said Lady Flora, looking at me as though pleading for understanding. 'I was still in the school-room, being taught French by my governess. I was a child. I had never met anybody, except my family and servants and other children. I . . .'

She stopped. She was blushing. Her eyes were lowered.

'Go on, Flora,' said Avington gently. 'I think you would prefer me to leave you. I think I would prefer to leave. This story makes me too angry. I will not go far.'

Lady Flora nodded.

We sat on tumps of heather by the croft, with a huge blue sky above us, and a brisk wind blowing along the hillside.

In one way, what I heard was not as bad as what I had been led to expect I would hear. In one way it was much worse.

'I suppose the first man in any young girl's life,' she said, 'can easily make a deep impression on her. She has read romantic novels, you know, and dreamed of a knight on a white horse . . . In the ordinary way I would scarcely have met him. I might never have met him. But I went to the

129

library for a book, as he went to the library for a book. I thought it was by accident that we met. He was as shy as I was. Shy and gentle, quite unlike the terrifying gentlemen of my brother's age, that I had only seen at a distance . . . We arranged secret meetings, and went for secret walks. I was flattered, and excited. I was not used to having my face and figure admired. I was not used to being kissed, except by my aunts. It was exciting to feel wicked. He lost his shyness, but not his gentleness. I could not feel afraid of him, of anything he would do. I lost my shyness. I lost my modesty. Not my virtue,' she added quickly, looking at me anxiously, to make sure I did not misunderstand. 'But I am ashamed to remember what − liberties − I allowed him − I allowed myself . . .'

Her face was scarlet.

I said, 'It is brave of you to tell me all this.'

'He said he wanted to marry me. He said he could not face a lifetime without me. I was so proud! And he made me feel − kissing me, and so forth . . . But there was not the slightest chance of my brother consenting, then or ever. I was in despair.'

'So he suggested you elope?'

'He was cleverer than that. He crept into my bedroom, late, knowing that my maid was out for the evening. He embraced me. He recited a poem.'

I had a dreadful premonition.

'It ended with a line about "thy silvery feet". I thought that was so beautiful that I cried. He said, "I yearn and burn for you". I thought that was even more beautiful than the poem. And so it was I who suggested that we elope.'

'I can understand that,' I said. 'Those words had almost the same effect on me.'

'*Those same words?*'

'Yearning and burning, and silvery feet. Actually mine are usually pink. Except when I have been going barefoot, when they are black . . . What happened? Why didn't you elope?'

'My maid came back early from her mother's. She saw Simon coming out of my room. She rushed to the housekeeper, who rushed to my aunt, who rushed to my brother. So that was the end of that.' She looked at me again with an air of asking me not to judge her too harshly. 'I was younger than you are now,' she said.

130

'My great-grandmother was not much older than I am now,' I said. 'And she got into much worse trouble.'

Lady Flora did not understand this reference. She had not been told the full story of my ancestry, not because it was false but because it was true.

She said, 'My brother made enquiries after that, by way of lawyers and so forth. He found that Simon had tried to do the same thing at least twice before. One very young girl who was an heiress. And a rich widow of about forty. That was when he was a student at Aberdeen.'

'Do you suppose the widow had silvery feet?' I asked.

To my joy, Lady Flora began to giggle; and in a moment we were both laughing helplessly. It was not what either of us in the least expected. Perhaps there was a note of hysteria in our laughter. At least, it had the effect of exorcising the spirit of Simon Donaldson from us both. If we could laugh about it, we were not so likely to cry about it.

Still laughing, we embraced.

For myself, I had known quite well in a part of my mind what Flora was going to tell me. Therefore I had known which of them to believe, Simon or Avington. Therefore, when I refused to be convinced, I was lying to the others and to myself. That was, perhaps, because I was unwilling to admit, to them or to myself, how royally, how totally, I had been duped. I had accepted Simon's caresses with joy, and his words of love with pride. I had remembered them first with doubt, and then with embarrassment and anger. Now I could laugh at them, because Flora had started me laughing.

I could have forgiven him a little, for the wonderful 'silvery feet' poem. But he had quoted it as part of his method for securing heiresses. It came out so wonderfully glib, because it was well rehearsed. It became outrageous and comical.

I had a new friend, which was good, because I had lost my greatest friend.

Seeing us laughing and embracing, from a distance, Avington rejoined us.

'I thought you might have been at blows,' he said. 'I stayed within sight, so that I could catch your sword-points in my cloak.'

'Why should Leo and I be at blows?' said Flora. 'Nothing divides us.'

131

Well, that was nice, but perfectly untrue. She had forgotten, it seemed, that I was still after claiming her family's castle and estate. Perhaps she thought I had forgotten.

'A question that exercises me,' said Avington, 'is where Leonora goes now. Until – things are a little clearer.'

He meant: until the lawyers have decided who owns Glenalban. It would not have helped the friendliness of our group to have come out and said so.

'I think I cannot ask you to Glenalban, Leo,' said Flora. 'I know you now, and I know that, whatever was planned, it was not by you. Since I was – bewitched – like you – I can understand how it all came about. But my family . . .'

'Will not, as things stand, extend a cordial invitation to Leonora,' said Avington. 'Unfortunately, I do not know this neighbourhood well. If I had been brought up here, I daresay I would know a dozen kindly and discreet farmers' wives who would hide Leonora, and feed her, and wash her clothes.'

'I know some like that,' said Flora. 'One in particular.'

'I hoped you would say so,' said Avington. 'I did not like to suggest it. I did not like to invite you to defy your family.'

'I am not defying them, exactly,' said Flora, wrinkling her brow. 'I think I am doing my Christian duty. But I am doing it without telling my family. Is that defiance?'

'It is casuistry,' said Avington. 'Don't you think so, Leonora?'

'I do not know quite what casuistry means,' I said. 'But I will accept Flora's offer of a kind farmer's wife who will give me a bed and a bowl of porridge. She need not wash my clothes.'

'She shall certainly wash your clothes,' said Avington. 'You are . . .'

Again he did not come out and say what I was, or might be.

Flora rode ahead with her groom, to make sure that Mrs McPhail would receive a lodger at Achmore, and keep very quiet about that lodger. Avington and I followed in the carriage. The coachman thought our destinations increasingly peculiar.

'What were you laughing about?' Avington asked me suddenly.

'Silvery feet,' I said.

132

He did not know what I meant. He did not know the poems of Robert Herrick. I would not tell him. He knew that Flora and I had both been bewitched, as Flora said. I did not want to admit that we had been bewitched by the identical words.

I felt like the Chosen People; I was introduced into a land of buttered oat-cakes and honey. Achmore, on low ground near Loch Grannom Side, might have belonged to a different planet from the bleak little croft we had left, though both were on the Glenalban estate. There were fat sheep and cattle, a steading full of ducks and hens, a barn bursting with the new season's hay, and fields of wheat and oats and barley ripening towards the reaper.

I suppose payment was offered. I suppose it was accepted. It was not mentioned when I was by.

No questions were asked. It was enough for the McPhails that I was Lady Flora's friend. They thought she was an angel. There was a long, intricate story about an ill child, and the trouble and expense her Ladyship had been to. I agreed that she was an angel. But I knew how very nearly she had been a fallen angel.

Oddly, this knowledge increased my affection for her. I was thankful to find that I was not the only fool. I was grateful to her for that. I was grateful to her for opening my eyes about Simon; and, for that, there was a little part of me that would never forgive her.

Avington, meanwhile, was to re-establish contact with the Barone di Vigliano, which he could quickly and easily do by way of the Edinburgh lawyers. The point was to see where we stood, and so to decide where we went.

While this happened, I was to wait. I waited for six days.

How greatly did I miss Lord Avington? I simply could not tell even so much. He was kind, amusing, attentive, considerate, gallant, sufficiently handsome. (Simon had been all those things.) He said deeply flattering and exciting things about myself, and his feelings for myself. (Simon had said all those things, and – better rehearsed – had said them better.)

I think I had the wit to realize that I was once again in danger of confusing gratitude with love. But was I not also in

133

danger of suppressing a love which was real, because it was mingled with gratitude? I found that, instead of feeling older as I approached my eighteenth birthday, I was feeling younger. I had thought that, as an adult, I knew my feelings. I now knew that, scarcely adult, I did not.

Flora came to see me on the sixth day. The McPhails treated her like royalty – as her aunt Lady Lochinver had pretended to treat me like royalty.

She showed that she was pleased to see me, and I was very pleased to see her. But she was puzzled, and inclined to be worried. Things were going on she did not understand. There were developments, among the lawyers. She knew this not from Avington, whom she had not seen, but from her brother. But that was all he had written, from Edinburgh, where the business kept him: that there were developments. She wanted to know if I knew more. But I had not seen Avington, either. I assumed that he too was in Edinburgh, if he was needed there, or catching salmon a long way off if he was not. I was hurt that I had heard nothing from him.

For the first time, I thought, Flora was becoming fully aware of what the rest of her family had known all along. I might dispossess them all. I wondered if this would change her loving attitude towards me. I did not see how it could fail to.

I wondered about my own feelings towards Avington; I wondered about Flora's. It was dreadful that such a gentle creature should be hurt twice – by a villain, and then by a man of honour.

My coming into her life was already a calamity.

And yet – and yet – if he fell out of love with her the moment that he met me – utterly amazing as this still seemed – would he not have fallen out of love with her anyway? Perhaps after a few months of marriage? Was that not worse? Had I not, in sum, done her a kind of favour?

I could not lie to myself on these lines for long.

Avington came, in a carriage.

The McPhails knew that he was another friend of Flora's, and everything in the house was his. Indeed he ate a gigantic

134

tea, in which I heartily joined (my experiences had not reduced my appetite). He was hungry, because he had come straight from Edinburgh, by train to Crianlarich, and then by this hired carriage.

He was aburst with news, but it had to wait until we were alone together. The McPhails were torn between curiosity, hospitality, and the good manners of the Highlands. In the end, we were free to go out into the fat farmland, and he told me his news.

'Things have been going forward apace during the last few weeks,' he said. 'Don't ask me exactly what things. Many of the words involved are Latin, which I have thankfully forgotten. And I know less than nothing about the strange Scottish laws of succession and property. So the fine details of what I heard went largely over my head. However, I think I understand the gist.

'Glenalban's lawyers challenged the very existence of the various deeds and charters which established the Grieves in their stewardship of the castle and estate. There were no such documents to be found in the castle. Of course there were not – Simon Donaldson had stolen them. The Barone's lawyers either had them, or had copies which were attested as genuine. First significant point to the Barone. Glenalban's lawyers then challenged the existence of your great-grandmother's journal, of the marriage certificate, of your grandfather's baptismal record. Or, they said, these things are forgeries. They were shown the originals, at Millstounburn, in the presence of experts. They heard Miss Sophia Grant's account of the discovery of the papers. Second significant point to the Barone.

'Well then, on the face of it the claim looks good. But is there a claimant? Where? She must be produced, or there is no case at all. So everything grinds to a halt. Processes about to be served, if that is the correct phrase, go back into the deed-box. Appointments are cancelled. Actions are struck off the rolls of forthcoming cases. The College of Arms rolls up its parchments.

'Now then, we come to the interesting part.'

'You have not bored me yet,' I said.

'Thank you. You remember that, the very day after you escaped from the asylum, the Barone was away, from early

135

morning until late evening. Except that it was urgent business, you did not know what he was about. I have since heard, from him, that he was most of the day travelling – the route I have come today, but both ways. He had little time between trains in Edinburgh. He dashed across the city – you can imagine that he makes a droll account of that – and spent a few minutes with his lawyers. What he had to say was extremely simple, and of the highest importance. You were found. You were safe. You were you. You see the significance of that?'

'Yes,' I said, 'but before you go on, did he say what had become of Simon?'

'The Barone doesn't know. Simon has disappeared. I expect it is a thing he has had to do before. I hope he is nursing a sore chin, but I daresay he is quite recovered now.'

'Like Edgar Smith.'

'Did he have a sore chin?'

'No, but he disappeared. That is two people who were quite important in my life, that I shall never see again.'

'Well, you will see the Barone again. He is to be invited to Glenalban. So am I, more or less forgiven. And so, of course, are you.'

'I do not like going to Glenalban. They lock you in wardrobes.'

'Not this time, Leonora. Not this time. You diverted me from my purpose, prattling about Simon Donaldson –'

'Not prattling,' I cried. 'I just asked what had happened to him . . . Very well. I am sorry. Please go on.'

'If you wish further discourse about Donaldson, shall we have it now, and dispose of it once for all?'

'Please go on,' I said, in what I hoped was a dangerous voice.

'Very well. As I was saying, you exist. You can be produced. You can be proved to be Miss Leonora Albany, by, for example, doctors and Ministers in East Lothian. There is a Glenalban claimant, and she has a good claim. It follows that, first, you will probably be Countess of Albany before the end of the year; and you will probably also be owner of Glenalban. It follows that, second, the present Earl of Glenalban, and his aunts, and their retainers, are now aware of the appalling injustice they did you. They are agog to make amends. I

136

think, if I were you, I should let them. That is why I came here in a carriage, instead of saving time by riding.'

'Why is it why?' I asked inelegantly.

'Because I am taking you away in the carriage, dear goose. I am taking you to Glenalban.'

'This turnabout is a little sudden for me.'

'It is not a complete turnabout. Glenalban will fight you in the courts. The issue is by no means certain. I would fight you myself, in his place.'

'Why could they not have, in the beginning . . . Oh yes. Of course. I was Simon's accomplice. I was branded.'

'Even Flora believed that,' said Avington. 'Even she thought it was right to lock you up. You have forgiven her, I think. Do you suppose you can forgive the others?'

'Not Lady Lochinver,' I said. 'I do not think I can forgive her.'

So, for the second time, I arrived at Glenalban in a travelling carriage, in the evening. The great hills were the same, and the frowning complexities of the castle. As to everything else – dear God, what a difference! No piper this time; no odious play-acting of reverence; no assembled regiments of servants imitating Arabs at their prayers. Just Flora at the foot of the great steps, embracing me, and leading me indoors by the hand.

It was strange to be sitting, in the evening sun, on the terrace which I had seen only from directly above. It was strange to be talking, almost calmly, to the Earl of Glenalban.

I remembered thinking, weeks before, how much Flora resembled her brother. I was struck now by how much Glenalban resembled his sister – tall, slim, with glossy black hair and wide-apart eyes. There was a further similarity. She had been deeply embarrassed, telling me about Simon Donaldson. Now he was deeply embarrassed. She had avoided my eye. He made himself meet my eye, when he embarked on his apologies.

His apologies were a little stilted. I thought it was because he was unused to apologizing. I could not yet judge whether that was because he did not usually stoop to apology, whatever he had done; or because he did not usually do

137

anything that called for apology. Both, perhaps? He was both arrogant and priggish?

I realized that I knew nothing about him at all, except things that were presumably completely false. Simon Donaldson's account of him, given for one reason. Lady Lochinver's, given for another. Avington had said that he was not really a close friend, but simply an old acquaintance. Flora simply revered him; her account of him would be perfectly truthful, and perfectly untrustworthy.

Like Avington, I would think as I found. What did I find? A very handsome man, with a severe, humourless face, telling me awkwardly that he was sorry for what he had done.

I could not even tell if he meant it.

He changed the subject, to my relief as well as his.

'I have been to Edinburgh,' he said. 'I think you know why.'

'To try to save your estate from an adventuress,' I said.

He smiled, but very briefly.

It was the very first time I had seen him smile. I had seen him contemptuous and coldly angry; I had seen him deeply embarrassed. The effect of his smile was interesting. But I did not have time to think about it, because he was telling me important things.

He said, 'I returned only a little before you arrived. Consequently, I had not heard until a few minutes ago my sister's account of her meeting with Jack Avington and yourself. I understood about the marriage which Jack rescued you from. We have some experience of that here. But what is this about a lunatic asylum?'

'You did not know?'

'Do you think I would have permitted such a monstrous thing?'

'You permitted me to be locked up here.'

'I could not bear to hand a creature like you over to the police for attempted fraud. I hoped you could be persuaded to come to your senses. I hoped especially you would listen to my chaplain and to my sister. Well, you know all that.'

'I would have put it differently,' I said. 'I thought you hoped to terrify me. What did you think Lady Lochinver had done with me?'

'We thought she had succeeded where we had failed. We thought so because she told us so.'

138

'Did she say she had paid me? Threatened me? Prayed at me? Or simply persuaded me?'

'All four. She said she had convinced you, finally, that your ploy could not succeed, that you were infallibly bound for prison if you persisted with it.'

'You believed her.'

'Why not? It seemed so very probable. She is a convincing lady.'

'She is,' I agreed.

'She convinced us she had convinced you. That you had returned to obscurity, with Donaldson or without him. Remember that we had thought you an impostor. Of course, an honest person might not have been swayed by the arguments my aunt said she used. But an impostor – a tyro imposter, a girl not turned eighteen – oh, we readily believed she had convinced you.'

'She did not even try,' I said.

'But tricked you into workhouse and asylum. Oh my God. I knew we owed you reparation. I swear I did not know how much. I swear that none of us heard a single word about my aunt's manoeuvre. It was unplanned, I am sure. She thought your arrival required action from her, and she conceived what must have seemed a brilliant stroke. It took her a few days to prepare things – that, I suppose, is why you were there for a week. What must have pleased her most was that there was nothing to pay, except a guinea for the doctors. The whole charge of removing you from the face of the earth was transferred from us to the ratepayers of Lochgrannomhead.'

'Well, it was clever.'

'It was devilish. I think she now knows it. That is why she is not here.'

'I did wonder why. I did have an odd feeling, at the thought of meeting her.'

'She had a more than odd feeling about meeting you, I think. I was not here, but I gather the household was much surprised when, almost the moment she heard that Avington was bringing you here, she remembered an engagement somewhere in Fife.'

'I am surprised to have frightened her away.'

'It is more, I think, that you have embarrassed her away. That is a peculiar use of the word, but I think you know what

139

I mean. She could not face you. It will never be easy for her to face you. I think it will be a long time before she does. She was embarrassed to face us, too – myself, my sister, her sister, Avington. At the time, no doubt she thought she was acting in the best interests of us all, as she had throughout. But I think she was appalled at what she had done, the moment she had done it. She would never have told us, and we would never have known. Then, suddenly, she was faced not only with meeting you, but with meeting our knowledge of the atrocity she had committed. I think it will be a long time before she comes back here.'

'She told me she stayed here only to protect your tenants against you.'

'She need not feel obliged to come back here on that account. Can you believe me, Leonora, that none of us here knows anything about that part of it?'

'I will try,' I said. 'But recently I have been asked to believe so many things. I was good at believing things two months ago. Too good. Now I am becoming bad at it.'

'You must believe, Leo,' said Flora. 'My aunt came back, saying that my cousin was better and that you were gone. She said she had paid you some money – fifty pounds. My brother gave her back the fifty pounds. Gracious, he must be cross about that! Not because of fifty pounds, you know, but because of being cheated by his aunt. I don't think she has ever done anything like that before, but being horribly clever once gave her a taste for horrible cleverness, I suppose . . .'

Suddenly, the fifty pounds convinced me. It was not a detail Flora could or would have invented. The Earl must indeed have given Lady Lochinver fifty pounds, and it must have been because she said it was the bribe she had given me.

'I am getting back into bad habits,' I said to the Earl. 'I am beginning to believe people again.'

For the second time, I saw his quick smile.

Once I stood with Aunt Sophia at Prestonpans on the Lothian coast, looking north-eastwards towards Gullane. It was mid-morning, on a day in March of high wind and fitful sunshine. The sea was grey. It looked cold and hostile and dangerous, like the Earl of Glenalban's face when first I saw him. Over Dysart and Kirkcaldy there were black clouds carrying rain out into the North Sea. Suddenly the wind tore the clouds apart, and a broad shaft of sunlight kindled the sea to silver. It was a transformation, a miracle. It was beautiful beyond words. When the clouds closed over the sun again, and the sea darkened, it was not as it had been before. There was something permanent in that momentary change. One could not look at the dark sea with fear or dislike, because one had seen it, for a moment, a sheet of fretted silver.

That was the transformation wrought in the Earl's face by his smile. And, though his face returned again so quickly to its usual severity, I could not look at it as I had looked at it before. I could not be frightened or repelled or angered – never again, by a face which could be lit by such a smile.

Yes, I was getting into bad habits again. I was becoming dangerously credulous. And I was not only believing in the truth of plausible words. I was letting myself believe in the truth of a smile.

'We were so astonished and delighted, my dear,' said Miss Louisa Frith, 'to learn that you were telling the truth.'

She was still awesomely elegant and fashionable. But she had her nephew's smile.

'Even though . . .' I began.

'Even though you are trying to evict us from Glenalban? But I don't think you will. My nephew has the best lawyers in Edinburgh and London. They will fight fair, but they will fight. What you will find yourself, dear, is not owner of Glenalban, but welcome guest. My own position, more or less. Given all the responsibilities and worries, I think in your place I should actually prefer that. Meanwhile, my sister – my unforgivable and unforgiven sister – made some promises to you about clothes. The very least I can do, by way of making some kind of reparation, is to honour those promises. I shall try to get my sister to pay, but I don't suppose I shall succeed . . . A dressmaker is coming here, from Perth, the day after tomorrow. She is French. You would not think she is provincial. She made this confection. It serves, for the country.'

It did, indeed.

'When you came here, you know,' said Miss Frith, 'our first notion was to hand you at once over to the County Police. It is a very good thing for us we did not. You could afterwards have sued us for I don't know what – false arrest, defamation of character, a whole roster of felonies.'

'I still could sue you,' I said, 'but I think I will not.'

'I will buy you off, with a wardrobe of clothes. As my sister pretended she had bought you off, and cheated my nephew of fifty sovereigns . . . That time you tried to escape, did you hang outside the window by your dress?'

'I nearly died of fright.'

'I don't think you did. But I did, when I concluded that was how you must have managed it. That was why bars were put over the window. I did not want you plunging to your death on the terrace. You hung outside that window, so high about the ground, clinging to your dress? You really did that?'

'I had no rope, Ma'am.'

'You deserve to be Countess of Albany. I don't think you will be, but you would grace the title. You are more of a man than your alleged great-grandfather. You would grace Glenalban, too, but I don't think you'll get that, either.'

She smiled her nephew's smile. We were enemies, and we were friends.

I met the servants who had been my goalers – Mary MacAndrew and Kenneth Doig.

I had seen the Earl's smile for the first time; I had seen Miss Louisa Frith's smile for the first time; and so I had learned something about them. With Mary MacAndrew it was the opposite. That stone-faced, silent creature, who had never shown any expression at all, burst into tears. I found that I was comforting her, which I had not at all expected.

Of course she had only done as she was told by Miss Frith; and she understood the reasons. She thought it was right that I was not at once handed over to the police, right that they should try by all means to persuade me to give up my attempt at fraud; she understood why she was to treat me as she did, and to answer no questions. And she hated every moment. She was thankful when Lord Avington took me away, as it relieved her of a horrid duty.

So she told me, her face wet with tears. I believed her. I was believing tears, as well as smiles.

I had seen Kenneth Doig's smile, come and gone in a wink, like the flame of a dark-lantern, at our first moment of meeting. Now he had no need to switch it off, and did not.

For him, the worst thing about his gaoler-duty was his own enforced silence. He was naturally a voluble man – words fairly tumbled out of him. What he wanted to know, was how I got out of a locked room – or, if I had not got out, how I had contrived to disappear. When I told him, as little boastfully as I could, the torrent of his words was quite shut off. He stared at me with his mouth open, like a fish.

There was one happy but ironic outcome to all this. Mary MacAndrew and Kenneth Doig had known one another only little, before they were thrown together by being my guards. In that time, they were constantly together, and so came to know one another well. And now they were betrothed. It was still a secret, because Mary's father was away, and had not been asked; but they wanted me to know.

'What would you like as a wedding-gift?' I said; and Mary MacAndrew burst into tears again.

I was not put in the King's Room, but an ordinary sunny bed-chamber among other rooms. Mary MacAndrew was to maid me, because she asked to.

And the wheel almost came full circle, because once again I was treated as royalty.

# 8

High summer on high ground was new to me, and beautiful beyond anything I had imagined. I had been confined; I made up for that. I had been undernourished; I made up for that. I had been treated as mad and bad; all the world seemed to be in a conspiracy to make up for that.

People were in the conspiracy, and animals, and Nature herself.

More than anybody else, naturally, I was with the gentle Flora. Though in company she was shy, and seemed somehow soft, she was most active and vigorous when she was walking the hill or riding the glen. She chose me a pony from the stables, a near thoroughbred of the kind they used to call a Galloway, a fast and bold little horse called Peregrine. He was short of exercise when first I rode him, and so was I, so we had a bumpy and perilous time of it. And then he grew used to me, and I to him, and when I went into his loose-box he blew on my cheek, and rested his chin on my shoulder; and I learned that what he liked best was to have his brow scratched with a fingernail. I should not have liked that, but I respected Peregrine's preference in the matter, and every ride began and ended with my scratching him interminably, while Flora and the grooms laughed over the box's half-door.

Flora and I talked about every subject under the sun, while we rode or walked or sat on the terraces; except three. We never talked about Simon Donaldson. We never talked about my impending claim to the castle where we were. We never talked about Lord Avington.

We had no news of Simon Donaldson, and did not expect any. We supposed he was gone forever, out of both our lives.

144

The legal processes were shortly to be in abeyance, because the courts would be in recess and the lawyers on vacation. Solicitors might still be preparing briefs, but Counsel would not be there to plead them. It was no matter. There was no hurry. With Michaelmas all would march again.

Lord Avington had left Glenalban immediately after he had carried me there. He was welcome, and his breach of the laws of hospitality most heartily forgiven; but he had engaged himself with other friends.

'I am torn,' he said softly to me, as he left. 'I want to be where you are, but I am not sure it is kind to be where Flora is. I wish I could stop feeling like a beast.'

I thought he was not a beast. I thought I was not one either, but, like him, I wished I could stop feeling like one. I did not know how deep Flora was hurt. I did not ask her. I was glad and sorry that Avington was gone. Flora treated me with loving friendship, though it seemed I had stolen her lover, and I was like to steal her home.

I resolved that, if Glenalban ever did become mine, they would all always be as welcome there as I was, while it was still theirs. This was not a thought to be put into words, to Flora or anybody else.

Miss Louisa Frith was as good as her promise. A French dressmaker arrived, and measured me, and we picked over drawings and designs and samples of material. The dressmaker said, in a mixture of French and English, that mine was the smallest waist she had ever measured. I thought she had made this remark to a great many young ladies, and probably to many ladies not so young. In an astonishingly short time, hampers of gowns began to arrive, as well as silk underclothes and stockings and hats and shoes; and I was able to enter rooms full of strangers without embarrassment.

'Fashion is a fraud, dear,' said Miss Frith. 'We should not value it. But we do. You look better even than I thought possible. You were beautiful before. Now you are scarcely credible.'

I had one truly absurd new dress, with gigantic leg-of-mutton sleeves, and a gigantic crinoline. It made me feel like an overdressed doll, and like a clown. When first the Earl saw it, he gave his rare brief smile, which was like the sudden sunlight on the Firth of Forth.

'It is *meant* to be comical,' I said. 'At least, I think it must be.'

'I was not smiling in derision, Leonora,' he said, 'but in startled admiration.'

His smile had come and gone. It came again, and stayed longer than I had ever seen it stay. I felt myself smiling back. I felt myself blushing. I felt self-conscious in my ridiculous sleeves. I felt hugely pleased with myself, to have aroused startled admiration.

Dear Aunt Sophia answered a letter from Miss Frith, as well as many from myself, saying that she would come to Glenalban in August.

The Barone Lodovico di Vigliano answered a letter from the Earl, saying that he would come to Glenalban in August.

Lord Avington wrote saying that he would come, in time for the first of the grouse shooting.

There was no word from Lady Lochinver. Her daughter wrote to Miss Frith, to say that her mother had gone south into England.

And, week after golden week, the sun blazed on the bare tops of the big hills, and on the shrunken waters of the Alban River; and the wind from the west sobbed in the trees of the lower ground, and combed the dry grass of the hillsides, and set the roses of the formal gardens nodding. The birds fell quiet, but the air of Glenalban was full of laughter and the sound of the hurrying river, and hoofbeats, and the excited barking of dogs.

Riding with Flora, I was astonished at the number of crofts and little farmhouses on the estate. Of course there were great tracts of emptiness, on the high ground where nobody could have lived, but where any kind of farming was possible, farms there were.

There had been no evictions, no threat of evictions. There were some feckless crofters, and some drunken, and some suspected of poaching and of making illicit whisky; but they had wives and children, and those children were safe. The Earl could not be called the best landlord in Scotland, because there were some equally good; but he was as good as the very

146

best. His supposed cruelty was another lie of Simon Donaldson's, told out of spite; another lie of Lady Lochinver's, told out of policy.

Often we stopped at those crofts, Flora and I and our groom – too often, for Peregrine's taste – because the folk came running out of them, calling to us to have home-made barley-water, or tea, or cake. Everywhere Flora was welcomed, because she was loved; and children tumbled round her feet like puppies, and sheepdogs nuzzled up to her like children. I was welcomed, for her sake. I thought that, after a little, I was welcomed for my own sake.

I thought that, all unconsciously, Flora was teaching me how to be mistress of Glenalban.

I thought that I did not want to be mistress of Glenalban. It was in good hands. I had believed lies, which I now knew to be lies. I had believed that it was desirable, necessary, that I should claim my birthright, for the sake of the poor folk on the estate. I now knew this to be needless. I did not want to make so shabby a return for hospitality.

I said to the Earl, 'Sir, I think it is silly for any of us to spend any more money on law-suits. We will tell the Barone to stop. He has spent enough.'

'He has stopped,' said the Earl.

'But the lawyers must still be sending bills?'

'Of course they are. It is a way lawyers have. I never knew such fellows for itemizing every detail of their services. "To writing one letter, one guinea." '

'If they are sending them, the Barone must be paying them.'

'No longer. That responsibility has been transferred. Your case will proceed, Leonora. It is too late to stop now. Why, you would be assassinated by the entire legal profession, as well as the College of Heralds and the House of Lords.'

'But who . . .? If the Barone is not . . .?'

He would not say who was paying the legal reckonings.

The obvious truth dawned on me, in the middle of the night. The Grieves were indeed making reparation.

I said, 'Sir, this is ridiculous.'

I was wearing again the dress with the enormous sleeves

147

and the crinoline. I had taken a great fancy to it, because it was intensely fashionable, as well as comical.

The Earl assented cordially. 'It is quite ridiculous,' he said, to my surprise. 'Those sleeves are frankly absurd. However, the extremes of fashion suit you, I suppose because you wear them with an air of such confidence.'

'I was *not* talking about my dress,' I said.

'It goes from the ridiculous to the sublime without moving,' he said.

'I am *still* not talking about my dress. Are you paying my lawyers?'

He would not say. He would not discuss it at all. He became almost brusque, in his refusal to speak about it. There was a hint in his manner of the arrogance with which he had first treated me. By this I knew that he was paying the bills, because if he had not been, he would have said so.

He was paying to have himself evicted from his own castle. It was as ridiculous, and as sublime, as the leg-of-mutton sleeves of my dress.

Almost overnight, I was transformed from a girl wearing dowdy provincial clothes, into a young lady dressed in the height of fashion. More people looked at me, more often, and in a new way. Flora began looking at me in a new way; and Miss Louisa Frith; and the Earl of Glenalban. I thought this was because of my new clothes. Then I thought it was something else.

I thought they all knew something I did not know. Well, to be sure, they all knew a vast number of things I did not know. The Earl and his aunt were widely travelled, and widely read. Flora was nearly two years older than myself, and had been to London, and met all kinds of clever and important people, and had started by being far better educated than I was. But there was more to it than that. There was some immediate knowledge they had, relating to immediate circumstances, which they were keeping from me.

Flora said, when I taxed her, that the odd looks I had seen were looks of admiration and astonishment. She said that she and her aunt were amazed that I could carry off such audacious clothes, because I was so very small, and usually only tall women could dress in such a style; but the dressmaker had understood that I could be successfully biz-arre; and they both envied me, and that was the look I saw.

Well, it was all possible; but I thought that for the first time Flora was telling me less than the whole truth.

The oddest looks, that I caught least often, came from the Earl. I could not begin to guess what he was thinking. His face was the opposite of mine – except when he smiled his rare smile, and often even then, his features gave nothing away. Perhaps it was natural; perhaps he had schooled himself, in politics and public affairs, to hide his feelings under a mask of impassive severity.

I caught him frowning at me, when he thought I was not looking. I thought it was not a frown of disapproval or of rage, but of calculation. Yet he was paying my lawyers!

I would have been uneasy. I should have been uneasy. But the weather was too glorious, and the high country too beautiful; and, when Peregrine galloped across the mown hayfields, the rush of warm air scoured all uneasiness out of my mind.

Aunt Sophia came, brought in a travelling-carriage sent by Miss Frith. The family left us alone together, for the whole of her first afternoon, with great kindness and tact, so that we could bring one another up to date without any reserve. I had told her in my letters such of my adventures as I thought would not give her palpitations; I still blotted out many of my memories.

She asked me, hesitantly, how much I had been upset, to find out that Simon Donaldson was a cold-hearted rogue. I said that the wound had healed. I thought it had. It was an itch rather than an agony, like a cut that is mending healthily.

'I think the Barone was quite as wounded as you were, dear,' said Aunt Sophia. 'He has been to see me, you know, and he could talk of nothing else! He is vexed at having been duped, because he prides himself on his judgement of people. What a good soul he is! I am glad he is to come here. I shall feel braver, and more at home, when he is with us.'

I also was keenly looking forward to the Barone's coming; I was amused at the thought of his exuberant gallantry, set against the sober reserve of the Earl, and the infinite correctness of Miss Frith. At least he would not be overawed.

149

Aunt Sophia was, of course. It was obvious to everybody that she was not accustomed to castles; it was also obvious to everybody that she was a lady of breeding, as well as a gentle and lovable creature. Miss Frith took her under her supremely competent wing, and the two of them went off to see local beauty-spots in an open carriage. Aunt Sophia grew pink from the sun, and there were freckles on her temples I had never seen there before.

I asked her what she and Miss Frith found to talk about, on those expeditions in the victoria which sometimes lasted all day.

'You, dear, principally,' said Aunt Sophia. 'Dear Miss Frith is inexhaustibly interested in your childhood, your education, the family, and so forth. I myself supposed that we had exhausted the subject, after our first conversation. But no such thing! Her questions had barely begun!'

Aunt Sophia did not quite say that there were, after all, other topics of conversation quite as interesting as myself; and that she would have preferred Miss Frith to embark on some of them. She could have said so, without wounding me; I would have agreed. I had myself answered a good many questions about myself, from Miss Frith. I did not know why she should want still more details of my uninteresting history.

I caught glances of special oddness when she looked at me, after these examinations of Aunt Sophia. They might have been expressing admiration and astonishment at my new appearance, as Flora said, but I thought not.

'I do not mind Jack Avington coming,' said Flora unexpectedly, when we were riding over a low hill in a bend of the river.

The meadow-pipits flitted before our horses, going *peep-peep-peep* as they settled for a moment on rocks or clumps of heather. Over the hillside beyond the river, a buzzard wheeled, mewing, like a crucifix against the sky. In the river below us I saw a salmon leap. Nature was showing us her handsomest, most generous face: and suddenly Flora was making embarrassing remarks, which I did not want to listen to.

I looked at her anxiously. If she wanted to tell me about the state of her heart, I would listen, because it was my duty as a

150

friend to do so; but I would have preferred another time and place. It was the first time either of us had mentioned Avington in private, though his name had cropped up in general conversation.

'Truly, Leo,' said Flora, 'you are not to worry on my account. Consider your own feelings, and don't be bothering with mine.'

'I don't know my own feelings,' I said.

And she gave me a look quite as odd as any of Miss Louisa Frith's.

Avington, when he came a few days later, showed that he knew his feelings.

He had two private interviews, each lasting a long time, before ever I exchanged a word with him. The first was with Flora. They walked up and down the terrace for an hour. I could see them from my bedroom window, where I sat having my hair cut and dressed by Mary MacAndrew. I could not well see their faces, nor hear a word of what was said. But I thought I knew pretty well what they were talking about. Avington was making sure that in coming back to Glenalban he was acting without dishonour or cruelty; and Flora was telling him what she had told me.

And presently, I supposed, I would be telling him what I had told her: that I did not know my own feelings.

Immediately afterwards, Avington sat for half an hour with Aunt Sophia. I watched them while my hair dried in the afternoon sunshine. He might simply have been amusing her, and passing the time for them both. I thought not.

I thought Aunt Sophia would approve of his suit, because she must find it impossible not to approve of him. For one thing, it would not matter for my future what happened in the courts of law. For another, his courtship of me would heal as nothing else would any wound I still carried made by Simon Donaldson. For a third, I was fast approaching my eighteenth birthday.

I came face to face with Avington at last, on the terrace where I had been watching him for most of the afternoon. He waved a greeting, and started hurrying towards me. Twenty

151

paces away from me, he stopped dead, with an expression of comic amazement

'Everybody laughs at this dress,' I said, 'but let me tell you it is the last word of fashion.'

'You simply take my breath away,' he said slowly. 'The jewel is properly set at last. I see that you are Countess of Albany. Nobody could doubt it. They could have, you know, but not now. I wonder Duncan Glenalban bothers to fight the case in the courts. Now, I was going to postpone a proposal to you, until I had adroitly established myself in your good opinion, by catching a salmon, and shooting a lot of grouse, and so forth, manly exploits which would oblige you to view me as a champion, but contemplation of you now simply pulls the words prematurely from my throat. From my heart, I should say. I must try to be elegant as well as passionate. Will you do me the honour to accept my hand in marriage, you unbelievable miracle of grace, beauty and courage?'

'What were you and Flora talking about?' I said.

'You. Myself. Herself. Did you not hear a question I put to you? Is your perfection marred by deafness, or by a perverse refusal to hear?'

He was smiling. He was joking. But he was in earnest. There was no shadow of doubt about that. And he knew that I knew it.

I was elated. He was a truly decent, honourable, kindly and most diverting man. I would be incredibly lucky to meet one I liked better. Sunburned and windblown, radiating health and humour, he seemed to me supremely attractive. He was in every single regard a man I could most happily contemplate sharing my life with. But I was not certain that I wanted to – not quite certain, not quite yet.

'You must give me time,' I said lamely.

'Why? I'll give you all sorts of other things, of course, trumpery affairs like rubies – but why time?'

'First of all, time to hear what you and Flora were saying. Then time to hear what you and Aunt Sophia were saying.'

'How do you know that I have been having these conversations?'

'I watched you.'

'All that age? I am more than flattered. Prolonged contemplation. That suggests that you do not find me repulsive.

152

You may even have detected in me a classical beauty which, as a matter of fact, my mother is the only person to have observed. Also that vigil would have given you time enough. But I daresay your mind was on other things?'

'I was having my hair done.'

'Whoever did it is a master.'

'And so,' I said, 'I was imprisoned in my chair, and I was obliged to watch you walking up and down with Flora, and then sitting beside Aunt Sophia. And I wondered what you were saying, and I still wonder.'

'I like your aunt very much.'

'Well, we can come to that later, and you can tell me exactly what you like about her. First you must tell me about you and Flora.'

'You know, you have changed more than your style of dress. Your character has changed. You are growing rapidly into your new role of tyrant, châteleine, empress. Even a thought too rapidly, if I may inject a note of nervous criticism into a conversation which I intended to be an anthem of praise and supplication on my part, and an almost immediate acquiescence on yours. You are not supposed to give me orders. You are not an Amazon. Or, if you are, I think they would say you were undersized for battle. I am supposed to give you orders, but I doubt whether I shall ever have the courage to do so.'

I burst out laughing. He laughed too. That was what was so very good about him – the laughter that he generated and that we shared. That was one of the most attractive aspects, of the prospect of sharing a life with him.

We bickered amicably, in the golden sunlight of early evening, often making one another laugh. I thought afterwards that it was the most extraordinary conversation I had ever had – even odder than the one in which Avington unmasked Simon Donaldson, outside the little square Kirk. For he was, even as he bantered and bickered, pressing me to reply to a proposal of marriage; and I was pleading for time, and demanding to know how matters stood between himself and Flora, and what Aunt Sophia had said on the subject I was sure they had discussed.

A footman came out on to the terrace, with the gong that was beaten there every evening. It told us it was time to go indoors, to dress for dinner.

153

'We have by no means completed our discussion,' said Avington.

'We have weeks to finish it in,' I said, 'if you are going to stay here as long as that.'

'My present plan is to stay until I have extracted an acceptance from you, which I shall do by force if necessary. One of those halberds or partisans which Duncan Glenalban so ostentatiously hangs in his hall. A few good jabs with a spear, and I'll soon have you saying "Yes". Of course I shall try first to secure your surrender by means of peaceful persuasion. But I must warn you that my patience wears thin very quickly. I am a most impulsive fellow. Don't be surprised to receive your first stab-wounds about the middle of tomorrow afternoon, if you have not by that time given me a satisfactory reply.'

'There are shields in the hall, too.'

'None that would protect me from the piercing impact of those amazing brown eyes. Inherited, as we know, from your great-grandfather. Really they make all ordinary eyes insipid, colourless, vapid.'

'We must go in and change, or we shall be late for dinner.'

'I rhapsodize, practically in poetry, about your eyes, and all you are thinking about is your dinner.'

'Being proposed to gives one an appetite,' I said.

'Come to think of it, so does proposing. I would have expected to turn away in disgust, from great platters of rich food. But I think I shall fall upon them with every circumstance of gluttony. I beg you will not watch me eating my dinner. I shall revolt you. You will contemplate with abhorrence the prospect of sharing a dinner table, all the rest of your life, with so obscene a spectacle.'

We both laughed, and laughing parted, with nothing decided, least of all what my answer would be.

As I went into the castle from that west terrace, where we had been amusing and enraging one another in the evening sun, I saw the Earl. He turned and strode away, as though to avoid me. He had been watching us. I was sure of it. Watching us as intently as I had watched Avington with Flora, and Avington with Aunt Sophia.

Though he turned away quickly, I had time to glimpse his

face. There was no trace in it of the smile I liked so well. It wore a black frown – another of his expressions which I had cause to know.

Had we angered him, by hooting with laughter outside his windows? Had we been boorish and rustic? I thought not – at least, not very. Other people laughed at Glenalban, and dogs barked, and pianofortes were played, most expertly, and with plenty of loud pedal, by Miss Frith and by Flora, and most inexpertly by me. It was a place full of bustling life, and all the mixed noises of activity and sociability. No one had objected to noise before, as far as I knew.

Mary MacAndrew helped me to dress. I was becoming used to being pampered, and it would be stupid to deny that I liked it, because nobody had ever pampered me before. Mary was prattling about her still-secret betrothal to Kenneth Doig, and it was glorious to see the happiness in her narrow face.

As though a coin spun, I saw the other side of Mary's happiness, the exact reverse. I saw misery, in my mind's eye. Not anger, but misery on the Earl's face. It had been a frozen frown. The Spartan boy whose vitals were eaten by a fox would have worn such a frown, and so prevented himself from crying out in anguish.

It came to me that I had been seeing less and less of the Earl; and, when I did see him, it was at meals, or in one of the drawing-rooms, in company with all the others. I was sorry for this, because his conversation was always interesting, and his compliments were welcome because they were rare and because they were meant. It came to me that it was no accident, that we no longer found ourselves talking together, or strolling together.

His misery might be on his sister's behalf, knowing her heart to have been bruised, and seeing Avington enjoying my company. I thought not. I thought it was on his own. The Spartan boy would not have worn such a mask of frozen misery, because that fox was eating someone else's vitals.

And so an astonishing theory jumped into my head. It had simply never occurred to me before; and the Earl had given me no grounds for supposing any such thing.

He was so learned and travelled and experienced. Though he could smile, he was generally serious to the point of severity. He had gigantic responsibilities. Though the same

155

age as Jack Avington, he seemed to belong to a different generation.

If he felt as he looked as though he felt, then my happy comradeship with Jack would, indeed, turn knives in his heart. But why should he, a sophisticated gentleman, a great nobleman, lord of this place, well able to express himself – why should he stand and suffer? He did not know my heart. I did not know it myself. I was not yet Avington's property, and might never be. I might have hated the Earl, for what he had done to me; but he knew very well that I did not. He could have spoken. He could have made a sign. But, instead, he avoided me as though I were a leper.

The supremely obvious explanation came to me, when I lay wakeful in the small hours.

He was drawn to me, but he was repelled by me.

He thought I was beautiful, and he liked my new clothes. But he found me a silly, shallow, ignorant and worthless child. And, indeed, I was. I was inconceivable as his companion, as mistress of Glenalban at his side; I was inconceivable as hostess of political receptions in London, and of great dinners with Prime Ministers and Dukes. Though my face and figure attracted him, my personality and conversation filled him with boredom and disgust.

That must be it, I thought. That explained everything. Nothing else explained anything. I could imagine being torn by such an internal conflict. I could imagine Simon Donaldson arousing physical passion and moral disgust, all at the same moment; I could imagine the misery that one might feel and that one might show. One would find oneself driven to stare upon the cause; but one would have sense enough not to torture oneself, perhaps, by private conversations with the cause.

I felt very wise, making these deductions with flawless logic. I felt very puzzled, and sorry. I felt flattered and angry. I was not, on second thoughts, so very stupid. If I was intolerably young, time would put that right. If I was fairly ignorant, he could put that right. Other clever people had managed to listen to me, without screams of irritated boredom – dear Jack Avington, and dear Aunt Sophia, and Miss Louisa Frith.

But still he was paying my lawyers' bills, with the object of having himself evicted from Glenalban.

It was a great puzzle, and a great muddle; I did not sleep until dawn, and then Mary MacAndrew had much difficulty in waking me.

'I had a long talk to Lord Avington, dear,' said Aunt Sophia after breakfast. 'I have been waiting to talk to you about it, but I had trouble in deciding what to say.'

'Say if you like him,' I said.

'Oh! Yes! That is an important point. I do like him, very much, on brief acquaintance. He has those very pleasant easy manners, and he is full of kindness and consideration! A gentleman, as well as a nobleman, which I think is not invariably the case . . . I understand that he has, ah, conversed with you also. That he has, ah, declared himself to you.'

'Did you give him leave to do so, Aunt Sophia?'

'He said that he could not stop himself from doing so. I was struck by his sincerity, you know. I think he has a true heart! I demurred about the difference in age, but he quite brushed that aside! He said many most generous things about you, which I shall *not* repeat, because those astonishing new dresses of yours are making you disgracefully vain already . . . He agrees that there can be no formal arrangement until your eighteenth birthday –'

'That is only a few weeks off.'

'I demurred also about the *very* short time you have known one another. To be precipitate in these matters may breed the most dreadful unhappiness! But he quite brushed that aside too! Never, he said, had he been more certain about anything! All the while he was in the way of laughing at himself, you know, in that amusing fashion he has, and obliging me to laugh also . . . But, at bottom, I am convinced he is in earnest.'

'Yes, I know.'

'He made the excellent point that while he knew you quite well enough, even after so short a time, for such certainty, he quite saw that you might not feel that you knew him well enough, but that the next few weeks could put that right. To that I had *no* answer.'

'I have no answer, either,' I said, 'to any of it.'

'That is as it should be, dear. Rush into nothing. Think most carefully, and consult your heart and your conscience.'

157

All this, of course, was quite the proper thing for Aunt Sophia to say. But I was sure she was sure that I would marry Avington; and I was sure that she would pray nightly that I did. Avington had one matchmaker firmly on his side.

I thought there was constraint between Flora and Avington, although they did not seem to avoid one another as the Earl avoided me. There was no change in Flora's attitude to me. She bore no grudge. I thought she deserved to be loved as she was, by all the folk of the countryside.

Avington was in undisguised pursuit of me, of which nobody at Glenalban could have been unaware. The upshot was reckoned a foregone conclusion, in the Servants' Hall, as Mary MacAndrew reported to me. I suppose that Flora's maid reported it to her, too, in all innocence.

Jack was not always at my side. The castle was filling up with shooting guests and their wives, for the Twelfth of August and the first of the grouse drives. He had to fish with some and ride with others, out of civility to them and to the Earl. He had to engage ladies in conversation after dinner, and turn the pages of their music, and take a hand at cards. These were the absolute duties of a bachelor staying in a great house as a member of a large party; and Jack performed them beautifully. All things considered, it was amazing how often he *was* at my side.

He did not, point-blank, repeat his declaration, his proposal. He made it clear, in a joking way which was perfectly serious, that he *would* repeat it. He paid me many compliments, joking and perfectly serious. But what he was really about was bringing the two of us closer together, so that we knew one another every day more deeply. It was just what Aunt Sophia would have advised.

Though there was nothing arrogant or complacent in Jack's manner to me, it was obvious that he did not entertain the possibility of my refusing him. And indeed, the possibility seemed to be shrinking. Everything was pushing me in the same direction – Avington himself, Aunt Sophia, some of the other guests, who made broad and sentimental hints, even the whole Servants' Hall.

This had a curious effect on me. I did not care to be pushed. Though Jack never *said* anything directly that showed he took

158

my acceptance for granted, he *did* without words show that he took it for granted. And so did everybody else; and I did not care to be taken for granted.

In an odd way, the exceptions to this universal pushing of me towards marriage with Avington were Flora and Miss Frith. When others winked and hinted, or even openly approved, they were silent. They were apt to glance at me, involuntarily; and the odd looks I had seen before came and went in their faces.

The Earl was engrossed in the sporting entertainment of his guests. I hardly saw him at all. Of course he knew about my friendship with Jack Avington. Of course he heard the romantic rumours which kept everybody busy and amused. Of course he had reason to know that they were true. Of course he did not know the outcome. Nobody knew the outcome, though everybody thought they did. I guessed that he was glad to be distracted. I even guessed that Jack was, in a way of drastic surgery, solving his own problem for him.

There were not only rumours about my approaching betrothal to Jack Avington. There were also rumours about my claim to Glenalban Castle. Though nothing had been published or publicly announced, such sensational matters could hardly be kept secret. It amazed some of the visitors that I was kindly entertained in a castle that I was trying to grab from its occupants of three and a half centuries. But other visitors knew better. There was no hope of my claim succeeding. This was, it seemed, the confidential news from Edinburgh. It was colourable; it was not fraudulent; it had been worth bringing; but it was based on flimsy evidence and uncertain law. That was the accepted view in Glenalban, in the first week of the blazing August.

I thought they were probably right, and I thought I was probably glad.

I did not precisely have conversations with anybody about it, because these were kindly and well-bred people who would not have embarrassed me for the world. But I overheard a good many snippets and wisps of other people's conversations.

'It's preposterous, the idea of that chit being owner of all this.'

159

'Preposterous it may be, dear boy, but damned attractive.'

'The idea, or the little claimant?'

I did not hear the answer: not because I was suddenly ashamed of eavesdropping, but because the two resplendent gentlemen strolled away out of earshot.

It was another foregone conclusion in all their minds, like my marriage to Jack. Still they were all, in varying degrees, agog to know what would happen when the courts sat again and the causes were pleaded. And I understood that there was widespread curiosity, thoughout the country, derived from things which were babbled by solicitors' clerks in Edinburgh taverns. This was something that was bound to have happened; but it shows how ignorant I was, that it came as a complete surprise to me.

Jack said, 'What will you do, Leo, if you find yourself owner of Glenalban?'

'I think I would give it back to the Grieves. But the question is academic. They all say that my cake is dough.'

'I wonder what I hope?' he said. 'Morally I think you ought to win, but I'm not at all sure I want you to.'

That was my position, exactly.

There was a great gala and a great slaughter on the Glorious Twelfth, the opening of the season for shooting grouse. All the gentlemen went off quite early, in knicker-bockers and shooting-boots. All the ladies joined them on a hillside, going by wagonette or dog-cart or Highland pony, for a monster picnic. It was still very hot. The men were purple, and had taken off their coats. The beaters and flankers and stops – the army of men and boys who put their lives at risk to make the sport possible – lay panting and scarlet on the heather, but were gradually revived by barrels of beer brought up the hill on donkeys.

I had never seen one of these lavish Highland sporting picnics before, but I had read in the illustrated papers about the Queen's great feasts on the hills above Balmoral. I thought the standard on Albanside must be quite as high as that on Deeside. I was agape, and so was Aunt Sophia. I could not imagine how so many servants, so perfectly point-device, had been transported to this wild place, with white gloves uncrumpled and buttons agleam; nor so much ice, and wine, and linen, and silver, and chairs, and cold salmon; but all the rest took it as a matter of course – or, if they did not, they were better at pretending than I was.

'Are you enjoying yourself, dear?' Miss Frith asked softly.

'Yes, Ma'am, very much. But I am amazed to see that the whole Glenalban dining room is carried all the way up here. Have you a herd of pack-elephants hid somewhere behind the stables?'

She laughed her moderate laugh – not unamused, but not precisely uproarious. 'Ah,' she said, 'there are a great number of improvisations and short-cuts, you know, which nobody is supposed to notice. The idea is to achieve the maximum of effect with the minimum of hard labour. The servants enjoy it, but not if their backs are broken.'

Miss Frith, like Flora, was unconsciously giving me lessons in how to be mistress of Glenalban.

Two days later there was a greater gala – the arrival of a circus, of a conqueror, of a clown. The event had the air of being attended by military bands and cheering crowds.

The Barone Lodovico di Vigliano came.

He was by now the friend of Jack Avington, Aunt Sophia and myself, and the friendly enemy of the Earl. To all the rest he was completely unknown. He was totally exotic in that place – yet, because he was as always completely himself, he was totally disarming to almost everybody almost at once.

He arrived in his notion of clothes for a Perthshire August – a pale-coloured silk frock-coat, trousers like chequerboard balloons, but pinched in at the ankles, brown button-boots instead of black ones, a scarlet cravat as big as a pillowcase, and a straw hat with a brim a yard broad. Among the sober tweeds and worsteds of the Glenalban party, he looked like a peacock among daws.

He kissed Miss Louisa Frith's hand. I was not sure how she would take an action which, in Perthshire, was as peculiar as it was in East Lothian. But she was pleased. She smiled. I took it that it had happened before, on her travels abroad, but not often. He greeted Aunt Sophia as an old and honoured friend, and kissed her hand. With most of those present, her stock, which had been only moderately high, immediately rose. He bowed deeply to Flora, and less deeply to me. He did not kiss my hand. He called me not *piccola Contessa* or *cara Contessina*, but Signorina Leonora, as though we had never shared adventures and betrayals, and planned my coronation in the Palace of Holyroodhouse. I was surprised, and a little put out. It was the kind of thing which should not matter, but does, when you are not quite eighteen, and long afterwards.

There were some strict gentlemen in the party, and stricter ladies, who were not immediately captivated by this affable eccentric. I think none of them held out beyond the end of the Barone's first evening. He talked much; he listened also. He exclaimed in amazement at the castle, the views from the terraces, the beauty of the ladies present; and at every story he was told. He became effortlessly, and without any apparent intention, the centre round which the party orbited. Everybody wanted to talk to him, men as well as women. I thought his beard was even bigger and glossier than before.

He once or twice smiled at me, that first evening of his conquest of Glenalban, and made little gestures indicating friendliness. But he was constantly surrounded, and we had no chance to talk.

Somebody asked him, as I had done, if his prodigious cane were a swordstick. He said, as he had said to me, that a man needed protection against the *ladroni* of his undisciplined country. He was asked if he had used it; indeed, he said, he had been more than thankful for it; it was not too much to say that it had saved his life. I waited for the story of the melon which he had cut with his sword on the banks of Lake Como. But he told a perfectly different story, about a large Bologna sausage which he wanted to cut into slices. There was a roar of laughter about him, in which Miss Louisa Frith joined, laughing more unreservedly than I had ever seen her do. It was good to see.

I thought that the truth was, that the Barone had used the sword in earnest, to save his own life or somebody else's; but he would never tell a story that glorified himself, but invent one to make himself ridiculous.

I wanted to tell them all the story of the way he rescued me from the Lochgrannomhead Asylum. But the story involved Simon Donaldson, and Lady Lochinver; and so this was not the place to tell it.

He did not join the gentlemen on the grouse-moor in the morning, though he was offered tweeds, and boots, and a pair of guns, and a loader. I did not hear the reason he gave, but it made the solemn Earl laugh as hard as his aunt had laughed.

He joined me instead, where I was sitting with some sewing, among terrifying ladies, on the terrace. He bowed all round; he requested permission from the company to take me for a stroll, since we were old friends who wanted news of one another; he apologized for his intrusion and for taking me away, with a droll humility that made even the grimmest ladies smile.

We went round a corner, so that we were out of sight of the terrace.

'Now,' he said, 'I can kiss your hand, *bellissima e piccolissima reina*.'

And he did so, bowing low.

'I could not speak so, or act so, before all those peoples yeterday,' he said. 'It would not have been *gentile*, I think, to show that I think you are Contessa d'Albini, and *proprietario* of this big house.'

'Oh, I see,' I said. 'Yes, of course, that is right. You do not *have* to kiss my hand, even in private . . .'

'Yes, I do,' he said. 'Now, you do not have to tell me your news, because I have heard it all last night, and again this morning, from one thousand peoples. First, you are even more beautiful than peoples thought, because now you have nice *vestiti*.'

'That is all thanks to Miss Frith.'

'The Signorina Louisa? So? She is kind and generous? That is good. I find her very handsome. But in a different style from you. So – I hear also that you are *spiritosa* – amusing – and not too shy, but also not too bold, so that you please all peoples very much. And I hear that you will marry the Milor' Avington. That is good. I like him. *Mi piace*. You will be rich and a *Miladi* even if we lose the case. And that is good, because I think maybe we lose him.'

'I don't care so very much,' I said, 'but why, when everything seemed so certain?'

'The lawyers have explain, and I have not understand.'

'Why is Lord Glenalban paying our bills?'

'He is *uomo d'onore*, that one. His family owes you much, in

163

*riparazione.* That is first. Another, he thinks I have paid enough, in an affair which is not my affair.'

'Well, that is true.'

'Yes, it is true. It is become quite difficult to get more *soldi* from Italia. They are there, but they are not here. Well now, I have more news. You know your friend, Signor Maitland, with the *negozzio* in Edimburgo. His is now my friend also. That is from Simon Donaldson, of whom we will not talk. Well now, you remember also the *banditto* Edgar Smith, who call himself a different name and come to your house?'

'Yes, of course. But I don't think Edgar Smith is his real name, either.'

'That may be. Such a man has one thousand names. But always he has the *uccello*, the *voglia* —'

He groped for the English word. I looked at him blankly.

'The marks of birth,' he said.

'Birthmark.'

'*Giusto.* So when he is caught he is known. He has been caught. He is in the prison. That is a little bit of good news, to put next beside my large bad news.'

'I think they're both good news,' I said. 'At least, I think I think so.'

# 9

Jack Avington had to go away again.

'I accepted the invitation months ago,' he said, 'before I met you. I have been wondering whether to make an effort to get out of it, but it could only be done by tellings lies. Remember Lovelace?

' "I could not love thee, dear, so much,
Lov'd I not honour more." '

'That's a better poem than the last I heard,' I said. 'No, you must not lie to your old friends.'

'I will be back in good time for your birthday.'

Aunt Sophia was very pleased to hear this.

The party dispersed; people went home or to other parties. Aunt Sophia said that she and I were outstaying our welcome. Miss Frith said that if we stayed for thirty years, we would not outstay our welcome. Flora said so, too. I thought she truly wanted me to stay. The Earl said the same, in private, to Aunt Sophia, which left her in a flutter of awestruck gratitude. I did not understand why they were determined to make themselves miserable. Left to myself, I would have gone home to Millstounburn, not because I preferred it, but because, in staying, I felt as Jack had said he felt – I felt a beast. But Aunt Sophia was happier than she had ever been, and it was happiness she deserved.

The Earl and the Barone went together to Edinburgh, very friendly and full in one another's confidence. They came back after four days, and the Barone found me on the terrace.

'The news is bad,' he said. 'Still bad. Worse than before. You shall be Contessa if you want, but you shall not have Glenalban.'

A few minutes later the Earl astonished me by proposing a stroll down through the park to the river-bank. He was not a man who strolled. He was always busy. When he walked, he strode briskly, and it was always in order to do something which had to be done.

There was a great constraint in his manner. He seemed to have difficulty with his voice, although, at first, we were simply chatting about the people who had been staying, and about his journey from Edinburgh.

He stopped. He seemed to force himself, as once before, to look me in the face.

He said, 'I think Vigliano has told you. I am fulfilling my legal obligation to you by making you free of this castle and estate, by entertaining you and yours, and by giving you what you require. Your own lawyers have confirmed the opinion of my lawyers as to the effect on your claim of the great period of time during which we have occupied this place, of the impossibility of distinguishing what King James II notionally owned and what we have added since, and of the fact that you demonstrably do not need a castle for political or military exigencies.'

'I think that is as it should be,' I said.

'I believe I can be forgiven for thinking so too. For obvious reasons, and for a much stronger reason which is not obvious. While there remained a possibility of your becoming one of the richest women in Scotland . . . While there was that possibility . . .'

He seemed to dry up. His words stuck. I had never before seen this formidable and splendid nobleman at a loss.

He blurted out, 'Now that I may speak, I can't.'

I stared at him, completely puzzled.

He was scarlet. I had never seen him blush. He made weak, flapping gestures with his hands, like the Chaplain when he was trying to persuade me to repent.

He said, 'You understand, don't you? You surely understand?'

'No,' I said, distressed to see anybody so distressed.

'If you were suddenly rich, and I suddenly poor . . . How could I speak to you?'

'Well,' I said stupidly, 'just by opening your mouth, you know.'

166

He dragged his eyes from the ground, and stared at me.

'How could I declare myself? Declare my heart? Make love to you?'

'Is that what you wanted to do?' I asked, having difficulty now with my own voice.

'It is what I have wanted to do ever since I first saw you.'

'Oh,' I said. 'That was not the impression you gave, when we first met . . . But of course you thought I was a criminal then. How awkward for you, to fall in love with a criminal.'

'No more awkward,' he said, 'than falling in love with a millionairess.'

'I am beginning to understand. That is as absurd as . . . the sleeves of that dress you laughed at.'

'What would the world say,' he burst out, 'if I, newly poor, went trailing after a great heiress? What would my friends say? What would you say? What would I say, myself, to myself? You would never know – never be entirely sure – that I was not another Simon Donaldson. And, worse still, I would never be entirely sure. I love this place . . .'

'So do I.'

'So I thought. How could I dishonour myself, prostitute myself, by marrying for it?'

'It might not strike me like that.'

'The suspicion would never be entirely absent from your mind. Thank God, it no longer arises. You love Glenalban. It is yours, Leonora.'

'Is that what you are offering me, Sir? Glenalban?'

'Glenalban comes with my offer. I am offering you my heart. The lawyers have at last made it possible for me to say so. I have been suffering the agonies of the damned, hiding my feelings so that you would never guess –'

'You did not quite hide your feelings. I knew them. At least, I thought I did. I saw your face –'

'When I had been watching you with Avington? I wondered if you had. I wonder if you can imagine what I went through, watching what I wanted most on earth being publicly and cheerfully taken from me, and powerless to make so much as a gesture – morally forbidden to do anything at all, until the lawyers made up their minds.'

'Oh,' I said. 'I thought I repelled you.'

'*What?*'

'By being so ignorant and silly and young.'

'Time will put the last right. If the first needs putting right, which I do not think, where lies the problem? The castle is full of books, and the world of places you can see.'

'Well, I did think that myself.'

'And silly? You are the least silly person I have ever known.'

'Even to my choice of sleeves?'

He managed an uneasy smile.

'What gives me agony now,' he said, 'is the thought that I have had to leave it too late. May I ask you . . . I have no right to, but I must . . . may I ask you, how stands your heart with Avington?'

'I don't know,' I said.

'Is that true? Forgive me. The question is unasked. Of course, if you say it, it is true . . . There is then hope for me?'

I thought of the gigantic prizes he was offering me. I thought of his handsomeness, popularity, kindness, sense of duty. I thought of what he had said about himself – about the impossibility of even the appearance of marrying for money.

I looked at him sadly – tall, handsome in a style I had once not liked, usually so immaculate but now, because of the expression on his face, somehow crumpled and woebegone.

'No,' I said.

In spite of what I had been thinking, hearing this word in my own voice startled me so much that I bit my tongue. Was I demented?

'No,' I said again. 'Because of what the world would say, and your friends, and your family, and you, and myself to myself. If I were rich, and you either poor or rich – or if you were as poor as I – then . . . Then I do not know what. I find that the rules you make for yourself apply to me. Everybody knows that I started by trying to take Glenalban. Everybody will know that I failed. Everybody would think, that having failed in one way I took another. Probably they would think that you asked me out of pity, because my disappointment was so bitter. I would never be sure that it was not so, myself. You would never be sure. Everybody knows that Jack Avington has been – courting me. Everybody predicts the result. How will they think, when suddenly I drop him, and grab the chance of a still richer and grander suitor? How would you not suspect that I was mercenary? How would I not suspect it?'

'But this is – as absurd as the sleeves of that wonderful dress!'

'Why is it absurd in me and not in you?'

'I am a man, dearest Leonora!'

'Is a woman no greedier than a man?'

'When a poor man marries a rich woman, there is always a suspicion, usually just, about his motive. When a poor girl marries a rich man, she is suspected of nothing worse than good fortune.'

'If she has just been trying to dispossess that man? The world will know very well what to think.'

'Do you care what the world thinks?'

'I care what I think, and what you think.'

'I utterly absolve you from greed. You yourself suggested to me that you drop your case.'

'Why did you insist on going on with it, Sir?'

'My name is Duncan.'

'To me you must still be "Sir", I think. Why?'

'Because there had to be a resolution, one way or the other. For my sake and for yours. For the sake of tenants and servants, men of business, neighbours. For the sake of the future. We had to know where we stood, now and in perpetuity. If we had let matters drop, then the next generation or the next could have recommenced the whole unsettling and expensive process, with unpredictable results. Nobody's tenure of anything would have been secure. And, supremely, I had to know which one of us two was rich. So that I could lay my heart and my castle at your feet.'

'I could never take your heart, Sir, in case I was confusing it with your castle.'

'I could abdicate here – abdicate all wealth and position. If I got you by doing so, it would be cheap at the price.'

These were the most amazing words that had ever been said to me. I was speechless. But, when I found my tongue, it was to say, 'That is magnificent. But you would never cease blaming me for your loss of everything.'

'I would never cease thanking you for honouring me. Do you think that, if I could make a straight choice between you

169

and Glenalban, stones and mortar would weight heavier than flesh and blood and spirit?'

'*If* you could? Could you not?'

'Of course not. Do you know how many people depend on me? I am bound to offer myself as I am, warts and wealth and all.'

'Do you suffer from warts, Sir?' I asked, startled that such a topic should enter such a conversation. 'You need a gravestone and a hair from a horse's tail and a night of full moon, or so my old nurse told me . . .'

He smiled briefly – the sun on the dark sea. 'It was a remark of Oliver Cromwell's, when his portrait was about to be painted . . . My talk of abdicating my responsibilities is completely empty, the merest oratorical flatulence. What I am asking you to do, Leonora, is not to share the life of the raggle-taggle gipsies, but to share my responsibilities. We work, people like myself. At least, we should. Only so do we justify our inheritances, the monstrous inequity of our good luck at birth . . . Great Heavens, I did not mean to give you a lecture on political economy, or the morality of inherited wealth. But what I do *not* offer you is a life of pampered indolence.'

'That is what I have been living, though, since I came here . . . Sir –'

'Duncan.'

'Sir, I owe it to you to be completely honest, if I can.'

'You can. Only if you tried to be less than honest would you fail. But I dread what follows such an opening.'

'You need not, because it is what I have already said. I am young and ignorant, even if I am not silly, and so I do not know what I truly feel about Jack Avington. But I do know that I could not live with myself, if I had to suspect myself of having married for a castle and a fortune.'

He opened his mouth to say something – even to shout something – but I went on before he had a chance.

'It is no more absurd in me than it would have been, than it was for those weeks, in you,' I said. 'I did think it was absurd in you, until the positions were suddenly reversed. Men have no monopoly of honour or pride. Oh, how pompous that sounded. We are lecturing one another, you on political economy, and I on whatever I am talking about, only I have lost the thread . . .'

170

'Answer me one last question, Leonora. Could you love me if I were poor?'

'I don't know. I have thought myself in love. I think I am too young for all this. And I do not think a magic wand is waved on one's eighteenth birthday. I think your question does not exist. You are what you are, and part of what you are is being lord of –' I waved at castle, park, river, farms and hills – 'all this.'

He heaved a great sigh.

He said, 'You are letting a moral scruple stand in the way of my happiness and, perhaps, your own.'

'You have been doing so for weeks.'

'You *must* admit, in spite of what you said, that there is a difference between men and women.'

'Oh yes. I could not grow a beard like the Barone's . . . We have only walked a hundred yards. They can all see us, if they are looking this way. What would they be thinking?'

'My sister and my aunt will be hoping for a different outcome to our talk.'

'They know?'

'They have known all along.'

'Oh! That explains some things I found odd. Odd looks. The way they did not seem to take any notice, when everybody was talking as though I was bound to accept Jack's proposal. Miss Frith examining Aunt Sophia about me. Was that on your behalf?'

'Yes, of course, though it was not at my request . . . I do not think, at this moment, I can bear to continue this walk.'

I could not, either. I did not know why I found that I was weeping.

'I can understand you refusing my brother because you did not like him,' said Flora. 'But just because he is so rich . . .?'

'Ever since all this began,' I said, trying as I spoke to understand myself, 'I have been simply – greedy and ambitious. What was it all for, if not for honour and position and wealth? At your expense – all at your expense. That was how it started, and that is how it has gone on. And now I am sickened at myself that I wanted those things so badly. It seems to me that you were all right about me, when I first came here.'

171

'No, Leo, no!'

'Your brother told me that he could never have – made love to me – if he was poor and I was rich, because he could never have been sure, in his own heart, whether it was me or his money that he wanted. It is exactly the same for me.'

Afterwards I thought: either I am in love with Jack Avington, or I have lost my reason.

Now it was, beyond question, time I went away from Glenalban.

Miss Louisa Frith said that she would lock me in the wardrobe again, rather than let me go before my birthday, which was two weeks off.

The Earl said that Avington had had weeks upon weeks; and it was only fair that he should have those two weeks, to get me to change my mind.

Aunt Sophia had heard in private from Flora what celebrations had been planned. She was appalled at the thought of our leaving, after what had already been done and spent, for me, secretly behind my back.

So I was overruled, and still I felt a beast.

I was preoccupied with my own concerns – with my feelings and conscience, and in regard to Flora a guilt I could not shake off, and in regard to my moral scruples a suspicion that I had gone crazy – so that I was not at once aware of what everybody else had noticed immediately. It was as obvious, as public, and as popular, as Avington's pursuit of myself.

It was something Mary MacAndrew said, indefatigably carrying the Servants' Hall gossip to my bedroom, that first made me lift my eyes from my toes. I saw what she meant. There was a change in Miss Louisa Frith. Though she kept her awesome elegance, she had lost her severity. She took to relaxing and to laughing. She smiled at the sky and at the trees and at whatever person was by.

Everybody understood the reason except, at first, myself. And then I understood, with a shock of delighted astonishment.

There was a maze of clipped yew-trees below the south terrace, part of a formal Italian garden laid out in the eighteenth century. Once you were well into the maze, you were lost to the world – invisible, almost inaudible because of the denseness of the ancient trees and the mossy paths underfoot. I was once half a morning trying to find my way out.

One day, about noon, I was going with Flora to the herbgarden. We were to pick some aromatic plants, which would be dried, and sewn up in muslin bags, to scent our wardrobes. We passed one of the green, growing arches which led into the maze. From it as we passed emerged Miss Louisa Frith. Her smile was as broad as the archway, and her eyes were dancing. Her hat was a little askew, and her hair a little disordered – amazing and unprecedented sights. She looked a little guilty and self-conscious, and sublimely happy. It was impossible not to smile, at the sight of such happiness.

The Barone Lodovico followed her out of the maze. He was bubbling, chuckling, beaming.

Flora giggled.

I saw that there was a pink flush on one side of Miss Frith's face, on her right cheek. I was puzzled for a moment. People did not blush on one side only; at least, I thought embarrassment sent a blush equally over both cheeks; it always did over mine. And then I glanced at the Barone's beard, and understood what Flora had seen at once, and which made her giggle.

The Barone's noble beard, of which he was so proud, had rubbed against Miss Frith's cheek, and raised that pink flush. He had been kissing her, in the maze. All her new exuberant happiness was explained.

I wondered what the Earl would make of it.

The Earl was delighted. He was so happy to see his aunt happy. He had an immensely high regard for the Barone, like everybody else at Glenalban. He was not only disarmed by the Italian's ebullience and manifest goodwill; he was also – after several long and private conversations – reassured by the antiquity of the Barone's family and title, and the extent of his Piedmontese estates. He had not one castle only, but three, acquired by the judicious marriages of his ancestors. One of the three was high in the Alps; at another he made, he said, most excellent red wine. He had also a town house in Turin, and a villa made out of an ancient tower on the coast near Mentone.

173

'You have a fourth castle now, Lodovico,' said the Earl. 'You have Glenalban, for as often and for as long as you want it.'

Miss Frith kissed her nephew, a thing I daresay she was in the way of doing, but which I had never seen her do before.

Flora told me that, some time before, her brother had made private enquiries about the Barone. He did so by letter to a British consul in Italy whom he knew. It was not that he mistrusted the Barone, but all that anybody knew about him came from his own words, and was unsupported by any document or by any other person's report. And the Earl had reason to see fortune-hunters behind every bush, after his experience with Simon Donaldson, and with myself.

The report came back from Turin. There was indeed a most authentic Barone Lodovico di Vigliano, a man of scholarly interests, noble beard, extensive estates, and ancient family. He was at present away, believed travelling abroad, as he often did.

There was no bar to the immediate announcement of the betrothal. The celebration would coincide with my imminent eighteenth birthday.

'There is a new fashion here, Leo,' said the Earl, who had taken to abbreviating my name as his sister did. 'You must have observed it. The fashion is for people to fall in love. It is all the rage this summer. My aunt and Lodovico and I and Jack Avington have all done it. You are so desperately fashionable in your dress – I cannot think how you can bear not to join this other fashion too.'

'Sir –'

'Duncan.'

'Duncan,' I said, suddenly finding that this was right. 'I have been wearing fashionable clothes, which make you laugh, because of your aunt's kindness. But I am not the *slave* of fashion.'

What he said was a kind of serious joke, like some of Jack Avington's remarks. It was not entirely ridiculous. The Barone and Miss Frith gave a daily example of happiness which it would have been delightful to follow.

I saw temptation, smiling ever so sweetly. If I could but

imagine myself in love with Duncan Glenalban, then I was on a shining highway to a glorious future – a magnificent man, in every regard, my husband – an angel my sister – a palace my home. Since I was marrying for love, I was forging the happiness of my beloved, and money and greatness were irrelevant.

And why should I not be in love with a man whom everyone admired and trusted, and whom I had come to like so very much? Why should I not be in love with a man whose smile was like a shaft of sunlight on the sea? Was not my reluctance to say 'Yes' to the entirely delightful Avington, to be explained by the fact that all along, unrealized by myself, I was really in love with Duncan?

Oh, it would have been very easy to slide down that treacherous path; and I thought, if I did it, I would be more contemptibly prostituted than the lowest drab in the Gorbals.

That night, at dinner, the Barone was looking comically downcast. He was visibly, if tacitly, begging to be asked the cause of his unhappiness; and it was most obvious that this would be another of his hilarious explanations.

I thought that if Miss Frith continued to laugh so heartily at his ridiculous stories – and I saw no reason why she should not, because they were all ludicrous and always new, drawn from an inexhaustible fund of invention which he pretended was memory – then her married life would be enjoyable indeed.

Usually somebody rose to his bait, and give him the excuse for his matchless foolery. But that evening we joined in a conspiracy, to tease the poor clown; nobody asked him the question he was waiting for; nobody appeared to notice his histrionic misery.

His betrothed at last took pity on him.

'You are all wondering,' she said, 'why Lodovico is wearing the tragic mask, although you are pretending not to be wondering. I will tell you the reason, because it will take much less time than if he tells it. I have issued an ultimatum. It is me or his beard. He cannot have both. I do not know which way he has decided. It is a close run thing, I think. Either he is moping because he is going to shave off his beard, and so keep me, or lose me, and so keep his beard.'

175

Flora caught my eye. She touched her right cheek, and giggled. I understood and burst out laughing – Miss Frith did not want a marriage devoid of kisses, but she did not want to lose the skin of her face, by having it rasped away by that great beard.

The Barone groaned, like a victim of the Spanish Inquisition, buried his face in his hands, and caused his shoulders to heave with pretended sobs.

'He has been my companion through all my life,' he said, through his hands, and through his sobs. 'I grow him as soon as I am able, to the despair of *mia povere madre*. And now *questa tiranna*, this lady tyrant . . . *Non posso piu*, no more, I cannot speak for my tears. The day he is cutted off, *caro* Duncan, your river will rise for two metres, because of the tears I will drop out of my eyes – there will be the dangerous floods, many peoples drowned, trees and houses and cattles washed down to the sea – all the faults of *questa crudele*, that lady without heart or pity . . .'

Miss Frith caught my eye and Flora's. She stroked her own cheek, and giggled, which I would not have believed if I had not seen it.

Imagining the Barone Lodovico without his beard was like imagining Duncan Glenalban without his castle, Aunt Sophia without her fluttering and moaning, me without the bright hair and brown eyes of Prince Charles Edward. It was part of him, like button-boots and broken English.

But I saw Miss Frith's point. Her cheek had looked quite sore, the day she came happily and guiltily out of the maze.

The Barone had another few days in Edinburgh, on business of his own. I supposed it was to do with the transfer of money, in view of his approaching marriage.

He came back with news that appalled Aunt Sophia and myself. He had looked in to see Mr David Maitland, our old friend, shopkeeper and antiquary, whom he had got to know in the spring. He had found a police officer on the door, and saw others, through the window, in the shop. Mr Maitland had been killed – murdered, in the middle of the night. His one living-in servant, an elderly man who had been with him for many years, had been struck down with a heavy club, in

176

the near darkness at the foot of the stairs which led from the shop up into the living quarters above. He had barely seen his assailant; he could only describe him as big. Mr Maitland was found lying in the doorway from the stairs into the back of the shop. He had been stabbed. He could have had no chance to resist or escape.

The Police had compared an inventory of the stock, which the servant believed was complete and up to date, with what was actually there. A few small but valuable objects were missing – snuffboxes, miniatures and the like. It was obvious that Mr Maitland had surprised the burglar. But why should the robber have killed him? Why not simply have clubbed him down, like the servant? He was an elderly man, not tall. He represented no threat to a big man armed with a cudgel.

The answer might be, as an Inspector of Police told the Barone, that Mr Maitland knew the intruder. Although it was late, and the shop's shutters up, there was light from the street coming in through the fanlight over the door: enough, perhaps, to recognize a man by.

An oddity was, that the shop door had not been forced, but unlocked with a key. Who could have a key to Mr Maitland's door, other than his servant and himself?

The answer might be, someone who had worked in the shop, and who had taken a key with him when he left. If so, either Mr Maitland had not noticed the disappearance of a key, and so not had the lock changed; or he felt safe in assuming that he would never see that erstwhile employee again.

What employee had there been, who was big, and audacious, and capable of shocking violence?

Edgar Smith, alias Doctor Nicol and who knew what else; a one-time employee who might have stolen a key, or borrowed one and had it copied; who was recognizable even in a bad light by his birdshaped birthmark; who had stolen just such small, valuable objects from that shop before; who was likely to hold a grudge against Mr Maitland for informing against him, and testifying against him at his trial, as the Barone was told he had done.

But was not Edgar Smith in prison? He was not. He had escaped, while being taken from one prison to another.

This was guesswork, but it seemed extremely likely. I

remembered the shocking blow with which he had felled the policeman, when he ran away from Millstounburn. It was easy to imagine that man clubbing down an old servant, and stabbing his master to death in revenge, in fear, in greed.

Edgar Smith was at large. No doubt he would commit some other crimes, and violent crimes. Perhaps he would not go to the gallows for the murder of Mr Maitland, but it was easy to imagine that one day he would feel the noose about his neck. It was not easy to imagine that anything would bring him anywhere near Glenalban.

We mourned David Maitland, a man of gentleness, scholarship, and the greatest kindness. We remembered how he had sold things for us, to keep Millstounburn afloat, and taken no commission on the sales.

Now he would never examine the papers in our attics. Aunt Sophia and I prayed for his soul.

The Barone had other news, for my ears only.

Though he was no longer employing the lawyers who had been preparing my case, he was still in their confidence – or thought he was.

They confirmed to him that my cake was dough, but not quite for the reasons Duncan Glenalban had given me. It was not only because the Grieves had held Glenalban for so long; not only because it was impossible to draw clear lines between what had been James II's and what was their own; not only because I did not need a castle to defend anything. These points weighed, but they were not conclusive. Much more simply, and much more seriously, some vital papers were missing.

'Simon Donaldson and I gave those papers to those people,' said the Barone. 'I am sure of it. Those, with the others. All the papers that we had, we gave them.'

'Do lawyers lose papers?' I asked.

I was not as concerned as the Barone, because I had for some time realized that I did not want Glenalban, and could not have shouldered the weight of such a responsibility; and Duncan Glenalban did, with the utmost competence and humanity.

I thought it strange that I was quite reconciled to not being a millionairess; and my friend, who stood to gain not a penny, was not reconciled at all.

'I think laywers do not lose papers,' said the Barone unhappily. 'But I think one clerk, maybe with little *soldi* and a large family – I think one poor man can be *corrotto* – corrupted.'
'Bribed.'
'Yes. Bribed.'
'But who would . . .?'
'That is why I am unhappy,' he said. 'Who?'

Who stood to gain from my case being lost? Well, who? The answer was supremely obvious, and totally impossible.

But I had thought Simon Donaldson a man of honour.

Suddenly, perversely, I found I was ready to change my whole mind about the whole affair.

I did not like being cheated.

I could not for a second accept that the obvious cheat was the real one. But I *had* been very certain that Simon Donaldson was a man of honour . . .

It was as though my thinking of Simon Donaldson was prophetic. He was seen, some three miles from the castle.

Two stalkers were out, with spyglasses and rifles, looking for a stag which had been wounded. They saw instead a man, by a little ruined croft. I thought, from the description, that it was the one where Jack had taken me, for my secret meeting with Flora. They were a long way away from him. Only with their powerful stalking telescopes could they have recognized him.

Of course they knew him. He had spent many months at Glenalban, and he was given to outdoor exercise and sport. And his height and yellow hair made him distinctive. They were in no doubt.

And of course, after so long, he knew that ruined croft, as a place which nobody went near, as a safe place to hide.

The stalkers made their best speed to the croft. But, from where they were, they had to go far down to cross a burn, and climb again; and by the time they reached the croft there was no sign of their quarry. He had seen them coming down the bare hillside to the burn, and disappeared over the skyline. Only a buzzard could have found him then.

Why was he here? We all asked ourselves, and one another. Not to steal more documents from the muniment room. It was

179

certain he would not dare come near the castle, let alone enter it. Not to repeat his so-very-nearly successful attempts on Flora and myself, with or without the poem about silvery feet.

To meet someone? Who? Had he an ally in our midst? Was he trying to make an ally, with money he had stolen from somebody? Why here, where he was known and hated?

All the folk on the estate were warned to keep an eye out for him; and the few who did not know him were given an exact description. It seemed impossible that, if he stayed anywhere nearby, he could escape the eye of a shepherd or a stalker, or the nose of a sheepdog.

I did not like the feeling of him near. It reminded me of my childish gullibility. Of which I might have been the victim, all over again, with a different liar who had the same motives.

Two days later he was found. He was in the river. He was dead.

His body was found where a fast and deep burn joined the main water, lodged against the pier of a little stone bridge. It seemed that he had been washed down the burn, but no one could guess how far. He had been in the water some time before he was found, but no one could tell how long. They said he had had a knock on the head.

It could have happened in many ways. He could have fallen, knocked his head on a rock, tumbled into the water, and then drowned because he was unconscious. He could have fallen into the water, perhaps trying to cross that dangerous burn, and then knocked himself out on a rock, and so drowned. These accounts of his death were possible, but they did not seem to us likely. He was lithe and active, and he knew how to cross burns.

I thought he had been hit on the head, and pushed into the burn to drown. Probably he had been held under, until he did drown.

Until his body was found, nobody had seen him, since the stalkers with their spyglasses glimpsed him by the croft. He had lain hid, and come out, probably by night, probably to meet somebody. That person, or another, had struck him down and drowned him. That person might be in Glenalban, of Glenalban, part of the household or the estate; or a person

180

from somewhere quite different; the murderer might have followed Simon, and come to Glenalban only because Simon was there. The brother or father, perhaps, of a girl he had seduced. It was possible.

But the possibilities were infinite. The probability, I thought, remained the same. Simon had come to have a secret meeting with a person in or about Glenalban. And that person, his ally, had turned his coat and killed him. Perhaps because Simon had betrayed him, or was about to do so. From all I knew of Simon, there might be many motives for murdering him.

And everyone on the estate was most strictly asked again, by the Procurator Fiscal and the County Police; and no one admitted having seen him.

I felt strange, that two people I had known should be murdered within a few days of one another. And they had known one another. It was in Mr Maitland's shop that Simon Donaldson had seen Charles Edward's sword, which had sent him to Millstounburn and to me.

It seemed impossible that there should *not* be a connection between the murders – two victims who had known one another, killed days apart. Had Edgar Smith a grudge against Simon, too? They had met, I thought, in Mr Maitland's shop. There was that link between them; there might be a far greater link. They were both villains. Had they planned some villainy, and had Simon betrayed Edgar Smith, as he tried to betray everyone he met?

This was wild guesswork, and we were all at it all the time.

Once again the Barone shed a new and horrible light on everything.

Once again he drew me aside. His face was deeply troubled. There was no trace of his usual ebullience.

'Leonora *cara*,' he said, 'I am troubled in conscience. I do not know what to do, to speak or keep silence. I cannot talk with any peoples here except only you. I cannot ask my *promessa sposa*, my own Louisa. Nor *sua buona zia*, the good Signorina Grant. And Duncan least of all. Milor' Avington, perhaps, if he was here, but he is not. A man we know was a *ladrone*, a thief and a traitor, is dead. That is good. It was a bad

181

way to die but it is good that he is dead. Probably he was killed for another treachery.'

'That is what I have been thinking.'

'Anybody who knew him would think so. So somebody has treaded on the head of a *serpente*. We are not sad. Almost we praise and thank the man who did it.'

'Almost . . . I think it depends why he did it, whether we praise him.'

'That is exact. Still I say, *il serpente e morto*. It should not destroy the happiness of many peoples.'

'Why should it do that?'

'I will show you why, *carina*. You know that the day after those men saw Simon, I went out with a *telescopo* and a gun and a man.'

'To stalk. Yes. You met Duncan on the hill. I thought it was odd that you should have been stalking in the same place. You might have shot each other.'

'No. We were not hunting the stags.'

'You were hunting the man. I ought to have thought of that.'

'He said he wanted to catch Simon. I knew he had good reason. I wanted to catch him. You know I had good reason. He started early. I did not know which way. I then decided to go also. By chance it was the same way. My man and I, we lay in a place where we were hidden from the stags and from peoples. And with his *telescopo* he stare to one side, and with mine I stare to the other. Up and down, and this way and that way, to search every inch of the ground we could see. I saw *una cerva*, a hind, in a little hollow like our hollow. But it was not a hind. It was a man. It was a hat of tweed on the head of a man of *capelli gialli*, gold hair.'

'Simon.'

'He came out of the hollow and crawled away, like a man stalking. But he was not stalking. He was crawling to be not seen. But with my big *telescopo* I saw him well. I said to the man that was with me, "*Eccolo!* There he is." But my man was not with me. He had gone to another place. I did not hear him move, because of the loud wind on that hill. And then another man, he come from that same hole in the ground. He looks slowly all round. He does not see me, because I am hidden in my hole, and my *telescopo* only is push through some

182

grasses. He walks towards me. Soon he will see me. I stand up. He looks very hard at me. I shrug my shoulders. I say I have not seen any peoples, any Simon. He says he has not. I do not tell my man that is with me, or the *polizia*, or Louisa. If I tell them, horrible troubles come. Why should I make horrible troubles, to destroy my marriage that is not yet, to destroy my friend, when a very wicked man is dead?'

'Who was talking to Simon, in that hollow?'

'Duncan Glenalban.'

# *10*

I put a hand to my head. It was not that I had not been expecting that answer, but that I had.

The Barone and I discussed the implications, from every side, hour after hour: what had happened, and what he should do. I had never before seen him so serious for so long.

It was, at last, clear to us. Much guesswork was included, but we thought our guesses were good.

Simon Donaldson knew that firm of Edinburgh lawyers very well – the ones who had been preparing to evict Duncan Glenalban and install me in his place. He had been to see them first, about my affairs, long before the Barone had even come to Scotland. If there was a dishonest clerk in their offices, then Simon's trained nose would have sniffed him out. Possibly he discovered some misdeed of the clerk, and so had him in his power if he needed him.

Things progressed, and my case looked strong. It was strong. Duncan Glenalban took over the responsibility of paying the lawyers, with the very convincing explanation that matters had to be brought to a permanent conclusion, for everybody's sake – an explanation which had totally convinced me and, I suppose, everybody else. He had probably not found the dishonest clerk out – the clerk had found him. The clerk had abstracted the vital papers. Duncan either had them now, or had destroyed them.

Simon Donaldson extracted from the clerk, who was in his power, the facts about the theft of the papers, about the bribe the clerk had been given. We wondered what had given Simon the idea that such a thing had happened; we concluded that Simon had put the clerk up to the whole thing – the removal of the papers, and their sale to Duncan. For this put not only the clerk in Simon's power, but Duncan also.

Simon, we thought, wrote to Duncan by the penny post. It was a letter which was not seen by Duncan's secretary or by anybody else. It was blackmail. Duncan was holding his millions, by dint of the stolen papers. He could spare a few thousand for Simon.

Duncan replied, probably to an accommodation address in Edinburgh – a tobacconist or bookseller or solicitor. Duncan said that he agreed to pay, to buy Simon's silence. He told Simon to come to Glenalban. He appointed a meeting place. It was unfortunate that Simon was seen by the stalkers, but not fatal. Duncan knew every inch of his lands, and could arrange to meet Simon quite safely. What he could not do, or said he could not do, was to produce overnight the amount of money in cash that Simon was demanding. That seemed to us a likely reason for their having a second meeting.

They must have thought they had a narrow escape – the Barone, they thought, had very nearly seen Simon. But the Barone was a good actor. He convinced Duncan that he had seen nobody. By this time they had arranged their next meeting, for the following night. Duncan said he would bring the money. Instead he brought a club. They met, and Duncan killed the blackmailer, by hitting him on the head and drowning him.

Where was Duncan believed to be, when Simon was killed? Why, asleep in his bed. He could get out of his own castle in the middle of the night, unobserved. Avington and I had done it.

Why had Duncan sought to make love to me? It was a subtle version of his aunt's strategy, of Lady Lochinver's passionate Jacobite vapourings. She had put me off my guard, and caused me to trust her completely. He had done exactly the same thing. He could not have shut me up again, in wardrobe or asylum – the Barone and Jack Avington knew too much about all that. So he sought to trap me in a different prison, one that was inside my own head.

Would he in truth have married me, if I had accepted him? Yes, perhaps he would. For two reasons, each on its own perhaps enough. I thought he *did* think me beautiful; physically he *was* attracted to me. I thought that there he had spoken the truth. He was in consequence prepared for me to share his life at Glenalban, as his property; he was not

185

prepared for me to own it. That was one reason. The other, we thought, was that as his wife I *was* his property. I could never again make legal claims against him. I was a spent force. He was permanently safe.

We debated, the Barone and I, which of these two reasons would be the stronger to the Earl. We took unexpected sides, perhaps. The Barone thought my beauty would have been the stronger reason; I thought my legal helplessness would have been stronger by far.

I wondered drably how far Miss Louisa Frith – how far even Flora – had been privy to the Earl's stratagem.

And we could not make out what the Barone ought to do. Anything he did would almost certainly be purposeless – cause misery, bring about no justice. The Earl would flatly, and apparently incredulously, deny having met Simon Donaldson. Surely he would be believed, against a comical foreigner. It would go ill for any policeman who thought otherwise. The Barone might not be suspected of malice, but of faulty eyesight, or of seeing what he wanted to see, because he was obsessed by the desire to see it.

I wondered if Miss Frith's surrender to the Barone were not another example of the same stratagem. Even Flora's regard for Avington. Were they all Simon Donaldsons, treacherous manipulators of other people's feelings?

He had said that, if he had been poor and I rich, he could not have spoken to me. He had said that, if he could have forgotten his responsibilities, he would have thrown away Glenalban to have me.

I was sickened not only because he had said these things, but because I had believed them.

And then a thought struck me, which had been amazingly slow in coming. He had connived at my being put in the Lunatic Asylum. He, involved with Hospital Managements and Lord Lieutenancies and such, would have been far better qualified than Lady Lochinver to arrange it all. What had happened, I thought, was that I had run to her; she had sent immediate word to him; he had found the doctors; and all else followed.

186

Lady Lochinver was not far away in England because she was too embarrassed to face me. She was away on his orders, in case she gave his part in it away to me.

I could not leave, without giving the reason. With my birthday imminent, with all the preparations so far advanced, I could not get up and go from Glenalban, taking Aunt Sophia with me, without the reason. I could not give the reason, because the Barone and I had excellent guesses, but no evidence.

He said that he would get the evidence. I did not know where he would find it, with Simon dead and the dishonourable clerk keeping as quiet as a mouse. I thought that, if he found it, his heart would be broken; because he would find that the whole family were of the same kidney.

Meanwhile I was committed to my birthday party, the horrible charade of rejoicing. I dreaded it. The worst was to see Aunt Sophia innocently looking forward to it, excited as a child; and Flora and Miss Frith and the Earl pretending to look forward to it.

The Barone had asked the Earl, some time before, if there were any empty croft or little farmhouse he could use as a retreat. I had not heard about this. There was no reason that I should, although it was no secret. It was not to be a place for assignations with his beloved, because everything between them was public and above-board; it was a place for assignations with his Muse. He was writing an epic poem about the *Risorgimento*. He had been coy about this, except to Miss Frith, for fear of mockery. There was no mockery, when his reason came out. It seemed likely that he would write a marvellous epic, since he was so learned, and felt so strongly and generously. I was not certain I would read quite all of it, as my recent experience of poetry had not been happy.

It would have been possible to find the poet a room in a tower somewhere, quite isolated, in a place as big as Glenalban. But such a thing would not have served in the same way. He would have been conscious of crowds of people near, even if he could not see or hear them. He would have wanted to join them. He would have joined them. He needed to be somewhere where he could not join anybody, where

187

there was no temptation to drop his pen and rush out to make people laugh.

There was no empty but habitable house on the estate when first he asked, but now there was one. It had been rebuilt after a fire, and was now ready. It was to be occupied by a new tenant, but not until the spring. Food and drink could be sent by Miss Frith; probably, I thought, taken by her. He would not be there all the time, but he was desperate to be there some of the time, or his epic would never be written.

He said that, however much glorious poetry was pouring out of him in his solitude, he would be back for the celebration of my birthday. He said this because other people were by. He knew very well how I felt about that celebration.

The Earl of Glenalban proposed to me again; and I refused him.

I found I had forgotten that though his mouth was broad, his lips were thin; that though his eyes were fine and wide-set, they were a cold cruel grey.

I found that his smile was a fraud. It was not sunlight on sea, but gaslight on a stage illusion, such as I had seen with Aunt Sophia at Christmas entertainments in Edinburgh.

'I beg you to reconsider, Leo,' said Flora. 'I beg you to accept Duncan, for your own sake as well as for his.'

Once again, I thought she knew something I did not know.

'You will tell me if this is final, Leonora,' said the Earl. He no longer shortened my name. I did not know why.

'It is final,' I said. I no longer called him 'Duncan'. I knew very well why.

Flora, understanding that my answer was final, was in pitiful distress.

What did she know, that I did not know?

They told me Jack Avington was come back to Glenalban, to my relief and joy and confusion. He seemed to me one rock in a heaving world. The Barone was my only other rock. All the rest were traps, or painted canvas.

188

As once before, I saw him talking to Flora before he talked to me.

But he saw me very soon. He looked to me better than ever – a miracle of health and humour and sanity.

I asked him about his grouse-shooting and his deer-stalking and his friends in Argyll. He waved away my questions, because he had more important things to talk about.

He said, 'I hear that Duncan Glenalban has done a turnabout, a somersault, a spin.'

'I think he has done more than that,' I said.

'The moment my back is turned, he declares himself your suitor. Flora tells me he would have done it long ago, but for not knowing who was rich and who was poor. I thought she must have got it the wrong way round. I thought a fellow would woo a rich girl if he found he was poor, but Flora says not. I suppose he has cut me out.'

'Why do you suppose such a thing?'

'Because he can offer you ten times my modest competence.'

'No. You can offer me what he cannot.'

'Better trout fishing than his. I can't think what else.'

'Well,' I said, embarrassed, 'I mean honesty, and sincerity, and so forth. I like those things.'

'Yes. So do I. So does Glenalban.'

'You know him to be honest?'

'I believe him to be so. Why not?'

'You said you did not know him very well. Not well at all, you said, although you were at school together.'

'Come to think of it, that is quite true. After spending so much of the summer here, I came to think he and I were intimates. I like and respect what I see, but I daresay I don't see very deep. Often it's better not to, I find. You'd lose half your friends if you knew their depths. Better not dig too deep. Awful things crawl out.'

'You have to dig deep, when you are thinking about marrying somebody.'

'Have you dug any distance into me, Leo?'

'Yes. To the bottom. Nothing has crawled out.'

'Will you marry me, my dearest girl?'

I opened my mouth to say 'Yes'. The words that came out were, 'I don't know.'

He sighed. 'Absence has not made the heart grow fonder. The barrel-organ plays the same tune. Well, you are not yet eighteen. And at least I am back, to counter the sinister efforts of Duncan Glenalban.'

'I am glad you are back.'

'That is absolutely the first unreservedly amiable thing you have ever said to me.'

I laughed; but it was a short unhappy laugh.

I wanted to confide in him. I could not do so, without asking the Barone; and the Barone was away in his retreat, composing Alexandrines.

'I wish my conscience allowed me to seize you and kiss you,' said Jack. 'I am staggered at the moral strength which stops me doing so. You're so beautiful I want to scream. I am mad with love for you. I must go and swim in the river, to cool my blood. Speaking of which – I have been out of reach of newspapers – is it true, this rumour I hear, of Simon Donaldson being found in the river?'

'Yes. We think he was killed.'

'The police, Flora says, are quite sure he was killed. I should think he had a thousand potential murderers, including you and Flora and myself. But what in the world brought him here?'

'We think we know,' I said. 'I will tell you, but only if the Barone gives me leave.'

'The epic poet. I suppose he is writing in Italian? I hope so, because I shall not be obliged to read it, because I shall not be able to read it. He has become your uncle, Leo. It's a very good thing. He is more use to you than your aunt, much as I like Miss Grant. What have I become? Your cousin? If you say that I shall go and swim in the river.'

I laughed; but it was another short, unhappy effort.

Jack was a haven, the still centre of the storm, asylum most unlike that in Lochgrannomhead. I felt safe when I was with him and when I thought of him. I felt comforted and confident.

And so I had opened my mouth to say 'Yes', and the words that had come out were 'I don't know'.

I had a new hat in which I much admired myself. It was a

kind of overgrown Highland bonnet, in a bold check of brown which matched my eyes and red which was supposed to intensify their brightness. From it stuck, directly upwards, a bunch of tail feathers of a cock pheasant, a foot and a half long, so that, when I wore the hat, I felt like not one but several members of the Company of Archers in Edinburgh Castle.

Jack Avington said my hat was by a Tam-o'-Shanter out of an opium-eater's dream. The Earl of Glenalban smiled at it, in the days when he smiled in my direction.

When I was happy, putting on that hat made me burst out laughing. When I was sad it cheered me up. That day was eminently a day to be cheered up by an extravagant bonnet, so I wore it for an afternoon walk.

It was a solitary walk. Flora had letters to write; Jack had salmon flies to tie; Miss Frith had a conference with the housekeeper in the linen room; Aunt Sophia had a croft to visit, with an illustrated Bible for the children (she had brought the missionary zeal of East Lothian to the heathen of West Perthshire); the Barone Lodovico his epic to write, in his remote retreat.

It was no longer possible for the Earl and me to walk together. He had in any case gone off alone with a gun to shoot pigeons, wearing his rust-coloured shooting coat, and with a Labrador retriever at his heels.

The sun was bright, but there was a cold east wind – the first cold wind of the autumn. It was a day for brisk walking. Hard exercise was what I needed; I hoped it would take my mind off my doubts and dismals.

But it did not. Try as I might to concentrate on the little scurrying clouds, the thrashing branches, the flocking peewits and the piping titmice, I could not rid my mind of the things that weighed it down.

As I walked down through the trees of the park towards the river, I thought about the enormous merits of Jack Avington, and my inability to say 'Yes' to him, as though some bit of my mind snapped on the word like a mousetrap. He was lovable, but I had to suppose that I did not quite love him, and never had, and I did not understand why. I questioned myself, and got no answer. I thought there was no answer. I did not quite love him, and that was how it was. It was such a pity.

191

My thoughts turned from my own unimportant affairs to larger matters, to conspiracy and murder. I brooded about the theory which the Barone and I had constructed, which answered everything as nothing else could. I examined it again, trying to be perfectly logical, which did not come easy to me.

There were some guesses in our theory, like the dishonest clerk in the lawyers' office. But these guesses were not essential to the theory. Duncan Glenalban, or some creature of his, could have stolen the vital papers in some other way; and Simon Donaldson could have found out about it in some other way. The central facts which we knew to be facts stood firm in the middle of everything. The papers were missing. The Earl had met Simon in secret, and denied doing so. Simon was dead. It was nearly certain that there was a connection between all these, and that the connection was the reason for Simon's death. Any other explanation was terribly far-fetched.

Would the Earl of Glenalban commit murder? Almost anybody would, who had as much at stake as he had. Almost anybody would, to silence a blackmailer. He was a tall, powerful man, a sportsman. He could murder. He was about to be blackmailed, by a deeply treacherous man. He had to murder. He did murder. I did not see how this conclusion could be avoided.

I came down into the belt of trees by the river, out of sight of the castle. The birds and I had the world to ourselves. The ground rose steeply to the east, and suddenly I was out of the wind, and the sun was hot. I realized that my racing thoughts had caused my legs to race. I had not noticed how hot and exhausted I was getting, because I was preoccupied, and because of the keen wind. I sat down, collapsing at the foot of an ancient oak tree, like a half-empty flour sack. My glorious and ridiculous hat felt like a feather pillow on my head, suddenly intolerable. My brow tickled with the woolly stuff. I tugged off my hat, and felt the sun on my temples. I put my hat on a small, dense bush of holly which had seeded itself amongst the roots of the oak – deposited it on top of the bush, which gave it an air of raffish vanity. The bush became a green and prickly young lady – like myself, in both regards – making shameless advances to the oak tree.

I closed my eyes, seeing and feeling the sunlight through the lids. I was glad to have the oak tree for my back, and glad that it was so old that many of its branches had fallen off, and let the sunlight through.

I heard the shrill shriek of a blackbird, as something startled it in the undergrowth of the wood. I wondered idly what had alarmed it. It was supremely unimportant; it was not a fox, at this time of day. Not a hawk, when the blackbird was in the shelter of trees. Not a wild-cat, on this low ground. Perhaps a farmyard cat that had gone wild, or a stray dog. Perhaps a person. But I had seen and heard nobody. I wondered why anybody would be in that piece of wood-land in the middle of the afternoon. Somebody going to the river, somebody the Earl had asked to fish? But it was not on the way from anywhere, the castle or the main road or the village. Someone shooting? But the grouse lived in heather on the bare hillside, not in trees; and the partridge shooting was still a week away, and the pheasant shooting two months.

A gamekeeper? But this little bit of woodland was not preserved. The nearest pheasant coverts were a mile away.

All that could bring anybody here was the chance of a wood-pigeon. Destructive vermin in the cornfields, and deli-cious eating in a pie or on a piece of toast . . .

The Earl was out after pigeons. This wood was a place he might try. He would enter it as stealthily as possible, hide himself, and keep perfectly still; for wood-pigeons are shy and clever birds, who seem perfectly aware of the difference between a walking stick and a shotgun. Perhaps he had just come into the wood, and startled the blackbird. That would annoy him, because it would alert the pigeons in the tree-tops.

I did not want to share the wood with the Earl of Glenalban. If I got up and left it, I would scare the pigeons, and spoil his sport. Did I care if I spoiled his sport? I did not care to be mean-minded, petty, vindictive; he might be all that I thought him, but I could not be childishly spiteful to a man who had asked me to marry him, the very day before. It was best if I sat quite still. It was best if he shot or did not shoot, but in either event went away out of the wood without seeing me.

There was a shot, much nearer than I had expected – the great boom of a sporting shotgun. And another, immediately. Both barrels of his gun. Shot tore through the leaves beside me. I heard the patter of pellets on twigs and leaves. I shrank back, startled. I had been nearly in the line of fire, though safe behind my oak tree. He had seen a rabbit. A rabbit, five feet above the ground?

I saw that my hat had exploded. It was shredded, by two charges of shot. Its tattered remnants had been knocked by the second barrel off the holly bush.

Whoever fired thought the hat was on someone's head. My head. No one else had such a hat. Whoever fired thought he had blown my head open, when he saw the hat disappear.

Would he reload at once? Would he come and inspect his handiwork? I could not run and hide, without making a noise he could not fail to hear. There were dead twigs and dead leaves everywhere. If he heard them rustle, he would know I was not dead. The undergrowth was not thick. He had a trained dog with him.

I was very frightened. I made a plan. If I heard his footsteps crunch over the wood's floor towards me, I would jump to my feet and run. I would run in a zig-zag through the trees, like a snipe over a bog. I would be very difficult to hit, and soon I would be out of range of a shot-gun. He could run after me. No doubt he could run faster than I, because his legs were longer. But if I ran directly towards the castle, he could not follow me far, shooting as he went.

I heard a crunch, of feet on twigs and leaves. I tensed myself, to jump to my feet and run, if they seemed to be coming towards me. They were going away. He was content. He was sure he had done his business.

I suppose his idea was to dispose of the body later, or get someone to do it for him. Or let me be discovered, and supposed the victim of an armed poacher whom I had surprised setting a deer-trap in the wood. It was likely enough. Every year, somewhere in Scotland, a keeper was killed by a poacher.

I peeped round the trunk of the oak, through the leaves of a clump of hazel.

I saw, disappearing through the wood, exactly what I expected to see. A rust-coloured shooting coat.

194

I crept out of the wood. I ran all the way back to the castle, my chin on my shoulder. I saw no sign of the rust-coloured coat. Of course, he would make sure it was seen a very long way away, as soon as possible.

I ran across the courtyard and into the great hall. I was hatless, my hair wild, my face crimson. My breath came in deep, shuddering gasps. I passed an astonished footman. I passed Flora, coming out of a morning room. She gave me a shriek, and put out a hand to me. I brushed passed, wordless. I ran to the smoking room, where Jack had been tying his salmon-flies. I burst in. He was there. I thanked God. He gave me a look of utter astonishment, and jumped to his feet. I collapsed into a leather chair. I struggled to get breath enough to speak.

He said, 'Whatever has happened, Leo, you are safe here with me.'

As soon as I could I said, 'Yes. I feel safe. Duncan Glenalban has just tried to kill me. He thinks he succeeded.'

Jack sat down suddenly, as though he had been hit on the head as hard as Simon Donaldson was. I thought he believed me immediately, not because what I said was probable, but because I said it.

I told him exactly what had happened.

He said slowly, 'It was an accident. It must have been. Obviously he was not shooting at a pigeon. They never go near the ground in a wood. Or a rabbit or any other ground-game. A squirrel. Possibly a rat or a weasel, but I should guess a squirrel.'

'How could he have thought my hat was a squirrel?'

'It was half obscured by leaves – in the shade of the trees . . .'

'It was perched right on the top of a holly, in full sunlight. Do squirrels have pheasant-feathers sticking out of their backs?'

'It was *that* hat? In full view, in full sun? But he could not have supposed anybody was wearing it.'

'Yes. Because of where I had put it, it would have looked from where he was exactly as though someone was wearing it.'

'In any case, who but a raving madman would wantonly destroy a hat with both barrels of a shotgun . . . I find it

195

difficult to get to grips with this, Leo. Duncan Glenalban is in love with you.'

'He is more in love with Glenalban. He said to me once that he was not, but today shows otherwise, I think. Oh. I have just realized something, and I wish I had not.'

'Tell me.'

'I think I had better tell you everything. What I have just realized is about Flora.'

'You *cannot* suppose Flora knew about such a shocking thing?'

'She came to me yesterday. It was after I had refused Glenalban. After I had said it was final. She said I must reconsider. I must marry him. It was for my own good. She was trying to warn me. She was telling me that if my refusal was really final, then I was signing my death warrant. I am sure she didn't want me killed. But she couldn't come out and say that is what would happen, if my refusal was final.'

'If she didn't want you killed, that is exactly what she should have done.'

'No, Jack. Think. She wanted me alive because she likes me. She wanted me to marry her brother, so I would stay alive. But she would hardly say, "Marry him or he will murder you". I mean, it is not endearing, in a prospective husband.'

'I see your point . . .'

'And she gave me another of those odd looks.'

'I can see how she might do that. Assuming that you're right about what happened, was it a *crime passionnel?* Was it that if he was not to have you, no one was?'

'No. It was this.' I waved round the big, dark, comfortable room.

'But he has this safe. Your case is lost.'

'I wonder. We have the fact that my case is lost only from Duncan Glenalban himself, and from lawyers he is paying.'

'If your case is *not* lost, and you will *not* marry him, he does have a motive. My God, he does have a motive. Little as I can bear to think it of a friend. Anyway, he will hardly try again in front of me.'

'I am quite safe now. I am as safe as I feel.'

'But, Leo, I cannot be at your side all day and night.'

196

'Not all night, no . . .'

'I think I should take you to the Barone, now at once.'

'I think that is a really good idea.'

'We'll creep out, as we did once before. Nobody will know where we're going. When I come back, nobody will know where I've been. You won't want to hide in the croft for ever, but it will serve for a day or two, perhaps. And we can make a plan. The important, immediate thing is to get you to safety. If Glenalban tried once he will try again. I still can't quite believe any of this –'

'You would if you saw my hat.'

The Barone was extremely surprised to see us. But he seemed glad, although we were interrupting his epic poem.

His quarters, the little rebuilt farmhouse, were cosy rather than spacious, but perfectly comfortable. The food which Miss Frith brought or sent him was mostly already cooked – I saw half a cold roast turkey on the scrubbed kitchen table – and he was perfectly capable of frying a rasher for his breakfast, and of making coffee. He said he made much better coffee than the servants at Glenalban, because he made it much stronger. A woman came in for an hour each morning, to clean the house. He would not have her more than an hour, he said, because she broke his concentration with her mopping and scrubbing.

The epic was progressing, but slowly. A table in the parlour was covered with sheets of foolscap paper, themselves covered with very bold black writing, full of alterations and crossings-out.

'The civilities having been performed,' said Jack, 'let us get down to business. First your story for the Barone, Leo; and then, I hope, the other things you wanted to tell me.'

The Barone was, of course, as stunned as Jack had been. But, instead of sitting down as though hit, he bounced up, charged out of doors, and plunged about the steading like an angry bull. He roared like a bull, too.

At last he calmed down enough to say to me, 'This proves we were right, *cara*.'

'Right about what?' said Jack.

'All the rest,' I said. 'Simon Donaldson, and the stolen papers, and so forth.'

197

'You've left me behind,' said Jack. 'Do you know why Donaldson came here, and why he was killed?'

'*Credo di si*,' said the Barone.

And so we told him what I was morally sure had happened. And in the telling I became more sure, because I had been thinking about it so much, and the pieces fitted together better.

It took a long time, partly because the Barone from time to time plunged out of the house again, to relieve his feelings by charging and bellowing; partly because Jack interrupted with a lot of questions. They were good questions, and we had good answers to them.

When at last we finished, Jack sat in silence for a long time.

He said, 'It is all horribly convincing, even to Glenalban arranging for your committal to the asylum, Leo. But there is one weak link. One unanswered question. One serious flaw in your theory.'

'No, there isn't,' I said.

'Listen. Documents have disappeared which, if produced, would provide Leo with a strong case in the courts. Their disappearance destroys her case. I accept the probability that Glenalban caused them to disappear. I suppose he either has them or has destroyed them. That being so, *what need to kill Leo?*'

'Well,' I said, 'as I said before, it must be that my case is really much stronger than they say. Or would be, if the lawyers weren't being paid by the Earl. And, if that's so, I might one day get different lawyers and start all over again. I might do that tomorrow. It *must* be so. If not, I'd still have my hat.'

'Then the missing papers are *not* crucial to your case.'

'Perhaps important rather than crucial,' I said. 'If they're not there, Glenalban has a good case, one that's worth fighting. If they are there, he has no case at all. Something like that.'

'If they're not there, Glenalban has a good case,' Jack quoted back to me. 'And they're not there. Why kill you?'

'I should think it's like getting at a horse before a race,' I said slowly. 'I have never been to the races, but I heard all about a dreadful episode at Musselburgh, from our gardener at Millstounburn. The man who owned the favourite had the

198

second favourite poisoned. Just to make extra certain, you know.'

'Improving the odds,' said Jack. 'A prudent course, if disgusting. And Duncan Glenalban is an outstandingly prudent man. Yes, I suppose it comes out like that. I'm not completely satisfied by your logic there. It still seems to me a weak point in your theory. There must *be* vital documents in the business, as well as those which are no more than important. Why not steal them?'

'Because the truly vital ones have all been copied,' I said, 'and the copies countersigned by bishops, or something.'

'Steal the copies too.'

'But they're spread all over the place, in the College of Arms and the University and so forth.'

'You have an answer for everything, Leo, but a trace of puzzlement lingers in my mind.'

'Not in mine. I was shot at by a man in a rust-coloured coat.'

'I can see how that increases conviction. Nothing like the rattle of musketry, to rid the mind of doubts. What do we do now, Barone?'

'You go back to the *castello*, and you very secretly bring back to this place the Signorina Grant.'

'Aunt Sophia?' I said. 'She won't like it here as much as Glenalban. And I don't see why anyone should want to murder her. Or is there a Grant claimant for Glenalban?'

'You must have a chaperone, Leo,' said Jack. 'It was stupid of me not to have thought of that.'

'I am not so *very* old,' said the Barone. '*La mia carissima* Louisa will not be happy if I am alone, all one night of summer, with the most beautiful girl in Scotland. And you, *cara*, would have no *reputazione*. You would be as dead as though Glenalban had shotted you.'

Of course it was true. He was not old, and I was almost eighteen. Being shot at, and so forth, had driven the social rules out of my mind. But Aunt Sophia would make everything respectable. Besides, she was devoted to the Barone. Under all the circumstances, she would be reconciled to the farmhouse for a day or two.

'How will you get her secretly out of the castle?' I asked Jack.

'I shan't try to. We will go publicly. I will be taking her to a croft which she would never find on her own, where the children are in instant need of an illustrated Bible.'

'What will you say when you come back alone?'

'That she is returning later, in another carriage, with a doctor or some such. I shall not have met the doctor, nor heard his name. I shall merely have heard that he is to visit the croft, to examine a child suspected of measles, and that Glenalban lies on his way home. The arrangement will have made itself.'

'Come to think of it,' I said, 'how will you explain leaving with me and coming back without me? Several people saw us go.'

'I took you, at your request, to the main road between Lochgrannomhead and Crianlarich. You were to be met by a friend with a vehicle, who was to take you to one of those places, or perhaps somewhere else. I do not know the identity of the friend, or how you communicated with him, or where he is taking you, because you refused to tell me any of these things. I did not wait for your friend's carriage, but left you by the side of the road. You insisted on this improper arrangement, because, I thought, you did not want me to see who your friend was. I think it is all convincing. I think it will add a nice touch of mystery and confusion, to divert everybody from the truth.'

'That is quite good,' said the Barone, in a tone of grudging approval.

'Won't Glenalban be amazed,' I said, 'when they tell him I was running about the castle after he'd killed me.'

'Perhaps he'll think it was a ghost,' said Jack. 'Like Banquo's, you know, after Macbeth had him killed. Perhaps Glenalban will expect you to shake your gory locks at him at his dinner table, but nobody else will see you, and they'll think he's gone mad . . .'

The Barone, on whom this reference was apparently lost, was becoming impatient. Jack drove away, in the dog-cart he had borrowed. I waved until my arm ached.

It was still early evening. The disc of the sun was only now being nibbled by the hill-tops. It was extraordinary that so much had happened in so short a time. Jack had driven like the wind from the castle to the farmhouse; I hoped he would come more sedately with Aunt Sophia, because she was a nervous passenger.

The Barone said that he had made a plan. It would involve our going immediately to Edinburgh. It would mean my missing my eighteenth birthday celebrations. I did not mind at all. We would have a much better party, in Edinburgh, or at Millstounburn – just me, Aunt Sophia, the Barone, and Jack Avington.

The Barone would have to go back to Glenalban, before setting off for Edinburgh. This was reasonable. The clothes he had at the farm were those of an epic poet and Italian patriot. They were sufficiently bizarre there; in Prince's Street they would have caused a crowd to gather, and the Barone to be arrested for a breach of the peace.

He said that Aunt Sophia and I would be quite safe for a few hours on the following day. He showed me the massive lock on the farmhouse's single outside door, and the padlocks on the heavy shutters. Coming from the peaceful Lowlands, I might have thought these defences absurd on a little farmhouse. But I knew now that things were different in the wild Highlands. There were roving bands of tinkers, brutal, greedy, almost inhuman; some said that they were mongrel gipsies, some that they were the savage descendants of the small, desperate clans proscribed after my great-grandfather's hopeless rebellion of 'forty-five. They preyed on isolated farms, stealing everything, sometimes killing, then melting away into the hills. Especially they were dangerous at this time of year, when the harvest was in, the meat hung, and the brine-barrels full of fish. And Highland farmers had to travel a long way with beasts or produce to market, leaving their wives and children unguarded for days and nights. Those great padlocks and bars of iron were very necessary. It was comforting to see them. Aunt Sophia and I could withstand a siege, if Glenalban chose to besiege us.

As to the Barone's plan, he would not tell me. It would not be complete until we had reached Edinburgh. Obviously it involved lawyers. It involved Jack Avington, on whom we knew we could rely. I thanked God for two such friends.

It was dusk when Jack came back with Aunt Sophia. She

shrieked when she saw me, because Flora had told her of seeing me run like a madwoman through the castle, scarlet and hatless and with a shocked expression on my face. Jack had told her a little, as they came along in the dog-cart; but, as he told me aside, he thought she should be sitting safely in a chair when she listened to the whole, not perched on the seat of a dog-cart.

He had already told his story to Duncan Glenalban, about leaving me beside the road. He said Glenalban had been utterly dumbfounded. Well he might be, that I was alive and well.

Jack had to get back at once, to make his story about Aunt Sophia credible. He pressed my hand as he left. I was never nearer loving him.

The Barone said that, before he went back to Glenalban, he must shave off his beard. It would be a lengthy and agonizing process, as well as heart-breaking. But we knew of his betrothed's ultimatum, and the baring of his face could no longer be delayed. He put a great kettle of water on the kitchen range to heat. He said he would need that and more, and that he would have to sharpen his razors fifty times.

Before he withdrew, to make this terrible sacrifice on the altar of love, he locked the door, and closed and barred and padlocked all the shutters. He said we would have no visitors in the night, but it was foolish not to take such simple precautions. He had no weapon, because he had left his swordstick in the castle.

As soon as his water was hot, he went out into the kitchen to shave. I told Aunt Sophia as much of the story as I thought she could stand. She did not at all want to go to Edinburgh. She was appalled that I would miss my party. But I could not give her the full reasons, without shocking her more than I could bear to.

She still wanted me to marry Jack Avington. We were on safer ground, when I tried to explain to her my feelings for Jack. She was distressed on his behalf and on mine. But she owned, in the end, that one could not commit oneself for a lifetime without perfect certainty.

Every so often, our conversation was punctuated by a howl of agony from the kitchen. He called out that he was not

202

slashing himself, but merely removing layers of skin.

I noticed that he had taken the keys out of the front door and out of all the padlocks on the shutters. I wondered idly why he should have done so.

He came at last, beardless, back into the parlour. His face was not unpleasing. It was perfectly familiar to Aunt Sophia and myself. We had seen it in the spring, at Millstounburn. It had a birthmark, resembling a bird, beside the left ear.

# 11

Edgar Smith said cheerfully, as though I had asked a question, 'Yes. Those padlocks keep people in as well as keeping them out.'

His voice was as I remembered – pleasant, educated, with no trace of any foreign accent.

He said, 'There were just four people who could have exposed me. Mr David Maitland. Poor foolish Simon Donaldson. And your good selves. I would not have had to kill anybody, if my dear Louisa had not insisted on the nudity of my face. But, once I discovered the extent of her private fortune, I was quite resolved to marry her. Besides, I have contrived to convince myself that she pleases me. She will not visit my castles in Italy, because I have none. Fortunately, I no longer need castles in Italy, or even in Spain; I have the unfettered use of a castle in Scotland. It is the culmination of a career in which effort and talent have been only intermittently crowned with the success they deserve. Of my many marriages, only one produced the dividends I expected. Do I bore you? I think not. You know, there is that in the artist – and I am indubitably an artist – which requires recognition and applause. But the nature of my art forbids my allowing anyone to see the fulness of it. Simon Donaldson knew most about me, but he was in the same line of business – indeed, we were once rivals, which was how we became acquainted – and he was never more than grudging in his appreciation of my skill. I cannot expect you to applaud me, but I cannot resist this unrepeatable chance to extract your recognition of my achievements. I can speak to you freely because, as you will already have realized, you will not repeat what I say. Except perhaps in Heaven, which I do not expect to visit.'

I cannot analyse my feelings. I had no feelings. I was numb.

I knew that Aunt Sophia and I were dead. We had to be dead, because we knew that bird-shaped birthmark.

Suddenly I said, surprising myself, 'Have you killed the policemen who came to arrest you at Millstounburn?'

'No, Leonora, if you will allow me to continue to call you so. One saw me only in the distance, and running away. The other I hit while he was rushing at me. I was deliberately contorting my face. There is no possibility of his identifying me, on oath, in a courtroom. It is not so with the four of you. I quite regret the implications of that. I was sorry to kill poor Simon, and sorrier to kill David Maitland. I shall be sorrier still to kill the amiable Miss Grant, and as for you, dear Leonora, I shall be disconsolate. Not inconsolable. Louisa and her bank-books will console me. But I shall be sad. Oh yes. For a poet to destroy a thing of rare beauty – I shall be sad.'

During this chilling rubbish, I was trying to think. The keys of the door and padlocks were in his pocket. They could be got only if he was unconscious. If Aunt Sophia created a diversion (as he and Simon Donaldson had, at the lunatic asylum) I could perhaps jump for some weapon, and hit him on the head . . . Could I, hardly more than five feet tall, and weighing no more than a squirrel, knock unconscious a big, powerful and healthy man?

I could try. Our last state would not be worse than our first, because our first was as bad as it could be.

There was a poker by the fireplace.

Edgar Smith's eye darted very quick from me to Aunt Sophia and back again. He was alert, wound tight as a fiddle-string. Nothing would pass him by. He saw my eye on the poker.

He excused himself, with a show of elaborate courtesy, and put the poker next door in the kitchen. I half rose to my feet, and sat down again. There was nothing in the parlour that made a weapon of any kind.

He had said he was unarmed, as a reason for all those padlocks. I did not now believe him. I was right. From the kitchen he came back into the parlour with both hands full. In one hand was his swordstick, in the other a double-barrelled shotgun.

'Was it you who tried to shoot me?' I said.

'Your beautiful hat. I was so sorry about the hat. I do not think I quite hid my surprise, when you knocked on my door this afternoon.'

It was true. He had not hidden his surprise, but he had hidden the reason.

He put down swordstick and gun where he could reach them and I could not. He stretched behind, to a cupboard, and pulled out a rust-coloured coat.

'It is amusing to reflect,' he said, 'that I acquired this coat on Duncan Glenalban's recommendation. He told me that, for rough shooting in August and September, the colour was ideal. It matched turning leaves and dying bracken. I followed his advice with some reluctance. A coat of this hue did not suit my performance as an eccentric Italian aristocrat. It was altogether sensible, practical, conventional, and I was being none of those things. But, pressed by dear Duncan, I allowed the little tailor in Lochgrannomhead to make me a coat of this stuff. Which enabled me to impersonate him to anybody who saw me, from a distance, by the river. Including yourself. A pretty irony, I think.'

'Quite pretty,' I said.

There were two things uppermost in my mind. I clung to them, in case my courage suddenly went from me, and I blubbered and knelt and pleaded. I did not wish to do that, in front of Edgar Smith, in front of Aunt Sophia.

She seemed calm. She knew exactly what was happening, and why. She had the courage of her steady faith. If I had courage, I thought, it was not quite of that sort. She stretched out a hand towards me, and I took it. Edgar Smith's hand flickered towards his shotgun; but he dropped it.

The two things in my mind were that I would *not* break down in cowardice or despair. And that we must keep the man talking – boasting – revealing himself – as he said he longed to do, and as he would never have such a chance to do again. While he talked, we were alive. When he stopped, we were dead, because if he did not want us as an audience, he did not want us at all.

He would talk vaingloriously, because he was proud of himself. He might relax his alertness, in clouds of self-esteem. From that, something might come. It was a very small chance, but it was our only chance.

Aunt Sophia's fingers, squeezing mine, said that we must be wide awake and brave. Mine, squeezing hers, said that there might be something else to hit him with, besides the poker.

I said, as firmly and as graciously as I could, 'Will you tell us the story of your life, Mr Smith?'

'With pleasure,' he said heartily. 'No one has ever heard it. You are privileged. I would say uniquely privileged, but as there are two of you, I think that would be a kind of solecism. I should start by correcting you. My name is not Smith.'

'We did not suppose it was.'

'What is it, you ask? I have none. So begins my story. My mother was English, governess to the children of a banker in Turin. Her employer, by her own later account, was a man of solid affluence, but without charm or culture. It was scandalous that a creature of her breeding and education should have been the vassal of such people. Unfortunately she had had to leave England somewhat hurriedly, and seek employment very far away. She told me scraps of that story, during my strange childhood, but never the whole story. She had been employed in a similar capacity, but in infinitely better circumstances, in London. The family of a judge. She was caught stealing. She ran away before she could be arrested. The same thing happened subsequently, in Italy. She was not so quick. She was arrested, and went to prison. I was quite sad, because it was embarrassing for me to have a mother in prison. That is one half of my inheritance – a superior and educated voice, a wide and general culture, an admiration for poetry and art, and a disposition to steal.'

'Do you steal papers in important law suits?' I asked, to make sure that he went on, and on, and on. Also, I was interested in the answer.

'Yes, of course. I could not have my Louisa deprived of her fortune – myself deprived of my fortune. But that comes much later in my story. I am telling you of my parentage, so that you will understand how triumphantly I have overcome the disadvantages of my birth. My father was a groom employed also by the banker. I never met him. The union was not blessed by the Church, since my father was already married. I believe he was a fellow of great adroitness, great charm, and his chief diversion was causing young females to fall in love with him. Others prefer manly sports, cards, the theatre, wine. My

207

father liked women. He was very successful, by my mother's somewhat embittered account. Behold the other half of my inheritance. The two together dictated my choice of career which, as you know, has now reached its triumphant culmination.'

'Not quite yet,' I said.

'Aha! Will you try to stab me with my swordstick, as I stabbed David Maitland? Club me with this knob it has, as I clubbed his servant, and Simon Donaldson? Or shoot me with this fowling-piece borrowed from the gunroom at Glenalban, as I shot your delectable hat? I know you have courage and resource and quickness of mind, Leonora. Without those qualities in you, we would never have got out of the lunatic asylum. But abandon any such ideas, child. I am much stronger than both of you together. And I move much quicker than you would think, to look at me. I have had to move quick, many times ... My mother was dismissed by the banker, of course, as soon as her condition became evident. She was naturally deserted and disowned by the groom my father, who thought the destruction of one life was sufficient penance for the sin they had committed. My mother was in some distress, until my birth and for some months after it. Then she fed herself and me by earning silver in the only way open to her. There were times when she found a protector, and we lived in moderate comfort. There were times when she had to put me in the care of some old woman, and take to the streets of Turin. In some ways, perhaps, an undesirable upbringing for a child. In others, richly educational. As a one-time governess, my mother *was* a woman of culture, and her voice was educated. Culture and speech she most assiduously taught me, when the exigencies of her profession allowed. Though my life was in the back streets of Turin, I could pass as an English gentleman. In those back streets I learned Italian also. I spoke both languages with equal fluency. It has been most useful to me. I would recommend any young fellow embarking on my profession to master at least two languages. It gives one so many choices of personality.

'So I grew up, developing my talents in all directions. I would have liked to have been slim, to have displayed the elegance of figure of a Simon Donaldson. I was not made in that mould, so I made the best of what I was, and became

208

instead a lovable clown. It does quite well, I think? I am the licenced buffoon of Glenalban? I adopted – perhaps by inheritance, perhaps by her example – my mother's taste for stealing. It is something I have always enjoyed. Ordinary, humdrum mortals can have no idea of the sheer exhilaration of a successful theft. I adopted, at the same time, my mother's enthusiasm for the arts, which was quite genuine in her and is quite genuine in me. It is, perhaps, my greatest enthusiasm, after money. As soon as I was old enough – and it would seem astonishingly young by Northern standards – I mounted my father's hobby-horse. But I saw that he had misunderstood his own life – underestimated his own talents, perhaps. He was always an amateur. I became a professional.

'I travelled widely. This was agreeable, and also necessary, because I was repeatedly married. With one exception, my marriages were a grave disappointment. The fortunes I had expected to control had either been grossly exaggerated to me, or they were under the noses of trustees and lawyers.

'I grew a beard. It had the effect of hiding the little blemish which you will have observed, beside my left ear. It had the effect of making me resemble the great Garibaldi, who was and remains my hero.'

'I thought I recognized you, when I saw you with your beard,' I said, because a silence had fallen, and silence was dangerous.

'You did recognize me, even though I had a beard. I told Simon Donaldson what to say. He was to say that you had, of course, seen engravings of Garibaldi in the illustrated papers, and that the likeness you saw was to them. I expect he laughed a little at my vanity. You would have liked me more, rather than less, for my harmless desire to resemble my hero. And you forgot Edgar Smith.

'Well, I found I had too many wives in Italy, and too many names. I went to France. I spoke a little French, as many of the people of Piedmont do, but only a little. France was a struggle. I found myself in Rouen, a dreary grey city but a place of much wealth. My beard was at its biggest and my manner at its merriest. I adopted a splendid name, and presently identified and pursued the spinster sister of a great merchant. I did not know or care what he bought and sold; only that there was a great deal of it, and the sister had

209

remarkable jewels. I became aware that, between the secret meetings she was having with me, she was having secret meetings with somebody else. A man in my profession develops what is, perhaps, a sixth sense in these things. I waylaid him with my swordstick in an alley. He said that he had been aware of me, too, and suggested that we be not rivals but allies. He said there was enough in that treasure-house to be divided. He was tall, with yellow hair. He cultivated a shy and gentle manner. In all respects he and I complemented one another. Any lady who recoiled from one of us might embrace the other. At that time he called himself Sir Gordon Crocker. Under this alias, he was as careful to avoid persons from Britain, as I was to avoid any Italians. I lent him a little money. We went into partnership. We failed with the merchant's sister, owing to the malignant intervention of her brother; but by this time, and to a qualified extent, we trusted one another.

'He told me an astonishing story.'

'About Glenalban,' I said.

'He was very angry. He had been within a whisker of securing a fortune beyond his dreams, or even mine, and the purest bad luck – the premature return of a servant – had cheated him of it. He nursed a bitter grievance. However, while there he had made a number of quite authentic historical discoveries, of which you know. He was sure some use could be made of them.

'I devised the use that could be made of them. Poor Simon was a clever lad, in some ways far more highly educated than myself, but he did not have my breadth of vision. Or, of course, my experience.'

Aunt Sophia sniffed. Our hands were still clutched together. I was not sure if the sniff was simply a sniff, or a comment on what Edgar Smith (or whatever he was called) was saying.

He smiled blandly in her direction, as though taking the sniff to be a comment on his words, and welcoming it.

He went on, 'The documents Simon had taken from Glenalban proved, as you know, that the castle was the property of any legitimate heir or heiress of King James II. Very good. We had to produce one. We wanted a man, or a woman, who looked like the portrait of any of the Stuart

210

princes – as close a resemblance as possible. James I, Charles I, Charles II, James II, the Old Pretender, the Young Pretender. Any of these faces would do. Our candidate could be of any age, and come from any country. The other thing we needed, of course, was documentary evidence that our candidate *was* a legitimate descendant of James II. It was fortunate that we had Simon's expert knowledge.'

'His knowledge of old documents?' I said.

'A knowledge of old documents which enabled him to simulate them.'

'Forge them.'

'It is not always necessary to call a spade a spade, Leonora. It is not always desirable or prudent.'

There was a hint of harshness in his voice. I felt the pressure of Aunt Sophia's fingers on mine. This was the man who had killed David Maitland and Simon Donaldson, and who had fired two barrels of shot into my hat.

'What form our simulated documents would take,' continued Edgar Smith, once again bland and cheerful, 'would naturally depend on our candidate. If an elderly Frenchman with an uncanny resemblance to James I, for example, we would construct one set of evidence of his legitimacy. If a middle-aged lady in Rome with a startling similarity to the Merry Monarch, another. Our search for a candidate might take years – we recognized that. But we need not be idle in the meantime. We could scrape incomes in other ways. We were bound to be obliged to do so, and we agreed that we could do so better in partnership. It was desirable that we should trust one another, up to a point. It was impossible that we should trust one another completely. Nobody but a madman would trust either of us completely.

'We agreed to go about the world, as we had been doing, but with the difference that we would be looking, always looking, for faces like the faces we had studied. It made a new interest for us both – almost a kind of game. In Paris I thought we had arrived. I saw a lady of about thirty, who looked, I thought, much like Charles II – those bold eyes, those black curls . . . She was a Levantine, wife of an importer of almonds and dates. We were days trying to make her understand what we wanted of her, and when at last she understood she began to scream and scream . . .

211

It was one of the times when I have had to move rapidly. Her husband had a very fierce moustache, like an Albanian bandit . . .'

He chuckled richly, remembering. Another silence fell. To fill it, I said, 'But you went to a professor. At Aberdeen, I think. The professor recommended Simon.'

He laughed. 'That was our account of how Simon and I became acquainted, yes. You heard that account from him and from me. That I wrote to a professor with whom I had been corresponding for years, on matters connected with my own historical researches. That he replied, recommending Simon as a colleague or assistant. That Simon came to Italy to meet me. I had not been corresponding with any professor. I did not know any professor. I was not engaged in any historical research. Nobody recommended Simon. Nobody would have recommended him, after what had occurred at Glenalban. But you heard the same story from two people, so you completely believed it. Indeed you had no reason to doubt it. If Simon and I were plausible, then so was the story of how we met. What was necessary was that we should tell exactly the same story. We took care to do that.'

'You were very clever,' I said, putting a sickening note of admiration into my voice.

'I don't think you mean that,' he said, 'but, if you do, you're right. We were very clever. I was very clever, and I made use of particular advantages which Simon had. Education, for one. A tall, slim figure. Attractive yellow hair. An air of shyness, so that he seemed disarming and trustworthy. Great advantages.'

I felt angry, because I had been the dupe of all these things.

'However,' Edgar Smith went on, 'in October of last year, exactly ten months ago, neither his advantages nor mine were profiting us. Our fortunes were at their lowest ebb. We were in Brittany, where people keep their purses buttoned. We had gone there in pursuit of two sisters, one widowed and one unmarried . . . That story I shall not tell you, as it ends in failure and humiliation. Well, having got to Brittany, we could not afford to leave it. We found ourselves in a little town called Lamballe, near the coast, not far from St Malo. We had rooms in the Tour d'Argent. After a week they presented us with the reckoning. We could not pay. It was highly embarrassing.

'We had heard of another Italian, who had taken a villa outside the town. I kept well out of his way, for good and obvious reasons. It was easy to find out everything about him that anybody knew, in that small place. He was a grandee, a baron. He was rich, he was Piedmontese, like myself. He was a big man, with a big beard. He was some kind of scholar – a thing I had never been, nor pretended to be – and he was in Brittany to study the stone circles of the Druids. Apparently there are many such things in Brittany. I would not give sixpence for a sight of all of them, but this Barone Lodovico di Vigliano was reported to be fond of them.

'I observed him from a safe distance, going out of his nice rented house, by himself, in a pony-trap. He went to measure and examine these idiotic bits of stone, which everybody made such a fuss about. In appearance he was not really at all like me. But we were about of an age, about of a size and shape, and we both had full black beards. There all similarity ended. I was disappointed, because a very good idea had entered my head . . .

'By this time the landlord of the Tour d'Argent had impounded our belongings. Things were desperate for us. I had a pistol.

'Simon was engaged in seducing a chambermaid at our hotel, so that we could with her help rescue our possessions. That was a necessary task. I undertook the other necessary task. I entered the rented house, when I knew its occupier was out in his trap. I knew from days of observation that there were three servants only. I threatened them with my pistol, and locked them in the coal-cellar. I searched the house, and found a useful number of gold coins, as well as other portable and saleable objects. Most unfortunately, the Barone returned and surprised me. He rushed at me, with a chair held over his head in order to smash me to the ground. He was far too brave. I was compelled to shoot him. I ran away, with my new possessions. I was quite stupid. I should have shot the servants too. They could describe me. Eventually they would get out of the coal-cellar, and then they would describe me. So I altered my appearance. It was extremely simple. I shaved off my beard. The change, you know, is total. It is quite remarkable. It is more difficult to recognize a man you have known with a beard, when you see him clean shaven, than the other way about. I was safe from arrest for a little, but for hours rather than for days. So Simon and I went to St Malo, and took a boat to England. It was all a new world to me. I was prepared to love it, for my poor mother's sake.

'Simon was homesick for Scotland, so we took the train from Portsmouth to London, and from London to Edinburgh. The gold coins made everything easy and pleasant, but they would not last for ever.

'From Edinburgh, I wrote to a friend in Turin, asking for all he could find out about the Barone Lodovico di Vigliano. He was most helpful. I was in a position to describe accurately the Barone's possessions and interests. I was in a position to be the Barone, when a suitable moment arrived. For the time being, in Scotland, I was a Scotsman, or an Englishman, speaking in the educated voice my educated mother had taught me, which you are listening to now. At any moment I could become Italian, or a mixture of the two.

'We looked in the windows of jewellers' and goldsmiths' shops, but stealing from them would have been extremely dangerous. To have been employed by one of them – that would have been helpful. But none would employ either of us. We met an attitude of suspicion which bruised our feelings. We looked in the window of Mr Maitland's shop of antiquities. It was as full of valuable things as any jeweller's. I secured a position with Mr Maitland, telling him an excellent story, and pleading misfortunes which were not entirely fictitious. I used the name Edgar Smith.'

'Why?' I said.

'Why not? What have you against such a solid, unpretentious, respectable name? Well, after I was established as an employee of the shop, Simon came in the character of a customer. Together, as was natural in our two roles, we examined much of the contents of the shop. Simon was by now an expert in all matters connected with Prince Charles Edward, in order to prosecute our grand design the moment we had found a candidate. He spotted the sword which you had sent. He knew what it was. I, working in the shop, knew where it had come from. It was I, in fact, who had opened the parcel in which you sent it.

214

'I also knew, from Mr Maitland, about the chests of papers in your attic. I did not know what they were – nor did he – but I knew of their existence, because he had told me how he looked forward to examining them. I should explain that my manner to Mr Maitland was not like anything you have seen. I was an eager and docile pupil, diligent, respectful, hard-working, grateful for his trust in me. I was ignorant about antiquities, but not about poetry and painting. On these subjects, I impressed Mr Maitland with my knowledge and enthusiasm, which were perfectly genuine. For all these reasons, Mr Maitland told me more than he would have told an ordinary assistant in his shop. He told me about those papers; and he instructed me in the value of various antique articles. I was interested in those which I could put in my pockets, and sell without risk.

'Now you see the advantage of the collaboration between Simon and myself. The sword would have meant nothing to me. Simon could never have discovered where it came from. But put our knowledge together . . .

'For a time it seemed to me an intervention of Providence, an extraordinary coincidence, that Simon and I, of all people, should find such a relic, considering the plan we had. But really it is not. We had been looking for anything that would help us, for a year and a half. We were alert, all the time, for any useful face and for any useful object. It would, I think, have been odd if we had not found something, in the end. It is even odd that it took us as much as a year and a half to find something. I do not include the Levantine lady in Paris . . .

'Why did you come first, and alone?' I said.

'Ah. I had not intended to come so soon, and I had not intended to come alone. I had not intended to be dismissed from Mr Maitland's employ, but to leave it at a moment that suited me. But he caught me taking some coins out of the cashbox, when I was certain I was alone in the shop. He dismissed me. I left, with my pockets full. If I was to come to Millstounburn, it must be at once, that same day. I came, I saw, I almost conquered.

'Of course, what I found was our candidate – a young lady with an unmistakable look of the Young Pretender. Called Albany, a name Simon had told me the Prince used. Who had

215

sent that sword to Mr Maitland to be sold . . . I am sure I looked wildly excited. I was. There was no need to conceal the fact, if I was Dr Colin Nicol, the antiquary.

'But I had to go and hide, after that unseemly brawl with the policeman, and Mr Maitland's knowledge of the contents of my pockets. If I had been caught, I would have been sent to prison. That would have been highly inconvenient, as well as uncomfortable. Also, it would have given Simon a clear field, without either my guiding hand or my participation in the profits. I had to remain in touch with Simon, but out of sight of anybody else.'

'So Simon came to Millstounburn instead.'

'He had been away, on projects of his own. I believe there was a widow in Stirling . . . By the time he returned, I was out of sight, waiting for my beard to grow. Nobody in Britain had seen my beard. I was not sure how long it would take for my beard to transform me back into what I had been. That is why Simon told you that he did not know – that I did not know – how soon I could leave Italy. By this time, of course, we had reinvented me, as his patron and colleague and fellow-scholar. He told you all about me, I believe. When you met me, I was much as you expected. Of course I adopted the name and style of the man I had killed. This was partly because, if enquiries were made to Italy about the cheerful Barone, the answers would be satisfactory. Partly because I was in possession of some small pieces of precious metal – a flask, a watch, that kind of thing – with monograms and crests which fitted my new identity. This impersonation would not have done in Italy, or even in France. But it did admirably in Scotland. There was a very faint chance that some Briton, travelling in Italy, had met my original. I decided to ignore the chance. It was a small risk. I was more likely to be exposed as a fraud if I adopted a completely fictional identity.

'So Edgar Smith, in hiding, died a slow death during the winter, and Lodovico di Vigliano was reborn. As soon as my beard concealed my face, and more especially my birthmark, you had the pleasure of receiving me at Millstounburn. And listening to a style of speech which I had devised, perfectly comprehensible to you, yet continents away from the voice of Edgar Smith.'

216

'By this time, we knew that we did not need to forge any papers. Simon had examined those journals, with you, while my beard was growing. He had established that the journals were authentic – that you were authentic. We felt like men grubbing in the earth for pennies, and being handed sacks of gold on golden trays.

'We began the legal business. It made serious inroads on my stocks of gold, but it was a necessary investment. And the rewards would be incalculable. We had always adopted a flexible approach, prepared to adjust our strategy to circumstances. The relevant circumstance here was that Simon's skill caused you to become attached to him. And I suppose you know the law – if all had worked out as we planned, Simon would not have been consort of the mistress of Glenalban, but himself master of Glenalban. It is an excellent law, I find – the instant and automatic transfer of wealth from bride to bridegroom, at the moment of their marriage. I am about to benefit from it myself, to a scarcely credible extent. I hope they never change that law . . .

'Most calamitously, Simon had meanwhile allowed himself to be outwitted. Over a long period, and totally. Yes, by Lady Lochinver. I feel a reluctant admiration for that pestilent woman. She knew – they all knew – that Simon was vindictive, as well as – we need not blink the word – avaricious. She rightly feared future trouble, an attempt at revenge. As an insurance against it, she pretended she stood his friend, prepared to betray her own nephew on Simon's behalf. He confided in her, confident of her support. It was a dreadful mistake, but it was not altogether foolish of him. Her support would have been an enormous help. It appeared that it was being just that, until the moment you were locked in that cupboard . . .

'I have said that Simon and I trusted one another, but only to a qualified extent. With your knowledge of him, you will appreciate my need for prudence. It was entirely possible that, when the prize was in his grasp, he would suddenly decline to share it. For that reason I abstracted certain documents from those which we handed to the lawyers. The lawyers assumed that those documents, which they had seen but not copied, were amongst those which we gave them. They proceeded on that assumption. The documents were to be produced at the proper time – at a time when I had made quite certain of my own legitimate share of Simon's wedding portion.'

'Legitimate?' I said.

Aunt Sophia's fingers tightened on mine. His temper was not quite predictable.

'Well, I had worked for it all as hard as he had. I was the mastermind throughout. I accept that "legitimate" was an ill-chosen word, though I question your wisdom in pointing that out. Let us say "equitable". At any rate, as I told you with perfect honesty, without those papers your claim to be Countess of Albany remained unanswerable, but your claim to Glenalban became thin to the point of disappearance. With the papers, that too approaches the unanswerable. In effect, having those papers enabled me to control Simon.'

'Where are they now?'

'Here.'

'Safe?'

'Safe in that box on the table. But to be burned in the morning. I no longer wish claims to be made on an estate part of which belongs to my betrothed. Besides, tomorrow there will be no legitimate descendant of King James II. The deeds will have become irrelevant, except as historical documents which hold no interest for me. We are jumping about. Let us return to the chronological. The date of the abstraction of the papers was about that on which Lady Lochinver lured you to the castle, and my beloved Louisa locked you in the cupboard. We knew nothing about that at the time, until Avington told us. What an agreeable fellow he is! So very trusting. And you know how necessary he was to your abduction from the asylum. The account we gave you of that was exactly true. I prefer truth, when possible. One cannot be caught out by it.

'And then it seemed, to Simon and myself, that your incarceration and liberation would work powerfully in our favour. You were hunted; as his wife you were safe. And you were so grateful! He had been so gallant! Our visit to the Kirk followed immediately and inevitably. What we did not know was that Avington had followed us; and we did not know that Lady Flora had told him her story.

'The effect of Avington's intervention, there at the Kirk, changed everything. It put Simon entirely out of the running.

But not myself. Rather the contrary. Like you, I had been Simon's dupe. I knew nothing of the episode with Lady Flora, nothing of his other conquests. I was as shocked as you were. You were even sorry for me. I could continue to fight our battles, Simon's and mine. I could go as a welcome guest to Glenalban, vouched for by you and by Avington, and, as to the rest, relying on my performance, which I had now polished, of a rich, eccentric and affable buffoon.

'Simon had wit enough to see, even while Avington was destroying him in front of you, that I must not be destroyed. I could salvage almost everything, as inmate of the castle and friend of its owner. But he did not want things to proceed on those lines, if he could possibly prevent it. He did not want to lose you.'

'Is that true?'

'He did not want to lose the future owner of Glenalban.'

'That does not answer my question.'

'With Simon? Yes, I think it does. He thought there was a chance he could retrieve himself, recover your good opinion. But not if Avington took you to Lady Flora. Hence my pistol, which I really didn't know he had. I can understand why he did it, but it was a mistake. I had to hit him with my stick. That proved me your ally. In fact we all gained something from his folly, although all Simon gained was a bruise . . .

'When I had duly been made welcome at Glenalban, I told you Edgar Smith was in prison. I did not say which prison, or under what name he had gone. That was so that no busybody could make any useful enquiries in the matter. My purpose was to reinforce, more surely than ever, the division between Edgar Smith and myself, our absolute separateness. There had always been a chance of your recognizing me. Small, but there. I might have a mannerism of which I was unaware, of rubbing my nose in a certain way when I was listening, or a way of crossing my legs in an armchair. I have observed such things in others. One does not observe them in oneself. Such a thing would possibly light a spark of memory in your mind, and then you would stare and stare at me . . . I mention this to show you how careful I have been, what trouble I have taken, how richly I deserve to succeed.

'Soon after I came to Glenalban, another factor entered the situation which profoundly affected my plans. I discovered

219

that Miss Louisa Frith could be rendered fond of me. I amused her, intrigued her. She had never met anybody like me, in Scotland or on her travels. I should think not, indeed! I made private enquiries, and discovered the extent of her personal fortune. Well, you know, in the profession from which I have now retired, there are times for siege and times for assault. This was a woman to be swept off her feet. It was a time for boyishness. I was *very* boyish.

'I now, Leonora, lost all interest in your affairs. You could marry Avington, or Duncan Glenalban, or who you liked. If you found your crock of gold, I was rather pleased than sorry, so long as my own was not threatened.

'And then it was threatened.

'My Louisa surprised and delighted me by her enthusiasm for kissing. There has not been much of it in her life, I suppose, and she was making up for lost time. The Scottish are energetic people, and their vigour on the field and the deer-forest is carried into their caresses. I was expected to respond with equal vigour, and did so, knowing that each hearty embrace made more certain my comfortable old age. But my beard scratched her cheek. It had happened before, but not to such a painful extent. Northern women have more sensitive skins than Latins, and my Louisa's is like a rose-petal. I could not refuse her request. Especially as it was not a request but, as she herself defined it, an ultimatum.

'Action had at once to be taken. Most of it, fortunately, was simplicity itself. It was entirely possible that I should be taken, at some moment in my married life, into Mr Maitland's shop, or meet him under some other circumstances. After all, I expect to frequent artistic circles in Edinburgh. There was a substantial risk that he would see me. If he did, he would undoubtedly know and expose me. Naturally I had had a copy made of the key of his shop door, and naturally I had taken it with me when I left him. I thought it might one day come in useful, and it did. I still had my beard, of course. He did not know me. How could he? He thought I was an intruder, as, indeed, I was. I did not give him time to raise the alarm. I was not troubled by his servant, who hardly saw me. Once again I took a few articles – things I could conceal about my person – to make it appear that robbery was the whole motive of the crime.

'I was a little worried that you might reflect on the coincidence that I was in Edinburgh, on a very brief visit, on the very night Mr Maitland was killed. I reinvoked the ghost of Edgar Smith, caused him to have escaped from prison, caused him to have a grudge against Mr Maitland, for the latter's non-existent evidence at a non-existent trial. All this provided, or confirmed, by a fictional conversation with a non-existent Inspector of Police. You believed me completely, did you not?

'I turned to the problem of Simon. He would not immediately expose me, but he would blackmail me by threatening to do so. You will agree that that was an intolerable prospect. So I sent for him. We remained in constant touch. He could write to me freely at Glenalban. It is not a house where people read the private letters of others. At least, I do, but I am exceptional in that as in so much else. I liked him writing to me here. Each letter addressed to the Barone di Vigliano reaffirmed my new identity.

'I told him I could smuggle him into the castle, and he could help himself to miniatures and silver. It was a chance he had been pining for, ever since his expulsion. Revenge as well as profit. But he was right not to risk attempting it without a friend in the garrison.

'The silly fellow let himself be seen. It did not greatly matter. Indeed, it probably enhanced the credibility of the story I told you, that I had seen him in secret conference with Duncan Glenalban. I made a rendezvous with Simon. I emerged quietly from the castle, which I had not attempted before; but I knew it could be done, because you had done it. I met him. He was enthusiastic about stealing the miniatures. He was also enthusiastic about sharing my new fortune with me. I held him under, with my stick. Thus I did not even get my boots wet, which might have been hard to explain.

'Then I came to you with my story, and with my distress. I did that well, too, I think? My motive there is probably obvious to you.'

'No,' I said. This answer would still keep him talking. Besides, it was true.

'If I could persuade you to suspect Duncan Glenalban of named and nameless crimes, then you would be on your guard

221

never against me, but always against him. Together we formed that theory, that Duncan had stolen the documents, that Simon had found out and threatened to blackmail him. You know, that theory was so good, I was almost believing it myself.

'Meanwhile this farmhouse had been rebuilt and furnished, and Duncan lent it to me.'

'Why did you want it?' I asked.

'Why,' he looked at me in surprise, 'to write my poem.'

'You really are writing a poem?'

'It has been in my mind for years. I have never had leisure or peace of mind enough to tackle it. I assure you, I have never been so happy as in my solitude here, producing what I believe to be a work of beauty. I would like to paint also, but that talent is denied me. Also I could come and go as I pleased, observed only by the birds of the air, carrying a gun and a spy-glass if I wished. This afternoon I did so wish.'

'How could you know I was going for a walk?

'On a fine afternoon, have you ever not done so, since you have been here?'

'How could you know I would be alone?'

'I did not. But I know the routine of Glenalban. Naturally, by now. I know that on Wednesday Lady Flora devotes the afternoon to letters, and my Louisa devotes it to some housekeeping task. I knew you would not walk with Duncan Glenalban. There remained only Avington.'

'Suppose I had walked with Jack?'

'Then you had longer to live.'

Aunt Louisa's fingers now clutched mine so tight they hurt. She was hearing things we had not told her.

'How did you know,' I asked, 'what road I would take?'

'I did not need to know, in advance. That is the merit of a spy-glass, together with the knowledge that from Glenalban most walks start from the terrace.'

'You must have entered the wood as I did, or after I did. How did you cross it so quietly?'

'Ah. You do not know a tithe of the advantages of an upbringing like mine. To write an epic poem, yes, I am capable of that, because I was brought up to it. To enter the bedroom of a sleeping man, even of a man not quite asleep – to cross it – to leave the room with his watch and money, yes, I am capable of that too, because I was brought up to it.'

'You wore that reddish coat so that I would think you were Glenalban, if I saw you?'

'Not at all. I did not intend you or anyone to see me. I did not think, after I had fired, that you had seen me. I did not think you would see anything, ever again. That is why I was so surprised when you came here. I wore that coat when I went out with a gun, because it is the coat I wear when I go out with a gun. That you should think it was Glenalban who shot at you merely provides an amusing irony. It is not at all credible that Glenalban should try to kill you.'

'Yes, it is, I mean it was.'

'No, child. Avington put his finger precisely on the weak point of the theory which accused poor Duncan. If he had stolen documents that destroyed your case, he had no need to murder you. He might have done one or other, to keep Glenalban, but it was absurd to suppose that he would do both. I had not suspected Avington of so much intelligence. His objection was unanswerable. You did your best to answer it, which was most amusing for me to listen to, but your logic was not good. His was better. It should have led you to conclude either that somebody else had stolen the documents, or that somebody else had pulled those triggers, or that somebody else had done both those things. I was in some fright that Avington would follow his own argument to its logical conclusion. But you beguiled him out of his logic, child. Whether permanently or not I don't know. It will not matter. There will never be a charge of attempted murder brought, because there will not be a witness. Just hearsay from Avington and from me. And, of course, Duncan can probably prove he was five miles away, full in view of a dozen people.

'Well, well. When Avington brought you here, I was surprised not only that you were alive. Also that I was being given a second bite of the cherry, as my poor mother used to say. And he fell in immediately with my idea that he should bring Miss Grant here also. It shows how completely he trusts me, doesn't it? My one fear now is that my dearest Louisa dislikes my birthmark. Perhaps I shall be allowed moderate whiskers – enough to cover it, not enough to lacerate her cheek. I shall suggest that. There will be many things to discuss between us.'

'I don't think,' I said, 'those discussions will take place.'

He looked at me, his eyebrows raised over the big, bland, not unpleasing face which I remembered so well from so long ago at Millstounburn.

He wondered what I meant. I wondered what I meant. I meant nothing at all. I simply wanted to keep the conversation alive.

While it was alive, we were alive.

I had an inspiration. I said, 'We are not the only people who can recognize you.'

'Yes.'

'Customers, in Mr Maitland's shop. Are you going to kill them all? How will you find them? One day one of them will see you.'

'I was not employed in the public part of the shop. I was at the stage of being a sort of apprentice, learning the trade. My duties lay in the storeroom and workroom behind. The only customer with whom I dealt was Simon Donaldson.'

'There is Mr Maitland's servant.'

'He was on holiday, throughout the few days I was there. That should have been obvious to you. He is alive.'

'Oh . . .'

The little parlour of the farmhouse was bright and comfortable. It had three ways out. One was the open door into the kitchen, in which an invisible lamp was shining. One was the incongruously massive front door, the key of which was in Edgar Smith's pocket. The third was the archway at the foot of the narrow, winding stairs. There was no hall or passage – simply the arch and immediately the dark staircase. The bottom two steps were visible from the parlour. Then the staircase twisted to the right, beyond the back wall of the parlour. Upstairs, I supposed, there were two bedchampers – one for the farmer and his wife, when they took occupation in the spring, and one for their children. In one, Edgar Smith had made himself comfortable, with fine linen and blankets from Glenalban. There was no possibility of us reaching those upstairs rooms. There would have been nowhere to go, if we had reached them.

In the parlour, the oil-lamp on the table spread a golden

light on the pages of the epic poem; and on the cheerful moonlike face with the bird-shaped birthmark; and on the narrow features of Aunt Sophia, who sat straight-backed and dignified in her wooden chair, as she always did, and as she had unsuccessfully taught me always to do ... My mind unaccountably sped backwards down through the years to my childhood, my happiness, her love and care for me. Her reward was a dingy and secret end at the hands of a monster. And she was here entirely because of me – because of my ancestry, because of my ambition and greed. It was not to be borne. It was not to be allowed.

'You will not discuss your whiskers with Miss Frith or anyone else,' I said, 'because you will go to the gallows. We shall send you there.'

'From the grave?'

'From the witness box.'

'Brave words, Leonora. And, like most brave words, the purest nonsense. Well well, I have indulged my hunger to tell somebody my story. The hour of my dinner is approaching. Talking so much has given me an appetite, to match the thirst which it has also given me. I shall eat and drink more comfortable in the knowledge that there now stands no impediment to my future luxurious felicity. How elegant my language has become, suiting its subject. My poor mother would be proud of her last pupil.'

He picked up the shotgun. It was pointing between Aunt Louisa and me. I wondered which he would shoot first. I hoped it would be me.

'There will be bloodstains,' I said, my words coming out a little high and strained, try as I might to be brave. 'They will catch you by the bloodstains.'

'How you are struggling to postpone the inevitable. I scarcely blame you. Miss Grant is more stoical. She has hardly contributed to our little symposium. The chairs need repainting, as you see. The paint is quite chipped. I have a pot of paint and a brush, sent up here at my request by my dearest Louisa. Had that not been the case, you would be sitting elsewhere. I shall paint the chairs. I shall enjoy doing so. It is a rewarding task, because so pleasant an effect is achieved with so little labour.'

'The floor.'

225

'Your chairs are standing, as you can see, on a little piece of shameful rug. It is all holes and frayed ends, bare patches and stains. I have been intending for days to burn it.'

'Lord Avington knows we are here.'

'Avington will be told that you have gone, on my advice and at my charges, to Edinburgh. I suppose he will continue to believe that Glenalban tried to kill you. It will be interesting to see what comes of that.'

'You will find our bodies hard to dispose of.'

'With the whole of the Scottish Highlands for their reception? With all night to spend? With a pony and cart? Do you know how deep some of the peat-hags are? No, and nor does anybody else, because when a sheep stumbles into one it is never seen again. The mud closes over its head, and it sinks, and sinks, and sinks, and within minutes the mud has oozed itself smooth again, and you would have no idea that anything had fallen into it. Duncan Glenalban was kind enough to warn me most particularly against the peat-hags. That is how I know what they are called.'

He pulled back the two hammers at the breech of the shotgun, cocking it. The gun was one of the new breech-loaders, invented in France only a dozen years earlier, and arrived in Britain hardly five years before. The new gun could be reloaded in seconds. It was a good gun for a murderer.

The two clicks of the hammers sounded as loud as shots, in the quiet little room.

# 12

'That will be enough, Mr Smith,' said the Earl of Glenalban.

He came down the last two steps of the little dark staircase. He was wearing a rust-coloured shooting coat, and carrying a shotgun.

Edgar Smith spoke the truth when he said that he could move very quick. He spun round in his chair, and at the same moment fired. The boom of the gun was shattering in that small space. But Glenalban moved equally quick. He must have been expecting Edgar Smith's spin. He dropped to the floor. Not knowing what I was doing, not having the smallest notion of a plan, I jumped out of my chair and threw myself at Edgar Smith – not at his person but at his gun. It was just as he fired again. I spoiled his aim, but not enough. Glenalban gave a cry. He was hit. I could not tell how badly. He was not dead. Edgar Smith threw me off, so that I crashed into a corner of the room. All the breath was knocked out of my body. To my absolute amazement, and still in the same blink of an eye, Aunt Sophia had also jumped up, faster than I had any idea that she could move, and seized the sword-stick.

Edgar Smith broke his gun at the breach, and pulled two fresh cartridges out of his pocket. In a matter of seconds he would be ready to fire again, at the injured and helpless Glenalban. I was fighting for breath, winded, powerless to move. Aunt Sophia pulled the sword out of the swordstick.

Even as Edgar Smith reloaded and cocked his gun, Aunt Sophia stabbed him in the thigh, as hard as she could, with the sword. He gave a great shout, and dropped his gun. I managed to crawl forward towards it, but before I reached it Glenalban, crawling also, had reached it and thrust it away

227

out of Edgar Smith's reach. On his knees, he pointed his own gun at Edgar Smith's stomach.

Edgar Smith was clutching his wounded thigh, looking at it incredulously. Blood was oozing between his fingers.

Speaking through clenched teeth from the pain of his own wound, Duncan Glenalban said, 'Between you, you saved my life. Thank you.'

I tried to speak. I could not. I was still winded.

Aunt Sophia said, 'You saved ours, Sir. Thank you.'

'Are you all right, Leo?' said Duncan, not taking his eyes off Edgar Smith.

'No,' I managed to say. 'But soon yes.'

And soon I was almost as good as new, though stiff and bruised from crashing across the room.

'Are you strong enough to hold this gun?'

'Only just,' I said, taking it from him without shifting its aim from Edgar Smith's chest.

Duncan was still on his knees. He could not stand. He reached out for the chair that Aunt Sophia had been sitting in. He dragged it across the floor, and put it in front of me, so that I could rest the barrels of the gun on its back. And still the aim of those barrels was Edgar Smith's bottom waistcoat button.

Duncan said to Aunt Sophia, 'Please see if you can find a clothesline, or any bit of rope in the kitchen.'

'You are wounded,' she said. 'Is it your leg? We must look at that first.'

'Not first but second,' said Duncan. 'We must truss our fowl first.'

Obediently Aunt Sophia trotted out into the kitchen. She found at once what every farmhouse kitchen had, a coil of hempen line for the washing to be pegged to. Duncan made two tight turns round Edgar Smith's chest and upper arms, and tied him to the back of his chair.

Edgar Smith was still clutching the wound Aunt Sophia had given him, and watching the blood ooze, with a kind of stupid blank expression, as though he had been cheated, and could not make out how it had been done.

'I think you had better keep hold of the gun, Leo,' said Duncan. 'But, if you have reason to shoot, make it his legs. He must be alive for the gallows. Besides, you are too brave and too adorable to be killing people with guns.'

228

'Adorable?' I stammered, as stupid as Edgar Smith.

'Yes. Will you marry me?'

'Yes,' I said.

'First things first,' said Aunt Sophia severely, coming back from the kitchen again. 'I have put some water on the heat. We must cut away the leg of your trousers, Sir.'

'But they are new trousers.'

'You can get other trousers, but not another leg.'

They were both quite calm. I did not understand how they managed it. My heart was still thudding from the wild terror and excitement of those few seconds of violent action; and from the Earl's proposal; and from my unexpected 'Yes'.

I was as astonished by my own sudden certainty as by anything else that had happened.

Aunt Sophia cut away Duncan's right trouser-leg, just above the knee, with a knife she had found in the kitchen. I did not watch them afterwards. I could not, without taking my eyes of Edgar Smith. I was thankful, though I despised my squeamishness. I heard grunts of pain from Duncan, which he tried to suppress. Each one tore at my heart.

'We must get all the shot out at once,' said Aunt Sophia, in the tones of a strict teacher of infants. 'Each of these pellets could fester, and then you would lose your leg.'

They were a long time about it. Aunt Sophia would not let Duncan tell us his story until she had finished. She said it would distract her from digging out the pellets. There were not so very many pellets. A full charge, at point-blank range, would have blown his leg off, if it had not blown his head off.

Suddenly Duncan said, after stifling a yelp of pain, 'I don't want you to say "Yes" just because of the events of this evening, Leo.'

'I seem to have changed my mind about a lot of things,' I said, trying to concentrate on the job I had been given.

Aunt Sophia found a clean linen sheet in a press, and tore it . into strips. She bandaged Duncan's leg. He was easier. His face was drawn with pain, and he could put no weight on his leg.

He said, 'I suppose we had better minister to the wound you so gallantly made, Ma'am.'

'I suppose so,' said Aunt Sophia without enthusiasm.

229

'The rules of war, you know. Humane treatment of prisoners.'

'Pooh,' said Aunt Sophia. 'But he should be able to walk to the gallows.'

There was not much she could do with a deep and narrow stab-wound. She staunched the bleeding by bandaging a pad very tight over the place. Duncan held the shotgun. But it seemed to me needless. Edgar Smith was a man in a stupor; he was like one of the silent, motionless lunatics I had lived among.

Eventually he was done. The furniture was put back on its legs. Aunt Sophia and I heaved Duncan into a chair, from which he could watch Edgar Smith. A little blood was mopped up, and the swordstick wiped. Duncan pushed a rag through the barrels of Edgar Smith's gun, which was his own gun; he said that, if it were left fouled overnight, the metal would be corroded.

'One of us could get back to Glenalban,' said Duncan, 'to set their minds at rest, and to bring a conveyance to get us home. But . . .'

'Out of the question, Sir,' said Aunt Sophia, who had adopted an air of authority I remembered her attempting ten years before. 'You are in no state to move an inch, except in a comfortable carriage. Nora has had both mental and physical shocks. I would never find my way! We must resign ourselves to staying here until morning. That creature said that a woman comes in to clean the house, daily, in the morning. She shall take a message to the castle.'

Duncan smiled.

The sun came out over the iron-grey waves of the sea. It was no fraud. I reached out suddenly, shamelessly, and took his hand. He squeezed my fingers as Aunt Sophia had squeezed them, when we were in the Valley of the Shadow of Death.

'All that horseplay,' said Aunt Sophia, 'has given me an unaccountable appetite.'

Duncan laughed. I had a great desire to kiss him. I could not make out what had happened inside me.

Dubiously I said, 'Shall I cook something?'

'No, dear,' said Aunt Sophia. 'You had better leave it to me.'

Aunt Sophia continued to forbid Duncan to tell his story, until we had eaten. She said it would be bad for our digestions, after so much excitement, and lead to inflammation of Duncan's injuries. He and I obeyed meekly. We stared at one another, as though in discovery, and held hands like children.

We had some cold bird, and potatoes which Aunt Sophia fried, and excellent cheese. We had one glass each of Duncan's own best Burgundy, which Miss Frith had sent up to the farmhouse.

'Any more would be dangerous for us all, for different reasons,' said Aunt Sophia. She firmly put the cork back into the bottle, and the bottle away in the kitchen.

And at last I was permitted to hear, and Duncan to tell, what had happened to bring him to the bottom of the farmhouse stairs.

'I came back from shooting,' he said, 'to find odd things going on. Flora told me that Leo had come rushing along the passages like a tempest, in a state of distraction, and many degrees below the usual level of her formidable chic. Almost immediately afterwards she disappeared with Jack Avington in a dog-cart. It did not seem like either an elopement or an abduction. I could not see why it should be in the nature of an escape. What had Leo to escape from? She had the love and protection of too many people, rather than too few. Nobody knew where they had gone. We assumed they would return. Meanwhile nothing could be done about it.

'Jack did return, after a long time, alone. He had a story ready. Two stories. One about Leo, one about you, Miss Grant. I would not be here if Jack were a better liar. His stories were simply no good. He had taken you to the main road, Leo, to meet an anonymous friend, who was to take you to who knew where? What friend? Communicated with by what means? Taking you away for what purpose? And Miss Grant had to go without a second's delay to a croft, of uncertain locality, inhabited by a family of unrevealed name, with an illustrated Bible for which the children could not wait until morning, thence to be brought back by an unnamed doctor, on whose way home Glenalban lay . . . This was all so ridiculous that I almost believed it, except for the uneasiness

231

in Jack's eye. So truthful a man shouldn't attempt such tactics.

'I couldn't begin to imagine what any of this meant. But I decided to follow your dog-cart, Miss Grant, and some instinct made me bring my gun. It soon became obvious where you were headed – the road to this place goes nowhere else. I was able to follow you at a safe distance, because I knew where you were going, and to double round and get here ahead of you, because I was on horseback.

'I was completely baffled, as you may imagine. There was no reason why you should not visit Lodovico in his retreat. But why in the evening, and why make a secret of it? I scented some very peculiar conspiracy. I couldn't begin to tell you, from sheer embarrassment, some of the wild theories that went through my head.

'Because I knew where you were going, Miss Grant, I was able to get here before you. I let my horse go, ran a little, and walked a little, and crawled a little, and was under the walls of his house when you arrived. I could do no more until the commotion of your arrival, or I would have been heard. I climbed in an upstairs window, while Lodovico was banging about, locking the shutters and so forth, covering any sound I made –'

'Climbed in?' I said. 'How?'

'Have you ever heard of a farm without a ladder in the steading? How do you suppose they make stacks of their hay and ricks of their straw? Also this house has just been rebuilt, after it was gutted by fire. I supervised the rebuilding. I know it inside out. I knew which upstairs window I could break without being heard from the parlour. I crept down the stairs under cover of Lodovico's voice, when he was boasting of his exploits. In that vein, he would drown a platoon of soldiers crossing a barrack-square paved with broken glass.'

'You sat there listening,' said Aunt Sophia, 'all the time he was talking?'

'In one sense I owe you an apology, Ma'am,' he said. 'I could at any moment have ended your discomfort and peril.'

'That would have been *quite* wrong,' said Aunt Sophia. 'You would have cut short his confession.'

'That is what I concluded. The more the better from him, I thought. Even to his plans for, er, eliminating the two of you, and disposing of your mortal remains.'

'Then you were so brave,' I said, very close to tears at remembering the lovely shock of his sudden appearance.

'I had this gun. It is easier to be brave when you hold a gun. You had no gun, Leo, when you jumped like a fury on an armed man. You had no gun, Miss Grant, when you ran and took his sword.'

'You were braver than I was,' I said.

'No. You were braver than I, both of you.'

'This is a sterile argument,' said Aunt Sophia, as dry as when she told me she would not treat me as a Queen.

'We can continue it in private, darling girl,' said Duncan, smiling at me; so that my fingers wriggled in his, like eels in love with their trap. 'Can you now overlook my fortune and my castle?'

'Yes,' I said, with difficulty. 'I will be brave about them, too.'

'What was the theory this fellow was talking about? That you and he worked out together? About my stealing documents from the lawyers, and having secret meetings with Simon Donaldson? And then trying to shoot you?'

'I cannot possible tell you, ever,' I said. And immediately told him.

He whistled, when I had finished.

Aunt Sophia looked gravely disapproving.

'And you had Jack Avington believing it, too,' said Duncan. 'I thought his manner to me was odd, this evening. You had him whisking you away from the awful dangers of Glenalban to the safety of this fellow's protection . . . I can see why you turned a little chilly towards me, dearest goose. One minute cheating you of your birthright, the next murdering Donaldson . . .'

'It is unkind of you to make fun of me,' I said, with an attempt at dignity. 'It was a very good theory.'

'Oh yes, my love,' he said quickly, '*very* good . . . I can tell you what I am dreading. Telling my Aunt Louisa what we have heard tonight.'

'I think you may leave that to me,' said Aunt Sophia.

'Would you do that?' he said, startled.

233

'As a woman, I can better understand her feelings. I can better soften the blow, the many cruel blows.'

'It would be an uncommon kindness.'

'A common one, Sir, I think.'

He bowed his head, rebuked by a goodness even I had not fully understood.

'I have just realized something,' I said. 'Duncan, what do you really think of Jack?'

'A very good fellow indeed,' he said instantly, 'Kind, decent, generous, courageous.'

'Yes, that is what I think. And he saved me from dreadful things, and he thought he was saving me from even more dreadful things, and I liked him very much, and he made me laugh, and I never quite fell in love with him. I could *not* understand why. I do now.'

Duncan looked at me, eyebrows raised, almost but not quite understanding.

'You were partial to Lord Glenalban from the beginning, dear,' said Aunt Sophia. 'I knew. I was quite sorry, because I am very attached to Lord Avington.'

'You *knew*, Aunt Sophia?' I said. 'How did you know?'

'By the fact that you refused Lord Avington, without being able to give a reason,' said Aunt Sophia. 'A man you knew to have every admirable and amiable quality. With whom you were on terms of intimate friendship. Why should you refuse him, if you were not in love with somebody else?'

'That's what Flora thought,' said Duncan.

He moved his injured leg, unthinking. He let out a gasp of pain.

'Please be still,' I cried, clutching his hand as though one of us was drowning.

'I will, when I remember . . . Flora was sure you would come to me in the end, dearest Leo. I tried to share her optimism. There was almost no moment when I honestly did share it. She will be happy. You did say "Yes", didn't you? It wasn't a trick of the sound?'

'Flora,' I said, remembering. 'She almost warned me not to refuse you. She said, for my sake. I thought . . . Dear God, I thought she meant you would kill me if I refused, because you might lose Glenalban. And she was quite against my being killed, I thought . . .'

234

Duncan laughed. Aunt Sophia looked shocked.

'She is so much in the way of admiring a much older brother,' said Duncan deprecatingly, 'that she convinced herself that your happiness depended on me as much as mine on you.'

'It does,' I said. 'Another thing has come clear to me. I would never have believed that I would actually attack, bare-handed, a man as big as that, with a loaded gun in his hands . . . But his gun was pointed at you. I think, if it had been pointed at anyone else in the world – even you, Aunt Sophia, even Flora, even dear Jack – I would never have had that – fit of madness. But I wanted you alive. I wanted you. Oh dear, I am as selfish and greedy as ever I was . . .'

'I can't get up and kiss you, curse it,' said Duncan.

I threw myself to my knees by his chair. He kissed me. My arms were tight round his neck. First our lips and then our cheeks were pressed together.

Into his cheek I said, 'I see what your Aunt Louisa meant. Please don't grow a beard.'

I felt his smile on my own lips, when he kissed me again.

When I emerged at last from the heaven of that awkward embrace – and I only did so because my beloved was beginning to hiccup from the pain of his wound – I saw that Aunt Sophia was sedulously looking away, stiff as a ramrod, like a seated statue entitled 'Tact'.

Edgar Smith was looking inwards, I thought, at the future he had lost and at the future he had gained.

We sat up for all that remained of the night. None of us slept. I could not have slept, for happiness and excitement. Duncan could not have slept, for the pain of his leg. Aunt Sophia would not allow herself to sleep, because convention demanded that Duncan and I, together in the small hours of the morning, be respectably chaperoned. Edgar Smith did not sleep, I thought, because of the monsters in his head.

Mrs McGill, a bustling little body, arrived on foot at nine o'clock. She shrieked when she saw how large a party was sitting having breakfast in the parlour. She shrieked at the bandage on Duncan's leg, and that on Edgar Smith's.

She hurried away to tell her man to run to Glenalban for two carriages. She was to tell them to get the County Police, and the Procurator Fiscal from Lochgrannomhead.

Edgar Smith ate no breakfast, though we offered him what we had. He did not seem to hear our voices, or see our faces.

The carriages arrived. The coachman and four footmen were saucer-eyed with curiosity. In the dog-cart came Jack Avington with Flora. Flora gave a little scream when she saw the bandage. Then she saw that Duncan held my hand. She looked from his face to mine. She laughed with sudden happiness. It was moving to see that gentle creature so joyful at another's joy.

Jack followed her eye, and saw what she had seen. He grinned ruefully, and shook Duncan by the hand that was not holding mine. I burst into tears, grieving at another's grief.

Two footmen lifted Duncan into the first carriage. He tried to stifle a grunt of pain, too proud to show weakness in front of his sister and friend and servants.

He called to me, as though suddenly remembering, 'Smith said something about a box. The missing papers. You should have them, Leo.'

I had entirely forgotten about the box, the papers, my claim, and all. There had been more important things on my mind. There still were. But Duncan insisted that we salvage the papers, and send them to the lawyers. I thought I had better begin as I meant to go on – I had better obey, as well as love and honour, as presently I would swear to do before an altar.

The papers went on my lap, as I sat beside Duncan in the carriage. I did not look at them. I did not care about them.

Of my days in the Lochgrannomhead Asylum for Pauper Lunatics, I recorded that I did not remember a continuous passage of the days, but a series of distorted lantern slides. So it is of the days that followed the autobiography of Edgar Smith, the battle of the farmhouse parlour, and my unexpected betrothal to Duncan.

I see myself contemplating the strength and symmetry of Duncan's face, and wonderng how I could ever have supposed it any but the most perfect in the world.

236

I see dear Flora's selfless joy, as she welcomed me as a sister.

I see the fallow deer flicking through the shadows of the great elm trees of the park.

I see Miss Louisa Frith, emerging after two days spent in the solitude of her room, faultlessly elegant as ever, her head held high. I marvel at courage greater by far than any I showed, when in a moment of madness I threw myself at that gun.

I see Jack Avington leaving, his smile a little twisted, but firm on his face; and Flora's smile sitting no easier, as she watches his carriage away.

I see my own unhelpful tears, as I learn that not every story can have a happy ending; and that, for there to be a silver lining, there must be a cloud.

I see Duncan's first attempt to walk, with a stick; and his smile, when he found he could.

That smile – that smile. My mind held an album of pictures of that smile.

The last day of August was my birthday. I wished that Jack had stayed, but I understood why he did not. That was the only shadow on a day and night of gold. Blurred gold, for me; I was drunk for twenty hours, not with wine but with happiness.

I remember the beginning. Mary MacAndrew gave me a birthday gift, when she called me in the morning. It was a little needle-case, delicately embroidered with tiny flowers and birds. I wept and embraced her. I was weeping and embracing people, thereafter, for twenty hours. Never can a small and undeserving female person have been shown such love and goodwill.

There was formal announcement of our betrothal. I remember no word of the kindly speech made by the Earl of Draco, when he proposed the toast to us; I remember only the smiles and cheers, and my sensation of being carried through warm starlight on a chariot drawn by swans.

'Leonora,' said Duncan.

I had gone out to join him on the terrace, after breakfast. It was two days after my birthday – thirty-five hours of official betrothal. He had been up very early, about farming business. I had not. I had gobbled my breakfast, most unladylike, because time was wasted that was not spent with him.

With Simon and Jack I had wondered how one could recognize authentic love in one's own heart. The question no longer arose. It answered itself. I would have done murder for Duncan, committed treason, flattened cities.

Why did he call me 'Leonora'? Why had he no smile for me?

He stood, holding his stick, which he still needed. All the marks of pain had been gone from his face. All of them had come back.

'The lawyers,' he said.

'The lawyers,' I repeated stupidly, the words meaning nothing to me. 'Is your leg hurting? Have you done too much this morning? I keep begging you, darling, not to tire yourself.'

'The lawyers have met together, yours and mine,' said Duncan. 'With the papers we sent. The ones Smith took. The result is a foregone conclusion. I am advised not to go to court.'

I looked at him blankly. The most horrible suspicion jumped into my mind. He was a man of scrupulous honour. Too scrupulous. He carried it to absurd lengths. Before, he had not made love to me, although he loved me, *in case* I was rich and he poor. Now he *knew* I was rich and he poor.

'It doesn't make the slightest difference,' I said. I tried to speak lightly, reasonably, although I was scared to death. 'It is as Edgar Smith said, that night in the farmhouse. The moment we're married it's yours. All the documents and deeds and arguments are aca-academic.'

'You refused me,' he said drably, 'in case the world confused love with greed, in case you yourself did.'

'When I refused you, I did not know I was in love with you. You do know you are in love with me. It is very astonishing that you should be, but you say you are, and I believe you, if only because I want to . . .'

'Do I, now, know I am in love with you? That was the point you made about yourself. You said that men have no monopoly of honour.'

238

'Since we are repeating old conversations,' I said, 'you said to me, after you were shot, that I must forgive you for being so very rich, and overcome my scruples, or something like that, because we loved one another. If you could say that, why can't I?'

'We must repeat yet another conversation,' he said. 'When a penniless girl marries a rich man, the world gives its blessing. When a penniless man marries a rich woman, the world sneers behind its hand. How could I know, in my heart why I married you?'

'Because you asked me when I was penniless.'

'No. I had heard Edgar Smith. The missing documents were on the table in the parlour.'

'Oh. That is true, but . . . Are you accusing yourself of asking me to marry you, with your poor leg full of shot, because you knew I might win Glenalban?'

'How can I not accuse myself? At any rate suspect myself? I did know you might win Glenalban. And in that knowledge I asked you.'

'And in that knowledge I accepted you. I admit I wasn't thinking of it at the time . . .'

'I did not think I was thinking of it,' he said. 'I thought I thought of you. Now I cannot know what I was thinking then, or what I am thinking now.'

'Try thinking of me again.'

'You and Glenalban are fused now, inseparable. You must grasp the central point. Suppose the case were fought and I won it. In marrying me, you would not become owner of anything, except what I specifically gave you. Put it the other way about. In marrying you, I would become owner of everything, and you would be left with only what I specifically gave you.'

'I shall be happy with what you give me,' I said. 'If I may wear dresses with sleeves that make you laugh . . .'

'It would be your own that I would be giving you! What fairness is there in that? It would be obscene, dishonourable, humiliating!'

'Am I to understand, Sir,' I said, drawing myself up to my full height, and trying, with terror in my heart, to be as dignified as an archbishop, 'that you are withdrawing your proposal of marriage? Is that honourable?'

239

'You know it is.'

He turned and limped away, his face as full of pain as in the moments after he was shot.

My mind was numb with misery. I ought to have foreseen all this, and I had not. He ought to have foreseen it, and he had not. Both of us had known, if we thought about it, that with the missing documents restored, my case was good, and perhaps unanswerable. Both of us had put the whole matter out of our minds – I because I did not care, he because of his wound and because of his love. Now a letter from the lawyers had jolted him out of his happy oblivion, reawakened that prickly conscience, so that it filled him with poisoned pins.

The trouble was that, in his own terms, he was right. To withdraw his proposal was honourable. In defiance of all logic, and of all the things I had said, there *was* a difference – a poor girl could decently marry a rich man, but not the other way about. A hundred years hence it might not be so; but in that year it was profoundly so.

I tried to make a plan, though my mind was not in a state for making plans.

Could I make all my property over to him, by irrevocable deed of gift? Secretly, so that he did not know I was doing it until after I had done it? I thought not. I was old enough to be married, but I was three years short of my legal majority. I did not think a minor was allowed to give away the moon.

Could I convince him that I loved him so much that his tender conscience was breaking my heart, that I would die of misery without him? I thought not. My heart would break. But I would not die. He knew that. And if by any such means I lured him into marriage, he would still never be sure of his own motives.

Could I convince him that he loved me so much, that Glenalban was no more than icing on the cake? Devise a situation where he must rescue me from a treacherous river or a savage bull? And thus reveal his heart to himself?

He had already done that.

And he was still lame. He could walk only slowly, with a stick. Heroics would be impossible, for many weeks yet.

I stared sightlessly at the sunlit park, sloping down to the Alban Water. It was mine, and it was death to me.

Luncheon took place normally, which somehow amazed me. After such a morning, life could *not* continue in its accustomed grooves; but it did.

I had no appetite. This was so rare that Aunt Sophia looked at me anxiously.

Duncan had not yet said anything to anybody. Nor had I.

I did not want to go down to dinner. But I thought I should imitate Miss Louisa Frith. I decided to dress with special care, and to hold my head high.

By a familiar magic, no less mysterious because it happened so often, the Servants' hall knew the story by evening. Mary MacAndrew looked stricken. I truly believed that my happiness had become as important to her as her own. Hers was assured; mine had been assured, and it was in ruins.

Next day at luncheon Duncan quietly announced that he was going to Edinburgh. There was to be a meeting between himself and both sets of lawyers. What was to be arranged was the transfer of property deeds from his name to mine. They would be put in the hands of Trustees.

Everybody nodded. Nobody could believe that it was actually happening. Nobody could think of anything to say.

Breaking a silence that had become painful, Miss Frith said to me, 'Congratulations, dear.'

'But I don't want it!' I said.

'I know. But we all know that it is your right.'

'I don't want my right,' I said. 'I want . . .'

I did not finish my sentence. I did not need to. They all knew what I wanted.

Duncan excused himself, rose, and went to the door. He turned, and said, 'I shall not be coming back. They can pack my personal things and send them on. I shall see you all again. Or perhaps not all.'

Flora suddenly said, 'Shall I come with you?'

'No!' I almost shouted. 'Because one person goes mad, the rest need not. This is your home.'

Duncan went through the door with no further word. The footman closed it behind him. It did not signify that we were playing this scene in front of half a dozen servants. Anything

241

they did not know about it, they soon would. It was their right to know; it was their home too. And none of it could be any sort of secret.

'It is a very moral form of madness, dear,' said Miss Frith presently.

'I know,' I said. 'It is duty and conscience and pride and so forth. I wish none of those words had ever been thought of.'

'From duty he has maintained the Glenalban that you see.'

'Yes. And from duty I shall have to try to do the same, if I must, but I had much rather he went on doing it, and then I could help, if he told me what to do, but now he never will . . .'

And then I did exactly what I had vowed I would not do. I collapsed my forehead on to my arms on the table, and burst into violent sobs.

'If I were you, Nora,' said Aunt Sophia, speaking loud so that I could hear over my sobs, 'I would find that dreadful man's swordstick, and stab Lord Glenalban in the leg – his good leg, I think it ought to be – and go on doing so until he gives up this nonsense.'

I raised my head, to stare at her in amazement. My face must have looked horrible.

'I do not like seeing you unhappy,' said Aunt Sophia, by way of explanation of her advice. 'I do feel that you and Lord Glenalban are ideally matched. I feel a duty in the matter quite as strong as his, to promote your future happiness. It has been my responsibility, ever since your dear mother left us. I feel a sense of responsibility for this betrothal, also, since I had the honour to be present at its inception.'

She was making excuses. She knew her suggestion was monstrous and unthinkable.

'I would use a pin, rather than the swordstick,' said Miss Frith. 'A good long hatpin.'

'You had better do it at once,' said Flora. 'He's leaving directly.'

I goggled at these amazing ladies.

'We don't care who owns what,' said Flora. 'We want you to marry Duncan.'

'The pin of this brooch,' said Miss Frith, removing a jewel

from her bosom. 'Two inches long, and something to get a good grip by. Hurry, child, you'll miss him.'

So I rubbed away my tears with my knuckles, most unlike the mistress of Glenalban, and ran down into the courtyard. A travelling-carriage was waiting. Duncan had not yet come out. He was expected any moment. I jumped into the carriage. I thought I saw a look of understanding on the stolid face of the footman who held the door. I even thought I saw the suspicion of a wink.

I drew the curtains over the windows of the carriage, to darken it. I made myself as small as I could, in the corner. He might not get into the carriage, if he saw from the ground that I was in it. Once he was in, and the door shut behind him, I could follow Aunt Sophia's plan.

I could not believe I had heard what I had just heard. I knew Flora was fond of me; I thought Miss Frith also. It jolted my heart to realize how much they loved me.

And, in Aunt Sophia, duty, morality, conscience were the stars she steered by. She should have approved of Duncan's rigid adherence to his code of honour. When she pretended to speak from a sense of duty, she was fibbing, and she knew it. She suggested the swordstick!

Duncan was helped in. He murmured surprise at the unexpected darkness of the carriage. He leaned out of the open window, to call a last instruction to his valet, who was to follow in another carriage with the boxes; he was still leaning out when the carriage started. Then he relaxed back into the seat. Thinking himself alone, he allowed himself to groan at the pain of being hoisted in. Then he saw me.

'Leo,' he said, 'this is only more pain for both of us –'

'No,' I said, 'only for you. I am to stab you with this pin until you promise to marry me. Again and again and again. It was supposed to be in your good leg, but it will have to be in your bad leg. It will hurt horribly. Wouldn't it be best if you promised straight away, so I don't have to stab you, which I am not looking forward to, although I can see it is a good plan . . .'

'You're demented,' he said. 'You've stumbled over the edge into lunacy. The real thing, this time. I shall have to take you back to the asylum in Lochgrannomhead. You were to stab me again and again and again, until I promised . . .'

243

I heard that his voice had changed. I saw that his face changed. He was smiling. I burst into more tears, and dropped my pointed weapon.

He took me in his arms, and I wept over his waistcoat.

'I'm defeated,' he said. 'I cannot withstand the threat of torture. I do promise to marry you. But it is simply to save you from the sin of stabbing me in the leg.'

And he called to the coachman to turn round; and we rattled home to Glenalban.